The Marketing

of

P

C

and Cases

The Marketing of Tourism Products: Concepts, Issues and Cases

A.V. Seaton
Director of the Scottish Tourism Research Unit,
University of Strathclyde, UK

M.M. Bennett
Lecturer in Tourism and Marketing,
Department of Management Studies,
University of Surrey, UK

THOMSON ™

LEARNING

Australia • Canada • Mexico • Singapore • Spain • United Kingdom • United States

THOMSON

LEARNING

The Marketing of Tourism Products: Concepts, Issues and Cases
Copyright © 1996 A. V. Seaton and M. M. Bennett

The Thomson Learning logo is a registered trademark used herein under licence.

British Library Cataloguing-in-Publication Data
A catalogue record for this book is available from the British Library

First published 1996
Reprinted 1997, 1999 and 2000
Reprinted 2001 by Thomson Learning

Printed in Croatia by ZRINSKI d.d.

ISBN 1-86152-302-5

Thomson Learning
Berkshire House
168-173 High Holborn
London WC1V 7AA
UK

http://www.thomsonlearning.co.uk

Contents

Dedications

To V.H.S. and in memory of F.M.S. with love

and

To L.C.B. and I.M.B. with love

Preface

This book attempts to do something new as a managerial tourism text. Through its three-part structure it provides: (a) a condensed account of the principles of tourism marketing; (b) an examination of a number of important current issues affecting tourism marketing; (c) five extended cases drawn from key product fields of the tourism sector – airlines, hotels, travel agencies, tour operators and destination marketers.

This three-part structure was developed after an audit of the major texts on tourism marketing in the UK and America. Many of these are excellent (we've used and referenced a number of them in this book) but we felt, from our own professional and academic experience, that there was room for a slightly different kind of text which condensed the theory, increased the emphasis on current special issues and extended the practical applications, particularly into the **international** field since most existing marketing texts use cases from their countries of origin.

We have therefore used a diverse variety of international examples to illustrate the main ideas. These range from short, anecdotal snapshots and mini-cases (the boxed exhibits featured throughout Parts 1 and 2) to longer industry studies (presented in Part 3). The case materials are based on academic and industry research derived from visitor studies, trade surveys, conference papers, journal articles and, not least, interviews with people in the industry. We have tried to show the close relationship between research and marketing throughout. We believe that this book offers a wider range of cases and research than any previous one and, through the diversity of materials presented, it is hoped that the text captures the essence of tourism marketing as an industrial activity, and brings to life how people in it go about doing their jobs.

The book is directed at both tourism executives and students at the undergraduate and postgradute levels, (with whom we have tested much of the content) and presents established principles of marketing, as well as new ideas and critical perspectives which challenge some existing orthodoxies. Our most important concern has been to impart useful knowledge. Marketing is an applied business discipline so we have emphasized ideas with a practical application which can be demonstrated by precedent. Where we have felt it necessary to discuss ideas which have achieved academic currency but, in our view, more limited industrial application, we have said so.

Acknowledgements

This book owes a considerable debt to many individuals and organizations, most notably for the case materials and research which are widely scattered throughout the text. We have tried to reference every source as accurately as possible but where, through ignorance or oversight, we have failed, we would like to offer our apologies in advance.

We would like to express our particular thanks to the organizations upon which we and our contributors have based the extended case studies in Part 3 and the longer or recurrent examples throughout the book. These include:

American Express
Association of British Travel Agents
Austrian tourist organizations
Best Western Hotels, Canada
British Airways
Bord Failte (the Irish Tourist Board)
British Tourist Authority
CACI
Canadian Pacific Hotels
Direct Holidays
Edinburgh International Conference Centre
English Tourist Board
Florida Department of Commerce
Forte International
Gloucestershire Tourism
Going Places
Hilton Hotels
Indiana State Welcome Centers
Intercontinental Hotels
London Arts Board
Lunn Poly
M & C Saatch: Maison de la France
Marriott Hotels
Northwest Airlines
Northern Ireland Tourist Board
The Scottish Tourist Board
Singapore Airlines
The Thomas Cook Group Ltd
Thomson Holidays
Virgin Atlantic Airways Ltd

Virgin Enterprises Ltd
Virginia Beach tourism administration

We would also like to thank those organizations and writers, too numerous to list individually, who facilitated our use of their materials by disseminating them in publicly available reports, academic journals and research studies.

List of contributors

CONTRIBUTING AUTHORS

Tony Seaton is Senior Lecturer in Tourism and Director of the Scottish Tourism Research Unit, University of Strathclyde. After taking an MA in English at Wadham College, Oxford he worked in hotel management, followed by marketing and brand management with Procter & Gamble. He took a further degree in Social Sciences and taught marketing and tourism at the University of Northumbria until coming to Strathclyde in 1991. At Strathclyde he founded the Scottish Tourist Research Unit which has done work for many public sector organizations. He has published three books, and broadcast and written widely on tourism in academic and professional journals. His teaching and research interests include: tourism marketing and promotion, tourism consumer behaviour, tourism history and the cartography of tourism. He has been Visiting Professor at the Universities of Innsbruck and Alicante and undertaken research and consultancy for many organizations including the BBC, the Northern Ireland Tourist Board and the Scottish Tourist Board and Scottish Enterprise.

Marion M. Bennett is a Lecturer in Tourism and Marketing at the Department of Management Studies, University of Surrey. She has a First Class degree in Geography from the University of Nottingham where she won an Exhibition in 1985 and The Edwards Prize for Human Geography in 1987. She obtained her PhD in 1991 from the University of Reading for research into the application of information technology to the travel trade. Upon leaving Reading, she joined the American Express Graduate Development Programme and gained a position in marketing. In 1991 she was appointed to a lectureship in tourism at The Scottish Hotel School, University of Strathclyde before taking up her current position at the University of Surrey in 1995. Her research interests which are reflected in her publications are in the travel trade, distribution, airlines and information technology.

CONTRIBUTING AUTHORS

Don Anderson is Senior Instructor and Director of the Bachelor of Commerce Program in Tourism and Hospitality Management in the Faculty of Management at the University of Calgary, Canada. In addition, he also serves as Director of Advanced Management Programs for the World Tourism Education & Research Center at the same institution.

With 11 years of operating experience in the tourism and hospitality field, Mr Anderson has held a number of senior management positions directly related to tourism/hospitality operations and marketing management. His management positions have included President/CEO of a city convention and visitors bureau, manager of an international exposition pavilion, hotel general manager and director of marketing and planning for a resort inn chain.

With a particular focus on urban tourism, Mr Anderson's main teaching and research interests include leadership and human resources development; tourism destination marketing and management; tourism competitiveness and economic development; hotel and restaurant operations; tourism mega-event planning and development; and tourism and hospitality executive development.

Rob Davison was formerly Education and Training Manager at the British Tourism Authority. He is now a freelance consultant and lecturer in tourism based in France.

Apart from a diverse range of consultancy activities he has spoken widely at international tourism conferences and is visiting Lecturer in Tourism at the Universities of Montpellier, Lyon and Lille.

He has published three books on tourism: *Tourism, Tourism in Europe* and *Business Travel*. He is currently researching a book comparing the structure and organization of tourism in France with arrangements in other parts of Europe.

J. John Lennon MPhil, BSc(Hons), MHCIMA is a Senior Lecturer in the Department of Tourism and Leisure Management, Glasgow Caledonian University. He has responsibility for all income-generation activities within the department and has undertaken consultancy and research projects in Russia, Poland, Romania and the Czech Republic. He is also the author of two texts and numerous articles within the hospitality/tourism fields and has a background in hotel and catering management.

Alison Morrison is Lecturer in Hotel Management at the University of Strathclyde, having taken her first degree in Hotel and Catering Management there in 1977. Over the next seven years she gained wide experience of hotel and hospitality management in Canada and Britain. She was appointed lecturer at Queen's College, Glasgow in 1984 and in 1989 moved to Napier Polytechnic, Edinburgh. She gained an MSc in Entrepreneurial Studies at Stirling University in 1990 and has recently completed a PhD in the small firm in the UK hotel industry at the University of Strathclyde. She has diverse consultancy experience in hotel and catering operations, exhibition provision and tourism, and retains a direct involvement with a Glasgow restaurant. Her teaching and research interests include small business management, entrepreneurship, marketing, customer care and hotel and restaurant operations. She is a Fellow of the HCIMA and a member of both the Institute of Management and the Institute for Small Business Affairs.

Barry Pitegoff graduated Valedictorian Summa Cum Laude from the Baruch School of City College of New York with a Bachelor's Degree in statistics. He received his Master's degree with Distinction in Business Administration from Adelphi University in Garden City, New York.

Since January 1981 he has served as Tourism Research Administrator for the Florida Department of Commerce. He manages a staff responsible for researching travel and tourism trends, for understanding Florida's tourist today, and for identifying key tourism marketing strategies for tomorrow.

Barry Pitegoff describes himself as one who blends a dedication to the tourism industry with a concern for his own community. In the Tallahassee community, Mr Pitegoff is involved in volunteer activities, mostly dealing with grief, bereavement and interfaith issues. He was a finalist in Tallahassee's 'Volunteer of the Year' program, and was featured in a November 1991 article in *Tallahassee Magazine* on volunteers in the community. Prior to relocating to Tallahassee, Barry conducted advertising and product research for Publishers' Clearing House in Port Washington, New York.

He has been a regular speaker at international tourism conferences including those of the Travel and Tourism Research Association of America and the Society of Travel and Tourism Educators.

Udo Schlentrich is Visiting Professor at the the Hotel School, University of Strathclyde. A graduate of both the École Hôtelier, Lausanne in Switzerland and Cornell University Hotel School, he has had held a number of senior executive roles in the hotel industry including: Vice President of Omni International and Stouffer Hotels; Managing Director of the Regency Hotel in New York; Managing Director of the Dorchester in London; Managing Director of the Stakis Hotel Group; and executive board member positions at Marketing Director and Vice Presidential level with Preferred Hotels and the Steigenberger Organization.

His consultancy has included work for the governments of Jamaica and the Bahamas as well as hotel and conference centre development projects in Europe. He is currently working on leisure and estate development in Berlin.

Ronnie Smith is a Lecturer in Tourism at the University of Strathclyde, having first taken an honours degree in German and Modern History at Glasgow University and winning a two year scholarship to the Free University of West Berlin. Acquiring a teaching qualification he took up a career in secondary education, including an exchange year in the USA. He developed his interest in tourism by taking the MSc in Tourism at the University of Strathclyde in 1987 and then joining the consultancy department of Heritage Projects, the York-based company which grew out of the highly successful Jorvik Viking Centre. After a spell as tourism officer with a Scottish local authority he joined the staff at Strathclyde in 1990. His main research and teaching interests are in resort development, Scottish tourism, heritage issues and visitor attractions.

Part 1

ncepts

f the main concepts and
managerial practices. Part
it came from and what it
ment of the marketing mix.
short, boxed cases which

The marketing concept in tourism

A.V. Seaton

1

OBJECTIVES

This chapter provides an overview of the tourism marketing process and is designed to act as a framework within which the individual elements of marketing, discussed in the chapters that follow, can be situated.

By the end of this chapter the reader should:

- have an appreciation of the dimensions of the tourism sector and the role of marketing within it;
- have an understanding of the five essential elements of marketing as: a philosophy of consumer-orientation, a set of analytical procedures and concepts, a body of data-gathering techniques, a managerial planning programme and an organizational orientation;
- have an understanding of the ways in which tourism marketing, as a service, differs from other kinds of marketing and also from other kinds of service marketing;
- have an awareness of how marketing developed.

TOURISM – INDUSTRY OR SECTOR?

This book is called *The Marketing of Tourism Products* because, although tourism has been called an industry, it encompasses a wide variety of products which, while sharing some similarities, display many differences in market characteristics and consumer profiles.

In Britain during the 1980s tourism was widely promoted as a coherent entity, rather than a multi-product sector, for political and economic reasons. Calling tourism an industry was a method of unifying a hetero-geneous and diverse number of different businesses which, individually, had little lobbying power, compared to more homogeneous industries such as transport and agriculture. Packaged together, however, as 'the tourism industry' they were able to achieve greater visibility with governments and the public. The bonding together of many different business areas as tourism and the lack of a rigorous definition of tourism has allowed tourism organizations and promoters to claim it as the first or second biggest industry in the world.

The main businesses which have been subsumed under the tourism label include: hotels and the accommodation sector, airlines, ferry and cruise companies, restaurants, travel agencies and tour operators, tourist attractions, car hire firms, etc. Their only common denominator is that they involve provision for people undertaking activities in places other than their place of residence. Even this apparent common denominator has been contested by some who argue that, in reality, much of the business generated by restaurants, hotels, transport firms and other tourism providers should not be designated tourism, since it includes the patronage of local people who cannot be described as tourists (Lieper, 1991). Libraries, museums, nightclubs and licensed clubs are included in official statistics on tourism in Scotland although much of their business is clearly local.

On the other hand tourism promoters might have included at least part of the output of other industrial sectors in their inventory of tourism. The oil industry, for example, sells much of its production for tourism purposes in the form of air fuel, coach fuel and, massively, as petrol for touring motorists. In the 1920s and 1930s oil companies such as Shell and Esso, and tyre companies such as Goodyear and Dunlop, invested considerable funds in tourism through guidebooks, maps and countryside books to promote the driving habit, realizing that the domestic use of the car for necessary journeys was a limited one and that the biggest expansion in petrol consumption lay in stimulating a well developed touring habit. Clothing could also be included within tourism since people buy new and/or special clothing for their holidays, as well as a wide range of pre-trip accessories such as sunglasses, books, medications, etc. Indeed all forms of shopping are now not just an element of tourism (over 90% of UK and US tourists claim shopping as an activity) but, in some instances, a prime motivator (British day trips to France to buy cheap wine and food; Norwegian trips to Britain for cheap clothes and cosmetics).

In summary then, tourism is not a homogeneous market like that, say, for breakfast cereals, cars or cat food. It is a heterogeneous sector which consists of several product fields, albeit ones which have a degree of linkage. Following Smith (1988: 183) we shall define tourism as:

> . . . the aggregate of all businesses that directly provide goods or services to facilitate business, pleasure, and leisure activities away from the home environment.

The heterogeneous products mean that a wide variety of organizations and firms are involved in tourism management and marketing know-how varies. Marketing principles may be applied to any tourism enterprise but there are differences between organizations in operational scope and impact arising from differences in financial resources, control of the market, degree of integration with other tourism enterprises and customer volumes. The organizations with large budgets – airlines, international hotel chains – are further advanced than most regional tourist boards and many smaller organizations whose marketing planning often looks primitive by the side of the detailed operational strategies of the giant private sector organizations.

WHAT IS MARKETING?

Before attempting to define tourism marketing let's begin by offering a small-scale example which shows it in action.

A married couple whose children have left home are thinking of entering the tourism business by investing some of their savings in a hotel business in the south west of England. At the moment the building is unoccupied and seems to be very cheap. How should they proceed in deciding whether to buy it and what will be involved in making it work if they do? What do they need to know in order to decide on whether it is a good move?

First and foremost where will its customers come from? This will partly depend on where it is located. If it is close to a main communications centre – an airport or main road – then it is likely that the hotel will get a good passing trade. Why will guests want to come – for an overnight stay to break a journey? a weekend break? a longer holiday? Who will they be – will they be foreigners? will they come from within Britain? will they be locals just using the place as a bar/restaurant? How many will there be? – how many beds does the hotel have and what level of occupancy will be necessary to sustain profitability? How will customers learn that the hotel is there (if it is not on a main route then some form of promotion will be necessary to create awareness)? What services should the hotel provide to satisfy the visitor? What kind of accommodation? What should the charges be for the hotel to run profitably? Will the business be seasonal or can the owners rely on some trade throughout the year, assuming they want a year-round business? What other kinds of accommodation are there in the area and how will they compare for price, quality of service and image?

Assuming that these questions have been answered satisfactorily and the couple go ahead with the purchase what must they do to make the operation work? How much should they spend on publicity and how should they achieve it – through adverts? media relations? word of mouth? Who might they need to influence or liaise with apart from customers to create awareness of their hotel – tourist boards? The media? incoming coach firms? What special offers might be necessary at different times of the year to achieve some degree of business spread rather than high-season occupancy? How should they plan their hotel's development over five years?

This book comprises an examination of many concepts and methods associated with the marketing process but, at the end of the day, marketing essentially involves confronting and finding answers to the questions just outlined. Marketing is an **analytical orientation** which involves knowing what questions need to be asked and answered to determine the business potential of a tourism enterprise in relation to: its past, present and predicted customers; the business environment in which it exists; the societal and social environment in which the business must operate. At the centre of marketing lie questions about consumer demand and the measures that are necessary to identify, influence, satisfy and manage it profitably. Once consumer needs and the various environments in which the business has to operate have been identified marketing then involves **managerial action** in the form of developing products for the market, pricing them correctly, promoting them effectively, distributing them to the final customer and then evaluating the results of the total programme – at which point the whole process starts again.

How shall we define the activity embedded in these processes? Nearly twenty years ago, in an article on the exact meaning of marketing, one writer (Crosier, 1975) reviewed 49 different definitions. He grouped the definitions into six categories of emphasis which included the following four main interpretations of marketing as:

- a directive, management function **targeted at** consumers in order to generate profit. This emphasizes the importance of identifying the target consumer but suggests that the customer is merely a passive stooge to be aimed at;
- a directive management function **for** consumers rather than just targeted at them. This puts more emphasis on offering services that meet consumers' needs rather than just setting them up as passive targets;
- a transactional **exchange** in which consumer needs, as well as those of the enterprise, must be balanced. This increases the focus on marketing as an **interaction** based on reciprocal rewards and mutual self-interest between an organization and its customers;
- a **philosophy** or state of mind. This emphasizes marketing as a broad **orientation** to business which involves putting the consumer at the centre of things.

From these broad categories we can move to two general definitions of marketing (1(a) and 1(b)) and two specific definitions of tourism marketing (2(a) and 2(b)):

1(a) 'Marketing is the management process responsible for identifying, anticipating and satisfying customer requirements profitably' (Chartered Institute of Marketing, UK).
1(b) 'Marketing (management) is the process of planning and executing the conception, pricing, promotion, and distribution of ideas, goods, and services to create exchanges that satisfy individual and organizational objectives' (American Marketing Association).
2(a) 'Tourism marketing is a management philosophy that, in the light of tourist demand, makes it possible through research, forecasting and selection to place tourism products on the market most in line with the organization's purpose for greatest benefit' (Coltman, 1989: 11).
2(b) 'Tourism marketing is a directed, goal-oriented activity that balances

the objectives of the tourist destination, or supplier within it, with the needs of tourists' (Coltman, 1989: 11).

Building upon the features embodied in these definitions marketing can be characterized by five essential features. It is:

- a **philosophy of consumer orientation**;
- a number of **analytical procedures and concepts** used to develop the philosophy;
- **data-gathering techniques** which act as the tools for operationalizing the procedures and concepts;
- a sequence of **strategic decision areas and planning functions**;
- an **organizational structure** for implementation of the planning.

Let's look at each of these.

MARKETING AS A PHILOSOPHY

Marketing, as a philosophy, means that, ideally, an organization produces nothing which is not known to be consistent with customer tastes, habits and wants:

> The key aspect of marketing is an attitude of mind. It requires that, in taking 'marketing' decisions, the manager looks at these from the *viewpoint of the consumer*. These decisions will thus be driven by what the consumer needs and wants.
>
> (Mercer, 1992: 11)

In tourism planning consumer orientation means understanding the needs, desires and perceptions of the visitor/tourist. For the destination marketer it requires a knowledge of who the potential visitors are, what services they require while making a trip and what they expect to get out of the whole experience. For the airline operator it requires knowing who the likely flyers are, what they are flying for (business? pleasure?), and what facilities they expect in flight (and, increasingly, while checking in, waiting to fly and on leaving the plane).

Tourism marketing involves another kind of consumer – the resident population at the destinations in which tourism is to be marketed. Tourism is a highly intrusive activity which involves the temporary presence of large numbers of people in environments which are not their own and the transformation of physical environments (high-rise hotel development, airport buildings, the annexation of land previously dedicated to local use, etc). Responsible tourism marketing should, and will increasingly be compelled to, take account of the needs of host populations if it is not to produce the negative environmental and sociocultural effects which have been widely documented and deplored in the past (see, for instance, Smith (1977 and 1989). Even the promotion and publicity of destinations to tourists may produce conflicts with local communities. The image of a place held by its residents is often different from that which must be promoted to attract holidaymakers from outside the area. Destination marketing frequently involves presenting simplified stereotypes about a place and its features which may annoy local residents. In Scotland and Wales tourism planners have had the dilemma whether to promote the aspects of their countries **their inhabitants would like to see**, or whether to promote the **more stereotypical aspects** (in Scotland bagpipes, kilts and haggis, for example) which foreign tourists tend to be attracted by (see below, Chapter 14).

ANALYTICAL PROCEDURES AND CONCEPTS

The marketing audit

Customer orientation is merely a philosophical idea. To be operationalized successfully it requires the application of a number of procedures and concepts.

At the outset the organization needs some kind of **stocktake** to assess its degree of consumer-orientation. This stocktake should determine who existing customers are and who future ones might be; to what extent the organization's capacities and products meet customer requirements; and what developments in society as a whole might affect both its customers and its own performance in the future. One of the distinguishing features of marketing management is that it is a dynamic process which involves anticipating change and planning for the future.

This stocktake is called a **marketing audit** which is an attempt to appraise the current performance and future potential of an organization (hotel, destination, airline, etc.) in relation to its existing and predicted capacity, its current and future customers, and predicted social and societal trends. It consists of three procedural steps:

(a) market and consumer analysis, including quantification of the total current and future markets and detailed analysis of the main customer segments within them;

(b) an organizational audit, including a SWOT analysis of the tourism organization and its products, assessing their potential capacity to meet identified market needs successfully;

(c) an environmental scan of the external forces likely to affect the tourism organization's operations in the future, including a thoroughgoing appraisal of competitors.

Market and customer analysis

Marketing is fundamentally a process of supplying products to meet a determined demand. Demand can be viewed in both a macro and micro sense. At a macro level it is the aggregate demand for tourism or specific tourism products (visitors to Spain, customers for skiing holidays, budget hotels, long haul travel, etc.), quantified in terms of people, trips or monetary value. This quantitative data is gathered to assess current markets but also, critically, in order to produce forecasts for the future since all marketing planning must be underpinned by forecast targets for the future.

At the micro level demand analysis is about understanding the bases of tourist choices, customer tastes, needs, preferences and motivations which drive the broad macro pattern of aggregate demand. Aggregate demand involves **market analysis** designed to determine the value of the total tourism market and the major sectors that constitute it in order for an organization to know what markets are worth entering. Micro analysis involves **customer analysis** to prioritize specific customer groups within an aggregate market and understand 'what makes them tick' so that marketing programmes can be designed which closely match their product needs, values and decision patterns. A major element of micro-demand analysis is **market segmentation** which will be explained along with other forms of demand analysis in Chapters 2 and 3.

The organizational audit

Once some idea of current and future demand has been achieved an organization must then assess its capabilities to supply it. This involves an organizational audit which should include an appraisal of every aspect of an organization's structures and activities: managerial expertise, image, people, its innovative ability and, crucially, its product capacity. The culmination of this audit should be a SWOT analysis which inventories the *S*trengths, *W*eaknesses, *O*pportunities and *T*hreats confronting the firm and its products in relation to the markets identified in the market and customer analysis. In Chapter 4 we shall look in detail at some of the ways in which an organization can assess its potential capacity to satisfy its markets.

The environmental scan

One of the most useful analytical orientations marketing brings with it is the assumption that businesses do not exist in isolation and that, in managing them, it is necessary to assess a number of external forces or **environments** which affect operations in the present and will do so in the future. Marketing is the ongoing and systematic acquisition of data gathered in order to better understand the paramaters in which strategy and plans for the future must operate. (See Barry Pitegoff's account of how the Florida Chamber of Commerce uses research to monitor external environments in Chapter 23 of this book.)

An environmental scan has been defined as: '. . . an early warning system of the environmental forces which may impact on a company's products and markets in the future' (Jain, 1981). This rather negative formulation suggests that scanning is a reactive process undertaken to pick one's way through some futuristic minefield. More recent strategic management thinking approaches scanning more proactively, seeing it not just as an early warning system of dangers, but as the identification of opportunities to be managed (see Chapter 9 for more on strategic management).

An environmental scan involves the appraisal of six external environments: technological, economic, ecological, political, sociocultural and competitive.

The technological environment

Writers such as Alvin Toffler and Robert Naisbitt have written influential books on the speed at which technological developments will revolutionize life as we approach the third millenium. Although some of their predictions have critics (e.g. Roszak, 1994) of their validity it is indisputable that technology has produced transformations in all aspects of daily life – and tourism is no exception. Scanning the technological environment is about assessing the future impact of technology on tourism development in general and marketing in particular. Some of the technological innovations that have had and are having impacts on tourism include the following.

- **Databases and computer reservation systems (CRS)** IT has transformed travel agency practice, made accommodation databases possible, and mechanized many forms of booking and reservations. CRS systems are no longer just a convenient luxury for the organizations that utilize them – they are a crucial form of competitive advantage. In Italy, for example, some regional destinations which have not appeared on CRS systems do not effectively exist and have been called 'lost cities' (Perugia, 1991).
- **Home video and TV video texts** The march of video as a consumer good and teletext as a TV medium has already influenced tourism. Video ownership has greatly increased holiday recording (which has made tour operators, for instance, aware of the importance of photostops on conducted tours). Video has also expanded tourism promotional opportunities: many holiday property companies and time-share firms now use video to sell their products. TV teletext services now provide on-screen tourism information on international destinations (exchange rates, road conditions, petrol prices, etc.) as well as providing TV viewers with direct booking opportunities. One of the most interesting is the BBC's Ceefax service 'Travel Advice Countries' which provides several on-screen pages of information on safety/security factors in a range of international destinations. Table 1.1 shows data on ownership of home video and teletext in selected European countries.
- **Transport innovations** Innovations such as high speed trains and the Channel Tunnel between Britain and France will change travel patterns, creating opportunities for some tourism organizations and threats to others. The Pas de Calais region in northern France has begun extensive tourism initiatives designed to capitalize on the

Table 1.1 Ownership of home video and teletext

	Video recorders (%)	Teletext (%)
France	52	—
Germany	44.2	32
UK	67	43
Switzerland	50	51
Netherlands	57	60
Belgium	55.8	14.1

Source: Adapted from data in *European Marketing Pocket Book* (NTC Publications, 1994).

Tunnel's projected impact, but on the negative side, Boulogne lost its main Sealink Ferry with Britain when the firm closed it in anticipation of having to concentrate its services to complete when the Chunnel opened.
- **Virtual reality** This technical innovation may ultimately offer travel simulations as a way of selling tourism destinations or, even, as substitutes for them. Already virtual reality is featuring as an attraction in resort amusement arcades, a souped-up development of the cinematic slot machines that used to feature at resorts in the past. Accounts of the possibility of virtual reality in future tourism can be found in Williams and Hobson (1994), and an account of the overall implications of IT in tourism in Chapter 17 of this book.

The political environment

Politics at regional, national and international levels profoundly affects tourism supply and demand. Governments and country blocs may pass laws affecting the provision of tourism, e.g. European Union regulations on package companies and travel agents. Governments may support certain kinds of tourism through grant aids for development, or restrict it through entry quotas (as in the Galapagos Islands or Burma until recently).

Political unrest, wars and terrorism can destabilize tourism overnight as in Lebanon during the 1970s and the former Yugoslavia during the late 1980s. London lost over 50% of its American visitors in the summer of 1986 following the bombing of Libya, and Jordan lost most of its tourists during the Gulf War. Since 1993 some package companies have stopped operating in the former Soviet Republic. As the Pitegoff article in Chapter 23 shows, murders of tourists in Miami in the summer of 1993 produced a serious tourism crisis in Florida. There is an increasing trend for minority opposition parties opposed to governments in power to attack tourism targets – e.g. in Egypt and the Basque areas of Spain and France – to weaken the tourism economy. In Northern Ireland between 1969 and 1985 there was an inverse relationship between the scale of terrorist incidents and tourist arrivals but now that a ceasefire has taken place part of the 'peace dividend' is expected to be an increase in tourism.

Evaluations of political developments in tourism destinations and assessments of political measures likely to affect tourism operations are thus an essential element of environmental scanning.

The ecological environment

Tourism both affects and is affected by the ecological systems in the areas in which it is developed. Tourism development can degrade natural environments (as in Aviemore in Scotland and the Spanish Costas where mass tourism resulted in the destruction of once attractive regions). Conversely ecological disasters arising from factors outside tourism can deter visitors (e.g. algae in the sea water of the Adriatic, ozone depletion and sun risk in Europe and Australia, and increasing pollution of the coasts of the Mediterranean and inland areas of Eastern Europe). Scanning the ecological environments in potential tourism regions can reveal threats to successful tourism marketing but also opportunities for alternative products (e.g. providing all-weather leisure complexes in unpredictable climatic environments as CenterParc have done in Britain and Holland).

The economic environment

Tourism demand is strongly affected by prevailing economic conditions. Economic factors which bear on tourism demand include:

- average wage rates and levels of disposable income;
- unemployment rates;
- fuel costs (which affect travel and transport costs);
- interest rates (when mortgage interest rates are high disposable income decreases);
- exchange rates and currency devaluations which can make some countries cheaper or more expensive in relation to competitors;
- the price of substitutes (as a luxury good tourism competes with a wide range of potential substitute purchases).

Economic analysis and prediction is thus a major element in environmental scanning in order to assess the conditions for future marketing planning.

The sociocultural environment

Marketing, as the old cliché has it, is a 'people' business. Monitoring the sociocultural environment is about understanding changing trends in populations, lifestyles and values: 'The social (and cultural) environment is a complex of demographic (population size, age structure, location) and cultural (social values, attitudes, education) variables' (Sanderson and Luffman, 1979: 16).

Some of the variables that would be included in a sociocultural scan would include the following:

- **Age structure of population** The western world (America, Europe and

Japan) is, for instance, experiencing an ageing of its populations (the 'Grey Panther' syndrome). This is likely to result in increasing levels of tourism by people who are over 50, still fit and comparatively rich.

- **Education levels** Tourism activity is strongly related to years in education so that when more people stay on into higher education (approximately a third now do so in the USA and UK) future tourism activity is likely to increase among the most educated.
- **Geographic distribution** In Europe, for instance, it has often been observed that tourism patterns reflect a broad movement of urbanized, northern populations to destinations that are southern and rural. In general tourism propensity – like murder and schizophrenia! – is greatest in areas of high urban concentrations of population.
- **Wealth and income distribution** As a luxury good it is not surprising that tourism is pursued more by the affluent than the less affluent. In Britain, for example, the three top social grades, the ABC1s, are much more likely to be travellers than the lower three (see Chapter 2). The same correlation between income and tourism propensity exists in America and other Western European countries.
- **Composition of family and working population including the male/female workforce** The number of earners in a household can affect tourism demand, a fact which makes the growth of dual income families of significance.
- **Ethnic subcultures** Little has been published about the impact of ethnic subcultures on tourism. One of the reasons for this is that most ethnic subcultures in Europe and America have been poor and thus low consumers of tourism. There are now signs that ethnic populations are increasing their tourism presence. In the UK travel agencies in Birmingham, London and Bradford now specialize in holidays for Asians. In America the black publishing company African-American Visions has recently produced a 500-plus page guide to black heritage sites in America (Chase, 1994) which will surely influence black tourism patterns over the next decade. After apartheid began to collapse in South Africa unprecedented numbers of black tourists began to take holidays at coastal resorts formerly reserved for whites.
- **New tastes and social trends** Tourism is affected by fashion and social

CASE STUDY 1.1

Dual incomes in the USA

In the USA in 1992 70% of all married women worked compared to 31% in 1960. Working couple households – about 30 million – accounted for 50% of discretionary income. Of dual income earners 60% were in the 25–44 age group; 38% were graduates; 54% earned combined incomes of $40 000.

Source: Mason (1993).

trends as well as being one of the forces that produces them (e.g. the increased demand for foreign foods in Britain and America which can be seen as partly due to people's international holiday experiences). Over the last decade some of the social trends that have affected tourism have been:

- **expanded interest in sport and fitness** (which has created a growing market for activity holidays and health tourism);
- **increasing leisure rather than work orientation** which has, for many, increased tourism propensity, particularly for short-break and second holidays (which are examined in Chapter 12);
- **increased internationalism of outlook** which has expanded foreign travel from Britain by a factor of over ten times since the war and produced a massive decline in traditional, domestic seaside holidays;
- **increasing media influence** – there is now a much increased output of specialist tourism coverage in Europe and America in both the broadcast and press media. In addition fictional presentations can popularize destinations as the film *Crocodile Dundee* and TV soap operas did for Australia and Peter Mayle's *Year in Provence* did for Provence (the impact of the media on tourism is discussed in Seaton (1994b) and Riley (1994));
- **increased tourism supply and promotion** – tourism activity has also been expanded by the cumulative effects of supply-led initiatives by the industry itself which have shaped social practices. The supply of cheap charter flights by tour operators in the 1960s triggered the great British summer exodus to Europe and developments such as Disneyland have popularized Florida among people who would have not previously thought of going there.

The competitive environment

Nowadays the consumer is faced with a multiplicity of products offered at bewildering speeds onto the market. In packaged goods markets (washing powders, confectionery, pet foods, etc.) companies have routinely devoted considerable efforts to the analysis of the performance of their competitors in product terms, promotional patterns, sales and market share. The same need for competitive analysis applies to tourism. In the last 10–20 years many newish destinations have been heavily promoted in Europe (Portugal, Turkey, the Far East, Africa and the Caribbean); other destinations have risen (eastern and central Europe) or fallen (Yugoslavia, Russia) for political reasons beyond the influence of tourism marketers.

Chapters 10 and 11 explore some of the further dimensions of tourism in Western and Eastern/Central Europe.

Any tourism marketing audit by a tourism organization must take account of the future competitive environment. Competitors do not just pose a threat; they may provide an opportunity. The collapse of tourism in the former Yugoslavia has, for example, enabled destinations like Spain

CASE STUDY 1.2

Competitive trends in Europe 1985–1994

Between 1985 and 1994 tourism in Europe continued to grow by an annual average of 4.6% in total arrivals and by 11.76% in terms of revenue. Within these overall levels there were significant sub-regional differences (see Table 1.2) which showed that Eastern/Central Europe and the East Mediterranean had grown fastest on a yearly basis, showed greatest increases when 1985 levels of tourism were compared with 1994, and had increased market share most – all at the expense of those other parts of Europe which had been the traditional heartland areas of European tourism.

to maintain a buoyancy they might not have otherwise achieved. National tourism organizations thus need to analyse in detail competitive trends in tourism worldwide. Hotel developers need to be aware of hotel patterns in the areas and countries in which they operate. Airlines need to assess the impact of new carriers entering or leaving particular routes and destinations. In the late 1980s and early 1990s British Airways attracted adverse, worldwide publicity for the 'dirty tricks' they were deemed to have used to try to limit the impact of Virgin Airlines on routes between Britain and the USA (see Chapter 15).

Marketing audit summary

The marketing audit provides intelligence on the factors that influence the markets for tourism products. In the context of destination marketing the audit has been summarized in the following terms:

Table 1.2 European and European sub-regional tourism trends by annual average changes, ten-year differences and European market shares 1985–1994

| | Average annual change 1985–1994 | | 1985 vs. 1994 (1985 = 100) | | Share of tourism in Europe (Arrivals = A; Receipts = R) | | | |
	Arrivals	Receipts	Arrivals	Receipts	1985		1994	
Europe	4.6	11.76	151	277	100		100	
Western Europe	3.77	11	140	277	39	(A)	36	(A)
					40	(R)	40	(R)
Southern Europe	3.49	11.8	129	270	35	(A)	30	(A)
					34	(R)	33	(R)
Central & Eastern	8.5	29.5	239	801	13.6	(A)	21.6	(A)
					2.2	(R)	6.6	(R)
Northern Europe	3.91	10.3	138	222	10	(A)	9	(A)
					19	(R)	15	(R)
East Med. Europe	11.8	16.0	230	294	2	(A)	5.2	(A)
					5	(R)	5.2	(R)

Source: STB/STRU (1996: 4), based on WTO, *Market Trends in Europe 1994* (Madrid, 1995).

CASE STUDY 1.3

Factors likely to affect the tourism market

In 1993 David Edgell, working on behalf of the Travel and Tourism Administration Division of the US Department of Commerce, assessed the external factors likely to affect the market for US tourism by the year 2000. Table 1.3 outlines the major variables identified.

> The essence of the tourism marketing audit . . . is 'knowledge' of the underlying sources of the critical strengths and weaknesses of a national tourist organization which provides the groundwork for strategic and tactical agendas for action. In addition, knowledge identifies competitive 'forces' and clarifies potential threats and opportunities.
>
> (Papadopoulos, 1989: 36)

Table 1.3 External factors likely to affect US tourism market

Economic
- strength (or weakness) of the US dollar
- currency devaluations
- international inflation
- disposable income levels
- health of the world economy: income and income distribution
- level of international airfares
- supply of facilities: transportation, accommodation infrastructure, etc.

Technological
- introduction of new electronic communication and transportation technologies: computerized reservation systems (CRS), electronic destination marketing, customs and immigration systems, etc.
- airline capacity and route agreements
- deregulation, standardization and privatization
- intellectual property rights: ownership, control, access.

Sociocultural
- availability of leisure time
- US promotion abroad (private and public)
- travel barriers (international and domestic)
- political relations with source countries
- socio-demographic changes
- a more knowledgeable and demanding consumer
- growth in retiree tourist flows (ageing of certain populations).

Environmental
- population changes and ecological capacity
- government regulations on pollution and ecosystem degradation
- sustainable tourism development.

Source: Edgell (1993: 65).

DATA GATHERING TECHNIQUES

All the elements of the marketing audit depend upon a marketing information system through which the various external environments can be appraised and quantified. Marketing research provides the basis of the information:

> Marketing research is the specification, gathering, analysing and interpretation of data by management about its environment, with the goal of better understanding that environment and developing and evaluating courses of marketing action.
>
> (Aaker and Day, 1991: 21)

Intensive market analysis and research into people's tastes, preferences and attitudes are now the backbone of marketing planning. Market research grew up before the Second World War with the rise of public opinion polls which offered ways of researching consumer tastes. As early as the 1920s and 1930s advertising and marketing texts recommended the need to analyse markets and understand tastes but it was only after the Second World War that marketing research became a major industry routinely utilized by the large consumer goods companies in Europe, America and Japan in planning and evaluating their marketing programmes.

The sources of information on broader environmental trends include government statistics, surveys, research reports and articles in specialist and popular papers (although these must be regarded with caution since the media tend to pick up on startling or striking trends without investigating the way in which they were identified or evaluating their long-term importance).

Arguably the main change in the last two decades has been the IT revolution (see Chapter 17) which has speeded up and increased the volume of data it is possible to obtain and process on every aspect of the marketing process, from consumer profiling, distribution, sales, promotional performance and employee performance. As a result far more can be known about products, purchase patterns, tastes and competitive trends than ever before. In Chapter 4 some of the main market research techniques used in tourism marketing are presented.

STRATEGIC DECISION AREAS AND PLANNING FUNCTIONS

Once the tourism marketer has a clear idea of the market, its requirements and the organization's capacity to supply them based on analysis of past and previous performance (the marketing audit), future objectives and a programme for implementing them can be set. Marketing involves systematic, periodicized planning. At the heart of marketing planning is the development and management of the **marketing mix**.

The marketing mix

The marketing mix is the most fundamental concept in marketing. The concept draws the marketer's attention to the fact that, in offering anything for public consumption, it is necessary to manage four key decision areas.

- **Products** What is/are the product(s) to be offered? What are its features and benefits? How will it serve the needs of its customers? What are its competitors?
- **Price** At what price or prices should the product(s) be offered to the market(s)?
- **Place** Where should the product be distributed? Most packaged consumer goods and durables are distributed via retail outlets (supermarkets, chain and department stores, etc.). Tourism, as we shall see in Chapter 7, is a service which cannot be distributed in the same way.
- **Promotion** How should the tourism product(s) be publicized?

Table 1.4 The marketing mix for an airline: basic decision questions and mix features

---

Product: *What should the tourism product(s) be to attract and satisfy the defined audience(s)?*
- **Product mix:**
    - *Basic product features:* routes, frequency and direct/stop-over flying times.
    - *Point of delivery features:* location of airline terminals; appearance of terminal and age/appearance of planes; position and facilities for embarkation/disembarkation (e.g. fast boarding and fast customs clearance facilities).
    - *In-flight features:* plane design – external and interior; availability of space; acoustic experiences; catering options; crew livery and service standards; inflight facilities (films, teleconferencing, fax facilities, laptop computer terminals, etc.).

Price: *How should the product(s) be priced to create the desired level of demand among the defined audience(s)?*
- **Pricing mix:** basic ticket price(s); price levels compared to direct competitors (other airlines) and other carriers (e.g. rail, coach, ships operating between same destinations); differential prices for different target markets including loyalty programmes.

Place: *Where should the product be made available for purchase?*
- **Distribution mix:** location and character of booking options (own offices, travel agent, direct line, inclusive tour operator); ease and speed of booking methods.

Promotion: *How should promotion be managed to reach defined audiences with the right messages in the right media at an affordable cost?*
- **Promotional mix:** budgetary choices and allocations by promotional options; corporate identity/image programmes; advertising decisions (creative and media); public relations campaigns; sales promotional incentives; salesforce decisions. (N.B. Promotional decisions can be summarized as the 3 Ms – *M*oney, *M*essages and *M*edia.)

Promotion refers to the ways in which a product is made known to its target markets, and also to other groups who may influence the decision process.

These four Ps are central to marketing. Table 1.4 indicates the key questions that need to be asked in planning each part of the marketing mix and indicates some of their elements for an airline.

How many Ps are there in the tourism marketing mix?

Some tourism writers argue that in tourism there are more than four Ps which need to be managed. The table below itemizes how two other authors, Middleton and Morrison, have extended the marketing mix for tourism to seven Ps and eight Ps respectively.

Basic mix	Middleton	Morrison
Product	Price	Price
Place	Place	Place
Price	Product	Product
Promotion	Promotion	Promotion
	People	People
	Physical	Packaging
	Evidence	Programming
	Process	Partnership

Both Middleton and Morrison include **people** as a fifth element of the marketing mix in recognition that tourism provision crucially depends upon personal service. Customer service is now a focal issue in tourism marketing which is why we have devoted a special chapter to it (Chapter 18). **Physical evidence** consists of the tangible features of a tourism organization (furnishings, colour, noise). **Process** concerns the interactions that happen in service provision (customer involvement etc). In addition to people, Morrison's additional Ps comprise: **packaging** and **programming** (the way in which several products may be put together as a conceptual entity – an inclusive tour offer, for instance – and organized for the consumer into a programmed sequence of delivery), and **partnership** which draws attention to the fact that tourism marketing frequently involves collaboration and cooperation between several organizations (hotels, airlines, travel agents, tourist boards, etc.).

However, all the additional Ps can be seen as aspects of **product** design and delivery, so, for the purposes of this book, we shall focus on four Ps rather than extending the list. In Chapters 5–8 we shall discuss in detail the planning of each of the main four elements of the marketing mix.

MARKETING AS AN ORGANIZATIONAL REQUIREMENT

Marketing requires an organizational structure which identifies everyone with its philosophy and goals. It is not enough for marketing executives to understand marketing programmes – marketing can only be effective when **everyone** in the organization is identified with its goals and their roles in implementing the marketing programme. This may be particularly difficult to achieve in public sector organizations (national and local government) where conflicts of interest and opinion may arise out of the division of responsibilities between departments. In local government agencies tourism tends to be managed alongside many other public sector functions by different people. The leisure services department of a local authority may be anxious to promote tourism but the planning or environmental department may be against such essential tourism measures as signposting or creating access to fragile sites, while financial officers may be against spending any significant money on tourism which may be regarded as a 'soft' or undesirable option. Moreover, tourist board officials often come, not from a marketing background, but a civil service one, which may lead to ignorance of standard marketing practices.

One mechanism for establishing organizational integration and support for a marketing programme is the preparation of a **marketing plan** which is circulated for discussion and agreement to all people with a participatory role to play. The marketing plan and other aspects of marketing's organizational needs will be discussed in Chapter 9.

ORIGINS OF MARKETING

Many texts suggest that marketing is a comparatively recent idea and trace its development through a three-stage evolutionary process. According to this account business evolved through three phases:

- **The production era** In the early days of mass production when manufactured goods were still a novelty and suppliers were few, the firm produced what it thought was wanted and the consumer was glad to buy what was on offer. As a result, according to this version of business development, customers beat a path to the manufacturer without much need for the firm to adapt either its products to specific tastes or engage in heavy promotion to make the consumer aware of them. The firm was confident it could sell the goods it made and concentrated on maximizing production while minimizing costs of distribution and promotion.
- **The selling era** As competition multiplied and production capacities increased the firm could no longer rely on a guaranteed demand for everything it made. Instead it had to influence demand through intensive selling efforts to get its products distributed and bought in the face of competition. This created the so-called selling era which was marked by widespread use of high-pressure selling and advertising to generate demand for goods the manufacturer made.
- **The marketing era** As competition among suppliers increased still further and consumers multiplied and grew richer (particularly after

the Second World War) the problems of trying to sell what the company chose to make, even with intensive selling campaigns, grew greater. The consumer had many more choices and the opportunities to pick and choose between a wide variety of goods and brands. As a result, the manufacturer had to increasingly take into account the tastes and specific needs of customers in the **design** as well as the promotion of products. This required extensive knowledge of customer tastes and preferences before the introduction of the final products that would satisfy them. At this stage, according to the evolutionary orthodoxy, customer orientation became necessary and the emphasis shifted to the design and manufacture of goods tailor-made to consumers' tastes, rather than trying to bludgeon the customer, through sales and promotion, into buying what the firm had decided it wanted to sell. This process began in the 1930s with the development of the marketing research industry to assist in tracking consumer tastes, but was only extensively deployed in America and Western Europe (and later Japan) after the war, mainly by multi-national firms. One author believes that marketing had fully blossomed by 1964 (Stavely, 1989: 86–9).

This periodicization has been challenged by a number of writers. Summarizing their criticisms in any detail, or the alternative accounts of marketing development they propose, is outside the scope of this chapter. (A good summary of them can be found in Gilbert and Bailey (1990: 6–13).) However, it is worth observing that the marketing concept is not a new one. It is a great condescension to firms and individuals who built businesses before the mid-twentieth century to suppose that, before multi-nationals began to apply the marketing concept and the business schools and universities to theorize it, mainly after the Second World War, that it did not previously exist. The notion that it pays to give people goods which meet their needs and wants is as old as commerce itself. If we relook at the features of marketing identified by Crosier (1975) in his review of marketing definitions presented earlier, it is obvious that even the smallest supplier (say a corner shop or baker) has always:

(a) **targeted** products at specific consumers, even if only those people who live close;
(b) produced or offered goods **for** them;
(c) been a party to some kind of **transactional balance** in which the seller's interests and those of the consumer have had to be weighed (since customers do not buy things simply to please sellers and sellers do not stay in business as philanthropists to please buyers);
(d) has applied some kind of **orientation** to the consumer's needs.

In short, marketing, with its essential emphasis on serving customer needs, had always been an element of transactions between buyers and sellers but, until the growth of mass markets in which the seller became physically separated from the final customer, it tended to be an **informal,** personal understanding based on first-hand knowledge of customers and markets. Marketing as a **formal** philosophy, explicitly emphasizing the design and production of products that fitted customer needs and tastes, became necessary when firms were supplying mass, consumer markets over wide areas in expanded competitive environments, and where there was little first-hand knowledge of customers by marketing managers who increasingly became located in company headquarters far away from the 'coal face' where purchases took place. Even this did not happen for the first time in the twentieth century – it had already begun in the eighteenth century with firms such as Wedgewood whose ceramic goods were produced with a very clear understanding of different consumer needs and tastes, even though the markets for them were far removed from Wedgewood's factory in Stoke. In early tourism development entrepreneurs such as Thomas Cook and Arnold Lunn devised their early packages with a clear understanding of the requirements of the groups for whom they catered.

The central problem became distance from the consumer and market spread. When sellers and suppliers were in personal contact with their customers they knew their tastes, could assess price and product requirements, and they were generally aware of who, if any, their competitors were and what was necessary to match them in product terms. In such conditions of close contact marketing was responsive common sense. Once firms lost direct contact with their customers, their tastes, preferences and competitive temptations were less easily determined. The marketing concept was most prominently associated with large multinational, packaged goods companies selling a diverse variety of products and brands in highly competitive mass markets that were geographically spread over wide areas (typically a whole country or across many countries).

The concept of **customer orientation**, then, was not a major discovery but rather a rediscovery. What was new was its **systematic application to mass markets** supported by a developing range of the procedures, concepts and data gathering methods we have discussed earlier.

MARKETING SERVICES – INCLUDING TOURISM

Modern marketing originally developed in the markets for mass, consumer packaged goods and durables. Its applicability to services has only been recognized in the last two decades. One of the focal issues in service marketing theory has been the extent to which services differ from physical products. A number of differences have been identified:

- **Intangibility**. You can't see, feel or handle a service before you commit yourself to it. Compared to physical goods, services are difficult to measure, pre-test or demonstrate. This means that the promotional task assumes a greater importance since it is promotion that must create the product in the consumer's mind prior to purchase.

Promotion includes the management of evidence of a product through images, words, facts and figures, etc. The brochure is often the key vehicle of evidence management for tour operators.

- **Heterogeneity**. It is difficult to standardize a service since it will differ because of variations in customer experiences and variations in people's performance in delivering the service. Macdonald's, British Airways, Forte and other large tourism organizations attempt to overcome the latter problem by standardization of operational procedures and training methods in order to reduce variations in the human performances that constitute the service act. Chapter 18 looks at customer care and total quality programmes that address the problems of trying to standardize a service product.

- **Temporary ownership**. The consumer only owns a service temporarily (e.g. in renting a holiday cottage, buying an aircraft seat, paying for time in a museum).

- **Perishability** A service 'dies' if not consumed within a given time. It cannot be stored. A package holiday, an air seat or a hotel room which have not been booked at the time they are available are lost for good. Hence rapid demand shifts, typically through last minute price-cutting, are necessary to reduce the lost revenue accruing from unused capacity.

- **Inseparability**. Services are produced and consumed simultaneously in interactions between the customer and service provider with no delay between the two. As a result the tourism provider has only one chance to 'get it right' – the option of replacing or returning the product which exists in relation to physical products is excluded.

HOW TOURISM DIFFERS FROM OTHER SERVICES

As a service tourism is different from the marketing of physical products. However, it also manifests differences from other services. These differences include the following:

- **Tourism is more supply-led than other services**. Classically, as we have seen, marketing begins with a bottom-up sequence of planning that starts with detailed analysis of the consumer, the market and the environment and only then does marketing planning begin. Tourism marketing often reverses this pattern. Tourism tends to be supply-side rather than demand-side led. Whereas products in other service sectors such as finance and communications may be designed after intensive research into consumer requirements, tourism marketing is often a matter of taking an existing place product and then determining who might be interested in purchasing it. In the real world few organizations have the luxury of starting from scratch with consumer needs (though developers of the Channel Tunnel, EuroDisney, and CenterParcs were nearer to it than most destination promoters). The typical pattern in destination marketing is for national or regional authorities first to decide that they wish to develop tourism in their areas, and only **after** that decision to begin thinking about the potential customer/tourist.

The result is that destination marketing in particular has tended to be promotion-focused rather than consumer driven. Even today when tourism managers talk about the need to market tourism they often equate marketing with promotion rather than the thorough-going consumer orientation that underlies this book. And in many cases they are right. It is doubtful, for example, whether tourists would have vociferously campaigned for holidays in Portugal, Turkey or Thailand if national governments had not decided that they wanted to develop a tourist industry and then promoted it aggressively. These issues will be discussed at greater length in the chapter on product development (Chapter 5) and the chapter on destination marketing (Chapter 14).

- **The tourism product is frequently a multiple one involving cooperation between several suppliers** Tourism is often a combinatory product which requires the deliberate or non-deliberate collaboration of several different parties in providing the tourism product(s). An inclusive package holiday, for example, involves a partnership between, at minimum, a tour operator, an accommodation supplier, a transport carrier and, often, a range of destination organizations (car hire firms, attractions). Thus there may be variations in competence, expertise and safety standards, and clashes of vested interests among the organizations involved. Control over the product is thus dispersed and the shortcomings of one organization may adversely affect the reputation of others (e.g. poor hotel food or airport delays may bring criticism on a tour operator who set up a package holiday). This lack of product control is particularly evident in destination marketing by public sector bodies where the tourism organization may have little or no control over **any** aspect of the product. A national tourist board, for instance, cannot dictate what attractions should be launched in their areas or how hoteliers design their product, though it may be able to exercise some influence on accommodation standards through grading awards (see Chapter 14).

  Moreover, consumers plays a decisive role in the design of the tourism product by the way in which they experience it (e.g. through the friends made at a hotel or the activities they choose to do at a destination). In some cases a tourism experience may require little product structuring of any kind by a tourism organization (e.g. a camping/hiking holiday).

- **Tourism is a complex, extended product experience with no predictable critical evaluation point**. Tourism experiences can extend over several weeks and involve long phases of pre-trip anticipation and post-trip retrospective reflection. There are no obvious points of evaluation. In banking the service is rated when the loan comes through; a car repair firm is evaluated when the car comes back mended or not; but a holiday is often appraised and reappraised at different moments before, during and after it has taken place.

- **Tourism is a high-involvement, high-risk product to its consumers**. People's holiday decisions are very important to them and they are fraught with a number of kinds of perceived risk:

They involve committing large sums of money to something which cannot be seen or evaluated before purchase. The opportunity cost of a failed holiday is irreversible. If a holiday goes wrong that is it for another year. Most people do not have the additional vacation time or money to make good the holiday that went wrong . . . [Holidays] involve encounters with the unknown in terms of destinations, accommodation, transport, food and, increasingly, crime and all these involve risk.

(Seaton, 1994a: 373)

The degree of perceived risk involved in holiday decisions means that an important element of tourism marketing is about reassurance and security building (see Chapter 8).

- **Tourism is a product partly constituted by the dreams and fantasies of its customers** Services such as banking, medicine and car repair are consumed for rational, functional purposes. Tourism is often bound up with fantasies of self-realization, personal transformation, exotic escape, romantic sublimation and other transcendental yearnings. Tourism organizers need to understand these kind of motivations and reflect them in the 'dream' content of their promotional efforts. Morrison (1989) has commented on the more emotional and irrational buying appeals that underlie tourism choice, and the greater emphasis on 'stature and imagery' necessary in promoting it.

- **Tourism is a fragile industry susceptible to external forces beyond the control of its suppliers**. All service organizations are affected to some degree by external forces but tourism is prone to them more than any. A war, a terrorist outbreak, a hurricane or a health scare at a destination or a sharp dip in the economy in a tourist-originating country can gravely damage tourism overnight. The result is that tourism organizations sometimes have to make rapid responses to crises in the form of product redesign, price reductions or promotional damage limitation to combat sudden adverse trading conditions.

SUMMARY

This first chapter has attempted to provide a broad overview of what marketing is about and its particular application to tourism management. We have identified its characteristics as: an orientation to the consumer; a set of procedures and concepts for achieving consumer-orientation; data-gathering techniques for acquiring the information necessary for following the procedures and applying the concepts; an action planning programme built around the management of the marketing mix; and an organizational requirement. The whole marketing process can essentially be summarized as a six-step sequence:

1. Identify customers (current and predicted) and determine their wants and needs.
2. Audit the organization and scan its external environments including competition, finishing with a SWOT analysis.
3. Set quantified, periodicized strategic objectives.
4. Plan and implement a marketing mix to meet them by:
   - creating the right product;
   - pricing it right;
   - distributing it effectively;
   - promoting it to the consumer.
5. Make the necessary organizational provision for implementing the marketing programme.
6. Evaluate the results.

Over the course of the next eight chapters we shall analyse these elements in more detail.

REFERENCES

Aaker, D.A. and Day, G.S. (1991) quoted in Crawford-Welch, S. Marketing hospitality into the 21st century, *International Journal of Contemporary Hospitality Management*, **3**(3), 21–7.

Chase, H. (1994) *In Their Footsteps*, Henry Holt, New York.

Coltman, M.M. (1989) *Tourism Marketing*, Van Nostrand Reinhold, New York.

Crosier, K. (1975) What exactly is marketing?, *Quarterly Review of Marketing*, Winter, pp. 21–5.

Edgell, D. (1993) *World Tourism at the Millenium*, US Dept of Commerce, US Travel and Tourism Administration, April.

Gilbert, D. and Bailey, N. (1990) The development of marketing – a compendium of historical processes, *Quarterly Review of Marketing*, Winter, pp. 6–13.

Jain, S.C. (1981) *Marketing planning and strategy*, South Western Publishing, Cincinnati, Ohio.

Leiper, N. (1991) Deflating illusions of the tourism industry's size implications for education, in *New Horizons in Tourism Research*, University of Calgary, pp. 157–170.

Mason, P. (1993) 1993 outlook for leisure/family vacation travel, in *Proceedings of 18th Annual Travel Outlook Forum*, US Travel Data Center.

Mercer, D. (1992) *Marketing*, Blackwell, Oxford.

Middleton, V. (1988) *Marketing in travel and tourism*, Heinemann, Oxford.

Morrison, A.M. (1989) *Hospitality and Travel Marketing*, Delmar, New York.

Naisbitt, J. (1982) *Megatrends*, Warner Books, New York.

NTC Publications (1994) *European Marketing Pocket Book*, NTC Publications, Henley on Thames, Oxon.

Papadopoulos, S. (1989) A conceptual tourism marketing planning model: Part 1, *European Journal of Marketing*, **23**(1), 36.

Perugia (1991) *Computer Networking and the Public Tourism Organization*, Centro Italiano di Studi Superiori sul Turismo, Assisi.

Riley, (1994) Movie induced tourism, in Seaton, A.V. (ed.) *Tourism: The State of the Art*, Wiley, Chichester, pp. 453–8.

Roszak, T. (1994) *The Cult of Information*, University of California Press, Berkeley.

Sanderson, S.M. and Luffman, G.A. (1979) Strategic planning and environmental analysis, *European Journal of Marketing*, **22**(2), 16.

Seaton, A.V. (1994a) Tourism and the media, in Witt, S.J. and the Moutinho, L. (eds), *Tourism Marketing and Management Handbook*, Prentice-Hall, Hemel Hempstead, Herts, pp. 135–9.

Seaton, A.V. (1994b) Promotional strategies, in Witt, S.J. and and Moutinho, L. (eds), *Tourism Marketing and Management Handbook*, Prentice-Hall, Hemel Hempstead, Herts, pp. 371–6.

Smith, S. (1990) *Tourism Analysis*, Longman, Harlow, Essex.

Smith, V. (1977, revised edn, 1989) *Hosts and Guests: The Anthropology of Tourism*, University of Philadelphia, Philadelphia.

Stavely, N. (1989) The rise and rise of marketing, *ADMAP*, November, pp. 86–9.

STB (Scottish Tourist Board)/STRU (Scottish Tourism Research Unit, Strathclyde University) (1996) *The Comparative Evaluation of Tourism Destination Performance: Scotland and European Tourism 1985–1994*, STB, Edinburgh.

Toffler, A. (1970) *Future Shock*, Bodley Head, London.

Williams, A.P. and Hobson, J.S.P. (1994) Tourism – the next generation: virtual reality and surrogate travel – is it the future of the tourism industry?, in Seaton, A.V. (ed.), *Tourism: The State of the Art*, Wiley, Chichester, pp. 283–90.

REVIEW QUESTIONS

1. What do you see as the main differences between services marketing and the marketing of physical goods?
2. What particular features does tourism have which distinguish it from other services?
3. Take a tourism product for which you have access to data and try to work out the main elements of the marketing mix which support it.
4. What factors might be examined in performing an environmental scan for UK seaside resorts?

2 The analysis of tourism demand: market segmentation

A.V. Seaton

OBJECTIVES

By the end of this chapter the reader should:

- understand the meaning and purposes of market segmentation;
- understand the main criteria for the successful deployment of market segmentation;
- have a working knowledge of some of the major kinds of segmentation used to classify and understand tourists and the kinds of tourism they engage in;
- be aware of general segmentation approaches to host populations, as stakeholders, in the tourism process.

SEGMENTATION AND TOURISM PROPENSITY

Since marketing is centrally concerned with consumer orientation the starting point for the tourism planner must be the identification and understanding of the customer. In this chapter and the next we shall look at some of the types of analysis and data that can be used to profile customers. We shall also consider a kind of consumer ignored in most tourism marketing texts – the host population in tourism destination marketing, and look at ways of classifying them as **stakeholders** in the tourism process.

There is virtually no product which is equally consumed by all sectors of the population. Consumption tends to be skewed in such a way that a minority of the population consumes a majority of the product. This is sometimes known as the **Pareto effect**, after the Italian sociologist who observed that 80% of the wealth of Italy in the late nineteenth century was owned by 20% of the population. In travel and tourism a similar effect means that some people exhibit a greater **propensity** to travel than others. Propensity to travel in a particular country can be calculated by dividing the number of people making a trip by the size of the total population and multiplying by 100:

$$\frac{P \text{ (persons making on trip)}}{\text{Total population (country or group)}} \times 100 = \text{Net travel propensity}$$

In America only about 11% of the population have passports so 100% of international travel is undertaken by 11% of the population (though not necessarily in the same year). In the UK only 60% of the population goes on holiday in any year, between 30 and 35% go abroad and only about 25% take two or more holidays a year.

Travel propensity can be applied to sub-populations. For instance, it would be possible to calculate travel propensity among 18–25 years olds, senior citizens or women business executives provided their total numbers/proportions in a country were known and also the number/proportion who engaged in travel activity over a specified period. Travel propensity can also be calculated on a regional basis (e.g. in the USA the state of California has a higher international tourism propensity than Indiana, and the 'home counties' of the south-east of England a greater propensity than the north-west). Travel propensity thus provides a broad indicator of travel potential in relation to defined populations. A number of general characteristics are known to be regularly associated with populations evincing high tourism propensity and a number with lower travel propensity. Table 2.1 contrasts them.

Travel propensity provides a broad, base-line indication of variations in tourist demand. But it is only a start. Neither all high propensity travellers nor lower propensity travellers are the same. Though they may share some features in common, in many other respects they may be different. More refined measures are required to provide more precise profiles on travellers for successful marketing planning. This brings us to the main subject of this chapter, market segmentation, which may be defined as: '. . . the task of breaking the total market into segments that share common properties' (Kotler, 1988: 69).

Table 2.1 Tourism propensity – general characteristics

Higher propensity	Lower propensity
Higher income groups (ABC1 groups in UK)	Lower income groups (C2DE groups in UK)
With higher education	Secondary education only
Urban populations	Rural populations
Own one or more cars	No car
Executive occupational status	Non-executive occupational status
West European, Australasian, American and Japanese nationality	Nationals of other countries
Four or more weeks paid holiday	Two or less weeks paid holiday

Market segmentation is the attempt to pinpoint homogeneous consumer groups within broad, heterogeneous populations in order to develop and implement marketing programmes specifically designed for their needs. It is thus using a sniper's rifle for precise target marketing rather than shotgunning the whole population. It recognizes that all people may be equal but some are equaller than others in the eyes of marketers trying to identify the most viable markets to compete for.

Segmentation is essential because even large tourism organizations can rarely afford marketing programmes aimed at the entire tourist market. The large tour operators commonly target three main markets: young singles and couples, the family market and the older market, but they do not, for example, produce a diverse variety of products for special interest groups. Segmentation enables tourism organizations to prioritize and focus their efforts on a few customer groups. It is thus both a response to markets and a necessary form of resource limitation. As Mercer remarks:

> In one sense segmentation is a *strategy* used by vendors to concentrate, and thus optimize, the uses of their resources within an overall market. In another sense it is also that group of *techniques* which are used by these vendors for segmenting their market.
>
> (Mercer, 1992: 252)

WHAT MAKES A CONSUMER SEGMENT WORTHWHILE?

A number of criteria need to be met before a market segment is worth targeting. These include the following.

- The market must be **measurable** and **substantial**. The number of people in a segment will determine whether or not it is worth a tourism enterprise developing marketing programmes directed to it.
- The market must be **cohesive** and **discrete**, one that can be identified as sharing a number of common characteristics. Unless a segment can be exactly **specified** and **differentiated** from both the population at large and other segments, it is unlikely to be a useful one.
- The market must be an **appropriate** one for a tourism organization to target. Not all identified segments, however substantial and well defined, are viable for every tourism enterprise. The segment has to be considered in relation to the products the tourism organization can offer and also the number of competitors already targeting the segment. It would not, for instance, be in the interests of a specialist tour operator to target the mass market, however substantial it might be.
- The segment must be **accessible** through distribution and promotional channels. An essential requirement for effective market segmentation is the need to **communicate** to the target group effectively. This means that communication channels must exist for reaching the group and the organization must be able to afford to use them.

THE MAIN KINDS OF MARKET SEGMENTATION

Segmentation is the most extensively researched area in tourism marketing. Both academics and practitioners have produced thousands of studies specific to particular markets on what tourism consumers are like. There are few tourism organizations of any significance which do not now periodically carry out visitor studies to profile their customers. Large organizations such as airlines, hotel chains and tour operators maintain sophisticated IT databases so that it is possible for them to make ongoing longitudinal analyses (i.e. analyses of their customer profiles over time) and many companies, in addition, carry out continuous consumer satisfaction studies (hotel room questionnaires, in-flight surveys, end-of-tour self-completion forms, etc.) which allow them to amass extensive data on the perceptions and attitudes of tourists to their products.

There are many different ways of segmenting tourism markets. Smith (1990a) has grouped them into two broad categories:

- segmentation based on **trip descriptors**;
- segmentation based on **tourist descriptors**.

Trip descriptors

This category of segmentation breaks down the total tourism market by different types of trip. It concentrates not on describing the person but the kind of trip taken.

Many tourism studies divide trips into four basic types: (a) recreational/pleasure; (b) visiting friends and relatives (VFR); (c) business; (d) other. Table 2.2 shows domestic tourist trips within the UK by the four categories in 1992.

Once the four basic categories have been identified it is then possible to gather further details about each kind of trip.

Recreational trips

Recreational trips are the core of the travel and tourism industry. They consist of all those voluntary trips undertaken as holidays. It is essential for most tourism organizations to know in considerable detail their

Table 2.2 Purpose of domestic travel in the UK 1992 (% of total trips)

	UK	England	Scotland	Wales	N. Ireland
VFR	22	24	17	11	15
Pleasure	63	60	65	80	71
Business	11	11	12	6	10
Other	4	5	7	4	4

Source: UKTS (1993: 7).

structure and composition. Recreational trips can be subdivided along a number of additional descriptors which include the following:

* destination: long haul, European, domestic, local;
* how booked: direct/through a travel agent;
* organizational form: full package/part package/independent;
* package type: mass or specialist;
* package cost: cheap/premium;
* transport used: car, air, train, etc.;
* accommodation used and gradings: hotel, bed and breakfast, self catering, etc.;
* trip duration: day trip, short break, long stay;
* travelling distance;
* timing: season, month, week, day, time of day.

Visitor studies commonly include questions designed to elicit data on some or all of these descriptors. A regional attraction such as a museum may analyse what proportion of the trips made by its visitors are local and how many come from outside the area. A national tourist board will attempt to quantify its visitors in terms of domestic/international trips, package/independent trips, seasonal distribution of trips, etc.

Business

In America business tourism accounted for 158 million trips in 1992 and involved 35.5 million travellers. An American Express study of ten European countries in 1993 calculated the total market as $141 billion, 31% of which was spent abroad. Germany accounted for 28% of the total at $38 billion with the UK and France at $30.3 billion and $25.3 billion respectively.

Although the numbers of people taking business trips is smaller and the trips are usually shorter than recreational trips, the daily expenditure per head is higher. As a result tourism promoters are eager to attract business trips to their destination. Business trips do not have the same seasonal peaks as much recreational tourism, although they are often affected by economic conditions. The number of business trips often declines in times of economic downturn but the total number of people taking them, the business community, remains more stable:

> . . . the number of trips a traveller takes can be increased or decreased depending on the so called 'tides of fortune' but the number of business travellers is fairly constant even in periods of economic boom.
>
> (Stewart, 1992: 86)

Once the total market for business travel has been identified it can be analysed through further trip descriptors which include some of the ones we saw in the analysis of recreational tourism trips. These include:

* destination/venue;
* how booked: by company, in-house travel agency, external travel agency;

- duration of trip;
- accommodation type;
- transport.

Business travel is a mixture of voluntary and unavoidable travel. Many trips have to be taken in the day-to-day management of businesses but things such as conventions and exhibitions are less constricted. As a result a particularly important differentiation to make in segmenting business travel is that between convention, conference and exhibition trips and others. Many cities in the developed world now have their own convention bureaux whose job is to attract fairs, exhibitions and conferences to their destinations. (The business market is discussed in detail in Chapter 13.) Table 2.3 provides some descriptors of business travel in the USA.

Visiting friends and relatives

The third major category of trip descriptor is the VFR category, those people travelling to visit friends and relatives. In the past this market has tended to be downgraded since VFR tourists spend less than recreational and business tourists. However, set against this is the fact that they stay longer, and are more widely spread throughout the year and thus less prone to the seasonality patterns of recreational tourists (Seaton, 1994). In some locations such as N. Ireland and the Pas De Calais in northern France VFR travellers may be the major kind of tourist. An unusual effect of the World Cup soccer tournament of 1994 was heavy bookings of VFR flights from Britain to Dublin; this was not because the World Cup was being held there – it was being staged in America – but because many Irish expatriates

Table 2.3 Some trip descriptors on business travel in America

	%
Length of trip	
2–3 days	38
6+ days	12
No stay on most recent trip	16
Transport used	
Car	48
Air	31
Company car	11
Rental car	4
Kind of business trip	
Conventions	48
Company operations	11
Consulting	10
Management reasons	7

Source: US Travel Data Center's National Survey 1991.

wanted to return to their country to see their team on television with their friends and relatives!

A particular sector of VFR travellers of growing interest to tourism marketers are 'ethnic' tourists – emigrants returning to their former home countries and relatives visiting them in their new ones. There is a thriving VFR market between Britain and former colonies such as Australia and Canada, and between European countries and America, derived from previous migration patterns. There are specialist travel agencies in Britain serving the needs of immigrants from Asia, and Holloway and Plant note that in Germany specialist travel agencies now exist to service the travel needs of 'Gastarbeiters', guest workers from Turkey and the former Yugoslavia (Holloway and Plant, 1992: 52).

One of the most recent findings in VFR research is the discovery that there are differences within the VFR category between those people visiting friends and those visiting relatives. Following preliminary work indicating the possible advantages of splitting the VFR category (Seaton, 1994), a study based on international VFR trips to N. Ireland (which accounts for about 40% of tourism to that country) between 1991 and 1993 found that almost 80% of VFR trips were actually made to relatives, and that there were major differences in the profiles of relative- and friend-oriented trips (Seaton and Tagg, 1996). In Britain a pilot test is being run in 1995/6 by sponsors of the UK Tourism Survey to determine to what extent domestic VFR trips differ among three groups: those visiting friends, those visiting relatives and people doing both.

Tourist descriptors

The second major kind of segmentation focuses not on the trip but the person making it. A way of approaching the diverse forms of tourist descriptors is through a series of simple questions: 'Who wants what, why, when, where and how much?' The answers to them indicate some of the common methods of segmentation:

- Who? socio-demographic data.
- Wants what? benefit segmentation.
- When? segmentation by season, time and occasion.
- Where? benefit by geography (destination, country/region of origin, etc.).
- How much? benefit by volume of usage (e.g. frequent vs. regular travellers).

We shall now consider some of the techniques involved in these questions in more detail.

Socio-demographics

Socio-demographic segmentation is an attempt to describe populations by a range of physical or social characteristics including income, occupation, family size and lifecycle, age, location, etc.

Social grading

For many years UK advertisers and marketers have used social grading as an indicator of behaviour. Six main classifications of social grading have been commonly used. They are as follows (with population proportions in each in brackets):

A   Upper middle class (3.1%): higher managerial, administrative and professional.

B   Middle class (15.7%): intermediate managerial, administrative and professional.

C1   Lower middle class (25.7%): supervisory, clerical, junior managerial, etc.

C2   Skilled working class (26%): skilled manual workers.

D   Working class (17%): semi- and unskilled workers.

E   Those at level of subsistence (12.6%): state pensioners, widowers, etc.

Social grading does not necessarily predict any specific tourism choice but it acts as a major indicator of the most likely market for many kinds of tourism. An article reviewing social stratification in tourism choices and behaviour over the last fifty years in the UK found that, though total tourism volumes among all classes had increased significantly, the proportion of participation among the different social groups remained significantly biased to ABC1 groups. They were more likely to travel abroad, take more than one holiday a year and also more likely to participate in wilderness tourism and visit art galleries (the latter two activities suggest that class is as much about educational and cultural access as income since neither are expensive) (Seaton, 1992). Some destinations exhibit strong class profiles: 70% of UK visitors to France come from the top three social grades (ABC1s) and a visitor study carried out in the Shetland Isles in 1992 found that 75% of visitors were ABC1s.

In 1989 Touche Ross, the management consultants, carried out a national study into museum visitors which showed that people in the ABC1 social grades were more likely to be museum visitors than others. In the same year nine museums and art galleries in the North-East of England also carried out visitor surveys which again showed that people in ABC1 social gradings were far more likely to be visitors than those in social grades C2DE. The results of the two studies are summarized in Table 2.4 (including the 36% of those surveyed who did not supply occupational data on their questionnaires).

Though America does not officially have a class system, income and education are powerful influences on travel, as they are in Europe. Davidoff and Davidoff, using data collected by Travel Pulse Opinion Research Corporation between 1978 and 1982, showed that the proportion of *non-travellers* increases in inverse proportion to household income with the majority of non-travellers, 36%, coming from those earning less than $15 000 and the lowest number among those of $35 000+. The same study

Table 2.4 Summarized results of visitor studies

	Touche Ross 1989 national survey %	Museum visitors, Tyne and Wear %	population %
AB	22	17	18
C1	43	30	23
C2	7	7	27
D	4	5	18
E	5	5	14
No answer	19	36	—

Source: Touche-Ross/Tyne and Wear Museums, 1989/1990.

showed that 40% of those who finished their education after high school were non-travellers, while only 5% who had attended graduate school (Davidoff and Davidoff, 1983: 10).

Family and family lifecycle

The family supplies the central market for recreational tourism (between 70 and 80% of it in the USA). Thus family profiles are important in tourism planning. One method of understanding family behaviour is through the family lifecycle concept. First developed by sociologists in the 1950s, it is based on the hypothesis that people pass through several stages of family life each of which is associated with different patterns of activity and consumption. The stages comprised:

*   Bachelor stage: young singles not living at home.
*   Newly married or coupled persons without children.
*   Full nest I: couples with youngest child under 5.
*   Full nest II: couples with youngest child 6–11.
*   Full nest III: older couples with dependent children 11–18.
*   Empty nest I: older couples, no children at home, head of family still working.
*   Empty nest II: older couples, no children at home, head of family retired.
*   Solitary survivors in labour force.
*   Solitary survivor retired.

These original groupings now look rather dated since they were implicitly based on the nuclear family. With greatly increased levels of divorce and single parent families (single parent mothers have tripled in Britain since 1979), and also the increase in gay couples, lifecycle phases in the 1990s could be extended to include:

*   Single parents with children: this group includes both unmarried single parents as well as divorcees, whose children may get two holidays taken with each parent at different times of the year.

- Gay couples: a group that includes, not just the young, but older couples whose joint earning power may make them high consumers of tourism.

Position in family lifecycle affects tourism expenditure-per-head (smaller for full nesters than empty nesters), facilities necessary (e.g. creches for full nest I and II families, bars/discos for young singles, etc.) and many other aspects of tourist provision. Family lifecycle segmentation is used in tourism in the product planning of mass tour operators who commonly market to several of the main life stage groups: young un-marrieds, families with children and the older market. The American travel market to Europe is strongly made up of empty nesters.

Age

It is obvious that age affects recreational and vacation choices. Package operators such as Twenties, Saga and Club International design holidays which are strongly based on age. Age will be an important factor in tourism forecasting over the next two decades because the age structure of the population is undergoing major changes in the West. In America the 50+ is the fastest growing population group. As one commentator has observed:

> These new mature travellers are better travelled, more highly educated and in better physical and financial condition than their predecessors. They will be more demanding of the unique and more demanding of convenience. For these travellers, vacations are opportunities to pamper themselves with treatment and surroundings they have not realized in their day-to-day lives. This group controls over 50% of the nation's wealth and more of the national expendable income.
>
> (Frenkel, 1992: 111)

In Britain the picture of an increasingly older population is similar. 15–19 year olds declined from 3.8 million in 1987 to 3.2 million in 1991 and are forecast to diminish to 3.1 million by 1996. Between now and 2000 the two fastest growing populations will be the middle aged and over 75s. There will be more consumers over 45 than under 30 in 1995. By 2030 deaths will exceed births and the population will begin shrinking. There will be 3.4 million people aged 80 and over, three and a half times more than in 1961. This ageing of the population is why 'Grey Panthers' are becoming a high-interest segment to marketers of the 1990s as Yuppies were to those of the 1980s. One consultancy, Development Business in the UK, has segmented the older population into life orientation groups: Retirement Aware, Wind-down, Lifestyle Adjustment, Leisure Years and Inactive (Gwyther, 1992).

Gender

Recently some tourism organizations have become increasingly interested in special provision for women travellers, particularly in the business travel market. According to some estimates women business travellers now account for 13% in Europe and 23% in the UK (Davidson, 1994: 378–9). Other estimates put the UK figure for women business travellers as high as 35% with an increase to 50% predicted by the end of the century. Some hotel groups have introduced facilities for business women. Forte hotels have Lady Crest rooms which are provided with ironing boards, spyholes and deadlocks on doors, special clothes hangers, women's magazines and baskets of fresh fruit. Holiday Inn offers Ten Absolute Standards for women guests which include: assistance with luggage, prompt service in bars, choice of tables and choice of room location (Churchill, 1994: 5).

Geographic data

Geographical data on tourists, both in terms of the generating regions from which they come and the destination regions at which they arrive, has always been central to tourism analysis. At a global level 70% of tourists come from Europe with four nations – the UK, Germany, France and Holland – accounting for the majority. At the micro level of the individual trip, distance and travelling time can influence choices of destinations, attractions and accommodation. Luxury hotels are frequently located within 30 mins–1 hour from a main airport, conference centre and/or major resort areas. One of the first tasks of segmentation for any tourism organization is that of examining the geographic origins of its visitors or potential visitors. This can be done by collecting data on the number of visitors, trips or bednights generated from a particular place, e.g. the USA and Germany are the two main sources of overseas visitors to Scotland.

Generating population development indexing

Geographical analysis can be extended by calculating **generating population development indices (GPDIs)** for tourism products, particularly destinations. The technique was first applied in packaged goods marketing by such organizations as Procter & Gamble to assess the relative strength of different geographical markets. In its adapted form it can be used to appraise the *comparative potential of different generating populations* in relation to specific destinations and other tourism products. To produce a GPDI it is necessary to know two things:

- the percentage and/or numbers of customers/tourists for a product/ destination who originate from one population group (country, town, region, socio-economic group, etc.);
- the percentage and/or numbers which that population group occupies within the total population which generated it.

The GPDI is then arrived at by dividing the one by the other and multiplying by 100:

GPDI =

$$\frac{\% \text{ generating population group at destination/using tourist product}}{\% \text{ of generating population group within total generating population}}$$

EXAMPLE 2.1

GPDI: Expenditure by generating region

In 1993 the main tourism revenue in Scotland was generated from English visitors, but there were variations in the English regions which generated it. Table 2.5 shows what proportion of tourism revenue was generated from different areas of England and what the GPDIs were.

These kinds of regional analyses can be applied to many destinations and attractions. In America, for example, the proportion of overseas tourists generated from the state of California is higher than that which its total population occupies as a proportion of the US population.

GPDIs can be applied not just to physical geographic analysis but also to social geographic analysis, as in Example 2.2.

EXAMPLE 2.2

GPDI by social grading

The main generating country of tourists to Scotland in terms of trips is Britain. Of those British tourists who make trips to Scotland 60% are in social categories ABC1 and 40% in the lower C2DE grades. Nationally, ABC1s are 42% of the British population and C2DEs 58%. The GPDI for the two groups is thus:

$$\text{ABC1 GPDI} = \frac{60}{40} \times 100 = 148$$

$$\text{C2DE GPDI} = \frac{40}{58} \times 100 = 69$$

Table 2.5 Proportions of tourism revenue generated by region

	% of UK population	% of tourism expenditure in Scotland	GPDI
South East	30.5	24	79
North	5.3	7	132
Yorkshire/Humberside	8.6	6	70
South West	8.2	5	61
Midlands	16.1	9	56

GPDIs are useful because they highlight the fact that it is not just the *absolute* proportion/amount of tourists/revenue generated from a population group which is important but the proportion/amount relative to the populations from which the group comes. In Example 2.1 above the GPDIs suggest that the North of England may have more market potential than the Midlands for Scottish tourism, even though it generates 2% less expenditure, because its GPDI is much higher, suggesting that further development will be easier than in the Midlands where the GPDI is lower.

The examples show how GPDIs may be produced to index populations on the basis of geography and social grading, but they can be produced to quantify other population variables in tourist generation provided data is available on both the population group's presence at the destination *and* its proportionate presence in the originating population. GPDIs can usefully be applied to age groups (e.g. cruise passengers consist of a disproportionately large per centage of people over 50 relative to the proportion of over-50s in the general population).

Once GPDIs are calculated for a range of population groups and the actual numbers of people in each are known, the tourism marketer will become aware that four market patterns of tourism population group generation are possible:

(a)   high population index, large group;
(b)   high population index, small group;
(c)   low population index, small group;
(d)   low population index, large group.

Once the four kinds of market pattern have been identified for specific population groups the marketer then has to decide how to prioritize them as market segments. The priority market will always be market group (a) which is both numerous and has a high index while the least attractive will always be market group (c) which has both a low index and a small total number of people in it. However, markets (b) and (d) may also be viable segments, the first because a high index in a limited population may be the basis for a successful niche market; the latter because, though the index may be low, if the market is numerous, it may still be a viable segment that can be developed further.

Generating population development indexing is particularly valuable when maintained over time. By recording GPDIs on a year-by-year basis marketers can identify which generating areas are strengthening and weakening. GPDI analysis can also be performed on competitive products, e.g. by destination promoters. A country marketer (e.g. a national tourist board) can calculate GPDIs for other national destinations using international visitor data and population statistics on the generating countries.

The GPDI principle has been developed for tourism in the USA using slightly different terminology by a group at Florida State University. A good account of its strategic implications can be found in Bonn (1994).

Geodemographic data

Another variation of geographic segmentation is geodemographics. Based on the premise that people living in similar residential areas may share common consumption characteristics, it is an attempt to use residential data based on postcode addresses (zip codes in the USA) and census data, often combined with further survey data, to provide profiles of neighbourhoods. In the UK, for instance, there are 22 million postal addresses, 1.3 million full postcodes, 170 000 postcode groups and 9000 postal sectors. This means that there are approximately 17 households at postcode level, 130 per postcode group and 2500 at postal sector levels.

Geographic data can be obtained by buying area profiles from a number of commercial companies which have analysed countries and supplemented it with additional data on consumption patterns, tastes, etc. There are several market research firms offering geodemographic data, the oldest of which in the UK is CACI, developers of the ACORN system, established in 1979. Geodemographic data can also be generated by individual tourism enterprises through recording the post codes of their customers and visitors when they survey them, or when they 'pass through the turnstiles' as customers making a booking or trip. Yorkshire National Parks have identified from what residential areas their main visitors come through progressive data-basing. As a result their manager now broadcasts on a local radio station which reaches the residential areas known to generate the most visitors.

Geodemographics can be used to help with: the selection of retail location (e.g. where to open a travel agency or restaurant); the preparation of mailing lists for direct marketing campaigns; and for assessing the catchment areas of likely visitors to tourism attractions.

There are some problems with geodemographics including the following:

- **Up-to-date address listings**. People move house in the UK on average every seven years. This need not be an insuperable problem, unless

---

CASE STUDY 2.1

ACORN

CACI's ACORN system has been applied in several tourism markets. In 1993 CACI reported that customer analysis based on ACORN and customer surveys had been used to supply Forte with data on their Harvester Restaurant chain. The research provided information which was used to assist in 'marketing on a site by site basis, promoting the brand, targeting different customer types, and tailoring sites to fit local potential and extending the network to new profitable areas'.

In the same year CACI also provided database assistance linked to ACORN to the Sally ferry line which runs cross-Channel ferries between Ramsgate and Dunkirk. The database included customer data on frequency of travel, length of stay and value of booking.

Source: *Marketing Systems Today*, Vol. 7. No. 2 (Winter 1992 – Spring 1993).

specific names and addresses are essential for direct mail shots. If it is only the *general residential profiles* that are important then the validity of ACORN studies holds provided an area does not change its social character.

- **Relating classifications to product behaviour and specific product choice**. Simply knowing the approximate profile of residents within an area, even assuming they are accurate, does not mean that a planner can predict specific product usage (e.g. likelihood to book with a particular tour operator or choose a specific destination). Residential data has to augmented with other kinds of data linking residential profiles to product usage. In the UK CACI augments its residential data with Target Group Index (TGI) data, a major national study of product usage, media habits and activities. In the Forte case described earlier CACI augmented the data by carrying out questionnaire research on the premises of Forte and then analysing the residential profiles of the customers who filled them in.
- **Non-homogeniety of areas**. ACORN is based on the assumption that consistent groupings of consumers exist within residential areas. In reality few neighbourhoods have such clone-like, identikit homogeneity in their residents.
- **Mass market applications**. For the mass tour operator and other mass tourism organizations ACORN may be too refined a measure to be useful, although for small specialist tourism products (up-market ski holidays, special interest holidays and business travel) geodemographic segmentation may provide leads on niche markets associated with residential patterns.

Psychographics and lifestyle

Psychographics and lifestyle segmentation is based on personality traits, attitudes, motivations and activities.

Lifestyle segmentation was the 'flavour of the month' in marketing circles in the late 1970s and through much of the 1980s. First described by Plummer (1974), lifestyle segmentation was an attempt to combine data on the interests, activities and opinions of consumers with standard demographics in an attempt to study them 'in the round', instead of on the basis of a few discrete characteristics (age, class, occupation, etc.). Its potential value has been summarized as follows:

> Psychographic segmentation is exceptionally useful, employing a range of variables which measure respondent activities (manner of spending time), interests (what are their priorities in life), opinions and attitudes (about themselves and the world) and fundamental characteristics (income, stage in lifecycle, education, place of residence).
>
> (Weber, 1992: 118)

Psychographic segmentation depended upon carrying out enormously detailed questionnaires with representative populations of consumers (national or grouped according to some homogeneous feature) and then identifying lifestyle groups within them through statistical analysis.

One of the problems with lifestyle segmentation was that it often set out to identify broad lifestyles within *the general population* rather than *product-related* lifestyles (e.g. types of flyer, types of hotel guest). One lifestyle grouping which was product- and market-specific was that developed by the British Tourism Authority (BTA, 1994: 9) to segment American travellers to Britain. It identified four kinds of American visitor to Britain:

1. **First-time visitor:** stays in London and concentrates on traditional attractions. Occasionally visits outside London (Windsor and other well-known sights).
2. **The traditionalist:** divides time between London and established regional locations (Oxford, Chester) using train and occasionally staying B & B. Seeks enriching vacation.
3. **The explorer:** wants to know country better. Stays outside London for most of time using cities as base for touring Wales, Scotland, etc.
4. **The Britophile:** knows a lot about Britain, returns regularly, stays in upmarket inns and B & Bs, and probably has friends and relatives in Britain.

Another tourist-specific grouping is that developed by Plog (1974) in America. Plog proposed that tourists could be broadly categorized on a continuum between two extreme personality types based on their motivations, destination and activity preferences. At one end of the spectrum were *psychocentrics* and at the other *allocentrics*. The general difference between the two groups was that the former were more cautious and conservative in their holiday tastes compared to the latter: 'Simply stated, allocentrics are much more venturesome and exploring than their conservative counterparts' (Plog, 1990: 43).

Pearce has developed Plog's ideas to provide the typology of the two shown in the diagram overleaf. The typology has been widely reproduced in the literature of tourism but there are a number of questions about it, namely:

- The dichotomous contrasts between allocentrics and psychocentrics seem extremely clear-cut. In fairness it should be said that Plog accepts that the typology should be seen as a continuous scale with few people at either extreme and most occupying *mid-centric* positions.
- Many people may fall into both categories at different times, particularly now that many people are taking more than one holiday each year. The same person who takes an allocentric short break, walking or activity holiday might also take a more passive sun, sea and sand psychocentric package holiday later in the summer. If this is the case is it possible to refer to a 'personality type'?
- In a British context the contrasts seem much more likely to be the result of sociological or demographic factors, particularly social grading and education, rather than psychological characteristics. As we have

Psychocentrics	**Allocentrics**
Prefer the familiar in travel destinations	Prefer non-tourist areas
Like commonplace activities at travel destinations	Enjoy sense of discovery and delight in new experiences, before others have visited the area
	Prefer novel and different destinations
Prefer sun 'n' fun spots, including considerable relaxation	
Low activity level	High activity level
Prefer destinations they can drive to	Prefer flying to destinations
Prefer heavy tourist accommodations, such as heavy hotel development, family type restaurants, and tourist shops	Tour accommodation should include adequate-to-good hotels and food, not necessarily modern or chain-type hotels, and few 'tourist' type attractions
Prefer familiar atmosphere (hamburger stands, familiar type entertainment, absence of competitive atmosphere)	Enjoy meeting and dealing with people from a strange or foreign culture
Complete tour packaging appropriate, with heavy scheduling of activities	Tour arrangements should include basics (transportation and hotels) and allow considerable freedom and flexibility

Source: Pearce (1987: 15)

suggested ABC1s tend to allocentric tourism choices while C2DEs often resemble psychocentrics in their tourism behaviour. Plog's observation that allocentrics are more likely to use print (Plog, 1990) as a medium, while psychocentrics use TV, is also consistent with sociological factors rather than psychographic since ABC1s are known to read more than C2DEs.

- In addition, some of the individual variables associated with the two types of traveller are *culturally specific* to America, particularly flying and long-haul travel as allocentric features. In the UK holidays such as walking and rambling which can be done 'on the back doorstep' with a modest travel component would be allocentric, while a flight-based holiday in Florida would most likely be psychocentric in most of its features.

Very little critical examination of Plog's typology has been made, partly one suspects because Plog never published details of his methodology or full results of his findings. Plog was able to produce a robust refutation of one critique of his theory by Smith (1990b) mainly on methodological grounds, but the two critical questions still remain: is it a sociological rather than a psychological theory, and is it culturally specific to American travellers?

Behavioural segmentation: benefits and product usage

Tourism markets can also be segmented on the basis of the kinds of tourism people choose and the amounts they consume.

Benefits

Benefit segmentation has been described by one writer as: 'an approach to segmentation whereby it is possible to identify market segments by causal factors rather than descriptive factors' (Haley, 1968: 30).

In tourism terms benefit segmentation means attempting to establish what things the tourist wants to get out of a trip and the services necessary to support it (e.g. hotel specifications, desired characteristics of the transport component and recreational or business facilities, etc.). Tourism consists of many kinds of product and benefit (e.g. cultural tourism, health tourism) all of which have their own kinds of customer. They can be inventoried by market research studies into specific tourism products and destinations and by visitor studies which elicit motivations and activities pursued at the destination.

Benefits segmentation can and should be augmented by other kinds of segmentation data, particularly socio-demographic. A Touche Ross activity study provided socio-demographic data on activity holiday seekers in Scotland which identified them as made up of equal numbers of men and women who were likely to be younger rather than older and skewed to upper social grade people, ABC1s, rather than lower social grades.

Product usage volumes

Another useful form of segmentation for tourism organizations is by volume of usage, including heavy, medium and light users. Data on number of trips taken, frequency of travel and expenditure of traveller can be vital in identifying prime travel segments; a numerically large tourist base may not be worth as much as a smaller, higher spending, frequent traveller – a fact that airlines and hotels have focused on in prioritizing the

---

CASE STUDY 2.2

Holidays in Scotland

A Touche Ross study in 1994 found that 5–10% of all holidays to Scotland were activity holidays and up to 25% of holidaymakers claimed to have taken part in some form of activity during their holiday. It was estimated that approximately 425 000 trips were generated each year by activity holidays in Scotland, the most common of which were walking, golf and fishing. The market is predominantly domestic – 85% of holidaymakers were British.

Source: Mckie (1994: 33).

regular, business traveller and cruise companies in targeting the regular cruise taker as prime audiences.

Past behaviour

Any segmentation process should start with the past and present. The most reliable indicator of what someone will do in the future is what they have done in the past. A consistent finding of customer research in general, and tourism research in particular, is that past and present customers are most likely to be future ones and, if they are not, then people with similar profiles may be. The repeat purchaser is a more lucrative prospect than the new customer, because it costs less to find him/her. Thus analysis of current and previous customers is critical to existing tourism organizations and new ones should attempt to assess the past profiles of customers for similar products. This is now much easier with the database opportunities offered by IT. Many tour operators and travel agents know that their customers come back. CenterParcs International which lets villas in holiday villages in the Netherlands, Belgium, France and the UK found that 28.3% of its customers had stayed at one of its villages five times or more and 56% of these repeat visitors had returned within a year (Fache, 1994: 465). There is also evidence that, even when they do not repeat the specific tourism experience, they repeat ones like it; cultural tourism, in particular, tends to attract the same kind of higher income, educated people time and again.

In the late 1980s and early 1990s garden festivals were a major kind of urban attraction in Britain developed to create interest and regenerate post-industrial centres. In 1990 the Gateshead Garden Festival organizers had to decide who to target for their event. They began their analysis of the probable market for the Gatehead festival by looking at the profile of visitors to three *earlier* festivals in Stoke, Liverpool and Glasgow compared to the total population of those cities. They were particularly interested in three consumer characteristics: the age, gender and socioeconomic grouping of potential visitors. The results of the previous festivals are shown in Table 2.6.

On the basis of this analysis the organizers concluded that, though the Gateshead Festival would draw some visitors from all of the population, its most likely customers would be: (a) in social Classes ABC1; (b) in the age groups 35–65 years old; (c) women more than men.

The organizers also analysed the distance travelled by visitors to past festivals into three bands: within 15 miles, 15–75 miles and 75 miles+. They then allocated a visit-per-head probability for people located in the three zones based on previous attendance figures. The weightings were as follows:

Visits per head: Zone 1: Less than 15 miles   1.1
                    Zone 2: 15–75 miles   0.1
                    Zone 3: 75 miles   0.02

They thus concluded that the Garden Festival was likely to be primarily a local affair of people travelling 15 miles or less rather than a national one.

Table 2.6 Social grades, age and gender of (a) residents in Liverpool, Stoke and Glasgow; (b) previous visitors to garden festivals/in Liverpool, Stoke and Glasgow

	National* %	Liverpool %	Liverpool G.Festival %	Stoke %	Stoke G.Festival %	Glasgow %	Glasgow G.Festival %
Social grades							
AB	17	12	25	12	26	15	27
C1	23	21	29	19	28	19	28
C2	28	26	24	26	30	24	21
DE	32	41	22	43	16	42	24
Age							
−14	21	NA	23	NA	14	NA	19
15–24	16	NA	9	NA	7	NA	12
25–34	14	NA	13	NA	12	NA	20
35–44	12	NA	15	NA	16	NA	16
45–54	11	NA	13	NA	16	NA	13
55–64	11	NA	13	NA	18	NA	13
65+	15	NA	14	NA	17	NA	7
Sex							
Male	49	47	42	48	44	47	47
Female	51	53	58	52	56	53	64

*National = social grades, ages and gender of UK population.
Source: Data based on exit studies from the garden festivals.

How did these predictions turn out? Visitor surveys conducted during the festival showed that as expected: (a) there was a dominance of ABC1 visitors (60% of the total) with more females than males, and that almost two-thirds of visitors came from within the area in which the festival was staged.

The case is one of many that could be used to illustrate the importance of analysing previous visitor/customer data in appraising future market profiles.

Segmentation by time

Tourism is notoriously seasonal and time skewed. Resort visitors tend to be concentrated in a few months rather than year-round. Some restaurants do better on weekdays, others at weekends; museums and galleries may be fuller in the morning than the late afternoon. A useful exercise for tourism firms wishing to obtain detailed knowledge of time segments is to compile data on: (a) monthly patterns; (b) weekly patterns; (c) daily patterns; and then use this as a basis for future planning (e.g. developing low-season destination offers; early evening 'happy hour' incentives in hospitality, etc.).

The importance of multiple segmental measures

The most effective market segmentation involves multi-dimensional measures. Depth and diversity of analysis are necessary to identify the niche markets that may exist in apparently homogenous mass markets. Studies by large tourism organizations often include a number of trip and tourist descriptor categories. The United Kingdom Travel Survey, based on an in-home survey of 80 000 people every year, for instance, collects the following information on tourists:

- country/region of residence;
- purpose of trip;
- types of holiday trip (main/secondary);
- party composition;
- transport used;
- inclusive package/independent;
- UK regions visited;
- activities undertaken;
- accommodation used;
- length of stay;
- type of location (coastal, urban);
- categories of expenditure;
- demographic details.

The Canadian results below show some points of similarity with a Belgian study reported by Vanhove (1994: 307) which identified seven main types of holidaymaker derived from cluster analysis:

- active sea lovers (5%): activities at sea and beach;
- contact-oriented holidaymakers (10%): want social interaction;
- nature lovers (12%): landscape and scenery, but passive experience;

CASE STUDY 2.3

Segmenting Canadian travellers

One of the most sophisticated attempts to combine several segmentation techniques was that carried out by the Angus Reid Group for the Canadian Pleasure Market Study of 1992. The study combined benefits sought, travel products, travel behaviour and psychographics in arriving at seven kinds of tourist:

- culture and nature seekers;
- knowledge and experience travellers interested in cultural experiences but more civilized and urbanized than C and N seekers;
- history and hospitality travellers interested in sampling local history through group tours;
- active players interested in games and sports;
- packaged sun and services travellers;
- family value travellers predictable in terms of low-budget accommodation and arrangements;
- no surprises travellers who were 'risk-averse' wanting all arrangements made for them.

Source: Cameron (1992: 154–67).

- rest seekers (26%);
- discoverers (10%): cultural enrichment;
- family-oriented sun and sea-lovers (27%): especial attraction to Southern Europe;
- traditionals (10%): safety, no surprises, familiar surroundings.

The secret of successful segmentation is to identify the most relevent categories of segmentation that account for the principal business of a tourism enterprise. Identifying the relevant dimensions of tourist attributes is itself a creative process since the most important ones may not be immediately obvious.

SOURCES OF TOURISM SEGMENTATION

Any tourism organization, however restricted its resources, can compile data profiling its market segments. There are several methods of gathering data:

Direct observation

Restaurateurs, museum curators and other small tourism organization executives can form a good impression of their customer base by simply spending time on the spot making observations on their numbers, gender, party sizes, etc. Chatting to customers often reveals interesting information on their backgrounds, motivations and satisfaction levels.

Staff perceptions

In larger organizations where the owner or managers don't spend much time 'at the coal face' valuable feedback on customers and their problems can be gained from the staff who do (waitresses, receptionists, admissions attendants, couriers, tourist information centre staff, etc.). In large organizations the people responsible for day-to-day service delivery tend to have a more extensive, up-to-date idea of customers than managers more removed from the operation who are often implementing company procedures initiated elsewhere at corporate headquarters. Employees' contributions can be elicited through regular staff feedback mechanisms such as quality service sessions, a suggestion book and competitions – but most of all through being motivated by the feeling that they are valued and that their views count.

Databases of past customers

With the widespread diffusion of IT in booking and reservation systems it is now easy to amass much data on customer profiles. But it requires an effort of will to analyse it on an ongoing basis. Even in small organizations not wired to sophisticated IT systems guest/visitor books may be kept and analysed. Guest analysis records can be compiled which may inventory such data as: names, party size and type, place of origin, arrival and departure dates, what number of trip it was (first time or more), reason for visit, activities engaged in, etc.

Surveys

The most extensive segmentation data is gathered through specially designed and conducted surveys and visitor studies. These may be financed and/or collated by international organizations such as the WTO which provides extensive data on international tourism flows, or by NTOs many of which carry out annual tourist monitors. Large private sector companies (airlines, ferries, attractions) carry out their own surveys using personal interviews or through self-completion questionnaires delivered to customers in transit (in-flight surveys) or at destinations (hotel room questionnaires).

THE APPLICATIONS OF MARKETING SEGMENTATION

Segmentation is one of the most extensively studied concepts in tourism, which reflects its importance and also the fact that it is relatively easy to gather segmentation data. Before looking at its uses a few comments of caution are in order. Market segmentation data is not a panacea and three of its limitations should be specified.

- Segmentation data often only tells **what** happened, not **why** it happened. It is just as important to understand the reasons behind discovered segmentation patterns (e.g. why so many ABC1 groups enjoy walking and rambling, and what they get out of it; the perceptions of place and attraction that impel some groups but deter others). This is why the next chapter looks in more detail at the behavioural factors that lie behind the descriptive classifications of many segmentation forms.
- Most importantly segmentation analysis only tells a tourism organization **what is** rather than **what could be**. A country park may find that most of its existing visitors are local, but that does not mean that marketing activity could not be used to widen its appeal to tourists from outside the area. In short segmentation analysis always reveals a status quo rather than highlighting possibilities for the future (although, as we have observed, in many cases past and present consumer patterns often do provide reliable predictors for the future).
- Thirdly, segmentation analysis can lead to erroneous planning that suffers from the the 'fat cat fallacy'. This fallacy is the result of extensive consumer analysis by tourism organizations which identifies the most lucrative tourist groups, followed by the assumption that the

organization should then target them for its products, regardless of whether the products are suitable. In the late 1980s and early 1990s NTOs around the world, including those in Britain, identified the Japanese and Americans as high priority targets because they constituted expanding, high spending markets. In some cases the NTOs set up specialist, budgeted sections for developing these markets only to find that the results failed to live up to expectations (the Scottish Tourist Board, for example, has recently dramatically cut its budgets for Japan and America, because of its lack of success in increasing visitor numbers).

So how should segmentation be used? Provided the limitations are recognized segmentation assists strategic planning in a number of areas. In general terms segmentation is undertaken in order **to develop marketing programmes appropriate to identified groups**. This involves the following.

- Matching media to known targets: it is impossible to select the right media for delivering promotional messages without knowing what audiences need to be reached and ensuring that the profiles of the media used (the viewers of particular TV programmes, the readers of a particular newspaper, etc.) match them.
- Choosing retail outlet locations that conform to customer traffic patterns (e.g. for travel agents).
- Suggesting creative approaches (e.g. a cover for a brochure which is designed for a specific target market).
- Estimating and forecasting the likely volume and value of a market.
- Estimating the catchment area for an attraction.
- Above all, in designing or improving the product to the known needs and preferences of particular customer groups (e.g. providing facilities for children in hospitality establishments if the family market is a desirable segment).

There are no ready-made formulae for determining how to segment tourism markets. Skill, judgement and creativity need to be applied to determine the relevent dimensions which most differentiate the submarkets that lurk in overall markets. This can only come from a close knowledge of the market concerned. The ones inventoried here represent a sample of some of the commonest forms of segmentation which have been used in the past. Segmentation methods come and go into fashion. In a recent review Brent Ritchie has commented on some of the diverse market segmentation variables that have been 'flavour of the month' in the past, including segmentation by involvement, activity sets, frequency of usage, benefits sought, type of destinations, customer loyalty, lifestyle and psychographics (Ritchie, 1994: 18).

Market segmentation is a dynamic process because customer trends never stand still. It is thus important to carry out regular, preferably continuous, tracking studies to monitor changes happening in the market. One of the most repeated predictions about tourism markets of the future is a trend to 'demassification' in which a greater number of niche markets will replace the mass ones of the past:

> 'Demassification' means that hospitality corporations are having to become increasingly sophisticated and precise in the simultaneous segmenting and targeting of mutiple target markets. The future of hospitality marketing will not be mass marketing but micro-marketing.
>
> (Crawford-Welch, 1991: 25)

If that prediction is correct market segmentation will become an even more essential requirement of effective tourism marketing than it has been in the past.

Stakeholder segmentation

Finally segmentation analysis can be extended to a kind of consumer of tourism often disregarded by marketing planners – the people in the regions in which tourism is supplied. Though they do not consume tourism as a leisure commodity, they consume its effects as the host communities in which it takes place. Responsible tourism planning will increasingly have to take account of the social, cultural and environmental impacts it creates. Segmentation can be used to identify some of these potential impacts by canvassing the opinions of those most likely to be affected, and then using the data gathered to minimize the negative consequences and maximize the positive ones. The concept of **stakeholder** is emerging as a vital bridge for relating tourism planning to the wishes of resident populations. Stakeholders may include: (a) local residents and host communities; (b) local businesses; (c) local and national governing bodies; (d) specific interest groups. Once the major stakeholders in a tourism development have been identified their opinions can be gathered through surveys, public meetings and other kinds of consultation. In public sector planning major projects such as airport developments and road building programmes are often accompanied by public inquiries, but the private sector has been slower to adopt mechanisms of consultation, particularly in third world countries.

SUMMARY

This chapter has looked at the principles behind market segmentation, its aims and objectives and reviewed a number of the common techniques used by tourism planners to analyse their customers. It has also suggested how segmentation can be applied to host populations in order achieve socially responsible tourism planning in the destination regions affected.

REFERENCES

Bonn, M.A. (1994) *Identifying market potential: the application of brand development indexing to pleasure travel*, paper presented at conference on 'Tourism: The State of the Art', University of Strathclyde, Glasgow, Scotland.

British Tourist Authority (1994) *Annual Report*, BTA.

Cameron, B. (1992) Who wants what – and why? An overview of the Canadian Pleasure Market Study, *Conference Proceedings of the 23rd Annual Conference of the Travel and Tourism Research Association*, 14–17 June, Minnesota, pp. 154–167.

Churchill, D. (1994) Rooms for improvement, *The Sunday Times*, 18 September, Travel Section, p. 5.

Crawford-Welch, S. (1991) Marketing hospitality in the 21st century, *International Journal of Contemporary Hospitality Management*, **3**(3), 21–7.

Davidoff, P.G. and Davidoff, D.S. (1983) *Sales and Marketing for Travel and Tourism*, Prentice-Hall, Englewood Cliffs, New Jersey.

Davidson, R. (1994) European business travel and tourism, in Seaton, A.V. (ed.), *Tourism: The State of the Art*, Wiley, Chichester and London, pp. 377–82.

Fache, W. (1994) The shortbreak market, in Seaton, A.V. (ed.), *Tourism: The State of the Art*, Wiley, Chichester and London, pp. 459–67.

Frenkel, T. (1992) *Proceedings of the 18th Annual Travel Outlook Forum*, Washington, 1992, p. 111.

Gwyther, S. (1992) Britain bracing for the age bomb, *Independent on Sunday*, 29 March.

Haley, R.I. (1968) Benefit segmentation: a decision oriented research tool, *Journal of Marketing*, **32**, 30–5.

Holloway, J.C. and Plant, R.V. (1992) *Marketing for Tourism*, Pitman, London.

Kotler, P. (1988) *Marketing Management*, 6th edn, Prentice-Hall, Englewood Cliffs, New Jersey.

Mckie, L. (1994) Signs of activity, *Leisure Management*, **14**(9), 33.

Mercer, D. (1992) *Marketing*, Blackwell, Oxford, UK.

Pearce, D. (1987) *Tourism Today: A Geographic Analysis*, Longman, Harlow, Essex.

Plog, S.C. (1974) Why destination areas rise and fall in popularity, *Cornell Hotel and Restaurant Administration Quarterly*, November, pp. 13–16.

Plog, S.C. (1990) A carpenter's tools: an answer to Stephen L.J. Smith's review of psychocentrism/allocentrism, *Journal of Travel Research*, Spring, pp. 43–5.

Ritchie, J.R.B. (1994) Research on leisure behaviour and tourism: the state of the art, in Gasser, R.V. and Weiermair, K. (eds), *Spoilt for Choice*, Kulturverlag, Innsbruck, Austria.

Seaton, A.V. (1992) Social stratification in tourism choice and experience since the war, *Tourism Management*, March, pp. 106–11.

Seaton, A.V. (1994) Are friends relatives? Reassessing the VFR category in assessing tourism markets, in Seaton, A.V. (ed.), *Tourism: The State of the Art*, Wiley, Chichester and London, pp. 316–21.

Seaton, A.V. and Tagg, S.K. (1995) Disaggregating friends and relatives in VFR tourism research: the Northern Ireland evidence 1991–1993, *Journal of Tourism Studies*, **6**(1), May.

Smith, S.L.J. (1990a) *Tourism Analysis: A Handbook*, Longman, Harlow, Essex.

Smith, S.L.J. (1990b) A test of Plog's allocentric/psychocentric model: evidence from 7 nations, *Journal of Travel Research*, Spring, pp. 40–3.

Stewart, E. (1992) Outlook for business travel, in *Proceedings of the 18th Annual Travel Outlook Forum*, Washington, p. 86.

United Kingdom Tourist Survey (1993) *The UK tourist*, ETB/STB/NITB/WTB.

Vanhove, N. (1994) Market segmentation, in Witt, S.J. and Moutinho, L. (eds), *Handbook of Tourism Marketing and Management*, Prentice-Hall, Hemel Hempstead, Herts. pp. 305–10.

Weber, S. (1992) Trends in tourism segmentation research, *Marketing and Research Today*, **20**(2), 116–23.

REVIEW QUESTIONS

1. What do you think would be the most important segmentation dimensions in analysing the likely demand for:
   (a) a regional transport museum?
   (b) a major international destination such as Florida?
   (c) A new hotel development by a major chain to be sited near an international airport?
2. Obtain a visitor study for an attraction, destination or other tourism product and identify the main segmentation data it monitors.
3. Identify the main factors necessary for a market segment to be a viable one for a tourism organization.

The analysis of tourism demand: tourism behaviour

3

A.V. Seaton

OBJECTIVES

By the end of this chapter the reader should:

* be familiar with the two main domains of tourism behaviour: macro-demand and micro-demand;
* have a broad grasp of the social influences on tourism behaviour, including culture, class, the family and group factors;
* have a broad grasp of the part played by individual factors in tourism behaviour including motivation and perception;
* have a preliminary grasp of the methodologies for measuring tourism behaviour.

INTRODUCTION

In the last chapter we looked at market segmentation and assessed the ways in which tourism marketers can identify and describe target customer groups through the analysis of the kinds of trip they take and their broad characteristics such as class, age, gender, etc. In this chapter we look at the ways in which tourism marketers can extend their knowledge of tourists and their reasons for purchase of different kinds of tourism product.

Market segmentation is primarily an attempt to classify populations into broad behavioural groupings, derived mainly from quantitative surveys. Tourism behaviour is also about attempts to understand the social, psychological and cultural bases of their behaviour, often through qualitative as well as quantitative research. Segmentation analysis may reveal that business travellers are mainly male, come from the AB social grade and habitually travel by air, but not what they feel about travel, how they perceive the destinations and hotels they use, or why they should prefer one airline to another. A package operator selling tours to Britain may know what proportion of the total market is likely to be made up of Americans and Japanese tourists but it does not tell them how the two nationalities may differ in the way they go about choosing a destination, their motives, perceptions, expectations and service requirements.

Understanding tourism behaviour involves two different levels of analysis: **macro-analysis** which seeks to identify the patterns and determinants of aggregate demand, and **micro-analysis** which involves insight into individual tourist behaviour.

MACRO-ANALYSIS

Macro-analysis is concerned with examining collective tourism movements in terms of numbers of visitors, trips and revenue generated from them. It deals with data such as arrivals per country, attraction admission numbers, flight loadings, hotel occupancy rates, visitor spending and so on.

A tourism organization is often interested in two basic aggregate demand types:

(a) **Total demand within a tourism market**. The market may be the whole world, a country or a particular tourism sector such as the cruise market, the European ski market, the cheap package holiday market, etc.

(b) **Sectoral and product market shares and volumes of the commercial or public sector organizations satisfying that total demand**. A package company will be interested in its market share relative to others, and transport organizations will be interested, not just in total passenger flows between destinations for which it runs services, but in its own proportionate volume/revenue from those flows and those of its competitors. Market segments constitute sub-aggregate components of these differentiated sectoral/product markets.

Macro-demand data underlies all marketing planning. Marketing organizations need access to quantitative market information in order that they may understand the past, cope with the present and forecast the future. In traditional economic terms the demand for tourism can be seen as a function of four factors (Edgell, 1994: 65):

• the price of the commodity;
• the price of competing and complementary commodities;
• the level of personal disposable income;
• the tastes, habits and preferences of potential buyers.

The data on macro-demand can be derived from many sources: governments, international tourism organizations such as the WTO and OECD, national tourism organizations and private organizations. Discussion of them lies outside the scope of this chapter (though in Chapter 14 we will briefly look at some of them).

Aggregate demand for tourism is influenced by many forces. Schmoll (1977) identified six major general features that account for the instability of tourism demand at all times:

- a high degree of elasticity of demand in relation to price and income;
- the strong seasonal variations in demand;
- the pronounced, often sudden and unpredictable impact of external and environmental factors on demand;
- the low level of consumer loyalty in respect to travel destinations and, to a lesser degree in respect of travel modes, types of arrangements and travel trade intermediaries;
- changes in demand structure, whether quantitative or qualitative in nature;
- the wide range of heterogeneous and often contradictory and incompatible motivations and expectations which underlie tourism demand.

Ryan (1991) has summarized the following five economic factors as key demand determinants:

- total income;
- prices of other factors that determine 'discretionary income';
- economic structure of industries relevant to tourism and their profitability (cost of accommodation, travel, etc.);
- inflation in the host and generating countries;
- rates of exchange.

Aggregate tourism demand is also influenced by many other factors including: growth of business travel, car ownership, demographic changes and particularly increases in wealth, age and education. The range of influences on aggregate demand means that tourism organizations, particularly large ones, need to monitor social and economic environments as part of the ongoing marketing audit in order to keep up to date with trends that may impinge upon their markets.

MICRO-ANALYSIS

Micro-analysis is concerned with the social and psychological factors that lie behind disaggregated group and individual tourist choices. These include such questions as:

- What makes people engage in tourism – what are their motivations? How do motivations differ for different kinds of tourism activity?
- How do people make their tourism choices and what influences them?
- What affects their perceptions and images of destinations, attractions and other tourism offerings?

- How can their satisfactions with tourism experiences be measured?
- How do people look back on tourist experiences?

Micro-analysis is more concerned than macro-analysis with **intra-personal** and **interpersonal processes** – the things that go on inside the heads of people or happen between people – that influence the behaviour of the individual or tourist group. Micro-analysis, then, is more concerned with the **why** and **how** of tourism behaviour whereas macro-analysis is more concerned with **who, where, how many and how much**.

Understanding tourism behaviour involves knowledge of factors that are by no means obvious because the influences that shape tourism tastes and activities are often so deeply embedded in the individual's personal and cultural biography that the subject is unaware of how they were formed. For example, sun-seeking is a major contemporary motivation for travel and seems 'natural', yet it barely existed before the 1920s.

TOURISM AS CONSUMER BEHAVIOUR

The main approaches to macro-analysis derive from economics and demography; those to micro-analysis come from a field of marketing theory called consumer behaviour. Consumer behaviour or economic psychology, as it is sometimes called, first developed in the late 1950s and 1960s as an attempt by marketers to understand why and how people bought things and what they did with them once they had done so. It developed as an essential supplement to economic models of buying which assumed that purchase was largely a function of rational calculation about price, supply and demand and could be studied independently of more subjective factors behind how people choose and consume products. What economics left out – tastes, habits, usage and experience, etc. – consumer behaviour put in. The subject developed largely by applying social science concepts, particularly those from psychology and sociology, to the world of marketing.

One of the earliest approaches to consumer behaviour was made by Katona (1954). He identified five sets of conditions that influenced and preceded the purchase of products. The five conditions were:

- **Enabling conditions**. These comprised basic financial access (to income, assets, credit) without which purchase was impossible.
- **Precipitating circumstances**. These could be an increase or decrease in purchasing power, change of family conditions, move to a new house, etc. These were contingent circumstances that might suddenly set a person off towards a purchasing decision or inhibit it.
- **Habit**. Katona recognized that many purchases were not deeply considered each time that they were made but might proceed from sheer force of habit. In some kinds of tourism there is evidence that people repeat their choices by, for example, going back to the same tour operator.
- **Contractual obligations**. Here Katona recognized the effect of

disposable income on purchase behaviour. Rent, life insurance, taxes, hire purchase, loans, interest rates could all inhibit expenditure on other things, particularly luxury goods like tourism which are only affordable after basic provisions have been taken care of. Tourism is highly price and income elastic (see Chapter 6).

• **Psychological state**. Katona was certainly not the first to recognize the importance of psychology in selling (the first book on the psychology of advertising was written as long ago as 1903 by Walter Dill Scott) but he was one of the earliest to put psychology alongside other variables in a comprehensive model of consumer behaviour.

Since Katona's formulation marketing theorists and researchers have developed more complex ways of depicting consumer behaviour, identifying many variables which affect the purchasing process and attempting to model their relationship (Howard and Sheth, 1969; Engell Blackwell and Miniard, 1990). However, most consumer behaviour books tend to see consumer behaviour as a function of two basic factors – **social influences** and **personal traits**. Moutinho (1987) has modelled the influences as in Table 3.1.

In a chapter of this length it is impossible to provide a detailed examination of all these variables but we shall attempt to sketch out some of the main ones.

SOCIAL INFLUENCES

No man is an island. People live in societies, communities and groups and the pattern of social networks through which they grow and develop influence their tastes, habits and values. We shall briefly examine four kinds of social influence which bear on tourism behaviour.

Culture

There is no universally agreed definition of culture. Anthropologists, sociologists, literary historians and academics from many other disciplines have defined culture in different ways. In 1952 Kroeber and Kluckholm examined more than 150 definitions of culture (Boechner, 1982: 6) and many more have been added since then.

Table 3.1 Factors influencing consumer behaviour

Social influences	Personal traits	
Culture and subculture	Personality	$\rightarrow$
Social class	Learning	$\rightarrow$ Individual
Reference groups and influentials	Motivation	$\rightarrow$ tourist
Role and family influence	Perception	$\rightarrow$ behaviour
	Attitudes	$\rightarrow$

Two main approaches to culture offer useful insights into the tourism process:

Anthropological 'whole-way-of-life' approaches

These are based on the idea that culture consists of patterns of behaviour including habits, ideas and values of communities. Society itself – a nation or state – is the largest community or social grouping, so that culture may be seen as the way of life of a society. Levi-Strauss, following Tylor, has defined culture as:

> ... that complex whole which includes knowledge, belief, art, morals, law, custom, and any other capabilities and habits acquired by man as a member of society.
>
> (Levi-Strauss, 1978: Vol 1, p. 18)

Anthropology originally developed in the late nineteenth and early twentieth centuries through the study of small societies outside Europe (e.g. in India, Africa and Polynesia) but in recent years writers have come to focus on the culture of modern, westernized societies and there is a growing literature on the social meaning of goods, including tourism:

> In every case the kinds of activities in which people engage are culturally determined; nearly all purchases of goods are made ... either to provide physical comfort or to implement the activities which make up the life of the culture.
>
> (Duesenberry, 1987: 298)

Tourism can be seen as a distinctive product of developed, industrialized societies which is why the main generating countries are in Western Europe, North America and Japan. As Krippendorf has observed in a stimulating critique of tourism:

> The travel needs of the modern age have been largely created by society and shaped by everyday life ... The motivation of the individual person to travel to look outside for what he cannot find inside, is produced not so much by an innate impulse – but develops primarily under the influence of the social environment, from which the individual draws his norms. The individual decision is socially predetermined, especially as regards travel and holidays. What our society offers routine-weary people is tourism, a variety of holidays outside the everyday world, extolling them as escape-aids, problem-solvers, suppliers of strength, energy, new lifeblood and happiness ...
>
> (Krippendorf, 1987: xix, and 17)

Tourism as elite culture

The anthropological approach to culture conceptualized culture simply as the way of life of **all** members of a society. A second approach to culture conceptualizes it, not as the way of life of a whole society, but as a special, almost sacred, body of knowledge (including knowledge of the arts and humanities), the acquisition of which **by some** confers a kind of moral distinction upon the initiate. This narrower interpretation of culture as civilized knowledge developed in the nineteenth and early twentieth centuries through the writings of critics and educationalists like Matthew Arnold, Walter Pater, John Ruskin, T.S. Eliot, F.R. Leavis and others and it has largely been incorporated into the Western education system. It was enshrined in the notion of the 'cultured' person, someone implicitly superior to those who have not become cultured.

Travel was an important element of this cultural competence. It did not just broaden the mind, it provided a liberal education which marked off cultured sheep from uncultured goats. The achievement of culture through travel and the aesthetic experiences associated with it (architecture, art galleries, museums, appreciation of landscape, etc.) became major goals of tourists. These links between tourism, morality and education can be seen in many kinds of tourism past and present. In the 1930s the Cooperative Travel Organization and the Workers Educational Association in Britain organized packaged holidays that included hymns and recitations as well as sightseeing and bracing walks. The institution of the 'school trip' worldwide from the 1930s onwards incorporated implicit ideologies of moral improvement and mental growth associated with sightseeing and cultural tourism. Today the concept of culture as access to knowledge and conspicuous appreciation of art, sculpture, opera, etc. exerts a powerful purchase on the tourism industry which can be seen in the reverential crowds assembled at museums, galleries and churches all over Europe and elsewhere.

Social class

Within every society subcultures and stratified groups exist with distinctive patterns of behaviour. In many developed industrialized societies social class and occupational gradings produce differentiated patterns of behaviour which have great impact on tourism consumption. In the previous chapter we saw how business tourism is largely consumed by the three top UK social grades, the ABC1s, and how these groups often constitute the main markets for many kinds of recreational tourism including heritage and cultural tourism, wilderness tourism and long-haul travel (precisely because it is the middle classes who have promoted and been most influenced by concepts of elite culture). Social class in the West is primarily determined by income and education both of which, either individually or together, are associated with both higher and different levels of tourism activity (see Seaton (1992) for an examination of some of these differences).

A less easily determined relationship between tourism and class is the possibility that certain kinds of tourism may enable people to act above or below their own class. Paul Fussell has suggested that people engage in tourism to raise social status at home, to allay social anxiety, or even to derive secret pleasure from posing momentarily as a member of a social class superior to their own (Fussell, 1989).

Gottlieb (in Davidoff and Davidoff, 1983) has suggested that there are two kinds of tourists – those who travel to be king or queen for a day and those who travel to be peasants for a day; the first seek a pampered lifestyle beyond their means in everyday life while the latter, having access to material luxuries in their everyday life, seek simpler, more primitive contacts in their leisure (e.g. on safaris, 'roughing it' on adventure holidays, etc.).

A related idea is the **inversion thesis**, propounded by Graburn (1983), which conceptualizes tourism as the pursuit of the 'other', that which is opposite and different from 'normal' life. The idea has a venerable pedigree. In sixteenth and seventeenth century Europe one of the great themes of popular culture was 'the world turned upside down', an imaginary vision of life that was the opposite of the actual one in which, for example, masters were servants, the rich were poor and animals ruled humans rather than vice versa. In Elizabethan England it was customary on Twelfth Night (6 January) for servants to be waited on by their masters. It is possible to view tourism as a cultural legacy of this 'world turned upside down' – a flight to places with features which contrast with everyday life at home. Table 3.2 presents some of the binary contrasts which can often be observed to underly patterns of movement between originating cultures and those of the destinations to which tourists travel. The promotion of tourism targeted at tourists from developed nations is almost invariably structured by some, or many, of these underlying mythic contrasts in which travel is presented as the attainment of a paradisal Shangri-la where everything is different from the 'here and now'.

In the 1960s and 1970s some British sociologists offered a **compensatory** view of leisure which suggested that people doing active, manual jobs would seek more passive leisure experiences while those in white-collar, sedentary jobs would prefer more active, physical ones. This view has also been offered as a basis of understanding tourism choices:

Table 3.2. The cultural contrasts of tourism with everyday life

The everyday world: features of originating culture	The other: features of destination culture
Uniformity	Diversity
Complexity	Simplicity
The modern	The antique/traditional
High-tech life	Low-tech life
Urban life	Rural life
Alienation	Fulfilment
Man-made environment	Unspoiled nature
Sophistication	Innocence (e.g. noble savage myth)
Secular, profane existence	The sacred (the earthly paradise)
Northern	Southern

Persons experiencing less stimulation in their lives than they desire expressed a preference for greater novelty and stimulation in the ideal vacation. On the other hand individuals experiencing more stimulation than they desired preferred a more tranquil and structured ideal vacation.

(Mannell and Iso Ahola, 1987)

All these theories are perhaps too simplistic to account for the complexity of leisure/tourism patterns but they do provide relevant insights into the relationship between tourism choices and people's position in the social structure of the societies from which they originate.

Family behaviour

Another kind of social influence is the family. The family market is the biggest one in recreational tourism. As shown in Table 3.3, in 1992 tourists from all three of Spain's main generating countries – France, Germany and the UK – were more likely to be travelling in family parties than any other (Consultur, 1992). In the same year data from the US Travel Center suggested that the family vacation market accounted for 70–80% of all leisure vacation travel in the USA (US Travel Center, 1992).

Family parties have different needs and activity patterns from non-family ones. In America, for instance, the three main motivations behind family travel have included: to be together as a family; the need to get away from the stress of balancing a home and career, and rest and relaxation (US Travel Center, 1992).

The family is not one thing with a uniform set of needs. It will vary according to the age of children and parents within it and, increasingly, by whether or not it includes both parents. A useful concept for examining family tourism behaviour, as we saw in the previous chapter, is the family life cycle (FLC).

Family structure affects how holidays are chosen. Since the family is a group all of whom share the outcome of a holiday it means that there may be joint consultation in the choice of what kind of holiday to have and where to have it. The family can be seen as a decision-making unit (see Chapter 8 for a discussion of this concept). The research study below suggests some of the dimensions of joint participation in family holiday decisions.

Table 3.3. Visitors to Spain 1992: with whom trip was taken*

	France %	Germany %	UK %
Alone	17.9	16.3	16.4
With family	41.7	45.5	52.3
With friends	34.0	30.5	24.7

*Balancing figures were non-responses.

CASE STUDY 3.1

Family holiday decisions in Europe

In 1992 children from four European countries (the UK, Belgium, Italy and France) were asked a number of questions about their last main summer holiday designed to find out (a) to what extent they were consulted about the decision; (b) how big a part they played in the final decision; (c) who made the final decision.

Most children in all four countries claimed to have been consulted about the holiday decision but there were variations between them with 78% of French children and 74% of Italian children claiming they had been consulted vs. 67% in UK and 61% in Belgium.

Of Italian children 48% thought they had played a 'big part' in the vacation decision, a figure over four times that for UK children (11%) and twice that for Belgian children (22%). UK and Belgian children were much more likely to see their decisional inputs as smaller with 50% of all UK children claiming they had only a 'small part' or 'none' in the family vacation decision. French children scored higher than Belgian and UK children but less than Italian.

There was striking agreement (60% or more for all countries) among European children that the final vacation decision was most commonly a joint one between mother and father (Italy 75%, France 64%, Belgium 63% and UK 60%). In those cases where the holiday was not seen as a joint decision, the mother was slightly more likely to be seen as the final decider.

Source: Seaton and Tagg, (1995a)

Finally the family can be seen as the motivating object of much tourism in the form of visiting friends and relatives trips (VFRs). During the 1990s 40% of all tourism to Northern Ireland was VFR tourism and, of this total, nearly 80% was actually visiting relatives. There are good reasons to think that the movement of people across borders following immigration/emigration patterns, refugee displacement, liberalization of travel, etc. will expand the VFR market in Europe and elsewhere (Paci, 1994; Seaton and Tagg, 1995b).

Groups and reference groups

Tourist behaviour is also influenced by the groups to which tourists belong. School groups, business groups and many kinds of peer groups consume tourism together (tour operators often offer discounts and free places to school teachers and other educational group leaders for parties over a certain size, normally 15 or more, because they are aware that educationalists can act as **opinion leaders** who initiate group travel). Even where people do not travel in pre-existing groups they often become part of one on the trip (as members of a coach party or package tour) and one of the skills of couriers, drivers, guides and other tourism organization representatives is managing the group dynamics of the party which can affect satisfaction at the end of the trip.

Reference groups are groups which people may not actually belong to but aspire to be like and, as a result, may base some of their behaviour on. A tourist may visit Mustique or Bhutan because he or she thinks it is a place smart people go to. Tour operators targeting their products at young singles often rely on publicity which suggests that their products are patronized by people like themselves or people such as they would like to be (normally attractive, fun-loving groups).

BARRIERS TO TRAVEL

So far we have appraised social influences as positive determinants of tourism behaviour. Social and physical factors also constitute negative influences which limit people's ability to travel. Barriers to travel, which produce negative tourism propensity, include low income and unemployed status, physical disability, non-ownership of car and single-parent status.

INDIVIDUAL FACTORS

Travel and tourism are thus induced or limited by social influences as much as by uniquely individual factors. Nevertheless, at the end of the day individuals choose, experience and evaluate tourism products and, however much the results may be affected by their social environment, it is

---

CASE STUDY 3.2

Using alumni groups as tourism targets

The University of Oxford, like Harvard and Yale in the United States, is an old-established British university with a flourishing alumni organization supported by ex-students who commonly share some degree of collective *esprit de corps* and – more to the point for marketing organizations – generally achieve a higher level of income and wealth than the average. Some tourism organizations have recognized that former graduates of the university constitute a lucrative market for premium tourism products and have developed programmes promoted through the alumni network. The Oxford Society, the prime alumni society for members of the university, distributes a quarterly magazine to its members in which more than 40 hotels and hotel groups offer special discount privileges to members among which are the Hilton, the Hôtel Belle Epoque, Paris, the Hôtel du Lac, Interlaken, and Randolph Hotel, Oxford, and Euston Plaza Hotel, London, the Royal York Hotel and the Imperial Hotel, Harrogate. Car hire firms and attractions also offer special deals to members and the Society has its own travel club which, in November 1995, offered packages on the Orient Express and a week at Reid's hotel on the island of Madeira. In early 1990 a new free, glossy quarterly, *The Oxford Magazine*, was launched and sent to all Oxford graduates, which has included advertising from specialist tour operators.

Source: Oxford Society (1995)

CASE STUDY 3.3

Barriers to travel

In Easter 1995 an eight-day Arts Fest was held in the Eastwood district of Renfrewshire in Scotland. It comprised over 30 separate events including classical and jazz concerts, exhibitions, children's entertainments, firework displays and puppet shows. A visitor study based on a sample of over 1200 visitors revealed that only 3% unemployed people attended and that more than 60% of attendance came from the top income groups, the ABs. A higher proportion of lower-income people attended some of the individual, free-entry events within the Festival.

Source: Scottish Tourism Research Unit Report, June 1995.

---

important to understand their individual perspectives. In this section we shall examine two major aspects of individual behaviour – motivation and perception.

Motivation in tourism

All tourism planners must know why people want their products.

Motivation has been defined as '. . . the driving force within an individual that impels him to action' (Schiffman and Kanuk, 1978: 24). It is a state of arousal of a drive or need which impels people to activity in pursuit of goals. Once the goals have been achieved the need subsides and the individual returns to equilibrium – but only briefly because new motives arise as the last one is satisfied. One theory of motivation, that of Abraham Maslow (1967), conceptualized motivation as a hierarchy or ladder of needs up which people progress beginning with basic physiological ones (food, shelter) and moving through to the highest needs, self-actualization, with its climactic point – the peak experience.

Tourism has been seen near the top of Maslow's hierarchy, since as a luxury item it may only be sought after other needs have been satisfied. The peak experience may be seen as the ideal object of tourism – the exotic fantasy, the dream of perfect place and personal fulfilment. However, tourism may also be a method of serving lower order needs, e.g. social needs for love and companionship, status needs and self-esteem, even basic needs for warmth and shelter (e.g. a mountain hut during a climbing holiday).

The problems of determining tourism motivations

Before we look at more specific formulations of tourism motivation it is important to understand that there are many problems involved in trying to identify and measure it. These include the following.

- **Tourism is not one thing**. Tourism is a diverse range of products that meet a diverse range of needs:

> Tourism demand does not represent a homogenous group of people striving to travel pushed by identical motivations. It is a complex of various, and sometimes conflicting desires, needs, tastes and dislikes.
>
> (Wahab, 1975: 16)

At one level tourism may be little more than a desire to pursue an interest or hobby – say, fishing or golfing – away from home, with the particular location or mode of travel little more than incidental facilitators. At a higher level it may involve transcendental expectations of particular places:

> Tourist-travel experience . . . can mean more than simple fun and recreation . . . It can also be a parallel voyage of the spirit to its own centre, a place where one can satisfy one's existential needs, accomplish one's highest values and ideals, change the state of one's consciousness . . . live through mystical and transcendental experience.
>
> (Comic, 1989: 8)

In some instances the destination may be less important than the *process of going* (e.g. walking/hiking holidays or trekking safaris).

- **People don't necessarily know why they do things and if they do, they don't necessarily reveal them**. People rarely think about the underlying reasons for their actions, particularly for well-established patterns of behaviour such as tourism which may come to seem like a natural activity. In other cases the motivations for activities may not bear too much self-critical scrutiny. Sex tourism in places like Thailand may spring from one form of inadmissible motivation. Another range of tourism may spring from morbid, voyeuristic curiosity (e.g. pilgrimages to the death spot of celebrities such as the book depository in Dallas from which John F. Kennedy was shot).
- **Tourism motives may be multiple and contradictory**. Tourism motivations often include contradictory impulses. Two such sets of opposing desires can be typified as follows:

Seeing and doing (sightseeing and activity)	vs.	Being and relaxing (sunbathing by beach or pool)
Novelty and adventure (exploring a new place)	vs.	Familiarity and security (staying in a hotel with familiar comforts)

Tourism motivation has sometimes been conceptualized as a balance of **pull–push** factors – the first being those factors which make people wish to get away from one place, the second the positive attractions that draw them to a new one. For example:

Push factors	**Pull factors**
Avoidance of work	Seeking leisure/play
Lack of autonomy	Freedom and escape

Poor environment	Attractive environment (e.g. good climate, beautiful landscape)
Cultural/social pressures at home	Positive attractions of host culture
Impact of tourism publicity	Impact of tourism publicity

- **Motives may change over time and occasion**. Cohen (1974) noted that when tourists first visit a place they do a lot of sightseeing but on later trips they do less. Moreover, over the course of a year people may engage in different forms of tourism for different reasons.
- **It is often difficult to distinguish individual motives from socially constructed and induced vocabularies of motives**. People often give the reasons for doing things that they have been programmed to give. This is particularly likely if they have been exposed to extensive social influence through promotion and publicity encouraging them to view particular kinds of activity as a function of specific motives ('take a well-earned rest in Southport', 'explore your industrial heritage at the Museum of Transport'). The problem of the production of socially induced vocabularies of motive may be encouraged in visitor studies which require tourists to tick one or more of a predetermined set of motivational statements, none of which may constitute the real reason for a trip (e.g. a visit to a transport museum may be less motivated by a desire to study industrial heritage than a need to find something for children to do on a wet afternoon during the school holidays).
- **Motivation may be inextricably bound up with many other factors of human behaviour including perception, learning, personality, culture**. Though academics parcel out human behaviour into discrete packages marked 'perception', 'learning', 'culture', etc. they are inextricably linked in practice. The reasons people have for doing things are linked to the society in which they live and their perceptions of the options available to them.
- **Needs can be satisfied in a number of ways**. Knowing why people do things does not automatically indicate what they will do. Many kinds of tourism may offer solutions to the same drive/need.
- **It is sometimes necessary to distinguish between different levels and kinds of motivation**. One useful distinction is that between primary tourism motivators and hygiene motivators: the former are the major reasons that determine a holiday or destination choice (rest, escape, cultural interests, etc.); the latter are needs to do with the provision of services (safe air travel, clean lavatories on a camp site, drinkable water in the hotel) which may be *necessary* but *insufficient* conditions of a successful stay.

Some approaches to tourism motivation

Tourism motivation has been extensively written about and many inventories have been produced classifying the principal needs. Historically tourism in its early forms was often the result of two general impulses – religion and health.

- **Religious motivations**. The origins of tourism have been said to lie in the religious pilgrimages taken by the devout to shrines such as Compostella del Santiago, Canterbury and Rome. More recently it has been argued that tourism is a latterday form of secular pilgrimage (Graburn, 1977), one of whose goals is sun worship (with long periods of trance-like state at the shrine of the sun god, with anointing rituals and the final goal of redemptive attainment – the tan). Another goal of the tourist/pilgrim can be seen as cultural experience; indeed, as the elitist conception of culture we looked at earlier suggests, art and cultural acquisition have been pursued with a semi-religious fervour by many educated initiates.
- **Medical reasons**. Many resorts in Britain and Europe from the seventeenth century onwards were coastal or inland spa towns where people went to take the waters to recover or improve their health, and by the nineteenth century holidays in general were being seen as medically beneficial as at least one Victorian doctor observed:

There must certainly be something more than mere fancy in the sudden improvement which many experience in their feelings and general state of health by leaving England for a tour on the continent. I have now had opportunities of witnessing its beneficial effects on the constitution of invalids whom I accompanied during such an excursion, and speak therefore from experience.

(Granville, 1866: xxxi)

Yet set against this convalescent/recuperative view it can be argued that tourism produces more physical wear and tear than being at home through the sheer slog of tourism activity – long journeys, heat fatigue, unpredictable climates, unfamiliar diets, etc. In more modern days the emphasis is more likely to be put on mental rather than physical improvement:

A holiday is undertaken in response to a sense of internal damage or depletion and represents a period of replenishment and restoration.

(Hills, 1965)

Neither religious or medical factors go very far in explaining the enormous variety of modern tourism. Probably they never did. Pilgrimages, as Chaucer described, were characterized by conviviality, carousing and sexual licence en route as much as a quest for religious enlightenment. Spa tourism at places like Bath and Baden-Baden were not just about health; they were also opportunities for social display, romantic liaison, marital matchmaking and partying for many who were already in the best of health.

In the past forty years many other motives for tourism, besides religion and health, have been offered by tourism planners and academics. One early approach to leisure/tourism motivation was Dumazedier's (1957) 3-D formulation:

- *délassement* – relaxation;
- *divertissement* – entertainment;
- développement – improvement.

A fourth D, *dépassement*, meaning surmounting or overcoming, was added by Comic (1989).

Macintosh (1978) also identified four basic groups of motivators, which owe something to Maslow's ideas:

- physical motivators – health, tension reduction, etc.;
- cultural motivators – art, religions, ways of life, etc.;
- interpersonal motivators – visit with or to friends and relatives;
- status or prestige motivators – esteem, personal development, e.g. business conference, conventions.

Other theorists have produced much longer inventories of tourist motivation. Hudman and Hawkins (1989) listed ten main ones: health, curiosity, sport (participation), sport (watching), pleasure, VFR, professional and business, pursuit of 'roots', self-esteem, religion. Schmoll (1977) grouped motivations into six combinations:

- educational and cultural;
- relaxation, adventure, pleasure;
- health and recreation;
- ethnic and family;
- social and competitive (including status and prestige).

Perhaps the longest inventory of all was that of Thomas (1964) who listed no less than 18:

Education and cultural motives:
1. To see how people in other countries live
2. To see particular sights
3. To gain a better understanding of what goes on in the news
4. To attend special events

Relaxation and pleasure:
5. To get away from everyday routine
6. To have a good time
7. To achieve some sort of sexual or romantic experience

Ethnic:
8. To visit places your family came from (e.g. Americans and Canadians in Scotland and black Americans in Africa)
9. To visit places your family or friends have gone to

Other:
10. Weather
11. Health (sun, dry climate and so on)
12. Sports (swim, ski, fish, sail)

13. Economy (inexpensive living)
14. Adventure (new areas, people, experiences)
15. One-upmanship
16. Conformity (keeping up with the Joneses)
17. To participate in history (ancient temples and ruins, current history)
18. Sociological motives (get to know the world – or other classes)

What are the problems with these inventories? Though these motivational catalogues shed some light on tourism behaviour they are too broad
to be of much practical use. For most tourism planners the key question is
not 'what makes people take part in tourism in general' but 'what needs
does my specific product (short-break package, cruise, airline) meet and
how successfully will it do so/is it doing so/has it done so?'

Answering these questions demands some knowledge of research techniques that can be used to explore tourism motivations.

Researching tourism motivation

Multiple-choice inventories
The commonest method of motivational investigation by the tourism
industry is based on survey research using questionnaires administered by
interviewers or self-completed by the respondent (guest, flyer, visitor).
Motivational questions are often included as multiple-choice inventories
in which the respondent is encouraged to choose one or more options from
a list of alternatives ('Which of these is your main reason for visiting
Butlins?' 'Tick from the following list the things you want from a skiing
holiday', etc.). In 1970 the Canadian government carried out a study which
listed 26 reasons for travel (CGTB, 1970).

The popularity of multiple-choice inventories is that they produce neat
quantifiable hierarchies in which motives can be clearly ranked. Statistical
tests can also be performed on the ranked motivations (cluster analysis,
factor analysis) so that they can be converted into broader groupings of
motivations that occur together.

There are, however, major problems with multiple-choices inventories.
Firstly, since the categories of choice have been determined by the
researcher it is difficult to assess to what extent the answers are merely
responses to the categories offered and so may omit important factors the
researcher hasn't taken into account as possibilities. Secondly, the verbal
items offered in multiple-choice inventories are usually simple ones, often
a sentence or even a word, which may not do justice to the complexity of
tourist motives. The Spanish visitor study carried out in 1992 asked tourists
'Why have you chosen Spain?' but included only six one-word options in
a multiple-choice inventory which comprised: 'climate', 'prices',
'entertainment', 'kindness', 'quietness' and 'others'.

Open-ended self report
One method of avoiding the dangers of multiple-choice questions is to
include open-ended questions which invite the respondent to use *their own*

words and categories in responding to broad questions ('What do you most want from a weekend break?', 'How could executive flying be improved?'). Open-ended questions may be focused on a specific product ('What did you like/dislike about Boston?', 'How do you think British Airways compares with other airlines?') or posed about more general tourism issues. Open-ended questions may be included in survey questionnaires or used as prompt questions in group discussions and individual depth interviews.

Direct observation

This involves watching what people do or getting them to record their activities and then inferring the motives that lie behind them. Some tourist boards inventory long lists of holiday activities and then try to assess the proportion of people who engage in each and thus their motives. A recent study of holidaymakers in four European countries indicated that French and UK families took part in more activities on holiday than Italians, and that the latter were more passively motivated than others (Seaton and Tagg, 1994). The problem is that such inferential techniques rely on the judgement of an external source and do not necessarily represent the subjective perspectives of the people whose motives are being inferred; the same action may derive from different motives, so knowing what people do does not produce an unambiguous picture of their motives for them. A variant of this is **participant observation** where the researcher joins the group under scrutiny (a coach party, package tour) and observes the motives of the group as one of its members. Research methods are discussed in more detail in the chapter following this.

Conclusions

Two conclusions may be ventured at the end of this brief discussion of the complicated issue of motivation:

- For tourism planners, as opposed to academics and theorists, the most useful way of identifying or measuring motivation is **in relation to specific tourism offerings or potential offerings**, rather than poring over inventories of general tourism motivations.
- For practical purposes it is often more realistic to concentrate on the **choice criteria** that govern tourist decisions rather than underlying motives which people may not know, won't admit or can't articulate. It is, for instance, more important for an airline to know that executives want short embarkation and disembarkation times than that such wants spring from embedded status concerns, competitive aggression or anxiety about schedules.

Tourism and perception

Perception is critical to tourism behaviour before, during and after the tourism experience. Long before the trip is taken perception will determine destination choice. Once the trip has begun perception is involved in sightseeing, attraction visiting, and satisfaction with accommodation and hospitality. However, perception, like motivation, is a vast field so all we can do is cover some basic concepts and indicate, where possible, their applications.

Perception starts with sensations – messages that come to us via our senses. There are five main sense modes – sight, sound, taste, touch, smell – and in addition four others – pain, cold, warmth, kinesthesis (sense of movement and position in space) and vestibular (body balance, position, movement).

CASE STUDY 3.4

Sounds and music in perceptions of destinations, attractions and restaurants

Southworth (1969) explored city sounds inventorying over 40 different kinds of noise, the commoner ones including: traffic, people, birds, echoes, water, planes, bells and doors slamming; the less frequent ones included: horse clopping, motorcycles, people kicking ash cans, boats creaking, kitchen sounds, dogs and telephone bells.

One tourism attraction in Britain which has explicitly recognized the value of the aural environment is the open air heritage museum at Beamish:

> Sounds are particularly nostalgic and bring reality to our recollections: ducks and hens, rattling tramcars, crackling fires, creaking vehicles, brass bands . . .

(Beamish souvenir guide).

Music has been demonstrated to affect commercial transactions. A study by Burleston (1979) in America found that 76% of managers in 52 retail stores thought customers bought more as the result of background music, while 82% thought it had a favourable effect upon the customer's mood. Milliman (1982) compared the effect of slow vs. fast tempo music on purchase patterns and found that slow-tempo music significantly increased sales volumes and made people stay longer.

At attractions music can be used to create the appropriate atmosphere. The London Museum plays barrel organ noises to evoke Victorian England and the Jorvic Museum in York uses sounds to bring to life the world of the Vikings. Music can also be used to make people feel relaxed (important, for example, for airline passengers in flight) or more revved up (loud disco music on board a floating nightclub, for instance).

In restaurants music is an important signifier of atmosphere. A study by Milliman (1986) carried out in the Dallas/Fort Worth area of Texas examined the effect of slow vs. fast music on several variables including: service time, customer time at table, amount of food and drink purchased, and estimated gross margin. The results suggested that people stayed at table on average 11 minutes longer (56 mins vs. 45 mins) and ordered an average of 3.04 more drinks when they were exposed to the slow music. Moreover, gross takings were on average 55.82 dollars for the slow music vs. 48.62 dollars with the fast. As Milliman noted at the end of the study, similar experiments could be carried out isolating other variables apart from music (carpeting, wall decor, temperature, etc.).

During a prolonged experience such as a tourist trip all of these senses will be incessantly activated in new environments: taste may be involved in trying regional food specialities; smell in responses to such things as sea air; the ear will catch street sounds and natural phenomena (wind, rain, cicadas chirping); touch may involve the texture of brick or the feel of wind or sun against one's cheek, etc. The kinesthetic and vestibular senses may be invoked in a turbulent air passage, a bumpy bus trek or a choppy channel crossing.

Smell is one of the most evocative of senses and a great memory trigger, particularly evocative of nostalgic pasts. Beamish Open Air Museum in Durham has capitalized on the smells of yesteryear to bring to life industrial and rural heritage including animal smells in its farm area and, in its 1920s dentist's surgery, the smell of clove oil connotes dental practices of yesteryear.

Sensation is not the same as perception. Sensations are the raw material of experience but the way we react to them is perception. Perception has been defined as:

> . . . the process by which an individual selects, organizes, and interprets stimuli into a meaningful and coherent picture of the world. A stimulus is any unit of input to any of the senses . . . The study of perception is largely the study of what we subconsciously add to or subtract from our raw sensory inputs to produce our private picture of the world . . .
>
> (Schiffman and Kanuk, 1985: 59)

Perception is *dyadic*, an interaction between two things: the observer and what is observed. In more formal terms we can define the two interacting factors as follows.

The Object Stimulus
What we perceive is affected by the thing itself – the object 'out there' in the 'real world'. In tourism terms stimuli might include skylines, a beach colour, the texture of a wall, the sound of an accent or a song on a foreign radio station, the look of a meal, the setting of a house, the height of a cliff. In promotional terms they might include packaging, brand names, brochures, commercials, as well as a whole range of representational features such as adverts, travel books, films, etc.

These object stimuli have physical properties such as size, shape, colour, tone, intensity, weight, height, texture, etc. The characteristics of stimuli help to determine the degree of perceptual impact.

Not all object stimuli lie outside the observer. A stimulus may be internal as well as external. A thought, an idea or a memory which comes to us may produce its own response, as when we smile at the recollection of a good time, go hot to remember an embarrassing situation and so on. The anticipation of a tourism experience may provide many pleasant perceptions before setting a foot outside the door, and many fond memories may linger after the return.

These stimuli can often be manipulated in tourism planning. A park may be landscaped; a museum can be given a certain colour scheme, an exhibition a themed layout; an airline may choose a particular livery. In promotional terms, an advert can be made up of certain elements of colour, size and symbol to try to maximize its impact. However, the stimulus is, of course, only partly within the control of the tourism provider. A tourist board cannot create a mountain range, a seaboard or snowscape, but it can finance the landscaping of a lakeside, or renovate an old building, while in the Dordogne tourism authorities have created sandy beaches for inland lakes.

Certain stimulus properties improve the chance of perception. Other things being equal big is more impactful than small, bright than dull, colourful than dowdy, and movement is more eyecatching than static features etc.

Perceiver factors

Perception is not simply a matter of the stimulus involved. Perception, like beauty, is significantly in the 'eye of the beholder'. Both the perceiver's physiological and psychological make-up (i.e. his or her physical condition and mental state) play a big part in what is perceived. There may, for instance, be circumstances when the biggest may be ignored and the smallest singled out. In a page of names written in different size type a person will notice and attend closely to his or her own name, even though it may be in the smallest type. Similarly a dull pub sign may be noticed by a thirsty football team while a bright revolving advert for an international airline next to it may be ignored. In short, the characteristics of the individual perceiver – the motives, attitudes, past experiences, mental traits, etc. – influence what is perceived.

The stimulus and perceiver factors that might influence the perception of a tourism experience can be inventoried as follows:

Stimulus factors	Perceiver factors
Intensity	Education
Size	Intelligence
Temperature	Needs
Novelty	Interests
Sounds	Expectations
Movement	Personality
Colour	Group factors
Shape	Culture
Multiple sensory inputs	Class

Selective perception

Perception is not a passive, automatic response, but involves an active effort of decoding in which some parts of a stimulus are attended to and emphasized while others are not. People don't respond to the total field of stimuli around them; they respond to a fraction of stimuli. It has been estimated that the individual has the sensory apparatus to experience about 50 000 impressions per minute, but in reality only takes in a limited number. In arriving at a new place, for example, we may be bowled over by a few immediate impressions but ignore many more. The perception of landscape is an immensely selective process that involves one's whole history – including education, place of origin, aesthetic preferences and many more. People filter what they 'take in' but their strategies for doing so become such second nature that they hardly realize it.

Selective perceptions are involved from the moment that a tourist is first motivated to see a sight (perhaps months or even years before the actual experience) to the moment when he or she actually gazes upon it. Knowing what to see is a source of tourist anxiety which can be reduced by the provision of guidebooks and effective promotional materials or trained tour guides.

When people come from similar backgrounds they tend to perceive in similar ways. But in tourism this is not the case. The people who plan and offer tourism are often very different from those who consume it. This holds true as much for the residents of a country trying to attract foreigners as for the museum curator or nature park manager trying to attract the general public who don't share his or her specialist perceptions of art exhibits or fauna and flora. Tourists may differ in their perceptions of the same tourism events. What a middle-aged couple may find attractive about Italy may bore their teenage children; what may attract their children to Benidorm may deter others.

Perceptual set, readiness and expectation

One aspect of selective perception is the concept of perceptual set and expectancy which suggests that what we 'see' is often governed by previous experience rather than by what is there. Perceptual set has two meanings, (a) the one referring to the impact of immediate, previous experience on perception; (b) the other to the effect of more long-term factors in a individual's make-up which create tendencies to respond in a certain way. The two kinds have been defined follows (von Fieandt and Moustgaard, 1977: 524):

(a) '. . . relatively short-term temporary and personality-unintegrated states, due to preceding events in general . . .';
(b) '. . . relatively long lasting and personality-integrated, inborn or deeply anchored directive tendencies . . .'.

Thus the first kind refers to the manner in which people's immediate needs and motives can influence their perceptual set. It may include personal factors such as hunger or tiredness. A classic experiment demonstrated how people experiencing hunger differed in their perceptions of Rorschach ink blots from those who had just had a meal. States of mind such as anger, frustration and fear have also been demonstrated to alter perceptions. Manipulating people's prior emotional state affects their responses which is why many live TV shows begin with a warm-up artist to get the audience in a responsive frame of mind. Getting people in the mood may be important in the management of tourism trips and in the staging of entertainment events that may be a part of them. The promotion of tourism through advertising, brochures and other kinds of publicity acts as an attempt to delimit the characteristics of a tourism product – destination, attraction, transport form, etc. – to pre-establish the tourist's expectations ahead of the trip.

Type (b) is a much more difficult thing to demonstrate experimentally since it is about longer-term, often unconscious perceptual biases stemming from an individual's personality and social and cultural learning experiences. Some idea of how these more general predispositions may influence tourist behaviour can be gained from this description in a guidebook written over 150 years ago:

> . . . the pleasure of travelling depends at least as much upon the state of a man's mind as on the objects he beholds. Those who set out in good health, with light hearts, and a disposition to be pleased, will be likely to secure a large sum of enjoyment. A peevish or fastidious traveller will find sources of dissatisfaction amongst the highest beauties of nature or art; whilst the good-humoured man will draw amusement even from accidents and hardships . . .
>
> (Baines, 1834: 13)

Perceptual sets of both (a) and (b) varieties are important in tourism. At the moment a customer books a holiday the product does not physically exist; it is purely a matter of expectation and image. One of the major functions of tourism providers is to *prefigure* their offerings to consumers – i.e. create a perceptual set – not only to trigger the decision, but also to steer perceptions of the experience when they come to take the trip. MacCannell (1979) has identified 'marking' as central to the tourism process – the labelling of things and places in ways that construct its tourism significance. Perceptual expectation can be significantly affected by trained guides, couriers, travel books and promotional material. In Iceland, for example, where Viking heritage is a major cultural feature of the country but there are few physical relics to see, guides are extensively trained to bring to life the history of each area through verbal commentaries for the tourist. Research carried out at Prince Edward Island suggests that tourists stay longer, spend more money and evince greater satisfaction if they have read a guidebook than those who have not (Woodside et al, 1996).

Perceptions of tourist roles

The role of tourist is associated with many role expectations people would not hold in everyday life. These are implicit rather than formally specified but tourism providers ignore them at their peril. Here are some:

- expectation of being waited on and indulged;
- not having to speak the language;

- sensitization to aesthetic/cultural experience less salient for the rest of the year;
- expectation of new social encounters with both hosts/providers of tourism and other travellers;
- expectation of distinctive or increased levels of drinking and eating out;
- expectations of abnormal levels of sun;
- expectation of adventure and *liminal* behaviour ('off-the-leash' behaviour that goes beyond the normal limits of everyday life);
- expectation of daily novelty (the 'what-shall-we-do-today' syndrome);
- desire to recapture and make permanent the vacation experience;
- desire for participation in the myths of place and travel (to experience Byron's Italy, drink in Hemingway's bar, etc.);
- dream of existential transformation, a new you, etc.

Not all these role expectations may operate in all tourism but some of them will be present in any. It is important for tourism providers to be aware of them to make sure that the services they supply as part of the tourism experience live up to expectations.

Tourism is a peculiar business since, while ultimately a commercially, mass-provided transaction in which a customer pays for a product, it is most successful when it appears as a spontaneous, unique one-to-one relationship individually offered to a person rather than an organizational product sold to an anonymous paying client. The ambiguities of the word 'hospitality' highlight this paradox; in private life hospitality is something one person gives freely as a courtesy or gift to another, but in the public domain it is the name given to a set of commercial transactions. Research has suggested that some travellers implicitly seek a unique, one-to-one, personal relationship with staff in a hotel, on a plane or with the locals at a resort, and the closer that service provision simulates this the more successful the product will be seen to be.

CASE STUDY 3.5

How occasion and context affect perceptions of eating out

In a Canadian study of consumer perceptions of hospitality, June and Smith (1987) got diners to rank 18 restaurants on five attributes: price, atmosphere, liquor licence, service and food quality, and then to rank them in order of preference for four different occasions: an intimate dinner, a birthday party, a business lunch and a family dinner. There were marked dissimilarities for the four different contexts. Service was regarded as the most important factor for business lunches but second to liquor choice for an intimate dinner. Price was the least factor for an intimate dinner but the second most important factor for both the business lunch and the family dinner.

Source: June and Smith (1987).

Stereotyping

One form of perceptual set/expectancy which is particularly common in tourism behaviour is stereotyping. A stereotype is a simplified image of something based on fragmentary, often very limited information.

Stereotyping affects a tourist's response to people, places, food, etc. It is an important process in the formation of *destination images* (see Chapter 14 for a discussion of this important concept). Travel may be motivated by a desire to encounter stereotypes (to experience the 'real' Spain, for instance, conceived as a place for encountering heel-clicking flamenco dancers and slim-hipped bullfighters) or, for other travellers, a desire to get behind such stereotypes to a more 'authentic' reality (often a different set of stereotypes). In 1980 the French tourist authorities discovered that tourists had an adverse image of the French as arrogant and unhelpful, and mounted a publicity campaign to encourage tourism providers to be more friendly and welcoming.

Stereotyping is a two-way process. Just as tourists have stereotypes of their hosts, so hosts hold stereotypes of their guests. Pearce (1982) noted that the English were perceived as insular abroad and that young Australians were seen as gauche and sex-hungry.

Tourism providers need to identify and define the stereotypes that may affect demand for their products and then decide to what degree they need to be (a) reinforced; (b) changed; (c) added to. Reinforcement is easiest while change hardest, which is why Spain has invested large sums of money to reverse the 'cheapo, lager-lout' reputation parts of the Costas achieved in the 1970s and 1980s.

In general tourism deals in national stereotypes that are often out of date but important in attracting tourists. This may be deplored by people like the writer Robert Byron who once wrote: '*The human museum is horrible, such as islands off the coast of Holland where the Dutch retain their national dress*' (Byron, 1938: 22). However, for every Byron there are a hundred less sophisticated tourists who respond to such stereotypes. Stereotypes are often what tourists are travelling to see. This is why Paris will probably continue to be gay, bohemian and romantic, India exotic and mysterious, Ireland quaint, charming and easy-paced, despite the fact that such typifications may not correspond to the images their inhabitants have of themselves.

Effort after meaning

Humans finds ambiguity threatening and seek to reduce it by trying to organize and impose structure in new situations. This has been called the 'effort after meaning' by Bartlett, an early theorist/researcher on perception and memory. One of the implications of this 'effort after meaning' is the importance of first or early impressions. A classic experiment by Asch (1952) which involved reading out the same verbal character descriptions of a person to two audiences backward and forward showed very different impressions being formed depending on which descriptors were heard first.

The implications are considerable in tourism. The initial impact of a place may set the tone for the rest of the trip. Large airports and other arrival points can be designed to be appealing. Calgary Airport in Canada offers the arriving visitor a modern, clean, upbeat pathway from plane to exit, including well designed murals emphasizing sport and the Winter Olympics. The ferry terminal at Calais is, in contrast, a messy sprawl which does not create a pleasing first experience of France. The Glasgow Development Agency has considered ways of developing a prime route from the airport into Glasgow city centre which will avoid the less attract-ive features of the city and create a favourable image for international visitors on arrival. This 'first impression' principle can be applied to other tourism offerings – the initial welcome provided by a hotel or restaurant, the first sight of a landscaped promenade, the entrance to a new attraction and so on.

Perceptions of the travel agent

Travel agents are important mediators of holiday/vacation consumption but little work has been published on how they are perceived. One of the few studies that has was that by Kendall and Booms (1989) who found that consumers agreed there were differences between agents but found it difficult to specify those differences, although perceived differences in knowledge of travel alternatives and ability to offer the same or different prices were mentioned as two.

CASE STUDY 3.6

Perceptions of retailers

Though little work has been done on perceptions of travel retailers more is known about retail perceptions and store image in general. A particularly useful inventory is that of Lindquist (1975) who reviewed a number of studies and concluded that retail image involved nine major variables:

* merchandise: range of holidays;
* service: manner of staff, helpfulness, etc.;
* clientele: other customers;
* physical facilities: atmosphere, hardware etc.:
* convenience: closeness, queuing, service time;
* promotion: in-store and media;
* store atmosphere: colour, light, comfort, heat, etc.;
* institutional factors: reputation, reliability, old-fashioned, etc.;
* post-transaction satisfaction: follow-up after transaction decision and after trip.

Many of these factors also operate in forming the image of hotels, restaurants and attractions. They therefore form a useful basis for analysing all such products.

The measurement of perceptions

The only way these perceptual differences can be anticipated and managed is through observation and research, which is why people responsible for the administration of destinations, attractions, accommodation and other tourism products are moving to the notion of continuous tracking on how they are perceived by their clients. The tourism provider needs to understand the perceptions of the target visitor both before, during and after the tourism experience. In the next chapter we shall review some of the variety of research techniques which can be used to track perceptions and other aspects of tourist behaviour.

THE MEASUREMENT OF TOURIST SATISFACTION

Successful tourism marketing is about the development of tourism programmes which will deliver a level of customer satisfaction that will make the customer want to come back. The creation of the regular flyer with the same airline, the repeat visitor to a destination, the brand-loyal hotel guest, the client who returns to the same tour operator or travel agent – these should be the priorities of tourism organizations.

The monitoring of tourist satisfaction is thus a critical issue in tourism marketing, not just to determine the success of a tourism product but also, when problems emerge, to indicate areas for improvement. In the next chapter we shall deal with market research techniques which can be used to explore a number of tourism issues including the monitoring of tourist satisfaction. In what remains of this chapter we shall address three preliminary issues.

The dominance of the quantitative, questionnaire-based survey in tourist satisfaction research

Many approaches to tourist satisfaction research methods have been described and prescribed by both academics and practitioners in the literature on tourism research (Veal, 1992; Ryan, 1995) but in practice one approach dominates the industry – the quantitative, questionnaire-based survey using multiple-choice responses. The basis of such studies, like those we have described in tourism motivation research earlier, is a questionnaire administered through a face-to-face interview (e.g. a visitor study carried out at an attraction or in the home of the respondent), by phone or through a self-completion form (e.g. a questionnaire left in a hotel room for the guest to complete when he or she checks out). Such questionnaires are then analysed and the results quantified to provide data on what percentage of respondents were satisfied/dissatisfied with their experience and what things about it they liked or disliked. The dominance of the survey means that any tourism marketer needs to be thoroughly familiar with the major factors involved in designing, administering and analysing questionnaire surveys including sampling methods. These are explored in the next chapter.

The under-usage of qualitative and observational measures of tourist satisfaction.

The dominance of the quantitative, questionnaire-based surveys may be a barrier to determining some kinds of tourist satisfaction. Questionnaire surveys are used because tourism managers, like many others, feel safe with a methodology which everybody else is using and which can be easily transformed into neat columns of statistics which look like objective, scientific evidence. What most managers rarely see, because they are rarely part of the field force which administers them, is the amount of information which eludes surveys. Their limitations in satisfaction research include the following:

- For one-off, fast-exit events such as festivals there is often little time to get people to complete a questionnaire (e.g. when a concert finishes, or people leave a beach party).
- Satisfaction is often a function of a range of factors which can rarely be comprehensively anticipated before a tourism experience, however hard tourism researchers try to do so in the questionnaire design. (Anyone who has ever filled in a hotel or in-flight questionnaire will be aware of the comments they cannot make because of the structure of the questionnaire and, often, the irrelevance of the ones that they can.
- A survey may reveal broad satisfaction ratings but not the reasons for them.
- People's verbal responses to verbal surveys never adequately reflect the totality of their reactions to a tourism experience (or any other for that matter).

These limitations can be overcome in two ways:

- **through qualitative verbal methodologies** based on interviewing people individually or in groups on an open-ended basis, thus allowing them a greater freedom of expression, instead of being funnelled into responses dictated by the rigid categories included in the questionnaire;
- **through direct observation by trained observers** of people on a trip or at an event which can include a diverse range of non-verbal evidence impossible to gain via other methods. Recent work at Strathclyde University into tourist satisfactions at festivals and events staged by regional, public sector organizations in Scotland has resulted in the decision to augment all future questionnaire surveys with observational measures of tourist satisfaction (Seaton, 1996).

The impact of motivation and perception on tourist satisfaction

Though, in this chapter, we have kept motivation, perception and satisfaction separate they are highly interrelated. The degree of satisfaction with a tourism experience is affected by what the tourist wanted and expected to get out of it. This means that asking questions such as 'did you enjoy your trip?', 'what did you like/dislike about the trip?' 'what improvements would you like to see?' which seek to determine **general** levels of satisfactions, may be less useful than trying to establish pre-trip expectations and then assessing how they affect post-trip satisfactions. A number of satisfaction research programmes have attempted to do this through the use of pre and post surveys which determine first **what people are looking for** before the trip and **how important the different elements in the total tourism package are perceived to be**, and then going back to them after the event to see how the tourism experience stacked up against expectations.

Two interesting findings have emerged. One is that a quite moderate tourism experience might produce high levels of satisfaction if it greatly exceeds expectations that were originally low, whereas a more substantial tourism experience may produce a smaller magnitude of satisfaction if the tourist's expectations were high in the first place (Chon, 1989). Secondly, studies of festivals and events by Crompton and Love (1995) have found that, though individual components of a festival (the seating arrangements, the catering facilities, for instance) may be rated quite poorly, overall satisfaction with the event may be still high if the negatively rated components were not originally seen as centrally important to the event's success.

The practical problem with these approaches is the necessity of carrying out two surveys – the one a pre-study to determine expectations and then a post-study to determine the achieved level of success vs. expectations – which is sometimes difficult. A further problem is that tourists sometimes find it hard to say what they expect of a tourism experience before it has taken place, particularly if it is of a kind that is new to them.

SUMMARY

This chapter has provided a condensed account of a few of the main issues that lie behind tourism behaviour. More specialist treatment of some can be found in Pearce (1982), Ryan (1995) which has a particularly good chapter (Chapter 3) on tourist satisfaction, and Sharpley (1994) which offers a useful basic introduction to the sociology of tourism. For all tourism organizations understanding the nature of their markets, both quantitatively and qualitatively, is essential. Though tourism marketers do not consciously think in general labels marked 'perceptions', 'motivations', 'social influences' as we have done here, the concepts and issues they encompass underlie the bases of choice and experience of all tourism products.

By way of conclusion we will finish with a practical seven-point checklist for behavioural analysis of tourism markets:

- Identify customer and kind of trip sought (the segmentation analysis outlined in Chapter 2).
- Identify the main motivations.

- Identify relevent product choice criteria relevant to motivations.
- Identify perceptions and expectations of product.
- Identify decision sequence: how, by whom and over what period the decision is taken.
- Identify influences on decisions: family, groups, reference groups, influencers/opinion formers, etc.
- Check satisfaction levels and post-trip evaluations.

Trying to answer each of these questions will at least focus the organization on what makes their product chosen, used and enjoyed – and by whom.

REFERENCES

Asch, S. (1952) *Social Psychology*, Prentice-Hall, New York.

Baines, E. (1834) *A Companion to the Lakes*, 3rd edn, Simpkin & Marshall, London.

Boechner, S. (1982) *Cultures in Contact*, quoting Kroeber and Kluckholm, *Culture: A Critical Review of Concepts and Definitions*, papers of the Peabody Museum, No. 47.

Burleston, G.L. (1979) 'Retailer and consumer attitudes towards background music', unpublished PhD thesis, University of Texas at El Paso.

Byron, R. (1938) *The Road to Oxiana*, Macmillan, London.

Chon, K.-S. (1989) The role of destination image in tourism. A review and discussion, *The Tourist Review*, No. 45, pp. 2–9.

Cohen, E. (1972) Towards a sociology of international tourism, *Social Research*, **39**(1), 164–82.

Comic, D.J. (1989) Tourism as a subject for philosophical reflection, *Revue de Tourisme*, No. 2.

Consultur (1993) *Encuesta a no residentes*, Secretaria General de Turismo, Barcelona and Madrid.

Crompton, J.L. and Love, L. (1995) The predictive validity of alternative approaches to evaluating quality of a festival, *Journal of Travel Research*, **xxxiv** (1), Summer, 11–24.

Davidoff, P.G and Davidoff, D.S. (1983) *Sales and Marketing for Travel and Tourism*, Prentice-Hall, Englewood Cliffs, New Jersey. (This includes a brief account of Gottlieb's ideas on pp. 221–3.)

Duesenberry, J. (1987) Quoted in Assael, H. *Consumer Behavior and Marketing Action*, Kent, Boston.

Dumazedier, J. (1967) *Towards a Society of Leisure*, Free Press, New York.

Edgell, D. (1994) *World Tourism at the Millenium*, US Dept of Commerce, USSTA.

Engel, J.F., Blackwell, R.D. and Miniard, P.W. (1990) *Consumer Behaviour*, Dryden Press, Chicago.

Fussell, P. (1989) *Abroad*, Oxford University Press, New York and London.

Graburn, N. (1977) Tourism: the sacred journey, in Smith, V. (ed.), *Hosts and Guests: The Anthropology of Tourism*, Blackwell, Oxford, pp. 17–32.

Graburn, N. (1983) The anthropology of tourism, *Annals of Tourism Research*, **10**, 9–33.

Granville, A.B. (1866) *Bradshaw's Continental Railway Guide*, Bradshaw, London.

Hills, J.M. (1965) *Holidays: A Study of the Social and Psychological Aspects with Special Reference to Ireland*, Tavistock, London.

Howard, J.A. and Sheth, J. (1969) *The Theory of Buyer Behavior*, Wiley, New York.

Hudman, L.E. and Hawkins, D.E. (1989) *Tourism in Contemporary Society*, Prentice-Hall, Englewood Cliffs, New Jersey.

June, L.P. and Smith, S.L.J. (1987) Service attributes and situational effects on customer preferences for restaurant dining, *Journal of Travel Research*, Fall, pp. 20–7.

Katona, G. (1954) Economic psychology, *Scientific American*, October.

Kendall, K.W. and Booms, B. (1989) Consumer perceptions of travel agencies: communications, images, needs and expectations, *Journal of Travel Research*, Spring, pp. 29–34.

Krippendorf, J. (1987) *The Holidaymakers*, Routledge, London.

Levi-Strauss, C. (1978) *Structural Anthropology*, Vol. 1, Allen Lane/ Penguin, London, p. 18.

Lindquist, J. (1975) The meaning of image, *Journal of Retailing*, **50**(4), 29–38.

MacCannel, D. (1979) *The Tourist*, Macmillan, London.

Macintosh, R.W. and Goeldner, C.R. (1986) *Tourism: Principles, Practices*, Philosophies, Wiley, New York.

Mannell, R.C. and Iso Ahola, S.E. (1987) The psychological nature of leisure and tourism experience, reporting R.G. Wahlers and M.J. Etzel, *Annals of Tourism Research* **14**(3), 314–31.

Maslow, A. (1967) *Towards a Psychology of Being*, Van Nostrand, New York.

Mason, P. (1993) Outlook for leisure/family vacation travel, in *Proceedings of 18th Annual Travel Outlook Forum*, US Travel Data Center, Washington.

Milliman, R.E. (1982) The effects of background music upon shopping behaviour of supermarket patrons, *Journal of Marketing*, **45**(3), 86–91.

Milliman, R.E. (1986) The influence of background music on the behaviour of restaurant patrons, *Journal of Consumer Research*, **13**, September, pp. 286–9.

Moutinho, L. (1987) Consumer behaviour in tourism, *European Journal of Marketing*, **21**(10), 1–44.

Oxford Society (1995) *Journal of the Oxford Society*, November, pp. 38–44.

Paci, E. (1994) The major international VFR markets, *EIU Travel and Tourism Analyst*, No. 6, August, pp. 36–50.

Pearce, P.L. (1982) *The Social Psychology of Tourism Behaviour*, Pergamon, Oxford.

Ryan, C. (1991) *Recreational Tourism: A Social Science Perspective*, Routledge, London.

Ryan, C. (1995) *Researching Tourism Satisfaction*, Routledge, London and New York.

Schiffman, L.G. and Kanuk, L.L. (1978) *Consumer Behaviour*, Prentice Hall, Englewood Cliffs, New Jersey.

Schmoll, G.A. (1977) *Tourism Promotion*, IUOTO, Geneva.

Scottish Tourism Research Unit (1995) *Eastwood Arts Festival Report.*

Seaton, A.V. (1992) Social stratification in tourism choice and behaviour since the war, *Tourism Management*, **13**(1), 106–12.

Seaton, A.V. (1996) Mass observation revived: unobtrusive measures as a qualitative extension of visitor surveys at festivals and events, unpublished research report.

Seaton, A.V. and Tagg, S.J. (1994) The European family holiday: a lifestyle analysis, in Gasser, R.V. and Weiermair, K. (eds), *Spoilt for Choice: Decision Making Processes and Preference Changes of Tourists: Intertemporal and Intercountry Perspectives*, University of Innsbruck/Kulterverlag, Vienna and Munich, pp. 99–119.

Seaton, A.V. and Tagg, S.J. (1995a) The European family vacation: paedonomic aspects of choices and satisfactions, *Journal of Travel and Tourism Marketing*, **4**(1), 1–21.

Seaton, A.V. and Tagg, S.J. (1995b) Disaggregating the VFR category: the Northern Ireland experience 1991–1993, *Journal of Tourism Studies*, December.

Sharpley, R. (1994) *Tourism, Tourists and Society*, Elm Press, Huntingdon, Cambs.

Southworth, M. (1969) The sonic environment of cities, *Environment and Behaviour*, **1**(1), 49–70.

Thomas, J.A. (1964) What makes people travel? *ASTA News*, August, pp. 64–5.

Veal, A.J. (1992) Research methods for leisure and tourism: a practical guide, Longman/ILAM, Harlow, Essex.

Von Fieandt, K. and Moustgaard, I.K. (1977) *The Perceptual World*, Academic Press, London and New York.

Wahab, S. (1975) *Wahab on Tourism Management*, London, Tourism International Press.

Woodside, A.G., Macdonald, R. and Trappey, R.J. (1996) Measuring linkage-advertising effects on customer behaviour and net revenue, unpublished paper.

REVIEW QUESTIONS

1. What would be the main macro-demand data an airline company might analyse in developing marketing plans for scheduled flights between London and New York?

2. What are the main problems in determining tourism motivation?

3. Suggest some of the perceptual features which would be worth monitoring in developing a new cruise ship primarily targeted at UK tourists?

4. Collect a range of brochures from a travel agent and attempt to identify:
   (a) the effects of family life cycle in their targeting and presentation;
   (b) the ways in which they construct versions of the 'other' in implied or explicit contrast with the 'everyday world'.
5. What impact do you think reference groups play in the market for travel and tourism products aimed at young singles?

4 Marketing research in tourism

M.M. Bennett

OBJECTIVES

By the end of this chapter the reader should:

- appreciate the importance of research in an organization;
- understand the process in undertaking a research plan;
- understand the difference between quantitative and qualitative methods and primary and secondary data;
- be able to evaluate the advantages and disadvantages of each method for the collection of data;
- understand the principles of sampling;
- be able to formulate a research plan to tackle a given problem.

MARKETING RESEARCH: THE WHAT AND WHY QUESTIONS

What is marketing research? It is the design of a plan for the collection of data, the purpose of which is to answer a given question. Such a question might be 'What do passengers think of our new revamped service?' or 'Who is the competition?' or 'What is the profile of our hotel guests?' These questions and others are commonplace in any organization, answers to which are vital for an understanding of the market within which the organization operates. The type of research undertaken falls into two camps: either it can assume a descriptive role whereby the aim is to focus on what is happening by concentrating on the collection of factual data to provide a picture of the current situation, or it can assume an analytical role by shifting the focus to why things are happening in an attempt to explain the situation by seeking out reasons. There is a logical progression from the descriptive type of research to the analytical. In order to understand why a particular situation has arisen it is of course first necessary to delineate the actual situation.

Historically, in the development of the tourism industry much emphasis has not surprisingly been placed on the 'what' question in the collection of descriptive statistics, and only in relatively recent years has there a been move to complement such data with an understanding of the reasons behind the statistics.

It is at this point that it is worth distinguishing between market research and marketing research. The key difference lies in the former's more specific focus on consumer behaviour while the latter encompasses a much broader spectrum of research of which consumer behaviour is just one part. This includes research on the four Ps – price, promotion, product and place (distribution).

Attention can now be turned to why marketing research is needed. In order to develop a strategic plan for an organization, it is imperative that information is gathered on the organization's performance and the marketplace. In other words information is needed on how well a product is selling – if it is an established product how sales compare with previous years at similar times, and if it is a new product, what are the growth trends and who are the purchasers? There is also a need to know who the competition is and what it is doing. Linked to this is the need to assess price in relation to both sales and the competition. Distribution strategy needs to be monitored and assessed to evaluate its effectiveness in reaching the consumer as does the various forms of promotion implemented in terms of which offers, incentives and advertising yield the most success.

Answers to all of these questions are necessary as a basis for an organization to make decisions. Without such information any decisions taken run the risk of being bad ones which could prove very costly both financially and otherwise to the long-term health of the organization. Consequently all organizations whether large or small should undertake research and such research should be carried out on a regular basis. Changes within the marketplace, among consumers, within the organization, will all have an effect on the organization. Such effects need to be evaluated continuously to minimize the risks involved of any decisions taken. While information gathered from marketing research will not be perfect, if the research is well planned and executed it will mean that decisions taken will more likely prove successful.

THE RESEARCH PROCESS

In undertaking research there are a series of steps which should be followed. Depending upon author, the number of steps varies from six according to Reid (1989) to nine in Kinnear and Taylor (1991). Although authors are clearly at variance in the precise number of steps involved, the actual process remains the same.

Identify and define the problem

Before beginning the task of gathering information it is first necessary to identify the problem for which research is required. This is crucial to ensure that any information collected is relevant and not wasted. A failure at this stage to adequately define the problem will result in wasted effort later. As well as formulating an aim, specific research questions (objectives) should be stipulated at the outset. It is these objectives which will determine the type of information required.

Investigate available sources

There is little point embarking upon a research programme involving the collection of primary data if information is already available. Therefore the next step is to seek out the information which is available. This will involve a trawl of internal data generated and recorded by the organization and an examination of secondary sources of data available. Such information should then be assessed to establish the extent to which the research questions can be tackled using this information alone. It may well be the case that a partial answer is provided but that further research is needed to satisfy the full objective.

Determine research plan

Once all available sources of data have been evaluated, a plan is formulated to identify what further information is required and how it should be collected. This will involve generating hypotheses to be tested and determining the manner in which information is to be collected (methodology). Methods that may be used include surveys, interviews and observation.

Data collection

Upon development of a research plan, data should be collected using the method(s) selected. During this stage of the process, great care should be taken to avoid bias which if introduced could render any results meaningless. This is a particular problem associated with the interview and observation methods.

Data analysis

The methods used and the type of information collected will determine the analysis needed. For example, qualitative information will require a different type of analysis to information of a more quantitative nature. While the former may involve some sort of content analysis, the latter will almost certainly involve statistical analysis whether descriptive or inferential. The increasing application of computer programs to data analysis has quickened the actual process of number crunching although time still has to be spent on preparing the data for analysis. A general rule in the analysis of data is to begin with the simple before moving onto the more complicated.

Present research results

Information needs to be tabulated and interpreted such that recommendations can be made regarding an appropriate course of action to take. This will almost certainly involve the presentation of a report which summarizes the results of the research thereby enabling the management of the organization to make decisions based on the newly acquired information. The importance of such information, and in particular the manner in which it is collected, is thus evident.

SECONDARY VERSUS PRIMARY DATA

Data collected for research can be distinguished according to secondary and primary types. **Secondary** data is data which already exists for an established purpose. It is also referred to as **documents** and **desk research**. It has a number of uses including the following.

- **Background material** – seeking out existing sources of information provides background material for the study and reduces the chances of repeating a study which has already been conducted.
- **Substitute for primary research** – if the existing data is adequate this can replace the need to undertake a new study. Instead the secondary data can be re-analysed for the purpose in hand.
- **Use for its own merits** – in certain circumstances the use of secondary data may be preferable to the collection of new data. In particular the use of secondary data can overcome some of the problems associated with new data such as sampling error and bias.

Sources

Sources of secondary data include the following.

- **Government agencies**. Statistics on visitor numbers are produced on a regular basis, e.g. the United Kingdom Tourism Survey (UKTS), the International Passenger Survey. The four tourist boards responsible for the UKTS are a source of information as are particular departments of central government including the Department of Trade and Industry (DTI). As well as generating a considerable amount of statistical data at the macro level, government is also responsible for a number of tourism related publications.
- **Trade associations**. Hotels, travel agents, tour operators and airlines all have associated trade bodies which compile information on their members and the market.
- **Trade press**. *Travel Trade Gazette* and *Travel News*, for example, are regular sources of information.
- **Subscription sources**. This encompasses journals, periodicals and reports, e.g. *Key Note, EIU, Mintel, Tourism Management, Travel and Tourism Analyst*, etc.

- **The press**. Given the dynamic nature of the industry, much up-to-date information can be sourced from the regular press and weekly newspaper magazines, i.e. *The Economist*.
- **Internal records**. Company reports, sales figures, in-house surveys, etc. are all valuable sources of data.
- **International organizations**. Trade and government related organizations such as IATA, ICAO, UN, WTO, OECD, etc. generate information on an international scale which is difficult for an individual organization or company to compile.
- **Management/research consultancies**. These undertake research on behalf of tourism organizations. As their services usually command high prices, the research produced is not usually made available for general consumption by the public.

Considerations

While the biggest benefit of using secondary data is the low cost involved, there are a number of factors which need to be considered in assessing the suitability of secondary data for the purpose in hand:

- Is the information up to date?
- How was the data generated? Is the source credible?
- Is the data accurate? Can it be verified?
- Does the data 'fit' the current study?
- Is the data contamination-free and therefore bias-free?
- What is the population coverage?
- How was the sample chosen?
- Can data from different sources be reconciled?

CASE STUDY 4.1

Tourism in Cyprus: balancing the benefits and costs

As the title suggests, the research concentrated on tourism in Cyprus, in particular the economic benefits engendered and the counterbalancing environmental, social and cultural costs. Emphasis is placed on the Greek zone following the island's partition in 1974.

To understand the importance of tourism in Cyprus, the majority of statistical information is derived from publications of both the Cyprus tourism organization and the Ministry of Finance, Department, of Statistics and Research. Further sources drawn upon include publications of the international monetary fund and the world Tourism Organization.

The conclusions of the study are that tourism has helped engender economic prosperity but a concomitant has been environmental damage and stress being placed on the host community at peak tourist periods. However, tourism has also encouraged the preservation of historic sites and stimulated more traditional culture within Cyprus. Recommendations are also made to limit the damage caused by tourism.

Source: Witt (1991)

- Are definitions compatible?
- Are the results supported by the data?
- Can the results be believed and if so can they be used?

Answers to such questions are vital before decisions are taken committing the researcher to the use of secondary data. This is all the more important where results form the basis of decisions determining action. If there is any doubt about the validity of the data, the results will be questionable.

Primary data

When all potential sources of secondary data have been exhausted, attention turns to **primary data**. This involves collecting new data. There are numerous methods which can be employed including the survey, the interview, observation and the Delphi technique. Each of these methods are considered in further detail below.

THE SURVEY

The survey is one of the most commonly used forms of data collection. It is a particularly useful source for obtaining descriptive information and it is usually based on a questionnaire which can be conducted over the telephone, by direct mail or personal interview. Each method has associated advantages and disadvantages.

Telephone

The major benefit of telephone research is cost. No travel is necessary nor is there the same need to employ and train interviewers as the researcher alone can interview a lot of people in a relatively short period of time. This type of research is also very quick in that responses are instant and the researcher is able to exercise a considerable degree of control by probing and clarifying points. Telephone research tends to suit short, straightforward questionnaires. The major disadvantages are the lack of face-to-face contact which can discourage people from answering certain questions and bias which can result from sampling only those people who own a telephone. Due to such weaknesses, this method is better used in conjunction with other methods.

Direct Mail

A key advantage of this technique is also cost. Postage costs are lower than employing interviewers and paying for travel costs. However, if the response rate is low then the costs per response increase so undermining this benefit. A related benefit is the option of using a broad geographical area from which to draw the sample. Responses tend to occur quite quickly making it a relatively speedy method. However, there is a caveat in that if a follow-up mailing is planned, extra time has to be allowed for this. A further benefit is the eradication of interviewer bias as no interviewers are involved. The method also enables the respondent to consult other people or information elsewhere which might result in more accurate answers being given so helping to overcome the problem of relying on memory. This can, however, be a disadvantage if the question requires a spontaneous reaction. Questions of a more personal or sensitive nature tend to be answered more openly and accurately using this method as completion of the questionnaire is virtually anonymous. A final advantage relates to the issue of contact. By sending a survey through the post, the problem of finding the person 'out' is avoided.

The disadvantages of this method are equally numerous. If the survey is particularly long or if explanations or probing are required then the mail survey is less suitable. Linked to this is the quality of answers given. Opportunities for clarifying or probing answers are removed as is the opportunity for checking that all the appropriate questions have been answered. Question dependency creates a similar problem in that where questions are not independent, earlier ones become redundant. For example, if you were to ask which tourist attractions the respondent was aware of in the local area and later followed that by asking the respondent to tick those visited from a given list, the first question would prove futile. Consequently, if the survey aims to test the views of just one person or test their knowledge or if spontaneity is required, then this method is inappropriate. Furthermore, there is no opportunity to ensure that the 'right' person completes the questionnaire nor is it possible to use observation to enhance the data. The biggest drawback is the low response rate associated with this method. Not only does this make statistical inference hazardous but it can also introduce bias into the survey so weakening the validity of any results.

Personal interviews

This method allows the interviewer to probe, use open-ended questions, clarify answers and check that surveys are fully completed. More information can be acquired and response rates tend to be higher. The main disadvantage is that of cost. Interviewers may have to be employed and trained and their travelling costs paid for. The process can also be time-consuming not only in terms of the travel involved but also in the time spent on the actual interview. The presence of an interviewer may also discourage respondents from answering personal questions and the interviewer may be a source of bias in the manner in which the interview is conducted.

SAMPLING

In looking at the application of surveys, consideration must be given to sampling procedures as the results yielded from a survey are directly related to the manner in which the sample is chosen. Collins (1986) defines sampling as 'the attempt to learn about some large group, a population, by looking at only a small part of it, a sample'. The basis of sampling then is to infer to the population from a section of that population.

The procedure, using Kinnear and Taylor's (1991) framework, is as follows:

1. **Define the population**. This is all the units about which information is sought.
2. **Establish the sampling frame**. This is the list from which the units will be selected, e.g. employee list, trade directory, map, etc.
3. **Determine the sample size**. This is almost always one of the most difficult aspects associated with sampling. A lot depends upon knowledge about the population including the amount of variability. The greater the variability the greater the margin of error or level of accuracy. The margin of error deemed acceptable will in turn influence the sample size. While in general larger samples generate more accuracy than smaller ones, there is a point at which there are diminishing returns from an increase in sample size and finding this point is not easy. Other factors which affect sample size are time and cost constraints, the number of variables and data analysis procedures. The latter two are linked in that where cross-tabulation is used several categories per variable may be involved resulting in a large number of cells. If the number of units per cell is very small or non-existent this will affect the validity of the results. The estimated response rates will also play a role in that the lower the rate the greater the sample size needed. Finally, non-sampling error must be considered in that a correlation exists between non-sampling error and sampling size. As sample size increases so too do other non-sampling errors such as non-response, interview errors and data processing/analysis errors. Consequently, it is fair to conclude that there is no simple answer to the problem of sample size. It is dependent upon a whole host of factors thus making each case unique.
4. **Select sampling technique**. There are two types of method: probability and non-probability. **Non-probability** is the least scientific of the two in that the sample selection is based on judgement which means that there is no known chance of any unit being selected and as a result sampling error cannot be calculated. Three main methods fall into this category: convenience, judgement and quota. The more accurate form of sampling is known as **probability** whereby each unit in the population has a known, but not necessarily an equal, chance of selection. Techniques subsumed within this method are simple random, systematic, stratified, cluster, multi-phase and area sampling.
5. **Select the sample**. This is undertaken using one of the above techniques. The procedures, problems and uses associated with each of these techniques are outlined in Table 4.1.

The sampling procedure adopted will have a direct impact on the validity of the results so it is vital that if the survey is to be the principal

Table 4.1 Sampling techniques

Technique	Basic procedure	Problems	Use
Non-probability			
Convenience	Units selected through convenience, i.e. self-selected or readily available.	Sample not representative of population. Sampling error cannot be measured Cannot infer results to population.	Exploration. Inaccuracy acceptable
Judgement	Select units for particular purpose.	Extent to which 'typical' unknown. Sampling error unknown. Cannot infer results to population.	Exploration.
Quota	Control variables used to select sample, e.g. male/female. Variables can be interlocked: classification variables most common	Difficult to ensure accuracy in terms of units conforming to control variables. Relevant control variable(s) omitted due to insufficient knowledge. Practical difficulties arising out of too many control variables, i.e. filling cells. Bias in selection of respondents, i.e. those accessible or approachable.	Where time and cost constraints imposed.
Probability			
Simple random	Population enumerated. Sample size established. Arbitrary number selected from random numbers table. Select all units making up sample		Results inferred to wider population. Principal form of data collection.
Systematic random	Obtain list of population, preferably alphabetical. Decide upon sample size. Determine intervals by dividing population by sample size. Choose random point towards top of list. Select unit at appointed interval on list to make up sample.	If list not random, possibility of bias, e.g. arising from cyclical/ periodic listing.	Homogeneous group.
Stratified	Population is divided into strata which are mutually exclusive and collectively exhaustive. Selection within each stratum undertaken separately using random procedure.	Choice of strata can be difficult. Use of proportionate/ disproportionate stratification.	Important variables known at outset.

Table 4.1 *(continued)*

Technique	Basic procedure	Problems	Use
Cluster	Selection of established group clustered in time or place. Can involve more than one stage (multi-stage) or be stratified.	Homogeneity of cluster members.	No suitable list. Interviewing – cost and time constraints; low field costs. Where survey area is variable need to stratify.
Multi-phase	Locate sub-group within population. Sampling unit remains constant but questioning increases.		Focus on particular sub-group. No suitable list.
Area	Units chosen according to location. Every nth unit selected from random start.		No suitable population list. Expanding areas. High population turnover. Electoral register out of date.

tool for data collection careful consideration must be given to the technique employed and the sample size chosen.

QUESTIONNAIRE/SURVEY DESIGN

The value of a survey questionnaire rests with its design. As there are so many ways in which a questionnaire could be formulated to perform its task it is difficult to develop a set of rules. Each questionnaire is unique. Consequently, the design of questionnaires has been referred to as an art which is influenced by the researcher's knowledge of the population, the subject matter, common sense, experience and pilot work.

It is, however, possible to draw upon a set of general guidelines which will assist the design.

Length

Only questions relevant to the purpose of the questionnaire should be included. If the questionnaire is too long then this can be demoralizing for the interviewer and respondent, affecting both refusal rates and the quality of the data (i.e. missed questions). The acceptable length of a questionnaire will relate to other factors including how interested the respondent is in the survey and the time he or she has available. If the final product is too long the questions can either be prioritized or the entire questionnaire can be photo-reduced.

Wording

Questions that require specific answers should be posed in an equally specific format. For example, 'Are you satisfied with your hotel?' As it stands this question is too vague as the nature of satisfaction has not been defined. The criteria upon which satisfaction is based, whether service, facilities, rooms, etc., should be stipulated.

Language

The language employed should be simple so that it can be understood by all respondents. Every effort should therefore be made to avoid the use of slang, technical terms, jargon and sophisticated words. Examples of the latter include 'paradox', 'hypothetical' and 'proximity'. Gowers (1954) produced a list of alternative simpler words, i.e. replacing 'state' with 'say' and 'consider' with 'think'.

Sentences should be kept short and to the point. Asking two questions in one should be avoided, e.g. 'Where did you holiday last year?' could be replaced with 'Did you go on holiday last year?', 'How many holidays did you take?' and 'Where did you go?'

Ambiguous questions should be avoided, e.g. 'Do you like travelling on trains and buses?', as should vague questions which tend to produce equally vague answers. So words like 'generally', 'fairly' and 'often' should be eliminated from the researcher's vocabulary.

Questions to avoid

Avoid the use of:

- abstract concepts;
- presuming questions which assume information about the respondent;
- hypothetical questions;
- personal/embarrassing questions.

Bias

The phrasing of a question can bias the response given. For example, Moser and Kalton (1971) argue that if a question begins with 'you don't think do you' a negative response will be elicited whereas beginning a question with 'should not something be done about' will engender a positive response.

Bias can further stem from the use of examples. While such examples can assist clarification of a question it is more likely to lead to those examples being used in the answer. For example, 'Do you watch any of the television holiday programmes such as *Wish You Were Here* or *Holiday?*' The answer to this question will almost certainly make reference to one of the two alternatives given, perhaps to the exclusion of others not identified. The solution to this problem is therefore to either name all of the alternatives or none at all.

Memory

Questions that involve the respondent's memory can lead to accuracy problems particularly if the question refers to an event some time ago or if the event is an irregular one or is insignificant to the respondent. This is exacerbated by the problem of selective memory which can result in the activity under question being overlooked or wrongly included. Potential solutions to this problem include spending time with the respondent, using diaries and emphasizing the importance of accurate answers.

Open versus closed questions

Two types of question can be used: open-ended questions enable the respondent to write a free-form answer on a few blank lines beneath the question. This type of question is particularly useful at the exploratory stage where all potential answers are unknown and where more depth is required. The weakness is that completion can be slow thereby discouraging respondents; also respondents will differ in how fully they answer a question and in how they convey their answer.

Closed questions can assume two forms: either the respondent is presented with a list of answers or a question is posed by the interviewer who then assigns the respondent's answer a given code. The choice ultimately depends on how the survey is conducted, i.e. whether by mail or by interviewer. The main ruling here is that alternatives should be collectively exhaustive and mutually exclusive with the use of 'Other, please specify . . .' for possible undetermined answers. While closed questions are easy for the respondent (for example, the respondent may not know the exact cost of a holiday but would be able to assign to it a price range) as well as being relatively straightforward to analyse there are also disadvantages including having too many codes making it difficult for the respondent to choose, answers being placed in the wrong category, answers affected by order of presentation and the adoption of the neutral position for opinion questions. (For a greater explanation of the advantages and disadvantages of open and closed questions, see Kinnear and Taylor (1991) and Moser and Kalton (1971)).

Opinion questions

There are a number of problems associated with opinion questions:

- the respondent may not have thought about the issue and therefore may not have an opinion;

- opinions have many different aspects (e.g. green tourism can be viewed from economic, ecological and social perspectives) making it difficult to ascertain the genuine problem;
- opinions vary in strength between individuals.

To overcome the latter problem attitudinal scales are employed. The most common scale is that of the Likert scale which provides an equal number of positive and negative rankings, for example:

Very good	1
Good	2
Adequate	3
Poor	4
Very poor	5

Where the scale is adopted for several questions it is common practice to vary the order in which positive and negative categories are given to discourage the respondent from habitually circling the same category.

Other scales include:

- **diagrammatic rating scales** whereby diagrams such as faces are used as a scale;
- **Semantic differential scales** whereby statements are rated as a five or seven point scale with an adjective at either end, e.g. hot——cold;
- **alternative attitude positions** whereby respondents are given two or more statements from which they have to state a preference.

For more information on the different types of scales, see Marton-Williams (1986).

A final problem is that bias in the wording and sequence of opinion questions will invariably affect the nature of the answer given.

Layout

The most important point is that the questionnaire is presented in such a way that it encourages, and does not deter, the respondent to complete it. The following guidelines should be adhered to:

- Provide a short covering letter and clear simple instructions at the outset.
- Make early questions simple, factual and not personal.
- Leave sensitive questions to the end.
- Adopt the funnel sequence of questioning by beginning with broad questions before progressing to more detailed ones.
- Avoid too many 'go to' questions.
- Adopt a different typeface to distinguish between instructions and questions.

- Rotate lists of items if used on a frequent basis.
- Place classification questions at the end.

The overriding point in questionnaire layout is simplicity. The less complicated the approach, the greater the chances of the respondent not only completing it but completing it correctly.

Pilot

A questionnaire should always be tested before full implementation to rid it of any flaws which would affect the use of the data. Marton-Williams (1986) suggests that a pilot be used to assess:

- persuading respondents to take part;
- opening questions;
- length and sequence;
- actual questions;
- instructions;
- layout.

CASE STUDY 4.2

Exploratory analysis of information use at Indiana State Welcome Centers

The purpose of this exploratory study was to identify the nature and extent to which people use welcome centres and to ascertain the effectiveness of these information centres in influencing travel behaviour. The research involved two stages:

1. An on-site four-question survey was used to identify why people stopped at the centre and what information they obtained. The survey was conducted on two weekdays and at the weekends for each site during July and August 1990. Visitors were systematically sampled resulting in 604 approaches and 595 completed surveys of which 560 were usable.
2. A follow-up survey was mailed to 560 respondents asking about their trip, the information obtained and their socioeconomic characteristics. With the aid of a reminder a response rate of 71.9% was achieved.

The tabulated results showed that the visitor centres had been effective in their influence on visitor travel: 21% stopped at an Indiana Welcome Center to obtain sightseeing information while 71% collected travel information; 21% stayed longer than planned while 29% visited places they had not planned to before visiting the Welcome Center; 33% spent more money than planned and 50% said that they would used information from the Center to plan further vacation trips. While there are likely to be differences in travel behaviour between seasons, the study indicated that 'Welcome Centers are a very important source for visitor information and may have substantial impact on a region's economy' (Fesenaier and Vogt, 1991).

BBC Holidays

Luxury 4 day Getaway break for two in a Best Western Hotel

Dear Club member,

Here at the BBC Holidays Club we aim to bring you the very latest information on the holiday scene. By finding out more about you and your holiday interests, we will be able to provide you with the best service.

By taking a few minutes to fill in this questionnaire we can build up an accurate picture of what you want. There is a prize draw for a luxury mini break for two for everyone who replies. Drawn on 31st March 93'

Please return the completed questionnaire as soon as possible. We value your views.

Thank you.

Tick this box ☐ if you do not wish to receive information on new products from the BBC Holidays club or other relevant offers.

Q1 Q2 Q3 Q4

MUST BE WON in our draw

You and a partner could be spending four nights away in the luxurious Best Western Mollington Banastre hotel just one and a half miles outside Chester.

The hotel is set in its own beautiful grounds and is the ideal setting for a relaxing few days away.

Spoil yourself with the finest foods from the two restaurants and then tone up in the extensive leisure complex. The facilities you will enjoy include swimming pool, gym, squash courts, solarium and beauty salon.

If you would like a Best Western Getaway brochure featuring the hotel, as well as 600 inviting ideas for weekends and holidays in England, Scotland and Wales, phone 081 541 5767

Please state your Club membership number

Club membership number __ __ __ __ __ __

Use the box below if you have moved address since joining the Holidays club or have lost club number.

NAME Please print MRS./MISS./MR.	First .... Second ....
ADDRESS	....
TOWN COUNTY POSTCODE	....

ABOUT YOU

Q1. What is your sex?

FEMALE ☐1 (03)
MALE ☐2

Q2. What is your age?

UNDER 15	☐1	35-44	☐5	(04)
15-19	☐2	45-54	☐6	
20-24	☐3	55-64	☐7	
25-34	☐4	OVER 65	☐8	

Q3. What is your marital status?

MARRIED	☐1	LIVING TOGETHER	☐3	(05)
SINGLE	☐2	DIVORCED SEPARATED WIDOWED	☐4	

ABOUT WORK

Q4. What is the occupation of the main wage earner in your household?

PROFESSIONAL eg. ACCOUNTANT/LAWYER	☐1	(06)
DIRECTOR/MANAGER IN BUSINESS OR INDUSTRY	☐2	
ADMINISTRATOR IN BUSINESS INDUSTRY OR SOCIAL SERVICES	☐3	
OFFICE WORKER OR SALESPERSON	☐4	
OTHER NON-MANUAL	☐5	
SKILLED-MANUAL	☐6	
SEMI-SKILLED MANUAL	☐7	
UNSKILLED MANUAL	☐8	
UNEMPLOYED. NON PAID JOB. STUDENT. RETIRED	☐9	

Figure 4.1 Example of a questionnaire.

ABOUT YOUR HOLIDAYS

Q5. Which of the following will you use to plan your next holiday ? You may tick more than 1

Guide book	☐1	(07)
TV	☐2	
BBC Holidays Magazine	☐3	
Other magazines	☐4	
National press / supplements	☐5	
Travel agent	☐6	
Holiday company brochure	☐7	

Q6. How many holidays away from home have you had in the last 12 months?

NUMBER	UK		ABROAD	
	Up to 4 nights	More than 4 nights	Up to 4 nights	More than 4 nights
None	☐1 (08)	☐1 (09)	☐1 (10)	☐1 (11)
Less than three	☐2	☐2	☐2	☐2
Three	☐3	☐3	☐3	☐3
Four to six	☐4	☐4	☐4	☐4
More than six	☐5	☐5	☐5	☐5

Q7. When booking your holiday do you usually try and book?

Immediately after last holiday	☐1	(12)
At least 6 mths before	☐2	
At least 3 mths before	☐3	
Less than 3 mths before	☐4	
At the last moment	☐5	

Q8. What was the total cost of your last holiday per adult (excluding spending money) and what is the most you have ever spent per person on a holiday?

AMOUNT SPENT		Last Holiday	Most Expensive
UNDER	£100	☐1 (13)	☐1 (14)
£100 -	£249	☐2	☐2
£250 -	£499	☐3	☐3
£500 -	£749	☐4	☐4
£750 -	£999	☐5	☐5
£1,000 -	£1,749	☐6	☐6
£1,750 -	or more	☐7	☐7

Q9. Will you be taking any children on your next holiday? If yes, please indicate their ages. If no, leave blank.

	ONE	TWO	THREE +
Below 7 years of age	☐1	☐2	☐3 (15)
8-14 years of age	☐1	☐2	☐3 (16)
15-18 years of age	☐1	☐2	☐3 (17)

Q10. On which of the following types of holiday accommodation would you like more information?

ACCOMMODATION	UK		Abroad	
Own holiday home / timeshare	☐1	(18)	☐1	(19)
Rented villa/flat/cottage	☐2		☐2	
Ski chalet	☐3		☐3	
Holiday home swap	☐4		☐4	
Guest house	☐5		☐5	
Caravan	☐6		☐6	
Boat/Yacht charter	☐7		☐7	
Camping site	☐8		☐8	
Canal/river boat	☐9		☐9	
Cruise ship	☐10		☐10	
City hotel	☐11		☐11	
Country hotel	☐12		☐12	
Holiday camp	☐13		☐13	
Youth hostel	☐14		☐14	

Q11. On which of the following types of holiday activities would you like more information?

ACTIVITY	UK		Abroad	
Quiet/scenic beach or resort	☐1	(20)	☐1	(21)
Activity/lively beach or resort	☐2		☐2	
Animal type theme parks	☐3		☐3	
Disney type theme parks	☐4		☐4	
Singles type holidays	☐5		☐5	
Historical interest eg Homes, Castles, Temples.	☐6		☐6	
Classic Cities eg Paris, Rome	☐7		☐7	
Holidays by train	☐8		☐8	
Holidays by touring coach	☐9		☐9	
Places of religious significance	☐10		☐10	
Lakes and mountains	☐11		☐11	
Hiking/walking holidays	☐12		☐12	
Adventure type holidays	☐13		☐13	
Health farm/spa	☐14		☐14	
Self /Fly drive holidays	☐15		☐15	
Food and wine gourmet	☐16		☐16	
Safari	☐17		☐17	
Water sports	☐18		☐18	
Skiing	☐19		☐19	
Self plan or independent travel	☐20		☐20	

Q12. Do you agree or disagree with the following sentences.

	Strongly Agree	Tend To Agree	Tend To Disagree	Strongly Disagree	
I like holidays in Britain rather than abroad.	☐1	☐2	☐3	☐4	(22)
I would consider going to Paris for the day.	☐1	☐2	☐3	☐4	(23)
I try and go somewhere different every year.	☐1	☐2	☐3	☐4	(24)
I'm interested in reading about countries I never plan to visit	☐1	☐2	☐3	☐4	(25)

Figure 4.1 *(continued)*

ABOUT HOLIDAY DESTINATIONS

Q13. Have you have visited the following regions or countries in the past 5 years. Also, tick those you would like to visit in the foreseeable future?

DESTINATION	Visits in last 5 years	Like to visit
Austria/Switzerland	□1 (26)	□1 (27)
Belgium/Luxemburg	□2	□2
France	□3	□3
Germany	□4	□4
Greece	□5	□5
Holland	□6	□6
Italy	□7	□7
Malta/Cyprus	□8	□8
Portugal	□9	□9
Scandinavia	□10	□10
Spain (inc. Majorca,Canaries,etc)	□11	□11
Turkey	□12	□12
South Africa	□13	□13
Eastern Europe/Russia	□14	□14
North Africa	□15	□15
Central Africa	□16	□16
Middle East	□17	□17
USA/Canada	□18	□18
West Indies/Caribbean	□19	□19
Australia/New Zealand	□20	□20
South America	□21	□21
Asia/Far East	□22	□22

ABOUT WHAT YOU WATCH ON TV

Q14. How often do you tune into the following programmes?

PROGRAMME	NEVER	ALMOST EVERY EPISODE	AT LEAST 1 IN 4	LESS THAN 1 IN 4	
BBC Holidays	□1	□2	□3	□4	(28)
BBC 2's Travel Show	□1	□2	□3	□4	(29)
Breakaway / Radio 4	□1	□2	□3	□4	(30)
ITV,s Wish you were Here..?	□1	□2	□3	□4	(31)
Channel 4 Travelog	□1	□2	□3	□4	(32)
BBC 2's Rough Guide	□1	□2	□3	□4	(33)

ABOUT BBC HOLIDAYS MAGAZINE CLUB

Q15. How interesting would you find the following services from the club?

SERVICE	Very Interesting	Interesting	Not very Interesting	Not at all Interesting	
Competitions	□1	□2	□3	□4	(34)
Free upgrades	□1	□2	□3	□4	(35)
Discounts	□1	□2	□3	□4	(36)
Exhibitions/Shows	□1	□2	□3	□4	(37)
Free product offers	□1	□2	□3	□4	(38)

ABOUT OTHER PUBLICATIONS

Q16. Which of the following do you read regularly? By that we mean at least every other issue.

PUBLICATION		
Daily Express	□1	(39)
Daily Mail	□2	
Financial Times	□3	
Guardian	□4	
Independent	□5	
Mirror	□6	
Daily Star	□7	
Sun	□8	
Telegraph	□9	
Times	□10	
Today	□11	
European	□12	
Independent on Sunday	□13	
Mail on Sunday	□14	
News of the World	□15	
Observer	□16	
Sunday Express	□17	
Sunday Telegraph	□18	
Sunday Times	□19	

ABOUT BBC HOLIDAYS MAGAZINE

Q17. Please take a few minutes to look at the following features in the magazine and tell us what you think of them.
(They are listed in the order they appear in the magazine)

PAGE NUMBER & TITLE	Very Interesting	Interesting	Not very Interesting	Not at all Interesting	
06 What's New	□1	□2	□3	□4	(40)
10 Armchair Traveller	□1	□2	□3	□4	(41)
12 Letters	□1	□2	□3	□4	(42)
13 Penny Junor	□1	□2	□3	□4	(43)
18 TV Travel Fact Sheets	□1	□2	□3	□4	(44)

Q18. Apart from yourself, how many other people will read this issue of the magazine?

None	□1	(45)
One	□2	
Two	□3	
Three or more	□4	

Q19. When you visit a new country how important is it for you to:?

STATEMENT	Essential	Important	Not Important	
Understand the currency	□1	□2	□3	(46)
Know about local customs	□1	□2	□3	(47)
Learn the language	□1	□2	□3	(48)
Eat local food	□1	□2	□3	(49)
Find out about local history	□1	□2	□3	(50)
Understand local politics	□1	□2	□3	(51)
Get to know people	□1	□2	□3	(52)
Join in local festivals/events	□1	□2	□3	(53)

Figure 4.1 *(continued)*

Personal questions

Questions which ask about the respondent's age, employment, income, etc. are known as classification questions and these are usually asked towards the end of the questionnaire for the purpose of analysis.

Questionnaires in tourism

Questionnaires are most commonly directed at the consumer as it is an ideal way for an industry to amass a considerable amount of data about the consumers of their products. Hence, tour operators will give out questionnaires to holidaymakers on the flight home; airlines too adopt this approach capitalizing on having a captive audience whose views on the product/ service is at the forefront of their minds. The same rationale is applied to visitor surveys. An example of a questionnaire is given in Figure 4.1).

OBSERVATION

The observation method enables the researcher to gather information directly on an individual's behaviour thereby differentiating actual behaviour from stated behaviour. It tends to be undertaken as a forerunner to other methods for the purpose of obtaining background information or formulating hypotheses. A key use therefore is exploration. It can also be used to predict future behaviour as well as proving of value in the study of small communities and the physical aspects of a place. Either the researcher can be directly involved in the role as a participant, i.e. participant observation, or the researcher can assume a detached role by using tape recorders, cameras or even two-way mirrors.

There are numerous problems associated with this method which Gardner (1976) distinguishes according to 'observer' and 'control effects'. Errors arising from the **observer** include:

- selective observation: this can be a problem if the criteria for observation is not specified;
- bias: preconceptions tend to be supported by biased observations;
- drawing inferences: observation is affected by experience and knowledge;
- recording observations: this is time-consuming and linked to the problem of inferences;
- unsystematic observation: it is difficult to know what is typical.

Solutions include training observers to ensure consistency; using several observers and allocating different criteria for observations; providing clearly defined schedules to record information; and sampling by location and time.

The other type of problem is that of the **control effect** whereby people behave differently in the knowledge that they are being observed. The solutions to this problem include making observation a discrete process,

CASE STUDY 4.3

What can you see?

You say, 'What can you see on the horizon?' One man says. 'I see a ship.' Another says, 'I see a steamer with two funnels.' A third says. 'I see a Cunarder going from Southampton to New York.' How much of what these three people say is to count as perception? They may all three be perfectly right in what they say, and yet we should not concede that a man can 'perceive' that the ship is going from Southampton to New York. This, we should say, is inference. But it is by no means easy to draw the line; some things which are, in an important sense, inferential must be admitted to be perceptions. The man who says 'I see a ship' is using inference. Apart from experience, he only sees a queerly shaped dark dot on a blue background. Experience has taught him that that sort of dot 'means' a ship.

Source: Russell (1927) quoted in Gardner (1976).

possibly by becoming a participant, and supplementing information with other methods.

While there are many circumstances whereby observation is an appropriate method, such as finding out about actual behaviour, the method suffers from a number of disadvantages, namely the inability to grasp

CASE STUDY 4.4

Influence of tourism on handcraft evolution

The research concentrated on craftpersons in the region of Oaxaca, Mexico who had developed a tourist market for their handcrafted textiles. The aim of the research was to develop a classification system for an evolving product responding to changes in producers, vendors and consumers. The research concentrated on the relationship between the handcraft products and consumers and their impact on the product.

After a feasibility study had been undertaken in June 1986, screening interviews were conducted to identify the handcraft producers. A non-probability sampling method was chosen to ensure that the sample met the criteria specified. The target population was identified largely from interviews with Mexican buyers, educators and weavers. Ultimately 31 textile weavers were identified as the target population of which 27 participated in the research. During January to May 1988 market observations, home and workshop observations, in-depth interviews and participant observation were employed to gather information. The interviews were deliberately informal to allow for exploration. Analysis was based on content analysis and descriptive statistics.

A classification system was subsequently developed which described changes in products, clientele and consumer preferences. Three periods of product and market evolution were also identified.

Source: Popelka and Littrell (1991).

opinions or attitudes, the time involved, the frequency with which behaviour occurs, 'overheard' information which is difficult to qualify and the failure to understand why people behave in the way they do.

INTERVIEWS

One way of understanding the motives behind certain actions as well as the opinions and attitudes of individuals is to undertake qualitative research. Van Maanen (1993) describes qualitative research as 'an array of interpretive techniques which seek to describe, decode, translate and otherwise come to terms with the meaning, not the frequency of certain more or less naturally occurring phenomena in the social world'. The characteristics of this type of research are that it tends to involve a small number of people, the results are not statistically significant and it often serves an exploratory purpose.

The principal method used for the collection of qualitative data is the interview. Burgess (1982) describes the interview as 'the opportunity for the researcher to probe deeply to uncover new clues, open up new dimensions of a problem and to secure vivid, accurate inclusive accounts that are based on personal experience'. This can take many forms which are basically differing degrees of formality including **non-directive** or 'open' interviews, **conversational** and **guided/focused** interviews. The basic aim of these types of informal interview is to provide flexibility to reach the heart of the matter whether on attitudes, opinions or beliefs. To be successful in achieving the aim requires considerable skill on the part of the interviewer, particularly in the art of probing.

CASE STUDY 4.5

How 'we' see 'them': tourism and Native Americans

The aim of the research was to understand whether tourism actually enhances cultural understanding or merely serves to endorse enthnocentrism. The study was based on US tourists encountering Native American culture in New Mexico to ascertain the perceptions by visitors to New Mexico of Native Americans.

The method of enquiry adopted was that of a 'cognitive' approach using observation and conversations with both Anglo tourists and Native Americans at a total of 15 events in New Mexico pueblos between July 1988 and December 1989. In addition 130 formal taped interviews were conducted with tourists at various museums, a cultural centre and Indian market in New Mexico during 1988. The group interviewed largely constituted the American upper-middle class, a fact determined from a question on their occupation.

The findings suggested that cultural tourism, rather than enhancing understanding of different cultures, tended instead to 'convince tourists of the correctness of their own worldview'.

Source: Laxson (1991).

Problems associated with this method include interviewer bias, inadequate response and the difficulty of recording notes and conducting the interview simultaneously. Probing and the use of a tape recorder can help overcome such problems.

The basic interview can be supplemented in a number of ways:

- **Group discussion** brings together a number of individuals under the direction of a moderator.
- **Projective techniques** encourage the respondent to project their views onto other things and overcome inhibitions.
- **Protocol analysis** is used to understand the stages involved in the decision-making process after the event.
- **The repertory grid technique** is used to understand the constructs individuals perceive the world through.
- **The critical incident technique** may be used whereby procedures are implemented to observe behaviour so bridging the division between pure observation and motivation for action.

To summarize then, the advantages of qualitative techniques are that information on motivations and opinions not easily obtained through quantitative techniques can be explored; information not previously thought about can be uncovered; issues can be explored and more clearly defined; and personal or sensitive information can be more easily tackled. The disadvantages are that data is subjective and therefore difficult to substantiate; different researchers will elicit different responses; and the quality of information obtained is directly related to the skill of the researcher.

DELPHI

The final technique under study is the Delphi method. It has been described by Linstone and Turoff (1975) as 'a method for structuring a group communication process so that the process is effective in allowing a group of individuals, as a whole, to deal with a complex problem'. It was developed by the RAND Corporation for technological forecasting although it has also been used for environmental problems and tourism research. The key feature of the Delphi technique is that 'experts' are used who never actually meet face to face. The actual process has been prescribed by Richey, Mar and Horner (1985) as follows:

1. Select members for the monitor team responsible for identifying experts and persuading them to join the panel, and for communicating information to the panel throughout the process.
2. Monitor team to identify discussion issues which are formulated into a questionnaire.
3. First questionnaire is sent to the panel.
4. Monitor team assesses the results.

5. A second questionnaire is sent enabling respondents to reconsider issues.
6. Responses assessed.
7. Summary of results sent to panel.
8. Outcome: new information to help resolve problems.

The logic of the Delphi method is that the response of the group will increasingly reach a common consensus through successive rounds of questionnaires. It is therefore an exercise in group decision-making, the advantage being that the experts never have to meet. The strengths of the technique are that expertise is gathered from a number of individuals; responses are anonymous; peer pressure and the 'bandwagon effect' is eliminated; and it is cost-effective. The method's weaknesses are that its success is inherently linked to the choice of experts; objective presentation/ feedback of results is linked to the monitor team; respondents decrease in number throughout the process and the drop-out rate may not be balanced across the categories; the process can be time-consuming; it is difficult to ascertain the required number of experts; and experts can be swayed by the panel response.

As a result of these weaknesses, this method is best used in conjunction with one or more of the other methods discussed in this chapter.

CASE STUDY 4.6

Delphi

Dann (1991) undertook a study of Barbados in 10 and 50 years' time using Delphi. Ten experts from Barbados were identified to form a panel of which seven accepted. In the brainstorming session conducted a number of tabled issues were overlooked including alternative tourism, ecotourism and the impact of global warming; the reason for this was that the composition of the group comprised practitioners unfamiliar with all the arguments surrounding these issues.

The results showed that change in tourism would be progressive and not rapid, occurring over the 50 year period. It also became clear that there was a general reluctance on the part of the panel to look at future scenarios. The main problems in undertaking the study were that of the time constraints, the commitment of panelists, the unfamiliarity with tourism issues and the inward-looking nature of the panel members which was attributable to the culture.

Source: Dann (1991).

ROLE OF RESEARCH IN TOURISM

There can be little doubt that in an industry as dynamic and expansive as tourism and one which appears to be inexorably growing, research must play a vital role in its development. Not only should research be undertaken by every organization whether large or small to assist in the task of practical decision-making at a strategic level, but it should also be acknowledged as important at the academic level in shedding valuable light on the development of tourism on a global basis and bringing together the many different strands which comprise the tourism industry.

As an interdisciplinary subject, the scope for research over time and in content is endless. Buckley (1993), for example, divides tourism research into the following categories:

- tourism as a complex service industry encompassing the structure and scale of tourism; transport; leisure and recreation; attractions; and hotel and catering research;
- case studies in tourism;
- tourism information statistics and forecasting;
- environmental, spatial and design issues;
- tourist motivation, behaviour and marketing of tourism;
- tourism management and training;
- tourism politics, planning and policy analysis.

As the list highlights, there is no shortage of topics worthy of study. What is required is regular research conducted on all aspects to ensure that tourism development is a planned process not left to chance.

SUMMARY

While research cannot guarantee 100% success in decision-making it does at least reduce the risks of making a bad decision. So some research is better than none at all. However, the importance of consideration being given to the manner in which the research is conducted cannot be overstated. In short, the value of research lies in the approach or method adopted. If the data is of questionable quality or validity then the same will apply to the results. Hence the need to understand the strengths and weaknesses of each method in deciding upon which method or methods to adopt. Ultimately the choice will depend upon the nature of the research question and the time and resources available.

REFERENCES

Buckley, (1993) Role of research in tourism, in Witt, S.I. and Moutinho, L. (eds), *Tourism Marketing and Management Handbook*, Prentice-Hall, Englewood Cliffs, New Jersey.

Burgess, R.G. (1982) *Field Research: A Source Book and Field Manual*, Allen & Unwin, London.

Collins, M. (1986) Sampling, in Worcester, R. and Downham, J. (eds), *Consumer Market Research Handbook*, MacGraw-Hill, London.

Dann, G.M.S. (1991) How tourism professionals view the future: the case of Barbados, *New Horizon Conference Proceedings*, University of Calgary.

Fesenmaier, D.R. and Vogt, C.A. (1991) Exploratory analysis of information use at Indiana State Welcome Centers, *Tourism: Building Credibility for a Credible Industry*, TTRA, Bureau of Economic and Business Research, University of Utah.

Gardner, G. (1976) *Social Surveys for Social Planners*, The Open University Press, Milton Keynes.

Gowers, E.A. (1954) *The Complete Plain Words*, HMSO, London; Penguin (Pelican) Books, Harmondsworth, Middlesex.

Kinnear, T.C. and Taylor, J.R. (1991) *Marketing Research: An Applied Approach*, 4th edn, McGraw-Hill, New York.

Laxson, J.D. (1991) How 'we' see 'them': tourism and Native Americans, *Annals of Tourism Research*, **18**, 365–91.

Linstone, A.H. and Turoff, M. (1975) *The Delphi Method: Techniques and Applications*, Addison-Wesley, Reading, Mass.

Marton-Williams, J. (1986) Questionnaire design, in Worcester, R. and Downham, J. (eds), *Consumer Market Research Handbook*, McGraw-Hill, London.

Moser, C.A. and Kalton, G. (1971) *Survey Methods in Social Investigation*, Heinemann Educational, London.

Popelka, C.A. and Littrell, M.A. (1991) Influence of tourism on handcraft evolution, *Annals of Tourism Research*, **18**, 392–413.

Reid, R.D. (1989) *Hospitality Marketing Management*, 2nd edn, Chapman & Hall, London.

Richey, J.S. Mar, B.W. and Horner, R.R. (1985) The Delphi technique in environmental assessment: implementation and effectiveness, *Journal of Environmental Management*, **21**, 135–46.

Russell, B. (1927) *An Outline of Philosophy*, Allen & Unwin, London.

Van Maanen, J. (1983) *Qualitative Methodology*, Sage, London.

Witt, S.E. (1991) Tourism in Cyprus: balancing the benefits and the costs, *Tourism Management*, March, pp. 37–46.

REVIEW QUESTIONS

1. Why is research so important to an organization?
2. What is the logical order of steps in the research process?
3. How does secondary data differ from primary data?
4. What are the main tourism sources of secondary data?
5. What are the advantages and disadvantages associated with each method of primary data collection?
6. When is sampling appropriate? What is the difference between non-probability and probability sampling?

5 The marketing mix: the tourism product

A.V. Seaton

OBJECTIVES

By the end of this chapter the reader should:

- understand the main features of the product mix and the main features of a successful product;
- be able to apply the main forms of product analysis including: SWOT analysis; core, tangible and augmented product analysis; features and benefits analysis;
- appreciate the different options in managing existing and new products;
- understand the role of corporate identity programmes and branding in tourism;
- understand the utility of the product life cycle and tourist area life cycle in tourism analysis.

INTRODUCTION

As we saw in Chapter 1 tourism constitutes such a wide span of products that it has to be seen in terms of sectors rather than a single industry comprising:

- **the accommodation sector:** hotels, bed and breakfast, self-catering, camp sites, etc.;
- **the attractions sector:** museums, galleries, theme parks, festivals, etc.;
- **the transport sector:** railways, cruise lines, ferry companies, airlines, car hire, etc.;
- **the travel organizers sector:** tour operators, travel agents, booking agencies, etc.;
- **the destination organization sector:** national tourist offices (NTOs), area tourist boards, chambers of commerce, local authorities, etc.

Table 5.1 Product features in three tourism markets

- **Resort:** appearance of beach and promenade; impressions of built environment (houses, public buildings, etc.); environmental impressions (clean, dirty, etc.); climate; attractions and accommodation; services and facilities; visitor profile; history.
- **Hotel:** location; access; decor; business services; front-of-house people; fittings and furniture; guest profile; food and beverage quality; historic image, etc.
- **Museum:** contents/exhibits and their perceived interest and importance (e.g. major collection, unique items, etc.); interpretive techniques; external and internal architectural features of museum; services and facilities (e.g. restaurant, gift shop, etc.); perceptions of staff.

This diversity is matched by an even greater diversity of component features specific to each tourism product sector which need to be considered and managed in providing individual products for particular markets. Table 5.1 illustrates some of the different features which constitute the product in the hotel, attraction and destination sectors.

Given such a heterogenous array of products what common denominators can be identified? What makes successful tourism products such as CenterParc, Disneyland or British Airways? In this chapter we shall look at product planning and draw on some general approaches to product analysis and management. In Parts 2 and 3 we shall move to a closer inspection of particular tourism product types and their special markets.

Before we start it is worth noting two key feature of all products, but of tourism products in particular – the fact that they have both a **physical** and a **symbolic** form. A car, for instance, is a bundle of physical attributes (wheels, windows, engine, etc.) but it is also a symbolic object because its physical features, both individually and collectively, connote symbolic values to the consumer such as status, adventure, youth, etc. Jefferson and Lickorish (1991: 67) have defined a tourism product as: '. . . a collection of physical and service features together within symbolic associations which are expected to fulfil the wants and needs of the buyer.'

In tourism the symbolic features of products are crucial – a colour scheme in a hotel room may be perceived as restful or strident; a resort may be seen as traditional or modern according to the visitor's first impressions of its buildings; a flight may be seen as safe because of soft background music, smiling hostesses and the pilot's relaxed commentary; a restaurant may be perceived as upmarket because of the arty, visual appearance of its food (nouvelle cuisine in the 1980s was a singular instance of this). Tourism provision is as much about the **stage management of illusion** as the supply of physical goods (although, of course, physical stimuli provide the cues from which symbolic values are derived). Tourists are often motivated by fantasies and dreams (including the pursuit of the 'other' described in Chapter 3), by the desire to play roles away that differ from the ones they occupy at home, and tourism providers must supply them with the materials. There is often a need to separate the backstage – from which the provision is planned – from the front stage where it is performed. A hotel kitchen can be a frenetic, routinized assembly line of food production but, for the guest, the meal has to be delivered as a unique culinary offering presented by poised, unruffled serving staff. In Disneyland it is important that the machinery driving the different themed spectacles is hidden, and that the staff playing Mickey Mouse and his friends never reveal their true selves (some students who have worked at Disneyland recount the progressive deflation they experience as they become familiar with the backstage mechanics of the operation). Tourism experiences at destinations depend upon **performances and enactments** which are most successful when they are hidden. It can be a let-down to a tourist who has watched a medieval pageant in Italy to observe later one of the gloriously garbed pikemen riding away on his Suzuki motorbike!

PRODUCT PLANNING: THE BASIC ELEMENTS

The most basic decision a tourism organization has to make is deciding what business it is in and what product mix is appropriate to it. The product mix is the portfolio of products that an organization offers to one market or several. Five basic market/product mix options exist:

- **Several markets/multi-product mixes for each**. An organization targets several markets and devises a multi-product range for each (e.g. mass tour operators which offer a wide range of multi-destination packages to singles, families and older markets; travel agents offering a wide range of holidays and travel facilities to a number of markets).
- **Several markets/single product for each**. An organization targets several markets but offers only one product to each (e.g. hotel chains with branded products for different markets; airlines with a product for business and economy class travellers).
- **Several markets/single product for all**. A single product is offered to all markets (e.g. a national tourist organization promoting a country; a small ferry crossing in the Shetlands offering one standard service to all).
- **Single market/multi-product mix**. A tourism organization may be interested in one market but offers a range of products (e.g. a specialist tour operator with a range of cultural tours aimed at a wealthy, educated market).
- **Single market/single product**. The tourism organization manages a single product for a niche market (e.g. a riding school in the Lake District catering for equestrians or an elite independent hotel targeting the very rich).

The decision whether an organization should go for one market or several, offering a multi-product mix or a single one, depends upon several factors:

- forecast strength and value of consumer demand in the different markets;
- the degree of competitive product advantage it has over organizations offering substitutes;
- the distinctive competence of the organization concerned to service the products/markets adequately.

The start point in product analysis and planning is thus to analyse the consumer and competitive offerings in relation to the goals and product capacity of the tourism organization. The most successful products, whether single or many, emerge from:

- **identified needs** specific to
- **targeted markets** and are based on
- **distinctive positioning** in relation to
- **competitive offerings**.

Positioning is the bedrock of product management. As the name suggests positioning is how an organization positions itself and its individual products against competing products in relation to specific differentiated markets. It is a psychological process which is about establishing clear consumer perceptions:

> Positioning is what you do to the mind of the tourist. That is, you position your destination or attraction in the mind of your market segment . . . Positioning is considering competition directly and finding a niche in the traveler's mind not occupied by some other destination or activity.
>
> (Woodside, 1982: 4)

Burke and Resnick (1991) have identified four main positioning strategies:

CASE STUDY 5.1

A product mix portfolio

Tour operators commonly offer a range of products. Before its demise in 1990 Independent Leisure Group offered nine branded products in its product mix portfolio:

- Intasun: air holidays for the main middle market;
- Lancaster: lower priced air holidays;
- Global: concentrated on apartment based holidays;
- Skiscene: winter sports;
- Golden Days: for the retired market;
- Select: long-haul, upmarket holidays;
- Skyworld: seat only arrangements;
- NAT: coach centred holidays.

- relative to target market (e.g. business travellers; families with children under 10, etc.);
- by price and quality (e.g. a premium product such as Concorde);
- relative to a product class (e.g. a tour operator positioning his products within a sun, sea and sand product category);
- relative to competitors (e.g. the Hertz Rental campaign 'We try harder. . .', which drew attention to the fact that Hertz was not market leader and, as number two, would work all the more to catch up with bigger competitors, or Sealink Ferries promoting their 'Ferry nice prices' to differentiate themselves from more expensive carriers).

The four options are not mutually exclusive and may be used in combination.

Product development: can tourism products be developed through testing?

The best method of developing a successful product is through intensive product research and testing. In the marketing of physical products there are well established methods and procedures for doing this. Ideally the marketing organization identifies consumer needs and tastes through research, tests different product concepts that might satisfy them and ultimately develops several new product ideas before launching the best option into the marketplace. Very often new products are tested in blind test conditions on consumer panels against competitive products as well as previous versions of the same product in order to determine their superiority/acceptability to the target market. This procedure is rarely possible in tourism for a number of reasons, some of which have already been suggested.

- Firstly as intangibles tourism products cannot be pre-tested with consumers because they have no transportable, physical form for the consumer to examine to gain an exact measure of their acceptability. There is no way Hong Kong or a Marriott Hotel can be distributed to

---

CASE STUDY 5.2

Market positioning

Holiday parks and centres in the UK have adopted positioning in their marketing:

Each operator is now seeking to establish a clear 'positioning', reflecting competitive advantage which it can defend and develop over the years. These positionings vary from the provision of futuristic waterworlds, the quality of accommodation and on-site offerings for children, the choice of self-caterer products, the strength of the entertainment programme, etc.

Source: Allport (1990/1: 26)

a panel of consumers in order to elicit their opinion before they are marketed, even though visitor opinions can be canvassed after the event.

- Secondly the marketer is limited in the extent to which the tourism product can be designed, modified or improved in the way of physical products. Often the marketer has to take what is and the main field of discretion is how it is packaged conceptually through promotion. Only in rare instances does the tourism developer have the option of shaping the product from the bottom up. A destination marketer usually has to make the best of a given state of geographical nature (the climate of Scotland, for instance) or a long established man-made environment (an established city or town). Small bits of a destination may, perhaps, be modifiable (e.g. landscaping a sea front, pedestrianizing a centre – which is why development grants by public authorities may be used to upgrade or enhance a destination). One exception to this was the development of the French resort of Languedoc which from the 1960s was a created resort salvaged from mosquito-infested swamp land. The relative control of product features varies between tourism products. A theme park developer or an attraction marketer, starting from scratch, has much greater freedom for consumer-oriented product innovations than a destination promoter. The Channel Tunnel was started from scratch. Hotels and restaurants may be given major facelifts. An airline may change its livery, uniforms, catering or terminal features. But none of them can be fully pretested.

- The potential for **differentiation** in product design is often limited. A washing powder manufacturer can change the pack, add new ingredients to the formula, and experiment with new aesthetic features (powder colour, flakes rather than powder) whereas many tourism products are similar and the opportunities for differentiation limited. A sun, sea and sand destination is similar in basics whether in Spain, Greece or Italy. An aircraft is only capable of minor differentiation, particularly since many carriers buy their craft from the same manufacturers.

- It is also difficult to be **fully consumer oriented** in some markets. Normally a marketer attempts to find out the consumers' major likes and dislikes about a product and then design one that matches the former and avoids the latter. This is not always possible in tourism. For airlines a major consumer issue is fear of flying, shared by 20–30% of the population. But this is virtually impossible to overcome (though courses to cure people of it have been tried) except by creating an internal environment on a plane which is as reassuring as possible.

- Finally, individual tourism marketers rarely control the whole product as delivered to the consumer. We have seen how tourism products like package holidays depend upon the performance of at least three interrelated offerings: the transport, the hotel and the destination itself. But there is also a fourth imponderable – the fact that the consumer partly designs the tourist product by the way in which he or she experiences it.

The normal pre-testing procedures used in the marketing of physical products are thus difficult to replicate in tourism marketing, except to the extent that it may be possible to conduct surveys or hold interviews with potential customers asking them what they would like before developing a product. But it is rarely possible to expose them to different product blueprints. P&O did limited pre-testing on the interior design of their new liner *Oriana*, launched in 1995, which included building life-size mock-ups of the main rooms (cabins, bars, etc.).

One kind of testing can sometimes be achieved – test marketing. This involves a limited pilot run of a new product followed by a wider expansion if it is successful. A tour operator could include a new package in the brochure, or make it available to a limited number of travel agents on a regional basis, and then launch it nationally a year later. One of the most successful hospitality product innovations of the last decade has been that of Courtyard by Marriott Hotels in America. The Courtyard concept was developed after an intensive programme of market analysis and market research (including consumer questionnaires, product simulations and sophisticated market segmentation based on multivariate and inferential statistical analysis), ending in a test market of the concept in three hotels in 1983 which later led to expansion to over 200 units. A detailed account of this ground-breaking product development programme can be found in Wind, Green, Shifflet and Scarborough (1989) and Crawford-Welch (1994).

What are the elements of successful product management? Marketing offers no ready-made prescriptions but it indicates a number of analytical procedures for realistic product evaluation and planning.

CASE STUDY 5.3

Influence of travel agents on airline choice

Travel agents can be important influences on airline choice. In 1990 a study conducted by The Association of British Travel Agents investigated their members' attitudes to a number of airlines. It produced the following rankings on airlines:

% of travel agents who categorize
each airline as 'one of the best in the world'

1.	British Airways	65%
2.	Singapore Airlines	42%
3.	Qantas	25%
4.	Virgin Atlantic	14%
5.	Cathay Pacific	13%
6.	Swissair	12%
7=	Air New Zealand	8%
7=	Thai International	8%
9.	Lufthansa	7%

Source: UK Airlines Travel Trade Image Survey 1990 (in *Travel and Tourism Research*).

APPROACHES TO PRODUCT ANALYSIS AND PLANNING

SWOT analysis

The most basic start point for product evaluation is knowing how one's product is seen by customers and the people who might influence them, and how it ranks in relation to competitive substitutes. SWOT analysis is the start point for this. SWOT is an acronym for **S**trengths, **W**eaknesses, **O**pportunities and **T**hreats and it can be applied by any organization to both the organization itself or to its individual products. Two conditions must be met for effective SWOT analysis:

- It must be based on data not just impressions.
- It must be based on data from all relevent audiences, which may not just be the consumer. In the airline market, for example, the impressions of travel agents are an important element of any SWOT

Table 5.2   SWOT analysis of Iceland

Strengths:
- Distinctive and exotic natural environment (geysers, volcanic mountains, lava deserts, glaciers, midnight sun, abundant bird life)
- Established cultural and historic heritage (saga sites, Viking culture)
- Good access via Keflavik Airport and reasonable accommodation stocks, particularly in the capital, Reykjavik
- Well established profile with committed specialist tour operators

Weaknesses:
- Seen as remote and largely outside the average tourist's 'consideration set' as a destination
- Is an expensive destination
- Extreme seasonality of climate and travel conditions mainly dictate summer visitation, especially into the interior
- Poor family destination due to lack of things for children to enjoy
- Poor travel infrastructure (no trains, poor roads especially in interior)
- Poor historic built environment since little architecture survives from pre-1900

Opportunities:
- Excellent development possibilities for specialist interest markets including: green tourists, natural history enthusiasts, sporting enthusiasts (fishing, river rafting, climbing, etc.)
- Opportunity for short city break development with capital Reykjavik as a trendy centre for upmarket done-everything tourists looking for something different
- Opportunity to develop Reykjavik as conference centre (Gorbachev and President Regan held Reykjavik summit in the 1980s)

Threats:
- Other Scandinavian destinations
- Cost factor may put Iceland at a major competitive disadvantage to other resorts
- Continuing difficulty of finding funds to market/promote awareness/destination image (Iceland has a tourist base of less than 200 000, so expensive promotional budgets are impossible)

analysis since they act as intermediaries (or gatekeepers) who influence the traveller's choice of transport.

SWOT analysis can be applied to destinations. Table 5.2 provides an illustrative example of a SWOT analysis of Iceland as a destination for international tourists.

Features and benefits analysis

Another useful method of analysing the tourism product is to consider its features and benefits. Features consist of the objective attributes of a tourism product; benefits are the rewards the product gives the consumer. Features have to be translated into meaning as consumer benefits. The differences between the two can be seen in Table 5.3.

In some instances features may be the physical aspects of products and benefits the symbolic ones we discussed earlier. One of the most useful disciplines for tourism planners is to inventory as many features of their product as they can (destination, attraction, hotel, etc.) and then attempt to translate them into benefits in relation to their main target audiences. This procedure often reveals that what planners regard as significant features of their product may have little relevance for the specific visitors they are trying to attract. The exercise can also be done in reverse by finding out what benefits consumers want from a tourism product and then trying to identify what features would enable them to gain them.

A slight modification of features and benefits analysis was deployed by the Angus Reid Group in Alberta, Canada in carrying out the Canadian Pleasure Travel Study in 1991. In approaching the task of tracking Canadians' vacation choices and experiences in order to understand the basis of their destination choices Reid produced a three-component model of the tourism product: 'Any product can be broken down into what it is, what it does and what people get from it. In other words the **attributes,**

Table 5.3 Features and benefits analysis for an airline

Tourism product item	Product feature	Consumer benefit
Aircraft seats	Wider seats with more footroom	Passenger comfort
Museum interpretation	Includes interactive video	Educational value for school parties
Hotel suite	Has own bar and conference table	Enables executives to host business meetings in own rooms
Santa Monica pier, California	Includes old fashioned fun fair and amusements	One of last seaside attractions offering traditional family fun
CenterParc	Provides covered sports facilities, swimming pools and shopping areas	Guaranteed all-weather action for all the family

benefits and the values.' Reid applied this triple categorization to the Yukon region of Canada to produce this product analysis:

Yukon product:
Attributes: Wilderness, Gold Rush.
Benefits: Getting away from everything, learning, reconnecting with nature.
Values: Discovering yourself again, exploring and growing, etc.

Reid argued that positioning a place may start with its attributes and work through to benefits and values, or begin at the consumer end by trying to understand and locate the consumer values that the destination will answer and then work back to the benefits and attributes associated with them.

Core product, tangible product and augmented *(added)* product analysis

For many years packaged goods marketing theory has differentiated between three levels of product offering: core, tangible/formal and augmented. The three levels can be seen as a continuum scale with the product's most basic benefit at one pole and a range of add-on benefits, not directly related to the product's essential purpose, at the opposite pole. The three levels may be defined as follows:

- **Core product:** the basic need function served by the generic product. For hoteliers the core benefits offered are shelter and rest; for travel companies the need to transport customers from A to B; for travel agents the supply of a range of tourism bookings.
- **Tangible/formal product:** the specific features and benefits residing in the product itself: styling, quality, brand name, design, etc.
- **Augmented Product:** the add-ons that are extrinsic to the product itself but which may influence the decision to purchase. Augmented features may include credit terms, after-sales guarantees, additional services supplied with the product.

Conceptualizing the product in these three areas allows the tourism marketer to appraise the comparative advantages and consumer appeal of his or her product versus others. In highly competitive markets it is unlikely that any supplier will have an advantage in core benefit (most airlines fly as quickly, most hotels offer the same rest capacity, most travel agents supply booking opportunities for the basic markets). Differentiation is more likely to reside in the second and third categories, and where it does not, it may be developed through creative innovations developed to the known needs of the target market. Table 5.4 lists some ways in which an airline might apply the three-part classification of product features in analysing and developing its products for the market.

Tangible and augmented product innovations have been keenly pursued in the competitive field of hotel marketing in the 1980s and 1990s. Fifty Hilton International Hotels round the world have developed the *Wa No*

Table 5.4 Core, tangible and augmented product features for an airline

Core	Tangible	Augmented
Transport	Airline name (corporate/brand)	Computer terminals
	Fast check in/out	Chauffeur to airport
	Executive lounge	Frequent flyer club
	Food/drink quality	Teleconferencing
	Movie programme	Hotel add-on to flight
	Decor/livery	Airmiles offer

Kutsurogu programme (comfort and service the Japanese way), aimed at Japanese travellers. It comprises (Schlentric and Ng, 1994: 409):

- Japanese speaking staff;
- Japanese hotel information;
- an oriental food selection;
- bottled, still mineral water in hotel rooms;
- green tea service;
- slippers, bathrobe and yukata (a lightweight gown) available;
- dedicated Japanese assistance telephone line;
- two-hour pressing service.

Another example of tangible/augmented product offerings is the 'Office away from home' concept in European hotel marketing:

Hotels no longer aim to be home-from-home, but rather offices away from the office. Office-like efficiency for guests can be assured through the provision of laptop computers, modems, and fax machines in rooms, with translation services and more widespread 'business centres' which offer guests the full range of secretarial services.

(Davidson, 1994: 381)

A whole package of tangible/augmented products has also been developed by airlines for business travellers based on the 'Office in the air' concept including frequent flyer schemes, late and early embarkation facilities, executive lounges, on-board telephones, fax and computer links and air-to-ground teleconferencing facilities.

PLANNING STRATEGIES: THE PRODUCT LIFECYCLE

A widely used concept in product planning is that of the product lifecycle (PLC). The idea is that products have lives like people, and that it is useful to understand their patterns in order to assess their likely development in the future. It involves tracing the development of a product in time through five stages of growth – introduction, growth, maturity, saturation and decline. The hypothesized pattern of growth and decline for a particular product can be shown as in Figure 5.1.

The different stages are associated with different numbers of people in

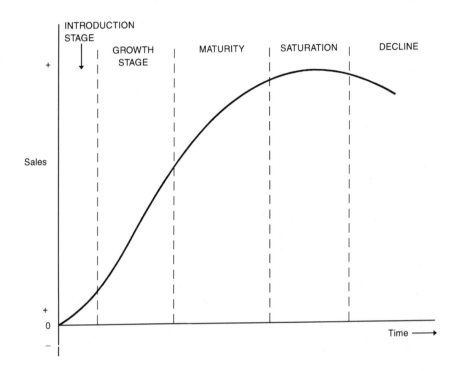

Figure 5.1 The product lifecycle.

the market, different levels of product volume sold and profitability, and different marketing and promotional strategies. Thus an airline might examine the product lifecycle of its executive class product by analysing sales over a ten-year period or longer and then try to identify what stage of the lifecycle it is at in order to plan marketing activities for the future.

However, the PLC is not as simple as it sounds. To begin with looking at the PLC pattern for a particular product has to take into account the market it is in. For example, if a product is showing no growth or decline, it may still be very successful if the market as a whole is in decline; thus the lifecycle **of the market** as well as the product have to be considered together. In fact it may be necessary to examine a product in relation, not just to the total market, but in relation to the product category in which a particular product exists. A package holiday operator offering cheap sun and sand holidays might want to look at the lifecycle trends in three product areas:

- product class: overall package holiday trends;
- product category: trends in budget priced sun, sea and sand holidays;
- product brand: trends for his or her own specific products.

For a travel agency in Britain one of the trends that would be essential in trying to operate the PLC would be the comparative growth of all

Table 5.5 Growth of the major multiples: number of outlets 1982–89

	1982	1987	1988	1989
W.H. Smith	88	126	200	202
A.T. Mays	124	233	266	287
Hogg Robinson	143	238	245	246
Thomas Cook	186	338	366	378
Pickfords	186	357	376	381
Lunn Poly	65	330	500	512
TOTAL	792	1622	1953	2006
Others	4141	5333	5425	—
% of total	16.1	23.3	26.5	

Source ABTA/Keynote (1989) *Market Review: UK Tourism and Holiday Travel.*

travel agencies and that of the major multiples vs. the smaller independents. Consider Table 5.5. The table suggests that though the travel agency market is growing, multiples are advancing at a much greater pace than others. Thus the PLC for each category may be different with the possibility that 'others' may decline still further as the multiples march on.

Another complication with the PLC is that a product which is in overall decline may be losing its customers from one market segment but increasing it or holding steady with another. For instance, a museum may see a decline in total visitors but find that, say, school parties are increasing. Thirdly, although the PLC is a neat concept on paper it is often difficult to determine, even from 10 or 20 years' data, at what stage a particular product is in. Finally, even assuming that a product's lifecycle position can be determined, it may be by no means obvious what should be done about it. If a product is in decline, there is nothing to stop a marketing manager taking action to stop it (through heavy promotion, launching an improved product or seeking new market segments). It is these problems with the PLC which have led one writer to comment: 'Its supposed universal applicability is largely a myth' (Mercer, 1992: 295).

However, despite these problems, the PLC is a valuable concept to operationalize since it forces the organization to analyse trends for its product in relation to the overall market and the segments within them in order to assess future marketing requirements. If, for instance, a hotel group is losing its business travellers while others are gaining, then action is essential. In consumer goods fields marketers constantly relaunch their products, seek new segments for them or, in some cases, find new uses for them.

A related concept for analysing destinations is that of the **tourist area life cycle (TALC)**. The idea is that destinations, like organisms, have a birth/growth/decline cycle which could be used as a basis for assessing their past development and future prospects. It will be discussed in more detail in Chapter 14 on destination marketing.

DIFFUSION AND ADOPTION MODELS OF TOURISM DEVELOPMENT

PLC and TALC were concepts about the development of products and resorts. A related concept is **adoption and diffusion theory** which is about the kinds of people/tourists who consume products/tourism and how they change over time as a market develops. When a new market emerges there are only a small number of innovative people in it but, as it grows, the number and kind of people who come into the market changes, culminating in market saturation when everyone who is going to be a consumer in a market is in it. The theory is premised on the idea that the curve of adoption follows a normal distribution pattern so that percentages of each adopter category are as follows:

Innovators	2.5%
Early adopters	13.5%
Early majority	34%
Late majority	34%
Laggards	16%

Ideally the marketing organization needs to know the profile of each of the adopter categories in order to target activities at each in sequence. If products are initially used by a small number of innovators and early adopters who later influence others, then it would be valuable to confine one's initial efforts to them. However, the problems are many:

- When is it clear that a market is saturated so that it is possible to look back and identify the sequence of adopter categories?
- Are there basic differences between all the categories, other than temporal dispersion, which would allow them to be differentially targeted?
- Can any of the categories be effectively isolated from others for discrete marketing activity?

Much research has been carried out into diffusion and adoption theory (see Rogers (1962) and Robertson (1971) for two important theoretical accounts) but the jury is still out about its practical application to tourism. Mass tourism developed so fast that nobody did any detailed studies to track patterns of diffusion, although there is an implicit model of tourist diffusion which is called **trickle-down theory** which hypothesizes that many kinds of tourism begin with small, often rich, elites and gradually broaden their appeal down the social scale to the mass tourist. It is certainly possible to tell with hindsight that resorts like Biarritz, Cannes, Nice and Spa were originally patronized by a rich elite and then gradually came down market in the course of time, but it is difficult to quantify the changes with any precision because of the problem of inadequate data. It is even more difficult to predict the patterns as opposed to recognize them with hindsight.

However, adoption and diffusion analysis remains an area that could be of interest to tourism organizations if they:

- carried out regular market segmentation studies from the moment their product was launched;
- used the studies to differentiate the profiles of people in each adopter category;
- monitored marketing activities carried out against each category;
- developed models of the interaction between the adopter category patterns and the marketing activities associated with each.

New products such as the Channel Tunnel and EuroDisney are in a position to track patterns of adoption among their customers but for long-established products such as resorts it may be too late.

CORPORATE IDENTITY: THE FIRM AS PRODUCT

The firm or organization is just as much of a product as the individual packages of offerings it makes to the markets it is in. How a company is perceived is particularly important for airlines, hotel chains, travel agencies and tour operators. This brings us to the concept of **corporate image and identity**.

The corporate image refers to the kinds of ideas and impressions people have of the organization in general . . . The corporate image may be of significance to consumers of the specific products by reassuring them of the responsibility and quality of the manufacture . . .

(Levy, 1983: 963-4).

The corporate identity is made up of the perceptions formed by external audiences of everything a company is seen to do: its employees, its services, its physical plant, as well as a whole range of promotional activities such as advertising, logos, stationary, etc. It is a symbolic entity:

An image is an interpretation, a set of inferences and reactions. It is a symbol because it is not an object itself, but refers to it and stands for it. In addition to the physical realities of the product, brand or corporation, the image includes many meanings – that is, the beliefs, attitudes, and feelings that have come to be attached to them . . .

(Levy, 1983: 964)

Olins (1989) has showed how, even in the nineteenth century, travel firms such as the great railway companies were aware of corporate identity and attempted to differentiate themselves from competitors by their architecture, rolling stock and the uniforms of their personnel (the North Eastern Railway actually produced a book entirely devoted to uniforms for all levels of staff). Firms such as Thomas Cook, Lunns and the great cruise lines of the 1930s established strong corporate identities before the war. Corporate identity can be particularly important in markets for tourism products which are high in perceived risk. People feel more secure in buying tourism products from well-known names like Thomsons than ones they know little about.

CASE STUDY 5.4

Forte: establishing a corporate identity

Since 1991 Forte has been undergoing a major corporate and branding operation to clarify the company's overall image and position the individual brands within it. The corporate aim was to produce an overall identity for Forte's 800 hotels worldwide, 74 airport shops, 1000 restaurants, 23 motorway service stations, 67 000 health clubs and 5000 catering contracts. This diverse portfolio was unified under the name Forte with the production of a lavish 45 second commercial designed to register the company name which was aired extensively in Britain in 1993/4.

BRANDING

Branding does, at the level of the product, what corporate identity does at the level of the firm. Branding developed in the field of packaged goods as a method of establishing a distinctive identity for a product based on competitive differentiation from other products. Branding was commonly achieved through naming, trade marking, packaging, product design and promotion. In the nineteenth century products such as Beecham's Pills, Cadbury's Chocolate and Eno's Salts were early users of branding and by the late twentieth century the market in packaged goods was dominated by brands. Successful branding gave unique identity to what might otherwise have been a generic product (tea, coffee, sugar, etc.). The brand identity produced a consistent image in the consumer's minds that facilitated recognition and quality assurance (before this modern buzz phrase had developed).

Branding had the effect of bestowing **added values** upon a product that could transcend its basic physical attributes. The added values were often created by advertising but, as Jones (1986: 29) has suggested, they are also generated by other factors including:

- people's experience of the brand;
- the sorts of people who use the brand;
- a belief that the brand is effective;
- the appearance of the brand.

The added values perceived in a branded good meant that it could often be sold at a premium price compared to unbranded substitutes. Brand names became financial assets that could be used as a basis for product diversification. Brand diversification sometimes used a corporate name (Cadbury's Fruit and Nut, Cadbury's Dairy Milk) but it could also be done without corporate identification, relying on the brand name alone to unite 'families' of products (Fairy Snow, Fairy Toilet Soap, Fairy Household Soap, etc.).

Initially branding was confined to packaged goods and durables but in the last 20 years its utility has been widely recognized in service marketing. In addition to the advantages just mentioned branding offers a solution to one of the most thorny problems in service marketing – consistency and product standardization. Branding can be a way of unifying services which is why it has been particularly developed in hotel marketing. For large hotel companies with a wide variety of properties grouping them into brands can:

- unify them into more easily recognizable smaller groups;
- enable each branded group to be targeted at defined market segments;
- enable product delivery, including human resource management, to be focused towards a specific set of benefits to a specific market.

The principles of hotel branding are no different from those governing other kinds:

> The success of a multi-brand strategy depends upon creating, and more importantly maintaining, a clear differentiation in the minds of the consumer. Each brand must stand for a unique combination or package of goods and services.

(Crawford-Welch, 1991a: 22–3)

The success of branding in hotel marketing is indicated by recent research by Horvath which showed that 88% of all bookings were to branded chains and that nine out of ten hotel users said they could distinguish between chains, franchise operators and independents (Gilpin, 1993).

Forte International has been a particularly energetic presence in corporate identity and branding operations in the 1990s. As part of the corporate identity programme described earlier Forte's have extensively branded their products. Three main hotel brands have been created: Forte Travelodge (mainly motorway and roadside hotels); Forte Posthouse

---

CASE STUDY 5.5

Examples of branding

In the 1980s Choice Hotels International (formerly Quality International) included the following brands in their product portfolio: Sleep Inns, Comfort Inns, Comfort Suites, Quality Inns and Hotels, Quality Suites, Clarion Inns and Resorts, Clarion Carriage House Inns and Clarion Suites brands.

In the 1990s ACCOR's portfolio included the following branded groupings: Sofitel, Mercure, Novotel, Compri, Ibis, Motel 6, Formula 1 and Hotelia.

Other international hotel groups such as Holiday Inn (one of the earliest branded hotels), Marriott, Sheraton and Ramada have developed branding with great success, and in many instances used it as the basis of franchise operations. Fast-food organizations like Macdonald's, Kentucky Fried Chicken, Burger King and Roy Rogers restaurants in the USA have also taken advantage of branding.

CASE STUDY 5.6

Forte Crest: product features

In 1991 Forte Crest, a 45-strong branded chain, was relaunched with a promotional campaign as 'the definitive hotel for business'. Its product freatures included the following.

- Set rate per room with no single person supplement, the whole chain having one of three standard prices (£95 for London, and £70 and £80 outside London).
- Introduction of a communications service including: message delivery in 10 minutes, free use of radio pager, access to fax, telex, photocopier and typing, 20 business support centres to provide word processing and secretarial support.
- A lobby manager to replace the concierge to give a more personal efficient service.
- A speedy 24-hour breakfast service due to irregular travel times.
- A single number to call for all services (which saves the customer looking up a directory for the right number).
- 24-hour hot and cold room service.
- Increase in number of Lady Crest rooms (rooms with dead lock, spy holes and better lighting).
- Increase in no-smoking rooms.

(three-star range products); Forte Crest (four-star business hotels). In addition, the company has also offered three collections: Forte Heritage (previously Trust House Forte hotels); Forte Grand (first-class international hotels); Exclusive hotels (the top-range hotels within the group). The product features associated with one of their main brands, Forte Crest, are inventoried in Case study 5.6.

In the past branding was often seen mainly as a matter of promotion – creating the right image through advertising and publicity, but there is now a recognition that successful branding involves the integrated deployment of product design, pricing policies and distribution selection as well as promotion. In short successful branding is about the deployment of the full marketing mix to create a differentiated product rather than a candy-floss dressing sustained by publicity. Jones's (1986) study of branding demonstrated that the most successful brands were not just me-too products with a distinct image imposed by advertising, but had real product differences that allowed them to achieve their dominance in the marketplace. The case for branding is strong for tourism products which offer the possibility of differentiation in several areas of the marketing mix. This is why branding has been particularly successful in hotel and restaurant marketing where the product can be physically differentiated (through architecture, design, food and beverage selection, company logos, staff uniforms and so on) and where price, promotion and distribution can be used to communicate and reinforce the differentiated brand images. Connell (1992: 29) identified four main differentiated features behind the Forte hotel branding operation of the early 1990s which resulted in three sets of hotels being put together into two branded groups:

- physical characteristics: modern or traditional;
- service style: formal or informal;
- location: city centre or out of town;
- principal use: business or leisure.

example ✓

The same holds true for airlines where differentiated brands can be developed based on differences in service provision, carrier design, pricing, etc. Doyle has forcefully underlined the essence of successful airline branding in the case of Singapore Airlines:

> Brands are rarely created by advertising. This concept is often misunderstood because the advertising is generally much more visible than the factor that creates differential advantage. Singapore Airlines is a strong brand and does some attractive advertising but the advertising is not the basis of the brand – rather the advertising communicates and positions it. The basis of the brand is the superior customer service provided by the cabin staff. This, in turn, is largely achieved by Singapore Airlines putting in more cabin staff per plane than do other airlines.
> (Doyle, 1990: 12–13)

Successful branding and corporate identity programmes can often lead to international market expansion through franchising operations which have made names such as Macdonald's, Sheraton, Marriott, Hyatt, Hilton, Ramada and Burger King well-known from Minneapolis to Moscow. (An excellent study on the franchising of hotels and restaurants in Europe and America can be found in Assisi (1995).)

Branding of restaurants, hotels and airlines developed extensively in the USA in the 1980s and early 1990s, and it is expected that this momentum will be matched in Europe in the future, particularly by large organizations which recognize that, to remain competitive, they may need to offer several products to different markets rather than relying upon a monolithic presence in one main one:

> Product portfolio management simply means that in post 1992 Europe corporations will no longer tend to be one-concept organizations. Rather they will operate several different brands.
> (Crawford-Welch, 1991b: 49)

The destination as brand

Branding is a superficially attractive idea with its connotations of clear image, distinctiveness, and perceived competitive advantage through a product which offers added values over and above its physical features. As a result branding has recently been bandied around as an idea by destination marketers, readily assuming that the concept is as applicable to places as it is to airlines, hotels, restaurants and attractions. There are, however, major problems with treating destinations as brands which will be examined in more detail in Chapter 14 on destination marketing.

NEW AND EXISTING PRODUCTS

Developing new products is different from maintaining existing ones, and both kinds of product planning will differ according to whether they are targeted at existing markets or new ones. Holloway and Plant (1992) provide a useful matrix to illustrate the permutations of market/product interaction that are possible and the product moves that might be suitable for each (see Figure 5.2). From this it is clear product management in tourism requires careful consideration of the product options in relation to the age of the market they are designed to satisfy.

One of the most critical tasks for tourism product managers is creating new or improved products. Where do new product ideas come from? There are no rigid formulae for finding them but the following include some of the options:

- from extensions of existing products – for instance, the new theme park in Orlando which builds on the existing success of Disneyland;
- from identifying dissatisfaction with existing products (e.g. the development of late boarding and early disembarkation facilities for business travellers by airlines to reduce 'hanging about' time);
- from growth in an existing market – where a tourism organization may expand its products or develop its own product in a market in which it has not previously operated;
- by seeking new markets for existing products as seaside resorts which were once holiday destinations, such as Brighton and Bournemouth, have done in developing their products for the conference/convention market;
- through finding solutions to unfulfilled or latent needs, e.g. all-weather, under-cover, CenterParc developments;

	Market	
	Existing	New
Product New	Introduce new product to present market	Launch of new product to new market
Existing	Modification to existing product for present market	Reposition present product to attract new market

Figure 5.2 Product options in new and existing markets.
Source: Holloway and Plant (1992).

CASE STUDY 5.7

Cruise product developments in Britain in the 1990s

In 1994 300 000 people took cruises in Britain, a 7% increase over 1993. The market is expected to expand to 500 000 by the year 2000. In response to this market potential P&O introduced a new liner aimed at the British market, the *Oriana*, in 1994 and another 77 000 tonne ship, the *Sun Princess*, was launched in Florida in 1995. Thirty new liners were in production by the end of 1995 with a combined value of almost £5 billion. The buoyancy of the market had also encouraged Airtours, a mass-market company which previously had not been in the cruise market, to introduce a low-price cruise product in the summer of 1994 which had a successful first season.

Source: *Sunday Times*, 19 November 1995.

- through technology-led innovations;
- through exploiting fashion and socio-cultural fashions (the nostalgia boom which for over a decade has produced a rash of industrial heritage products as different as Beamish Open Air Museum in County Durham, UK and Route 66 in the US);
- through brainstorming sessions designed to identify tourism trends and predict needs for the future.

These are only a few possibilities. All tourism organizations ought constantly to examine their products, looking for innovations and, if

---

CASE STUDY 5.8

Technology-led product innovation: Cyberia Internet cafés

One of the most successful new products to come out of the IT boom in the 1990s is Cyberia Internet cafés. In 1994 Eva Pasco and Gene Teare set up a wired-up café just off Tottenham Court Road in London with an investment of £50 000. As women they felt that IT had previously been dominated by men and identified an opportunity for reaching a wider market through the more user-friendly characteristics of the Internet in a coffee house setting. Within 14 months Cyberia had had 91 000 customers, had expanded in the UK through franchise operations in Edinburgh, Manchester, Kingston on Thames and Ealing, and had international operations imminent in Tokyo, Los Angeles, New York and Paris. Franchise charges were a flat rate fee of £10 000 and 8–10% of revenues from each outlet. In November 1995 the business was valued at almost £5 million.

Cyberia illustrates two aspects of good product planning: (a) the importance of a good name (the Cyberia name is now legally protected); (b) the importance of a well-chosen location. As Pasco commented: 'It [the Tottenham Court Road café] had to be on a street corner. Cafés and café culture tend to be on street corners because there is more light and a much more sociable environment.'

Source: Lloyd (1995).

necessary, cessations. Organizations as different as resorts, airlines, hotels and restaurants (which require refurbishing and presentation if they are to stay looking modern) have an ongoing requirement to update their products and services in relation to the developing needs of markets.

SUMMARY

This chapter has set out to evaluate some of the analytical procedures and concepts involved in product management in tourism. In Part 2 we shall look in more detail at specific products and markets.

REFERENCES

Allport, P. (1990/1) Holiday Parks/Centres, in *The Tourism Industry, 1990/1*, The Tourism Society.

Assisi: Centro Italiano di Studi Superiori sul Turismo (1995) *Il franchising nel settore alberghiero e della ristorazione*, FrancoAngeli, Milan.

Association of British Travel Agents/Keynote (1989) *Market Review: UK Tourism and Holiday Travel*, ABTA/Keynote.

Burke, J.F. and Resnick, B.P. (1991) *Marketing and Selling the Travel Product*, South-Western Publishing, Cincinnati, Ohio.

Cameron, B. (1992) Who wants what – and why? An overview of the Canadian Pleasure Market Study, *Conference Proceedings of the 23rd Annual Conference of the Travel and Tourism Research Association*, 14–17 June, Minnesota, pp. 154–67.

Connell, J. (1992) Branding hotel portfolios, *International Journal of Contemporary Hospitality Management*, **4**(1), 26–32.

Crawford-Welch, S. (1991a) Marketing hospitality in the 21st century, *International Journal of Contemporary Hospitality Management*, **3**(3), 21–7.

Crawford-Welch, S. (1991b) International marketing and competition in European markets, *International Journal of Contemporary Hospitality Management*, **3**(4), 47–54.

Crawford-Welch, S. (1994) The development of the Courtyard by Marriott, in Teare, R., Mazanec, J.A., Crawford-Welch, S. and Calver, S. (eds), *Marketing in Hospitality and Tourism*, Cassell, London, pp. 184–96.

Davidson, R. (1994) European business travel and tourism, in Seaton, A.V. (ed.), *Tourism: The state of the art*, Wiley, Chichester, pp. 377–82.

Doyle, P. (1990) Building successful brands: the strategic options, *Journal of Consumer Marketing*, **7**(2), 12–14.

Gilpin, S. (1993) *Branding in the hotel industry. Where are we now?* CHME Conference Paper, Napier University, Edinburgh.

Holloway, J.C. and Plant, R.V. (1992) *Marketing for tourism*, Pitman, London.

Jefferson, A. and Lickorish, L. (1991) *Marketing Tourism*, Longman, Harlow, Essex.

Jones, J.P. (1986) *What's in a Name: Advertising and the Concept of Brands*, Gower, Aldershot, p. 29.

Levy, S.J. (1983) Imagery and symbolism, in Britt, S.H. and Guess, N.F. (eds), *Dartnell Marketing Manager's Handbook*, Chicago, Boston and London, pp. 961–70.

Lloyd, E. (1995) Business, *The Sunday Times*, 19 November.

Mercer, D. (1992) *Marketing*, Blackwell, Oxford.

Olins, W. (1989) *Corporate Identity*, Thames & Hudson, London.

Robertson, T.S. (1971) *Communication and Innovative Behaviour*, Holt, Rinehart & Winston, New York.

Rogers, E.M. (1962) *Diffusion of Innovations*, Free Press, New York.

Schlentrich, U.A. and Ng, D. (1994) Hotel development strategies in Southeast Asia: the battle for market dominance, in Seaton, A.V. (ed.), *Tourism: The State of the Art*, Wiley, Chichester and London.

Wind, J., Green, P.E., Shifflet, D. and Scarborough, M. (1989) Courtyard by Marriott: designing a hotel facility with consumer-based marketing models, *Interfaces*, **19**(1), 25–47.

Woodside, A.G. (1982) Positioning a province using travel research, *Journal of Travel Research*, Winter, pp. 14–18.

REVIEW QUESTIONS

1. Perform a SWOT analysis on a town or city near you using, if possible, published studies and research which might be useful in assessing its potential as a tourism destination.
2. Working alone or in a brainstorming group with others develop some new product ideas that might augment the appeal of:
   (a) a local bed and breakfast establishment or guest house;
   (b) a small travel agent operating in your area.
3. Prepare a presentation comparing the corporate or brand image of two tourism organizations of your choice taking into account their products, publicity, premises, service standards and any other factors which you believe to be important.
4. How useful are the product life cycle and diffusion and adoption theory as approaches to understanding the market for coach travel?

The marketing mix: tourism pricing

A.V. Seaton

6

OBJECTIVES

By the end of this chapter the reader should:

- appreciate the variety of prices that exist between and within tourism product sectors;
- be able to analyse the main forces that influence pricing decisions at both the strategic and tactical levels;
- understand and evaluate the main pricing options commonly adopted by tourism organizations.

INTRODUCTION

One of the many distinguishing features of tourism marketing is the wide diversity of pricing policies adopted by tourism organizations and their susceptibility to rapid changes. Restaurants charge several prices for similar meals with, for example, dinner costing twice or three times that of lunch in some cases. Tour operators offer their packages at variable prices with reductions for early bookings and late bookings. Most carriers charge differently for the same journey with fares that show variations by time of year, position on the plane and time of booking. Hotels may charge up to eight different prices including: rack rate, seasonal rates, weekend vs. weekday rates, corporate rates, priviliged user rates (regular stayers, members of societies, owners of particular credit cards, etc.), conference rate, short break rate and tour group rate. This chapter looks at some of the factors that influence the prices of tourism products and the ways in which individual organizations can arrive at effective pricing decisions.

Before the development of marketing pricing was often seen a way of making a profit after costs had been taken into account. An organization calculated what the product cost and then added a margin on to this in order to arrive at the price to the customer. Price was seen as a discrete area of decision, fixed according to the needs of the supplier, with little appreciation of its wider implications within the total marketing process in relation to consumer perceptions, competitive requirements and, above all, to external environmental forces that might necessitate tactical price adjustments. Before the war, for instance, hotels and carriers produced price lists which tended to operate unchanged throughout the year or season and, in many instances, showed little movement from year to year.

The kind of price stability which existed for the first decades of the century now makes the period look like a golden age. Since the war high inflation levels, rocketing labour costs, increased competition and the general volatility of markets have tended to make tourism pricing decisions more complex, particularly since the 1970s as mass tourism has increased in the West.

IS PRICE STRATEGIC OR TACTICAL?

The development of marketing has also had a profound effect on the way price is managed by tourism organizations. Within the marketing orientation pricing is seen, not just as a monolithic device for making profit after the recovery of costs, but as a way of creating customers. Pricing is conceived as an inherent part of the product positioning which makes a statement to consumer groups about the nature, quality and competitive features of the product they are purchasing.

> A positioning approach for pricing decisions puts the customer front and center for strategic marketing planning. Positioning, by one definition, is the customer's perception, real or perceived, of a product's value or worth to them.
>
> (Shaw, 1992: 31).

Price is an important product cue, inseparable from the perceived identity of the product in the marketplace. Tourism is, as we have seen, an intangible which is difficult for consumers to evaluate on the basis of physical evidence. Though some tourism products such as hotels may have objectively determinable features (size of rooms, decor, position, etc.) many aspects of evaluation are more subjective and price can influence the image of a product upon which evaluations are based. Price acts as an indicator of product type and quality and a form of competitive differentiation. The role of price as part of a product's positioning can be illustrated by Stena Sealink's decision in 1994 to represent itself through an advertising campaign built around the theme 'Ferry nice prices', which had as its objective the aim of flagging the company's value-for-money compared to other carriers, particularly against the new Channel Tunnel which was opened in May.

For luxury products positioned to affluent markets a premium price may be an essential requirement to maintain an image of exclusivity. A golf

---

CASE STUDY 6.1

Pricing in the luxury cruise market

Classical Cruises is a company operating at the luxury end of the cruise market in the USA with customers who are above the average in income and education and are also older. Jamie Rosen, President of Classical Cruises, in 1992 defined his product as: '. . . cultural and natural history voyages aboard small luxury ships and offering unique itineraries that span the globe and the calendar year.' The market for the product was the older affluent market, typically retired. During the recession of the early 1990s Classical Cruises preferred to maintain prices rather than discount them in order to maintain the quality of their services and also because: 'Our market is not necessarily price sensitive, it is *value conscious*. In a recession it does not necessarily spend less, it spends wisely.'

Source: Rosen (1992: 231)

---

museum in Scotland charged a low price for admission and failed to attract many American tourists who felt that it could not be a very good museum if the admission was low.

In hotel marketing, classification and grading systems determine the broad parameters of price and positioning – a two-star hotel has to operate within a price band that is set by the quality of service specified in its grading and the prices of all other competing hotels within it. Luxury hotels, on the other hand, such as Reid's in Madeira and others in the south of France, derive an important part of their image and customer franchise from being seen to be more expensive ('If you have to ask the price, you can't afford it'!).

Price is thus one of the earliest strategic decisions to be considered alongside the other three major elements of the marketing mix.

THE MAJOR FUNCTIONS OF PRICE

Price has to evaluated against general organizational objectives and the marketing goals derived from them. For private sector organizations such goals as achieving market share and profitability will play a part in determining prices. For public sector organizations whose primary remit may be the free provision of services to the community, profit will be less of an issue, although in the developed world many public sector organizations are being pushed by governments to recover at least part of their costs through greater commercial orientation.

Price can be used in a number of ways to control consumer demand for a product. These include pricing to:

- *Maximize access*. This is often a major consideration for public sector organizations whose performance is judged on the levels of service they provide to the communities (whether national or regional) who

CASE STUDY 6.2

Free admission to nuclear power stations

In Britain an unusual tourism market has been created by the nuclear industry which, after Chernobyl, set about trying to allay public concern about nuclear plants through ambitious public relations programmes which included the creation of visitor centres with expensively produced interpretation displays. British Nuclear Fuels at Sellafield in Cumbria was a pioneer of this, spending around £2 million a year on advertising from 1986 onwards, and opening a free-admission visitor centre in 1988 at a cost of £5.4 million. Within a year it was attracting 200 000 visitors making it one of the top tourist attractions in the north. In Scotland a similar initiative was made at Hunsterstone B Nuclear Power Station where entrance is free, the sights are free, and a free bus will pick parties of 15 or more up from anywhere in Scotland – and when you leave you get a free drink!

ultimately pay their salaries (e.g. through taxation). A regional park or public museum may want to maximize local visitors and hence opt for free admission or low price entry. However, it is not only the public sector which may want to maximize access as Case Study 6.2 indicates.

Other private sector organizations may elect to maximize customers through low price policies in order to maintain dominance in a market. In the late 1980s major tour operators like Thomsons cut prices to the bone in order to maintain market share in their prime mass sun and sea holiday sectors.

- **Restrict access**. Conversely discriminatory pricing may be used to restrict access and limit it to customer segments an organization is particularly interested in at the expense of other groups. This is particularly common in the marketing of top-end of the market luxury

CASE STUDY 6.3

Eurocamp in Europe

Eurocamp operates in eight countries in Europe offering camping holidays at 300 destinations to 12 destination countries. It provides self-drive campsite holiday packages including Channel crossing, tent or mobile home and on-site service. It sells mainly direct to the customer and uses travel trade intermediaries to a lesser extent. It has four main brands but all of them are niche marketed products targeted at an affluent, middle-class market of families with children of school age. This basic corporate positioning, as an upmarket family product, drives everything the company does including its service quality, promotion and pricing. The company seeks to differentiate itself from competitors on the basis of core product quality and is able, as a result, to charge prices higher than many competitive products.

Source: Gareth Jones, Managing Director of Eurocamp, 1995.

products and in many kinds of niche markets (cruises, five-star hotels, business travel packages, Concorde, the Orient Express).

- **Control demand in time**. Price can also be used to manage consumer demand through time. Higher prices may be charged at times when demand is known to be strong with reductions to attract people during low periods of traffic. Many carriers such as ferry companies and rail firms offer reduced rates during low seasons of the year or at times through the day or week when people travel less. Intercity, the UK rail network, sets its peak travel rates early in the morning when business travellers are most likely to use its services and reduces them once the morning rush is over. Icelandair charge up to three times more for weekday flights to Iceland from Britain (mainly used by executive travellers) than for weekend ones (when the business market is absent). City hotels commonly offer reduced rates at weekends to fill bedspaces normally occupied by business travellers during the week. Bars and restaurants have introduced 'happy hours' (normally between 6 and 8 in the evenings) when drinks and meals can be discounted before the later evening rush.
- **Control demand in space**. At a destination price can also be used to disperse people away from the central areas. High admissions may be charged by attractions, restaurants and the accommodation sector in 'honeypot' locations (central Florence, for instance) while lower prices may be charged further 'off the beaten track'.

BASIC INFLUENCES

The three major influences on price are costs, competition and the consumer. Their relationship has been neatly summarized by Margaret Shaw (1992: 31): 'Demand sets the ceiling, costs set the floor, and competition determines where on the continuum the actual price will fall.'

The market

Like everything else in marketing price decisions must start with an analysis of customers. In general tourism is both price and income elastic. Thus raising price depresses consumer demand while lowering prices normally increases it. Similarly when people's earnings increase their tourism consumption increases, while when it drops, tourism as a luxury good may be one of the first discretionary expenditures to be cut. People tend to plan holidays against a fixed budget which may involve careful saving through the year. Before making a final decision they often closely compare brochure prices and make a choice which seems to offer best value against other options. Others may leave the holiday booking till the last minute in the hope of being able to take advantage of last minute bargain holidays. The tourism marketer must therefore understand the way in which the consumer makes the purchase decision in order to decide what level of pricing might be appropriate.

One implication of close analysis of consumer groups is the possibility of differential pricing for different consumer segments. At Madame Tussaud's in London higher prices have been set for high-season international visitors, and lower ones for school groups and other parties who visit all the year round. In other tourism markets separate prices have been offered to students, senior citizens, previous customers, first-time visitors (introductory offers), families with children and many more.

Price sensitivity was once thought to operate mainly in the recreational tourism market and to be less critical in business tourism. This has changed profoundly over the last five years as recession worldwide has made firms in the USA, Europe and Britain increasingly cost-conscious. One instance of this new corporate sensitivity to travel costs was a 1992 article published in the magazine *The Business Traveller* called '21 ways to cut travel costs' with recommendations to executives that included shopping around, using frequent flyer schemes, loyalty clubs in hotels, early booking discounts on car hire, two-for-one offers, introductory deals (including staying in new hotels offering low price as a means of market entry), using guides such as *Half Price Europe*, using trains rather than air transport in France and Germany, and airpass offers in Scandinavia and South Africa (McWhirter, 1992).

The lesson in both the recreational and business market is simple – the tourism organization must closely monitor customer attitudes to price and be prepared to make modifications to existing policies when occasion demands.

Competition

In many tourism markets competition provides an iron constraint on pricing options for individual organizations. The power of the 'going rate' can force organizations as different as tour operators, airlines and seaside landladies to adopt parity pricing policies.

In competitive mass tourism markets follow-my-leader pricing can lead to rapid adjustments as firms clammer to match or beat the market leader. One effect of this is that tour operators often publish several editions of their brochures with price adjustments as the season develops. In recent years operators such as Horizon, Thomson, OSL (Thomsons), Airtours, Aspro (Airtours), Falcon, Enterprise, Go Greek and Go Turkey (Owners Abroad) have published second, third and even fourth editions of their brochures with price adjustments, in efforts to establish competitive advantage or simply keep down with the pack.

In destination marketing, comparative price levels at destinations, often a function of such things as exchange rates, labour costs and stage of economic development, can be crucial in determining the relative attraction of a place. Bull (1991: 32), summarizing work by Edwards, suggests that:

The most significant variable by far in international destination choice appears to be relative prices. Research suggests that this explains at least 40% of variation in travel shares of destinations, and as much as 60% where those destinations are close substitutes.

The continuing strength of Spain as a destination through the early 1990s was bound up with its economic advantages to the tourist, particularly versus its adjacent competitor, France, where the strength of the franc meant that international visitors got less for their money than they did in Spain. Another factor which affects the relative price of a destination is the fiscal structure of countries. In Europe VAT rates (Value Added Tax) and other kinds of taxes on consumer goods differ between countries making some more expensive to tourists than others. France and Ireland have special low rates of VAT for some tourism products, notably hotels, whereas Britain does not.

It is therefore essential to monitor competitors' prices before arriving at a pricing policy. Such monitoring will reveal price structures within the market from which the individual organization can decide its own pricing policies.

Costs

Tourism product costs are less easy to assess than those in some manufacturing industries because they fluctuate, depending on the number of units sold. This is because tourism products such as hotels and airlines are high in **fixed costs** and low in **variable** costs. It does not cost much less to run a hotel with 10% occupancy than one with 70%. Similarly the costs of flying an aircraft are not that much greater whether it is full or half booked.

However, some assessment of costs has to be made in setting prices. These may include the following.

- **Distribution costs**. Different distribution methods are associated with different kinds of cost. For an organization using middlemen such as travel agencies, commissions of between 7 and 12% will have to be allowed for in the price. For direct-sell organizations promotional costs must be covered by prices.
- **Research and development costs**. A package holiday may take 1–2 years to put together by a tour operator and while this is being done no revenue will be coming in. For bigger, capital-intensive projects such as a new attraction or a hotel costs may have to be set for a payout period lasting several years. EuroDisney, which opened in 1993, lost £600 million because prices were set high in an attempt to recover the enormous costs of development too quickly. The Channel Tunnel is not expected to break even until well into the next century.
- **Wage costs**. In a labour-intensive industry such as tourism where the product depends upon personal service the wage bill is a major influence upon ultimate price.

In addition to these basic influences, external environmental trends (currency movements, political developments such as terrorism, health scares, etc.) may force organizations to review their prices in order to adapt to changed market conditions. The gap between brochure production, when prices are first published, and the provision of the holiday product may be up to nine months; in that time circumstances may change dramatically as they did when the Gulf War broke out shortly after holiday companies had issued their brochures in 1989/90. Price cuts are frequently used as a mechanism for reviving sudden falls in demand.

APPROACHES TO STRATEGIC PRICING DECISIONS

How then does a tourism organization go about setting its prices? The initial boundaries of price can be arrived at by a fairly simple ballpark exercise which involves two estimates:

- First determine what **minimum** price must be asked to cover costs.
- Then determine an upper limit, **maximum** price that might be possible given the organization's knowledge of market competition, costs and the consumer.

The final price will then lie somewhere between the two. This is, of course, a very broad start. Once some kind of upper and lower limits have been established it is necessary to refine the decision process through additional analysis.

Cannon and Morgan (1990) have developed a systematic methodology for setting price which involves consideration of six major pricing strategies:

- **Target-profit pricing**. This involves pricing to achieve a target rate of return in relation to forecast sales volumes.
- **Cost-plus pricing**. This involves a mark-up on unit costs, based on company or industry norms (e.g. £100 per holiday sold).
- **Perceived value pricing**. This involves charging what the market will stand based upon the customer's perception of the quality of the product.
- **Going rate pricing**. This involves charging the same or similar to what one's competitors are charging in similar markets.
- **Sealed bid pricing**. This involves responding to the buyer's invitation to submit a price for a contract or product against other (generally unknown) competitors.
- **Negotiated pricing**. This involves negotiation between a customer and his or her tourism supplier, generally to negotiate down from the prices the supplier publicly declares (e.g. the rack rate of hotels)

In order to decide which of the six to adopt Cannon and Morgan advocate a six-step analysis based on asking the following questions:

- Does the customer merit individual attention?
- Does the customer know monetary value?
- Does the price influence customer demand?
- Does the firm have demand-related information?
- Are there close substitutes against which price is compared?
- Will customers favour competitors for non-price/quality reasons?

The answers to the six questions can then be used as a basis for appraising which or what combination of the pricing techniques to adopt.

Although Cannon and Morgan's pricing framework was a general one not specifically developed for tourism markets, it has useful applications for tourism marketers. The commonest forms of pricing used in tourism of the six presented are perceived value pricing (luxury hotel rates, cruise charges, business air fares, specialist tour charges), and going rate pricing (business lunch rates, mass tour operator charges, travel agency commission levels, cross Channel ferry prices in Britain). The reasons why these two strategies are used in the different markets derive from the factors embodied in Cannon and Morgan's questions, particularly those about the effect of price on demand (important in mass markets; less so in affluent, specialist markets); the presence of substitutes (many in mass tour packages; fewer for luxury hotels); and the likelihood of the customer favouring competitors for non-price/quality reasons (likely for specialist tour packages and premium hotels; unlikely for mass tour packages and travel agency chains). Cannon and Morgan's criteria questions also suggest why sealed-bid pricing and negotiated price have been used by airlines and hotel chains in dealing with customers meriting individual attention, such as companies with large or frequent corporate travel budgets. The Marriott in Miami negotiated a special deal for the crews of Virgin Atlantic. A.T. Mays, the British travel agency chain, lost the travel account of Strathclyde Regional Council in a tender bid to Pickfords Travel (now Going Places) which is part of Airtours Group RC.

Another useful way of approaching price strategy is by assessing different price options in relation to product quality (actual or, better still, perceived quality determined from consumer research) with both price and quality being benchmarked against competitors. Six permutations of price and product quality are possible as shown in Table 6.1 together with the likely positioning within the consumer's mind associated with each. The table enables the tourism organization to decide its pricing policy in explicit relationship to competitive levels of product performance.

Another approach to price strategy is that noted by Crawford-Welch (1993: 52). He identified three basic price positions:

- overall cost leadership which can yield high profits through low prices, high sales volume and high market share (e.g. Thomson's pricing of its mass market holidays);
- differentiation which should foster high prices, margins and profits with a much smaller sales volume and share of the market (e.g. the pricing of flights on Concorde);

Table 6.1 Price vs. product quality

Price charged	Product quality offered		
	Superior to competitors	Parity with competitors	Worse than competitiors
More expensive than competitors	'Rolls Royce' product positioning	Expensive positioning	Rip-off positioning
Similar price to competitors	Excellent value positioning	Equal value ('going rate') positioning	Poor value positioning
Cheaper than competitors	Miraculous value positioning	Excellent value positioning	'Cheap 'n cheerful' positioning

- focus which may include a combination of low costs and some differentiation designed to appeal to a highly focused niche market. A firm achieving both low costs and high product differentiation should be in a position to dominate the market.

BASIC PRICING STRATEGIES

Having looked at some of the principles behind pricing we shall now look at two basic pricing strategies.

Market skimming

This is a pricing method based on setting a high, sometimes introductory, price aimed at attracting the cream of a market. It may be supported with or without heavy promotion depending on whether the product offered is or is not known to the potential market. It can be a way of maximizing profit in the short run. It is workable in the following circumstances:

- In high fashion markets with short lifecycle and/or when demand exceeds supply over a short space (e.g. accommodation pricing in Edinburgh during the period of the Edinburgh Festival, the cost of inclusive packages for sought-after hallmark events such as the World Cup, the Bayreuth Festival, Oberammagau, etc.).
- For products with highly differentiated or unique features, e.g. the £21 000 luxury world cruise which Thomas Cook offered as part of its 150th anniversary programme in late 1990.
- For one-off consumption where no consumer loyalty is expected (restaurants at major attractions or tourism centres, motorway services, etc.).
- In monopolistic or oligopolistic markets where the customer has little choice but to take the product at the price demanded (e.g. food prices

on British Rail trains, prices on ferry lines which are the sole carriers between specific destinations such as that running from Stranraer to Ireland). However, high pricing by monopolies or oligopolies has to be considered in relation to the ill-will it may create with the customer which will affect the organization's image adversely.

Market penetration

This pricing method is the opposite of skimming. It involves offering the product at a low price in order to make the product available to the widest number of people as quickly as possible. Once again it may be supported with high or low levels of promotion. It may be deployed in the following circumstances:

- When repeat business is a major consideration and customer loyalty is key (e.g. for restaurants anxious to win the daily lunch custom of workers in a city centre).
- When there are many competitive substitutes (e.g. for proprietors of bed and breakfast establishments in the same neighbourhood or street).
- When product differentiation is small (e.g. for sun, sea and sand resort packages to Spain, Greece, Turkey, Portugal). Generally speaking it is only possible to get away with a premium price when a product has a perceived added-value.
- When the product is inferior to substitutes (e.g. coach companies know that if they increase prices beyond a certain level customers may defect to forms of transport such as rail or air which are perceived as more congenial).

TACTICAL PRICING

Though the underlying price level set for a product or range of products is strategic, the volatility of tourism markets frequently demands short-term tactical adjustments necessitated by the need to generate rapid demand shifts in order to overcome unused capacity arising from the following:

- **Seasonality**. In markets subject to seasonal peaks and troughs the preferred strategic price can only be maintained in the high season and reductions are necessary outside this main period. In some cases even high season prices must be reduced at the last minute if an organization finds it is likely to be stuck with unused capacity.
- **Sudden market fluctuations**. These may be caused by the external events (terrorism, ecological disasters, economic factors) noted earlier.
- **Competitive activity**. As tourism becomes more competitive pricing becomes an increasingly important means of combating threatening moves by other organizations. Discounts and many other kinds of special offer may be introduced to 'spoil', or simply match, the

activities of competitors. Mass market tour operators constantly look over their shoulders to take into account of what their competitors are doing.

SPECIFIC PRICING TECHNIQUES

Camouflage pricing

This is a presentational method of concealing parity pricing, in markets where a number of organizations are adopting similar prices. It consists of the differential itemizing of services offered so that it is difficult for the customer to make direct price comparisons because they are not comparing like with like. Some ferry firms may change a flat rate price for a car by its size, while others may charge on a per passenger basis. Self-catering firms offering cottages or houses abroad may charge a price per person or, alternatively, charge a weekly or fortnightly price per unit. Presentation is an important part of pricing – the way an offer is made may make it perceptually attractive and different in the consumer's eye from others even though the underlying pricing policies behind them may be similar.

Decoy pricing

This policy depends upon offering two or more priced offers which includes one which is demonstrably poorer value than the others. The idea is that the poorer offer will act as a negative benchmark against which the attractiveness of the other offer(s) will be evaluated making consumers adopt the latter – the ones the organization wanted to sell in the first place!

Two-part pricing

Some tourism organizations with a desire to appear to offer good value to the consumer may charge a low basic price or none at all, but then charge

---

CASE STUDY 6.4

Camouflage pricing

In 1994 three hotels in a Scottish Tourist Board short-break brochure promoted their priced offers as follows:

- **Hotel A:** 'For an enjoyable break away, we will spoil you for choice. Buy two and get another two free, only £109 Dinner, Bed and Breakfast.'
- **Hotel B:** '£120 per person for 3 nights Dinner, Bed and Breakfast.'
- **Hotel C:** 'Rates from £35 per person per night for Bed and Breakfast.'

Which hotel offered the best value? How long did it take you to work it out?

CASE STUDY 6.5

Decoy pricing

Two American researchers collaborated with a US travel agent to offer three holidays to Las Vegas and three to Disneyland. The offers comprised three price/value relationships: a low price/low value holiday (an already existing option); a high price/high value holiday (the target option); a high price/low value holiday (the decoy offer). The results showed that the decoy price achieved a 9.2% shift in favour of the target offer for the Disneyland holiday but that there was no appreciable shift for the Las Vegas one. The research suggests that a high price/low value decoy price may have the effect of trading some people up to a high price/high value alternative.

Source: Josiam and Hobson 1993).

---

for additional services once the customer has purchased the basic product. Museums and galleries often admit visitors free but then may charge for temporary or special exhibitions staged within them. A funfair is an even better instance of an attraction where entry is free but the rides and amusements are all charged for individually.

The technique has its dangers. Customers dislike add-ons which they only find about after committing themselves to the basic offer. This can allow competitors an opportunity in some markets. Just America, a tour operator which competes in the outbound market to America from Britain, prominently advertises its no add-on policy, precisely because other packages may include hidden extras.

EVALUATING PRICE

Pricing decisions should ideally be **pre-evaluated** before final introduction in relation to the consumer and competitors. There are three main methods of doing this.

- **Through competitive analysis**. Obtaining brochures of one's competitors is an essential method of price comparison for tour operators (which is why many tour operators are increasingly reluctant to publish their prices first). For an accommodation supplier, knowing the rack rates (and where possible the special deals) offered by equivalent hotels and accommodation suppliers will determine a price range that should only be exceeded in special circumstances. Travel agents and attraction marketers can often gain competitive pricing information by judicious visits to competitive organizations and simply observing their advertised prices.

- **Through customer surveys**. It is possible to gauge consumer reaction to prices by surveying them beforehand. This may be done through

CASE STUDY 6.6

Charging admission to a regional park in Scotland

In 1994 a major regional park, Clyde Muirshiel, carried out a year long study into its visitors involving interviews with 2500 people. One of the objectives of the study was to explore the sensitive issue of introducing admission charges to a leisure amenity which had formerly been free. This issue was investigated through a key question: 'In principle would you be prepared to pay admission to use the park or parts of the park?' Results indicated that opinions were about equally divided on the issue with 51.5% saying that they would be prepared to pay and 48.5% saying that they would not. Admission charges have not yet been introduced.

Source: STRU (1994).

quantitative questionnaires administered by post, phone or personal interview with populations of target customers, or through qualitative studies, e.g. group discussions with members of a target market. The questions can be directed to establishing reactions to a particular price possibility or a range of potential prices.

- **Through market testing**. The most accurate method of pre-evaluating price is through a limited trial run based on a small number of consumers, or by trying the price in one area or geographical bloc (e.g. one city or town within a country). An organization may also arrive at an effective price through learning from past experience, as Euro-Disney has done in France where it originally priced itself out of the market at the time of its launch in 1993.

NON-PRICE REVENUE

In some public sector tourism, particularly attractions such as museums, galleries, parks and gardens, pricing may be a limited tool of revenue-generation because of a traditional commitment that such products should be made available free or very cheaply as a community service. However, this does not rule out revenue generation by other means. Entry prices are only one method of revenue generation. In the field of cultural attractions additional sources are particularly important. As Richards (1994: 373) notes in a recent article on cultural tourism: 'Entry prices are only one measure of increasing revenue generation by cultural attractions. Some studies also indicate that income from merchandising, catering and other secondary spend sources is growing.'

A study for the Association of Independent Museums in Britain on the marketing of museums suggests a number of alternative ways of raising revenue. These are summarized in Case Study 6.7.

With the public sector in many countries under increasing pressure to raise at least some of its funds commercially, there is great scope for the

CASE STUDY 6.7

Non-price revenue generation for museums

In 1980 a manual of marketing prepared for the Association of Independent Museums advocated the following methods of raising revenue instead of, or in addition to, admission prices:

- Admission free but added charges for admission to special exhibitions within the main attraction.
- Paid admission to special events.
- Mark-up on literature, merchandise and catering.
- Filming and TV facility fees.
- Copying of photographs, plans and documents for research.
- Hire of facilities for specific functions. In July 1994 Kelvin Grove Museum in Glasgow charged as the venue for the international conference, 'Tourism: The State of the Art' dinner which celebrated the 50th anniversary of the Scottish School at Strathclyde University.
- Loan of collection items.
- Consultancy, advice or valuation services.
- Endorsement, use of the museum's good name or reputation.
- Reproduction or copyright fees for commercial use of collection material.
- Charges for seminars or meetings.
- Use of research and library facilities.

Source: Bryant (1988: 65)

development of revenue-generating ideas where it is not possible to charge for admission. As Hewison (1991: 162–77) has noted:

> Museums are being forced into the market place. If they remain free at the point of entry they must do more than justify their existence by the volume of visitors passing through their doors, and once inside, these must be exploited through the sale of souvenirs, refreshments, and so forth.

REVENUE GENERATION BY CROSS SELLING

Another form of non-price revenue is **cross selling** where a tourism organization, instead of just selling its own products, sells ancillary products provided by other organizations. This is already widely used and is likely to develop even further. Travel agents and tour operators often offer a range of complementary products with their basic holidays (insurance, travellers' cheques, car hire, guide books, attractions vouchers, etc.). Motoring organizations and tourist information centres may sell guide books, maps, souvenirs or even arrange accommodation bookings taking a percentage of the booking charge. Large hotels sometimes have their own retail outlets or feature display cases of merchandise (cosmetics, antiques, jewellery, etc.) from which they derive a mark-up. The future possibilities of cross selling are great because it has advantages to both the consumer and the organization acting as agent. From the customer's point of view being able to buy everything for a trip at one stop (when the package is booked, when an airline reservation is made, etc.) is a great convenience. For the organization cross selling can be almost pure profit since all it has to do is distribute the products and take a commission or mark-up on the sales without having any/much responsibility for their production, promotion or their bulk warehousing (if they are physical products, e.g. guide books, souvenirs, etc.).

SUMMARY

This chapter has reviewed the role of price in tourism marketing, appraised some of the main issues that have to be taken into account, and indicated some of the specific methods commonly used in the trade. There are no ready-made solutions that can be instantly adopted by tourism organizations but the modes of analysis suggested will ensure that the right disciplines are applied in searching for an optimum pricing mix. And even then, as in all marketing activities, there is always a need for judgement and improvization in order to respond to the complexity of the market place:

Positioning on price, indeed, involves a bit of instinct, guesswork, and luck. It is also a learned art separate and distinct from the tactical or scientific side of pricing decisions.

(Shaw, 1992: 38)

REFERENCES

Bryant, J. (1988) *The Principles of Marketing: A Guide for Museums*, Association of Independent Museums, London.

Bull, A. (1991) *The economics of travel and tourism*, Pitman, London.

Cannon, H.M. and Morgan, F.W. (1990) A strategic pricing framework *Journal of Consumer Marketing*, **7**, 57–67.

Crawford-Welch, S. (1991) International marketing and competition in European markets, *International Journal of Contemporary Hospitality Management*, **3**(4), 47–54.

Hewison, R. (1991) Commerce and culture, in Corner, J. and Harvey, S. (eds), *Enterprise and heritage*, Routledge, London, pp. 162–77.

Jones, G. (1995) Marketing the niche product: case studies from Eurocamp, in *Latest Developments in the Marketing of Holidays and Leisure Travel*, Henry Stewart Conference Studies, London.

Josiam, B. and Hobson, J.S. (1993) Consumer choice in context: the decoy effect in travel and tourism, in Chon, K.S. (ed.), *Proceedings of Research and Academic Papers*, Vol. V, Society of Travel and Tourism Educators Conference, Miami, Florida, 14–17 October.

McWhirter, A. (1992) 21 ways to cut travel costs, *Business Traveller*, December, pp. 35–36.

Richards, G. (1994) Developments in European cultural tourism, in Seaton, A.V. (ed.), *Tourism: The State of the Art*, Wiley, Chichester and London, pp. 366–76.

Rosen, J. (1992) High end marketing in the new recession: Classical Cruises, in *Travel and Tourism Research Association, 'Tourism Partnerships and Strategies', 23rd Annual Conference Proceedings*, Minneapolis, 14–17 June, pp. 221–2.

Shaw, M. (1992) Positioning and price: merging theory, strategy and tactics, *Hospitality Research Journal*, **15**(2), 30–8.

STRU (Scottish Tourism Research Unit) (1994) *Clyde Muirshiel Visitor Study: Final Report*, Renfrew Enterprise and Clyde Muirshiel Regional Park, Glasgow.

REVIEW QUESTIONS

1. Collect a range of brochures for a number of tour operators selling in similar markets and produce price comparisons on the products they offer. Attempt to explain differences/similarities between the prices revealed in the brochures.

2. Visit a local museum (or gallery or other attraction) and assess to what extent cross selling and other activities are being used to generate revenue outside basic admission prices.

3. Carry out a survey of restaurants in your area noting their menus, location, decor and prices. Then assess to what extent their pricing policies are different or similar and why.

4. Why in general have cruise holidays been thought to be more expensive than inclusive, sun, sea and sand packages? Is it true? Obtain cruise materials to investigate the issue.

7 The marketing mix: tourism distribution

M.M. Bennett

OBJECTIVES

By the end of this chapter the reader should:

- be able to identify the channels used to distribute the tourism product;
- understand the role of the travel agent;
- appreciate the main issues facing travel agents;
- understand the importance of information technology to distribution;
- understand the distribution channels used in the UK.

INTRODUCTION

In the four Ps of the marketing mix, it is place which represents distribution of and access to the product. Here we can differentiate between goods and services. While in manufacturing goods are transported to the consumer, in tourism it is the consumer that is transported to the product. This difference is crucial having implications for the method of distribution. What is apparent is that information assumes a vital role. (As consumers are unable to physically inspect the product/service, they are forced to rely on information about the product.) As such, at the time of purchase/ booking the product can be seen as nothing more than a bundle of information (Suppliers therefore not only provide the product but they also provide information on price, quantity (number of beds and seats), flight/ferry times (arrival and departure), quality (class of hotel), supplements (single room, day flight, stopovers, rooms with a balcony, etc.)) conditions of purchase and booking procedures. Furthermore, this information needs to be communicated to the consumer, hence the importance of the information transmission mechanism. Here we are concerned with the methods used to distribute that information – principally travel agents but also tour operators and information technology (IT).

From a consideration of the choice of distribution mechanism, this chapter will focus primarily on travel agents which act as the key form of distribution for the travel industry. Within this chapter various marketing issues are reviewed and discussed including vertical integration, customer service and IT. The chapter concludes by speculating on the future of distribution within this constantly changing industry. Emphasis is placed on the UK situation, and while it must be acknowledged that there are differences in operations elsewhere in the world, for the purposes of consistency and continuity only the UK situation is looked at. Nevertheless the principles of distribution which form the structure of this chapter are applicable universally.

DIRECT SELL OR TRAVEL AGENCY NETWORK?

(A principal, that is a travel product supplier, is faced with a decision on choice of distribution channel) If the principal is an airline or a hotel, it has potentially three options: selling through a tour operator, selling through a travel agent or selling direct to the consumer. If the principal is a tour operator (that is a company packaging different products together to form a new travel product), two options confront it: again, either selling direct to the consumer or selling via a travel agent (see Figure 7.1).

Certainly from one perspective, the tourism product lends itself to this kind of selling. (The fact that the product cannot be seen, touched or physically inspected before purchase (in other words, its intangibility) means that the consumer is dependent on information. So you could argue that it is irrelevant whether the consumer receives information directly from the supplier or through a third party, in this case the travel agent. However, there are other factors at work here. Consumers like to have a choice, they like to be able to compare different companies' products and assess the range of options available to them, and it is a travel agent which can provide this. Furthermore, consumers like advice, for example on travel restrictions, inoculations, insurance, and it is the travel agent which

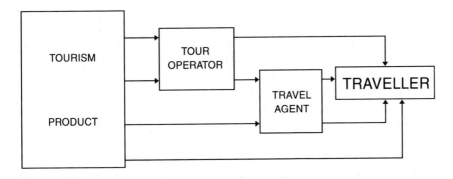

Figure 7.1 Industry structure: the distribution channels.

again provides that – it is, in short, the reassuring human face of the travel industry. The mentality of going out to shop, the high cost involved of most forms of travel and the fact that for many people the holiday is only a once a year event, all point to the need for a travel agent. So while the travel agent, as seen earlier, has a definite role in providing a convenient service, it is also offering a lot more in the way of a personal service which is perceived to be unbiased, a point which is tackled later.

So far the discussion has been general but a specific point in choice of channel relates to the type of product being sold. The growth of the inclusive tour to mass market proportions resulted in the emergence of the now famous 'Ss' (sun, sand, sea and sex) and holidays conformed to this identikit formula. Substitutability was the order of the day. Although the travel industry has introduced alternative forms of holiday and variations among package tours, the bedrock of mass market tourism (particularly from the UK) remains the tried and trusted inclusive tour by charter (ITC) to mostly sunny locations. The point here is that if the experienced package holiday taker wishes to choose a package, they may be less concerned about visiting a travel agent. The consumer will have fewer questions to ask and less need for reassurance or a personal service. But for complex itineraries and tailor-made bespoke packages, dealing with someone at the end of a telephone would be less than ideal. So type of product being sold assumes importance in determining suitability of distribution channel.

Estimates of the size of the market for direct selling in the UK are difficult to find but given the limited number of companies selling direct it is thought to be small. Companies that sell direct can be split into several categories:

- those that sell direct exclusively – an example is Direct Holidays;
- those that sell both direct and via a travel agent – Thomson Holidays is the obvious example with its direct sell wing Portland Holidays, but there are others including companies which sell the same product through both channels by using direct marketing (cruise companies are one such example). Also under this category are companies which advertise on teletext to offload late availability;
- travel agents selling direct – the most notable example is Thomas Cook Direct which operates a telesales unit to make holiday bookings for its own products as well those of other tour operators. Travel agents using teletext for late availability are a further example. Strictly speaking this category does not fall within the definition of direct selling in that the travel agent is still playing a key role;
- credit card companies selling direct – this type of selling usually involves a number of tour operators and can, in some cases, involve a travel agent. Normally, incentives in the form of discounts are offered to consumers to encourage them to use this route.

So from the principal's viewpoint, why should they go **direct**? Direct selling appears an attractive proposition because it eliminates the travel agent's commission and places the control over sales in the hands of the product providers. It also helps to induce brand loyalty since the company is advertising itself direct to the consumer. Cost advantages are debatable since the benefits gained from cutting out the travel agent are offset by the increase in advertising and organizational costs and the costs of setting up and maintaining a sales team within the company. Control over the entire sales process is thus a key factor encompassing information provision and customer service and also highlighting the powerful position of the principal over the travel agent's more vulnerable one.

Equally we can ask why a principal should choose to use the **travel agency network**. There are over 7000 agents in the UK thus in theory giving the principal an office in every town. This is a substantial advantage as the travel agent will assume a customer service role as well as administering the actual booking. However, the disadvantages include getting the brochure racked by the travel agent, servicing the agent (sales representatives, contracts, brochure provision, educational/familiarization trips), the commission fee, overrides and other incentives, and IT costs.

There is no easy answer to which is the best method as much depends on the supplier in terms of its size and turnover, the products it is selling and the costs involved. Ultimately, the decision to go direct or use the travel agent is based on cost.

THE TRAVEL AGENT'S ROLE

Implicit so far has been the travel agent's role in the chain of distribution. The agent's role is to act on behalf of both principals and consumers. The agent, therefore, by the very nature of the business provides information about other companies' products, not its own, hence the term 'agent' (see Foster, 1985; Burkart and Medlik, 1981). Furthermore, without information the agent's role is void. This is heightened by a unique feature of travel agents in that they do not purchase travel products or services in advance. Instead they merely act as an intermediary between principal and consumer thereby sharing in none of the risks associated with more typical retailers in buying in stock. The risks therefore lie with the principals which, in turn, are able to dictate the market opportunity available to travel agents (Goodall, 1988). By not buying in stock, it could be argued that the travel agent is less likely to develop brand loyalty towards a company or product. In such circumstances this aids impartial advice to consumers but it also poses a marketing problem for the principals who rely on the agents to sell their products (Holloway, 1985). This has resulted in vertical integration to solve the marketing problem (see later) but also serves to introduce bias into selling. Such bias is further heightened by override commissions, sales incentive schemes for staff and the link to preferred operators. It should be mentioned that tour operators may also be selective in travel agency outlets allowed to stock their brochures. Although the main role of travel agents may be seen to be to provide a convenient location for the purchase of travel (Holloway, 1992), the truth of the matter is that the information provided about products may be biased.

(In addition to providing information about products available in terms of product types, dates, times, location and availability, the agent's role is enhanced through its advice-giving capacity (even if this can be biased).) Agents are also able to provide information related to the products which is not supplied by the principals. Other information, such as that on travel insurance, travellers' cheques and foreign currency, all serve to broaden the scope of services provided. The travel agent's ability to optimize holiday choice can be furthered through knowledgeable, well-trained staff and the associated service they provide.

In the marketplace it is possible to distinguish between several types of travel agent. In the first instance we can differentiate between business and leisure agents, the former focusing on business travel for company employees, and the latter that of holidays and travel for pleasure. Business travel is dominated by the multiples. The major players in the UK in 1994 were Hogg Robinson Business Travel International, Carlson Wagonlit and American Express.

The major leisure suppliers can be separated according to multiples, miniples and independents. The main distinguishing feature is that of size in that multiples are nationwide organizations, their presence and influence sometimes extending into the international arena, e.g. Thomas Cook; at the other end of the spectrum are independents – essentially small businesses comprising one or a handful of units located within a 'local' area; and finally there are miniples – medium sized chains which are usually regionally based, e.g. Bakers Dolphin with around 40 outlets in the West Country. Differences extend beyond size to product range. Multiples, for example, operate a racking policy based on selected tour operators, usually the mass market ones (which offer incentives), while smaller travel agents tend to offer a greater range of tour operators, often including specialist independent ones. A distinction can also be made in terms of growth strategies. The large multiples in general have tended to opt for a policy of expansion in the quest for market share while small firms and independents have tended to remain small, exploiting the benefits of a more loyal and experienced workforce and the provision of a personal customer-orientated workforce.

CASE STUDY 7.1

American Express

In September 1994 American Express considerably strengthened its position in the business travel market with the acquisition of Thomas Cook business travel for $375 million. Although this effectively removes Thomas Cook from the market, it is still allowed to handle accounts up to $150 000 but it is barred from major involvement in business travel for four years.

Source: *The Financial Times*, 14 September 1994; *TTG*, 21 September 1994.

Table 7.1   ABTA-registered travel agents in the UK: year at 1 July 1989–93

	1989	**1990**	**1991**	**1992**	**1993**
Members	2967	2971	2828	2755	2671
Offices	7493	7431	7057	6850	6875
Offices per member	2.53	2.50	2.50	2.49	2.57
Members admitted	120	237	210	194	203
Members lost	122	233	353	267	287

Source: Key Note Report (1994).

In terms of overall numbers there are approximately 7000 travel agents in the UK. Table 7.1 distinguishes between companies and branches for the period 1986–93. What is clear is that the number of companies has declined reflecting a reduction in the number of smaller firms. The larger companies, however, have continued to show growth throughout this period as highlighted in Table 7.2; in particular the strength of Lunn Poly and the newly formed composite travel agency Going Places can be noted.

Figures for market share (Table 7.3) show that the top chains hold approximately 46% market share for leisure leaving 54% in the hands of the smaller travel agents. So while the major travel agents are able to secure prime locations in the major towns and cities and use the national media to project their company into people's homes, their actual share of the market and dominance of this sector of the industry is less than one might at first imagine.

Table 7.2   Number of branch offices of major UK travel agents: 1990–93

	1990	**1991**	**1992**	**1993**
Lunn Poly	503	510	578	705
Thomas Cook	330	330	330	365
Going Places	334	334	334	545
A.T. Mays	305[2]	287[3]	302[3]	317
Top four	1472	1461	1544	1932
Other ABTA travel agents	5959	5596	5306	4943
All ABTA travel agents	7431	7057	6850	6875

1. Going Places is made up of the combined outlets of Pickfords and Hogg Robinson Leisure in 1993. Going Places is the branded Airtours chain of retail outlets. Airtours took over 334 Pickfords outlets in September 1992 and 214 Hogg Robinson retail outlets in June, 1993.
2. Includes 30 business travel agencies which were excluded from 1991, 1992 and 1993 totals.
3. Estimate.
Source: Key Note Report (1994).

Table 7.3 Air inclusive tour market shares[1] of UK travel agents (% by volume): 1991–93

	1991	**1992**	**1993**
Lunn Poly	21.0	21.0	23.0
Thomas Cook	11.0	10.0	10.0
Going Places[2]	11.5	9.5	9.0
A.T. Mays	4.5	4.5	4.0
Top four	48.0	45.0	46.0
Other travel agents	52.0	55.0	54.0
Total	100.0	100.0	100.0

1. AIT summer market.
2. Going Places made up of the combined shares of Pickfords and Hogg Robinson Leisure.
Source: Key Note Report (1994).

INTEGRATION AND ITS IMPLICATIONS FOR TRAVEL AGENCIES

It can be argued that for a travel company to be successful it needs three parts: a tour operator to put together holidays, a travel agent to sell them and an airline to transport consumers to their holiday destination. The theory is certainly being borne out in the strategies of the major travel companies. This is known as vertical integration which in simple terms is the merger or takeover of firms at different stages of the production process. The rationale is equally simple. By integrating fully (i.e. airline/tour operator/travel agent), the company has complete control over the entire operation thereby conferring more power. Forward integration into travel agencies ensures that the tour operator has outlets for the sale of its products. Remember that, as already stated, travel agents have preferred tour operators and tour operators are equally selective in their choice of travel agents to sell through. Remember too that travel agents have limited shelf space and, crucially, do not purchase stock thus resulting in limited brand loyalty. An obvious way of overcoming that problem is to set up or take over a travel agent.

Integrating backwards into the airline industry has similar advantages. The company has control over the number of passengers being flown and changes in destinations can be accommodated more easily. In other words, the company has greater flexibility and control.

Full integration offers further advantages. Again relating to the issue of control, information supplied by one part of the firm can be used by another part. For example, information on sales can be utilized to monitor the market and formulate long-term business strategies. Information about consumers can be obtained at every stage of the operation which can ultimately be used for marketing purposes. The results of such information control are synergistic in that having the full picture, i.e. all the information, is of greater value than information collected individually from each part of the business. Furthermore, there are economies of scale to be gained encompassing the centralization of functions such as advertising, staff training and information technology. Control too is associated with power and that has benefits in the form of negotiations with principals regarding hotel rates, commission fees and incentives.

The top three tour operators in the UK – Thomson Tour Operations, Airtours Plc and First Choice (previously Owners Abroad) – each have their own charter airline and each own or have affiliations with a travel agency chain (see Table 7.4).

First Choice's link with a travel agent stems from Thomas Cook's 24.6% shareholding in the company in July 1992. Due to the size of these companies in the marketplace such integration has been the subject of debate as to whether it acts against the consumer's best interests. In particular there has been a question mark over the nature of advice given by the multiple travel agents. Indeed, in a study reported by *Holiday Which?* in September 1993 it was found that travel agents associated with the three tour operators actively skewed information towards the affiliated tour operator. As a result of the allegations of biased advice stemming from vertical integration, the Office of Fair Trading launched an investigation. The outcome of the inquiry announced in August 1994 concluded that the issue should **not** be referred to the Monopolies and Mergers Commission as the evidence did not support the allegation that there was anti-competitive practice in the travel industry.

The OFT looked into:

- the use of discriminatory rates of commission;
- travel agents' decisions not to carry brochures of certain tour operators;
- tour operators limiting the supply of brochures to travel agents;
- late season directional selling by leading tour operators.

The key issue tackled was whether any of these practices restricted the ability of independent travel agents or tour operators without shares in travel agents from competing. It was found that while vertical integration may make it more difficult for new entrants there was no evidence to show that the integrated companies could insulate themselves from competition. Indeed the vigorous competition associated with the brochure launch periods in 1993 further endorsed this view. The Director-General of Fair Trading, Sir Brian Carlsberg, stated:

Table 7.4 Vertical integration and the top three UK tour operators

	Company		
Tour operator	Thomson	Airtours	First Choice
Travel agent	Lunn Poly	Going Places	Thomas Cook*
Airline	Britannia	Airtours Intl	Air 2000

*Thomas Cook has a 24.6% stake in First Choice. This is termed a strategic alliance.

Our extensive review of the sector has shown that, despite ownership links between some tour operators and travel agents, there continues to be a wide choice of competitively priced packages available to holidaymakers from both new and established firms.

(OFT, 11 August 1994)

Interestingly, one aspect where action was deemed to be required was that of biased advice, in particular directional selling to the consumer. Although it was not felt that consumers were being 'deliberately misled' it was felt that holiday choice could be 'artificially restricted'. Consequently the Director-General called for links between tour operators and travel agents to be disclosed.

At the time of writing (November 1995) the OFT had reopened the case on vertical intergration due to pressure from smaller independent operators who argue that they are being squeezed out by the three largest companies. This indicates persistent concerns about the nature of competition in the travel industry.

In addition to vertical integration there is also horizontal integration. This is the expansion of a company at one level of the chain of distribution. So for a travel agent it would mean a growth in the number of outlets. This can occur in one of three ways:

* the setting up of new outlets;
* the acquisition of another company;
* merger with another company.

There is evidence of all these routes to growth being used by travel agents. One of the most significant examples of horizontal integration is the sale of W.H. Smith to A.T. Mays in 1991. A.T. Mays, originally a Scottish firm, was acquired by the Carlson Group in 1990.

CUSTOMER SERVICE

A main function of the travel agent is to provide advice to the consumer. Although on the surface this would seem a relatively simple thing to do, in

---

CASE STUDY 7.2

Airtours

Forward integration by Airtours began in September 1992 with the takeover of Pickfords Travel (333 retail outlets). This was followed in June 1993 with the acquisition of Hogg Robinson leisure and its 210 outlets. In December 1993 all outlets under the control of Airtours were renamed 'Going Places'.

Source: Key Note Report (1994).

practice there are a whole host of complications which affect the nature of the advice given. The root of the problem lies with the travel agent's position within the chain of distribution. To reiterate, the travel agent's role is to act on behalf of both the principal and consumers: to this end they can be seen as a 'double agent'. Herein lies the crux of the matter – can travel agents adequately serve both principal and consumer without introducing bias? From the principal's perspective, the travel agent, by not buying in stock in advance, has no brand loyalty so the aim of the principal is to get the travel agent to sell its products over other competitors. To ensure that this happens, the principal has two options – either it can vertically integrate into travel agency such that a guaranteed channel for its products is created (as we have seen, this has happened) or it can offer incentives or overrides to encourage loyalty.

Let us look at the latter in more detail. Special incentives are usually offered to counter clerks on the basis of number cf flights, holidays, car rental bookings sold or whatever it is that the principal happens to specialize in.

Alternatively, higher commission rates are offered. The commission fee is the basis of the travel agent's income and varies according to the product sold. Typical commissions are 10% on a package tour, and 9% on an airline ticket (see Table 7.5). The high rates for the ITC partly explain the growth in 'holiday' shops specializing in package holiday sales. An override commission is where the principal increases the commission fee paid (usually by Linsen 1–2%). Often this is linked to the volume of sales – the principal will set a sales target and if the travel agent reaches it, the principal will pay

---

CASE STUDY 7.3

Falcon

In 1994 Owners Abroad (now First Choice) offered £5 Marks & Spencer vouchers on every return Falcon flight seat to Canada booked between 19 January and 15 February 1994.

Source: *TTG*, 19 January 1994.

CASE STUDY 7.4

Cathay Pacific

In January 1994 Cathay Pacific offered a 'Dance with the Dragon' prize draw to celebrate Chinese New Year in Hong Kong. For every First Class or Marco Polo Business booking on the UK to Hong Kong route for travel between 27 January and 30 April, the travel agent would receive an entry to the prize draw. As an extra incentive a complimentary Chinese New Year T shirt was sent for the first booking each travel agent made.

Source: *TTG*, 19 January 1994.

Table 7.5 Travel agent's commission earned on sales of product, 1991

	%
IATA airlines	9
Domestic airlines	7
British Rail	7
Tour operators	10
Cruises	9
Ferries	9
Insurance	35–40

Source: Key Note Report (1991).

out the higher commission rate. Insurance is another high earner for travel agents with commission rates often exceeding 40% with the result that travel agents will tie in insurance with discounts offered on holidays such that the revenue gained from the insurance will help to offset the discount offered.

Directional selling, that is the active encouragement of sales of particular company's products usually associated with vertical integration, has been exacerbated with discounting. As a result travel agents tied to tour operators through integration have discriminated in the discounts offered on their parent-owning tour operators and those of their competitors.

For the consumer all of this amounts of biased advice. John Dunscombe, Chairman of the Travel Agents Council, in 1988 stated: 'There has been a popular misconception in the past that people are getting completely unbiased advice from their travel agents . . . We live in a commercial world . . . and it would be unrealistic to expect it' (*Holiday Which?*, 1989). This was further borne out in a survey of travel agents reported by *Holiday Which?* in 1993 which showed that of 37% of multiple agencies surveyed, only products of the parent tour operator were offered. Once again the link with vertical integration is brought to the fore.

The problem then for the travel agent is that it is also serving the **consumer**; indeed, without the consumer there is no sale and no travel business. As consumers use travel agents to obtain information and advice about products, it is vital that the travel agent is seen to be working for them which means providing advice which is in the consumer's best

CASE STUDY 7.5

Discounting and insurance

In the frenzy of discounting which has characterized the brochure launches since 1994 a consistent requirement associated with every discount offered is that of the travel agent's insurance being taken out (see Figure 7.2).

Figure 7.2 Examples of discounting and insurance.
Source: Various.

Figure 7.2 *(continued)*

10%OFF
Summer Holidays with Going Places.

"Play the Going Places game in the Daily Mail - up to £100,000 worth of holidays to be won."

THIS OFFER IS FOR A LIMITED PERIOD ONLY

We've got a really, really great offer for you **NOW** at Going Places, the new name for **Pickfords** and **Hogg Robinson Travel Shops**.

We'll give you a 10% discount off the brochure price when you book your overseas summer holiday at one of our Going Places shops.

Choose from a wide range of holidays from all the top operators to all the top destinations. And, you only need to place a **£5** deposit per person.

For a really, really great holiday call into any of the 546 Going Places shops nationwide or for credit card telephone bookings only, call our Holidayline on **061 474 7555**.

LOW DEPOSIT ONLY £5 PER PERSON

You get really, really great prices at

10% discount applies for overseas and Channel Islands inclusive Summer '94 holidays or charter flights costing at least £100 per person booked with Going Places, and is for a limited period only. Discount and low deposit available only when Going Places insurance is purchased at time of booking. Full deposit due by 31 3 94 or on cancellation. Full details from your local Going Places shop. Low deposit not available on telephone bookings. ABTA 47064

Figure 7.2 *(continued)*

ABTA 18057/E1800

Lunn Poly

HUGE DISCOUNTS ON EVERY OVERSEAS SUMMER HOLIDAY

OR GETAWAY WITH TWELVE MONTHS TO PAY

Don't book your summer holiday until you've checked our huge discounts. Take advantage of this fantastic new offer, and there's a flexible payback system to suit your needs. Pay in one lump sum, or make your repayments in four convenient, easy to manage instalments within twelve months. And with no hidden extras, all you pay is the brochure price. Just take out our top quality holiday insurance when you book. Too good to be true? This amazing offer applies to overseas holidays, cruises and brochured flights featured in Summer '96 brochures, and to departures between 1st April and 31st October in year round brochures. So race down to your local Lunn Poly Holiday Shop now or **call us on †01203 225888**.

Don't book your summer holiday until you've checked our huge discounts. Or for the first time ever, at Lunn Poly, you can purchase your holiday on easy pay terms.

EASY PAY Scheme

Subject to availability. Lunn Poly reserve the right to withdraw this offer without notice. †Lines are open Mon-Fri 8.30 am-8pm, Sat 9am-6pm, Sun 8.30am-5pm. Methods of payment accepted: Mastercard/Visa/Switch/Delta. Credit card payment surcharge of £1 per person applies. Easy Pay minimum spend £200. Subject to status. Full details available in store. Offer applies to new bookings only.

Figure 7.2 (continued)

CASE STUDY 7.6

Discounts and vertical integration

In August 1994 the three biggest travel agents Lunn Poly, Going Places and Thomas Cook engaged in a discounting war. At Lunn Poly 15% discount was offered on every 1995 overseas summer holiday including Kuoni and British Airways Holidays. At Going Places the discount ranged from 5–15% with only 5% off Thomson brands. Thomas Cook offered 8–15% off all companies except for Thomson where again the discount was 5%.

Source: *The Sunday Times*, 14 August 1994.

---

interests. Given the level of vertical integration in the industry together with incentives and commissions offered, it is questionable whether this actually happens.

A further layer of complexity is added in looking at differences between multiples and independents. Clearly the point about preferred tour operators, incentives and overrides disadvantages the multiples to a far greater extent in the service stakes. But the difference goes further and relates to the type of product sold and the quality of the staff. The holiday shops, in particular, i.e. those that specialize in selling mass market package holidays, have been criticized for the service they offer. The point is that to sell a package holiday does not require a great deal of skill or intelligence and this has been reflected in the quality of staff employed. Furthermore, given that multiples are going for volume in terms of sales, quality of service is, in theory, again going to suffer. Of course, it could be argued that if the consumer only wants a package holiday then he or she does not require a greater level of service than that which is provided and that, in this sense, the service cannot be described as poor.

Independents, in contrast, offering a greater array of tour operators and willing to put together tailor-made holidays, have relied on more experienced and knowledgeable staff and have thus built up a loyal clientele through the provision of a personal service extending from pre-sales to after-sales. Buck (1988), an independent agent, set out in his view the differences between multiples and independents on this service issue. While the service issue certainly helps to differentiate independents to their advantage, it remains a generalization and there are exceptions to every rule. That said, personal service is certainly one strategy for survival for independents and indeed travel agents in general, a point which is tackled later.

THE ROLE OF INFORMATION TECHNOLOGY

Distribution of the tourism product is intrinsically linked to information technology (IT). Indeed, IT has become a fact of life for the travel industry to the extent that it is difficult to imagine how the industry could survive today without it. But how has this situation arisen? To answer this we need to understand why the industry is suited to IT and what factors have led to its adoption. At the beginning of the chapter we looked at how information can be considered a representation of the tourism product. This is made more apparent when considering the nature or characteristics of the tourism product. It is useful to recap on some of those characteristics first introduced in chapter five.

Intangibility

The tourism product cannot be inspected, touched, seen or experienced prior to purchase. The only guide to suitability of the product in relation to consumer needs and desires is that of information – information on price, quantity (number of seats, beds, etc.), flight/ferry times (arrival and departure), quality (hotel/airline class), supplements (single room, day flight, stopovers, rooms with a balcony, etc.), conditions of purchase and booking procedures. Such information is conveyed by published material such as brochures and timetables but due to the dynamic and perishable nature of the tourism product it is also transmitted electronically.

Perishability

The product has only one life. Once the date has passed that product is dead. A flight half empty, a hotel half full, a tour operator's availability half filled all mean the same thing: a loss of revenue for that airline, hotel and tour operator. Information analysis and management help to minimize the number of perished seats, beds or places. Factors determining loads can be predicted such as season (weather), times and dates and thus availability can be altered. The product's availability can either be expanded if there is excess demand or reduced through lack of demand; consolidation is an example of the latter.

Such perishability also explains the increasingly common phenomenon of overbooking, particularly among airlines. It is now common for airlines to overbook a scheduled flight on the basis that not all of the passengers will appear for that flight, a key reason being that many of these passengers will be on business with tickets enabling them to alter flights. More frequently than otherwise the airline's predictions are accurate and so it is able to maximize returns and limit the number of perished seats. However, the laws of probability dictate that there will be times when all potential passengers turn up, hence the problem of 'bumping'.

All of this relates to the product's perishability and the need stemming from that for information to minimize the number of perished products and to maximize loads and thus revenue. As the tourism industry has grown, competition has increased and there has been a parallel expansion in information needs. The perishability of products, the products themselves being represented by information, has placed emphasis on the need not only for accurate information but also on the mechanism for communicating that information throughout the industry.

Heterogeneity

The inherent nature of the tourism product bringing together elements from all over the world creates an information problem. The industry is essentially fragmentary and lacks standardization, a problem stemming from competition within the industry which impinges upon tour operators, travel agents and ultimately consumers.

Volatility

The tourism product is constantly changing. External factors such as political troubles, the economy, air traffic control, weather, consumer tastes, etc. affect the actual array of products on offer. Changes in the market need to be monitored such that the industry is able to respond by withdrawing, altering or creating new products.

Volatility can also be considered from the point of view of availability. Once the product has been established it is available for sale but that availability is constantly changing as consumers purchase products or as principals alter the number of products supplied. Such information needs to be transmitted throughout the industry to avoid overbooking. For example, a tour operator will have a limited number of single rooms or day flight seats. It is therefore vital that, at this more detailed level, travel agents and tour operators and consumers are constantly updated on what has been sold and what is available. Such information can also be used for marketing purposes by the principal or travel agent but a means of monitoring and analysing that information is required.

Summary

All of this brings into focus the need for an efficient communication system. The dynamic nature of the tourism product is such that a mechanism is required to transmit information about products between the different sectors in the chain of distribution, i.e. principals, travel agents and consumers. Without such a mechanism the travel industry's operational efficiency would be severely restricted. Competition between suppliers further heightens the need for efficient, reliable and accurate information regarding the products and their availability. As a result the means of conveying that information in and around the chain of production and distribution becomes virtually as important as the information itself.

Based on information and driven by computers, IT is proving to be all-pervasive. Travel agents, tour operators, airlines and hotels are all heavy users of IT to the extent that Poon (1988) refers to it as a total information system. A distinction, however, can be made between intra- and inter-organizational adoption of IT. The former involves firms using IT internally for management and organizational functions, while the latter concerns the use of IT for external communication with other sectors of the industry. Travel agents, for example, utilize administration and accountancy systems which perform the back-office functions (intra-organizational) while reservation systems provide them with access to principals, notably tour operators, airlines and hotels, to make reservations and obtain information (inter-organizational).

What is apparent then is that IT has gradually eroded earlier mechanisms of information transmission such as post and telephone which were slow, less reliable and cumbersome. In their place is IT, a quicker, more efficient and reliable form of communication better able to cope with increasing demand and a constantly changing industry.

Not surprisingly, travel agents in their role as information providers have become a focus for IT. This, together with the use of IT by principals and the issues arising from it will be discussed in greater detail in Chapter 17.

EUROPEAN LEGISLATION

To understand the importance of European legislation on the travel industry it is first necessary to set out the regulations which have governed the operations of travel agents and tour operators. The Association of British Travel Agents (ABTA) has been the principal organization concerned with the operations of tour operators and travel agents. Set up in 1950 with 100 members, today it represents 90% of tour operators and travel agents in Britain. It is a self-regulatory body run by its membership and its aim is to ensure that a high standard of service and business is provided. This is partly achieved through codes of conduct developed for both travel agents and tour operators. A key role has been financial protection of the consumer should a company fail such that: (a) consumers are reimbursed if their holiday has not started; and (b) if the holiday has begun to ensure that the holiday continues as far as is possible and that holidaymakers are returned to the UK. As members of ABTA, both travel agents and tour operators are required to provide bonds as an insurance against financial failure. This was further assisted by the introduction of Stabiliser in 1965 which acted as a closed shop system by only allowing members to work with other ABTA members making ABTA, in effect, a licence to trade.

The European Directive on package travel (The Package Travel, Package Holidays and Package Tours Directive 90/314/EEC) introduced on 23 December 1992 has changed this situation. Under the terms of the Directive, all holiday companies are now required to safeguard client's money thereby making bonding mandatory but enabling greater flexibility in how it is provided. This reduced Stabiliser to a restrictive practice and as a result in October 1993 ABTA voted to abolish it. A key implication of this change to the rules is the opportunity that arises for outsiders such as financial institutions and retail chains to enter the travel selling marketplace and so challenge the role of the travel agent. A problem yet to be resolved is that of policing the Directive. Currently in the UK trading standards officers

---

CASE STUDY 7.7

Coach operator fine

The maximum fine in the UK for failing to provide financial protection for clients is £5000. In the first year and a half of the introduction of the Directive only one company has been prosecuted. Coach operator Simon Gray of Hull was fined £250 and ordered to pay costs of £289 for failing to provide a bond. This was viewed by the travel industry as a soft sentence which does little to deter other companies from ignoring the legislation.

Source: *The Sunday Times*, 6 February 1994; 29 May 1994.

---

are responsible for enforcing the Directive but they have admitted this is difficult due to a lack of resources.

The Directive also tackles information provided to consumers, notably that in brochures, in terms of the type of information conveyed and the accuracy. So in theory the brochure should be far more accurate in the description of a place it provides to the consumer. Consumer complaints about 'white lies' should therefore become fewer as honesty becomes the only policy.

For tour operators and travel agents alike, the Directive means an increase in responsibility ensuring that the client receives what he or she is entitled to and that this is made explicit. Misleading information on the package, price, description or conditions will result in the package organizer or retailer paying compensation to the consumer and a penalty for the offence. In turn this should result in a more professional industry to the benefit of tour operators, travel agents and consumers.

CASE STUDY 7.8

Brochure complaints

In 1993 the Advertising Standards Authority received 450 complaints about travel companies. One of the most common complaints concerned brochure descriptions: 'One said the beach was about 200 yards as the crow flies but failed to point out that for those of us without the power of flight it was more like a two mile hike.' As brochures for 1993 would have been produced before the introduction of the Directive, this should account for the high number of complaints.

Source: *The Sunday Times*, 29 May 1994.

DISTRIBUTION IN THE FUTURE

For the principals, their main concern is to distribute their products as quickly and cheaply as possible. Currently, this involves either selling direct to the consumer or using the travel agency network. The development of IT threatens the latter. The ability of principals to use IT to communicate with consumers in their homes or in other public places could ultimately cut out the travel agent. This is known as **disintermediation**. The worst scenario would be total elimination of the travel agent thus radically altering the current chain of distribution. For this to happen, a tremendous number of obstacles would need to be surmounted encompassing social, economic and political as well as technological factors. Until then the travel agent will retain its role.

To ensure survival in the longer term, it is vital that the travel agent focuses on the service it provides to the consumer. So long as consumers feel they are receiving good advice, they will continue to use the travel agent. For independents which often provide the service but are unable to compete with the multiples on discounts and incentives, etc., one strategy for survival is to band together to form consortia. Although not a new idea, it is one that has not been practised to its full potential in travel agency. This would enable independents to speak with one voice or at least a limited number of voices to gain preferential rates with principals and to market themselves more effectively to the all-important consumer.

Further separation within the retail division of travel agency may well occur. Currently, it is the large multiples which rack the large tour operators (this has been exacerbated by vertical integration) and the smaller travel agents which rack the independent tour operators. Potentially more independents may become specialists in different types of travel products such as activity holidays and destinations. Certainly there are examples of specialist successful independents in the market now such as Trailfinders specializing in long-haul trips and Travelbag with its focus on Australia and the Far East, but the practice could become more widespread.

A further potential change to distribution in the travel industry would be to encourage travel agents to purchase products in advance of sales. Not only would this ease the financial burden for principals but it would also mitigate the problem of brand loyalty. It is unlikely that the travel agents would embrace this idea since it directly affects the service they provide to consumers; bias would become more blatant and it would leave them financially weak.

In the short to medium term the pattern of travel product distribution is unlikely to change much but in the longer term IT and changes in both principals and consumer attitudes to distribution could well engender more radical change to the distribution of travel products.

SUMMARY

The chapter has outlined the different channels used to distribute the tourism product, in particular differentiating between direct selling and the use of the travel agent. Emphasis has been placed on the role of the travel agent in serving both consumers and principals and the associated difficulties arising from that. Linked to this is vertical integration in the industry and principal-driven incentives, both of which have led to allegations of biased advice. Two other issues were looked at: the role of information technology and the effect of European legislation on travel distribution. Finally the chapter speculated on distribution in the future and in so doing highlighted the threats posed to the travel agent's role.

REFERENCES

Buck, M. (1988) The role of travel agent and tour operator, in Goodall, B. and Ashworth, G. (eds), *Marketing in the Tourism Industry: The Promotion of Destination regions*, Croom-Helm, Beckenham.

Burkart, A.J. and Medlik, S. (1981) *Tourism: Past, Present and Future*, Heinemann, London.

The Financial Times (1994) Three-card trick from American Express, 14 September.

Foster, D. (1985) *Travel and Tourism Management*, Macmillan, Basingstoke.

Goodall, B. and Ashworth, G. (eds), (1988) *Marketing in the Tourism Industry: The Promotion of Destination Regions*, Croom-Helm, Beckenham.

Holiday Which? (1989) Travel agents, May.

Holiday Which? (1993) Travel agents, September.

Holloway, J.C. (1989) *The Business of Tourism*, Pitman, London.

Holloway, J.C. and Plant, R.V. (1992) *Marketing for Tourism*, Pitman, London.

Key Note Report (1991) *Travel Agents and Overseas Tour Operators*, Key Note Publications Ltd.

Key Note Report (1994) *Travel Agents and Overseas Tour Operators*, Key Note Publications Ltd.

Mail on Sunday (1993) 26 December.

Office of Fair Trading (1994) Press release No. 37/94, 11 August.

Poon, A. (1988) Tourism and information technologies, *Annals of Tourism Research*, **15**.

The Sunday Times (1994) Bargain battles, Style and Travel section, 14 August.

The Sunday Times (1994) Trade-offs, Style and Travel section, 29 May.

The Sunday Times (1994) Soft sentence, Style and Travel section, 6 February.

Travel Trade Gazette (1994) 21 September.

Travel Trade Gazette (1994) 19 January.

REVIEW QUESTIONS

1. What are the different channels that can be used to distribute the tourism product?

2. Why should a principal choose to sell directly to the consumer?
3. What role does the travel agent perform in the chain of distribution?
4. What are the implications of integration in the tourism industry for (a) consumers; and (b) travel agents/tour operators?
5. Why is the term 'double agent' applicable to travel agents?
6. Why does IT play such an important role in distributing the tourism product?
7. How has European legislation affected the role of tour operators and travel agents?
8. How might distribution change in the future?

The marketing mix: tourism promotion

8

A.V. Seaton

OBJECTIVES

By the end of this chapter the reader should:

- understand the role of information in consumer tourism decisions;
- be able to identify the main sources of information used by tourists in taking decisions and evaluate their main characteristics;
- understand the components of the promotional mix and the managerial applications of each;
- understand the main methods of evaluating promotion.

INFORMATION IN THE TOURISM DECISION PROCESS

How does a tourist know what a resort will be like? What gives a business traveller the idea that one airline is a better executive experience than another? Why do some hotel groups have a more modern image than others? What makes one museum or gallery rate high on a tourist's must-see list while others are passed over?

One answer to these questions is – previous experience. A person who has been to a resort, stayed in a particular hotel or flown with a particular airline will have formed judgements about them and these will be used as the basis for making future decisions to repeat or not repeat the experience.

A second answer, which brings us to the main subject of this chapter, is prior communication. For the person with no previous personal experience of a tourism organization any ideas about it will have been formed from previous information gained from a variety of sources. This brings us back to one of the key features of tourism marketing: the fact that the products are intangible – they cannot be seen, tasted, tested or demonstrated before the decision to purchase or make the trip is taken. As a result, for the

Table 8.1 The consumer information matrix: main sources of information

	Personal	Impersonal (mass media)
Commercial	• Travel agents • Tour operator reps • Tour guides • Tourist information centre staff • Telephone sales staff • Organizational employees • Etc.	• Advertising • Brochures • Tourist board leaflets • Videos and displays • Teletext • Etc.
Non-commercial	• Friends • Relatives • School teachers • Peer groups (e.g. business, students) • Hearsay • Etc.	• Media output: travel programmes, newspaper travel pages, guide books, news programmes, novels, films, *Holiday Which?* • Etc.

first-time visitor prior communication inevitably provides the basis of information on which the decision is taken. Prior communication creates the images upon which tourism decisions are based.

Promotion is part of this prior communication but not all of it. The sources of information which make up prior communication can be divided into four main categories:

• commercially provided information;
• non-commercially provided information;
• personally provided information;
• impersonally provided (media) sources.

The four sources, with examples of each, can be expressed in a **consumer information matrix** as in Table 8.1.

The sources of information are not mutually exclusive and may be used in different combinations by the consumer at different points along the path that leads to a decision. In considering a holiday in an unfamiliar destination such as Cuba the British tourist may be influenced by general media information on Cuba going back years (newsreels of Castro for instance), a friend's account of a visit there, a radio travel programme covering specific packages, and later by telephone sales information from a specialist tour operator providing details of costs, flights, hotels, etc. From the consumer's point of view the different sources of information have advantages and disadvantages, as listed in Table 8.2.

In planning communication programmes a tourism organization has to be aware of the many kinds of information that a consumer may use in making a tourism choice and work out ways of influencing or working within them. In the same way that the different kinds of information have advantages and disadvantages to the consumer, so each has

Table 8.2 Consumer information matrix: characteristic features of information from the consumer's point of view

	Personal	**Impersonal (mass media)**
Commercial	• Detailed and flexible • Easily available • Cheap to obtain • Message quality of informant may vary • Continuously available • Accuracy may vary • Low or high credibility – may be seen as expert but biased • Two-way communication • Good for obtaining information and completing booking (sale can be arranged on the spot)	• Limited, inflexible • Easily available • Cheap to obtain • Consistent message quality (well produced, glossy brochures, TV ads, etc.) • Continuously available • Factual accuracy covered by law • Lower credibility – advertising is known to be biased • Mainly one-way communication • Good for creating awareness and interest, less good at closing sale (though brochures and some direct sale adverts may do so)
Non-commercial	• Seen as trustworthy (would your friends lie!) • Non-expert • Detailed and flexible • Availability variable	• High credibility (seen as unbiased) • Possibly seen as expert • Limited, inflexible (you can't talk back) • Availability variable

strengths and weaknesses to the tourism organization. Some examples are given in Table 8.3.

The reason for looking at information sources in such detail is twofold. The first is that, given the diverse sources of information that might be used, it is necessary for the tourism organization to recognize the need not just of influencing the customer directly but influencing the influencers who can be seen as **gatekeepers**. A gatekeeper is someone who acts as a filtering/relaying medium between an organization and its final audiences. Two kinds of gatekeeper play a part in tourist decisions:

• **Opinion formers**. These are individuals or groups in public organizations such as the media and travel agencies who may transmit information to the consumer. The travel media, for example, pour out great quantities of information on destinations and holidays which may influence people in their tourism choices. Some gatekeepers are high in source credibility by virtue of their perceived expertise or prestige. A fashion-sensitive market such as tourism can be affected by

Table 8.3 Consumer information matrix: characteristic features of information from the organization's point of view

	Personal	**Impersonal (mass media)**
Commercial	• Requires organizational management to be effective (e.g. training/briefing/back-up literature) • Is more persuasive than impersonal info. • Extensive feedback/ feedforward possible • Can be used to close sale/booking	• Can be expensive to produce and run in the media • Content of message can be exactly controlled • Timing can be exactly controlled • Medium of exposure can be exactly controlled • Good for creating awareness and interest, less good at closing sale
Non-commercial	• Difficult to influence, except through previous customers' 'word of mouth' recommendations	• Difficult to control content (may be favourable or unfavourable) • Difficult to control exact timing • Difficult to control place/medium of exposure • May be highly influential

trendsetters such as celebrities known to take vacations in particular resorts and by well-known travel writers who create awareness of new destinations, as Eric Newby did with his account of the Hindu Kush region in the 1960s.

• **Opinion leaders**. These are different from opinion formers since they are not public figures or groups but influential people closer to home who share the same social networks as the people they influence. They may be friends, relatives or work colleagues who are seen as trustworthy sources of information on places and tourism products they have tried. Personal influence and recommendation is a stronger factor in tourist destination choice than any amount of commercially provided information. Many visitor studies have shown that family and friends are more often the source of information about destinations than mass media sources.

Secondly, it is possible to analyse the information sources of tourist decisions even more closely through the concept of the **decision-making unit (DMU)**. This idea, first developed in the field of industrial and consumer marketing, drew attention to the fact that the decision to choose a particular product may involve several parties as a buying unit comprising:

- **an initiator:** the person who starts off the decision path;
- **influencers** (personal or impersonal): children would be an example of a direct personal influence, while a TV holiday programme such as the Discovery Channel in the USA would be an example of the second;
- **decider:** the person who finally says 'Yes, we'll go there';
- **purchaser:** the one who pays over the money;
- **user:** the people who consume the final product.

The purpose of breaking up the decision among these potential participants is that it alerts the tourism marketer to the possibilities of having to influence several parties, either through separate communications or through materials that appeal to a number of people (e.g. a brochure which has something in it for husbands, wives, children). An IPC survey in the UK, reported by two UK authors, found that twice as many women as men were responsible for the planning and organization of a holiday, even though the whole family were users (Holloway and Plant, 1992: 60).

In summary, it is the total information sources used and the nature of the overall decision-making unit that that have to be considered before engaging upon promotional programmes. A tourism marketer can then devise communications targeted at the most important audiences (customers, travel agents, the media, etc.). It is important to know what the various audiences already know – or think they know – about an organization, what they still need to know, and what their likely sources of information will be.

Having looked at the total range of information that may be used in tourism decisions we can now focus on commercially provided sources of information which constitute promotion.

THE PROMOTIONAL PROCESS

The promotional or marketing communications mix consists of all those communications undertaken to achieve a desired level of tourism demand through delivering the right messages through the right channels to affect those audiences who constitute or influence demand in the short and long term. The mix consists of four primary options: advertising, public relations, personal selling and sales promotion. Before each is described in detail it is important to understand a number of general features about the promotional process.

Promotional objectives

Effective promotion starts, like any other marketing activity, from an analysis and clear formulation of strategic objectives. These involve:

- identification of the target audiences to be reached;
- identification of the communication goals to be achieved with each;

- formulation of messages designed to achieve the goals;
- choice of media for delivering the messages effectively to the designated audiences;
- allocation of a budget to achieve the production and delivery of the messages;
- evaluation mechanisms in terms of sales, direct action or communication measures.

Promotional objectives must be based on careful analysis of the current situation – which means that they should emerge from an analysis of research data, not on opinions and gut feelings. Research is required before, during and after promotion. It is used to define the target audience and the message needs, and to evaluate the success of promotional campaigns while they are running and after they have finished. Though most research in tourism tends to be quantitative (occupancy studies, visitor studies, multiplier studies, etc.) qualitative research is often helpful in promotional planning, particularly in developing advertising ideas. In the verbatims of qualitative research (single person interviews or group discussions) one often hears the direct voice of the consumer which is often muffled in the statistical tables of large-scale surveys. In August 1991 the Scottish Tourist Board carried out group discussions with people from England and Scotland to explore their image of Scotland as a destination. Here are some of the comments which illustrate the variety and richness of data that qualitative research may reveal:

> 'We go for long weekends up north but that's all, I wouldn't think of it for my main holiday'; 'One thing I notice in England is they cater for children in the pubs, they welcome them and often have play areas for them. You wouldn't get that here, most pubs don't allow children'; 'It seems so far away, you imagine the roads aren't very good but they are probably the same as here'; 'You'd go to Scotland to see all the history, people in kilts, it's what you'd expect'.

(STB, 1991)

The research was used as the basis for developing an advertising campaign addressing some of the issues revealed in the group discussions.

Because the definition, implementation and evaluation of promotional objectives are dependent on research, we have provided a detailed case to illustrate the relationships between research, objectives and promotional actions (see Case study 8.1).

The more carefully objectives are set the better promotion works. The worst mistakes are made by doing the wrong thing well, rather than the right thing badly. Promotional objectives can be divided into three main types:

- **Reinforcement**. The most important promotional function for many larger firms is simply hanging on to what they have got. Though promotion is often seen as the conversion of non-visitors into visitors,

---

CASE STUDY 8.1

Promotional planning and evaluation by objectives: Virginia Beach 1991

In 1991 the USA was experiencing the after-effects of the Gulf War, an economic recession and increased competition in the tourism market. Virginia Beach Convention Center marketers identified a number of developing trends likely to affect the tourism potential of their destination: a trend to shorter vacation planning times which made toll-free bookings important; a trend for consumers to travel shorter distances, 60% coming from within 300 miles of their home; a trend for shorter average vacation trips.

In the light of these conditions they planned a spring and summer promotion which had the following general objectives:

- to increase awareness with infrequent and non-visitors from relatively close to Virginia Beach;
- to create awareness of improved infrastructure;
- to increase toll-free phone enquiries;
- to improve total visitor figures above the existing 540 000 they had been achieving, and increase length of stay and spending.

The message goal was to position Virginia Beach as a 'nice clean beach resort with a variety of fun things to do – a great place for a memorable vacation'.

The prime *target audience* aimed at were adults aged 25–44 with incomes of $40 000 or over. They targeted these groups in over 30 cities which had been allocated to four classes of priority: (a) cities such as Washington, Pittsburgh and Cleveland which were thought of as high in new visitor potential (these received 53% of total budget spend); (b) the cities of New York and Ontario, thought to be lower in new visitor potential (these received 18% of the budget allocation); (c) and (d) classes were a number of cities designated for the lowest market spending, 30% of the budget allocation.

$1.3 million was spent on the advertising campaign. Its effects were measured by a range of research activities including: occupancy studies, sea-front interviews, advertising conversion studies and spending data.

The results were as follows: overall occupancy was up 2%; June occupancy reached a five-year high and September occupancy increased by 17%; length of stay increased by 2% to 4.7 nights; toll free 1–800 enquiries increased by 25%; spending per party increased by 2.4% to $925; the year also produced record hotel and restaurant revenues.

Source: Ricketts (1992: 230–5).

for highly successful tourism organizations such as British Airways and Disneyland and destinations like Blackpool, Spain and Florida the main objective is to retain their market.

- **The creation of new ideas and attitudes**. Another type of general objective is the creation of attitudes and behaviour that did not previously exist (e.g. creating awareness of a completely new tourism product such as the Channel Tunnel).
- **Change**. The most difficult task is attitude change and conversion –

stopping people doing what they are already doing or making them do something different. Destinations or organizations which have attracted unfavourable images may want to remedy the situation; for example the Spanish Costas have been trying to undo their reputation as 'tacky' and overdeveloped.

These three general kinds of influence can be refined by trying to specify more exactly what effect promotion is expected to have on consumer demand. Kotler (1972) has identified seven potential kinds of demand which promotion may be designed to affect:

- **No demand**. A tourism organization sets out to create something from nothing. South Tyneside, a post-industrial region in Northumberland, launched itself as a tourism destination in the 1980s by packaging itself as 'Catherine Cookson Country' after the best-selling novelist who was born there.
- **Latent demand**. Promotion may be used to trigger a promising but unrealized tourism opportunity, e.g. in Southern Italy, which has much to offer culturally and scenically but has lagged behind better known places in northern and central Italy.
- **Faltering demand**. The promotional task here is to revive demand for once popular tourism products, as in the case of the English seaside resorts which have been periodically marketed by the English Tourist Board in an endeavour to halt their decline as main holiday destinations since the 1960s.
- **Full demand**. Promotion, or lack of it, may also be used to keep things as they are for products that have reached their maximum, sustainable level of visitation. Holy Island, a small cultural island destination off the Northumberland coast of Britain, was not promoted in the 1980s because it was deemed to be 'full up'.
- **Overfull demand**. Promotion may even be used to turn people away or re-route them from destinations such as Venice which are facing environmental degradation from over-visits. For many years French tourism authorities have provided alternative 'green route' maps to avoid the congestion of main roads choked by tourists heading towards the southern sun in summer.
- **Irregular and seasonal demand**. One of the most common uses of promotion is to even out demand that would otherwise consist of sharp seasonal peaks.
- **Unwholesome demand**. Some kinds of tourism are being increasingly seen as dangerous. The cancer risk associated with sunbathing is already being addressed in Australia through educational advertising and beach warnings.
- **Negative demand**. Promotion may be used to turn around negative destination images (in the Lebanon and Northern Ireland, for long known as war-torn, dangerous destinations) or improve the acceptance of products such as time-share developments.

Promotion as the reduction of perceived risk in tourism decision-making

A useful way of looking at promotion is as a risk-reduction mechanism within a consumer decision-making process. Decision-making has been seen as a sequence:

- need recognition;
- information search;
- evaluation of alternatives;
- choice of product or service;
- post purchase evaluation.

At all stages of the sequence the consumer may experience perceived risk in trying to arrive at a satisfactory decision. The magnitude of perceived risk varies in proportion to two things:

- **The amount at stake**. The more there is at stake the greater the perceived risk. In choosing a major holiday there are many kinds of potential risk: financial (what will the total cost be? will there be surcharges? can we afford it?); physical (is the destination safe? can we drink the water? do we need to take special precautions?); and social (what will our friends/family think of the holiday? is the resort fashionable? will there be something for the children to do?).
- **The purchaser's confidence in his or her own competence to choose well**. The amount at stake does not matter if people feel sure of their ability to make a good decision. There are number of ways in which consumers try to improve their feelings of confidence in arriving at decisions. These include:
  - relying on previous experience, e.g. staying with a tried and tested tour operator or going back to the same destination year after year;
  - going to a known supplier, e.g. booking with well-known travel companies;
  - getting warranties or money-back guarantees (the problem here is that, even if a company is prepared to offer another holiday as compensation for an unsatisfactory one, it is often not possible to take it because of limited holiday allocations/school terms, etc.);
  - delegating the decision to a third party, particularly one seen as expert and unbiased. This might include following advice in a consumer magazine such as *Holiday Which?* or staying in accommodation given a five-star rating by a motoring organization or a tourist board;
  - reducing amount at stake and expectations, e.g. opting for a shorter, cheaper holiday than originally intended;
  - reducing options considered: perceived risk is greater the more options there are to choose from. Mass tour operators may confuse the consumer by offering too many options that are similar;
  - through intensive information search and acquisition, e.g. by studying alternative brochures in great detail, getting expert opinions, seeking advice from friends, etc.

In general the bigger the expenditure, the more major the holiday and the more unknown the destination, the greater the perceived risk. By a detailed understanding of the ways in which a consumer chooses a particular tourism product it is possible for an organization to identify the major kinds of perceived risk and then devise a communication programme of reassurance. There are several options.

The most effective form of risk reduction is to provide a good service that will make people confident in coming back. Repeat business is crucial to hotels, carriers, tour operators and many destinations. (Over half the visitors to Spain, Florida and Stratford-on-Avon have been before.)

Reducing perceived risk in order to attract the first-time customer can be done in two ways:

- Through addressing each form of perceived risk individually. The organization must first identify what the main forms are and then devise promotional solutions to them. This may be done by comprehensive guarantees, warranties, insurances, money-back offers or using the endorsement of credible authorities (e.g. trade associations like the Association of British Travel Agents). In 1982 Thomas Cook introduced its ten-point guarantee which was an attempt to cover the main worries customers had about booking package holidays.
- By corporate security building. Here an organization invests, usually through heavy expenditures, in building a high-profile reputation. People generally have greater confidence in a name with which they are familiar than in a lesser known one. Corporate identity campaigns and branding are examples of this kinds of approach.

Promotion as image building

It is useful for an organization to see every promotional activity, however minor, as part of the projection of a consistent image. Identity is not just about promotion – everything an organization does affects its image – but promotion is a big part of it. Every advert, letterhead, prospectus should incorporate a unified housestyle. A distinctive, relevent and appealing logo can be a major common denominator in promotional efforts.

The promotional time chain

A useful way of assessing promotional needs is as a temporal sequence of targeted information bundles which will address different goals at different times. Consumers use information for different purposes before, during and after a tourism decision. Though the temporal sequence will vary for different products and organizations four main influence phases are possible.

Influencing the purchase decision choice

The first phase of promotion is designed to take the consumer to product purchase (booking the package, hotel, flight, etc.). This has been theo-

CASE STUDY 8.2

The P&O logo

One of the original identifying features of the historic shipping line, P&O, had always been its house flag, first introduced in 1837. The flag was based on an amalgamation of the personal standards of the royal houses of Bourbon in Spain and Braganza in Portugal. Over the years, however, the flag had come to be given little special emphasis in corporate design, so in the 1970s, when P&O initiated a wide-ranging review of its corporate identity, it was decided, on the advice of the company charged with advising the shipping line, the Olins organization, to remove the flag from its relative obscurity and to relaunch it into prominent featuring in all of the company's activities. Since then the flag has been incorporated into fleet design, staff uniforms, advertisements and P&O's road carrier vehicles, and it was featured prominently on the cover of the company's corporate history in 1986.

Source: Olins (1989: 74–5).

rized as a sub-sequence itself through **hierarchy of effects** models of promotion which suggest that the consumer has to be taken through a sequence of progressive steps before making a final purchase. One such model is AIDA – which suggests that promotion must first generate Attention, then create Interest, then stimulate Desire and finally produce Action. Another hierarchical model is the DAGMAR formulation (named after a book by Russell Colley entitled, *Defining Advertising Goals for Measured Advertising Results*) which suggests that consumers must be moved through five phases of influence before they make a final decision to purchase a product: from unawareness to awareness; from awareness to comprehension; from comprehension to conviction; and from conviction to action.

There are other similar models, all of which stress promotion as a process of moving the consumer from little or no knowledge of a product to final purchase. A print advert might, for example, be used to create awareness and interest in a product (Disneyworld, a new CenterParc) and this might be followed by a send-away brochure providing more detailed information designed to generate more knowledge and desire; later a sales pitch from a travel agent might produce the final sales commitment/booking.

Hierarchy of effects models have been criticized on several counts (all presuppose the consumer knows nothing to begin with, has never before bought the product, and that the sequences happen in logical order, rather than, in some instances, all happening at once, as in a last-minute impulse purchase of a cheap package holiday on the strength of a shop-window offer). However, they have the advantage of forcing the marketer to assess the exact objectives of promotion over time, including how close to the final sale they are intended to take the consumer.

Consolidating the purchase through post-decisional confirmation

Promotion should not stop once a sale has been secured. For major purchases like tourism, which have a considerable time lag between booking and product experience (taking the holiday), it is often important to reduce **post-decisional cognitive dissonance**. This is based on the notion that after taking a big decision people still feel residual tension (cognitive dissonance) about whether it was the right one. Promotion, in the form of follow-up communications, can be used to make people feel good about their choice. A tour operator might, for example, supply further information about a destination or a hotel, or an airline might tell buyers of special privileges they can enjoy, e.g. that their flight has been upgraded etc. Tourists anticipating a holiday enjoy reading appetizing details that will whet their appetite still further.

Shaping the trip experience

Once the basic trip has been sold tourism marketers may want to influence how it develops. Specialist tour operators often supply reading lists about destinations, suggested itineraries and 'things to do' recommendations which have the aim of maximizing the customer's satisfactions on holiday. Tourist information centres (welcome centers in the USA) often play a crucial role in affecting trip patterns, length of stay and expenditure by providing information on where to stay and what to do in an area (Fesenmaier & Vogt, 1993).

Post trip promotion designed at encouraging repeat purchase influences

Finally promotion can be used to get people to come back. Tourism organizations, along with many other marketing firms, are increasingly interested in the concept of **relationship marketing**. One of the many nuances of this current buzz word is the desirability of building long-term relations with customers that extend beyond one purchase/consumption cycle. Direct mail firms have always used past customer bases as the launch pad for future sales, and tourism firms now regard staying close to previous customers as good business. Regular mail-outs with offers and news to customers on the database and the creation of loyalty clubs (British Airways Club Class programmes) are used by large organizations to keep their customers. Some tour operators offer Christmas reunions and other short-breaks for people who have travelled with them as summer holidaymakers. Even small organizations may provide reminders to past customers through goodwill gestures such as cards and calendars at Christmas, perhaps with preferential rates for the coming season.

THE PROMOTIONAL MIX

Having examined in some detail the main aims and functions of promotion we move now to an appraisal of the four main elements of the promotional mix:

[1]**Advertising**

Advertising has been defined as the paid-for sponsorship of a message in a commercially available medium.

In planning and managing advertising the start-point is, as usual, an analysis of objectives including the definition of target audiences and message requirements. Advertising in tourism has many uses. They include:

- creating awareness (e.g. EuroDisney launch in 1993);
- informing about special services (e.g. a new frequent flyers' club);
- creating a corporate image (Forte in 1993);
- influencing destination image (the primary advertising goal behind most NTO campaigns);
- advertising a special offer (e.g. a special weekend price for a hotel group);
- providing information on special services or seasonal deals (e.g. an autumn break hotel offer);
- direct selling to elicit direct response (e.g. a specialist tour operator selling cruises through the 'quality' press);
- soliciting consumer information (e.g. incentive questionnaires on a ferry designed to produce consumer profiles that can later be used as a database for direct marketing efforts);
- branding (see Chapter 4);
- improving distribution (e.g. a tour operator wishing to expand the racking of brochures with travel agents);
- overcoming negative attitudes (e.g. adverts designed to reassure people after a health scare at a destination);
- improving employee and organizational morale (advertising influences employees as well as external audiences);
- reaching a new target audience (e.g. a coach operator moving into the schools market);
- providing a new use (promoting health tourism in Cuba based on a clinic offering a unique treatment for people with skin problems);
- announcing a launch or relaunch (a hotel chain announcing that it has swimming pools/fitness centres in all its main executive hotels);
- reinforcement/reminder advertising aimed to keep an organization in people's minds;
- updating (e.g. reprints of brochures with revised prices);
- contributing to cooperative/partnership advertising ventures (e.g. a joint advert between a carrier and a hotel group for weekend breaks).

Once the objectives have been defined the advertising decisions are twofold: media and creative.

Media

The media task is essentially to choose and buy the most economical combination of advertising space and/or time to reach defined audiences sufficiently frequently and with sufficient impact to convey the agreed messages effectively.

The media planner appraises all the media options and then tries to match their profiles to the known media habits of the market segment(s) to be targeted. The circulation and readership of the press, the audience profiles of radio and TV channels and the characteristics of people passing by poster/billboard sites are studied in relation to the known numbers and characteristics of the audience(s) aimed at. Much of this involves number crunching. The media planner must know how many people read a particular newspaper or listen to a particular TV programme and what kind of people they are.

A number of technical, but relatively simple, concepts are useful in understanding media planning. These include the following.

- **Media class**: the basic, generic medium to be used, e.g. TV, radio, press.
- **Media vehicle**: the individual medium within a class (e.g. *The New York Times*, or the *Guardian* within the press class).
- **Media unit**: the specific purchasable unit within a vehicle (e.g. a half-page colour advert, a 30-second commercial, a 16-sheet poster).
- **Frequency**: an estimate of how often an advertising campaign should be delivered to the target audience over a given period. Two specific measures are used for TV and radio: OTS (opportunities to see) and OTH (opportunities to hear). Both OTS and OTH are based on calculations of the average number of times a viewer, reader, listener will be exposed to a campaign in a given period.
- **Reach or coverage**: the total percentage or number of people in a given target audience who see or hear an advert at least once over a given period.
- **Cost per thousand (CPT)**: the cost of reaching a thousand people through a particular medium. This is a basic benchmark used to assess the comparative cost-effectiveness of different media. It is arrived at by dividing the total audience for a medium (normally given in terms of readership, audience ratings) by the cost of the advertisement and multiplying by 1000. For example, if a TV spot cost £65 000 and was seen in a programme reaching 12 million people the CPT would be:

$$\text{CPT} = £65\,000 \times \frac{1000}{12\,000\,000} = £5.4$$

CPT calculations show how a media unit that is high in unit terms (e.g. the cost of a 30-second TV spot) may be more economical than a cheaper advert because of its reach.

- **Television rating (TVR)**: the percentage of a commercial TV station audience able to see an advert, i.e. a TVR of 25 means that a commercial went out in a programme to which 25% of the commercial TV audience were tuned. A TV campaign can be measured in total TVRs, the combination of rating points delivered by a given number of TV exposures.

- **Circulation and readership**: these two concepts are often confused. Circulation is the number of audited copies of a print medium sold. Readership is the number and characteristics of the people who actually read it – readership of a newspaper is often between 2–3 times higher than circulation. Readership is determined by questionnaire surveys which determine what vehicles people read and how often they read them.

Although media planning is traditionally seen mainly as a quantitative activity (conjuring up figures on audience sizes, media profiles, costs, frequency, etc.), it also involves more difficult qualitative issues about the way in which media are used and their impact. In the case of the press, for instance, basic circulation and readership figures only provide a start-point for evaluation. Other more difficult-to-measure factors might influence the success of the advert. Issues beyond readership and circulation data include: number of pick-ups (a weekly TV programme guide is picked up much more often than a daily paper), pass on rates, time spent reading, how much of the vehicle is read, the qualitative impact of message, the advert exposure (as opposed to the vehicle exposure), the effects of perceived editorial stance, where the medium is read and the 'drool effect' (how much of a persuasive bonus the medium offers creatively). A number of these issues have been researched separately (see Costerdine, 1990).

We can summarize some of the main factors in media appraisal as follows:

- readership or audience size;
- geographical reach;
- repetition and frequency;
- segment penetration;
- unit cost and cost per thousand (taking into account the cost of special positions, rate concessions and advertising package reductions);
- production costs;
- timing flexibility: how quickly can you place and run an advert?
- seasonal/period discounts;
- mood/atmosphere of the medium;
- exposure time and duration of message;
- availability (not all media can be booked quickly – prime poster sites, for example, may be prebooked for months, even years, by advertising agencies for their clients);
- competitive differentiation;
- qualitative characteristics (prestige effects, nearness to sale decision, creative scope, e.g. length of message detail, impact, exposure conditions);
- reproduction quality (glossy magazines produce better colour images than either newspapers or TV);
- marketing back-up (some advertising vehicles offer special facilities to advertisers such as reproductions of adverts for display in retail outlets);

- research data available on the media.

A number of things are likely to increase or decrease the chances of a medium getting an audience response:

- **Prior exposure of the target audience to campaign**. Adverts may have a build-up effect that starts by creating awareness of a product, then comprehension of its basic messages, after which further exposures may simply be reminders.
- **Category exclusivity for advertising subject**. If a tourism organization is the biggest or only one in a product category to use a specific media vehicle (e.g. the only hotel advertiser in a business supplement) it may achieve an area of dominant influence, as the airline British Airways has done on UK TV. On the other hand it may be necessary for a tourism product to be seen with its competitors (e.g. in one of the special travel sections of magazines and newspapers published in the winter to get bookings for the summer).
- **Receiver involvement**. Adverts in some media get closer attention from their audiences than others (e.g. special interest magazines). Media planners must assess the involvement factor in appraising media.
- **Delivery timing**. Media may vary in impact according to when their messages are delivered (which day, week, weekend, hour, etc.). For example, weekend supplements and magazines are read in a more leisurely and relaxed manner than morning papers. An advert heard over the car radio in morning 'drive time' will have less force for a person hurrying to work than one heard at home on a Saturday morning, even though the audience may be bigger. As one adman has written, 'Advertisers want the right type of person, in the most conducive environment at a relevent point in the purchase cycle' (Bill Patterson, *Admap*, October 1987, p. 52).

Media appraisal

In a general marketing text of this sort it is impossible to provide a detailed examination of every media option, so we shall be selective in presenting some of the features of the main tourism media. In 1992 £220.8 million was spent on holiday and travel advertising making it eighth in the top 20 advertising categories in the UK. Of this expenditure 72% was spent on press, 25% on TV and 2% on radio. However, only four individual tourism organizations featured among the top 100 individual advertisers in Britain (Macdonalds ranked 38th, British Airways ranked 51st, Lunn Poly ranked 63rd and Thomsons ranked 75th: *Marketing Pocket Book*, NTC, 1993).

These figures reveal two things about media use in travel and tourism advertising and conceal a third:

- Tourism is a large but highly fragmented advertising market made up of a few giant enterprises with large advertising budgets and many more smaller ones with less to spend on advertising.
- Print is the dominant medium in travel and tourism advertising. Few

Table 8.4 *Press/TV/Radio as % of travel tourism advertising by selected countries 1991*

	UK	Switzerland	Sweden	Belgium	Spain	Netherlands	Ireland	France	Italy
Print	72	72.3	92.2	70.5	76.8	55	68.0	61.2	73.6
TV	25	6.8	5.7	13.9	16.6	28.4	18.7	14.5	21.2
Radio	2	—	2.1	6.8	2.7	6.6	11.9	11.5	1.3

Source: Advertising Association/NTC, *The European and Media Yearbook 1993.*

advertisers can afford the expense of TV although it formed a large part of the total advertising of the bigger tourism firms, notably Macdonalds (88%); British Airways (40%); Lunn Poly (42%); and Thomsons (22%). Press is a more selective medium for reaching affluent groups than TV. The dominance of the press in travel and tourism can be clearly seen across Europe in Table 8.4.

• What the figures conceal is that in travel and tourism much advertising expenditure may not be spent on paid-for media space, but on direct marketing materials such as brochures, destination guides and point-of-sale displays. Tourist boards, tour operators and tourist information centres depend upon a vast quantity of printed (and sometimes audio-visual) material which is not reflected in media expenditure tables.

Press as medium
Press consists of a diverse range of general and specialist magazines and newspapers which cover a wide number of consumer social groups, interest groups, professional readers and trade interests. The 'quality' press (in Britain *The Times, Guardian, Telegraph, Observer, Independent,* etc.), primarily read by ABC1 readers, all offer weekly travel supplements. Some magazines stay around the house a long time and are read over a long period. The main advantage of press is its ability for precise segmentation of geographic, socioeconomic and interest groups. It is also popular with direct sell operators because of its capacity to deliver large amounts of detailed textual information, as well as inserted direct mail materials.

Broadcast media
TV is the most impactful mass medium. In the UK commercial TV reaches over 95% of the population in any one week and set ownership is increasing; 48% of the population has one set, 36% has two sets and 16% has three (BARB, 1994). It is particularly suited for reaching mass markets quickly and offers unrivalled opportunities for demonstration. However, it is a less selective medium with a higher wastage factor and expensive on a unit cost basis, and the cost of commercial production is high (although video offers a quicker, cheaper but poorer quality alternative).

Radio accounts for less than 2% of all UK advertising and has a young, downmarket audience except for Classic FM which is the only national commercial radio station with a predominantly ABC1 audience. In America it is a more diverse medium built around niche music markets (Morrison, 1989: 351). Radio is cheap in both unit costs and production costs and has the same advantages in frequency as TV. However, it is lower in impact and much lower in reach of mass audiences. Its lack of visual capability may be a disadvantage for 'dream' products like tourism yet it appeals much more to the imagination (a commercial, produced by the radio industry in the UK, selling radio as an advertising medium

Table 8.5 Press, TV and radio characteristics

Press	TV	Radio
• Immense range and diversity of vehicles (magazines, newspapers, etc.) • Precise segmentation without wastage • Frequency varies from daily to annually • Variable timing flexibility (e.g. daily newspaper good/monthly magazine poor) • Editorial atmospherics possible (e.g. from adverts in special positions/sections of paper/magazine) • Excellent colour reproduction • Reader controls order and pace of presentation • Lower impact • Planned exposure to adverts • Good geographic targeting (city, towns, small areas) • Can carry inserts, brochures, coupons, etc. • Prestige effects (e.g. print has prestige with upmarket, educated groups) • Poor at demonstration • Suitable for long, complex, detailed messages (e.g. direct sale of holiday) • Unit costs vary • CPT often high for general audience/low for specialist • Enduring message (adverts/articles can be saved, transported and consumed anywhere)	• Limited, though growing channel options through increasing satellite and cable options • Blunt instrument: mass audiences/limited segmentation • Frequency infinite (every commercial break for advertisers with money) • Variable timing (full production takes time/video quicker, cheaper) • Limited editorial atmospherics except in individual programmes (e.g. Discovery Channel in US) • Colour quality poorer • Exposure brief, dictated by medium • Highly intrusive impact • Unplanned, often ignored exposure • Poor geographic segmentation (only 16 major UK TV areas) • Limited marketing support • TV has prestige only in general sense and with lower income groups • Excellent demonstration medium • Best for image advertising or simple messages • Unit cost high • CPT low for general audience/high for specialist • Restricted exposure points, determined by location of TV set; multi-set ownership growing	• Limited, though growing channel options • Blunt instrument: small programme audiences/limited segmentation • Frequency infinite (every commercial break for advertisers with money) • Flexible timing (commercials are cheap and quick to produce and place) • Limited editorial atmospherics except in individual programmes • No visual capacity • Exposure brief, dictated by medium • Moderate impact • Unplanned, often ignored exposure • Good geographic segmentation (many local channels) • Limited marketing support • Poor prestige effects (radio seen as minor medium) • Audio demonstration and 'theatre of mind' evocative effects • Best for image advertising or simple messages • Unit cost low on local basis • CPT low for all audiences • Varied exposure points (radios are portable and many homes have several)

emphasized its creative possibilities in appealing to the 'theatre of your mind'). In 1993 £6.6 million was spent on radio travel and tourism advertising making it the sixth biggest category of advertising accounting for 4.5% of the total (MEAL).

TV and radio can sometimes be used synergistically to achieve 'image transfer' effects. A campaign established on TV may also be run in sound to evoke the visual effects of the original, particularly if there are distinctive musical or soundtrack features that can 'carry over' from TV.

Some of the main differences between the three media are summarized in Table 8.5.

Other media
In addition to the three media discussed above an advertiser may also use the following.

- **Posters/billboards**. Best for simple messages (one big picture and about 6–10 words) in locations with a large pass-by traffic, and preferably close to point-of-sale (which is why hotels/motels are often advertised on highways close to their locations, and airlines close to air terminals).
- **Cinema**. Even higher in impact than TV because of screen size, colour, sound quality and the captive audience, but poor in frequency, and miniscule in total audience sizes which mainly consist of young people (under 35 years of age).

The creative function

The most important thing in advertising is knowing **what** you want to stay and **to whom**. These basic strategic decisions override all lesser issues. Creative strategy should be agreed and written down before any advertising development takes place.

Creative objectives can often be seen as the provision of two major kinds of information.

- **Motivational**. One aspect of promotion is generating desire for the product – making people want to come to a destination, to visit an attraction, to fly with an airline, to buy from a tour operator. Much of this involves analysing the specific appeals to be emphasized and then implementing them through 'dream' copy. The essential principles of 'dream' copy have been known for years. This was written in 1928:

  The use of sunny landscapes and seascapes for travel publicity is obvious in its appeal to all, rich and poor . . . Artistic bias follows psychological bias closely; our natural desire for sun and warmth, in fine and pleasurable weather, is reflected in the conventions of selection prior to design. All seaside resorts are sunny, all seas smooth; all hotels are comfortable; all trains punctual and speedy.

We could also add that in selling airlines it is better to show the destination rather than the plane and if you do, always show it soaring upwards into blue skies rather than landing or on the ground.

- **Logistic**. The second type of objective relates not to motivating customers but providing the logistical details through which they can achieve their motivational goals. Tourism advertising requires the provision of detailed information on prices, routes, accommodation, visa information and methods of payment. With legislation now on both a European and national basis, it is important that brochures and adverts relay essential information accurately.

The motivational function involves imaginative arousal, the logistic one painstaking descriptive and prescriptive information based on checking, proofreading, legal compliances, etc.

Once the message goals have been defined, what makes good advertising? Here are some pointers.

- **Personal address**. It has been said that the most important word in advertising is 'you'. An advert should not describe the product but project it empathatically in terms of the audience's self-interest in a way that evokes the excitement and pleasures of the holiday experience as in this copy for Frontierland at EuroDisney:

  In the land of frontier romance and excitement you'll scream through Big Thunder Mountain on a runaway train, float down the river aboard the Mark Twain steamboat, shoot 'em up with roughriding cowboys and dance, if you dare, with Phantom Manor's 999 ghostly ghouls.

- **Competitive element**. In product categories where there are many substitutes (e.g. the mass package tour market) advertising should offer reasons why customers should choose the advertised product not its competitors.
- **Visual atmosphere**. tourism is about seeing things so visual images are important. Krippendorf quotes a psychologist's prescription for establishing visual atmosphere:

First and foremost, a 'holiday mood' or 'vacation atmosphere' has to be conveyed, i.e. the counter-image of everyday life, expressing on the one hand informality, abandonment, serenity, freedom, pleasure, and on the other hand peace, space, time standing still, relaxation, a certain 'romanticism', a return to nature, to our origins, or a special, extraordinary experience . . . It must show something beautiful, characteristic of holidays, certainly not something one can have at home (e.g. in the local swimming pool) or something that is reminiscent of the workaday life of the country of origin . . . Typical holiday symbols, e.g. the sun, a parasol, a beach basket and the like, can certainly be used to advantage . . .

(Krippendorf, 1988: 20–1)

The best advertising campaigns are single-minded, simple and unified. The American market research consultant, Schwerin, whose company has researched thousands of advertising campaigns, has suggested that successful advertising persuasion involves seven prescriptive elements (Schwerin and Newell, 1989):

1. There should be one unified impression.
2. Commitment should be to one dominant mood – either logical or emotional.
3. The visual and verbal elements should support each other.
4. Structure and order should be a simple as possible.
5. The story should be presented in the consumer's terms, not the product's.
6. The story should involve the right consumer.
7. Any entertainment values should have a purpose.

Some tried and tested advertising techniques

Anyone involved in advertising development should be aware of a number of basic, off-the-peg techniques which have been used extensively by advertisers over the years.

- **Slice of life**: a technique, often used in TV and radio adverts, that offers a mini-drama, involving fictitious but realistic characters, experiencing a product's uses/benefits.
- **Testimony**: one of the strongest methods of selling products is through the testimony of satisfied customers. It may be the testimony of a single person, a number of people or a famous celebrity (e.g. Rocco Forte's endorsement of American Express).
- **Problem solution**: this technique, often used with slice-of-life, sets up a problem, introduces the product and its benefits, and shows the problem resolved at the end. A TV commercial might begin by setting up the problem of choosing a holiday all the family would enjoy, introducing a particular destination and its attractions, and finishing with a satisfied family.
- **Demonstration**: where the main benefit(s) of a product can be demonstrated they should be, especially if TV is being used. A particularly competitive form of demonstration is the side-by-side demonstration which involves showing the benefits of one product against another. In 1993 Jersey promoted itself in print advertising as a short-break destination with photos comparing its clean, sunny beaches to the urban housing, grimy chimney stacks and TV aerials of major cities which were also marketing short-breaks.
- **Documentary**: this TV technique involves using real-life footage, as in a newsreel, to present a product. It is particularly appropriate for short promotional films for destinations.
- **Burlesque and fantasy**: this technique relies on larger than life exaggeration. It can also be achieved through animation and cartoon effects.
- **Presenter(s)**: a standard technique in radio and TV is the use of a

presenter to deliver the story. The presenter may be anonymous or a celebrity.

- **Animation**: cartoon and other animation techniques can work well, particularly with products aimed at the young. EuroDisney employed animation at its launch in 1993.

Direct marketing and the brochure

Tourism organizations make heavy use of promotional materials mailed out or given away to customers, or passed on to them by intermediaries (travel agents, tourist information centres, hotels, etc.). The brochure is the central direct marketing material for many organizations.

The first consideration is the target audience aimed at. What little research has been published into brochure effectiveness suggests that one of the most important considerations is the **cover**. The main function of the cover is to identify the target audience and achieve impact in doing it.

Organizing the internal contents depends upon a trade-off between the motivational goals to be achieved (a new destination will, for example, require greater selling than one to which the customer has already been, or has already decided to go) and the amount of detailed information necessary to close a sale, if that is intended (cost and accommodation data, conformity to legal requirements, etc.).

Photographs are a crucial element of mass tour brochures. It is important to show clear pictures of the exterior of the hotel, the bedrooms and the swimming pool since it is known that 80% of the time a tourist spends on a package holiday is in the hotel. Maps play a critical part in tourism promotion in generating interest in a destination, supplying logistic information for tourists once they are there, and providing take-home

---

CASE STUDY 8.3

Promotion in action: the BTA's D-Day campaign to attract Americans to Britain

In 1994, the fortieth anniversary of the D-Day landings was used by the British Tourist Authority as an opportunity to attract Americans to Europe. An advertising campaign built round the theme, 'Celebrating an alliance forged in war and dedicated to peace' was developed and run in five main American newspapers. A 16-page D-Day supplement, in conjunction with *Travel and Leisure* magazine, was also produced and included in the *New York* and *Los Angeles Times* reaching 1.3 million readers. The campaign also included: a slot on America's biggest breakfast show, *Today*; $300 000 of editorial coverage; an hour long radio tape broadcast on over 140 stations; a video news release that reached 12 million viewers; and a D-Day hotline that attracted 18 500 callers. The BTA estimate that as many as 100 000 Americans may have been influenced to visit Britain as a result of the campaign.

Source: British Tourist Authority Annual Report (1994: 15).

mementoes (which act as permanent destination image reminders) (Seaton, 1994; Seaton and McWilliam, 1995).

One of the most difficult things to achieve in brochures aimed at the mass market is competitive differentiation. Because most organizations find themselves having to deliver the same kind of basic information about similar resorts the leeway for creative innovation is limited – which is why the brochures in the average travel agency are often hard to tell apart except for the company name and logo. Specialist tour operators with distinctive, niche-market products often have greater leeway for creative innovations, particularly if they are selling direct, since the formats of their brochures will not have to conform to the relatively standard sizes and shapes required by travel agencies.

Public relations

Public relations has always been the 'Cinderella' activity of promotion compared to advertising in terms of the amount of attention it has attracted among marketing theorists and practitioners. Yet the effects of public relations can exceed those of advertising and, even when they do not, they may turn out to be a lot cheaper.

What is PR? Here are two definitions:

> PR in tourism is about how people who matter to a tourism organization think about it and how their perceptions, attitudes and behaviour can be kept or made positive.
>
> (Seaton, 1994: 389)

And this is the way the Institute of Public Relations in the UK defines the business it is in:

> PR is the planned and sustained effort to establish and maintain goodwill and mutual understanding between an organization and its publics.

Neither tell you much about what PR actually involves for the simple reason that PR is such a diverse and broad-based set of activities that it eludes instant summary. External PR involves everything an organization does that impinges on people's perceptions including: its products (what kind of planes, hotels, destination features, attractions it offers); its employees (how they look, dress, interact with the public); its communication programmes and media coverage; its overall corporate identity; its financial reputation; its promotional activities; the buildings in which it transacts business – in short everything that contributes to the **image** of an organization. PR also has an internal function – to build and maintain morale within an organization through such things as good communication practices, incentive benefits (e.g. concessionary travel), sports and activity provision, etc. Public relations thus involves issues that affect every level of organizational activity and should be a corporate, as much as a marketing, activity.

One of the key differences between PR and advertising is that it involves messages to a range of **publics**, rather than targeted campaigns to one or a few market segments. The targets of PR may include: customers, the travel trade, the media, the financial world, public sector organizations including national governments, local authorities and tourist boards, business communities, employees (recent and potential) and opinion formers.

Similarly the range of communications and media used in PR may be more diverse than those for advertising campaigns. Public relations may involve political lobbying, corporate hospitality with VIP support (e.g. the launch of a new visitor attraction at Blackpool with a dinner and an opening ceremony attended by the Queen), and a whole range of personal communications aimed at opinion formers who may act as important third person endorsers of a tourism product.

Media relations

The function with which PR is most commonly associated is media relations. In some quarters PR has been defined as 'free publicity' because it is partly about getting stories in the media. However, successful media relations requires organization and investment. Ways of getting publicity include press releases, press conferences and telephone briefings. Familiarization trips for journalists – the 'freebies' for which tourism marketing is famous – can also be used. All these activities involve expenditure, even though the results may far exceed the outlay.

Crisis management

In a volatile market like that for tourism PR is increasingly about 'damage limitation' following unforeseen crises. Over the last five years ferry disasters, crime or terrorism at resorts and plane crashes have adversely affected consumer perceptions of destinations, carriers and tour operators. Crisis management is about dealing with the fallout from such occurrences in order to reduce their negative impact and restore public confidence. The

---

CASE STUDY 8.4

Selling Britain to the Italians

In 1993/4 the British Tourist Authority targeted Italy as one of several main European generating markets for visitors to Britain. Since resources for advertising were limited the prime thrust was put on media relations and publicity. The BTA established a temporary public information office in central Milan within one of the country's top tour operators and conducted a vigorous media campaign which resulted in £3 million of coverage in Italy's newspapers and magazines. The travel magazine *Meridiani* ran a 185-page special issue on Scotland. The campaign achieved a 16% increase in enquiries about Britain.

Source: BTA Annual Report (1994: 13).

Florida case study in Part 3 (Chapter 23) illustrates crisis management in action.

Sales promotion

Sales promotion has been defined as:

> Those marketing activities other than personal selling and advertising and publicity that stimulate purchasing and dealer effectiveness, such as displays, shows and exhibitions, demonstrations and various non-recurrent selling efforts not in ordinary routine.
>
> (American Marketing Association)

This somewhat negative formulation emphasizes the point-of-sale role of sales promotion at the expense of some of its wider functions. A more positive way of looking at sales promotion is to view it as 'a short-term incentive offered to the consumer, sales force or trade to induce a booking, reservation or sale'. David Bernstein, a UK creative consultant, has emphasized the difference between advertising and sales promotion by arguing that advertising persuades with the product while sales promotion persuades with something over and above the product.

SP can have three main targets:

- consumers;
- the trade;
- the company.

Its aims and objectives are many and may include the following.

- **Gaining trial or awareness**: e.g. an introductory offer for a new restaurant or ferry service.
- **Encouraging early bookings**: tour operators often offer discounts at the start of the season to generate immediate bookings. 'Loss leader' offers may be used to generate impact when a new season's programme is introduced – in the 1980s Thomson virtually gave away a limited number of holidays at £25 as a way of launching their new-season product portfolios.
- **Encouraging repeat stays or visits**: e.g. frequent flyer clubs and air miles offers.
- **Spreading visitors across a wide area**: a group of attractions may join together to offer inducements for multiple visitation. In the US bicentennial year of 1979 Baltimore State gave away a free charm bracelet to encourage tourists to visit different attractions from each of which they could collect charms for the bracelet.
- **Combating competition**: tour operators and airlines may cut their prices to match or improve on deals being run by competitors.
- **Shifting seasonal and temporal troughs**: low season special offers and 'happy hours' drink reductions in bars and restaurants may be used to attract customers to come at times when demand would otherwise be low.

- **Motivating the trade**: e.g. through increased commission to travel agencies. In the early 1980s PanAm set up their World Club to reward travel agents selling a certain number of tickets and a coach operator sent coupons for free ice cream cones to 30 000 travel agents (Davidoff, 1982: 120).

The techniques used to implement these different objectives may include:

- money off deals;
- vouchers and coupons;
- competitions;
- two for the price of one/children go free offers;
- sweepstakes and prizes;
- gifts and premiums (badges, key rings, stickers, sets of items to be collected, T shirts, pencils, pens, diaries, calendars, etc. – there are now many firms specializing in making cheap corporate premiums);
- self-liquidators: these are free gifts (towels, T shirts, etc.) which depend upon the customer collecting several proofs of purchase or paying an additional sum on top of a single proof of purchase. They cost the organization nothing because the gifts have been bought in bulk at a price well below their value to the consumer;
- volume discounts, e.g. special hotel rates for block bookings;
- additional nights/ferry crossings at reduced rates;
- cooperative deals between different organizations, e.g. a carrier such as a rail company doing a tie-up with a group of attractions offering passengers reduced admission prices;
- point-of-purchase displays, slide shows, maps, etc.;
- merchandizing activities and giveaways, e.g. in-flight magazines, posters, leaflets, drink mats, place settings, illuminated displays, giveaway maps, etc.

In the past SP has been seen as a short-term tactical activity compared to the more long-term image investment in advertising and PR. Burke and Resnick (1991: 152) have suggested that 'the art of promotional pricing is to use discounts to attract customers initially to products they will buy

---

CASE STUDY 8.5

Sales promotion: the Virgin Freeway Membership Card

In March 1990 Virgin Atlantic announced the Virgin Freeway Membership Card to 3 million frequent air travellers allowing them to collect points which they could redeem against introductory gliding courses, free travel with Virgin and trips on the Orient Express. The points were added monthly. Other companies involved in the offer were Thomas Cook Direct, Chase Manhattan, Holiday Inn, Budget Rent-a-Car and London City Airport.

Source: *The Sunday Times*, 25 March 1990.

again at nondiscounted prices.' However, the regularity and frequency of sales promotional activity in tourism marketing makes this questionable. Few organizations can get along in a price sensitive market such as tourism without offering special rates, discounts, loyalty incentives and so on, and those who tried would likely be at a significant competitive disadvantage.

SP often requires effective advertising support (it is pointless running a special offer which nobody has heard about), either at point of purchase or in the media. The way in which an offer is presented can have a crucial effect on its acceptance.

Personal selling

Personal selling has been defined by Coltman (1989: 323) as 'an interpersonal process whereby the seller ascertains, activates, and satisfies the needs and wants of the buyer so that both the seller and buyer benefits.' In marketing physical goods, personal selling was once seen mainly as a method of influencing the purchase. Older sales manuals used to include long prescriptive inventories of things that made a good sales person (knowledge, appearance, enthusiasm, sincerity, personality, etc.) and techniques necessary to get a sale (the ability to listen to the customer, identify his or her needs, overcome objections, knowing how to open and when to close the sale, etc.). Although things have moved on from these kind of prescriptive checklists – particularly in recognition of the after-sales role – selling physical goods is still heavily oriented to getting the sale.

Selling has a much wider role in service marketing. Selling is involved not just in getting the purchase, but delivering the product to the customer. Selling in tourism can be many things: a travel agent's telephone manner, how TIC staff deal with enquiries, the product expertise of the counter assistant in a travel agency, the honesty of a taxi driver conducting the tourist from the the airport to the hotel, the appearance of the front-of-house team in a hotel, the attentiveness of a waiter in a restaurant, the manner of an airline pilot addressing his passengers, the commentary provided by a driver to a coach party, the personality and knowledge of a tour guide, even the way a deckchair attendant collects money from a beach party. Tourism is often stereotyped as the have-a-nice-day, 'smile' business and for good reason – the 'people factor' critically affects not just the sale of the product but customer satisfaction with it, i.e. the tourism experience itself.

The influence of organizational personnel on the delivery of the product means that in tourism selling is as much about **total quality management** and **customer care** as getting the order (the booking, reservation, etc.). Both will be considered at length in Chapter 18.

Selling skills have been divided into a number of general areas: telephone techniques, complaints handling, and written and oral communication including presentations. Coltman divides the selling sequence into prospecting and qualifying, planning and delivering sales presentations, overcoming objections and closing the sale. Detailed discussion of them is impossible in a general text of this sort but there are specialist books which examine them in depth (e.g. Burton and Burton, 1994).

One of the problems that can arise in selling in tourism is that an organization may not control the sales intermediaries making the sale. Tour operators may try to affect how their products are presented by travel agents (through educationals, briefings and the provision of brochures and other sales aids), but in the final analysis they are not there when the sales encounter takes place. Where control is possible the essence of personal selling in tourism depends upon careful training of all organizational personnel who will meet the public – a thing which bigger organizations such as British Airways and Macdonald's do but smaller ones often do not.

PROMOTIONAL EVALUATION

Most tourism organizations are light years behind packaged goods companies in researching promotional campaigns. This is often due to limited budgets but also, in the case of destination marketers, to the difficulties of determining the influence of promotion on trip taking. In general American tourism organizations have been more enterprising in trying to measure their success than those in Britain and Europe.

A number of techniques exist for evaluating promotion, as discussed below.

*   **Behavioural measures** (e.g. using visitor data as an indicator of success). The problem with this is that visitor figures may be affected by a variety of factors other than promotion (e.g. habit, friends'/relatives' recommendations). However, large carriers (rail, air and coach firms) and hotels prepare annual marketing plans which include forecast targets of passengers/guests which are used to judge the success of their efforts. Tourist boards are often shyer of committing themselves to visitor numbers/spending targets which can then be used as an index of their success, although in the mid-1980s the Northern Ireland Tourist Board did set visitor targets and measured its success on the increases.
*   **Advertising enquiries**. This involves trying to count how many people requested further information in response to media advertising. If an advert is accompanied by a code numbered coupon or a toll-free phone number it is possible to determine how many responses were gained to a particular medium or campaign.
*   **Conversion studies**. These go one step further than advertising enquiries in attempting to find out how many people made bookings on the basis of information received. The main problem with conversion studies is that it is difficult to assess to what extent other factors influenced a trip decision. In many cases people request information after they have decided to make a trip so that it is not converting them, (Pitegoff, 1991) only providing supporting material for a decision already made. (Good discussions of conversion studies can be found

in Ronkainen and Woodside, 1987; Silberman and Klock, 1986; Perdue and Merrion, 1991.)

- **Image awareness and attitude studies**. Both advertising and public relations may be evaluated by monitoring their communication effects on their target audiences. This may be done through quantitative surveys based on structured, multiple-choice questionnaires, or through qualitative techniques (mainly depth interviews or group discussions, like those carried out by the Scottish Tourist Board quoted earlier).

- **Media content analysis**. Public relations is also often assessed by editorial content counts of publicity achieved through the media. Press cuttings may be kept to audit newspaper and magazine coverage; broadcast time counts (number of hours/minutes of air time) may be used to assess TV and radio achievements. Many national tourist boards, in their annual reports, proudly inventory the number of media vehicles in which they have achieved exposure. However, amount of exposure is, by itself, an inadequate index of success; it has to be further analysed qualitatively to establish whether the content was favourable/unfavourable and, ideally, the degree to which the precise messages delivered conformed to the communication strategies set.

SUMMARY

This chapter has provided a condensed treatment of issues that could well have been the subject of chapters and even books in themselves (media planning, PR, sales promotion, etc.). Even so it has been a long chapter because, for many tourism organizations, promotion is the major element of the marketing mix. The chapter has attempted to specify the major general features of information in tourism decision-making, the role of promotion, and the more detailed features of the promotional mix.

REFERENCES

Burke, J. and Resnick, B.P. (1991) *Marketing and Selling the Travel Product*, South Western Publishing, Cincinnati, Ohio.

Burton, J. and Burton, L. (1994) *Interpersonal Skills for Travel and Tourism*, Pitman, London.

Coltman, M. (1989) *Hospitality Marketing Management*, Van Nostrand Reinhold, New York.

Costerdine, G. (1988) *Readership Research*, Gower, London.

Davidoff, P.G. and Davidoff, D.S. (1982) *Sales and Marketing for Travel and Tourism*, Prentice-Hall, Englewood Cliffs, New Jersey.

Fesenmaier, D. and Vogt, C. (1993) Exploratory analysis of information use at Indiana State Welcome Centers, in 'Tourism: building credibility for a credible industry', *Proceedings of 22nd Annual Conference of the Travel and Tourism Research Association*, Bureau of Economic and

Business Research, Graduate School of Business, University of Utah, pp. 111–22.

Holloway, J.C. and Plant, R.V. (1992) *Marketing for Tourism*, Pitman, London.

Kotler, P. (1972) *Marketing Management: Analysis, Planning and Control*, Prentice-Hall, Englewood Cliffs, New Jersey.

Krippendorf, J. (1988) *The Holidaymakers*, Routledge, London.

Morrison, A. (1989) *Hospitality and Travel Marketing*, Delmar, New York.

Olins, W. (1989) *Corporate Identity*, Thames & Hudson, London.

Patterson, W. (1991) *Admap*, October, p. 52.

Perdue, R.R. and Merrion, D. (1991) Developing low cost, but improved conversion methodologies, *Proceedings of 22nd Annual Conference of the Travel and Tourism Research Association*, Bureau of Economic and Business Research, Graduate School of Business, University of Utah, pp. 435–40.

Pitegoff, B.E. (1991) Accountability research: Florida tourism examples, in 'Tourism: building credibility for a credible industry', *Proceedings of 22nd Annual Conference of the Travel and Tourism Research Association*, Bureau of Economic and Business Research, Graduate School of Business, University of Utah, pp. 441–9.

Ricketts, J. (1992) Virginia beach spring and summer tourist campaign, in 'Tourism partnerships and strategies: merging vision with new realities', *23rd Travel and Tourism Research Association Conference Proceedings*, Minneapolis, Minnesota, pp. 230–5.

Ronkainen, I.A. and Woodside, A.G. (1987) Advertising conversion studies, in Brent Ritchie, J.R. and Gouldner, C.R. (eds), *Travel, Tourism, and Hospitality Research: A Handbook for Managers*, Wiley, New York.

Schwerin, and Newall, (1980) *Persuasion*, Heinemann, London.

Scottish Tourist Board/Market Research Scotland (1991) Advertising testing report.

Seaton, A.V. (1994) Tourist maps and the promotion of destination image, in Chon, K.S. (ed.), *New Frontiers in Tourism Research: Proceedings of Research and Academic Papers*, Vol. VI, The Society of Travel and Tourism Educators, Lexington, Kentucky, pp. 168–84.

Seaton, A.V. and McWilliam, F. (1995) Mapping for pleasure, *Geographical: The Royal Geographic Society Magazine*, **LXVII** (2), 38–40.

Silberman, J. and Klock, M. (1986) An alternative to conversion studies for measuring the impact of travel ads, *Journal of Travel Research*, Spring, pp. 12–16.

REVIEW QUESTIONS

1. Using an annual report or other documentation by a national tourism organization of your choice assess the promotional mix used to promote an international destination.

2. What are the main factors that determine an airline's choice of advertising media? If possible obtain details or exhibits of advertising by specific airlines to support your answer.
3. What kind of sales promotional programme might a hotel in an attractive historic city run to improve occupancy out of season?
4. Prepare a folder of destination advertisements and attempt to identify their main target audiences and the main strategic messages they are attempting to deliver.
5. What might radio offer to a tourism organization that TV does not?

9 Putting it all together: tourism marketing past and present

A.V. Seaton

OBJECTIVES

This chapter begins by trying to draw together some of the threads of the previous chapters by comparing the contemporary features of tourism marketing with those in the past. It provides a discussion of modern tourism marketing planning and strategic management including an account of budgetary decision-making. The second half of the chapter is more complex than much of the materials so far and should be re-read and studied closely.

By the end of this chapter the reader should:

- understand the differences and similarities between past and present features of tourism marketing;
- have a grasp of the purposes and elements of the marketing plan as a control and evaluation mechanism in tourism marketing;
- have a critical appreciation of the main ideas of strategic management and its relationship to marketing theory;
- understand some of the main methods of allocating budgets to tourism marketing.

INTRODUCTION

For the last eight chapters we have looked at some of the main concepts and methods of tourism marketing. In this final chapter of Part 1 we shall try to bring some of the strands together.

Marketing, as we saw in Chapter 1, is not new in its basic elements. Managers have always had to manage the variables of price, place, product and promotion, and to do so with some understanding of both consumers and markets, in order to prosper. However, in general tourism managers had far less knowledge of marketing as a systematic form of analysis, planning and control than present-day managers, and they had vastly inferior information systems on which to base decisions, compared to the range of marketing research techniques supported by sophisticated IT systems which are available today. But set against that they often developed greater entrepreneurial and judgemental skills that can get stifled under the torrents of data in our own days of more 'scientific' management. One way of appreciating the differences and similarities between older approaches to tourism marketing and more contemporary ones is to take a specific case study from the past and to reassess it in the light of marketing knowledge today.

We begin this final synthesizing chapter with a case history from 60 years ago – the launch in 1927 of The Mayfair Hotel in London by Gordon Hotels Ltd. The purpose of the case is twofold:

- to identify to what extent marketing approaches were utilized;
- to assess how adequate they were in the light of the principles and practices described in this text.

MARKETING THEN AND NOW: THE MAYFAIR HOTEL LAUNCH BY GORDON HOTELS, 1927

The launch programme

The Mayfair was the first new luxury hotel to be built in London for twenty years. The hotel was not a sudden idea. Sir Francis Towle, managing director of Gordons, had for some years wanted a hotel in Mayfair which would provide:

> . . . the possibility of offering to the cultured travelling public a temporary home in London, perfectly situated, distinguished by elegance and refinement, and planned on lines which we believe mark a forward step in the development of the British Hotel Industry.

The market

Towle had noted that Britain lagged behind both America and Europe despite the fact that foreign visitors to Britain were increasing:

> They come from every country on earth . . . Since the war interest in all things English has been stimulated to an extraordinary degree, not only in foreign countries but also in England, where the popularity of the cheap motor car is largely responsible for the enormously increased interest in our history, topography, antiquities and in the natural beauties which lie so thickly throughout our green shires.
>
> (Morton, 1927: 50)

The product concept and positioning

Towle aimed to differentiate the Mayfair from a style he called the 'palace style' which was common in France and America and consisted of attempts to 'perpetuate the gilded glories of Versailles'. He saw this as inappropriate for the English-speaking traveller and he wanted instead to introduce a concept that was distinctively English:

> ... it must carry to perfection the comfort, freedom and personal service, that good taste and 'rightness' in the small details of life which have made English home life famous the world over. Centuries of cultured living have evolved the English country house life with its leisurely, friendly atmosphere, its sure and unmistakeable touch of England. This is the manner of life from which great English hotels of the future will draw inspiration.

(Morton, 1927: 53)

Having fixed on the English theme Gordons executed it with great single-mindedness. The hotel was built on a prime site in the heart of London's Mayfair, facing where Old Devonshire House once had been. It was designed, built and managed by English companies and had a higher number of English staff than any similar company. Virtually all the fittings were manufactured in Britain: the carpets, the electroplate, the fabrics and the furniture. Over £1 million was spent with English firms on the building and furnishings. The hotel included a lounge, restaurant lounge, restaurant, ballroom and garden grill. It had 300 bedrooms each with central heating and phone.

Pricing

The Mayfair charges for rooms through the 1920s and 1930s were between 20s. (£1.00) and 30s. (£1.50) a night. Lunch was 8s. 6d. (43p) and Dinner was 12s. 6d. (63p). These rates were in the same premium price band as the ten most expensive hotels in London (including the Ritz, Claridges, Savoy, Grosvenor House and Berkeley).

Promotion

The hotel was launched with press publicity and a large commissioned brochure written by H.V. Morton, the most successful popular writer on travel of his time, and lavishly illustrated with drawings using the latest colour printing techniques. The brochure showed all the main features of the internal design. The hotel also produced promotional postcards. A major public relations coup was the arrangement of a visit by King George V and Queen Mary to open the hotel which achieved high-profile press coverage (Taylor and Bush, 1974: 157).

Programme evaluation

From this brief account to what extent were marketing methods applied to this major product launch? How well was the market defined? How good was the original product concept and positioning? Did it grow from identified customer needs? Did it take into account trends in the market? What environmental factors were monitored? Were viable market segments identified? Was the concept well implemented and promoted? How do you think the market responded?

- **The market**. Towle's account suggests that the hotel was indeed developed as a response to a market opportunity. He had identified a growth in rich, international visitors to London, a developing tourism habit, and a gap in the market based upon his judgement that existing English hotels were too similar to foreign ones and that there was thus an opportunity for a more differentiated product.
- **The product**. The product Towle aimed to introduce was based upon a distinctive positioning. He wanted to introduce a luxury hotel that had an English country house ambience (as many small UK hoteliers were to do again in the 1980s). He executed the concept single-mindedly by using English design and manufactures to equip it, and English staff to run it.
- **Pricing**. The premium pricing strategy developed by Towle was also a reasonable one given the luxury positioning aimed at, the competitive structure of the luxury market and the rich international visitor he sought to attract.
- **Promotion**. The publicity programme achieved considerable impact. In the 1920s press was still the main medium for reaching an affluent market and the royal visit (still used by tourism marketers to launch major projects such as the Channel Tunnel) generated the right kind of prestigious editorial coverage.

The launch then suggests a degree of marketing orientation. Yet a number of criticisms can be made of the launch judged against the principles adumbrated in the last eight chapters.

Firstly, on the basis of the information presented, it seems that most of the planning was made on the basis of judgement without any degree of quantitative analysis derived from hard evidence. What was the size of the market aimed at? How many international visitors were coming to London? By how much were they increasing?

Secondly, what evidence was there of dissatisfaction with existing hotel provision? Towle's judgement that 'the gilded glories of Versailles' style of hotel was flawed and that a more English style would be attractive may have been correct, but no evidence was supplied to demonstrate this. At worst his product could have been an example of producer-orientation, whereby the prejudices of the supplier rather than the consumer drove product development. Moreover, even if the English country house concept was a desirable option, to what extent was it necessary to implement it through English manufacturers unless the consumer was capable of differentiating between English and foreign craftsmanship? (P&O are currently developing a new liner for the English market which is built by Germans, and mainly designed by Scandinavians and Scots.)

The launch thus fell short of the full panoply of marketing analysis advocated in this book. Though Towle's planning suggests an awareness of the marketing mix, changing visitor/customer patterns and product positioning, most of it appears to have been based on judgement. Today an intensive marketing audit would be instigated, designed to produce greater knowledge of the market, the environment, the consumer and competition. This audit would involve greater quantification of everything, greater use of research to investigate the main parameters of marketing decision-making and include use of IT to mount the necessary information systems.

But did the hotel succeed? The answer to this is yes and no. Two years after the launch of the Mayfair a major international economic crisis, the Wall Street Crash and the Great Depression (which would probably have eluded an environmental scan, even had one been carried out), plunged Gordon's Hotels into financial difficulty but the hotel ultimately prospered and continues as a premier, luxury hotel to the present day (it is now part of the Japanese-owned, Saison Intercontinental group), still positioned as a traditional hotel, with its main market the international, particularly the American, traveller.

So what does the Mayfair case study tell us about marketing past and present? Perhaps three things.

Firstly, it suggests that many basic marketing principles were alive and well in the Mayfair launch seventy years ago, albeit combined with impressionistic evidence and subjective judgement. Inadequate as the marketing analysis might appear by the standards of those advocated in marketing textbooks like this one, many smaller hotel ventures in our own times have been launched or run with less clearly defined aims and less consumer orientation.

Secondly, it demonstrates by default that, although modern marketing has access to many data gathering facilities that can be used to improve formal knowledge of markets (research studies, consultancy reports, etc.), they are not the only ways of understanding them. Managers with a long knowledge of an industry may absorb considerable data on markets from their own experience giving them an intuitive 'feel' for new developments. Francis Towle was part of a dynasty which has been called 'the most distinguished family of British hoteliers' (Taylor and Bush, 1974: 115). His father had been chief executive of Midland Hotels, his brother later succeeded to the same position and founded Gleneagles, and their sister Marie Muggeridge wrote on hotel management (whenever hotel expertise was required in the first four decades of this century it seems that the answer was to 'throw in a Towle'). Through this experience Francis Towle was able to use judgement allied to experience to launch a major new hotel development without access to the volumes of data that would be deployed today.

Thirdly, marketing information systems are, in any case, a means not an end. The ultimate task of marketers is creativity and innovation in responding to market conditions. To paraphrase Marx, the ultimate role of managers is not to understand markets but to change them. One of the dangers of modern marketing is that so much data is collected it can produce creative paralysis and end up as a substitute for action. Almost anybody can be taught to initiate research and crunch data but deciding what to do as a result of the information gathered involves innovatory and judgemental skills. Tourism organizations are now generally wise to the benefits of research but less productive in the field of creative thinking. Entrepreneurs of the past like Towle were perhaps bolder and more original because they were less burdened by fact-fatigue. The Mayfair Hotel was an innovation-led development that was as much the result of creative thinking – the realization that the traditional, English style could produce a successful market entrant at a time when British imperial culture was a powerful influence on international consumer tastes – as analysis.

In summary, the differences between past and present marketing techniques, and the qualitative superiority of the latter, can be over-exaggerated. Despite the huge volumes of business information and theory, and the professional and academic industries that have grown up to export them since the war, it would be a brave person who would assert that business is now better understood and run than it has been in the past. In the 1980s and 1990s the incidence of Titanic-scale corporate disasters such as BCCI, Barings, PanAm in Britain, the International Leisure Group, the problems of the Channel Tunnel consortium, and the demise of many medium sized travel companies gives no reason for uncritical confidence in modern business theory, while the continuing success of long-established tourism businesses such as Forte and P&O, and resorts like Blackpool, suggest that those who did it right in the past may still be doing so. One of marketing's most recurrent faults is congenital neophilia – an assumption that modern business is superior to the dark ages of business that preceded it. The latest is always the best and different from the past. This fallacy springs from two causes:

- **Vested interest and the cult of the expert**. In the competitive world of business there is no percentage for either practitioners or academics in coming clean with the truth that basic marketing principles often go back years and that many new ideas are old wine in new bottles. Business executives, consultants and academics make their reputations by ignoring or undermining confidence in ideas of the past and prose-lytizing apparently new ideas that can be conspicuously and profitably associated with their names. In tourism management this tendency has been compounded by a worldwide trend since the 1960s for investment by the public sector in tourism planning, associated with lucrative funding for tourism research and know-how. Since many of those responsible for the public sector have often had little previous experi-ence of tourism, there is a natural tendency for consultants and aca-demics wooing them to promote a cult of the expert, based on the myth that experts have access to the latest and best in tourism thinking, whether or not much of it is derived from well-established precedent.
- **Ignorance**. Other consultants or academics may have little interest in

or knowledge of marketing and tourism history and may misrecognize old ideas as new ones. As the old calendar motto has it, 'When someone encounters an idea for the first time, he or she frequently thinks it is the first time it has been encountered.' This is particularly so in tourism planning. The interwar years (1918–1939) were, for example, a period of rapid and innovative tourism development and promotion. By simply studying some of the immense variety of marketing and promotional materials which survive in archives such as Thomas Cook, P&O and elsewhere, tourism executives would be surprised to find that very many of the tourism principles and practices seen as recent – partnership marketing, target marketing, business tourism (business tourists were formerly called 'commercials') and destination image promotion – go back a long way.

THE MARKETING PLAN

So far we have emphasized some of the continuities in tourism marketing past and present in order to qualify a dominant orthodoxy which emphasizes radical difference. For the rest of this chapter we shall try to identify the distinctive contributions of modern marketing to tourism planning.

As we have demonstrated in this chapter and in Chapter 1, marketing as a form of consumer orientation was not a new discovery. What was new was its systematic application across a range of integrated activities called the marketing mix using a range of analytical procedures and concepts described in Chapters 1–8, supported by extensive, research-based data on markets, consumers and the environment (described in chapters 1–4) and leading to quantified, periodicized managerial planning.

Of all the marketing ideas we have discussed the most important are the concepts of **systematic consumer-orientated planning** and **integration of the marketing mix**. Marketing only works when it is undertaken as a holistic process in which all activities (product design and manufacture, promotion, pricing, distribution) are planned as interdependent elements and subsumed within the overall goal of satisfying the consumer in a given set of environmental and market conditions.

The **marketing plan** is the central management mechanism for approaching and achieving integrated marketing planning. It is a document which consists of an annual, written statement of objectives and quantified, periodicized goals covering every aspect of future marketing activity over a specified period, normally 1–5 years, with the costs involved. In general terms a tourism marketing plan addresses four questions:

- Where is tourism now?
- How did we get there?
- Where do we want tourism to go?
- How do we get there?

O'Hanlon (1972: 45) has identified its key elements as follows:

- It examines the major facts in the marketing situation under consideration.
- It identifies the problems and opportunities inherent in the particular marketing situation.
- It establishes specific long- and short-range corporate objectives for the product.
- It proposes a long-range strategy to solve the problems and to capitalize on the opportunities.
- It recommends specific selling, advertising and promotional tactics to carry out short-range strategy and accomplish the objectives set for the next twelve-month period.

The marketing plan is thus a stocktake of the past and present from which the future is projected and planned. To meet the requirements just specified O'Hanlon (1972: 47) suggested that the plan should be in six sections:

1. situational analysis;
2. problems and opportunities (SWOT analysis);
3. company objectives;
4. strategy (long range);
5. tactics (short range);
6. evaluation.

How does one go about producing this master plan? There are no agreed documentary formats for producing a marketing plan in the way, for example, that there are standard accounting procedures in financial reporting. Every organization must undertake a marketing plan according to the nature of its own markets. Macdonald (1989) has produced a book-length study on formats for marketing plans suggesting some options. The main necessity is access to quantified data which can be used to answer a number of questions relating to the organization's past, present and future performance, including the following:

- How many current customers does it have? Who are they? (Mass markets? Niche markets? What are the main segments?)
- How are they likely to develop in the future? Whom does the organization want to retain, gain, jettison?
- How much revenue does tourism create for the tourism organization (hotel, airline, destination, etc.)? By how much should it increase in the future?
- Who are the competitors and what is their market performance? How might these change in the future?
- How does the organization's products rate against competition? What improvements are necessary?
- What infrastructure developments (if the organization is a destination promoter) are necessary to support market targets?
- Are the organization's prices competitive? (Has it got a superior

product to justify charging more? What are its reasons for charging less than/the same as competitors?)
- How well is the organization resourced in human terms to compete? How are its staff training techniques and management structures?
- How effective is its promotion?
- What partnerships might be necessary to support future plans (private and public)?
- What future developments will affect its markets (technological, political, social, environmental, etc.)?

These are just some of the issues which a marketing plan should address. How it does so will depend on the product, the company and the market. The elements of a marketing plan for a hotel will differ from those for a national tourist board but they will essentially address a number of common areas which may be summarized as:

- current position;
- threats and opportunities;
- objectives and issues;
- marketing strategies;
- action programmes;
- budgets;
- controls.

Buttle (1992: 55–67) has recently produced a detailed, systematized approach to marketing planning in tourism based on a five-stage flowchart which can be reduced to a one-page format consisting of the following elements:

1. SWOT analysis:
   1.1 Internal analysis
   1.2 External analysis

2. Mission statement

3. Objectives and strategies:
   3.1 Financial forecasts and objectives
   3.2 Market forecasts and objectives
   3.3 Demand management
   3.4 Target markets
   3.5 Positioning statement

4. Capsule marketing strategy

5. Budgeted marketing mix
   5.1 Product
   5.2 Promotion
   5.3 Place, channels
   5.4 Price
   5.5 Marketing organization
   5.6 Budget

Producing a marketing plan is a complex business since it involves extensive data gathering, time-consuming analysis and then often difficult, hotly debated decisions about future actions. This is why, for many organizations, producing the annual marketing plan is the high-stress, crisis point of the year. However, it is a vital activity since the marketing plan serves four essential functions:

1. It is a managerial control document which aims to ensure that clear goals and targets have been established in order that the organization does not drift about. A marketing plan is above all an action document with costed periodicized goals derived from analysis of the tourism organization's resources, customers and competition.

2. It provides a detailed inventory as to how the marketing budget is to be spent and why it has been allocated in the ways set out. All sales and revenue targets must be identified and justified.

3. It provides an agreed basis of action that can be circulated to every group or individual involved in its implementation. As a result it acts as a mechanism for ensuring that everyone is clearly identified with marketing aims. It is thus as much a communication device as a policy statement which helps the organizational integration which we identified in Chapter 1 as a central element of effective marketing planning.

4. It provides a set of benchmarks against which marketing programmes can later be evaluated and redefined for the future. Without explicit targets evaluation of tourism marketing is impossible.

In summary, marketing planning **directs** organizations to seek answers to a number of basic questions (involving market data, competitive analysis, consumer analysis, environmental anticipation, etc.); **enjoins** them to develop periodicized strategic objectives and produce a marketing mix for implementing them; **specifies** precise market targets and profitability forecasting tied to budgeted measures; **ensures** identification at all levels of the company with them; and **provides** evaluation mechanisms to measure performance in order to adjust and plan for the future.

Later in this chapter we shall illustrate these ideas with a state-of-the-art case study showing how these highly desirable, but so far rather theoretical, elements of marketing planning can be pursued in practice. But before we do so, we need to make a short detour into a related area – strategic management.

STRATEGIC MANAGEMENT AND CORPORATE STRATEGY

Strategic management (SM, or corporate strategy as it is also known) has been a management growth industry for nearly two decades. It emerged in the 1970s associated with the names of a number of consultants and academics including the Boston Consultancy Group (Morrison and Wensley, 1991), Porter and Ansoff. During the 1980s and early 1990s it was widely adopted in the manufacturing sector, the service sector, government, education and even religious organizations. In the last decade it has been increasingly debated in relation to the tourism and hospitality sectors. What is it all about? Here are two definitions from texts on its application to the hospitality sector:

> Strategic management is the process of examining both present and future environments, formulating the organization's objectives, and making, implementing and controlling decisions focused on achieving these objectives in the present and future environments.
>
> (Chon and Olsen, 1990: 207)

> Strategic management can be thought of as a consistent pattern of decisions made by an organization's management as it pursues its mission and objectives. These decisions include the types of products to offer and their appropriate markets, the allocation of resources to that end, the establishment of policies and procedures, and the control of, and responsibilities to, employees. The decision-making process is influenced by events occurring in the internal as well as external environments of the firm. Management's goal in employing strategic management is to match the resources of the firm to the threats and opportunities in the environment so as to achieve long-term viability for the firm.
>
> (Olsen, Tse and West, 1992: 1)

From these two broad definitions it is difficult to identify the features of SM which differ from marketing. Both definitions suggest that SM, like marketing, is concerned with product choices, market decisions, and environmental opportunities and threats.

What happens if we move from broad definitions to more detailed aspects of SM? Chon and Olsen (1990: 208) went on to identify a six-part strategic management process for tourism planning:

- tourism organization mission;
- environmental analysis (tourism impacts and internal and external environment);
- strategic analysis and choice (long-term objectives and grand strategy);
- annual objectives/operating strategies;
- implementation of strategy;
- control and evaluation.

Once again it is difficult to identify what is different from marketing planning in this list. The organizational mission is simply a statement of what business an organization is in and what it hopes to achieve in it. Environmental analysis is an element of the marketing audit (see Chapter 1). Strategic analysis and choice are essentials of marketing (see Chapter 1 again), though 'long-term objectives and grand strategy' are admittedly extensions, albeit ones about which we shall shortly express some scepticism in relation to tourism planning. Annual objectives and operating strategies are elements of any marketing plan as we have described earlier in this chapter. Implementation (through the marketing mix) is also a feature of marketing planning (see Chapters 5–8 on the marketing mix and the earlier part of this chapter). And control and evaluation are central requirements of marketing planning. The differences between strategic management and marketing are thus still hard to detect in Chon and Olsen's inventory.

A number of general features of strategic management have been emphasized in the literature in addition to those just inventoried. Some of them will now be presented with comments on each from the point of view of tourism planners.

The time period addressed in SM is longer than in other kinds of planning

Marketing plans normally cover periods of 1–5 years while strategic management planning may involve projections, forecasts and strategies for up to 10 or 20 years. The latterday strategic manager, often aided and abetted by corporate consultants, is enjoined to be a visionary and prophet, able to predict and shape the future. (The words 'vision' and 'future' are common in SM texts.)

Comment

Futurism has almost been routinized into executive thinking despite the poor record of prophetic attempts throughout human history. There is little evidence to suggest that such long-range analysis and the optimistic strategic choices based on it (no long-term analysis ever predicts failure!) works in manufacturing industry, let alone in tourism which is a sector so volatile that even short-term objectives are constantly confounded by developments none could predict (the collapse of the Soviet Union, the Gulf War, a fuel crisis, a freak summer heatwave in the UK, etc.). Thinking in short/middle-term perspectives – the main activity of marketing in practice – may be more realistic than devoting serious time and effort to long-term time spans, though more risky since executives may be held accountable for the plans they have developed in the short-term, whereas they may not be around when longer-term predictions come home to roost. (There is a saying that those who can't manage the present can always predict and manage a distant future.)

SM theory puts greater focus on corporate multi-product portfolio analysis rather than single products or brands

The early work of the Boston Consulting Group, in particular, emphasized SM as a high-level management function undertaken at the overarching level of the firm rather than that of the product or brand. SM was focused on the management of multi-product operations, including assessment of the relative importance of products within a company in terms of future profitability, market share and the allocation of the right priorities and funds to each.

Comment

Though portfolio analysis is obviously useful for multi-product organizations, particularly multinational companies, its application in tourism is more debatable. Tourism is a highly fragmented sector where many organizations are small, independent ventures (hotels, guest houses, attractions, etc.) operating in one country. Though portfolio analysis may help large hotel chains and airlines, it has less to offer smaller organizations and destination promoters.

SM centres competition as a major parameter of management planning

Another of SM's emphases is the notion of making competition a prime factor in strategic analysis, most famously associated with Porter's concept of **competitive advantage** as a crucial strategic issue in corporate thought (Porter, 1980). Competitive advantage, according to the theory, becomes a driving force arrived at after analysis of a number of force fields including the organizational players in the field, their resources and capacities, and the future environments in which they operate.

Comment

Again this is not a new notion. Marketing has always advocated producing products positioned for a competitive niche in the marketplace. An older marketing concept, the unique selling proposition, first formulated by Rosser Reeves in 1952, advocated that all products should seek to market a differential feature that could be seen as uniquely distinct from the competition. However, the level of importance ascribed to the competitive dimension by Porter certainly does have applications in tourism. Competitive advantage has been a factor in corporate planning in the accommodation sector (e.g. Marriott), resort developments (CenterParcs), and transport sector (Channel Tunnel planning). It could well be given more attention by destination agencies – in general regional and national tourist boards devote far less attention to comparative analysis and competitive positioning than organizations in other industries.

SM emphasizes the importance of assessing and managing the whole external environment in which business takes place

In the late twentieth century, organizations operate in highly complex environments, subject to rapid change. To cope with them involves detailed environmental scanning that lays emphasis on developments in technology, economics (including the predicted patterns of the financial/capital and labour markets); politics (including government action); and consumer tastes.

Comment

Environmental responsiveness is a critical area for all managers, particularly in a fickle, fashion-conscious sector such as tourism. However, as we have already seen, environmental analysis is an essential element of the marketing audit and is not unique to SM.

SM theory emphasizes organizational design and structuring as part of the SM process

SM theory has emphasized the organizational requirements of successful management, notably the need to shape the structure and culture of the company to its strategic mission and objectives. Some of the effects of SM programmes have been a reduction in the workforce, renegotiation of contracts and transformed work practices, often associated with elaborate training programmes and monitoring mechanisms.

Comment

Marketing theory has always stressed organizational structure and integration as a prerequisite for success. In SM this organizational emphasis is broadened to take in the whole enterprise, not just its marketing operation. Many SM ideas thus look rather like old marketing wine in new bottles. A number of consultants and theorists most prominently associated with SM were originally marketing advisors, and in many academic institutions marketing and SM are departmentally associated. SM was a revamping of marketing that had as much to do with professional development as business necessity. Relaunching marketing – commonly, although wrongly, often viewed as a relatively intermediate line management function – at the corporate level was a good career move for marketing advisors. Put baldly, corporate strategists (whether in-house or consultants) are remunerated better than marketing counsellors. The salary differentials between senior executives and line operators which have widened in the last ten years have often been justified on this SM presumption.

Where SM is not similar to marketing its distinctive emphases may have dangers in tourism management. SM widens the financial and status gap between management and employees by suggesting that all the really important and difficult stuff is going on at the top and that the workforce is just an 'internal environment' to be directed (despite a compensating rhetoric of 'empowerment' which frequently means no more than a freedom to do as one is told). Strategic management tends to disable the employee, because it locates all the important decisions as being from the top down – made up in the clouds by corporate strategists – and creates a language which invalidates employee perspectives by impersonalizing human decisions as inexorable, irresistible forces. ('Adjusting an organization to its environment' in the pursuit of 'windows of opportunity' is, for example, a more difficult thing for an employee to resist than redundancy, and it makes better PR-speak than saying 'we are firing people' or 'moving to a part-time workforce'.)

This developing gap between employees and management institutionalized at the heart of SM is particularly dangerous in tourism and hospitality. Tourism, as a service sector inherently dependent upon face-to-face transactions between people, is one of those markets where the 'coalface' workers in daily contact with the customer very often know more about the true state of the operation than grand strategists who get it filtered through research studies and consultants (many of whom have no specialized knowledge of the industry except through the data they can acquire, often at short notice, from reports, academics and other secondary materials). Many tourism organizations would be better off listening at ground-level to the realities of their current and short-term markets, rather than peering longsightedly into the stratosphere of corporate mission and millenarian prophesy. Over the years tourism has produced, and continues to produce, oceans of macro-forecasts – the current fashion is for predictions and punditry for the year 2000 and beyond. Delightful as such speculations may be there is little evidence that grand strategy derived from such long-term forecasting and analysis works in tourism.

Finally, it should be said that in the UK industry seems to have been slow to adopt SM. Two recent studies found little evidence of SM applications in the hospitality sector – the one which SM might reasonably be expected to assist since it comprises multi-product portfolio chains, often operating directly or through franchises, in international markets. Both studies found that the basis of hotel management was still founded on short/medium-range marketing planning rather than the more extended periods of SM. The first concluded:

> In the majority of the cases strategic planning was in reality no more than extended financial budgeting. The annual budget, supported by the sales and marketing plan, were the main documents used to outline the specific actions or initiatives for the future.
>
> (Phillips, 1994)

The second study of Swallow Hotels concluded:

> The management processes leading to the strategy were not found to be rigorously analytical and none of the tools and techniques associated with strategic management were used, with the exception of mid-range

---

1. More fancifully it may be that SM serves a particular kind of male executive orientation to power games, particularly in multinational organizational cultures, that was once channelled into war. Now that it is politically incorrect to aspire to military conquest of other nations, corporate executives in large MNEs can indulge fantasies of being commercial Alexander the Greats, planning strategy across continents and epochs, and have a dedicated praetorian guard of highly paid consultants, academics and well-wishers to both generate and sustain the fantasy that they are devising plans for the world for years to come. It would be inappropriate to remember Hitler's dream of a Reich that would last a 1000 years but disappeared after 12. The businesses that have lasted (the Mayfair, Cooks, P&O, Forte) seem to have done so with no grand, millenial strategy, only through a laborious, heuristic process of constantly updating their organization and products through monitoring their customers, keeping their eye on competitors, making product innovations and market analysis – all eye-level, marketing activities.

plans which were not found to be particularly significant to the actual running of the company.

(Webster, 1994)

This account of strategic management should probably have started with a health warning since it takes a somewhat sceptical view of SM. It has emphasized the problems of SM precisely because it is currently being so strenuously recommended by some to the tourism sector. Of course many of the ideas of SM, being essentially similar to marketing, are useful (the three pillars of strategic management – strategic analysis, strategic choice and strategic implementation – are good examples). But the more detailed elements of strategy often consisting of extensive prescriptive inventories (see Olsen (1991) for a positive and well-documented longer look at these) can become a distracting, bureaucratic game that tourism planners frequently have not got time to play, and if they do, find the market has moved by the time they arrive at their strategic choices.

To complete this comparison between marketing and strategic management we shall conclude this chapter with a look at one of the most detailed examples of planning ever published by a national tourist office – that of the Scottish Tourist Board.

MARKETING AND STRATEGIC PLANNING TODAY: THE SCOTTISH TOURIST BOARD, 1995

We began this chapter with a case history from the past. We end it with one from the present which exemplifies the systematic, integrated and quantified planning that characterizes modern tourism marketing.

Scotland is a country within the United Kingdom which has a population of just over 5 million and hosts over 10 million trips, gains over £2000 m in tourism revenue, and provides employment in tourism for 8% of its population. Because tourism is such an economically important sector the UK government has since 1969 supported it financially and the Scottish Tourist Board, the country's tourism marketing agency, is currently grant-aided by a budget of £10 m. Through this funding the STB's research department has been in a position to innovate and commission extensive research so Scotland is one of the best-provided countries in the world in terms of tourism data.

In the early 1990s Scotland's tourism experienced problems, particularly through the weakening of its principal UK markets (which have historically comprised around 70% of its tourism revenue) so between 1993 and 1995 the Board, under the direction of the Scottish Office, set about taking steps to reassess its position.

This began with a wide-ranging consultation with the Scottish tourism industry in which those who had an opinion on tourism development in Scotland were invited to submit their suggestions. Over 400 responded in writing including submissions from the public and private sector and academics. One of the views expressed (e.g. Scottish Tourism Research Unit, 1993) was that tourism planning in Scotland should include precisely quantified objectives and targets, and be capable of measurable evaluation.

At the end of the consultation the STB produced two major marketing policy documents:

* *The Strategic Plan*;
* *The Corporate Plan 1995/6–1997/8*.

The Strategic Plan

The Strategic Plan, which went through two drafts, consisted of a marketing audit which comprised a thoroughgoing analysis of where tourism was in Scotland and how it had developed over the previous ten years up to 1993. This included data and analysis of:

* tourism employment trends in Scotland;
* environmental trends likely to affect international tourism demand;
* Scotland's main markets from 1983 to 1993 by visitor expenditure, season, bednights and trips, including an analysis of domestic and international tourism to Scotland;
* Scotland's main tourism resources including accommodation, visitor attractions, the natural environment, sports and activities, training needs, visitor services and transport;
* public sector and private organizations responsible for tourism;
* SWOT analysis of Scotland as a tourism destination.

On the strength of the analysis the *Plan* identified seven main goals for the year 2000 (STB, 1994: 5):

* increase total visitor expenditure from £2090 m in 1993 to £2300 m in 1993 prices;
* increase total bednights from 60.6 m in 1993 to 65 m;
* increase the number of jobs in tourism from 171 000 in 1991 (latest employment census) to 195 000;
* increase low-season tourism (October–June) from 56% to 60% of total;
* increase the value of tourism outside the main areas (Edinburgh and Glasgow) from 71% to 75%;
* increase Scotland's market share of domestic tourism expenditure from 11.4% to 13%;
* improve visitor perceptions of Scotland, as quantified in market research survey ratings, using 1994 as a base.

These main targets were then translated into two sets of marketing objectives relating to domestic and overseas tourism to Scotland.

UK marketing objectives:

* increase overall levels of tourism expenditure, in particular holiday expenditure;

- increase tourist expenditure outside the main summer period, particularly in the second and fourth quarter;
- increase the percentage of touring holidays;
- increase the percentage of activity, cultural and special interest holidays.

Overseas marketing objectives:

- increase overseas visitors' intentions to choose Scotland as a destination;
- increase levels of visitor expenditure;
- increase the spread of visitor expenditure in Scotland;
- increase the seasonal spread of visitor expenditure in Scotland.

The Strategic Plan thus fulfilled the first two requirements of a marketing plan we discussed earlier, namely:

- it set out where Scottish tourism was;
- it indicated where it wanted to go through establishing broad marketing objectives for the future.

What remained was to declare how it would achieve its goals and how its marketing programmes would be evaluated. This was done six months later when the final *Corporate Plan* was published.

The Corporate Plan

The 53-page corporate plan constituted one of the most comprehensive, publicly available statements produced by a destination agency about its marketing planning. It is a model of how a national tourist organization can approach the task of identifying, quantifying and setting up evaluation procedures for its marketing tasks.

It opened with a statement of its central mission which is:

The generation of jobs and wealth for Scotland through the promotion and development of tourism.

The core of the plan was contained in two pages: a one-page statistical table which set out performance indicators and visitor expenditure targets for six years, 1992–1997 (Table 9.1) and another page which itemized the total budget allocation for the four years 1994–1998, broken down by expenditure category (Table 9.2).

The main budget expenditure was then allocated across eight sub-categories comprising: UK Marketing, International Marketing, Scottish Convention Bureau and Exhibitions, Visitor Services, Planning and Development, Press and PR, Finance and Administration, and Monitoring and Evaluation.

Each of these budgeted sub-categories were then further itemized into their component activities; for example, UK Marketing consisted of advertising, brand promotion, publications, consumer promotions, distribution, and research and development. Many of the activities

Table 9.1 STB's *The Corporate Report*: Scottish tourism main performance indicators and targets (1994 prices)

	Performance		Est.		Target	
	1992	*1993	**1994	1995	***1996	1997
Total Visitor Expenditure (£m)						
Scotland	385	550	460	465	475	480
Rest of UK	886	905	790	800	815	825
Overseas	644	750	765	805	845	885
Total	**1915**	**2205**	**2015**	**2070**	**2135**	**2190**
Holiday Visitor Expenditure (£m)						
Scotland	300	370	320	325	330	335
Rest of UK	615	655	580	590	600	605
Overseas	345	379	390	410	430	450
Total	**1260**	**1404**	**1290**	**1325**	**1360**	**1390**
Scottish Expenditure in Scotland as % of all Scottish Expenditure in the UK (all tourism)	43%	42%	43%	44%	45%	46%
English Expenditure in Scotland as % of all English Expenditure in the UK (all tourism)	8.3%	7.7%	7.9%	8.1%	8.2%	8.4%
Overseas Expenditure in Scotland as % of all Overseas Expenditure in the UK (all tourism)	7.9%	8.0%	8.1%	8.2%	8.3%	8.4%
% of New Visitors (UK only)	—	30%	34%	35%	36%	36%
Average Length of Stay (nights – all tourism)						
Scotland	4.0	3.6	3.7	3.7	3.7	3.7
Rest of UK	5.5	5.9	5.7	5.6	5.3	5
Overseas	10.2	10.2	10.2	10.2	10.2	10.2
Average Daily Spend (£ – all tourism)						
Scotland	22	32	31	31	31	31
Rest of UK	37	37	40	40	41	41
Overseas	35	36	36	36	36	36
Expenditure – Seasonality						
Jan to June & October to December (£m)	1068 (56%)	1235 (56%)	1128 (56%)	1160 (56%)	1215 (57%)	1250 (57%)
July to September (£m)	847 (44%)	970 (44%)	887 (44%)	910 (44%)	920 (43%)	940 (43%)
Expenditure – Regional Spread						
Outwith Edinburgh and Glasgow (£m)	1367 (71%)	1590 (72%)	1450 (72%)	1490 (72%)	1550 (73%)	1595 (73%)
Edinburgh & Glasgow (£m)	548 (29%)	615 (28%)	565 (28%)	580 (28%)	585 (27%)	595 (27%)
Occupancy						
Average % Hotel Room Occupancy	54%	57%	57%	58%	58%	58%
Average % Caravan Park Pitch Occupancy (April to October)	31%	33%	32%	33%	34%	34%
Average % Self-Catering Occupancy (April to October)	67%	72%	70%	71%	72%	73%

*1993 Overseas still Estimate.
**1994 Estimate.
***Targets based on UK + 1.5% p.a., overseas + 5% p.a., + 2.8% p.a. overall.

Table 9.2 STB's *The Corporate Report*: resource allocation – guideline figures (£000)

	1994/95	1995/96	1996/97	1997/98
Budgets for 1994/95 – 1997/98				
Block A				
Running Costs				
1&2 Salaries, Wages, etc.	2 681	2 813	2 650	2 535
3 Administration				
(a) General	1 587	833	833	681
(b) T & S	544	594	594	594
Sub-total	**4 812**	**4 240**	**4 077**	**3 810**
Block B				
Programme Expenditure				
5 Marketing				
UK	3 180	4 349	3 497	3 839
International	2 034	2 002	2 002	2 002
SCB & Exhibitions	833	770	770	770
Sub-total	**6 047**	**7 121**	**6 269**	**6 611**
6 Visitor Services	710	896	824	800
7 ATB Grants	2 755	2 755	2 755	2 755
8 Research	286	324	324	324
9 Planning	60	60	60	
10 Development	616	557	557	557
11 Press and Public Relations	294	454	304	304
Sub-total	**10 708**	**12 167**	**11 093**	**11 411**
Block C				
12 Quality Assurance (net)	270	270	270	270
Sub-total	**15 790**	**16 677**	**15 440**	**15 491**
13 Section 4 – Gross	1 685	200	51	—
– Receipts	(180)	(182)	(182)	(182)
– Net	1 505	18	(131)	(182)
Totals **Gross of S4 Receipts**	**17 475**	**16 877**	**15 491**	**15 491**
Net of S4 Receipts	**17 295**	**16 695**	**15 309**	**15 309**
1994/95 – 1997/98 Breakdown by Division				
UK and Ireland Marketing	3 800(22%)	4 968(30%)	4 091(26%)	4 391(28%)
International Marketing	3 144(18%)	2 947(17%)	2 915(19%)	2 863(19%)
SCB and Exhibitions	1 525 (9%)	1 359 (8%)	1 337 (9%)	1 302 (8%)
Visitor Services	4 927(28%)	4 975(29%)	4 860(31%)	4 765(31%)
Planning and Development	3 419(19%)	1 814(11%)	1 638(11%)	1 542(10%)
(incl. Section 4)				
Press and Public Relations	660 (4%)	814 (5%)	650 (4%)	628 (4%)
Finance and Administration				
Apportioned to Operating Divisions	—	—	—	—
Total Resources	**17 475**	**16 877**	**15 491**	**15 491**

Table 9.3 STB's *The Corporate Report*: UK Marketing

Key Consumer Objective
- To raise awareness of and propensity to purchase a holiday in Scotland.

Activities	Inputs (£)	Methods	Targeted Outputs
Performance Evaluation Summary 1994/1995 (Detailed)			
Advertising	1 707 000	TV campaign key questions:	
		1. First country mentioned as Scotland for holiday destination in Britain or Europe.	6% pre/8% post
		2. Scotland mentioned for holiday destination in Britain or Europe.	17% pre/20% post
		3. Seen any advertising recently for holidays in Scotland.	26% pre/35% post
		4. Likelihood of taking holiday in Scotland in next 12 months or 5 years:	
		(a) Next 12 months – very likely	8% pre/9% post
		– quite likely	7% pre/8% post
		(b) Next 5 years – very likely	15% pre/18% post
		– quite likely	24% pre/27% post
Performance Evaluation Summary 1995/1996 (Detailed)			
Advertising (net)	2 342 000	TV campaign key questions:	
		1. First country mentioned as Scotland for holiday destination in Britain or Europe.	8% pre/10% post
		2. Scotland mentioned for holiday destination in Britain or Europe.	20% pre/24% post
		3. Seen any advertising recently for holidays in Scotland.	35% pre/37% post
		4. Likelihood of taking holiday in Scotland in next 12 months or 5 years:	
		(a) Next 12 months – very likely	9% pre/10% post
		– quite likely	8% pre/8% post
		(b) Next 5 years – very likely	18% pre/19% post
		– quite likely	27% pre/28% post
		In addition, research will be carried out in 1995/96 to establish the extent to which consumers surveyed actually did holiday in Scotland in the next 12 months. It must be recognized, however, that STB cannot have responsibility for the conversion of intention into holidaying in Scotland as individual businesses have the key influence on this.	

itemized were assessed under four headings: activities, inputs, methods and targeted outputs, so that it was immediately clear what investments were being made in each, what they were designed to achieve and how their results were to be measured. Table 9.3 illustrates how much much was allocated to advertising in UK Marketing for 1994/5 and 1995/6, how its performance was to be assessed (through a number of consumer attitude measures), and what results were expected (quantified improvements in the attitudes measures).

In summary the STB *Strategic Plan* and the *Corporate Plan* which followed it fulfilled all the elements of marketing planning identified in this chapter: they provided a situational analysis of Scottish tourism; defined future marketing goals; specified exactly what marketing activities were going to implement them; what each of them was intended to achieve; the costs involved; and how the results would be measured at the appointed dates. As such they represent a particularly good example of best practice in **methodological approaches** to marketing planning. (NB: It is outside the scope of this chapter to evaluate the specific targets and expenditures set out.)

The Scottish Tourist Board was particularly well funded and provided with research-based information on which to analyse the present and plan for the future. Many marketing organizations will be less fortunate in their resources. Nevertheless, the approach offered by the Board is a model of the depth of analysis necessary for serious marketing planning. The Scottish Tourist Board has, of course, taken a commendable risk in being so upfront with its plans because it has effectively created the rope by which some may attempt to hang it if the targets are not met. In the past other destination organizations have been, and still may be, less ready to declare publicly their marketing intentions so specifically and risk being held to account by them. It is to be hoped that this will not be the case in the future. As we have emphasized in this text tourism marketing is affected by numerous factors outside the control of any marketing organization. (It may be, for example, that Scotland's tourism has suffered recently from inexorable competitive pressures from continental Europe, rising living standards which have meant that more people can go abroad, and changes in taste.) For publicly funded tourism organizations to come of age they must engage in the detailed marketing planning which has characterized other industries for decades instead of expressing their goals in the unmeasurable generalities and 'good news' hype which have too often been a feature of tourist boards in the past. Provided marketing plans are properly produced and based on the right kinds of analysis, even if the specific targets are not met, there is at least the basis for further refinement of objectives which is impossible if no measurable ones have been set. The purpose of a marketing plan is to provide a framework for managerial analysis and control, not to provide perfect predictions.

One final point may be made about the STB case. The Board's initiatives illustrate the blurred line between marketing planning and strategic management discussed earlier. Both the *Strategic Plan* and the *Corporate Plan* could equally be seen as examples of strategic management or marketing planning, suggesting that the ultimate differences between them are mainly semantic. Both were about short/middle-term planning, environmental responsiveness, strategic direction, market definition, resource analysis and organizational implementation – elements of both the newly fashionable concept of strategic management and the rather older one of marketing planning. Two things would lead us to suggest that they are best seen as marketing initiatives: firstly, the fact that they emanated from a marketing agency, the STB, which has sole public sector responsibility for marketing Scotland at the national level; secondly, the fact that they were produced under the direction of Derek Reid, the chief executive, who came to the STB from a major consumer marketing company, Cadbury Schweppes, and whose planning procedures have all the hallmark of practices widely used in mass consumer goods marketing, a fact that he has publicly acknowledged many times in proselytizing his concept of 'Scotland, the brand'.

Whatever name we give to the STB's recent activities they represent a sophisticated application of analytical marketing techniques and planning methods to destination development. Even Sir Francis Towle would have learned a few things from it.

BUDGETING TOURISM MARKETING

How much should an organization spend on marketing? The answer to this depends on what is included in the marketing budget. In packaged goods companies the marketing budget may include the costs of product development, consumer and marketing research, promotion and distribution. For many tourism organizations the marketing function is conceived more narrowly as research and promotion. The costs of developing a resort, hotel or attraction are, for instance, normally kept separate from the marketing function, even though product decisions are, as we have seen, theoretically part of the marketing mix.

The main budgetary decisions are four fold:

- How much in total should be allocated to marketing? The total marketing budget is sometimes called the **appropriation**.
- How much should be allocated to the main research and promotional options (e.g. to advertising, PR, sales promotion)?
- How should the budget be allocated in time (e.g. by season, time of year, etc.)?
- How should the budget be allocated geographically (e.g. by region, country, etc.)?

Main methods

There are no instant formulae for making any of these decisions but a number of rule-of-thumb techniques are widely used by marketing organizations in both tourism and other industrial sectors.

Affordability

This commonsense approach involves allocating marketing funds according to what is perceived to be affordable. For public sector organizations this may mean working within budgets laid down by local or national government; for others it may mean spending what remains when running costs and profits have been covered.

The problems with it are several. Notions of the affordable are always subjective, and have a tendency to be less than what is necessary. Affordability estimates are often based on 'left-over' amounts whereas marketing costs should be judged as investments for the future rather than residual amounts available from the past. Nevertheless, for many small tourism operators (small accommodation owners/small attractions/local authorities, etc.) affordability does provide a basic orientation to budget allocation.

Sales/profit ratios

This approach depends upon trying to decide a budget in relation to some level of sales or profit. As such it improves upon the earlier method which simply picks a figure out of the air. The ratio may be determined in relation to previous sales/profitability or projected future sales/profitability.

One of the problems is deciding what the ratios should be and, if based on expected sales/profits, adjusting them if they either exceed or disappoint expectations. Case study 9.1 below demonstrates the principle.

Competitive gearing

In a market where there are a number of direct competitors another method of allocating the appropriation is to benchmark major competitors. Knowing what competitors spend can be determined by consulting media expenditure data provided by organizations like MEAL in the UK

CASE STUDY 9.1

Advertising ratios and media in the US motel industry

A 1990 study conducted on advertising expenditures and media choice in the motel industry based on 269 motel owners and executives found that advertising/sales ratios ranged from 0.25% to 2.5% with the average being 1.25%. This was lower than that for hotels of 1.67% as reported in *US Lodging Industry*. The most used media reported by the organizations were: billboards (86%), travel guides (47%), newspapers (34%), brochures (30%), phone directories (21%) and direct mail (18%).

Source: Lowe and Kruger (1992).

or by observational appraisal of what media are being used. A seaside landlady will probably know where her competitors advertise and form some idea of what it is costing them.

Once a competitors' costs have been estimated the decision has to be whether to match them, exceed them or spend less. This will depend on the extent to which their goals are similar and their markets the same. (It would be pointless for a small hotel to try to spend as much as larger chains.)

A development that may improve the way in which international destination agencies monitor competitive budgets is a recent study by the World Tourism Organization which presented comparative data on total budgets and marketing appropriations of national tourism organizations between 1991 and 1993 (WTO, 1995). This allowed NTO planners to benchmark their spending against that by other countries. This study has already been utilized by the Scottish Tourism Research Unit at Strathclyde University (STB, 1996) in work for the Scottish Tourist Board designed to assess Scotland's marketing support needs in the context of the budgets of other nations.

Task approach

The task approach consists of identifying the goals of promotion, determining what media and materials are necessary to achieve them and then allocating money accordingly. For instance, a tourism organization might identify the total of number of prospects in a market segment, determine what media would reach them and then allocate money for using those media. Creative goals should also be considered since messages work better in some media than others (it would be difficult to promote a new long-haul destination without the use of colour advertising).

A mass tourist operator will have some idea of how many brochures must be produced and distributed to achieve a given level of sales and this will immediately dictate a level of expenditure on brochure production. A specialist tourist operator, distributing direct, will have to take into account not just the the cost of brochures, but the media advertising necessary to generate the requests for brochures from which final sales will flow.

The task approach depends upon defining the tasks to be achieved by marketing correctly and also a correct assessment of the mechanisms for achieving them (see Singapore Airline case study 9.2).

The four approaches are not mutually exclusive; indeed the greater the number of methods used to approach the setting of budgets, the greater the likelihood of a realistic decision.

SUMMARY

This has been a somewhat different kind of chapter from those which preceded it. It has attempted to draw together the threads of the previous

CASE STUDY 9.2

Singapore Airline's use of TV advertising in Britain: the task approach in action

Singapore Airlines (SIA) was one of the first major airlines operating in Britain to build its business with dominant use of television, an example which has since been followed by others, notably British Airways.

SIA first used TV as part of its business building in the early 1970s to achieve a number of basic strategic aims: to build an image which would give the airline stature, and provide reassurance and security (the promotional risk-reduction function discussed in Chapter 8, which is particularly important for relatively new entrants to a market). The campaign was designed to create a long-term corporate image rather than sell seats in the short-term. With a limited budget SIA initially confined its TV advertising to one TV area, London, because it was known to comprise a high proportion of SIA's prime target customers, business travellers. The campaign was designed to reach, not just the travellers themselves, but also influentials such as secretaries and travel business managers, who constituted part of the decision-making unit (also discussed in Chapter 8). TV was particularly appropriate for the creative message of the commercial featuring 'the Singapore Girl', which focused on the service quality provided by SIA's hostesses. The campaign was aired during summer, in and around the main evening news programme, which was known to be viewed by ABC1 executive travellers. Later the campaign was aired in Scotland.

Both campaigns were tracked after two years of TV advertising, using pre- and post-awareness studies, which compared results in the two TV test areas with UK areas which did not have TV advertising. The results were as follows:

London test: Awareness of SIA in London and UK pre and post TV campaign (%):

	Pre	Post
London	43	64
Rest of UK	25	30

Scotland test: Awareness of SIA in Scotland and UK pre and post TV campaign (%):

	Pre	Post
Scotland	19	46
Rest of UK	7	10

The success of the campaigns in achieving their initial objectives encouraged SIA to use TV again in 1978 to announce their joint leasing of Concorde, and in 1984 to launch new 'flagship' flights to the Far East and Australia.

SIA's use of TV illustrates the relationship between promotional objectives and implementational options – in short, the task approach to budgetary allocation and media choice.

Source: ITCA (1984: 8–11).

eight chapters by showing how marketing planning can be used to integrate the activities of the marketing mix. It has suggested that the main differences between marketing past and present are not conceptual, but differences in access to data, depth of analysis available to interpret it, and managerial methods used to plan from it. It has illustrated the differences through two longish case histories from 1927 and 1995.

It has also provided a critical comparison between marketing and strategic management with which many may disagree.

Finally, it has briefly reviewed some of the ways in which budgets are allocated to marketing planning.

This completes Part 1. In Part 2 we look at particular issues in tourism marketing.

REFERENCES

Ansoff, I.H. (1987) *Corporate Strategy*, Penguin.

Buttle, F. (1992) The marketing strategy worksheet, *Cornell HRA Quarterly*, June, pp. 55–67.

Chon, K.-S. and Olsen, M. (1990) Applying the strategic management process in the management of tourism organizations, *Tourism Management*, September, pp. 206–13.

ITCA (Independent Television Companies Association) (1984) *Viewpoint*, Spring, pp. 8–11.

Lowe, L.S. and Kruger, A. (1992) Motel advertising: practices and themes, *International Journal of Contemporary Hospitality Management*, 3(1), 17–21.

McDonald, M.H. (1989) *Marketing Plans*, Butterworth-Heinemann, Oxford.

Morrison, A. and Wensley, R. (1991) Boxed up or boxed in? A short history of the Boston Consulting Group share/growth matrix, *Journal of Marketing Management*, 7, 105–29.

Morton, H.V. (1927) *The Mayfair Hotel*, Gordon Hotels, London.

O'Hanlon, J. (1972) Making the marketing plan, *Marketing*, June, p. 45.

Olsen, M. (1991) Strategic management in the hospitality industry: a literature review, in Cooper, C.P. (ed.), *Progress in Tourism, Recreation and Hospitality Management*, Belhaven Press, London.

Olsen, M.D., Tse, E.C.-Y. and West, J. (1992) *Strategic Management in the Hospitality Industry*, Van Nostrand Reinhold, New York.

Phillips, P. (1994) An empirical investigation of the strategic planning practices of the corporate hotel sector in South Wales, *CHME Conference Paper*, Napier University, Edinburgh.

Porter, R. (1980) *Competitive Strategy*, Free Press, New York.

Scottish Tourist Board (1994) *The Strategic Plan*, Edinburgh.

Scottish Tourist Board (1995) *The Corporate Plan 1995/6–1997/8*, Edinburgh.

Scottish Tourist Research Unit (1993) *Making Tourism Work in Scotland*, Scottish Tourism Research Unit, The Scottish Hotel School, University of Strathclyde.

Scottish Tourism Research Unit (1996) *The Comparative Evaluation of*

Tourism Destination Performance: Scotland and European Tourism 1985–1994, The Scottish Tourist Board, Edinburgh.

Taylor, D. and Bush, D. (1974) *The Golden Age of British Hotels*, Northwood, London.

Webster, M. (1994) Investigating strategic management in context: Swallow hotels, *CHME conference paper*, Napier University, Edinburgh.

World Tourism Organization (1995) *Budgets and Marketing Plans of National Tourism Administrations*, WTO, Madrid.

REVIEW QUESTIONS

1. How different is modern tourism marketing from that in the past?
2. What are the essential features of a good marketing plan?
3. To what extent does the Scottish Tourist Board material presented in this chapter conform to the criteria you have identified in the previous question?
4. What are the differences and similarities between marketing planning and strategic management?

Part 2
Issues

This second part of the book moves from general principles to a number of specific issues of current importance in tourism marketing. They comprise four main areas:

- **Chapters 10–11** cover issues specific to the market development of two important geographical blocs, Eastern Europe (the fastest growing destination region in Europe) and the European Union (which remains the most important tourism generating region in Europe).
- **Chapters 12–13** cover issues specific to two major behavioural markets, the short-break market and the business market.
- **Chapters 14–16** cover applications of marketing to three important kinds of tourism organization – the small business, the destination agency and the airline company.
- **Chapters 17–18** cover two major operational issues of current importance to tourism marketers – IT and customer service management in the delivery of tourism marketing programmes.

Tourism marketing in Eastern Europe 10

J.J. Lennon

OBJECTIVES

By the end of this chapter the reader should:

*   Understand the major factors influencing tourism development in this region
*   Identify significant differential levels of tourism development
*   Appreciate factors influencing marketing of tourism in this region
*   Understand the significance of business tourism to the development of the region
*   Have a greater appreciation of difficulties of marketing and development in the context of Poland and the Russian Federation

INTRODUCTION

This chapter will consider the marketing of tourism in the emergent democracies of Eastern Europe. Inevitably such efforts at marketing destinations must be seen in the context of transition and development. Examples and discussion will be drawn from across Eastern Europe but in order to illustrate aspects of marketing and development detailed reference will be made to the contexts of two countries: Poland and Russia.

MARKETING AND EASTERN EUROPEAN TOURISM DESTINATIONS

Marketing Eastern European destinations to international visitors, who would introduce much required local currency and create demands for tourist goods and services, would seem to offer obvious benefits to those hard-pressed economies in the painful process of transition. Yet tourism development remains merely one aspect of emergent economies that requires investment and strategy. Infrastructure and transport systems require massive investment in almost all Eastern European and former Soviet states. Conditions for inward investment and economic and political stability vary greatly from nation to nation. In such a context of transition and reconstruction after communism, tourism planning and marketing has rarely been a priority of government policy. Developing a distinct national image for tourist marketing and an appreciation of the sustainable aspects of tourism development (now so critical in Western Europe) has rarely occurred.

The relationship between tourism development/marketing and the consequent effects on the environment is more complex in the emerging Eastern European and former Soviet states. The natural assets of Eastern European countries may be viewed as tourism resources which should be capitalized on. The development of tourism means that an infrastructure of transport systems, hotels and attraction developments must be imposed upon the current 'natural/original' state of these countries. A serious environmental dilemma is normally that to maintain a base of assets which are attractive to tourists the identity of a country is changed as a function of tourism development (Ryan, 1993). Such effects can be very positive; for example, in cities and towns urban regeneration can significantly enhance inner city areas and stimulate employment. Yet a concentration on urban development can focus tourist interest away form rural communities who would also benefit significantly from tourism development.

When tourism development is considered against a background of national reconstruction and transformation of the economy, the environmental argument becomes more problematic. In such a context the significant catalyst to development occurs primarily from business tourism (Lennon, 1994a, 1994b; Lockwood, 1993). Such demand is urban and often restricted to capitals. This frequently occurs in the context of a failing economy, rising unemployment and infrastructure which is extremely dated. Considering such critical developments against some of the worst pollution and environmental excesses on the planet (Woodward *et al.*, 1994) the arguments for protection of the fragile destination becomes more doubtful. Yet within Eastern Europe and the former Soviet states a considerable range of attractions and cultures exist which will inevitably suffer and change with the rapid transformation of the economies (Bauman, 1994). Tourism is increasingly being recognized as an important aspect of development in a number of these countries (Lockwood, 1993; Hall, 1993a). Growth in incoming tourists and increased resources to facilitate this are inevitably perceived as benefits. However, future tourist destinations are likely to be judged on the criteria of quality. Achieving a balance with the physical and social environments and developing a sustainable approach to tourism development may well be seen as inconsistent with the economic development initiatives of Eastern European countries. The appreciation that sheer growth in visitor numbers may be inconsistent with and harmful to the maintenance of quality environments has not been largely recognized. Further the need to consider carefully how tourist attractions and destinations are marketed has often been ignored. The concept of matching the type of tourist targeted (cf. Ryan, 1993) with a particular tourist zone has also often been ignored. In the following case studies and examples the context of such unplanned developments will be explored more fully. The role of long-term strategic planning over short-term maximization of profits is the dilemma that faces many countries emerging as destinations following the demise of the former communist regimes.

TOURISM DURING THE PROCESS OF TRANSITION

The qualitative problems of much of Eastern Europe's tourism is a legacy of its communist past. Both the quantity and quality of much of the accommodation throughout the region remains problematic (Hunt, 1993). Tourism development and growth was rarely at the forefront of economic development planning in the communist regimes. Invariably industrial development priority was towards primary and manufacturing sectors rather than services (Turnham 1993). Furthermore, infrastructure at almost all levels was extremely limited in both scope and quality. Yet, a number of Eastern European economies have embarked upon a programme of radical transformation of their economies and it is now becoming apparent that those who have grasped the nettle of reform fastest and most firmly are starting to show encouraging results. Poland, the Czech Republic and Hungary were very much the 'laboratories' or first attempts at market reform and are now starting to show continued improvements in GDP percentage growth (see Table 10.1 below). Tourism development is seen as important to the economic reforms of a number of these countries and this inevitably calls for investment in tourist accommodation, tourist attractions, general infrastructure and particularly transportation systems (Hall, 1993b). In the human resource area there is widespread agreement on the skill shortages which are particularly evident in service industries (see, for example, Hunt, 1993; Lockwood, 1993; Kennedy and Lennon, 1994). Clearly service quality aspects will similarly require investment in terms of training and education of staff at a range of levels.

The administration of tourism in the former communist countries of Eastern Europe in many cases remained locked in old communist structures and bureaucracy. This lack of administrative support is now further frustrated by the way former communist nomenklatura have managed to retain positions of legal or economic power (Sobell, 1993; Hall, 1993a). Against this background the currencies of many of the Eastern European countries are not internationally traded. Problems of conversion are further frustrated by excessive inflation rates and erratic financial measures introduced to alleviate the situation. Such financial instability creates uncertainty for investors at a strategic level (see Lennon, 1992, 1994a) and

Table 10.1   GDP growth year on year: Eastern Europe (%)

	1992	1993	1994
Bulgaria	−13.9	−5.0	0.0
Czech Republic	−6.9	0.0	2.0
Hungary	−4.0	−1.5	1.0
Poland	1.5	4.5	4.5
Romania	−10.5	−2.0	1.0
Russia	−20.0	−12.0	−6.0
Slovakia	−8.3	−6.0	−1.0
Slovenia	−6.5	−1.0	1.0
Ukraine	−14.0	−20.0	−8.0

Source: Economic Intelligence Unit (1994).

at an operational level for tour operators and travel agents who are attempting to price and sell holiday packages some 12–18 months in advance.

When financial and economic problems are combined with political instability then the tourism potential of whole countries can become problematic. The most obvious example here is the catastrophic effect the war in the former Yugoslavia has had upon international tourism to that region. Yet exceptions do occur – Croatia is starting to see the return of tourists following the Croat–Serb ceasefire. The country's national resources: a 5790 km coastline and some 718 islands, led to the development of a considerable tourism industry since the late 1960s. Some 570 000 tourists can be accommodated in hotels, campsites and other forms of accommodation. Indeed Austrian, Italian and German visitors are starting to return as the country invests some $13.4 m in promoting the country's tourism industry (Ojtojic, 1994). In addition tourists from the former Eastern European counties are also returning (see Table 10.2 and Figure 10.1).

It is apparent that Eastern Europe offers considerable tourism development and marketing potential (Lockwood, 1993; Hall, 1993a). These nations offer historical and cultural cities, winter sports centres,

Table 10.2   Visitors to Croatia by nationality (July to October 1993)

Czechs	15.6%
Slovenians	13.5%
Germans	13.5%
Austrians	12%
Italians	10.4%
Hungarians	5.8%
Others	29.2%

Source: *Business Central Europe* (1994).

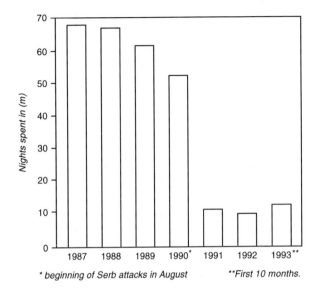

Figure 10.1 Tourist nights spent in Croatia 1987–93.
Source: National statistics.

areas of outstanding natural beauty, water-related tourism attractions, coastal tourism, spa locations and a growing base for business tourism (see Figure 10.2). However the profile, development potential and marketing for each of these countries is unique and merits individual consideration.

A further example of contrasting development and marketing issues is provided by Bulgaria. It has long capitalized on its natural tourism resources. Resorts were developed from the 1960s to capitalize on the sandy beaches and wooded coastline. Even in the confusion of post-communism Western European package holidaymakers (particularly from the UK and Germany) continue to be attracted to the low prices (see Table 10.3). Yet in marketing terms, although there is considerable awareness of the nature of the tourist resource, the image of this area is not great. Problems of quality in terms of accommodation and transport systems remain (Filipov, 1994).

The number of Eastern European tourists visiting Bulgarian Black Sea resorts has reduced dramatically. In 1987, more than 1.5 m tourists visited Bulgaria from Eastern Europe; by 1993 that figure had reduced to just 26 486. This must be compared with some 374 386 Western European tourists visiting the region in the same year. Such a change in tourist origin coincides with the demise in planned or state-influenced tourism and the reduction in Eastern European citizens' spending power.

Yet despite a growth in Western European tourists to Bulgaria, roads,

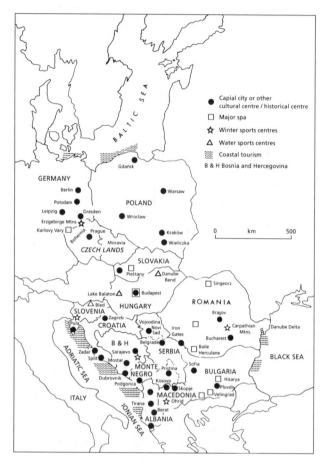

Figure 10.2 Eastern Europe: major areas for tourism.
Source: Hall (1993a)

air transport systems, water supply and telecommunications all require considerable investment. Furthermore, the lack of developed activities at the Black Sea resorts of Sunny Beach and Goldens Sands means that there are minimal activities for tourists to spend money upon. Furthermore

Table 10.3 Bulgaria's tourism sector (1993)

	Tourists	% change over 1992	Hotels	Beds
Sunny Beach	204 244	+11	112	25 000
Golden Sands	121 527	+4	80	14 000
Albena	112 613	+20	40	11 000
All coastal resorts	563 700	+7		

Source: Fillpov (1994).

problems persist with privatization strategies developed in Bulgaria's tourism industry. The large coastal hotels that accommodate many of the tourists and date back to the communist era are only now being considered for privatization. Tourism development lacks clear policy direction in Bulgaria with power and responsibility divided between:

- the State Committee for Tourism;
- the Privatization Agency; and
- the former state companies which operate the large coastal resorts.

As a consequence control of these large integrated accommodation, food and beverage, entertainment facilities remains in dispute. Despite the government undertaking valuation studies prior to sale, the hotels' management continue to lease out hotels to operators. In marketing terms this transfers to a lack of strategy and direction. What marketing that does go on is restricted to newspaper advertisements and brochure entries directed at low-cost package holidaymakers. In such a divisive case aspects of sustainable development and image review can only be considered as long-term future goals.

Clearly both Croatia and Bulgaria must be looked at individually in any consideration of marketing and development. Yet across Eastern Europe certain general trends are evident. For example, from an examination of privatization undertaken to date, hotels appear to offer a relatively attractive investment prospect. Indeed, in the first waves of privatization in Russia, Poland, the Czech Republic, Hungary and the Baltic states, it has been consistently one of the most popular sectors for inward investment by foreigners. Indeed, following the political changes in Eastern Europe at the end of 1989, almost every major international hotel company was considering expansion in the region. However, because of the high financial risk and the political and economic uncertainty there was a reluctance on the part of many to invest capital (Slattery, Feehely and Savage, 1994). The French international hotel company Accor, with their well-developed broad portfolio of brands, were amongst the few companies to risk large amounts of capital. As a consequence, their market share in this region has grown considerably, predominantly via joint venture developments. For example, Accor recognized the potential of Hungary at an early stage and made a major investment in the former state-operated Panonia Hotels.

The demand for quality accommodation (specifically hotels) has been both immediate and profitable. As a consequence this sector has seen investment since the profitability of hotel operations can be extremely high. Occupancy levels, achieved room rates, food and beverage yields and telecommunications profitability, all contribute to above average performance (Lennon, 1992). In some cases this has resulted in near saturation of demand, for example in Warsaw, where the Polish government's commitment to market reform coupled with the perceived demand for accommodation has heralded a sharp rise in international hotel group presence in Poland's capital. Indeed Poland represents a good example of tourism development in post-communist Eastern Europe and the case analysis below will hopefully illustrate a range of phenomena related to marketing and development potential.

POLAND: A CASE ANALYSIS

Since the advent of communist rule in Poland in 1945 inefficiencies within the planned system had gradually caused the slowing down and eventual stagnation of the domestic economy. The 1980s saw great economic and political changes which were initiated by 'Solidarity' (the trade union/ social movement for reform). The Polish government faced hyperinflation, falling Gross Domestic Product and a worsening balance of payment deficit (Polish State Office, 1992). This, combined with the severe domestic unrest, led to the fall of the communist government and the first partially free elections of 1989.

There was much hope in 1989 of a rapid transition to full political democracy and the development of a free-market economy via the massive privatization of large (formerly state-owned) companies (Lampe, 1992). It soon became apparent that if Poland were to successfully pursue its aims of creating a free-market economy it would need to look closely at reforming both its legal and economic infrastructure. The period of central planning (1946–86) had left a legacy of crippling foreign debt with a lack of financial resources from which to fund reforms. Furthermore, a vacuum existed in terms of personnel; few possessed the experience to guide the country through the necessary market-orientated reforms. By 1989 Poland faced rapid currency devaluation, galloping inflation, growing foreign debt and a worsening balance of payments deficit. In order to gain backing from the International Monetary Fund (IMF) and the World Bank (WB) it was conditional for the new government to embark upon a range of radical reforms. There was a pressing need to control money supply, restrain wage increases and reduce the budget deficit (Jackson, 1992).

A number of fundamental reforms were necessary:

- stabilization of currency/inflation;
- liberalization of the market environment;
- institutional transformation.

The Polish government choose the potentially high-risk strategy of simultaneously attempting all three – a strategy later to become known as 'shock therapy'. Such policies initiated stabilization of the spiralling inflation rate and rapidly engineered economic liberalization. Institutional reform in the form of privatization has followed. Significant success has been achieved: according to the Economic Intelligence Unit, Poland showed the largest GDP percentage growth in Eastern Europe during 1992 and is forecast to achieve the greatest growth in 1993 and 1994 in comparison to its Eastern European neighbours (see Table 10.1 above).

Recent indicators show that foreign investors remain encouraged by the potential of Poland. Factors such as a well educated workforce, a large potential domestic market of approximately 38 million, passable transportation links, historic ties to the potentially large markets in the east and relatively low wage costs combine to offer an attractive location for investment.

With cognizance of the above developments it is useful to focus on the tourism industry and how it is marketed since it remains a favoured sector for inward investment in Central/Eastern Europe, a region in which Poland is geographically at the centre (see Figure 10.3).

Tourism and Poland

Poland possesses many natural assets in terms of tourism development. There is a wide and varied topography with mountainous regions to the south, lake lands to the north and large forests to the east. Poland is a country steeped in history and culture that plays host to many artistic

Figure 10.3 Location of Poland and major capitals.
Source: Robinson and Bobinski (1994).

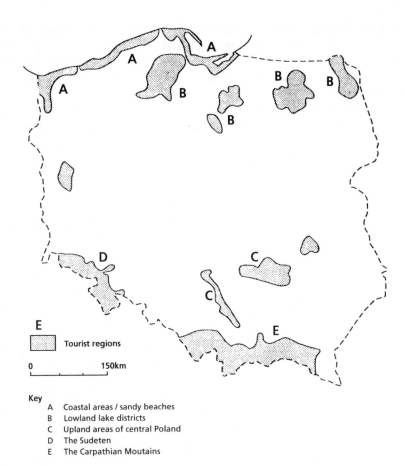

Figure 10.4   Tourist regions of Poland.
Source: Licinska (1985).

festivals. There are numerous attractive towns and cities with strong
cultural/religious and historical connections (e.g. Cracow, Poznan,
Gdansk). The former Polish authorities had recognized this, noting that
some 45.6% of the country was 'of tourist value'. Such areas included
forests, mountains, lakes and coasts (Dawson, 1991). Figure 10.4 identifies
the key tourism destinations with an annotated key.

During the period 1946–89 visitors to Poland consisted mainly of
tourists from within the former communist States. Indeed Poland, because
of its central European location, was an established destination for some
years for tourists originally from the former USSR.

This tourist profile has changed rapidly with the fall of communism in
1989. Now international visitors consist largely of Western business tourists who are used to, and expect, high standards of quality, facilities and
service. Yet the tourism infrastructure remains problematic. It is very
apparent that hotels must be upgraded and airports need to be expanded
and modernized. Yet the demand for quality accommodation is immediate

and it is the business market which has been the main catalyst to hotel investment and development in Poland. This relatively high-spending group have become regular hotel users in the region in the wake of the rapid expansion of foreign investment within Eastern Europe. Many companies expect their executives to be taking on average 20% more trips to the region (Hunt, 1993) over the next five years (1993–98). Such business tourism is especially concentrated in the capital of Poland, Warsaw, where most hotel development by international companies has occurred.

Warsaw is an important industrial city with up to 30% of its workforce being employed in the manufacturing sector. The Polish government is keen to establish the city as a gateway to Eastern Europe due to its central location. The rapid development of international hotels in Warsaw since 1989 is evidence of the astounding growth in business demand for quality accommodation (Panell Kerr Forster, 1992). As a consequence there have for some time been reports of over-supply and a reduction in the level of room rates and room occupancy achieved (cf. Menorca, 1991; Gordon, 1993). To date, the concentration of hotel development has been in the capital with Poland's other major cities Lodz, Cracow, Wroclaw, Katowice, Poznan and the ports of Gdansk and Szczecin experiencing much slower rates of foreign investment in the hotel sector (see Table 10.4). This trend is also reflected in the state of the business property market, with Warsaw constituting by far the most developed location (Jones, Lang and Wooton, 1993).

In addition to the business market other tourism markets have been identified: ethnic tourism and short-break accommodation demand. Ethnic tourism represents a growing sector. It may be defined as: 'Foreign travel to an ancestral home without the intention of settling . . . or undertaking temporary paid employment' (Ostrowski, 1991: 125).

Polish ethnic tourism is the result of the historical evolution of the Polish diaspora. The recent political changes and opening of borders have precipitated a considerable rise in incoming visitors (Ostrowski, 1991). This is sometimes disregarded by analysts since ethnic tourists are perceived to be low spending. However, exceptions do occur and many of the quality

Table 10.4 International hotel development projects in Poland 1989–93

Group	Location	Open	Rooms
Accor-Novotel	Warsaw	1993	250
Forte	Warsaw	1993	200 (renovation and extension)
Holiday Inn	Radom (Poland)	1994	119
Marriott	Warsaw	1989	484
Movenpick	Warsaw	1995	300 (at airport)
Radisson	Szczecin	1992	369 (in complex)
Vienna International	Warsaw	1994	320 (managed by Sheraton)
	Bydgoszcz (Poland)	1992	130

Source: Economist Intelligence Unit (1994).

njoyed buoyant trade during April 1994 from Jewish
country for the fiftieth anniversary of the Warsaw
tajczyk, 1994). It should also be noted that the utiliza-
es by the Polish domestic population has been recog-
nal operators such as Marriott. Local management at
ott claim that 60% of their food and beverage receipts
sh nationals at that property.

k market offers considerable short-term potential
gures are distorted by the influx of employment seekers
European countries who enter the country as visitors.
in Poland from Western Europe have risen from 18.0
rips in 1989 to 29.4 in 1992 (see Table 10.5).

noted that Poland faces significant competition from
pean destinations in the short-break sector. Indeed this
been more successful to date in Prague and Budapest.
In terms of attracting large numbers of tourists both Hungary and the
Czech Republic have been extremely successful even if the marketing
strategy has not always been totally effective. The main difficulty is that
the volume of tourists now flooding capitals such as Prague are of a
low-spend nature and outside of the business tourism sector, high-spending
tourists are still in a minority. However, Poland is also experiencing a
growth in coach-borne budget tourists who are more prepared to accept
the relatively low levels of accommodation that one finds in the state-
operated Orbis chain.

Marketing tourism in Poland

Printed media utilized for marketing purposes by the state sector hotels
has not benefited from updating. Brochures and hotel guides in the state-
operated hotel chains often remain similar to those utilized prior to 1989
(see Appendix 10.1). Clearly investment in marketing media has not been
seen as of critical importance. Photographs are poor, design is dated and
text is poorly translated. By comparison international chains locating in

Table 10.5 Visitors to Central Europe 1991–92

Country	Arrivals (m)		Change (%)		Market share (%)	
	1991	1992	91/90	92/91	1991	1992
Bulgaria	4	3.75	−11.1	−6.25	1.44	1.3
Czechoslovakia	8.2	8	1.23	−2.44	2.95	2.78
Hungary	21.86	20.18	6.58	−7.6	7.89	7.66
Poland	3.8	4	11.76	5.26	1.37	1.39
Romania	5.35	6.28	−17.95	17.16	1.93	2.18
Ex-USSR	6.89	6.9	−4.29	0.07	2.48	2.40
Central Europe	50.12	51	−0.26	1.82	18.03	17.75
Total Europe	277.90	287.53	−2.21	3.48	100	100

Table 10.6 Range of hotel ownership/management identified in Warsaw

Type of ownership	Hotel example
State-owned and controlled	Orbis, Grand, Novotel, Solec and Vera
Franchise with government control	Holiday Inn
Joint ventures between Western companies and the Polish government with Western management	Forte Bristol
Independent joint ventures with non Polish government involvement	Marriott

Poland have brought with them a professional and state-of-the-art approach to such media. For example, the most recent addition to the Warsaw hotel scene, the Hotel Bristol, has invested considerably in hotel-related marketing material. The Hotel Bristol, which opened in 1994, is part of the Forte Exclusive Hotel brand and is marketed as part of the worldwide Forte group, now part of Granada Plc. Printed material stresses the international standard of the property, its heritage and the high level of quality to be experienced in food, beverage and accommodation (see Appendix 10.2). Four main types of hotel ownership/management can be identified within Warsaw (see Table 10.6).

Essentially ownership is reflective of the approach to marketing. Where there is international involvement, either in the form of a joint venture or the presence of an international management contract, then the marketing function in terms of personnel and investment will be more developed. In the state sector in Warsaw such functions are rare and the level of expertise is not great.

Attempts have been made to market self-catering accommodation throughout the country via the Centre for Agricultural Counselling and the Centre for Tourist Information (1993). This is essentially an agro-tourism initiative aimed at generating increased revenue for rural inhabitants through offering self-catering or bed and breakfast facilities. However, the marketing media remain hampered by poor translation and unflattering photographs (see Appendix 10.3). The real problem here exists in the distribution of the brochure outside of Poland and the difficulties encountered in travel around Poland for the independent tourist. Areas such as the Mazury Lakes situated inland from Gdansk and Sopot are relatively undeveloped and of outstanding natural beauty, yet accessible accommodation remains at a premium and basics such as maps, guide-books and road signage are minimal (Simpson, 1994). Promotion of this area is seen simply as a non-priority and its relatively untouched beauty remains an undeveloped asset.

Poland's tourism development evidences clear urban bias to date. This is a pattern reflected across Eastern Europe since 1989 (see Table 10.7).

Table 10.7 Major international hotel projects signed since 1989

Group	Location	Open	Rooms
Accor-Novotel	Moscow	1992	488
	Hungary	1993	25 hotels
	Warsaw	1993	250
	Bucharest	1993	250
Forte	Warsaw	1993	200 (renovation and extension)
Holiday Inn	Brno (Czech Rep.)	1993	205
	Bratislava	1993	171
	Radom (Poland)	1994	119
	Budapest	1995	380 (renovation of Grand Hotel Royal)
	Lake Balaton (Hungary)	1995	380
Inter-Continental	Moscow	1991	403 (renovation)
Keminski	Budapest	1992	367
	Moscow	1992	235
Marco Polo	Gudauri (Georgia)	1989	122 (ski resort)
	Tbilisi	1991	n.a.
	St Petersburg	1993	288
	Nizhny-Novgorod (Russia)	1991	255
	Moscow	1991	64
	Moscow (Palace)	1993	370
Marriott	Warsaw	1989	484
	Budapest	1993	340 (formerly Duna Inter-Continental)
Movenpick	Warsaw	1995	300 (at airport)
Oberoi	Budapest	n.a	Conversion
Penta	Moscow	1991	n.a
	Prague	1993	309
Radisson	Szczecin	1992	369 (in complex)
	Moscow	1992	430 (in complex)
	Riga	1994	370
	Bucharest	1995	399 (in complex)
	Sochi	1994	400
	Budapest	1993	300
Rogner	Moscow	1993	n.a
	Tirana	1995	110
Sheraton	Tallinn	1993	365
	Tirana	1995	n.a
	Moscow	1994	450

Table 10.7 *(continued)*

Group	Location	Open	Rooms
Vienna International	Miedyzdroje (Poland)	1991	206 (resort)
	Warsaw	1994	320 (managed by Sheraton)
	Bydgoszcz (Poland)	1992	130
	Prague (The Savoy)	1993	61
	Prague (The Diplomat)	1990	374
	Karlovy Vary (Czech Rep.)	1990	87
	Plzen (Czech Rep.)	1994	204
	St Petersburg	1993	320

Source: Economist Intelligence Unit (1994); various media.

Poland gives a clear insight into the contradictions and difficulties to be overcome in tourism development. Whilst sustainable tourism developments are in evidence, e.g. the Green Lungs of Poland aimed at achieving ecologically sound tourism development in the forest areas of northern and central Poland (Kamieniecka *et al.*, 1993) their influence on international visitor numbers is minimal. The catalystic effect of business tourism and the development of an entrepreneurial class and the availability of cheaper forms of tourist accommodation has meant that short-term financial benefits are seen as the priority.

A further outcome of the activities of this entrepreneurial class is the diversion of tourism spending out of state coffers and into private hands. The largely unlicensed but rapidly expanding bed and breakfast industry of the Czech Republic and Hungary is a particularly good example of how the private entrepreneur can earn income (often in hard currency) without state interference through taxation registration.

IMAGE, ENVIRONMENT AND EFFECTIVE MARKETING

The problems of image in Eastern Europe are closely associated with environmental problems (Carter and Turnock, 1993). This has worked against tourism development and remains a considerable problem in marketing destinations. The communist system created the ecological problems that are only now becoming evident. The communist economic planners created a system that combined huge energy and raw material subsidies with an emphasis on greater industrial output. In order to achieve planned production targets environmental issues and the problems of waste were rarely considered. The region remained insulated from global trends towards greater energy efficiency through the availability of low cost/subsidized Soviet fuels. As a consequence countries such as Poland are now suffering alarming consequences:

> ... some 95% of Polish rivers are polluted, a third so badly the water cannot even be used for industrial purposes as it corrodes metal. Water from two-thirds of residential wells in Polish villages is undrinkable, mostly due to contamination from community sewage. The Baltic and Black Sea ecosystems are under serious threat form river-borne pollution, unmanaged fisheries and the dumping of toxic waste; 20 out of 26 commercial fish species have disappeared from the Black Sea since the mid-sixties, according to the World Bank.
>
> (Woodward *et al.*, 1994: 24)

The drinking water supply of the whole of Eastern Europe is under serious threat – a legacy from poor water resource management throughout the communist years. Pollution of surface water is acute and the polluted tributaries of the Danube, Vistula and Niva feed their impure water directly into the Baltic and Black Seas. Air pollution which affects much of Eastern Europe is a legacy of the overt relevance on low quality brown coal for heat and electricity generation. Accordingly the health of the population has been seriously effected (Carter and Turnock, 1993).

Albania is a particularly dire example of environmental and image-related problems. Water distribution is a major problem which means that few of the 3.3 million population have constant, let alone clean, water supplies. It is estimated that 40% of the water supply is wasted because of the dilapidated state of water pipes in the country (De Boerr, 1994). In places this results in the blending of drinking water and sewage. Furthermore, there is no treatment of sewage or waste water in Albania (Woodward *et al.*, 1994). Such environmental issues are seen as a lower priority than housing, unemployment and food distribution.

Albania's tourism statistics are remarkable by their absence. The relatively 'closed' status of the country under Enver Hoxha's regime meant visitor numbers were shrouded in mystery and were simply unavailable to organizations such as the WTO (see, for example, the lack of statistics for international tourism arrivals in *WTO Yearbooks 1991* and *1992*). However, it is very clear that tourism infrastructure is grossly inadequate. Tirana–Rinas airport is primitive, the road network is extremely undeveloped, and the rail service is also inadequate (Woodward, 1994). Tourist accommodation even in the capital is limited, although three further hotel development projects have been identified for the future (see Table 10.7 above). Once again business tourism located in the capital is seen as the first stage of an ambitious programme of tourism development. Nationwide development capitalizing on coastal, lakes, mountain and cruise based tourism is planned. However, in the short term the poor state of infrastructure coupled with food and fuel shortages, social unrest and problems related to the privatization programme have prevented Albturist (the state tourism organization) from developing marketing and promotion plans (Hall, 1993b). Consequently foreign tourists remain rare and inward investment is slow. The confusion that exists over ownership legislation and land restitution remains a deterrent despite the government's intentions.

The problems of environment and negative image are even more pronounced in the country which has the largest land mass and greatest potential for tourism development: Russia. To illustrate the complexities of the problems faced the following case analysis is included.

RUSSIA: A CASE ANALYSIS

Tourism development potential and the marketing of Russia

During the period of 'perestroika' (1985–91) international tourism to the USSR and latterly Russia saw great changes with decentralization and the partial dismantling of former tourism and hotel monopolies. Foreign visitors have now been granted greater access to areas of the world, long considered inaccessible. The change in attitudes was the result of three key policy aims:

* to develop access for tourists to almost all areas within the country;
* to increase foreign currency from tourism;
* to create more and better jobs in the service industry.

Yet the volume of tourist arrivals to Russia and Eastern Europe as a whole remains small. In 1992 Eastern Europe received just under 18% of total European arrivals, whilst the countries of the European Union received 65% (Hunt, 1993). Of this the former Soviet Union's share was 6.9 million in 1991. This constitutes a reduction of about 1 million on the previous year. The primary reason for this is the political instability and economic difficulties that Russia and the former Soviet states were experiencing and continue to experience.

Despite this, many oblast (regions) governments and cities see tourism development as an important development aspect. There are considerable and detailed plans for investment in hotels and foreign tourist facilities. For example, Moscow's tourism development plan details the potential for restoration of old hotels as well as the construction of new properties throughout the capital (Sorokin, 1993). However, the need for similar developments away from the main cities of Moscow and St Petersburg will also have to be addressed. In most secondary cities existing hotel stock is well below international standards and foreign investment in the form of new hotel developments have been slow to materialize (see Table 10.8 for an indication of the overt concentration of development in Moscow and St Petersburg).

The British Soviet Chamber of Commerce remains bullish on the future potential of tourism in the former Soviet states and particularly Russia. Even without the identified growth in business tourism, it is their belief that private trips and arranged tourism will also develop (see Table 10.9).

Table 10.8 Hotel projects in Russia since 1989

Company	Location	Opening date	Nature of property
Penta	Moscow	1991	500 rooms, joint venture
Metropol International Hotel	Moscow	1991	403 rooms, renovation, joint venture
Grand Hotel Europa	St Petersburg	1991	310 rooms, joint venture between Intourist, SIAB and Reso Hotels
Radisson Slavjonskaya Hotels	Moscow	1992	430 rooms, joint venture between Radisson Hotels International, American International and Intourist
Kempinski Hotel Ballshug	Moscow	1992	230 rooms, management contract by Kempinski
Accor-Novotel	Moscow	1992	516 rooms, joint venture between Sherotel and Aeroflot
Aerostar Hotel	Moscow	1992	407 rooms, joint venture between IMP (Group) Canada and Aeroflot
Marco Polo Nevskij Hotel	St Petersburg	1993	350 rooms, operated by Marco Polo
Marco Polo Palace Hotel	Moscow	1993	370 rooms
Vienna	St Petersburg	1993	320 rooms
Commodore Hotel	St Petersburg	1993	334 rooms, Effjohn of Finland
Sheraton Hotels	Moscow	1994	450 rooms
Grand-Otel	Moscow	1996	Joint-stock company, Infa-Otel
Taj Hotels	Moscow	n.a	Joint venture with Intourist
Oberoi	Moscow	n.a	400 rooms, joint venture
Holiday Inns	St Petersburg	n.a	

It is safe to assume that in the short to medium term business travel will continue to play the most significant role in tourism within Russia. As foreign investors explore the various and diverse market opportunities, the demand for quality accommodation will continue to grow. Indeed, it is the business market which has been the main catalyst to hotel investment and development in Russia. This relatively high-spending group have become

Table 10.9   Foreign travel to Russia (millions): current and projected*

| | Current | | Projections | |
	1990	**1991**	**1995**	**2005**
Arranged tours	2.1	2.0	2.4	4.5
Business trips	1.6	1.5	1.8	3.5
Private trips	1.3	1.2	1.5	2.6
Transit	1.5	1.4	1.8	3.2

*However, these figures raise a number of anomalies with regard to their calculation since Russia does not use the standard World Tourism Organization Categories and accordingly should be treated with caution. This is by no means a problem solely limited to Russia and data inconsistencies are not uncommon throughout Eastern Europe (Buckley and Witt, 1990).
Source: BSCC (1993: 9).

regular hotel users in the region in the wake of the expansion of foreign investment within the RSFSR economy. Many companies expect their executives to be taking on average 20% more trips to the region (Hunt, 1993) over the period 1994–98. Indeed international advertising placed on behalf of Radisson emphasizes the business and conference facilities and makes a virtue of non-Russian management (see Appendix 10.4). Such advertising is located in international business newspapers such as *The Financial Times* and specialist journals for the business community interested in the region (e.g. *Business Central Europe*). Clearly what is occurring is sophisticated targeted marketing capitalizing on a reliable high-spending sector. In such a context 'image' must convey efficiency and international standards.

Business tourism is especially concentrated in Moscow and St Petersburg (both of which are important transit points as well as political and economic centres), and in the regional capitals throughout Russia. However, the Greater Sochi coastline (the Russian Riviera) has been identified as an area with considerable growth potential by a number of commentators (see, for example, the Radisson conference and hotel complex shown in Appendix 10.4). This concentration of development in the Western and Central European region of Russia mirrors the pattern of concentration of accommodation and recreational facilities found in the former Soviet Union (see Figures 10.5 and 10.6). The maps identify the major areas of tourism to be:

- Moscow/St Petersburg;
- the Greater Sochi coastline;
- the former Baltic coastline of the USSR (now the coasts of Latvia, Lithuanian and Estonia).

Other areas with a history of international tourism such as Azerbaijan, Georgia and Armenia have been severely affected by the civil war that was occurring in the disputed region of Nagorno Karabakh. It has been suggested that the former 'closed' areas of Russia have significant

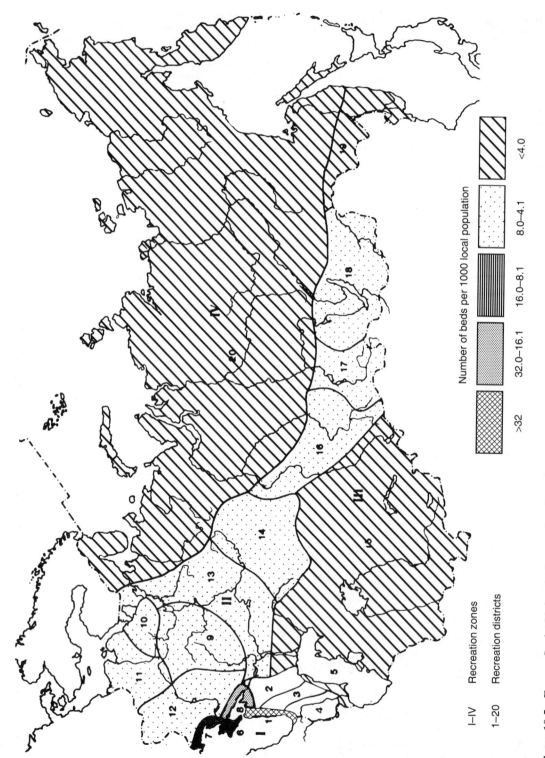

Figure 10.5 Former Soviet Union: bed spaces in official recreational accomodation, by recreational zone and district.
Source: Shaw (1991).

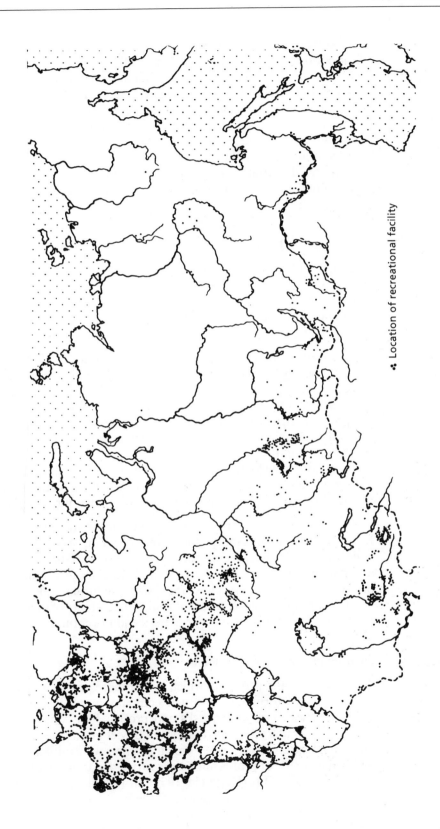

Figure 10.6 Former Soviet Union geographical distribution of official recreational accommodation.
Source: Shaw (1991).

long-term potential, e.g. the Murmansk region (Arctic Circle) and sections of the country bordering Kazakhstan and the Chinese border (part of the former 'Great Silk Road'). However, tourists will have to face the familiar problems of Eastern European transport systems: almost all aspects of air, road and rail transport from booking and reservations procedures to safety and accessibility (EIU, 1992). The short-break potential of the cities of Moscow and St Petersburg, which are within short flying distance, is negatively affected by the increasing lawlessness that now abounds (see, for example, Boulton, 1994). Until this situation stabilizes it is likely that quality hotel accommodation will be occupied by business tourists in the first instance.

Hotel supply in Russia

The supply of hotels in the majority of cities outside of Moscow and St Petersburg remains severely inadequate. Intourist (the former state hotel organization) still dominates with approximately 44 hotels capable of accommodating up to 32 000 people (EIU, 1992). Lockwood (1993) has offered the following classification of existing hotel stock:

*   old traditional hotels – mainly constructed prior to 1917 as purpose-built luxury properties now in need of considerable investment;
*   concrete/glass dormitories – many of these have been built since 1945 to accommodate Soviet tourists and visitors from other Eastern European countries. They were developed by city municipal governments and trade unions and played an important part in the supply of tourist accommodation prior to 1985;
*   new hotel developments – built or upgraded to international standards, mainly by international companies and located primarily in Moscow and St Petersburg and a small number of regional capitals.

Thus, despite the shortage of quality accommodation outside of Moscow and St Petersburg, the development in secondary cities and regional capitals remains dependent upon the political process rather than accommodation demand. At present the Russian government is giving priority to other sectors – agriculture, manufacturing, industry and residential housing which is considered vital to the stability of the country. The main form of hotel investment remains the joint venture.

Joint venture investment in hotels

A joint venture is a project in which two or more parties invest, normally resulting in the formation of a new company in which all parties have shares. Parties share assets, risks and profits. Joint ventures were first legalized in January 1987 by the former Soviet authorities as a means of attracting foreign investment. Foreign partners were initially entitled to a maximum of 49% of profits and were restricted in terms of ownership and repatriation of profits (Hertzfeld, 1991). In 1990 the legalization of 100%

Table 10.10   Foreign investment in Russia to 1993

Nation	No. of joint ventures	National investment as a percentage of hotel registered foreign investment
USA	1433	15.7% (of total)
Germany	1141	12.5%
UK	557	6.1%
Italy	511	5.6%
Austria	475	5.2%
Poland	438	4.8%
Finland	429	4.7%
China	347	3.8%
Switzerland	319	3.5%
France	283	3.1%
Sweden	238	2.6%
Bulgaria	237	2.6%
Canada	209	2.3%
Japan	173	1.9%
Hungary	164	1.8%

Source: British Embassy (1993a, 1993b).

foreign-owned enterprises gave investors a new opportunity to consider investment in Russia. Indeed, by 1992 foreign companies were allowed to obtain up to 100% of profits. The success of joint venture investment in the hotel sector is now documented. The Commercial Department of the British Embassy (1993a) reported that the most successful sector for joint ventures so far had probably been the service sector. The establishment of joint venture hotels and restaurants, and legal, accounting and consultancy firms are the areas which have attracted most inward investment. Indeed, by 1993 some 85% of foreign investment has been through joint ventures. Yet it is notable that the UK has not moved into the market with any great conviction (see Table 10.10).

The privatization reform programme in Russia is of an unprecedented scale and the potential for hotel and associated tourism development is contingent on how the transition of the economy progresses. Expansion of tourism necessitates basic tourism infrastructure and to a large extent this will depend upon Western investment and Western aid. Investment must move out of the main cities so that an evenly balanced tourism industry can be seen to be developing. Many obstacles must be overcome if the Russian government is to successfully attract foreign investors. Economic conditions, legal aspects, bureaucratic constraints and economic conditions must be addressed to prevent them hindering the process of inward investment. Fundamentally, political instability remains a major concern for hotel companies hoping to expand into this new market and this remains a major reason for the low concentration levels attained thus far. The expansion and growth of non-business tourism once again faces the

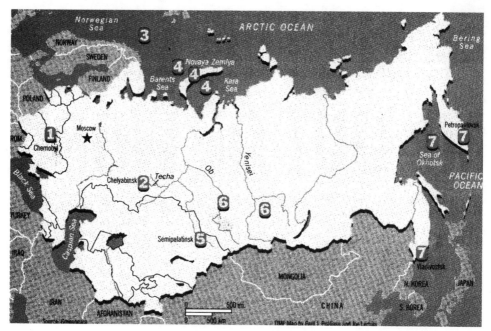

Figure 10.7 Indication of primary areas of nuclear contamination.
Source: Jackson (1992).

1 Chernobyl: Reactor meltdown in 1986 released heavy isotopes of plutonium and uranium, contaminating a large area around it. There are 19 similar reactors still in operation.
2 Chelyabinsk: A tank containing waste from a nuclear weapons plant exploded in 1957. Nearby Techa River is severely contaminated.
3 Barents Sea: Off Norway, a submarine sank with its reactor and nucleararmed torpedoes on board.
4 Novaya Zemlya: Nuclear test and dump site. Up to 17 000 lb of solid radioactive waste was dropped into the waters offshore and into the Kara Sea between 1964 and 1990. Nearly 165 000 cubic metres of liquid waste were dumped into the Barents Sea between 1961 and 1990, and at least eight submarine reactors, some with fuel, and three reactors from an ice-breaker were sunk off Novaya Zemlya.
5 Semipalatinsk: Nuclear testing area. More than 125 atmospheric explsions were set off before 1962, and some 300 underground tests have been carrried out since.
6 Ob and Yenisei Rivers: Contaminated by waste from nuclear weapons plants.
7 Petropavlovsk, Sea of Okhotsk and Vladivostok: Radioactive waste has been dumped in these areas by the Pacific Fleet.

dual difficulties of a dated and low quality image combined with serious environmental problems. Nuclear contamination is a particularly severe problem in Russia. Across this massive nation a legacy of the military industrial complex and the nuclear power industry will hamper tourism development for many years to come (see Figure 10.7). Accordingly it is as yet difficult for many involved in Russian tourism to attempt to plan for strategic growth of the industry against such a grave macro environmental picture.

SUMMARY

Marketing Eastern European tourism destinations is a process that is invariably linked to tourism development in the context of economic transition. Against a background of growing unemployment, decaying public services, rising inflation and pitifully inadequate infrastructure tourism development must be considered. Tourism is one among many industries requiring investment, renewal, strategic planning and ultimately marketing. The emerging picture is no longer of a 'bloc' but rather of a range of nations and emerging democracies all possessing differing tourism resources set against individual cultures, identities and traditions. Progress is evident but both development and marketing will be faltering and for the moment short-term returns are seen as preferable to long-term sustainable development.

APPENDIX 10.1 MARKETING BROCHURE FOR ORBIS
HOTELS, WARSAW, POLAND (JANUARY 1994)

ORBIS-GRAND
Hotel ****
00-522 Warsaw
ul. Krucza 28
tel. 29-40-51
tlx 813422
grand pl

Businessmen and tourists wishing to make a closer acquaintance of Warsaw are invited to stay in the Grand Hotel situated in the town centre.
The hotel has many single and double rooms with private baths, radios and telephones as well as several 2-3 room suites with TV sets. There is round-a-clock telex service which assures fast connections with the whole world, a barber's and hairdresser's. Newspapers in different languages are available at the kiosk. Three restaurants, two of them with dancing floors, feature continental and Polish style cuisine. The Olimp night club, on the top floor, provides not only a splendid panoramic view of the city but also good entertainment. There is also a cocktail bar and a great chance that you will take a fancy to our pastry.

We believe that your stay in our hotel will be a pleasant experience.

ORBIS-VERA
Hotel ****
00-366 Warsaw
ul. Wery
Kostrzewy 16
tel. 22-74-21
tlx 8116184
very pl

Welcome to our modern Vera Hotel.
It is located at the crossing of ul. Wery Kostrzewy and ul. Szczęśliwicka. The hotel has 146 single and double rooms and 6 suites, all with private baths, radios and telephones.

There is a good restaurant seating 150 persons, a cocktail bar seating 30 guests as well as a quiet and comfortable hotel lounge where newspapers in foreign languages are available. A multifunctional hall for 100 persons is suitable for holding banquets and conferences. On the ground floor, there is a branch of Intershop (PEWEX), a kiosk with newspapers, "it" tourist information centre, and a currency exchange desk.

The hotel car park can accommodate 70 cars. Vera Hotel provides rent-a-car services as well.

We believe that your stay in our hotel will be a pleasant one.

APPENDIX 10.2 MARKETING BROCHURE FOR THE HOTEL BRISTOL, WARSAW, POLAND (JANUARY 1994)

HOTEL BRISTOL

W A R S Z A W A

HOTEL ℬRISTOL

W A R S Z A W A

The Malinowa Restaurant

Bedroom

Salon

S E R V I C E S   A N D   A M E N I T I E S

Opened December 1992

Location Situated on the "King's Walk" - Warsaw's most fashionable street, 5 minutes from the old town, 20 minutes from Okecie Airport.

Restaurants The Malinowa with 56 seats. A selection of traditional Polish dishes with a French influence.

The Marconi with 160 seats. Informal Italian.

Cafe Bristol with 60 seats. Viennese light meals and pastries.

Column Bar.

Bedrooms and Suites 163 rooms and 43 suites.

Room Service 24 hours.

Air Conditioning In all rooms and public areas.

No smoking rooms 40%

Leisure Facilities Indoor pool, sauna and steam sauna.

Banquets and Conferences	Cocktails	Dinner	Conferences
Salon Moniuszko	60	35-43	30-55
Salon Chopin (1+2)	120	60-85	40-100
Banquet Foyer	150	------	------
Salon Kossak	------	------	10
Salon Curie	------	------	10-25
Salon Mickiewicz	------	------	10-25
Salon Reymont	------	------	15-30
Salon Kiepura	------	------	20-50

The Hotel Bristol, pictured in the early days of the century.

Business Centre	Translation services, secretarial services, Business Centre systems and software available for guests own use.
Car Rental	Through the concierge.
Parking	Off-street parking.
Credit cards	All internationally accepted cards.
Reservations	For your nearest Forte Hotels Reservation/Sales Office please call:
Germany	Toll Free 0130-2944
France	(1) 42-61-10-65
Italy	Toll Free 1678-20088
Sweden	(08) 663-01-15
United Kingdom	0345 40 40 40
Japan	0120-09-40-40
Australia	Toll Free 008-22-2446 within Sydney (02) 267-2144
USA/Canada	Toll Free 1-800-225-5843

HOTEL BRISTOL

WARSZAWA

Ul. Krakowskie Przedmieście 42/44, 00-325 Warszawa, Poland
Tel: + 48 2 625 25 25, Fax: + 48 2 625 25 77
Satellite link Tel: + 48 39 12 10 61, Satellite link Fax: + 48 39 12 10 67

An Exclusive Hotel
of the World
by Forte

APPENDIX 10.3 MARKETING BROCHURE AND
INFORMATION GUIDE FOR THE AGROTOURISM
INITIATIVE, GDANSK REGION, POLAND

35 | **KONKOL ZOFIA** | Sianowo 83-328; gm. Kartuzy; tel. 81-57-88

Budynek mieszkalny jednorodzinny dla turystów przeznaczone są 2 pokoje 2-osobowe. Możliwość korzystania z kuchni, łazienki, WC. W odległości 100m piękne jezioro otoczone lasem, zabytkowy kościół, sklepy. Miejscowość położona na terenie Kaszubskiego Parku Krajobrazowego. Możliwość zbierania grzybów, jagód, łowienia ryb i pieszych wędrówek. Najbliższa restauracja w Kartuzach - 12km. Dojazd autobusem z Gdańska i Kartuz. Możliwość zabrania psa lub kota.

2 chambres à 2 lits destinées aux touristes dans maison individuelle; accès à la cuisine, salle de bains, WC; à 100m - beau lac, forêts, église historique, magasins; village situé sur le terrain du Parc Naturel Régional de Cachoube; possibilité de récolte de champignons et myrtilles, de pêche et de randonnée à pied; restaurant le plus proche à Kartuzy (12km); accès par autobus de Gdańsk ou de Kartuzy; chiens et chats acceptés.

Einfamilienhaus. Zu vermieten 2 Doppelzimmer mit Bad und WC. Küchenbenutzung. Ca 100m entfernt ein schöner See von Wald umgeben. Im Dorf eine alte Kirche und Läden. Die Ortschaft liegt innerhalb des Kaschubischen Landschaftsparks. Es gibt Möglichkeit Pilze und Beeren zu sammeln. Fische zu angeln und Fußtouren zu unternehmen. Die nächste Gaststätte in Kartuzy 12km entfernt. Busverbindung von Gdańsk und Kartuzy. Hund oder Katze können mitgebracht werden.

2 double rooms in a detached house available to tourists. Access to kitchen, bathroom, WC. A beautiful lake surrounded by wood 100m away, old church, shops. Situated in the Kaszuby View Park. Mushroom and blueberry picking, fishing and walks. Nearest restaurant in Kartuzy - 12km. Can be reached by bus from Gdańsk or Kartuzy. Dogs and cats admitted.

36 | **PRYCZKOWSKA STEFANIA** | Sianowo 83-328; gm. Kartuzy; tel. 81-57-20

Budynek mieszkalny, piętrowy, 2 pokoje 2-osobowe na parterze przeznaczone dla turystów. Możliwość korzystania z kuchni, stołówki, WC. W odległości 200m piękne jezioro. Na miejscu sklepy ogólnospożywcze, zabytkowy kościół. Malownicze okolice, możliwość wycieczek pieszych i rowerowych. Lasy Kaszubskiego Parku Krajobrazowego, rezerwaty przyrody. Najbliższa restauracja w Kartuzach - 12km. Dojazd z Gdańska autobusem.

2 double rooms on the ground floor in a two storey house available to tourists. Access to kitchen, canteen, bathroom, WC. A beautiful lake 200m away. Old church, grocer's shops. Picturesque surroundings. Walks and cycling. Woods of the Kaszuby View Park, nature reservation. Nearest restaurant in Kartuzy -12km. Can be reached by bus from Gdańsk.

2 chambres à 2 lits, rez-de-chaussée, à la disposition des touristes - cuisine, cantine, salle de bains, WC; beau lac à 200m; en place - magasins, église historique, paysages pittoresques; possibilité de randonnées à pied et à bicyclette; bois du Parc Naturel Régional de Cachoube, réserves naturelles; restaurant le plus proche à Kartuzy (12km); accès par autobus de Gdańsk.

Wohnhaus 1.Stock hoch. Zu vermieten: 2 Doppelzimmer im Parterre mit Bad und WC. Küchenbenutzung, Mittagstisch. Ein schöner See 200m entfernt. Im Dorf Lebensmittelgeschäfte und eine alte Kirche. Malerische Gegend für Wanderungen und Fahrradausflüge. Wälder innerhalb des Kaschubischen Landschaftsparks. Naturreservate. Die nächste Gaststätte in Kartuzy 12km entfernt. Busverbindung von Gdańsk.

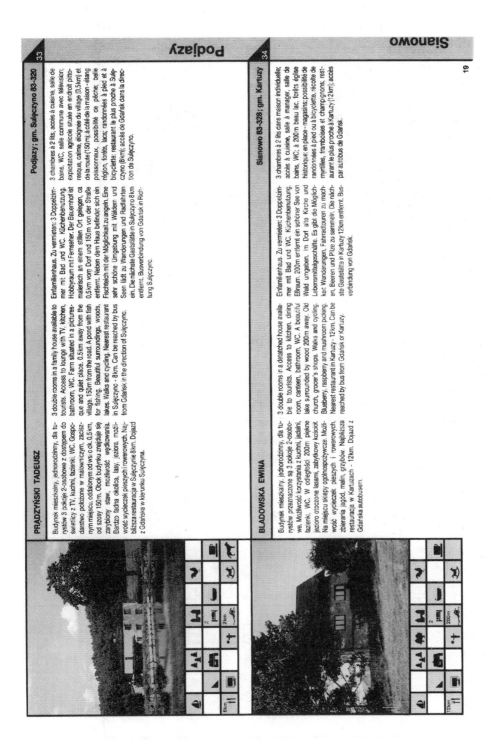

PRĄDZYŃSKI TADEUSZ

Podjazy ; gm. Sulęczyno 83-320

Budynek mieszkalny, jednorodzinny, dla turystów 3 pokoje 2-osobowe z dostępem do świetlicy z TV, kuchni, łazienki. WC. Gospodarstwo położone w malowniczym, zacisznym miejscu, oddalonym od wsi o ok. 0,5km, od szosy 150m. Obok budynku znajduje się zarybiony staw, możliwość wędkowania. Bardzo ładna okolica, lasy, jeziora, możliwość wycieczek pieszych i rowerowych. Najbliższa restauracja w Sulęczynie 8 km. Dojazd z Gdańska w kierunku Sulęczyna.

3 double rooms in a family house available to tourists. Access to lounge with TV, kitchen, bathroom. WC. Farm situated in a picturesque and quiet place. 0.5km away from the village. 150m from the road. A pond with fish for fishing. Beautiful surroundings, woods, lakes. Walks and cycling. Nearest restaurant in Sulęczyno - 8km. Can be reached by bus from Gdansk in the direction of Sulęczyno.

Einfamilienhaus. Zu vermieten: 3 Doppelzimmer mit Bad und WC. Küchenbenutzung. Hobbyraum mit Fernseher. Der Bauernhof ist malerisch an einem stillen Ort, gelegen, ca 0,5km vom Dorf und 150m von der Straße entfernt. Neben dem Haus befindet sich ein Fischteich mit der Möglichkeit zu angeln. Eine sehr schöne Umgebung mit Wäldern und Seen lädt zu Wanderungen und Radfahrten ein. Die nächste Gaststätte in Sulęczyno 8km entfernt. Busverbindung von Gdansk in Richtung Sulęczyno.

3 chambres à 2 lits, accès à cuisine, salle de bains, WC, salle commune avec télévision; exploitation agricole située en endroit pittoresque, calme, éloignée du village (0,5km) et de la route (150m); à côté de la maison - étang poissonneux, possibilité de pêche; belle région, forêts, lacs; randonnées à pied et à bicyclette; restaurant le plus proche à Sulęczyno (8km); accès de Gdansk dans la direction de Sulęczyno.

BLADOWSKA EWINA

Sianowo 83-328 ; gm. Kartuzy

Budynek mieszkalny, jednorodzinny, dla turystów przeznaczone są 3 pokoje 2-osobowe. Możliwość korzystania z kuchni, jadalni, łazienki, WC. W odległości 200m piękne jezioro otoczone lasami, zabytkowy kościół. Na miejscu sklepy ogólnospożywcze. Możliwość wycieczek pieszych i rowerowych. Możliwość zbierania jagód, malin, grzybów. Najbliższa restauracja w Kartuzach - 12km. Dojazd z Gdańska autobusem.

3 double rooms in a detached house available to tourists. Access to kitchen, dining room, canteen, bathroom, WC. A beautiful lake surrounded by wood 200m away. Old church, grocer's shops. Walks and cycling. Blueberry, raspberry and mushroom picking. Nearest restaurant in Kartuzy - 12km. Can be reached by bus from Gdansk or Kartuzy.

Einfamilienhaus. Zu vermieten: 3 Doppelzimmer mit Bad und WC. Küchenbenutzung. EBraum. 200m entfernt ein schöner See von Wald umgeben. Im Dorf alte Kirche und Lebensmittelgeschäfte. Es gibt die Möglichkeiten: Wanderungen, Fahrradtouren zu machen, Beeren und Pilze zu sammeln. Die nächste Gaststätte in Kartuzy 12km entfernt. Busverbindung von Gdansk.

3 chambres à 2 lits dans maison individuelle; accès à cuisine, salle à manger, salle de bains, WC; à 200m beau lac, forêts église historique; en place - magasins; possibilité de randonnées à pied ou à bicyclette, récolte de myrtilles, framboises et champignons; restaurant le plus proche à Kartuzy (12km); accès par autobus de Gdansk.

APPENDIX 10.4 EXAMPLES OF ADVERTISING FOR
RADISSON HOTELS, MOSCOW AND SOCHI, RSFSR

Stay in the comfort of our four Tsar Hotel.

24 hour room service? Business centre? Executive fitness club? English speaking staff? In the heart of Moscow? This can't be right.

For the business traveller to Moscow, the Radisson Slavjanskaya Hotel provides more hospitality than you dared hope for. Whereas other hotels still display the 'Nyet' approach to service, 'Yes I Can' sums up the attitude of our expertly-trained staff to make your stay a real pleasure.

Added to which, Russia's only American-managed hotel offers Moscow's *best* business facilities, including round the clock secretarial and translation services. (And the city's *only* colour photo-copier!)

After the sweat and toil of the day, we've a range of places to unwind: Skandia and Cafe Amadeus, for eating continental-style; The Exchange, where we serve steaks flown in from the USA; and The Lobby Bar, one of the places to be seen in town. So when your business takes you to Moscow, come to the place – the Radisson Slavjanskaya Hotel and Business Centre.

Radisson.
SLAVJANSKAYA HOTEL
AND BUSINESS CENTRE

MOSCOW, RUSSIA

For your confirmed reservation, call free on 0800 19 1991.

—— THIS MUST BE THE PLACE ——

AT YOUR CONFERENCE IN SOCHI, YOU MAY HAVE TO LOCK THEM IN.

Despite its obvious distractions, the key to a great meeting is the luxury Radisson Hotel Lazurnaya in Sochi. We have meeting facilities for as many as 400 people, with simultaneous translators and state-of-the-art A/V equipment. For smaller private parties or functions we have a choice of 5 smaller rooms. Not to mention the hotel itself: its dazzling restaurants, bars, pools, casino, rooftop nightclub, fitness centre and every thing under the Black Sea sun. Talking of which, it has a private beach with every recreation imaginable. The Radisson Lazurnaya Sochi is part of the world's fastest growing up-scale hotel group, (the folks who introduced 'feel good' into the Russian language). Put the wind in your sales. Call us now on International: (358) (15) 661 5999/ Russia and C.I.S: (8) (8622) 975 974 or fax Int: (358) (15) 661 5998/Russia and C.I.S: (8) (095) 956 1704.

Radisson
HOTEL LAZURNAYA - A RADISSON RESORT

BARCELONA · BERLIN · BUDAPEST · LAKE GARDA (OPENING JULY)
LONDON · MOSCOW · SALZBURG · SEVILLA · STOCKHOLM · SZCZECIN
RIGA (OPENING 95) · EUROPE · THE AMERICAS · ASIA PACIFIC

REFERENCES

Bashford, D. and Robinson, A. (1994) Poland Survey, *The Financial Times*, 30 November.

Bauman, Z. (1994) After the patronage state: a model in search of class interests, in Bryant, C. and Mokrzyck, E. (eds), *The New Great Transportation*, Routledge, London.

Boulton, L. (1994) St Petersburg's belief in better times fades, *The Financial Times*, 17 May, p. 17.

British Embassy (1993a) *Joint Ventures in Russia*, Commercial Department, Moscow, June (based on information published in *Izvestia*, 1993).

British Embassy (1993b) *The Russian Foreign Investment Environment*, Commercial Department, Moscow, June.

British Soviet Chamber of Commerce (1993) Editorial – Foreign travel to Russia, *BSCC Bulletin*, December, p. 9.

Buckley, P.W. and Witt, S.F. (1990) Tourism in the centrally-planned economies of Europe, *Annals of Tourism Research*, **17**(1).

Business Central Europe (1994) Country Indicators, *Business Central Europe*, April, p. 81.

Carter, F.W. and Tunock, D. (eds) (1993) *Environmental Problems in Eastern Europe*, Routledge, London.

Centre for Agricultural Counselling/Gdansk Centre of Tourist Information (1993) *Wies Polska Zaprasza*, Gdansk Centre for Tourism Information, Gdansk.

Dawson, A. (1991) Poland, in Hall, D.H. (ed.), *Tourism and Economic Development in Eastern Europe and the Soviet Union*, Belhaven Press, London.

De Boerr, H. (1994) Freedom to own and to pollute, *The Financial Times*, 29 June, p. 20.

Economic Intelligence Unit (1994) Facts and figures, *Business Central Europe*, February, pp. 64–6.

EIU (1992) *Commonwealth of Independent States – The Changing Political and Economic Situation*, International Tourism Reports No. 3, Economist Group, London, pp. 58–79.

Filipov, F. (1994) Stuck in the Sand, *Business Central Europe*, **2**(12).

Gordon, R. (1993) Warsaw packed, *Caterer and Hotelkeeper*, pp. 33–5.

Hall, D.R. (1991) New hope for the Danube Delta, *Town and Country Planning*, **60**(9), 251–2.

Hall, D.R. (1993a) Tourism in Eastern Europe, in Pompl, W. and Lavery, (eds), *Tourism in Europe: Structures and Developments*, CAB International, Wallingford, pp. 341–59.

Hall, D.R. (ed.) (1993b) Transport and economic development, *The New Central and Eastern Europe*, Belhaven Press, London.

Hertzfeld, J.F. (1991) Joint ventures: saving the Soviets from perestroika, *Harvard Business Review*, January/February, pp. 3–15.

Hunt, J. (1993) Foreign investment in Eastern Europe travel industry, in *EIU Travel and Tourism Analyst*, No. 3, pp. 65–85.

Jackson, J. (1992) Nuclear time bombs, *Time*, **140**(23), 48–49.

Jackson, M.R. (1992) Company management and capital market development in the transition, in Lampe, J. (ed.), *Creating Capital Markets in Eastern Europe*, Woodrow Wilson Centre Press, USA.

Jameson, S. (1993) Insider's guide, *Business Traveller*, September, p. 56.

Jones Lang and Wooton (1993) *Quarterly Investment Report: The European Property Market*, Winter, 1992/93.

Kamieniecka, J., Drewnowski, J., Kamieniecki, K., Kassenberg, A. and Wojicik, B. (1995) *Green Lungs of Europe*, Institute for Sustainable Development, Warsaw.

Kennedy, K. and Lennon, J. (1994) Staff recruitment and retention in quality hotels in Eastern Europe: a case analysis of Warsaw, Poland, *Proceedings of Third Annual Research Conference of the Council for Hospitality Management Education*, Napier University, April.

Lampe, J. (1992) *Creating Capital Markets in Eastern Europe*, Woodrow Wilson Centre Press, USA.

Lampe, J. (1992) *Creating Change Markets in Eastern Europe*, Woodrow Wilson Centre Press, USA.

Lennon, J. (1992) Opening the box: unlocking the tourism potential of the former Soviet states, *International Association of Hotel Management Schools Conference Proceedings*, Manchester Polytechnic, 7–9 May.

Lennon, J. (1994a) Hotel and tourism privatisation in Eastern Europe; Process and Progress in Leslie, D. (ed.) (1994) *Leisure and Tourism Towards the Millenium*, LSA.

Lennon, J. (1994b) Leisure and tourism privatisation in Eastern Europe: progress and process, *International Leisure Studies Association Conference Proceedings*, Glasgow, 5–8 April.

Licinska, D. (1985) *Geographia: Poliska*, Interpress, Warsaw.

Lockwood, A. (1993) Eastern Europe and the former Soviet states, in Jones, P. and Pizan, A. (eds), *The International Hospitality Industry – Organisational and Operational Issues*, Pitman, London, pp. 25–37.

Menorca, E. (1991) Warsaw hotel market update, *The Hotel Valuation Journal*, Winter.

Ojtojic, N. (1994) War, what war? *Business Central Europe* **2**(12), 27–8.

Ostrowski, S. (1991) Ethnic tourism – focus on Poland, *Tourism Management*, June, pp. 125–31.

Pannell Kerr Forster Associates (1992) *Eurocity Survey*, PKF, London.

Polish State Office (1992) *Poland Invites You*, Warsaw, Poland.

Ratajczyk, A. (1994) Ghetto ceremony – demand risen, *The Warsaw Voice, Polish and Central European Review*, **2**(272), 9 January, pp. 4–5.

Robinson, A. and Bobinski, C. (1994) Cleared for take-off, in Financial Times Survey – Poland, *The Financial Times*, p. 1.

Ryan, C. (1993) *Recreational Tourism: A Social Science Perspective*, Routledge, London.

Shaw, D. (1991) The Soviet Union, in Hall, D.R. (ed.) *Tourism and Economic Development in Eastern Europe and the Soviet Union*, Belhaven Press, London, pp. 119–40.

Simpson, P. (1994) Of water and woods, *Business Central Europe*, **2**(3).

Slattery, P., Feehely, G. and Savage, M. (1994) *Quoted Hotel Companies: The World Markets 1994*, Kleinwort Benson Research, Tonbridge Wells.

Smith, L. and Alexander, N. (1994) Poland Survey, *The Financial Times*, 30 November.

Sobell, V. (1993) Privatization in Central and Eastern Europe, *EIU Economic Trends*, 2nd quarter, pp. 71–87.

Sorokin, P. (1993) All flags are welcome – tourism department programme, *Novecon Delovoi Mir*, 15 July.

Turnham, D. (1993) *Employment and Development – A New Review of Evidence*, OECD, Paris.

Woodward, C. (1994) Call it, um, 'exotic', *Business Central Europe*, **2**(1).

Woodward, C., Lowenberg, S., Kinnear, A., Knights, S. and Koza, P. (1994) Environment survey, *Business Central Europe*, **2**(12), 33–47.

World Tourism Organization (1991) *Yearbook of Tourism Statistics*, WTO, Madrid.

World Tourism Organization (1992) *Yearbook of Tourism Statistics*, WTO, Madrid.

REVIEW QUESTIONS

1. What are the major factors influencing tourism development in Eastern Central Europe?
2. Identify one nation in Eastern Central Europe and conduct a brief tourism audit of its market potential in terms of tourism.
3. What are the main marketing problems facing the emerging tourism destinations of Eastern Central Europe?
4. Critically examine the view that Eastern Central Europe is primarily a business tourism market?
5. To what extent is risk, both financial and political, the major determinant of tourism development in Eastern Central European destinations.
6. 'Eastern Europe will not provide a substantial part of international hotel company portfolios for decades to come . . . we see no real hope of any real domestic market developing until well into the next century.' Critically review the above analyst's comment in respect of your knowledge of Eastern European tourism market potential.

The EU leisure tourist market

11

R. Davidson

OBJECTIVES

By the end of this chapter the reader should:

- gain an understanding of some of the main indicators used to assess tourism marketing developments in Europe;
- gain an overview of tourism marketing developments in five leading European generating countries: France, Germany, Spain, Italy and the Netherlands;
- be able to distinguish the different pace at which these tourism developments are happening in the countries inventoried;
- be able to identify the extent to which these European trends represent stability or change in relation to previous patterns.

INTRODUCTION

Western European markets dominate international tourism. With the exception of the USA, Japan and Canada, the other seven out of the world's top ten countries in terms of international tourism spending are in Western Europe. Five out of these big spenders (Germany, the UK, France, the Netherlands and Italy) are already members of the EU, and the other two, Austria and Sweden, are set to join their ranks.

Nevertheless, there are notable disparities within the EU in terms of international tourism spending. While smaller member states such as Greece, Ireland and Portugal account for only about 1% each of total EU tourism expenditure, Germany, the UK, France and Italy between them account for three-quarters of all spending on tourism by EU nationals.

But this situation is evolving rapidly and the traditional overview of European tourism patterns – an overwhelmingly predominant north–south flow during the summer months – is being blurred by new trends.

One of the most important of these comes as a result of the relatively new-found ability of southern Europeans to afford international leisure travel. As their economies expand (often as a result of EU intervention to spread European prosperity more evenly among member states) the Spanish, Portuguese and Greeks are increasingly finding themselves able to realize their long-standing ambitions to travel for leisure. In many cases, their first experience of international tourism leads them to explore the cities and culture of northern European countries, thus adding to Europe's growing south–north tourism flow.

What is the state of the Western European leisure tourism market in the mid-1990s? Some of the most useful information on individual countries' tourism markets is to be found in the different market surveys carried out periodically by the various national tourist organizations. The British Tourist Authority (BTA) and Maison de la France (MDLF) have the responsibility for marketing Britain and France respectively to overseas markets, most of these situated in Western Europe. The following profiles are based on the BTA's and MDLF's own guides to key continental tourism markets. They provide a snapshot image of the French, German, Spanish, Italian and Dutch leisure tourism markets in the mid-1990s, in the context of evolving trends in these countries' holidaytaking habits.

FRANCE

Market profile

The early 1990s' recession in France led to high levels of unemployment, with the professional and executive classes being particularly hard hit. Despite government measures designed to improve the situation, general unemployment has stubbornly refused to drop below the 12% level. Despite the general economic depression, several ongoing factors make the French tourism market one of Europe's most robust.

The French holiday entitlement is among the most generous of all European countries. The legal minimum leave entitlement for French employees is five weeks, but many companies now give six weeks as a result of individual employees' long service or collective agreements with trade unions.

There is a long tradition of holidaytaking. Fifty-nine per cent of French people take at least one annual holiday, almost the same as the proportion for the UK, which has approximately the same size of population. This means that in 1992, 34.6 million French people took one holiday or more, a substantial increase on the figure for 1975 of 27 million. Higher disposable incomes and increased leisure time across all social classes is largely the cause of this increase in France, as in other Western European countries.

There are certain categories of French people more likely to take holidays than others. In terms of age, for example, the under 20s and those

Table 11.1 Number of holidays taken by the French in 1992

	In millions	% of total
France	56.4	84.3
Abroad	10.6	15.7
Total	67.0	100.0

Source: INSEE (Institut national de la statistique et des études economiques) (July 1993).

between 40 and 50 years old have the strongest tendency to go on holiday. Residents of Paris and the surrounding region and those at senior management and company director levels are other groups taking frequent holidays. France's ageing population also plays an increasingly important economic role. They spend more than other groups on their food, health and leisure activities. In 1975, 36% of retired people took holidays; today this has increased to 50%. This market segment is heavily targeted by the retail travel trade offering them a multitude of special deals, and is recognized in France as having very strong future potential.

In 1992, the French took a total of 67 million holidays of four days or more, divided up as shown in Table 11.1. As can be clearly seen, the French have a marked tendency towards spending their holidays in their own country. In 1992, 84.3% of all holidays taken by the French were taken in France. And the reason for this is not difficult to understand. While the British and the Germans, for example, have to go abroad for guaranteed sunshine in summer and guaranteed snow for winter sports, France has a Mediterranean coastline and Alpine and Pyrenean ski slopes to satisfy the needs of its domestic tourist market.

In addition to the country's own inherent attractions as a tourist destination, the BTA *1994–1995 Market Guide to France* suggests several other reasons for the strong French tradition of domestic holidaytaking: 'the somewhat unadventurous spirit of the French, linked to a lack of foreign language skills and a certain apprehension about foreign cultures and – in particular – foreign food'.

Nevertheless, in 1992, one summer holiday in five taken by the French was spent abroad and total spending on foreign tourism that year amounted to US$14 700 million. The most popular destinations were Spain, which attracted 18.7% of French foreign holidaymakers, followed by Portugal (8.9%), Italy (8.9%), Germany and Austria (7.6%). Britain and Ireland were in fifth place with a market share of 6.6%. France's continuing links with its former colonies also have an impact on its tourist market profile: over 300 000 visits to Morocco were made in 1992.

How do the French get to their holiday destinations? As would be expected in a country where the car is king, the private vehicle features prominently as the major means of transport, as shown in Table 11.2.

Finally, it is useful to compare the different types of destination favoured by the French. Some interesting distinctions are highlighted in

Table 11.2 How the French got to their destination in 1990: % of holidays taken based on 63 million visits

Type of transport	In France	Overseas
Train	11.5	5.6
Car	81.3	40.2
Coach	2.5	10.2
Plane	3.1	41.0
Boat	1.1	3.0
Total	100.0%	100.0%
Based on	52 m visits	11.1 m visits

Source: INSEE (1992).

Table 11.3. Seaside holidays score highly, indicating a continuing French love of travelling to sun destinations for beach holidays. Touring holidays are much more popular abroad than in France, and foreign cities hold a strong attraction for the French.

Tourism trends

As holiday entitlement has increased, the French have tended to break down their holiday entitlement into several blocks of one, two or three weeks taken at different periods throughout the year. Thus, the traditional pattern of French holidaytaking – one long holiday lasting three or four weeks in July or August – has gradually been changing over recent years. Now, 27% of the population take more than one holiday a year. This compares with an average of 19% in the other EU countries.

Short-breaks are also becoming increasingly widespread, as more and more French people take advantage of bank holidays and extend them into mini holidays by adding weekends and extra days. A substantial proportion of these short-breaks are spent by the French in their own *résidences secondaires*. France has more of these holiday homes than any other country in the world, and even families on a fairly modest income

Table 11.3 What type of holiday destination the French preferred in 1992: % of holidays based on 67 million visits

Type of holiday destination	In France	Overseas
Tour	4.4	18.6
Sea	40.8	33.5
Mountains	19.1	6.2
Countryside	26.3	17.5
Town	9.4	24.2
Total	100.0%	100.0%
Based on	56.4 m visits	10.6 m visits

Source: INSEE (1992).

level may own a holiday flat by the sea or a simple country cottage in which to spend long weekends and other short holidays. General holidaytaking by the French is therefore becoming more frequent but of a shorter average duration.

According to the BTA data, all of France's top five destinations lost market share in 1992, indicating perhaps an increase in diversity and adventurousness in destination selection. At the same time, market share increases were noted in the cases of Scandinavia (up 0.7% to 2.8%), Turkey (up 1.3% to 2.6%) and the Benelux countries (up 4.4% to 5.6%). All in all, Western European destinations accounted for 68.1% of all foreign holiday visits made by the French in 1992.

Retail travel trade

Only 11% of all holidays taken by the French are booked using the services of a tour operator or a travel agent, a significantly smaller proportion than in Britain and Germany. However, this figure rises to 34% in the case of French holidays abroad, according to the Société Nationale des Agences de Voyages (SNAV, the French equivalent of ABTA). As might be expected, travel agencies tend to be used more for long-haul destinations and destinations not easily accessible by car. Even so, the domination of the market by powerful tour operators offering an abundant supply of foreign package tours is by no means as strong a feature of the French tourism industry as it is in Britain or Germany – as Table 11.4 shows: It is primarily younger holidaymakers, the management classes and retired people who book package holidays. There is a heavy concentration of travel agencies in the Paris region, where 25% of all the country's package holidays are purchased.

GERMANY

Market profile

With its population of 80 million inhabitants and its long, strong tradition of taking holidays abroad, Germany is Western Europe's major international tourism force in terms of spending. Approximately one-third of all EU spending on international tourism is German in origin.

Table 11.4 How the French book their holidays

	Germany	Britain	France
% of population taking a holiday	66.8	60.0	59.1
% of holidays abroad	67.6	34.8	18.0
Packages sold (millions)	14	10.5	3.5

Source: BTA, *Market Guide to France 1994–1995.*

Over 70% of the population take at least one holiday a year. In 1992, 29.3 million holidays (of four days or more) were taken abroad and 15.4 million holidays were taken by Germans in their own country.

The main foreign destinations visited by the Germans on holiday that year were as follow: Spain (5 million visits), Italy (3.9 million), Austria (3.4 million), France (2.4 million) and Greece (1.8 million). All in all, Germans spent a total of US$ 37 200 million on holidays outside their own country in 1992 (Studienkreiss für Turismus, *Reiseanalyse 1992*). The respective shares of Germany's top four foreign destinations are shown in Figure 11.1 in terms of percentages.

German reunification has been widely blamed for the economic slow-down of that country. According to the Federal Statistics Office, there was only 1.5% growth in the Gross Domestic Product (GDP) of West Germany in 1992, compared with an increase of 3.7% the previous year. However, there was 6.1% growth in the GDP of the new Länder in the eastern half of the country for 1992. The unevenness of these developments is reflected in Germany's tourism patterns: 1992 saw, for the first time since the 1988/89 season, turnover in financial terms increasing faster than actual reservations. The German retail travel trade recorded a rise in turnover of 22% for an increase in the number of clients of 17.6%. How much of these increases was due to the growth in tourism in ex-East Germany can be seen in Table 11.5.

The impact of former East Germany on tourism consumption will continue to grow, in line with the economy of that region. As for the country as a whole, although the cost of reunification has been immense, there is no doubt that in the long term it will benefit from the high level of investment currently being undertaken in its eastern half.

During the 1990s, German spending on tourism has been increasing each year, with close to perfect regularity, as the following figures from the Deutsche Bundesbank show:

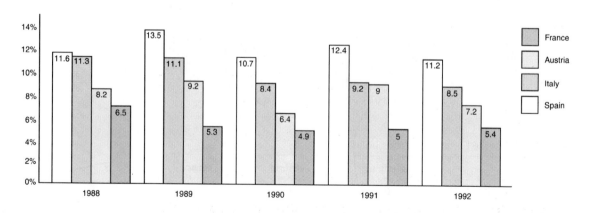

Figure 11.1 Germany's main overseas destinations (% share of market).
Source: MDLF, *1994–1995 Marketing Plan*.

Table 11.5 Changes in the market for German tour operators: 1992 compared with 1991

	Former West Germany	Former East Germany	Total
Clients	+13.22%	+108.0%	+17.60%
Sales of package holidays	+17.72%	+110.2%	+21.54%
Sales of other products	+6.16%	+88.5%	+11.50%
Turnover	+18.62%	+117.9%	+22.01%

Source: MDLF, *1994–1995 Marketing Plan.*

1989: 37 700 million DM
1990: 47 600 million DM
1991: 51 000 million DM
1992: 57 000 million DM

Every year is thus a record year for German spending on tourism – and also a record for the staggeringly high deficit of Germany's tourism balance of payments: of the order of 40 000 million DM in 1992.

Tourism trends

The 1990s have also seen substantial growth in the volume of long-haul tourism from Germany. In 1992 alone, there was an increase of 33.6% in holidays taken outside Europe, and an increase of 38.15% in visits by Germans to the USA. (For this single year, however, it must be borne in mind that not only was the dollar weak, making travel to the USA very attractive, but also that long-haul travel had been severely hit the previous year by the Gulf War.)

Nevertheless, there is no doubt that long-haul holiday destinations are being increasingly favoured by Germans, while traditional Mediterranean destinations are steadily losing their appeal for this market. As the German tourist shows a more and more marked preference for visiting 'unspoilt' destinations, Spain and Italy are gradually seeing their lead being challenged. And while to some extent the German market for Mediterranean destinations (including North Africa) has been sustained in recent years by the arrival of former East Germans, these tourists do not have the same spending power as their fellow countrymen and women from the western Länder. Tourism receipts per German tourist have, consequently, fallen in Mediterranean destinations.

The MDLF *1994–1995 Marketing Plan* for Germany highlights several other emerging trends:

- The length of the average main holiday is falling, and now stands at just under 16 days.
- But this is more than made up for by the current increase in short-breaks.
- Consumer expectations are rising, particularly in terms of standards of comfort, service and environment.

- This has resulted in a definite move towards independent travel as opposed to mass tourism. Flexible, tailor-made holidays are very much in favour.
- Cultural pursuits and the possibility of participating in outdoor activities while on holiday are increasingly sought after.

Retail travel trade

Just over 8 million Germans buy the travel products of the vast tour operators who between them control the lion's share of foreign tourism from that country. The largest European tour operator is TUI (Turistik Union International) which, with three and a half million clients a year, has a turnover of one and a half times more than its closest European rival, the Thomson Travel Group. TUI is followed by NUR (Neckermann und Reisen) with 2.3 million clients and ITS with 1 million. These giants among tour operators have a massive distribution network of their own: TUI alone has 7200 outlets in Germany.

SPAIN

Market profile

After decades of economic despondency, Spain has taken its place among the world's top ten economic powers. In the ten years between 1981 and 1991, its GDP rose steadily by 5% a year, at a time when the growth rate of most Western countries failed to go beyond 3%. This progress was due, to a great degree, to its entry into the EU, which enabled Spain to modernize its means of production, improve its transport infrastructure and train its workforce.

Despite this economic progress, still fewer than half of the Spanish population as a whole take an annual holiday. But certain regions show a much greater tendency to go on holiday: in Madrid, this is the case for 63% of the population, in Catalonia 58% and in the Basque Country 59%. And while foreign destinations are growing in popularity, nevertheless the market for domestic holidays still predominates, with only 19% of Spanish people going abroad in 1992. The Spanish tourist market for holidays outside that country is generally led by young people, who are particularly eager to explore foreign countries. In 1992, the Spanish spent US$ 4700 million on foreign tourism (World Tourism Organization).

Of the holidays taken abroad, 76% were taken in Europe, 9% in America, 6% in Africa and 4% in Asia. Regarding Europe, neighbouring countries are the most visited. France has about one-third of the market and Portugal has 20%. The other preferred European destinations for the Spanish are Italy (11%), Germany (5%), Switzerland (3%) and the UK (3%).

The popularity of neighbouring destinations combined with the relative ease of getting to them keeps down the average length of stay abroad – currently around six days.

Tourism trends

Their rapid economic and social development contributed significantly to the growth in foreign holidaytaking by the Spanish during the 1980s. Nevertheless, in this decade, two factors have played their part in considerably slowing down this growth: a series of devaluations of the peseta in the years 1990–92, and (as a result of the recession of the early 1990s) an unemployment figure sticking stubbornly around 3 million, 20% of the active population – a European record. As a result, Spain's main markets have experienced reductions in both the length of stay and levels of expenditure by their Spanish visitors.

Nevertheless, even if the market is showing no immediate signs of further expansion, the aspirations of the Spanish as regards their holidays have been undergoing subtle changes. The MDLF *1994–1995 Marketing Plan* for Spain points out that certain forms of tourism, in which the Spanish have shown little interest up until this decade, have been growing fast in popularity. This is notably the case for adventure and sports-related tourism (mountain biking, white-water rafting, golfing, etc.), rural tourism and health-related tourism products such as thalassotherapy – the use of sea water treatments to induce a feeling of well-being and relaxation.

Retail travel trade

The Spanish travel trade is highly structured, with different tour operators specializing in certain products (rural tourism, golf, health tourism . . .) and certain market segments (youth travel, senior citizens, etc.). For the neighbouring foreign destinations in particular, the travel trade has to fight hard to sell its services and products to a market which is highly independent and quite capable of organizing its own visits. For example, less than 15% of Spanish visitors to France use the services of travel agencies to get there.

ITALY

Market profile

Italy is the world's fifth most powerful industrial nation, with its wealth concentrated in the north of the country within the highly prosperous Lombardy–Piedmont–Liguria triangle.

About 55% of Italians take at least one holiday per year. In 1992, they made 40 million domestic trips of two days or longer and 16.6 million foreign trips, of which 86% were leisure trips and 14% for business-related purposes.

In 1992, the Italians spent a total of US$ 12 000 million on foreign tourism in 1992, representing an increase in 31% in spending on this item since 1987, when exchange controls were abolished in Italy. Over the same period, however, spending on domestic tourism remained static.

The socioeconomic changes which Italy has undergone since the late 1980s have manifested themselves in many fields, not least in Italian tourism trends. During that period, travel and tourism have established themselves as essential items of consumption for Italians, and now stand in second place in the list of items of family expenditure, after food and drink, according to the Italian National Statistical Institute (ISTAT).

The MDLF *1994–1995 Marketing Plan* for Italy suggests that, for Italians, travel means the search for new, unspoilt places. It also means the search for cultural activities and new acquaintances, as well as the need to enjoy themselves in an environment where the quality of life is better than that which they experience in their everyday lives.

According to a report by the market consultancy CENSIS, Italian tourists feel a strong need to express their personalities while on holiday and do not like to be regarded as anonymous members of a group. They are very demanding and are prepared to pay highly for quality tourism products with the individual touch. The same source claims that the elements of a holiday which Italians are prepared to pay the most for are, in order of importance: the quality of their accommodation, the level of comfort of their means of transport, the possibility of getting away from the tourist crowd, the quality of the food and drink, the warmth of the climate and good quality customer relations skills.

In their wish to avoid the tourist crowd, Italians are increasingly prepared to take their holidays outside the main tourist season, with the month of September becoming a more and more attractive time for their summer holidays.

Tourism trends

Figure 11.2 shows the progression of the market shares of Italy's main foreign destinations, given as a percentage of all Italian tourism abroad. The continuing popularity of Mediterranean destinations can clearly be seen. And, unlike the German tourist market for example, the appeal of the Mediterranean for Italians has actually been growing in recent years.

The three principal motivations which determine Italian tourism tastes were identified by the MDLF as follows:

- urban tourism, associated with the discovery of cities' cultural heritage, and activities such as shopping, entertainment and eating out;
- the exploration of nature, linked to their search for good quality, unspoilt environments;
- seaside tourism, which would appear to hold a continuing, if not growing, appeal for the Italians.

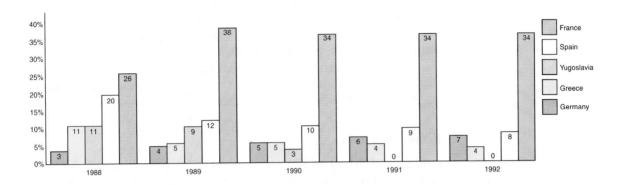

Figure 11.2   Italy's main overseas destinations (% share of market).
Source: MDLF, *1994–1995 Marketing Plan*.

To these three themes may be added the fast-growing number of foreign language study holidays taken by young Italians intent on preparing themselves early for their future professional lives.

Foreign destinations have been the main beneficiaries of the Italians' growing fondness for travel and tourism. MDLF explains this as being partly a result of Italians' wish to escape, albeit temporarily, their country's many political and economic scandals while on holiday, but also cites as contributory factors the following features of the Italian domestic tourism product:

Italian hotels are expensive, often shabby and unable to meet tourists' demands for quality accommodation.

- The environment is often polluted, poorly conserved and a victim of recent uncontrolled economic development.
- The transport infrastructure is poor and out of date.
- The Italian heritage has been largely neglected by the public powers with responsibility for its conservation and protection.
- The tourism industry as a whole offers poor value for money compared with neighbouring European destinations.

These factors must bear at least part of the responsibility for the recent drop in Italy's travel balance of payments, which, while still positive, fell one-third, from US$ 9000 million in 1987 to US$ 6000 million in 1992.

Clearly, though, another major contributory factor has been the Italians' apparently insatiable demand for foreign travel. Despite a severe drop in the value of the lira in 1992, a survey carried out in 1993 by the consultants Trademark Italia confirmed that the trend towards foreign holidaytaking was set to continue. The survey showed that:

- 97% of Italians said that, far from giving up their holidays in the near future, they intended to go away more often;
- 90% of those questioned said that they would be taking as many, if not more, holidays abroad, rather than stay in Italy where 'the domestic tourism product was no longer satisfactory';
- 93% said that they would not be reducing the amount they spent on holidays, but would most likely be spending more.

Retail travel trade

A high proportion of Italians (around 85%) use the services of travel agencies and tour operators to book their holidays abroad. Those in the +50 age group are particularly likely to book their holidays in this way, and in fact account for about 60% of the Italian retail travel trade's turnover. This sector is characterized by a multitude of small businesses, mainly concentrated in the north, and there are no equivalents to the giant tour operators and travel agency chains found in the UK and Germany. The biggest Italian tour operator, Alpitour, ranks only 21st by size of turnover in the list of largest European TOs, and the second, Aviatour, holds the 44th place.

THE NETHERLANDS

Market profile

With one of the lowest inflation rates of all European countries and a consistently strong currency, the Netherlands has benefited from its close economic alliance with neighbouring Germany, which is its main customer as well as its main supplier of manufactured goods.

Amsterdam, Rotterdam, The Hague and Utrecht, the four largest cities, define the borders of the highly urbanized 'Randstad' area which houses over 40% of the population and the majority of the country's manufacturing industries.

Economic prosperity is reflected in the Netherlands' tourism patterns. At 68%, the Dutch rate of holidaytaking is one of the highest in Europe, and is growing. Foreign holidays (of four days or more) generally outnumber domestic holidays at a ratio of about 2:1 – generally about 4½ million of the former to over 8 million foreign holidays in the mid-1990s.

Annual Dutch spending on foreign tourism during those years amounted to over US$ 9000 million, a tremendously high figure for a country of only 15 million inhabitants.

The principal foreign destinations for Dutch tourists are shown in Table 11.6. France is the clear favourite and appears to be building on its lead: up 3% in 1992. EuroDisney may have played its part in boosting the numbers of Dutch tourists visiting France. With their great love of theme parks, the Dutch have been eager to try out Europe's biggest.

Table 11.6 Main overseas destinations for the Dutch market

	Market share (%)	Number of visits (1000s)*	Average length of visit
France	21	1700	16.3
Germany	13	1034	11.2
Austria	10	773	12.1
Spain	8	647	14.7
Belgium/Luxembourg	7	553	9.8
Italy	5	373	15.6

* All figures relate to visits of four days or more by those aged 18+.
Source: NIPO, *General Report 1992.*

Consequently, in the first two years of its opening, EuroDisney had already attracted half a million Dutch visitors, who now rank third among foreign markets for the theme park. While France is gaining in popularity, Spain is losing ground: down from 10% in 1991 to 8% in 1992 (in 1988, Spain was the chosen destination for 14% of all Dutch foreign holidays).

Tourism trends

While July remains the preferred month for holidaytaking, there is a marked trend away from taking holidays in the peak summer season. In 1992, the number of those choosing July/August fell again, from 44% to 42%. For the UK as a destination, the regional spread is even better, with 70% of Dutch visitors to the UK arriving outside the peak third quarter.

At the same time, the general trend is towards the average holiday becoming shorter. The average has been falling from year to year, which underlines the growth of short second holidays taken by the Dutch.

A point which the Dutch have in common with their German neighbours is the attention they pay to the quality of the environment in which their holidays take place. 'Green' travel products, whether walking, cycling, camping or simply escaping urban life, are increasingly in demand. Even at the beginning of the decade, the Dutch, in a survey of holiday intentions, spontaneously cited the environment as being the current burning issue for them.

Retail travel trade

Of all foreign holidays taken by the Dutch, 53% are independent and do not use the services of the retail travel trade. This figure rises to 77% in the case of France, the favourite destination, and to 80% in the case of the UK, an easily accessible destination from the Netherlands. Nevertheless, these figures are falling as the Dutch increasingly turn to tour operators in their search for suitable holiday products. As an example, the MDLF *1994–1995 Marketing Plan* states that in 1979, 85% of Dutch visitors to France came as independent tourists. It is to their great credit that Dutch tour operators have proved so effective in responding to their customers' needs, in particular for adventure/activity holidays and tailor-made products.

The main Dutch tour operators are shown in Table 11.7. There is a trend towards independent travel agencies being bought up by the larger tour operators and chains. At the same time, the Dutch tradition of booking holidays through travel agencies' counters situated in their banks is dying out and most banks are in the process of closing down this aspect of their business. For example, in 1993/93, the bank ABN-AMRO closed down its 366 points of sale.

SUMMARY

The general picture which emerges from the above survey of selected national markets is one of a continent in flux, with different markets developing at different paces.

Increasingly, for the inhabitants of the wealthier, northern EU members, taking a break away from it all is no longer a once-a-year experience, but a regular and more frequent habit. A rising number of paid holidays and perhaps also the growing need regularly to escape the stress of modern life means that there is a significant trend towards taking shorter main holidays supplemented by various short-breaks dispersed throughout the year.

As well as being more frequent, holidays taken by Northern Europeans are also increasingly likely to be taken in long-haul destinations, to be 'greener' and to be taken independently.

At the same time, growing prosperity has brought more and more Southern Europeans into the holiday market, as the Greeks, Spanish and Portuguese are finding leisure travel more affordable.

A key question for the European tourism market is how much it can be expected to grow in the years leading up to the turn of this century.

Table 11.7   Market shares of the main Dutch tour operators (%)

	1982	1992
Arke	7	10
Holland International	19	14
Hotelplan	7	6
De Jong Intra	8	5
Neckermann	5	5
OAD	4	5
Vrij Uit	5	18
CenterParcs	0	10
Total	55%	73%

Source: NIPO, *General Report 1992*.

Northern European tourism markets – in Scandinavia, Germany, the Benelux countries and the UK – are relatively mature, so growth there should be steady rather than explosive. Although France is also a mature market in terms of the number of its residents who regularly take an annual holiday, the fact that most of them still prefer to spend this in France means that there is potential there for greater expansion into international tourism, but only at the expense of the domestic tourism product.

As for Southern Europe, the general economic stagnation which has characterized the 1990s in the continent as a whole means that that region is unlikely to see further expansion into leisure tourism in the immediate future.

However, the real area of expansion may well come from the hitherto travel-starved holidaymakers of Eastern Europe. Among the populations of the former Soviet bloc, there is enormous pent-up desire to visit the West, and the sharp rise in the numbers of tourist arrivals from the Eastern half of the continent is already a feature of many countries' national tourism statistics. One in every ten tourists on the Italian Riviera now comes from Eastern Europe, and in Britain alone their number has grown sevenfold in a decade – to 400 000 in 1994.

For the moment, their levels of expenditure are low compared with those of other international visitors: for example, Eastern European visitors spend an average of £15.20 a day in Britain, which compares with £55 a day spent by Americans, £68.50 by the Japanese and £69 by Norwegians. But if disposable incomes continue to grow in that region, east–west travel will increase significantly, and with it, tourism spending power. Indeed, one development which could, in the longer term, produce the economic circumstances favourable to creating greater prosperity in certain former communist countries would be their integration into the EU itself. Practically unthinkable at the beginning of the decade, six of these countries – Bulgaria, the Czech Republic, Hungary, Poland, Romania and Slovakia – came a giant step closer to membership when in 1994 their representatives were invited to attend all EU meetings as a preparatory move towards their full integration. The consequent impact on their economies of being drawn closer to the West's market-oriented norm may provide the ideal circumstances for boosting the new east–west wave of international tourists in Europe. And, with experienced Western European travellers being increasingly tempted by destinations in other continents, their Eastern counterparts could prove to be just what is needed to maintain a healthy 'internal' market for Europe.

REVIEW QUESTIONS

1. How might developments in the French market described in this chapter affect French demand for holidays in Britain?
2. How might developments in the German and Dutch market affect demand for short-break and long-haul travel in the future?

3. In the past European tourism movements have been primarily from north to south. How does the data offered on Spain and Italy suggest that this may be changing or will change in the future?

4. The review of the major European markets in this chapter concludes: 'The general picture which emerges from the above survey of selected national markets is one of a continent in flux, with different markets developing at different paces.' To what extent does this seem to you to be a fair summary of the data presented on European developments?

The UK short holiday market

12

R. Smith

OBJECTIVES

By the end of this chapter the reader should:

- understand how short holidays can be defined;
- be aware of the main characteristics of short holidays;
- be aware of the main characteristics of short holidaytakers and some of the key factors influencing their choice of destinations;
- have a working knowledge of some of the factors which will influence the future development of short holidays in the UK market.

DEFINITION OF A SHORT HOLIDAY

Short holidays are often said to be the fastest growing type of holiday in Europe today. But the statistical evidence which might support this view is difficult to gather and not at all easy to interpret. One of the reasons for this is because there are different ways of defining short holidays.

In the United Kingdom statistical reports have generally distinguished between 'long holiday trips', which last for four or more nights, and 'short holiday trips', which last from one to three nights (ETB *et al.*, 1994). However, at the present time there is a move towards a threefold division of holiday length. This means bringing in a new category of trips between 'long' and 'short' trips – that is, trips which last from four to seven nights. If this change were to be accepted, 'long trips' would have to be redefined as lasting eight or more nights. This would clearly be a sensible move. Many holiday trips are indeed undertaken for a single week (for example, during school half-term breaks). And it may well turn out on closer examination that trips lasting for four to seven nights actually have quite different characteristics from either longer holidays or short trips. On the other hand, some commentators (EIU, 1992) suggest that trips of three nights are more similar to those of four, and possibly also five nights, than they are to two-night trips. Either way, it would appear that a redefinition of short holidays is now overdue.

However, the way that the main set of statistics for British domestic tourism is presented makes it particularly convenient to think of short holidays in terms of trips of one to three nights. Therefore, although some other European countries and some British tourism researchers have used other definitions, this chapter will stay with this long-standing definition of short holidays. If any of the facts and figures quoted here refer to periods longer than three nights this will be made clear.

Apart from length, a second defining characteristic of short holidays has to do with the traveller's main motivation for going on the trip. Usually only holiday travel is included in the category of short trips. Business travel is excluded. Travellers frequently 'mix business with pleasure'. In other words, a business trip may contain elements of leisure travel. For example, a business person's partner may go along on a conference trip purely for a holiday, or an individual traveller may decide to stay on at a destination for a few days' recreation or sightseeing after a business meeting. Although this trend is growing, it does not yet present a serious problem in tourism research. Even if their travel motivation was mixed, people are certainly able to tell a research interviewer what their main reason was for taking a trip. However, mixed motivation has a particular relevance in relation to those trips which involve staying with friends and relatives. Sometimes people consider these to be holidays, sometimes not. Statistical reports therefore make a broad distinction between VFR holiday trips and VFR non-holiday trips. Again, it makes obvious sense that only VFR **holiday** trips can be considered to fall within the short holiday sector. Therefore, in the usual definition of short holidays, not only are business trips excluded, so too are visits to friends and relatives which are undertaken for what people consider to be non-holiday purposes.

Finally, the published material on short holidays presents us with a key issue of definition concerning accommodation. Although short holiday nights can be spent in a great variety of places, some studies deal only with short trips which are taken in paid-for accommodation. Such trips are sometimes referred to as 'commercial short-breaks'. The commercial short-breaks sector therefore includes all stays in hotels and guest houses. The problem is that some studies also include other forms of paid-for accommodation such as self-catering units. This can make meaningful comparisons between studies difficult. As we will see, most short holidays are taken in non-paid accommodation such as friends' homes. Yet short-breaks in commercial accommodation are of particular interest to many in the tourism industry – hoteliers, tour operators and tourism marketing organizations. This is because short-breaks are seen as a dynamic and increasingly valuable sector of the tourism industry. And in the UK this interest is all the greater because other sectors of the domestic holiday industry are either stagnant or in decline. However, in this chapter we will try to keep the focus on the big picture, examining short trips using all types of accommodation, not just those involving commercial premises. Where we are considering the more narrowly defined commercial short-break, this will be pointed out.

To sum up, in defining what we mean by short holidays, we have said that:

- they are trips of between one and three nights away from home (although some studies refer to trips lasting longer);
- the purpose of travel is a holiday;
- there is a distinct sector of the market, sometimes known as 'commercial short-breaks', which involves stays in hotels, guest houses and possibly other paid-for accommodation.

THE SIZE OF THE MARKET

Table 12.1 shows some of the key facts about short holidays (1–3 nights) and long holidays (4+ nights) taken by UK residents in the UK in 1993. The figures in this case include holiday visits to friends and relatives and stays in non-commercial accommodation.

Table 12.1 shows that short holiday taking by British residents in the UK produces a high aggregate expenditure. The sum of £2220 million represents about a quarter of all British spending on holidays in Britain.

However, short holidaytaking in the UK has not been as buoyant as is often thought. When we consider the trends since 1989, it is clear that short holidays have been just as vulnerable to recession as long holiday trips.

Table 12.2 shows a dramatic decline in trips and nights between 1989 and 1993. Contrary to what was expected at the time, 1992 turned out not to have been a turning point in this decline, merely a temporary recovery. On the other hand, Table 12.2 also shows a rise in spending on short holidays. The spending figures are given at current prices, but even if allowance is made for inflation, the 1993 spending figure still shows a remarkable increase on the previous year in spite of the lower volumes of trips and nights.

So what emerges is a rather confusing picture. Remember that we are

Table 12.1 Short and long holidays by UK residents in the UK

	Short holidays	Long holidays
Trips	24.6 million	30.3 million
Nights	51.1 million	223.2 million
Spending	£2220 million	£6205 million

Source: ETB *et al.* (1994).

Table 12.2 Short holiday trends 1989–93 (millions)

	Trips	Nights	Spending
1989	30.5	61.1	£1720
1990	26.7	54.3	£1740
1991	26.1	53.8	£1740
1992	27.4	56.6	£1945
1993	24.6	51.1	£2220

Source: ETB *et al.* (1994).

talking about short holidays in general rather than commercial short-breaks. The general trend in terms of volume is poor, but we may be seeing the beginning of a new development whereby total spending keeps up and even increases on a per trip or per head basis.

What we have to bear in mind is that short holidays are part of a changing pattern of holidays in the UK and in Europe. It is now well established that many British people prefer to take their main holiday abroad. These people often supplement their overseas holiday with a second or additional holiday in their own country. This trend bears unevenly on different destinations. Some traditional British destinations associated with long holidays are under pressure – seaside resorts, for example – whereas certain new types of destination which are particularly favoured for short holidays are doing relatively well. There are therefore both problems and opportunities tied up with the development of short holidays.

It may also be the case that the commercial short-breaks sector has weathered the recession better than short holidays generally. We can examine part of this proposition by briefly reviewing the UK statistics. In 1989 42% of short holiday trips were accommodated commercially. In 1993 the equivalent figure was 47%. In other words, in 1989 some 12.8 million short holidays were taken in commercial accommodation, whereas in 1993 only 11.6 million visitors were accommodated commercially. Overall, this represents a decrease of 9% for the commercial sector. But if we consider the figures for only one component of the commercial accommodation sector – licensed hotels – we find that the corresponding change of –4% was substantially less than the general decrease. In other words, in a shrinking market licensed hotels did rather better than self-catering units, caravan parks and other types of non-serviced accommodation.

These are only broad calculations. Examining this kind of development in much greater detail should be part of the research agenda for UK tourism over the next few years. For the moment, one thing stands out. Whereas in the late 1980s there was ample evidence to suggest that during the previous decade short holidays and short-breaks in commercial accommodation were growing faster than holidays as a whole (Beioley, 1991), in more recent years the dynamic of growth in the short holiday sector has definitely slowed down.

INTERNATIONAL SHORT HOLIDAYS IN THE UK AND EUROPE

Most of this chapter is concerned with short holidays taken by UK residents in the United Kingdom. But there is also the question of the British taking short holidays abroad. A study published by Mintel in 1993 examined holidays taken by UK residents overseas (excluding Ireland) of one to four nights involving all types of paid accommodation. The study found that this sector accounts for around 12% of the total overseas holiday market in the UK. Rapid growth between 1988 and 1991 was found to have given way to a levelling out since 1991. As a result, the overseas short-break market among UK residents remains relatively small, with only around 5% of the UK population taking a short break abroad.

Nevertheless, the estimates for 1993 were that about 2.73 million trips would be taken, worth £640 million. Fortunately for the UK domestic tourism industry there is to some extent a compensating growth of overseas interest in the UK as a short-break destination. Reviewing the size of the **inbound** short trip market, Beioley (1991) found that European short holiday visitors to the UK (1–4 nights) accounted for 1.3 million trips.

The general European trends are no easier to interpret. An Economist Intelligence Unit study of international short holiday trips taken by Europeans (EIU, 1995), drawing on surveys in 18 originating countries of Western Europe plus key East European markets, suggests that following a boom in the 1980s the international short-break market (i.e. 1–3 nights and excluding VFR) in Europe appears to be in decline. Thus, after a decade of unprecedented growth, the annual volume of short-breaks taken by West Europeans abroad is estimated to have fallen from a peak of some 29 million in 1991 to 25 million in 1994. However, this is admitted to be at odds with industry perceptions – and industry performance. The explanation offered is that the volume of international short holidays of around four or five nights (and therefore outside the scope of the study) has increased sharply. It is claimed that a great variety of new products are being offered and many specialist tour operators are entering the market and meeting with success. Therefore, if a somewhat wider definition of a short-break were to be used, the sector would be found to be performing well.

In the UK and other European markets it remains to be seen whether growth will be renewed as prosperity grows and consumer confidence returns. Will short holidaytaking once again outstrip the general growth in holidays? Or will other changes in the marketplace such as different attitudes to leisure spending inhibit renewed take-off? Some possible influences will be discussed at the end of this chapter. In the meantime we will try to understand as much as we can about the nature of short-break holidays and the people who take them.

Table 12.3 Accommodation used on short holidays

	% trips
Hotel/motel/guest house	25
Paying guest in:	
farmhouse	1
other private house/bed & breakfast	3
Self-catering in rented:	
flat/apartment	1
house/chalet/villa/bungalow	2
hostel/university/school	1
Friends'/relatives' home	41
Own second home/timeshare	1
Holiday camp/village:	
self-catering	1
serviced	1
Camping	5
Caravan:	
towed	6
static owned	7
static not owned	2
Boat	1
Other/transit	2
Total commercial accommodation	**47**
Total non-commercial accommodation	**53**
Total serviced	**30**
Total self catering	**18**

Source: ETB *et al.* (1994).

THE CHARACTERISTICS OF UK SHORT HOLIDAYS

Accommodation used

Table 12.3 shows the accommodation used by UK residents on short holiday trips taken in the UK in 1993.

Over half of short holidays (53%) take place in non-commercial accommodation. The main provision here is in friends' and relatives' homes (41%). Second homes and timeshare, although a growing sector, still only represent 1% of holiday trips.

Looking at holidays taken in commercial accommodation, the main type of provision is in hotels/motels/guest houses (25%), with farmhouses and B&B taking only 4% of the market. A lot of attention has been focused on some of the success stories in attracting leisure visitors to use 'off-peak' capacity in city centre business hotels.

Trinity Research (1989) point out that the short-break industry was founded on the concept of 'off-peak' availability. Packaged short-breaks make use of the services of hotels and often of public transport at periods of time when demand is low and premium prices cannot be charged. For commercial hotels and car-hire firms the relevant times are Friday night to Sunday night and the months of July and August; for tourist hotels the low season is October to the Spring Bank Holiday; for trains the off-peak times are weekends and Monday to Friday outside the rush hour.

The history of the commercial short-break began in the 1960s when Trust House Forte, Britain's largest hotel group, launched its 'Bargain Breaks' programme and British Rail set up the Golden Rail company, which sold rail transportation and hotel accommodation as a package (Trinity Research, 1989). The growth of some newly emerging city destinations was built on successful collaborative efforts between business hotel operators and other agencies, such as imaginative local authority marketing departments or newly established Visitor and Convention Bureaux. In the 1980s the astonishing rise of Bradford as a short-break urban destination came about as a result of this kind of public/private sector partnership approach. Since then, many major industrial cities have succeeded in attracting substantial numbers of weekend visitors with well-designed hotel-based packages.

But in fact, as the predominance of non-commercial accommodation in Table 12.3 makes clear, the most common type of short holiday is today what it always has been – a visit to friends or relatives. VFR trips can be undertaken for a wide range of social purposes and there can be no doubt that some of this 'family and friends' motivation also finds expression in the commercial accommodation sector. For example, attendance at a big family wedding might well involve a stay in a guest house, while many people undertake weekend trips to caravan sites or self-catering country cottages in diverse family or friendship groups.

One rather interesting finding set out in Table 12.3 is the relatively low incidence of stays in timeshare units. This is rather surprising since the UK has the highest per capita ownership of timeshare accommodation in Europe. It is certainly true that many homes owned on this basis are located abroad, but a substantial number are in the UK. So it may well be that the organizational pattern of timeshare occupation, usually involving allocations of a full week at a time, does not as yet encourage the use of timeshare units for short holidays of one to three nights' duration.

Another rather surprising fact to emerge from the UKTS statistics is the relatively small market share held by self-catering/serviced holiday camps and villages. During the 1980s a number of traditional operators in this sector began to remodel their product for the contemporary market. Butlins, for example, have invested heavily in revamping their old-style holiday camps and creating 'Holiday Worlds' with enhanced accommodation, catering and entertainment facilities. Several holiday centre operators have put a lot of thought and effort into developing niche markets through the creation and promotion of accommodation and entertainments packages designed to appeal variously to families with young children, senior citizens or special interest groups. There has also been a move away from reliance on the traditional one-week stay by the introduction of such innovations as themed weekends. These might involve any of a range of activities – a chance to try out a new sport, to take part in a bridge tournament, to rock the night away to the bands of the 1960s and 1970s. But while such initiatives may have proved valuable additions to the range of products which holiday centre operators offer, and may even have helped some companies to open up new markets, short-breaks are still a long way from becoming the mainstay of established holiday centres' business.

By contrast, one of the most talked about phenomena of the 1980s in UK domestic tourism, the success of the Center Parcs operation, is almost entirely based on short-break occupancy. The formula for Center Parcs was developed in the Netherlands and successfully exported across northern Europe. The key elements include quality self-catering villa accommodation, attractive woodland and water settings, a large leisure pool inside a heated dome, and lots of sporty activities for both children and adults. A holiday at a Center Parcs resort is not meant to be taken as an alternative to a main holiday in the sun, but rather as a complementary three- or four-night break in pleasant 'green' surroundings with easy access to a temperature and humidity controlled leisure environment. The product is pricey but convenient, and is very appealing to affluent families with children. The high occupancy rates achieved by the first Center Parcs resort in the UK at Sherwood Forest and the subsequent expansion of the chain has led to a flurry of interest by other developers. The National Economic Development Council's 1992 report *UK Tourism: Competing for Growth* doubled the English Tourist Board's previous estimate and argued that there was a need for twelve such holiday villages in the UK. However, the Center Parcs operation, which is now owned by the Scottish and Newcastle brewing company, has maintained a cautious approach to expansion. Other would-be developers of a similar style of product have found it difficult to make headway with their plans. This is partly because in a small country like Britain areas of attractive scenic beauty are the very areas where it is most difficult to get planning permission for new developments. At this stage a holiday village of the Center Parcs style needs a very large catchment population within easy driving distance in order to be reasonably sure of success. The capital investment required is very substantial. But the strength of the product has been recognized and the Rank Organization is about to go ahead with a variant of the basic concept to be known as 'Oasis Villages'.

Main mode of transport

The United Kingdom Tourism Survey (UKTS) also provides information about the main mode of transport used on short holiday trips by British residents in the UK. The favourite is the privately owned car (80%). Campervans and hire cars account for a further 2%. Public transport use is divided between trains (8%), regular coaches or buses (3%) and organized coach tours (4%). So although there are successful niche operators packaging short-breaks using public transport it is clear from this break-down that the convenience of personal transport is a vital facilitating factor in the short holiday market. With car ownership, a decision to take a weekend break can be left to the last moment, maybe allowing good weather to provide the final impetus to go. And the knowledge that a trip can be cut short without too much fuss if the weather turns bad is perhaps another important positive consideration when car owners are thinking of taking a break.

In Europe, the expansion of high-speed rail networks and the availability of special offers for off-peak travel are likely to encourage greater use of the rail system for short-breaks. Of particular significance for the UK are the extension of the Eurostar service to France and Belgium and the development of Le Shuttle car transport through the Channel Tunnel. Scheduled airline operators are also looking to build up leisure business by offering special deals involving discounted fares to European cities, to be taken outside peak periods. An increasingly common way for these to be offered is through such promotions as 'two-for-one' readers' offers in regional newspapers. The widespread introduction of 'air miles' incentive schemes for business travellers also encourages the use of airlines for leisure trips to destinations which might previously have seemed out of the question for a short-break.

There is of course a wide variety of short holidays available in Britain involving privately owned or hired vehicles – from cycling holidays to pony trekking to leisurely canal cruising in narrowboats. A strong growth market in North America and Europe is mini-cruising. As cruise operators target new market sectors, aiming to attract younger customers by providing a greater choice of on-board entertainments, it seems quite likely that this type of short holiday might be launched successfully in the UK.

Organization of trip

More than nine out of ten (91%) of UK domestic short holiday trips are independently organized, with bookings through a travel agent (both fully inclusive trips and any travel or accommodation items) accounting for only 3% of trips. Even for commercial short-breaks, the involvement of the travel trade is not high. Trinity Research (1989) calculated for 1987 that around a third of short-break trips and a third of spending of the total market for short-breaks in licensed hotels were bought in package form from a short-break supplier. The great majority of licensed hotel breaks were therefore booked unpackaged directly from the hotel.

The low level of travel agency involvement is often seen as a problem in UK domestic tourism. Unfavourable comparisons are made between the effectiveness of travel agency activity in selling package holidays abroad and the limited availability of British holiday products through high street or shopping mall retail outlets. The implication is that demand for British holidays could be stimulated by suppliers providing more commissionable items – or more generous rates of commission – to make it worthwhile for travel agencies to try to push British products more vigorously. However, the review by Trinity Research (1989) suggested that there were definite cost advantages to licensed hotel operators in cutting out the middleman and using direct response methods to sell their packaged breaks. However, there could also be disadvantages in withdrawing from travel agents, such as allowing vacated racking space to be taken over by competitors and the increased ahead-of-sales costs which other sales methods incur. According to Trinity Research, these problems in part explain the rise of cooperative marketing groups, such as Best Western, which provide a joint brochure and one central reservation system. This type of measure allows such groups to achieve a higher rate of penetration among travel agents than would be possible for individual hotels.

Tourism marketing organizations such as regional tourist boards also have difficult decisions to make as to how they wish to handle short-break business. There are complexities in the situation which we will not pursue – except to say, by way of illustration, that in 1995 the Scottish Tourist Board became embroiled in a row with the Association of British Travel Agents over the Board's attempt to sell its Spring Breaks promotions directly to consumers. The Board quickly changed its mind and reversed its policy. Its UK Marketing Director was quoted as saying:

> Every consumer-targeted brochure we produce from November this year will contain only products and accommodation which are commissionable to retailers. We are now set up to rekindle trade support, and view travel agents as a vital element in our strategy of reversing the downward trend in bookings from the domestic market.
>
> (Tim Hailey, quoted by MacBeth-Seath, 1995)

Yet the fact remains that in the domestic short-break marketplace what the UK tourist calls 'other commercial organizations' handle more trip bookings than travel agencies, and non profit-making organizations are not far behind them in market share. However much tourist board officials might profess their goodwill and retailers themselves might wish to enjoy a bigger slice of the cake, the travel trade does not as yet take a very substantial portion of the UK domestic short-break holiday market.

This is in marked contrast to the way in which short-break holidays abroad are bought by the British public. According to Mintel, some 40% of self-drive breaks abroad are purchased through travel agents, and between 90 and 95% of city breaks. Because customers prefer to book quite late, discounting in short-breaks is unusual. Mintel suggests that customers will not usually have time to gather together brochures from main operators but will tend to rely on travel agents for advice, often choosing their operator on the basis of such advice and according to what is available. Because availability at short notice is so important, the main operators have invested in computer reservation systems, giving travel agents direct access to holiday details and instant confirmation. Thus travel agents have begun to find that the short-break abroad sector is a valuable source of income in the off-season.

The leading operator in the UK for city breaks abroad is Cresta Holidays, owned by the Belgian group Sun International (EIU, 1995). Thomson Tour Operations is also active in this market. Cresta offers more than 60 city destinations in Europe, but has also widened its programmes to include options such as theme parks and countryside holidays. In 1994 Cresta expected to sell more than 90 000 short-break packages, or 200 000 including seat-only and hotel-only sales.

Type of location

The United Kingdom Tourism Survey identifies four main types of location for short holiday trips in the UK: the seaside; large cities and towns; small towns; the countryside/villages. The seaside of course traditionally exerts a strong pull on the British holidaymaker and it is seaside resorts which have been most worried in recent years about the competition from Mediterranean and long-haul sun destinations. But the concern has been mostly about consumers switching main holiday allegiances. Overseas destinations are too remote to have much effect on short seaside holiday choices, although the Channel Tunnel and increased Channel ferry competition may have some influence on the destination choices of people living in South East England. Some of the larger British seaside resorts have made efforts to attract short holiday business and a few have achieved remarkable success, effectively repositioning themselves in the marketplace. Blackpool remains uniquely successful. There is probably some scope for imaginatively managed smaller seaside resorts to maintain their position, provided they are able both to develop new products and play to their traditional strengths. The essential strength of 'the seaside holiday' was a theme picked up by a television and newspaper advertising campaign in the early 1990s sponsored by the English Tourist Board and some 35 participating resorts.

Large cities have always attracted business tourism. London sits at the hub of the transport system and has a huge variety of cultural attractions which draw leisure visitors from all over the UK and abroad. It also offers the best shopping facilities in the country, and an unequalled range of specialist exhibitions and sporting events which appeal to large numbers of short-break visitors. So, however unfavourably London might compare as an international destination with Paris or other world cities which have invested more imaginatively and to better effect in transport and cultural infrastructure, its domestic appeal for short holidays is likely to be perennial.

Over recent years several other British cities have consciously attempted to build up a tourism base. Birmingham has established modern exhibition and conference facilities to meet the needs of the business market but at the same time has gone for high-profile cultural developments such as a state-of-the-art concert hall and an impressive redesign of public spaces, all intended to help place the city more firmly on the national tourist map. Glasgow, like several other run-down urban areas in the 1980s, benefited from the opportunity to host a publicly funded National Garden Festival. This was the biggest consumer event of 1988 and was the occasion of strenuous efforts to promote the city as a short-break destination. These were renewed during Glasgow's reign as European City of Culture in 1990, helping the city to capitalize on its existing cultural assets and establish itself as a significant short-break leisure destination. In many places, such as Liverpool, Bristol, Leeds and Hull, the redevelopment of redundant docks or waterfront areas has been the focus for ambitious efforts to attract visitors by establishing a mix of museums and galleries, interpretive centres, leisure shopping and catering outlets. Manchester has developed the Castlefield urban heritage park along similar lines and has had the good fortune to have the enormously popular Granada Studio Tour open up on an adjoining site. It is not surprising that Belfast, long inactive in tourism promotion but with rapidly improving attractions, is now the latest city to consider a tourism marketing plan which refers specifically to the potential of the short-break market.

Small towns attract some 19% of short holiday trips in the UK. Since the 1970s these locations have undoubtedly drawn more visitors than ever before, partly as a result of the greater freedom of movement which widespread car ownership has conferred and the vogue for 'heritage' among some of the more affluent sectors of the population. Yet small towns are the places where the conflict between residents' and visitors' interests may be most acute. Occasionally, scepticism about the supposed benefits of more visitors in already crowded town centres may mean that local councils will adopt restrictive policies towards new tourist development and will decline to support promotional initiatives. In some cases councils have taken deliberate decisions not to promote a historic town to certain markets. This was a policy adopted by Cambridge in 1990. Low-spending day-trippers were therefore rather less welcome than the culturally sophisticated staying visitor or the high-spending conference delegate. In other small towns, such as Stratford-upon-Avon, the fame of the place may be such that the main focus needs to be on devising more effective visitor management techniques to direct and channel the large numbers who will inevitably come, whatever the preferences of the council.

There is a remarkable consistency in the popularity of the countryside for both long and short holidays – 24% of UK trips in each case. Again, there is a likely connection with greater car ownership over the last few decades and a consequent growth of bed and breakfast accommodation, self-catering facilities and caravan sites in the countryside to cater for the visitor. There are now many trends at work in maintaining the demand for short holidays in the countryside. These include a more widespread interest among the young in 'the environment' and a growing taste among various age groups for outdoor activities. One only needs to consider the phenomenal growth in mountain biking in the space of just a few years to realize how even commercial fads are likely to influence demand for access to the countryside.

On the other hand, there are several indicators to suggest that the

motivational force of such factors as car ownership and interest in outdoor activities are quite limited. Thus only 1% of short holiday trips in the UK are touring holidays, confirming that people tend to use their cars to take them to their destination, and possibly then for day trips into the country-side or to the seaside, rather than spending each night of the trip in a different place. The car is therefore a **facilitating** factor in short holiday planning. Also, the balance between those who say they had no particular activity in mind as the main purpose of their holiday, as opposed to those who gave **any** activity as their main motivating factor, is weighted quite heavily towards those who were not seeking to pursue any particular activity (78% to 22%). It seems, therefore, that in choosing to go on short holidays relatively few people set out on what might properly be described as an 'activity holiday'.

Activities pursued on holiday

There is, of course, a very wide range of activities pursued by short holidaymakers, whether they organized the holiday around them or not. About half of all short holidays taken by the British in the UK involve some kind of activity. The most popular are the activities grouped together by the UKTS as hiking/hill-walking/rambling/orienteering (12%), fol-lowed by visiting 'heritage' sites such as castles, monuments, churches, etc. (9%) and swimming (8%).

Seasonality

Whereas long holidays in the UK are quite heavily peaked in the third quarter of the year – about a quarter of trips are taken in August – short holidays taken by British residents in the UK are spread rather more evenly. The least popular months are January, February, March, September and November. No doubt this has to do with the colder weather in the first quarter of the year and in November. Short holiday activity rises to its peak in April and May (11% of trips in each month), falling back slightly in June and July (9% each), before regaining its peak in August (11%). Schools have resumed by September, which helps explain the decline in that month to 7%, while the revival in October (9%) is probably due at least in part to the half-term school holidays at that time of year. December (10%) is twice as popular for short holidays as November, reflecting Christmas holiday activity.

This more even seasonal spread of short holidays is an important consideration for the domestic tourism industry. While main holidays are likely to remain heavily concentrated in the summer months from May to September there are opportunities for tourism businesses to promote short spring and autumn breaks which will extend their operating season and ensure better use of capital. Achieving this is likely to be more realistic for some types of business than others. A country house hotel, for example, is more likely to be able to attract shoulder season business for a relatively luxurious and even cosy experience than more weather-dependent facilities such as a caravan site or an outdoor wildlife visitor attraction. For tourist boards and marketing organizations one of the essential problems is the difficulty of persuading operators that it is worthwhile experimenting with a longer opening season. In the first years of operation the returns may not immediately justify the additional costs – a familiar chicken and egg problem. But building up the shoulder seasons in a given destination area also calls for the exceptionally difficult task of orchestrating enough extra commitment across a range of operations to achieve an adequate range of services for the visitor. So there are many chickens which have to be hatched simultaneously – public transport, a variety of accommodation types, information services, visitor attractions. The problem is likely to be all the more intractable because many small operators in tourism have entered the industry in order to secure a lifestyle which allows them to relax or pursue other interests in the off-season. They may well have no desire to work over a longer season even if it means achieving better returns.

Geographical spread in the UK

Compared with other types of tourism the geographical spread of short holidays across the UK shows some interesting variations (English Tourist Board *et al.*, 1994). Whereas the West Country is by far the most popular destination area for long holidays, its 14% share of short holiday trips in England gives it only a fairly short lead over several other regions of the UK. No doubt this discrepancy in popularity comes about because the West Country is largely about seaside holidays – which enjoy twice as big a share of long holiday trips – and because of the region's distance from main markets. London takes a 10% share of short holiday trips which, rather surprisingly in view of the capital's huge spread of attractions, is no greater than East Anglia or Yorkshire and Humberside.

In Scotland, the former local government region of Strathclyde – which includes Glasgow – takes about a third of short holiday trips (0.7 million), followed by Lothian region – which includes Edinburgh – with 0.4 million. The Highlands and Islands of Scotland have, like the West Country of England, a proportionately much smaller share of the short holiday market (0.3 million) compared with long holidays. This suggests a concentration of short holidays in the central belt of Scotland, where the bulk of the population is to be found. The Scottish Tourist Board is now committed by the strategic plan for Scottish tourism to achieving a wider dispersal of tourism throughout the country.

In relation to its size and population Wales takes a fairly substantial proportion of short holiday trips in the UK, outperforming Scotland in terms of both the number of trips and the number of nights taken in short holidays. South Wales is the main destination for short holiday trips to Wales, in contrast to long holiday trips where North Wales is dominant.

Northern Ireland experienced around 0.5 million short holiday trips in

1993. There are special factors at work in the province, in particular its remoteness from the main UK markets, and there are political considerations relating to the relationship with the Republic of Ireland as well as largely misplaced perceptions of risk by potential tourists during the period of armed conflict between 1969 and 1994. However, difficulty and expense of travel between Northern Ireland and Great Britain works the other way as well, encouraging Northern Ireland residents to holiday close to home. It remains to be seen how effectively the opportunity created by the paramilitary ceasefires of 1994 and the attendant political developments, which have certainly produced a great upsurge of interest in holidays in Northern Ireland, can be translated into increased short holiday business from the UK and the Republic.

EUROPEAN INTERNATIONAL SHORT-BREAK TRAVEL DESTINATIONS

In continental Europe, most commercial short-break trips are between neighbouring countries with land borders (EIU, 1995). Germany is the most important country of origin, the Germans accounting for approximately a third of the total West European volume. Rather surprisingly, in view of Britain's island status, in 1993 the UK took second place in this market. That is, 10% of commercial short-breaks originated in the UK. This illustrates the comparatively high priority which many British people attach to their holiday habit.

According to EIU, the leading destination for European short-breaks (the figures exclude VFR) is France (18%), followed by Austria (11%). Much of the popularity of France can be explained by the appeal of Paris, now supplemented by the attraction for families and young adults of EuroDisney, but also by the country's wide range of cities, towns and countryside environments for short-breaks. Austria is particularly popular with the Germans and its fortunes fluctuate with the level of demand from Germany. But Austria is also a favourite destination with other nationalities for winter sports trips. It remains to be seen how quickly East European destinations can develop their appeal to Western markets. Among city-break destinations Prague and Budapest have already achieved some success.

CHARACTERISTICS OF UK DOMESTIC SHORT HOLIDAYTAKERS

Not only does the United Kingdom Tourism Survey gather a wealth of information about the characteristics of short holidays taken by the British in the UK, it also investigates the characteristics of the people who take short holidays. To understand more about the market for such holidays it can be a useful exercise to compare the characteristics of short holidaytakers both with the those of long holidaytakers and with the UK population as a whole.

Table 12.4 tells us that short holidaytakers tend to come from the upper socioeconomic groups. The AB grouping (professional and managerial workers) takes notably more than its 'fair' share. By contrast, the DE grouping (semi- and unskilled manual workers, state pensioners, casual or lowest grade workers, the long-term unemployed with no other earner in the household) takes a much smaller share of short holidays than its proportion of the UK population would imply. As a result we can conclude that short holidays are rather more unevenly distributed across socio-economic groups than long holidays.

When we look at short holidaytakers by age grouping, a discernable bias

Table 12.4 Profile of short holidaytakers in the UK – 1993 (by trips)

		Long holiday (%)	Short holiday (%)	UK Population (%)
Socioeconomic group				
AB	(Professional and managerial)	24	29	17
C1	(Clerical and supervisory)	28	30	25
C2	(Skilled manual)	23	23	25
DE	(Unskilled, state pensioners, etc.)	25	19	33
Age				
15–24		12	18	17
25–34		20	25	19
35–44		23	23	17
45–54		13	16	14
55–64		13	10	13
65+		19	8	20
Children present in household		44	41	31
Children not present in household		56	59	69
Lifecycle				
15–34	single with no children under 15	9	17	16
15–34	married with no children under 15	3	7	4
15–34	married or single with children under 15	20	19	16
35–54	married or single with no children under 15	13	18	18
35–54	married or single with children under 15	23	22	13
55+		31	18	33

Source: ETB *et al.* (1994).

emerges in favour of people aged between 25 and 44. It is very clear that the over 65s are seriously under-represented, in marked contrast to this age group's nearly proportionate participation in long holidays. And whereas the presence of children in a household is a strongly positive factor in terms of the propensity of those household members to take long holidays, this factor is somewhat less marked in relation to short holidays.

Motivational factors

Beioley (1991), in reviewing studies of the motivation behind short-breaks, suggested that there were two broad groups of reasons for taking a trip. One group is centred on a general desire 'to get away from it all'. This might include such commonly cited reasons as 'needed a break', 'wanted a change', 'opportunity to relax'. The other group of reasons could be described as 'trigger events'. These include reasons such as 'attend an event', 'a celebration/anniversary', 'holiday entitlement to use up', 'saw an advert', 'special offer'.

In 1992 the English Tourist Board commissioned a study of the domestic short holiday market. For the purposes of the study a short holiday was defined as lasting from one to five nights, although some investigation was undertaken into the differences between shorter and medium length holidays, and the research was restricted to adults aged 16 and over who had used or intended to use paid accommodation. This meant that the study excluded everyone who would be staying with friends and relatives – or in their own second home, own static caravan, a timeshare unit or under any arrangement where the accommodation would be loaned to them rent-free. The survey established that the key factors influencing the type of destination chosen were broadly similar for both long and short holidays (as defined by the study) in paid accommodation. Thus both types of holidaytaker are seeking one or more of such features as:

- facilities for children;
- things to do if the weather is poor;
- a good beach;
- lovely countryside;
- peace and quiet;
- lively holiday atmosphere;
- evening entertainment;
- range of places to eat and drink;
- good shops;
- history and culture;
- opportunity to pursue sports and hobbies.

While this may not seem all that surprising, one of the most important outcomes of the study was that it was able to take respondents' interest in different holiday destination features and define six key market segments for the commercial short holiday market. Two of the segments were 'seaside oriented' and were given the snappy titles 'Kids rule OK' and 'Out for a good time'. Together these account for around a third of the market. Three other segments were oriented on the countryside – 'Brogues & National Trust', 'Sport 'n' Interests' and 'Rural Recreation'. These were found to account for two-fifths of the market. A sixth segment, accounting for 15% of the market, had an urban orientation and was defined as 'Cities & Culture'.

The main features for each of the segments are as follows:

- 'Kids rule OK' is likely to contain working-class families. The choice of destination is determined by the range of things for children to do, covering all weathers.
- 'Brogues & National Trust' tends towards the top of the market. This group has a strong interest in holidays combining country pursuits, particularly walking, with visits to historic and cultural sights.
- The 'Rural Relaxation' segment wants peace and quiet and the opportunity to relax in attractive rural surroundings.
- The 'Out for a good time' group tends to be young working-class and is looking for a lively holiday atmosphere involving pubs and clubs.
- 'Cities & Culture' people have an above average interest in historical and cultural sights, in evening entertainment, shopping and eating out. They are therefore particularly interested in historic cities and towns. They account for a greater proportion of winter holidays than of holidays at other times of year.
- 'Sport 'n' Interests' people are generally upmarket. They have a wide spread of ages, but the single largest age group is adults aged 35–44. They are particularly likely to seek peace and quiet in attractive countryside, where they can pursue their sports and hobbies.

The relative market shares of these segments are given in Table 12.5.

Another objective of the ETB study was to examine the actual process by which short-break destinations are chosen. The study found that there seems to be less scope to influence the choice of destination in the 1–3 night holiday market than for 4–5 nights or long holidays. Of those taking a 1–3 night break 61% had one specific destination in mind from the outset,

Table 12.5 Short-break market segments – market share

| | Total | Market share 1–3 nights | 4–5 nights |
	%	%	%
'Cities & Culture'	15	20	10
'Brogues & National Trust'	12	14	10
'Kids rule OK'	16	14	19
'Out for a good time'	15	14	16
'Sport 'n' Interests'	10	9	12
'Rural Relaxation'	18	19	16

Source: ETB (1993).

compared to 43% of those taking a holiday of 4–5 nights and 45% of those taking a longer holiday.

On the other hand, all short-break takers were much less committed to particular accommodation than long holiday takers. Two-fifths of short holidaytakers had considered more than one possible place to stay. A further 29% had only considered one particular establishment or site but they had not stayed at it before. The remaining 25% had found an establishment/site they liked and were going back to it. As a result, 70% of short holiday takers did not automatically assume which accommodation/site they would be using. In this case there was little difference between short-breaks of 1–3 nights and those of 4–5 nights. What this means is that people taking commercial short-breaks are considerably more open to influence about accommodation choice than long holiday takers, a welcome finding for those involved in trying to promote and sell short holidays.

Information sources

The same ETB study also investigated the related matter of which information sources people use in choosing a short holiday destination. It found that more than eight out of ten short holidaytakers (84%) had seen or heard something which helped them decide where to go for their holiday. Four out of ten had looked at brochures or guidebooks and two out of ten at advertisements. Around a third had received information or advice from friends, relations or colleagues. Different groups of short-holidaytakers were found to make use of promotional information sources to a greater or lesser degree according to factors such as the type of accommodation, the ways in which the different accommodation suppliers promote themselves and whether the particular type of accommodation tended to be booked in advance. Not surprisingly, tourist board brochures were found to be a particularly important source of information for users of lesser grade hotels/guest houses and of bed and breakfast accommodation. Holidaytakers staying in holiday centres and medium to top grade hotels were more likely to make use of holiday companies' brochures.

In 1994 the Scottish Tourist Board carried out research to investigate the effectiveness of an 'Autumn Breaks' campaign. This had consisted of a television campaign shown in selected English regions and a series of press adverts in national newspapers throughout England. In each case, respondents could telephone for a pack of information about autumn breaks in Scotland. The research objectives were:

- to obtain an analysis of responses to the campaign, that is respondents' use of and satisfaction with the information sent;
- to obtain an indication of the effectiveness of the campaign in encouraging visits to Scotland.

Table 12.6 shows how far various factors were influential on those respondents to the campaign who subsequently took an autumn holiday

Table 12.6. Rating (%) of influence of factors on visiting Scotland

	Degree of influence					
	+2	**+1**	**−1**	**−2**	**Don't know no reply**	**Average score**
Previous holidays in Scotland	46	14	4	17	19	+0.86
Information pack	23	36	11	13	17	+0.52
Scottish holiday adverts on TV	21	27	10	17	25	+0.32
Personal recommendation from friends/relatives	20	22	7	21	29	+0.19
Scottish holiday adverts in newspapers/magazines	12	21	11	24	32	−0.19
Brochures obtained from local tourist offices	13	19	7	29	33	−0.28
Brochures obtained from travel agents	5	12	8	40	36	−1.04

Source: Scottish Tourist Board (1995).

in Scotland. Respondents were asked to rate the importance of each of a list of seven factors (including the information pack) in influencing their visit. The scores were applied on a scale from +2 (Very influential) down to −2 (No influence) in order to allow comparison between the seven factors.

As can be seen, the most influential factor was experience of previous holidays in Scotland – a total of 60% of respondents claimed that this had some influence or was very influential on their decision to take an autumn break. However, the second most influential of the seven factors listed was the Autumn Breaks information pack: 59% of respondents were influenced by the pack, 23% stating that it was **very** influential. Forty-eight per cent were influenced to some extent by TV advertising, which the Board concedes is unsurprising, given that half of the sample applied for information following the STB television advert.

This STB survey is interesting in that it provides a useful insight into the effectiveness of various media in relation to the promotion of short-breaks in a destination area. Previous experience and personal recommendation are clearly not factors over which a national tourist organization can be expected to have much influence, but the combination of TV (and to a lesser extent press advertising) and the information pack does appear to have been quite effective with those who came. The much greater difficulty would lie in trying to determine how the advertising and information pack went down with those who decided not to take an autumn break in Scotland.

Destination preferences

Other studies have explored destination preferences in the UK short holiday market. The previously mentioned English Tourist Board *Short-Break Market Study* (1993) tried to determine interest in 59 British holiday destinations for short holidays in paid accommodation. City breaks were found to be more popular for short holidays between October and April. By contrast, seaside and country breaks were more popular between May and September. Table 12.7 shows the five most popular destinations for each period of the year.

Table 12.7   Interest in specific destinations – most popular choices (1st/2nd/3rd choice)

October – April		May – September	
33%	London	41%	The Lake District
26%	York	40%	Cornwall
21%	Edinburgh	37%	Devon
21%	Blackpool	29%	The English Riviera
18%	The Lake District	26%	The Yorkshire Dales

Source: ETB (1993).

As October to April destinations London and York appealed to all the market segments identified by the study, although interest was highest among the 'Cities & Culture' group. Edinburgh also featured in the top five choices of all the segments except the 'Kids rule OK' group. Blackpool is interesting in that it is the most popular individual resort during the summer period (18%) but is even more popular as a destination choice during the October to April period, appealing to all except the countryside oriented segments.

As May to September destinations the Lake District, Devon/or the English Riviera were popular with each of the market segments. The 'Kids rule OK' and 'Out for a good time' groups also favoured the Isle of Wight as one of their top five destinations. The countryside oriented segments included the Peak District among their leading choices.

Using a definition of 1–4 nights trip length, Mintel (1993) found that city breaks represented the largest sector of the UK market for packaged short-breaks abroad. The most common form of transport for city breaks is air, followed by coach and then self-drive. City breaks seem to be particularly popular with couples – either young couples or empty nesters. Paris and Amsterdam are the most popular destinations. Mintel found that these cities, together with Bruges, account for around 75% of the city breaks market.

The other major segment of the short-breaks abroad market is regional self-drive. Relatively cheap, this type of break is attractive to families. Among the advantages of this type of break are: children under 11 are included either free or at greatly reduced prices; the lifting of duty-free restrictions makes it possible to take advantage of low alcohol and food prices on the Continent; and the great flexibility which car driving provides.

In this sector France, the Netherlands and Belgium are the most popular destinations.

Finding out more

Market studies are important for organizations which wish to promote particular destinations or particular types of short holidays to appropriate market segments. Clearly, if the timing of the decision-making process is better understood it becomes easier to identify the most effective period during which to promote the holiday product. If there is a defined market segment likely to have a greater than average interest in a particular type of holiday activity then it is an advantage to be able to select advertising media which that segment is more likely to see, or indeed particular newspapers which they might tend to buy more than other groups. Well designed research studies might also yield useful information for tourism destination organizations and others on whether it is worth promoting particular types of holiday rather than regional destination areas or individual resorts.

Newspaper and magazine publishers are well aware of the interest of holiday operators in reaching target markets. In 1993 the leading publishing company IPC Magazines inserted a total of 304, 500 six-page holiday surveys into no fewer than 21 of its magazines. The variety of selected titles included *TV Times*, *Marie Claire*, *Woman's Own*, *Golf Monthly* and *Cycling Weekly*. Weighting was applied to each title's primary readership sample to reflect the National Readership Survey primary readership profile in terms of sex, age, social class, working status, reading frequency and presence of children in the household. The sample base used was 4539. This was a self-selecting sample and the survey was obviously initiated by IPC with an eye to persuading potential advertisers of the value of magazines as a medium for advertising to consumers. Even so, the responses are of considerable general interest.

Defining a short-break as a holiday of 1–3 nights, the IPC survey found that three-quarters of respondents had taken a short-break of some kind in the previous year. One in five had taken three short-breaks or more. The socioeconomic profile of short-break holidaytakers among respondents showed that ABC1s were more likely than C2DEs to have taken a short holiday in the previous year. Even so, two-thirds of C2DEs had taken a short-break in the last twelve months. Younger respondents (15–24 and 25–34) were found to be more likely than older groups to have taken a short-break, with the lowest level of participation among those over 65.

A significant finding featured in the survey report was that advance planning is much less in evidence for short-breaks than for main holidays. The average period across the sample was found to be 1.8 months. Thus 61% of *Marie Claire* readers and 65% of *Motor Boat & Yachting* readers stated that they had planned their last short-break less than one month in advance.

While in general terms the findings of this study tend to confirm the

UKTS findings, the kind of focused information produced by the IPC survey is likely to be very useful for potential advertisers, organizers of promotional competitions and other tourism interests in planning their campaigns.

CASE HISTORY

An example of how a national tourist organization can attempt to capitalize on the potential of short holidays is provided by the Scottish Tourist Board's 1995 'Autumn Gold' campaign. As reported in the newspaper *Scotland on Sunday*, the target was to increase tourism in the months of October and November by 7%, equivalent to an extra £5 million in income.

> Covering the whole of Scotland, it will give individual companies a marketing hook to work with in return for contributions to the campaign.
>
> 'We needed something to hang it on and turned to America,' said David Michels, chief executive of Stakis plc, the hotels group, who heads the STB Seasonality Working Group set up to find ways of increasing visitor numbers and spending off-season.
>
> 'An awful lot of Americans go to New England in the fall. The weather isn't as good as they say it is, but it's caught on.' Michels said success or failure would depend on Scottish companies and institutions responding to the sponsorship 'begging bowl' and on hundreds of places agreeing to stay open a month longer.
>
> The initiative already had tacit agreement from Historic Scotland, the National Trust for Scotland and area tourist boards who might otherwise shut information centres and attractions at that time of year . . .
>
> . . . The key tool is the Autumn Goldcard, a 'lifestyle' card, offering users discounts on travel, accommodation, restaurants, visitor attractions and products such as crafts, jewellery and whisky.
>
> Goldcard booklets will be mailed out directly or in response to telephone calls through an Autumn Goldline allowing the Board to add to its already substantial mailing list and market intelligence.
>
> Participating companies are being offered a range of benefits – e.g. counter displays, promotional material, inclusion in the booklet, marketing and media relations advice, promotion inserts and use of the mailing list – depending on whether they make a £1,000, £2,000 or £5,000 contribution.
>
> (Stokes, 1995)

This campaign, and other initiatives aimed at stimulating domestic UK demand for holidays in Scotland, is crucial to the implementation of the 1994 National Strategic Plan for Tourism in Scotland. It is now recognized that Scotland has limited scope for presenting itself to the key English market as a main holiday destination. Of course, promotions of this kind can only be one element in the strategy, which will require to give attention to the many deficiencies in the Scottish tourism product. Nevertheless, the shift in thinking is very significant in that it recognizes the dynamism of the short-break sector and seeks to capitalize on it in a derivative but nonetheless creative way.

FUTURE DEVELOPMENTS

As we have seen, short holidays in the UK have not grown during the 1990s to the extent predicted. There are many underlying factors which will influence their growth in the future. It is often assumed that leisure time and disposable income will continue to grow in future years as they have done in the past. But there is some evidence that in the UK at least a significant section of the workforce is tending to feel obliged to work longer hours while enjoying less job security and suffering more work-related stress than before. Whether this is likely to result in less holidaytaking by those affected, or in substitution of short for long holidays – or conceivably in more 'impulse buying' of short holidays – is difficult to foresee. Likewise, the general underlying level of unemployment will affect demand for short holidays. So too will the trend towards part-time, temporary or notionally self-employed working patterns, with their associated loss of paid holiday entitlement and their peculiar psychological strains. Possible political developments in the later 1990s, such as the imposition of a minimum wage or the adoption of the Social Charter of the EU, issues on which the UK is out of step with the rest of the European Union, or moves towards the introduction of a single currency, could have incalculable effects on the aggregate demand for short holidays.

Also, even if disposable income does rise across the board, short holidays are only one product competing in the leisure marketplace. A revival in the housing market might prompt more spending on home improvements at the expense of holidays. Other economic factors might have contradictory effects. For example, low interest rates, while welcome to those with heavy mortgage commitments, also affect the savings income of those (generally older) groups without mortgages, thereby reducing their propensity to take additional holidays.

Changing demographics are another factor which may have an important influence on demand for short holidays. Here commentators generally consider the outlook to be favourable (Mintel, 1993; Beioley, 1991). For example, there will be more 'empty nesters' (middle-aged ABs with no dependent children), who make up the top end of the market for short-break holidays abroad. There will also be more fit and affluent over-65 year olds who are already experienced short-break holidaytakers.

Considering the market for commercial short-breaks abroad, there are a number of factors which seem likely to lead to rapid growth if and when consumer confidence returns. These include lower air fares, the successful operation of the Channel Tunnel and increased competitiveness among ferry operators. The lifting of duty-free limitations within the European Union in January 1993 provided a boost to self-drive cross-Channel traffic. Greater familiarity with Europe, the strong promotional efforts of Euro-Disney, Paris, and the staging of major one-off sporting or cultural events may also encourage more British visitors to take short-breaks to the continent.

On the supply side, it has been suggested (Beioley, 1991) that there will be a broadening out of the accommodation base for short-break packages. The pioneering role in the UK of Center Parcs has already been mentioned. An important part of the company's significance lies in its more flexible approach to short-stay bookings (Fache, 1994). Other sectors such as hire boats and holiday cottages are increasingly willing to offer short-breaks, creating competition for hotels but also expanding the market. Within the licensed hotel sector commercial short holiday breaks have been identified (Edgar, 1992) as shedding their old off-peak image and now offering the hotelier a highly attractive alternative to discounting. Thus it is possible to fuel demand by providing more product variations across a greater variety of market segments, more locations and a wider selection of accommodation standards. Hotel groups lead the field here, attempting to brand through brochures, while independent hoteliers competing on price and through destination marketing techniques tend to be squeezed. Although they hold a relatively small proportion of the total market, it seems likely that suppliers of special interest and themed breaks will increasingly tailor products to particular age, interest or lifecycle groups. It has also been suggested (Beioley, 1991) that short-break packages will become a more important source of business for travel agents, although with increasing sophistication a significant proportion of consumers will prefer to make their own arrangements. Perhaps travel agents will find it easier to capitalize further on the sector where they are already strongest – commercial city-break packages abroad, rather than in selling UK-based holidays. In the European context, it has also been argued (EIU, 1995) that, contrary to general opinion, direct booking accessibility for the public actually increases opportunities for travel agencies. Consumers could be encouraged to bypass the travel trade and put together their own packages meeting the need for freedom and flexibility. But those travel agencies equipped with the appropriate technology can provide consumers with a much wider choice of flexible programmes and options at attractive prices and thus gain competitive edge.

Many factors are likely to ensure that cities in the UK and Europe will continue to be active in trying to attract short-break visitors. The proliferation of special events such as the Tall Ships Race and of arts festivals and cultural extravaganzas of all kinds should extend the appeal of places not previously considered leisure destinations. Innumerable urban regeneration schemes are tied in to city tourism development and marketing perspectives. Many of the infrastructural improvements put forward by city interests in the UK for Millenium Fund support had a significant tourism dimension. Whereas historic towns may be ambivalent towards short-stay tourists, large cities are keen to promote themselves in the short-break marketplace.

SUMMARY

Short holidays are an important and increasingly significant element in the mature tourism markets of North America and Europe. Because of the long-term structural shift in British holiday preferences away from main holidays in the UK in favour of main holidays abroad, short holidays have a strategic significance for the UK industry as a whole. There are particular benefits to accommodation suppliers and other operators in the more even pattern of seasonality which short holidays provide. As the market for short holidays matures, a greater variety of types of holiday can be offered and more sophisticated products developed with consequent benefits for the health of the whole tourism industry.

REFERENCES

Beioley, S. (1991) 'Short Holidays', in *Insights*, English Tourist Board, London.

British Tourist Authority/English Tourist Board (1988) *The Short Break Market*, BTA/ETB Research Services, London.

Economist Intelligence Unit (1992) Market segments: the European international short-break market, *Travel and Tourism Analyst*, No. 5.

Economist Intelligence Unit (1995) Market segments: the European international short-break market. *Travel and Tourism Analyst*, No. 2.

Edgar, D. (1992) *Commercial Short Holiday Break Markets in Scotland. A Report for the Scottish Tourist Board*, Napier Polytechnic, Edinburgh.

English Tourist Board (1993) *Short Break Market Study*, ETB, London.

English Tourist Board *et al.* (1994) *The UK Tourist: Statistics 1993*, ETB/NITB/STB/WTB.

Fache, W. (1994) Short-break holidays, Seaton, A.V. (ed.), *Tourism: The State of the Art*, Wiley, Chichester, pp. 459–67.

IPC Magazines (1994) *Holidays: An IPC Magazines Survey of Consumer Behaviour*, IPC Magazines, London.

MacBeth-Seath, R. (1995) Scots 'U-turn' on trade strategy, *Travel GBI*, No. 199, May 1995.

Mintel International (1993) Short break holidays abroad, *Leisure Intelligence*, Vol. **2**.

Scottish Tourist Board (1995) *Autumn Breaks Campaign, 1994, Research Results*, Research Section, Planning and Development Division, STB, Edinburgh.

Stokes, R. (1995) Holiday industry taking a leaf out of the New England book, *Scotland on Sunday*, 5 February.

Trinity Research (1989) *The UK Short Break Holiday Market*, Trinity
Research.

REVIEW QUESTIONS

1. In what ways do people taking short holidays tend to differ from
   people taking long holidays?
2. Explain how these differences provide opportunities for certain tourism service providers.
3. Consider the Scottish Tourist Board's 'Autumn Gold' campaign.
   Drawing on your perceptions of Scotland and what you have learned
   about the short holiday market in the UK, suggest how a comparable
   scheme might be devised to attract visitors to Scotland either during
   one of the shoulder seasons (spring or autumn) or during the New Year
   holiday period.

13 Business travel marketing

U.A. Schlentrich

OBJECTIVES

By the end of this chapter the reader should:

- be able to identify the main constituents of the business tourism market;
- understand the distinctive features of and demands for each including: the conventions and meetings sector, and the exhibitions and trade fairs sector;
- be aware of current developments in accommodation, transport and incentive travel targeted at business travellers;
- be aware of research approaches to targeting the business traveller by city tourism marketers.

INTRODUCTION

The rapid growth of the service sector, comprising to date almost 75% of the total gross domestic product for the G7 nations (USA, Canada, Japan, Britain, Germany, France, and Italy), and the elimination of international trade barriers has resulted in a global marketplace making business travel one of the most important profit and growth sectors of the tourism industry. The recent conclusions of GATT (the General Agreement on Tariffs and Trade) and NAFTA (Northern American Free Trade Agreement) have resulted in further breaking down artificial trade restrictions and have set the stage for over 120 nations to compete freely internationally. The trend towards free market economies in the former Eastern bloc countries and the present move by China towards a liberalized market economy will further encourage favourable international business travel.

The *European Business Travel and Expense Management Report 1993* published by American Express (1994) ranks Europe as the foremost business travel market in the world, outspending the United States and Asia. In the ten European countries surveyed (Belgium, France, Germany, Hungary, Italy, Netherlands, Spain, Sweden, Switzerland and the UK),

Table 13.1 Private sector business travel and expense markets

	T&E (US $ billion)	% of GDP on T&E	% of T&E spent abroad
Germany	38.8	2.5%	24%
United Kingdom	30.3	3.5%	38%
France	25.3	2.2%	24%
Italy	16.0	1.9%	28%
Spain	8.8	1.9%	23%
Sweden	6.8	3.8%	60%

Source: American Express (1994).

there are over 94 million people in the private sector workforce. Private sector employment recorded an annual T&E (Travel and Entertainment) expenditure of $141 billion, amounting to 2.5% of GDP. Thirty-one per cent of European T&E is spent on international travel, primarily by sales staff and management. The largest private sector business travel and expense markets are shown in Table 13.1.

Of the total European T&E expenditure, 31% is spent abroad. The countries with the highest proportion of T&E spent overseas are Sweden with 60%, Switzerland with 50% and Belgium with 44%. Business travel is now reported by companies as the third highest controllable cost factor representing nearly 5% of total operating expenses. Table 13.2 details the spending breakdown by category. Air fares (26%), hotels (20%) and motor fuel/mileage (19%) constitute the largest T&E sectors.

The two major segments of travel categorized by purpose are pleasure/personal and business. Business travel is further broken into three broad segments:

- individual business travel;
- convention and exhibition travel;
- incentive travel.

INDIVIDUAL BUSINESS TRAVEL

Traditional hotels have primarily marketed their properties towards the lucrative business travel market. Through target advertising, hotels

Table 13.2 Percentage of T&E by type of expenditure

Air fares	26%
Hotels	20%
Motor fuel/mileage	19%
Meals	16%
Entertainment	11%
Car hire	4%
Rail	4%

Source: American Express (1994).

attempted to entice the individual business traveller to book at their respective properties. Advertisements focused on concierge services, club rooms, business libraries and an array of bathroom amenities.

The travel agent

Traditionally, it was the hotelier's belief that the business traveller was the primary decision-maker in choosing where to stay. However, recent research (American Express, 1994) indicates that the travel agent has taken a pivotal role in the decision-making process. European hoteliers have long had a love/hate relationship with travel agents, often not recognizing their right to a commission (10% on rooms) or having to be reminded to send payment. The role of the travel agent is rapidly changing and the hotelier must be aware of the transformation which this important marketing and operational link in the travel purchase sector is undergoing. Hotel marketing budgets have to reflect the change in the purchasing process from the individual to the travel agent. Above all, hoteliers need to redress their travel agent relationships and develop service strategies targeted to communicate effectively with this fast growing sector.

Corporations as well as individual business travellers are increasingly turning to the travel agent to organize all aspects of their business travel arrangements. Six major factors contribute to this reliance:

- **Efficiency and reliability**. With the introduction of on-line reservation systems, travel agents can make airline, hotel and car rental arrangements through speedy 'one-stop' purchasing transactions, thus freeing up valuable secretarial time.
- **Economies**. Travel agents can negotiate discounted rates on behalf of their corporate clients and help implement corporate travel policies resulting in substantial savings.
- **Deregulation**. Airline deregulation and complicated rate structures and purchasing conditions have made the advice of a professional travel planner necessary.
- **Overseas expansion**. International travel has continued to grow as corporations have expanded their overseas business networks. The need for business travellers to deal with foreign time zones, climates, customs and holidays has made it necessary for the travel agent to take on the role of advisor as well as booking agent.
- **Airline/travel agent partnership**. As a result of the efficient retail distribution system of airline ticket sales via travel agents, the partnership between the airlines and travel agents has grown in importance. In the United States, 95% of all overseas airline tickets are sold by travel agents.
- **Global reservation systems**. The airlines have invested in global reservation systems. Travel agents are valuable indirect suppliers to the system in the form of air, hotel and car rental reservations which

generate considerable additional income received through commissions.

Corporate travel managers

The 1994 American Express T&E Management Survey indicated that 38% of companies with a large number of frequent travellers have their own travel manager. Seventy-four per cent of European companies have at least one appointed travel manager. The executive secretary/personal assistant coordinates 54% of companies' travel arrangements. Companies which participated in the survey rated the importance of services provided by travel agents as follows:

Lower cost air fares	77%
Guaranteed booking of lowest rates/fares	74%
Bookings on short notice	74%
Rebates on volume	73%
Lower priced hotels	69%
Reconciliation of travel expense reports	33%

The latest US Corporate Travel Manager Study (1992) conducted by Plog Research Inc. estimated that Americans took 151 million business trips during the previous year with 115 million hotel bookings (US Travel Data Center). Total business T&E in the US amounted to $130 billion compared to $141 billion in Central Europe. Four out of ten US corporations in the study have either a formal travel department or an in-house travel agency. Corporate travel managers are responsible for 28% of all business-related hotel bookings and execute 33% of all conference reservations. Sixty-five per cent of the companies place restrictions on reservations such as choice of airline and/or class of service when booking air travel, the lowest restrictions being on the choice of hotel chains (51% were highly restricted, 37% had some restrictions). Four out of ten companies have negotiated corporate rates with an average of six hotel chains. It is projected that corporations will increasingly take advantage of their purchasing power to negotiate favourable rates with hotel chains, airlines and rental car companies.

As a result of the recent recession, many corporations have initiated zero-based budgeting procedures, examining all corporate policies, structures and expenses. As their third highest controllable expense, it is no surprise that corporations have identified T&E as a sector requiring rationalization and cost saving.

Global distribution systems

Travel agents are increasingly using global distribution systems (GDS) as a 'one-stop' tool for their client's air, hotel and car rental reservation requirements. American Airlines launched the first central reservation

Table 13.3 Percentage of travel agencies linked to computer reservation terminals

USA	96%	Korea	98%
France	85%	Australia	91%
Italy	85%	Japan	85%
Scandinavia	61%	Hong Kong	65%
Spain	53%	Singapore	56%
Germany	48%	Taiwan	50%
United Kingdom	23%	Malaysia	32%

Source: The Graycon Group, Inc.

system, SABRE, approximately 20 years ago. Other leading US systems are Apollo (COVIA) and WORLDSPAN PARS. British Airways launched the Galileo consortium in alliance with United's COVIA, Swiss-Air and others. Lufthansa and Air France followed with the Amadeus system. Future systems will be enhanced with product display features such as voice and video applications. The percentage of travel agencies using computer reservation terminals has rapidly increased and presently over 380 000 travel agents in 125 countries are linked to these systems (see Table 13.3).

The female business traveller

The female traveller has been the fastest growing segment of the business travel market. During the last decade, the number of female business travellers is reported to have increased three times faster than the number of male business travellers. According to the US Travel Data Center, nearly 13.5 million women took 444.9 million business trips in 1991, representing 25.4% of all business travel. It is predicted that by the year 2000 nearly 50% of all business travellers will be women. In the UK, Expotel reports that 35% of business travellers in 1993 were women.

Hoteliers have recognized the importance of this market and have conducted market research in order to determine female preferences in terms of services and facilities. In 1992, the Kempinski Hotel Group conducted a 'Female Business Traveller Survey' in each of its five properties in North America. Female travellers were asked to identify the five most important criteria when selecting a hotel. In order of importance the responses were as follows:

- a workout facility;
- a friendly and knowledgeable staff;
- an iron, ironing board and hair dryer in guest rooms;
- a large room and bathroom;
- complimentary shuttle to airport and city centre.

Other features mentioned by female business travellers for the ideal hotel included: low calorie food, quick/casual food outlet serving salads and sandwiches, fax machine in guest rooms, two-line phones, separate floors or wings for business travellers away from tourists and families, large desk with good lighting and valet car parking service.

THE CONVENTION AND EXHIBITION MARKET

The convention and exhibition market has experienced unparalleled growth during the past 20 years. This market can be divided into two primary sectors:

- conventions and meetings;
- exhibitions and trade fairs.

Quality convention and exhibition centres can now be found in virtually every major city around the world. Asian cities in particular (for example, Hong Kong, Jakarta and Singapore) have recently developed state-of-the-art facilities competing favourably with established centres in Europe and North America. National and regional governments have long recognized the economic importance of this tourism sector and have supported the development of most centres whether through direct subsidies, grants or the raising of supplementary taxes.

Conventions and exhibitions attract visitors from different parts of the world who often would not normally visit a given destination. This supplementary income creates the following primary benefits:

- **Delegate spending**. It is estimated that between $525 and $970 is spent per delegate staying in a host community on an average of 3.8 days. For example, the economic benefit to Scotland from conferences and meetings in 1990 was £300 million in total delegate spending.
- **Employment**. The IACVB (International Association of Convention and Visitor Bureaux) estimates that every $20 000 spent by conventioneers generates one new job. However, estimates vary greatly from location to location. An economic impact study conducted by KPMG Consultants on behalf of the NEC (National Exhibition Centre) in Birmingham projected 4.5 million visitors would spend £430 million securing 16 800 full-time jobs in the Midlands in 1993.
- **Positive image**. Convention centres often substantially enhance the urban image of a city. Atlanta, Providence, Birmingham and Glasgow are examples of cities where new facilities acted as a catalyst in the process of inner-city renewal by contributing to a new image of vitality and regeneration. World trade centres, hotels, shopping, leisure facilities and restaurants are often part of the master plan which, as a result of the new infrastructure, reignite inner-city economies. Cities such as Chicago, Boston, Singapore or Las Vegas would not have experienced such phenomenal growth had it not been for their convention and exhibition market.
- **Indirect benefits**. Economists do not entirely agree on the exact value of the tourism expenditure multiplier. The Horwarth 1989 Annual

Convention Center Report suggests that the multiplier for indirect spending increases the impact of initial spending from 1.5 to 2.5 times. Local municipalities and state governments benefit from delegate spending through increased tax revenues estimated to be between 3% and 6% of total revenues.

Conventions and meetings

This segment of the hospitality industry has rebounded strongly after the recent recession and the Gulf War. This market is estimated to account for $97 billion in revenue globally:

North America $48 billion
Europe $22 billion
Asia $16 billion
Africa/Middle East $7 billion
Latin America $4 billion

Meetings and Conventions magazine (1990) reported that over 186 000 association meetings were held in 1990 with 22 million delegates in attendance. The corporate meeting market represents meetings held by companies outside of their offices primarily for the following purposes:

- management meetings;
- shareholder meetings;
- training sessions;
- sales and marketing meetings;
- product introductions.

According to a 12-month study in the US, the corporate meeting market accounted for over 866 000 meetings with a total expenditure of over $9.5 billion.

In the early 1960s, conventions and meetings were nearly always held in hotels. This changed with the explosive growth of the association market which virtually doubled from 12 000 meetings per year in the 1970s to over 22 000 meetings per year in the 1990s. As associations grew larger and more international in scope requiring not only meeting but also exhibition space, the stage was set for purpose-built conference and convention centres. Sophisticated, integrated convention facilities were developed in order to meet the needs of this rapidly developing market. The facilities developed in Birmingham are a case in point:

- **The Exhibition Centre** – with a capacity of 158 000 m^2 and parking for 15 000 cars;
- **The International Convention Centre** – capable of handling conferences from 50 to over 2 000 people;
- **The Symphony Hall** – which is home of the Birmingham Symphony Orchestra and available to meeting planners for special occasions such as opening sessions for up to 2 200 people;

- **The National Indoor Arena** – with an international standard sporting arena having a seating capacity of up to 13 000. Larger conventions make use of this facility for their opening plenary sessions.

A unique feature of these superb facilities is that they are managed by one management group on behalf of the Birmingham City Council, thus providing efficient marketing and operating expertise.

The city of Edinburgh has also initiated the development of an international conference centre in order to further boost the city's income from UK and overseas visitors.

Association Meetings

In order to attract the important association market, it is imperative for the hotelier and convention bureau executive to understand the different organizational and meeting requirements which apply to the various association sectors. The purpose of an association is to advance their members' interests which, according to the American Society of Association Executives (ASAE), can be broadly defined as to:

- advance the status and image of the members;
- provide for peer interaction and exchange of information;
- evaluate and project future trends;
- lobby and advance the association members' interests (political, economic, social);
- evaluate and project future trends;
- emphasize the value of membership;
- provide entertainment and informal interaction.

Members of associations elect local, regional, national and international boards who, on a voluntary basis, direct the affairs of the association, representing their members' views. Larger associations employ a full-time staff at their national or international business office. The elected board members usually serve for a limited time period (one to three years) since they also hold full-time positions in their respective professions.

An association's main board is primarily concerned with the setting of policies and the direction which the association should be taking from a strategic point of view, whereas the full-time executive staff is responsible for the implementation of policy and the running of the association on a daily basis. The organizational structure of an association's main board is typically mirrored by the structure of the paid executive structure of the organization. An association's organizational structure might look as illustrated in Figure 13.1.

Types of associations
Associations can be classified into the following categories:

- **Trade and professional associations**. These associations are primarily interested in improving the image and economic and trading environment of their members. Educational and networking sessions are an

CASE STUDY 13.1

The new Edinburgh International Conference Centre

The destination

Edinburgh is one of the world's most beautiful cities, renowned for its unique heritage, architectural grandeur and cultural vibrance. The city's worldwide reputation as host to major global events such as the Edinburgh International Festival, the Military Tattoo and the European Council Meeting is now to be further enhanced by the development of the Edinburgh International Conference Centre.

- The City offers over 15 000 hotel beds with accommodation to suit every budget. Two of the city's premier hotels are adjacent to the Centre.
- The range of social programmes on offer includes private tours of the Palace of Holyrood, river boat and canal cruises, and tours of distilleries or The Scotch Whisky Heritage Centre.
- There is a choice of 69 art galleries and museums.
- 28 golf courses can be found within the city boundary and international sports events are frequently held here.
- The city is a gateway to the breathtaking beauty of Scotland, and is within an hour's drive of the Highlands.

The economic impact

The EICC – a £38 million investment.

It is no surprise, in fact it is exceedingly well researched and documented, that hosting conventions and conferences makes money for the city in question, a fact that did not escape Edinburgh District Council and the City's enterprise company, Lothian and Edinburgh Ltd. The Edinburgh International Conference Centre has moved their search for an economic boost to Scotland's capital from dream to reality.

Before the first architect's drawing could be finalized, further research was required. Who were to be the beneficiaries, what impact would the development have on the City's infrastructure and where would the income come from? 'The results were quite outstanding', says Jim McIntyre, Executive Director of EICC Ltd. 'We are aware that the economy of Edinburgh and Scotland would receive a significant boost once the facility was open. However, even at their most conservative, the economic benefit assessment results are incredibly encouraging. In round figures, the conference centre will generate £19 million of net additional expenditure income to Scotland each year. It was when we examined some of the individual statistics that we truly realized the benefits of constructing the conference centre,' admits McIntyre. Each year the centre will generate more than 100 000 new business tourists with over £3.5 million spent on accommodation, a multi-million pound boost to the city's hotel trade. Annually £1.75 million will be spent in bars and restaurants, up to £450 000 in local travel. Most importantly, the city will enjoy an employment boost of nearly 1000 jobs generated from conference centre business.

The venue

Opening Autumn 1995 the Centre will provide international standard purpose-built meeting facilities of the highest quality, right in the heart of the city. The unique feature of the Centre, designed with the needs of the conference organizer in mind, is the main auditorium. Providing raked seating for 1 200 delegates theatre-style, this main auditorium can be subdivided, in moments, into three separate, self-contained auditoria for 600, 300 and 300. Supported by spacious well appointed foyers, exhibition and catering areas and a range of breakout rooms, the Centre will also offer the latest in presentation and communications technology.

Source: Adapted from ECCI (1993).

---

integral aspect of the association meeting schedule. Members regard belonging to their association as a vital part of their profession. Conventions are held during non-vacation periods and budgets for hotel accommodation, entertainment and meetings are in the upper tier. National and international meeting dates and locations are often set three to five years in advance.

- **Government organizations**. Political parties, regional municipalities, and military and police organizations all belong to this segment. These meetings are usually held during fixed, predetermined dates. Meetings are often held in the same location annually. Expenses incurred are generally reimbursed, based on per diem guidelines. Entertainment is normally rather limited for these events.
- **Labour unions**. Union conventions and meetings are usually held in the summer or the beginning of autumn. All expenses are generally borne by the local or national union on behalf of their delegates. These conventions would only be held in venues which are unionized.
- **Scientific and medical associations**. As a result of the continuous rapid changes in technology and the sciences, this sector organizes frequent conventions and meetings at the national and international level. Meetings comprise the presentation of papers, demonstrations, plenary sessions and exhibits. Main sessions involve all participants, require large theatres and are nearly always followed by smaller special interest symposiums which often involve sophisticated audio-visual equipment such as rear screen projection, closed circuit satellite television or multi-media presentations. The medical field is divided into twelve major associations, each serving a particular aspect of the medical profession. These meetings are prestigious and the participants usually stay in upmarket accommodation.
- **Religious organizations**. There are two major groupings of religious conventions: those held for clergy and support staff and those held for individuals practising a particular religion. Meetings for the first group are scheduled on a regular basis and are attended by approximately the same number of participants from year to year. Meetings for the

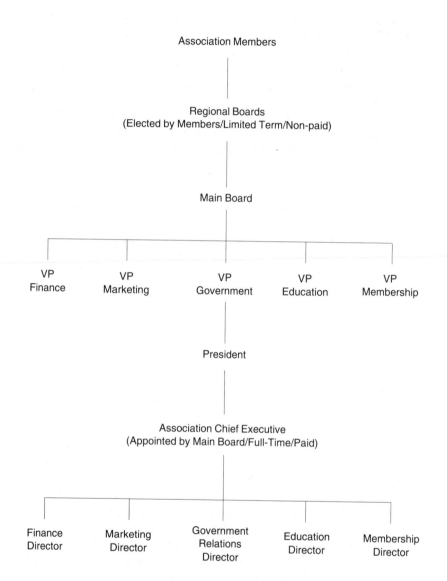

Figure 13.1 Example of the organizational structure of an association.

second group are primarily family affairs and are therefore often scheduled during school vacation periods. As participants at these conventions finance their own attendance, hotels in the lower budget category are in higher demand. Participants often stay with local church members or use university student accommodation.

- **Educational associations**. These conferences are generally held on university campuses and require a large number of breakout meeting rooms for plenary sessions and the presentation of papers. Meetings are usually held when universities and schools are not in session.

Budgets are relatively modest and associations attempt to obtain sponsorship for meal functions and social gatherings. Publishers often exhibit at these conventions.

- **Avocational associations**. These associations span a broad sector of interest groups. In contrast to members of the previously mentioned associations who generally share vocationally related interests, members of avocational associations comprise members sharing sport, recreational, hobby, fraternal, cultural, civic or other social interests. Meetings are held at local, national and international levels and usually take place on weekends and during holiday periods. Members pay for their own expenses.
- **Charitable associations**. These organizations are divided into two primary groups. The first group supports and raises funds for the advancement of a particular cause such as the arts, human rights or the fighting of poverty or disease. A major source of fund raising is the staging of charity gala events and raffles. The second group is represented by research, lobbying or support organizations (for example, the Red Cross) who are actively involved in the operational aspects of addressing particular problem areas. These groups meet frequently both nationally and internationally to set the stage for future strategic development.

Association marketing strategies

Venue selection for the more prestigious national and international conventions is basically a two-step process. A joint study by the ASAE (American Society of Association Executives) and the IACVB (International Association of Convention and Visitors Bureaux) confirms the important role which the paid association staff and executive team hold in the process of site selection. This study indicates that 58% of the time the association executive conducts site inspections, and 28% of the time it is the meeting planner. When the final choices are presented to the association's main board, 57% of the time the paid association chief executive is involved in the decision-making process to award the convention to a particular venue. Given the permanence of the paid staff versus the continuous change in composition of the main board, it becomes evident that the function of the full-time staff is extremely important and the convention centre or hotel needs to establish credibility with these professionals.

The bid to host a convention usually requires the cooperation and support of different partners:

- local/national association board;
- local convention/visitors bureau;
- national tourist bureau;
- the venue itself (convention centre/hotel);
- local community leaders (council, lord mayor).

International associations plan their site selection on a geographic rotation schedule, changing year to year from continent to continent. City selection within a region depends largely on the following criteria:

- site and standard of convention and exhibition facilities;
- accommodation mix and standard;
- transportation/access;
- security and health;
- quality of recreational facilities, shopping, restaurants and amenities;
- reputation of site management and staff (professionalism, stability, management/union relations);
- value for money.

The bidding for a larger convention requires strong support, especially from the local association chapter. Critical support in the preparation of a bid document is provided by the national tourist authority. In the United Kingdom, the BTA (British Tourist Authority) offers financial and technical assistance to associations and venues in the preparation of bid documents.

The BTA stages and/or participates in trade missions aimed at promoting the UK conference market. In 1994, for example, the events listed in Table 13.4 took place. Individual cities and venues can participate in these missions targeted to reach the association executive and meeting planner. Furthermore, the BTA coordinates the following activities aimed at this important market:

- **Familiarization trips** are launched for potential overseas association clients to gain first-hand experience of locations and venues. Transportation companies, local hoteliers, conference organizers and officials from the conference and visitors bureau participate in hosting 'fam trips' to showcase their respective cities and facilities.
- **Meeting and incentive travel workshops** are staged in different parts of Britain, bringing together overseas conference and incentive buyers with hotel and conference operators.
- **Publications**, including directories such as *Britain – Where the Business World Meets*, are distributed to potential buyers all over the world via

Table 13.4 1994 UK trade missions

Event	Location
EIBTA	Geneva
Meeting World Exhibition	New York
Meeting and Incentive Travel Show Symposium	Toronto
ASAE Annual Conference and Exhibition	San Francisco
Meetings Management Exhibition	Washington, DC
BTA Missions	Frankfurt
	Hamburg
	Oslo
	Stockholm
	etc.
CONFEX	London

Source: 1994 BTA Business Travel Marketing Initiatives.

BTA. The *British Business Bulletin* is another excellent vehicle to promote a conference venue. This newsletter is distributed to all BTA and overseas trade offices. It is a regular digest reporting on business travel events and news updates.

The BTA works closely with the regional and national convention bureaux in order to achieve maximum market penetration. In 1991, the Scottish Tourist Board (STB) relaunched a dedicated bureau, The Scottish Convention Bureau, with the aim of increasing Scotland's share of the international conference market. For the purpose of market networking, both the BTA and the STB maintain membership in relevant industry associations. The most important are:

- ASAE – American Society of Association Executives;
- ACE – Association of Conference Executives;
- ICCA – International Congress and Convention Association;
- MIA – Meeting Industry Association;
- SITE – Society of Incentive Travel Executives.

The membership of the above professional associations is responsible for the selection and staging of conventions and exhibitions throughout the world.

Convention and visitor bureaux

City governments and civic leaders have long recognized the importance of tourism as a vital link to employment, prosperity and overall positive city image and have therefore established convention and visitor bureaux to promote their cities. Convention and visitor bureaux coordinate and promote the diverse interests of city governments, travel suppliers (such as convention centres, hotels, restaurants, transportation companies and attractions) and trade and civic organizations. Bureaux act as information centres and promotional agencies. Probably the best known convention and visitor bureau campaign was centred on the 'I love New York' slogan and symbol:

This campaign created civic pride and accomplished a radical change in New York City's image.

By joining the International Association of Convention and Visitors Bureaux (IACVB), bureaux have access to the association's valuable database which contains industry data on organizations that hold conventions, a history of past conventions and up-to-date attendance records. This information is of immense value to convention and visitor bureaux in formulating their marketing strategies. In addition, IACVB assists its members by publishing up-to-date convention research data and by staging educational workshops and seminars.

Individual convention centres and hotels employ marketing staff whose aim it is to promote their facility. The blueprint for a facility's marketing activities is the annual marketing plan. This plan contains detailed action and budgetary targets aimed at maximizing the marketing strategy of a venue. Participation at trade shows, membership in industry associations, advertising strategies, direct mail campaigns, telephone sales and special promotions are developed and booking goals established.

Although most publicity is given to the larger national and international association meetings, over 90% of all association meetings have less than 1000 participants and more than 50% are attended by less than 100 participants. Associations hold only one major annual convention but innumerable smaller information, social, training and board meetings throughout the year. The market for smaller association meetings is of interest not only to larger hotels and convention centres but also to smaller properties.

Corporate meetings

Corporate meetings represent the other major meeting sector. This market has also expanded rapidly during the last decade. The removal of trade barriers has resulted in the internationalization of business ventures. Through mergers and joint ventures, corporations expanded both their manufacturing and service base, thereby increasing the need to communicate with their staff and clients. Although rapid communication methods such as fax, satellite conferencing and e-mail have gained in popularity, the most effective method of communication is still the personal meeting. Many companies which rely heavily on training have developed their own dedicated conference centres (i.e. McDonald's, Holiday Inn, Exxon). However, the vast majority of corporate meetings take place in hotels or purpose-built conference centres.

The primary purpose of corporations, as opposed to associations, is to be profit oriented by either producing products or delivering services. The opening of borders and the establishment of free trade agreements have encouraged what were once national companies to target their products and services towards the global community. British companies, for example, are now the largest foreign investors in America. Furthermore, the rapid advances in information technology and the growth of the service sector have resulted in cross mergers and expanded distribution networks. These trends are expected to continue well into the future. In their latest book, *Competing for the Future*, Hamel and Prahalad state: 'The future is to be found in the intersection of changes in technology, lifestyles, regulations, demographics and geopolitics' (Hamel and Prahalad, 1994).

Whereas attendance at association meetings is voluntary, attendance at corporate meetings is mandatory. The agenda for the corporate meeting is set by one person or an executive committee whereas the agenda for an association meeting is developed largely in consultation with its membership. The billing for corporate meetings includes all room, meal and entertainment expenses under one master account billed to the company whereas association billings for rooms and meals are paid for by the individual association member. The lead times for corporate meetings is relatively short, often governed by previously unknown events such as new product launches, changes in strategy, new legislation or acquisitions. Association meetings, on the other hand, are usually held annually as required by their constitution and are planned years in advance.

A survey by *Meetings and Conventions* magazine identified the types of meetings which corporations hold most frequently as listed in Table 13.5:

- **Management meetings** typically last two to three days and are attended by 10 to 25 participants. Their main purpose is to determine and communicate corporate budgets and products, and marketing and service strategies. Increasingly, however, meetings are being used to form motivational links between management teams. One reason why management elects to hold meetings away from the corporate offices is to create a non-hierarchical environment. Although meetings are often held in an informal setting, they usually require state-of-the-art facilities and high service standards. Recreational or informal 'get togethers' are often integrated into the meeting agenda. Activities might include a round of golf, a cycling tour, a rafting trip or a round robin tennis tournament. After the evening meal, participants often gather into smaller groups for case studies or team projects with activity breaks such as darts, table tennis or snooker.
- **Training seminars**, typically last from three to five days and are usually attended by 30 to 50 participants. These meetings are very focused, involving classroom style presentations, small teamwork groups and individual projects to be completed by the participants. Organizers of these sessions are looking for a high standard in the quality of food, up-to-date conference rooms and audio-visual equipment.
- **Marketing and sales meetings** are held primarily to motivate, familiarize and educate participants about a company's products and

Table 13.5 Most frequently held corporate meetings

Management meetings	25%
Training seminars	23%
Regional sales meetings	16%
New product introductions	10%
Professional/technical meetings	9%
National sales meetings	6%
Incentive trips	4%
Shareholders meetings	3%
Other meetings	4%
Total meetings	100%

Source: Taken from *Meetings and Conventions* (1986).

services. Meetings often comprise award ceremonies for high producers, promotional presentations by advertising or public relations agencies and peer interaction along the lines of a theme or a particular marketing slogan. National marketing meetings often require elaborate audio-visual support and are usually attended by 180 to 400 participants.

- **Product introductions** are often attended by a company's top management and technical, marketing and service staff. Existing and potential customers are invited together with trade press. These launches are generally elaborate events booked at upmarket conference venues or deluxe hotels. The primary purpose is to celebrate, educate, stimulate interest in and promote the new product.
- **Professional and technical meetings** are similar to training sessions, often involving experimentation and product demonstrations.

A survey of corporate meeting planners revealed that their primary requirements for corporate meetings are as listed in Table 13.6.

Corporate marketing strategies

Whereas it is relatively easy to target the executives responsible for arranging association meetings, corporations generally do not employ a full-time executive responsible for planning corporate meetings. Corporate executives from the human resource, marketing, finance or research department could be involved in planning meetings. It is often the department head's secretary or executive assistant who is responsible for negotiating meeting details. The level of their understanding of event planning can vary greatly

Table 13.6 Factors influencing hotel selection

Factors	% of respondents rating as very important
Quality of food service	78
Meeting rooms	69
Previous experience with facility and staff	48
Sleeping rooms	47
Efficiency of billing procedures	46
Assignment of one staff person to handle meeting	41
Efficiency of check-in/check-out	41
Meeting support services	38
Convenience to transportation	23
Proximity to airport	23
Special meeting services	19
Exhibit space	17
On-site recreation (golf etc.)	16
Suites	12
Convenience to shopping etc.	9
Newness of facility	6

Source: Schlentrich (1993).

from being highly professional to requiring personal assistance during each step of the planning process.

The most productive corporate meeting sales strategy is that of target marketing. Target marketing involves research into a company's meeting patterns such as when and where meetings take place, who makes the decisions, what the budget is, what services are required and what type of facilities are preferred. In 1972, Omni International Hotels pioneered the concept of market research targeted to the meeting market. A data base was established with input from the local, regional and national sales offices. Marketing research coordinators communicated detailed 'lead data' to sales executives who contacted decision-makers at a particular company. This approach resulted in effective conversion rates (sales effort versus bookings). Post-conference information was fed back to the market research coordinators thus keeping the database up to date.

Advertising in trade publications such as *Meetings and Conventions* serves primarily as a tool to promote new facilities or marketing programmes. Telemarketing has increasingly become an integral part of a hotel group's direct sales marketing strategy. Telemarketing is targeted towards the smaller, short lead time group meeting market. Hotel chains promote this service by advertising a toll-free telephone number and publishing a group meeting brochure detailing a daily delegate price (including guest rooms, meeting rooms, meal functions and meeting breaks). Hotel chains also use in-house newsletters to communicate with their target market. For example, in the winter 1994 issue of their newsletter, the Savoy Group of hotels and restaurants featured the launch of their new high-tech meeting room at the Lygon Arms Hotel. The 'Tradition meets tomorrow' article heralded this purpose-built facility and specialized services which the hotel provides for the corporate market.

It is also becoming common for larger hotel chains to brand their conference facilities. Hilton International, for example, promote their 'Meeting 2000' product, a facility and service concept which was developed after extensive research and user consultation. All aspects, from room design, lighting, projection and communication equipment to meeting chairs, coffee breaks and meal preferences, were researched. Operational training and service standards were established in consultation with the hotel's conference managers to ensure consistency of services offered (Hilton, 1994).

In North America, purpose-built urban and resort conference centres have recently experienced strong market acceptance. In 1981, the IACC (International Association of Conference Centers) was formed. The organization today has more than 285 members. In order to join, over 60% of the centre's business must be derived from meeting-related activities. In addition, centres must provide a 'total and balanced meeting environment' including high-quality meeting rooms which are designed and furnished for comfort, productivity and endurance, guest rooms with adequate work space, dining facilities that ensure flexibility and privacy, a full range of audio-visual equipment, a fully trained staff as well as recreational and leisure facilities to create a balance between work, relaxation and inter-action. The primary reason why these centres are so popular is that they provide a custom-designed meeting environment served by specialized professionals. A conference coordinator is the meeting planner's primary point of contact within the facility. The conference coordinator assists in all aspects of the meeting. Another special servicer of these conference centres is the conference concierge who acts as a central information source handling services such as typing, messages, group registration and coordination of leisure programmes. The 'Complete Meeting Package' (CMP) is a unique element of the pricing and service package which these centres promote. While hotels usually have different charges for guest rooms, meeting facilities, meals, coffee breaks, supplies and audio-visual equipment, the CMP rate is a daily rate that includes all of these charges, thus eliminating the element of surprise inherent in the 'à la carte' method of pricing.

Exhibitions and trade fairs

Exhibitions are increasingly held in conjunction with the annual meetings of associations. They permit suppliers and manufacturers to directly reach a target audience which otherwise would be difficult and expensive to contact. According to a study by the ASAE (American Society of Association Executives), more than 50% of association meetings hold exhibitions to supplement their income. Fifty per cent of the time, exhibitions were held in hotels and 42% of the time they were held in convention centres.

A trade fair is a marketplace for commercial suppliers of products or services which are of interest to a specific profession or market segment. Trade fairs are the most dynamic of all direct media marketing, the only situations in which customers and prospects come to the seller intending to place orders for purchase. Initially, marketing executives dismissed the idea of trade shows as an 'educational enterprise' but they soon realized that trade shows are a cost-effective means of reaching a broad spectrum of customers. Trade fairs or shows are usually held during the same period and in the same location each year. There are closed trade fairs which are open only to the professional trade and open shows which are targeted to a sector of the general public. Popular open trade shows, such as the annual car, travel or home shows, attract millions of visitors each year around the world and are a profitable and important element of the business travel market.

Trade shows may be organized by trade or professional associations, exhibition centres, exhibitors themselves and private or public companies. Trade shows such as the annual hotel show in Paris, the ITB (International Travel Mart) in Berlin and COMPLEX (the world's largest annual computer show) in Las Vegas each attract from 100 000 to more than 200 000 visitors every year. Trade shows are so successful because they unite under one roof during a limited period of time (3–5 days) exhibitors and buyers from different parts of the world, making them a cost-effective marketing and sales vehicle.

The marketing of trade shows is becoming more and more sophisticated. The organizer's objective is to identify potential buyers through market research and to interest them in attending a particular show. Visitor statistics are recorded for each event by market segment and customer origin. Exhibitors fill out confidential order and purchasing reports allowing venues to quantify the total value of orders placed.

In 1993, the NEC in Birmingham held over 108 separate exhibitions (more than any other exhibition centre in Europe), registering £2 billion worth of orders. Over 2 million visitors (69% from outside the West Midlands) and 34 000 exhibitors attended these shows. Hotels registered 1.3 million bednight bookings, representing 23% of hotel space in the region. The NEC is by far the largest exhibition centre in the UK with 158 000 m^2, followed by Earl's Court in London with 59 000 m^2, Olympia in London with 42 000 m^2 and the SECC in Glasgow with 20 000 m^2. The largest European exhibition centres are listed in Table 13.7.

Trade shows are a $21 billion a year industry with over 9000 shows held annually attracting over 45 million visitors worldwide. In 1992, approximately 190 000 business visitors from overseas attended exhibitions and trade fairs in the UK, spending on average £707 per person. By contrast, the individual business traveller spent on average £481 per person.

INCENTIVE TRAVEL

Incentive travel has long been recognized by companies as a motivational tool to reward their employees for outstanding accomplishments. The largest share of the incentive market is derived from insurance companies and car dealerships. Companies reward achievements such as attaining customer satisfaction, reaching financial targets or reducing staff turnover with incentive travel awards. It is expected that incentive travel will

Table 13.7 Largest European exhibition centres

	Area (m^2)
Hanover	475 600
Frankfurt	273 000
Cologne	260 000
Milan	249 000
Paris (Porte de Versailles)	222 000
Dusseldorf	198 000
Basel	172 000
Paris (Nord Villepointe)	164 000
Birmingham	158 000
Utrecht	120 000

Source: NEC Ltd Annual Report (1994).

continue to grow as companies find this to be an effective and personal way to reward their staff.

In the UK, this market is estimated to be worth more than £150 million, whereas in the USA incentive travel generates over $2 billion annually. Incentive trips are usually organized by travel agents or destination management companies. The average incentive group comprises 60 participants. Spouses are usually invited to take part in the trip at the expense of the company. The average length of an incentive trip is one week and is usually scheduled when a company's business will allow participants to be absent.

Incentive travel organizers seek venues (hotels, cruise ships or country estates) which offer quality facilities and will create a memorable experience. The BTA incentive publication states, 'The ultimate incentive trip requires a unique blend of ingredients to fulfil corporate objectives and achieve expectations' (BTA, 1994). Almost all incentive programmes involve special entertainment, themed food and beverage functions and either spectator or participative events (such as visits to a theatre or rafting, shooting, etc.). It is not uncommon for larger companies to charter jets, cruise ships or an entire hotel for their incentive programme. Companies also stage hospitality functions and shorter incentive weekend programmes planned around prestigious sporting events such as Ascot, Henley or Wimbledon. Hotels such as The Gleneagles or Turnberry in Scotland have developed special incentive programmes. These properties offer golfing, fishing, shooting and luxurious spa surroundings to the discriminating corporate client.

The BTA and national tourist boards have targeted the incentive travel segment by providing marketing support to venues and destination management companies. The BTA annually invites European, American and Pacific Rim incentive clients for workshops and site inspection visits to Britain. The 1994–95 full-colour brochure *Britain – the Great Incentive Venue* was published by the BTA to feature hotels, unique country houses, estates and castles.

BUSINESS TRAVEL SERVICE PROVIDERS

Transportation (air, rail, ship and automobile) and accommodation (primarily hotels) represent by far the largest components of the T&E budget. Following Parker (1990), both sectors are undergoing continuous change as a result of the evolution experienced within:

- **the remote environment** – economic, social, political, legal, technological, ecological;
- **the industry environment** – entry barriers, supplier power, buyer power, substitute availability, competitive rivalry;
- **the operating environment** – competitors, creditors, customers, employees, suppliers.

Transportation

There is no doubt that the rapid evolution of reliable and secure travel modes has greatly impacted on business's ability to expand beyond regional horizons. Initially, major centres of commerce grew around distribution hubs such as harbours (Amsterdam, Liverpool, Hamburg) or rail centres (San Francisco, Montreal), linking production and manufacturing plants with consumer markets. The invention of the jet engine and the end of the Second World War led to an explosion of international business travel. The 1993–1994 American Business Travel Survey indicated that transportation expenditure represented 53% of total T&E.

Air travel

The business traveller is of great importance to the airlines as this market represents 20% of all traffic, but accounts for 60% of total revenue. As a result of the recent recession, corporations are increasingly requesting first-class passengers to cut back to flying business class and business class flyers are scaling back to economy class. Airlines are challenged to offer services and marketing concepts which will prevent this type of erosion. Many airlines are now replacing first class (costing about twice the price of business class) with a new upgraded business class adding ground support services. British Airways took the unusual step of creating a brand management department responsible for conducting research into traveller's needs and expectations. In 1992, British Airways invited 80 frequent business travellers to a weekend of 'focus group' sessions to determine how the airline could create distinctive market-driven customer care and service programmes. Marketing strategies of the past, such as competing on price and barrages of promotions (two for one, upgrading, or double frequent mileage credit) launched by one airline would almost certainly be quickly copied by its rival thus negating its initial competitive advantage.

Most international airlines are now investing millions to introduce interactive communication services for long-haul business travellers which would permit direct dialling, fax services, destination news, movies and video games through seat-back screens. Increasingly, ground services are also being improved by extending customer care, such as valet parking, speed check-in, airport lounges with business centres and facilities allowing business travellers to shower and change after long flights and proceed directly to business meetings without having to check into their hotel first. A recent survey of more than 2000 frequent travellers carried out by VISA International found that the majority of travellers worked harder while travelling but only one in five would willingly give up travelling. The business traveller, however, demands increasingly better service and efficiency with less hassle while on the road.

It is not only the airlines which are undergoing drastic changes, airports are also in the process of being restructured. ACI Europe (Airports Council

International), an association of operators and owners of airports, projects that its 261 member airports will be spending over $22 billion on new facilities comprised mainly of terminals and runways between 1993 and 1997. Airports with a daily presence of a captive audience are turning into shopping, restaurant and conference centres. From mid-1993 to mid-1994, BAA, owner of several UK airports, handled 74.2 million passengers deriving half of its revenue from non-airline operations. BAA's research indicates that Heathrow is Europe's busiest airport with nearly 48 million passengers providing employment for 70 000 people.

Airports without efficient ground transportation feeder systems are increasingly placed at a competitive disadvantage. Road transportation to or from airports can often be more stressful and time consuming than the actual flight itself. Furthermore, passengers arriving at an airport who require rail or bus connections object to the lengthy transfer time required to reach ground transportation terminals. Airports such as Frankfurt, Charles de Gaulle or Geneva are directly linked to a rail network system making transfer to the final destination relatively easy.

As an effective marketing tool, the value of the frequent flyer programme has now been firmly established. Although schemes are expensive to administer, they have become a necessity, especially for international carriers. The OAG Business Travel Lifestyle Survey of 1994 provided data on the habits of travellers from Britain, France and Germany. It reports that 86% of business travellers belong to at least one frequent flyer programme. Seven out of ten regular flyers would opt to travel with the airline to whose scheme they belong.

Rail travel

The railway networks spanning Europe and North America were at the root of those continents' economic growth. The railroad's commercial and passenger transportation heydays lasted approximately one hundred years, from 1830 to 1930. Since the mid-1920s, however, the automobile has replaced the railroad as the most popular mode of transportation.

As a result of increased gasoline prices, overcrowded roads and seemingly endless road repairs which make travel by car more stressful and lengthy, the railroads have been staging a comeback. Business travellers across the world are increasingly using intercity rail networks which provide reliable and comfortable service from city centre to city centre. Japan has led the way in connecting its major cities with high-speed rail links and thereby dramatically reducing dependence on the automobile and the plane for intercity travel. In Europe, the French TGV rail network was launched in 1981. The network achieved an increase in passenger usage of more than 90% with average train occupancies of 70% to 80%. In Germany, the ICE rapid rail network has gained a 5% market share from the airlines and 9% from individual automobile usage since 1991. The EU Commission has identified 26 projects valued at over $100 billion which are aimed at the development of efficient speed rail networks. Within the European

Union, auto traffic has doubled since 1970 and air transportation increased fivefold. The less flexible, slow and obsolete rail networks lost market share which rail systems are now trying to regain through the implementation of European-wide speed rail linkages. The latest statistics released by the UIC (International Rail Service Association based in Paris) show that during the past ten years, speed rail usage has increased from 5.7 billion passenger miles to 30 billion passenger miles. At present, the European high-speed rail network spans 1367 miles of new high-speed lines with high-speed trains travelling over an additional 6000 miles. An article in *The Daily Telegraph* reported that a 'master plan' for Europe, partly spurred by the needs of the business traveller, aims at a high-speed network of more than 18 650 miles by early next century (Knutton, 1994). The recently launched Eurostar service will enable business travellers to journey via the Channel Tunnel at speeds close to 200 mph linking London with Paris or Brussels in about three hours. Not only are these intercity train connections less time consuming and generally more reliable than air routes, they also place less strain on the environment.

For rail travel, however, to regain its market dominance, substantial capital investments and visionary leadership from governments will be required. Scientists are presently developing technologies for new rail systems which will allow trains to reach speeds of up to 450 km/h. The latest such venture exists between the German industrial groups, Thyssen, Siemens and AEG. This venture, subsidized by the German government, seems to be the most promising in re-establishing rail service as a credible alternative to both auto and air travel. The German group's 'Transrapid Project' has been in development for the past ten years. It is presently undergoing extensive field trials. What makes this rail system so promising is that trains glide on a magnetic field, virtually noise free. The first commercial link is planned for completion by the year 2010, connecting Berlin with Hamburg and requiring only 53 minutes from city centre to city centre.

Efficient speed rail links will not only benefit business travellers but may also provide an impetus for the regeneration of inner cities. Inner cities have been overburdened with traffic, negatively affecting the business environment. As a result, many companies have relocated to the suburbs making business travel more difficult and inefficient. The decay of the inner city, as seen primarily in America, has resulted in urban ghettos deprived of their tax base with little chance for renewal. If European cities are not to follow this American pattern, effective transportation systems which substantially reduce car usage must be put into place.

Ship travel

Sir Samuel Cunard pioneered the first scheduled trans-Atlantic sea crossings in 1840. Just as the automobile led to the demise of the rail network, so the introduction of commercial airline flights led to the rapid decline of ship travel as a scheduled passenger transportation mode. The past decade, however, has seen a phenomenal increase in the cruise ship industry. The industry predicts that more than 5.5 million passengers will have sailed on 200 cruise ships in 1994. This number is projected to double within the next ten years. Businesses are increasingly using attractive purpose-built liners for conferences and incentive travel. Fly/cruise packages took off in the United States in 1978 when the deregulation of the airlines resulted in lower air fares. Florida-based cruise operators developed affordable packages targeted at the 'snow belt' states and Canada for warm weather cruising.

Automobile travel

All travel surveys show that the automobile is the dominant travel mode used by business travellers. US intercity travel surveys indicate that 84% of all travel is by automobile. The predominant reasons for choosing the car for business travel are:

- ease of travel from door to door;
- control of departure time;
- freedom to use car once destination has been reached;
- low cost (especially if used by more than one passenger);
- provision of corporate car by company.

However, business travel by car is increasingly seen as stressful, time wasting and dangerous, particularly for longer distances.

According to data from Hertz Corporation, the rental car industry is a $4 billion a year business. The rental car industry's growth has paralleled that of air travel. Over 75% of the car hire market is derived from the business traveller. The four major car rental companies (Hertz, Avis, National and Budget) dominate the airport rental locations, accounting for 95% of the market. These car hire giants compete fiercely for the profitable market of business accounts. Most car rental agencies are owned by leading car manufacturers who use the agencies to introduce their latest models in the hope that satisfied customers will purchase their cars for private and business use.

Car hire companies are turning towards information technology in order to speed up the process of check-in and check-out. Business travellers with corporate accounts or membership in frequent user programmes such as Hertz No.1 Club can virtually drive out of the airport with their rental car within minutes after their planes touch down. Similarly, return of cars is greatly facilitated by car hire staff recording mileage via hand-held computers at the drop-off point.

Accommodation

Increased competition and the sophistication of the business traveller has led individual hotels and chains towards the development of hotel brands and the launch of product and service strategies in the search for a sustained competitive advantage. Branding, market segmentation, total quality management and frequent stay programmes have become the cornerstone of recent hotel business traveller marketing strategies.

Branding and market segmentation

Only a few years ago, hoteliers hotly debated the issue of whether their property should be branded or whether they should continue to be marketed as individual hotels under a corporate umbrella. Today we know that those companies which identified their hotels through strong product branding achieved increased market share, superior financial results and accelerated growth when compared to non-branded competition.

In many instances, these companies merged with under-marketed competitor groups achieving spectacular turnaround results. The question, therefore, is not whether branding is beneficial to the hospitality industry, but how one can achieve dominance in a given market segment.

Benefits of branding

The objective of hotel branding is to achieve increased market share through heightened public awareness, thereby resulting in higher occupancies and average rates. A clearly positioned brand has a distinct competitive edge by offering to its target market value-added services and desired amenities.

The benefits of hotel branding apply to the following areas:

- **Financial**. A strong brand will achieve superior operating results and thus more easily be able to attract favourable financing, joint venture capital or franchise partners. In addition, economies of scale usually will reduce costs such as construction development, centralized purchasing, accounting, marketing and information technology services.
- **Marketing**. The key objectives of brand marketing are to achieve brand recognition and to convey a distinct image of the brand to the potential guest. Guest loyalty is achieved by offering and providing value-added services which clearly distinguish the brand from the competition. A strongly branded hotel group catering primarily towards the business traveller also provides the opportunity to cross-market promotions and programmes, such as conference packages, health and fitness events, family vacations, short-breaks and personal-enrichment or teaching packages.
- **Operations and personnel**. Branded property management allows for the standardization of management and operating systems which will ultimately result in increased guest satisfaction, greater efficiency and higher standards of service. Uniform services and operating procedures will greatly facilitate the training and development of both management and staff. Clear career ladders can be developed permitting promotion and transfer of employees which would be considerably more difficult to achieve in groups where operational systems

differ from property to property. As a result, employee motivation, productivity and retention are increased.

These advantages of branding will become even more significant in years to come.

Total quality management

Hotels primarily distinguish themselves through their service quality. While business travellers might be initially impressed by a hotel's decor, long-term success is the result of quality management. TQM is not about reaching short-term goals and objectives; rather its focus is on continuous improvements and responding to the ever-changing market. To attract and maintain the business market, it will not suffice for a hotel to merely satisfy the customer. The hotel must be able to create a bond by exceeding guests' expectations.

Many hotel companies are presently redesigning their organizational structure from the multi-layered, 'top to bottom' hierarchy to one which promotes an open, participatory style of management. Hotels will need to create new job structures rewarding teamwork, adaptability and willingness to learn new skills. Companies which have been willing to create learning organizations and to invest in continuous training and the teaching of new skills reap the benefits by obtaining an increased share of the business travel market.

The Ritz-Carlton hotel company has achieved a sustained competitive advantage by focusing on product and service quality. Today the company rates highest in the market business traveller and conference market.

Management together with its employees must develop a shared vision of how to organize and manage for change and competitiveness. Operating procedures and customer care programmes should be developed by the respective departments and not imposed from the top. Results and performance must be measurable and be communicated openly. Achievement of targets and special efforts should be recognized, celebrated and rewarded accordingly.

CASE STUDY 13.2

The Ritz-Carlton Credo

The Ritz-Carlton is a place where the genuine care and comfort of our guests is our highest mission. We pledge to provide the best service and facilities for our guests who will always enjoy a warm, relaxed yet refined ambience. The Ritz-Carlton experience enlivens the senses, instils well-being and fulfils even the unexpressed wishes and needs of our guests.

Source: Ritz-Carlton Corp., Atlanta.

Table 13.8 Estimated 1995 frequent stayer hotel membership subscription

Marriott	6.0 million members
Holiday Inn	4.2 million members
Hilton Hotels	2.8 million members
Hyatt Hotels	2.5 million members
Sheraton	1.5 million members

Hotel loyalty programmes

Increasingly hotel groups have adopted the airline strategy of rewarding frequent travellers with bonus points in order to secure repeat business and loyalty. Virtually all major hotel chains have now established their own frequent stayer programmes. Guests subscribed into such a programme earn points for room accommodation, gift certificates or in-house purchases. Larger international chains thus have a competitive edge over smaller groups or independent hotels. It is therefore no surprise that the larger hotel chains have established a significant membership base (see Table 13.8).

Although frequent stayer programmes represent a substantial cost in terms of investment in technology, administration and promotional expenditure, hotel chains claim that the additional income by far offsets expenditures. Hilton considers its 'H-Honours' programme to be its best strategic weapon in the battle for the lucrative individual business market. Its 2.8 million members contributed more than 4.7 million room nights in 1993, a 32% increase over the previous year. Hilton attributes the success of its programme to allowing its members to earn both hotel points and airline miles for the same stay, whereas most other hotel programmes require their customers to choose either hotel points or airline miles.

Many hotel companies are establishing strategic alliances with airlines, car rental companies and credit card companies thus providing a powerful data and client base for purposes of joint promotions and cross marketing (see Table 13.9).

A survey of *Frequent Flyer* magazine readers (December 1991) found that 56% chose to stay at full service hotels, 23% chose mid-price properties, 9% stayed in deluxe hotels, 4% selected suite or extended-stay hotels and the remaining 8% frequented economy and airport accommodations. Almost 90% of the frequent travellers were enrolled in at least two hotel chains' frequent stay programmes.

Table 13.9 Hotel group frequent stayer programme affiliation

Marriott Hotels	**Hilton Hotels**
British Airways	Delta Airlines
US Air	United Air
Hertz Rental Car	Avis Rental Car
Natwest Visa Credit Card	American Express Credit Card

CASE STUDY 13.3

Marriott Hotels loyalty marketing programme

Simple   Easy to understand and participate in
            – 'Stay credit' linked to spending
            – Painless redemption

Relevant   Benefits must be highly desirable
            – Valuable options
            – Destination and price

Attainable Benefits must be reasonably achieved in the near term
            – Quick rewards
            – Higher awards to drive sustained participation

Marriott attributes the success of its loyalty programme to its clarity and structure stating that for a loyalty programme to succeed it must be perceived by the customer to be simple and relevant, offering attainable awards.

Information technology

Information technology in particular has a significant influence on business travel service providers and on how the practice of business is continuing to evolve. Advances in information technology (IT) are emerging in multiple forms throughout all sectors of the tourism industry providing direct and indirect benefits to the business traveller. Airlines, hotels and car rental companies are looking to information technology to provide a competitive edge in their quest to achieve increased market share. IT support services play a major role in increasing back-office efficiency and improving personal service standards extended to the business traveller.

Marriott Hotels and Resorts are considered to be a leader among the hospitality firms in effectively using IT in their marketing and service strategy (see Table 13.10). Marriott's primary marketing strategy focuses on:

- consumer marketing;
- distribution and intermediary marketing;
- direct sales;
- revenue maximization systems.

All of these components are dependent on IT for their full and efficient integration.

Smaller independent hotels can also cost effectively use IT to drastically improve their guest services and marketing strategy. The arrival of the microchip and desktop PCs allows small businesses to establish guest histories and a database marketing system at a reasonable cost. The latest PC with the 586 microchip now costs approximately £2500. In the 1980s,

Table 13.10 Keys to Marriott's marketing strategy

Consumer marketing	• Honoured guest awards • Strategic alliances • Advertising • Guest satisfaction report
Distribution and intermediary marketing	• Marriott reservation system • Global Airline CRS/GDS • Travel agency relations • Sales agent network
Direct sales	• International sales network • National transient sales • Telesales • Sales technology
Revenue maximization systems	• MARSHA central reservations system • Demand forecasting/yield management • Directors of reservation sales • Property diagnostic process

Source: Adapted from Hanks (1994).

an IBM mainframe with the same capacity cost £180 000. The evolution of the microchip and the development of multi-media PCs will continue to evolve at a fast pace.

A marketing database is 'an organized collection of data about individual customers, prospects or suspects that is accessible and actionable for marketing services such as service sales or maintenance of customer relationships' (Kotler, 1991). The development of such a database and its continuous updating should be viewed by hotels as an essential marketing tool. Hotels with such a database can provide a higher level of personal service by maintaining a detailed guest history with information such as previous number of stays, preferred room rates, birthday, room preference, billing instructions, hobbies, etc. The database can become a valuable tool for cross-marketing promotions such as meeting packages, corporate rate programmes and special events.

Furthermore, technology can greatly enhance a business traveller's hotel stay by providing speedy in-room check-out, multi-lingual video and TV channels, room service order placement via TV, 'smart' telephones provided with multi-lines and automatic dialling, jacks for faxes and PCs, a voice mail message system, in-room mini-bars with automatic billing and computerized key lock systems.

By the year 2010, the development of multi-media, virtual reality and satellite conferencing will dramatically change the way business is conducted. The race to link every home in the Western world to a fibre optic network during the next ten years has already begun. Telephone companies and cable television operators are presently replacing copper wires with fibre optic cables. One fibre optic strand the width of a human hair is capable of delivering up to 300 000 simultaneous telephone calls or 150 high quality video channels. In November 1994, Bill Gates, the founder of Microsoft which brought personal computers within reach of hundreds of millions of households around the world, announced the launch of his firm's new venture offering interactive on-line database services via this information superhighway. Business men and women will have direct access to rail and air timetables, hotel booking services, on-line share dealings and electronic newspapers.

SUMMARY

This chapter has introduced various facets of business travel marketing. The tourism industry has changed from an operation-driven to a marketing-driven industry. The rapid changes which the industry is experiencing in the external and internal business environment require service providers to continually assess their product and service offerings. Peter Drucker (1974) states: 'What the customer thinks he is buying, what he considers "value" is decisive – it determines what business is, what it produces and whether it will prosper.' In addition to creating a customer, the purpose of service marketing is to keep the customer. Ultimately, successful service strategies will depend on the quality of human interaction between business traveller and service provider.

Business travel has experienced phenomenal growth during the past decades. The foundations laid and the trend of free market economies will continue to provide a stage for future growth. The technological advances and improvements in communication and transportation networks will ensure that during the next century the business travel industry will be one of vitality and exciting challenges.

REFERENCES

American Express (1994) *European Business Travel and Expence Management Report 1993*, American Express, Brighton, UK.

British Tourist Board (1994) *Britain – The Great Incentive Venue 1994–1995*, BTA, London.

Brymer, R.A. (1991) *Hospitality Management – Introduction to the Industry*, Kendall/Hunt, Dubuque, Iowa.

BTA/ETB Research Services (1993) *Overseas Conference Visitors to the UK 1992*, London.

Drucker, P. (1974) *The Practice of Management*, Harper & Row, New York.

ECCI (1993) *Conference Call*, Summer issue.

Emmer, R.M. *et al.* (1993) Marketing hotels using global distribution systems, *The Cornell HRA Quarterly*, **34**(5), 80–9.

Hamel, G. and Prahalad, C.K. (1994) *Competing for the Future*, Harvard Business School Press, Boston.

Hanks, R.D. (1994) *Marketing Means 'Customers First'*, EUHOFA International Conference, Providence, RI.

Hilton (1994) *Initiatives for the Year Ahead*, Hilton Hotels Corporation, Beverly Hills.

Horwarth (1989) *Annual Convention Center Report*, New York.

Knutton, M.C. (1994) Airways for the second age of railways, *The Daily Telegraph*, 15 November.

Kotler, M. (1991) *Marketing Management: Analysis, Planning, Implementation and Control*, 7th edn, Prentice-Hall, Englewood Cliffs, New Jersey.

KPMG Peat Marwick (1993) *The Economic Impact of the ICC, the NIA and the NEC on Birmingham and the West Midlands*, Birmingham.

McIntosh, R.W. and Goldner, C.H.R. (1986) *Tourism – Principles, Practices, Philosophies*, John Wiley & Sons, New York.

Meetings and Conventions (1986) 'The meetings market', 31 March, p. 52.

Mill, R.C. and Morrison, A.M. (1992) *The Tourism System*, Prentice-Hall, Englewood Cliffs, New Jersey.

National Exhibition Centre Ltd (1994) *NEC 1994 Annual Report*, NEC, Birmingham.

Partlow, C.H.G. (1993) How Ritz-Carlton applies 'TQM', *The Cornell HRA Quarterly*, August, pp. 16–24.

Plog Research Inc. (1992) *US Corporate Travel Manager Study*, US Travel Data Center.

Porter, M.E. (1990) *Competitive Advantage of Nations*, Free Press, New York.

Robinson, R. and Kearney, T. (1994) Database marketing for competitive advantage in the airline industry, *Journal of Travel and Tourism Marketing*, **3**(1), 65–81.

Schlentrich, U.A. (1993) Trends in world hospitality, *Hospitality Management*, December–January, No. 135, pp. 1146.

Scottish Tourism Board (1993) *Marketing Plan*, STB, Edinburgh.

REVIEW QUESTIONS

1. What are the main factors which have increased the role of travel agents in business travel decisions?
2. What are the main differentiating features of:
   (a) the conventions and meetings sector?
   (b) the exhibitions and trade fair sector?
3. Assess the importance of the incentive travel market to tourism planners.
4. What are the main ways in which city tourism marketers can go about research and promotion designed to attract conventions and exhibitions to their destinations?

14 Destination marketing

A.V Seaton

OBJECTIVES

By the end of this chapter the reader should:

- understand the distinctive features of destination marketing and its central place in all tourism marketing;
- be aware of the main approaches to international tourist profiling and forecasting in destination development and the problems of the data from which they are derived;
- understand the main elements of destination auditing including resource analysis, destination image analysis and representational scanning;
- understand the role and functions of the public and private sector in the organization of destination marketing.

INTRODUCTION

Destination marketing is the heartland of tourism marketing. The destination is the catalyst link that precipitates all the other industries in the tourism sector – transport, accommodation and attractions. Unless people want to go somewhere provision for transporting them, resting them, feeding them and amusing them will be in vain. 'Being there' – the destination factor – is the *sine qua non* of tourism.

WHAT IS A DESTINATION? HOW DESTINATIONS VARY

A destination is a complex and peculiar animal:

- It is one product but also many. A destination is at once a single entity (we speak of 'Spain' or 'Boston') but it comprises every kind of tourism organization and operation in its geographical area (hotels, transport, attractions, etc.). It can literally include everything in a region – the people, the other industries, the landscape, etc. – which may be be part of the destination experience, the 'local colour' to the tourist, even though they are not specifically part of the tourism economy.

- Though a destination is the central tourism product that drives all others there may be no central agency or organization responsible for marketing it. Even where there is such an organization (e.g. a national or regional tourist organization) it may have limited powers and resources and its efforts may be affected by the activities of many other tourism and non-tourism organizations. Destination marketing is **always** an intentional or unintentional collaboration simply because all the tourism organizations marketing themselves in an area have some impact upon perceptions of the overall destination. Destination marketing at its best involves planned cooperation, coordination and linkages between tourism organizations in a country or region, not least in generating or obtaining funds through which the destination can be promoted coherently to its target markets.
- A destination is both a **physical** entity (a geographical location with spatial, physical properties) but it is also a more intangible **socio-cultural** entity (made up of its history, its people, its traditions and way of life).
- A destination is not just something that actually exists; it is also what is thought to exist, a **mental concept** in the minds of its tourists and potential tourists. This is why the concept of destination image is an important one.
- A destination can be affected by current events happening within its own boundaries but it can also be affected by events happening elsewhere (e.g. an economic crisis in big tourism originating countries such as the UK or Holland may affect the appeal of destinations 2000 miles away).
- It can be affected by the present (a hurricane hitting a Caribbean island, a terrorist outbreak in Egypt) and it can be affected by historical events (Pompeii, the Roman city destroyed by a volcano and rediscovered in the eighteenth-century).
- It can be affected by real events (Shakespeare being born in Stratford, President Kennedy being shot from the book depository in Dallas) and it can be affected by myth and fictitious events (Loch Ness, Universal Studios, Hardy's Wessex and many other locations made popular through fiction, film, poetry, etc.).
- Destinations are thought of as expensive or cheap and yet there is no single index for putting a precise value to them. Comparative surveys on relative destination costs can be carried out, as the British Tourist Authority did in 1993 when it surveyed the costs of 16 international cities (Tokyo, Stockholm and New York were the most expensive with London 11th, better value than Rome and Sydney: BTA 1994). However, in general perceived price is more likely to be a subjective evaluation made by tourists through an appraisal of the combination of all expected or actual expenditures made getting to and in the area relative

to others, which will be affected as much by external factors such as exchange rates as by the deliberate pricing policies of tourism suppliers.

- Destinations differ in many respects including the following.
  - **Size**. Destination marketing may be a large tourist board promoting a whole country, or a small, voluntary group of local people in Hucqueliers, Northern France, opening up a small shop in their village and filling it with postcards, photographs and memorabilia to interpret its history and traditions for tourists. Between the two extremes a destination may also be: a state driven by a Chamber of Commerce (Florida); a big city with its own marketing agency or convention bureau (Edinburgh marketed by the Edinburgh Tourist Board); a seaside resort marketed by its local government authority. Some destinations have specialist tourist boards to market one tourism sector, e.g. London Arts Tourist which concentrates on London's arts products.
  - **Physical attractions**. A well established destination such as Italy may be rich in cultural and heritage attractions, seaside resorts, inland spas, mountain areas, etc. while others may consist of little more than created enclave products (the Gambia).
  - **Infrastructure**. A country like Spain may be well served with accommodation and transport access (rail, road, air) while others, such as Iceland, may have no railways, few main roads, and only one or two cities of any size.
  - **Their benefits to visitors**. Destinations also offer different benefits to their tourists. Some meet the needs of mainstream recreational tourists (Spain) while others may appeal primarily to business travellers and shortbreak markets (many cities in the UK).
  - **Dependency on tourism**. Tourism is a more important strategic issue to destinations with a limited economic base than to those with a more diversified economy. In Cuba and the Caribbean tourism is a more vital economic activity than in most West European countries.

CASE STUDY 14.1

Marketing Blackpool

Blackpool, a famous UK seaside resort, is primarily marketed by its city council. In 1991–92 its budget was £883 000 and in 1992–3 £650 000. The resort is promoted through a 196-page holiday guide to its attractions and accommodation. It is also promoted at fairs and exhibitions in the UK and abroad. Its main tourist information centre handles 370 000 public enquiries during the year and answers 250 000 replies to information and brochure requests

Source: Blackpool Borough Council Report 1992/3, p. 12.

CASE STUDY 14.2

Route 66

Route 66 in the USA once ran, as the song says, 'from Chicago to LA, over 2000 miles all the way', crossed nine state lines and passed a diverse variety of places and attractions. In the late 1970s it was effectively killed off as a working route by the building of a giant interstate highway which ran parallel to it. Over the last five years lobby groups and enthusiasts in the states through which the road used to run, arguing that Route 66 constituted a major part of American heritage – it was called 'the mother road' – have succeeded in reviving it as a tourist attraction sought not only by Americans but Germans, Dutch and Japanese. The promotion of Route 66 has come from numerous small or local initiatives, often enthusiasts, in the form of books, maps, state promotional materials, badges and stickers and, not least, from publicity for those cultural works based on Route 66 – Steinbeck's *Grapes of Wrath*, Kerouac's *On the Road* and the song itself. The route was featured in a tourist package by Just America in Britain and, in early 1995, as a theme of a Macdonald's promotion.

• A destination may not even be a single place, but a conceptual entity which incorporates several destinations and locations, e.g. Route 66 in America which crosses nine state boundaries but is perceived as a totality.

THE PRACTICE OF MARKETING OF DESTINATIONS

How does one go about marketing such a complex entity?

At the end of Chapter 1 we drew up a summary outlining the main steps in general tourism marketing planning. Here it is again:

1. Identify customers (current and predicted) and determine their wants and needs.
2. Audit the organization and scan its external environments including competition, finishing with a SWOT analysis.
3. Set quantified, periodicized strategic objectives.
4. Plan and implement a marketing mix to meet them by:
   • creating the right product;
   • pricing it right;
   • distributing it effectively;
   • promoting it to the consumer.
5. Make the necessary organizational provision for implementing the marketing programme.
6. Evaluate the results.

How appropriate is this general planning model to the specific problems of destination marketing? Before we answer this question it is worth

Table 14.1 Main steps in marketing destinations: two approaches compared

United States Department of Commerce/University of Missouri (1991)	Wall and Heath (1990)
• Inventory social, political, physical, environment	• Situation analysis: environmental and resource analysis
• Forecast/project trends	• National goal and strategy formulation
• Set goals and objectives	• Regional strategy formulation
• Examine alternatives to reach goals and strategy objectives	• Target marketing strategy
• Select preferred alternatives	• Regional positioning strategy
• Develop a strategy to reach goals	• Regional marketing mix strategy: product, pricing, distribution and promotion strategy
• Implement the plan	• Regional organization design
• Evaluate the results	• Management supporting systems: regional information, planning and evaluation systems

looking at two different models of destination marketing planning offered in two specialist texts focused on destination marketing. The first of these, *Tourism USA*, was produced by the University of Missouri for the United States Department of Commerce (1991) and was intended to provide a practical guide to tourism destination development in the USA. The second was produced by two academics (Wall and Heath, 1990) applying strategic planning theory to destination marketing. The main steps proposed in the two texts are summarized in Table 14.1.

How do the two checklists compare? Though the the naming and ordering of the steps show some differences the underlying actions involved are essentially similar. Both describe how destination marketing emerges from an analysis of markets and destination resources, followed by strategic decision-making, organizational design, implementation and, finally, evaluation.

If we now compare our original sequence from Chapter 1 with the two alternatives just presented it is possible to depict destination marketing as five major operations:

1. Assessing the current market(s) and forecasting future market(s) (taking into account general environmental trends).
2. Auditing the destination and analysing its appeals to the markets (again taking into account environmental trends).
3. Developing strategic objectives and a marketing mix.
4. Creating an organization for implementing the objectives.
5. Carrying them out and evaluating the results.

Let's look at these in more detail.

ASSESSING CURRENT TOURISM MARKETS AND FORECASTING THEIR FUTURE DEVELOPMENT

Destination marketing begins with an appraisal of the likely total consumer market and an analysis of the major segments which will constitute it (see Chapter 2). It is necessary to know who the visitors are/will be, why they are likely to come and what they will do. Once a destination is developed it will later be necessary to keep three kinds of regular data on trips: their total number, total staying nights and average expenditure per day and/or per trip.

For established destinations this information can be obtained from analysing current visitors based on existing data or through specially designed visitor studies. For new destinations it has to be derived from an analysis of similar destinations (e.g. a new city convention bureau may look at visitors at other major cities), or ones targeted at similar tourists (e.g. a new resort hoping to develop skiing might look at the profile of skiiers in a variety of other places).

For national destinations and major ones within individual countries (Florida or London, for example) which attract international visitors, tourist trends worldwide will have to be analysed and projections made for the future in order to plan successfully. This raises two particular problems.

The problem of data

Tourism destination data is unlike that for any other marketed goods. Manufacturers of physical products know exactly how much they have made and shipped from their factories, and can audit retail organizations to find out how much of it has actually been bought by the customer. Providers of many services also have a good idea of their markets: lawyers know how many clients they have and how much money they have taken; doctors know how many patients they treat. Destination marketers are not so fortunate because the recording of tourism activity is problematic and varies between different destinations, so that it is often difficult to compare total tourist volumes, let alone specific segmental volumes. In any one destination a number of different organizations may be keeping their own records of tourists: carriers may be counting and analysing how many people travel with them by air, sea or rail, to and from a destination; tour operators may be recording and analysing packages sold to different destinations; hotels may be registering and analysing guests and bednights; attraction managers may be counting people through the turnstiles; tourist information centres (welcome centers, as they are called in the USA) may be auditing people who arrive in their offices. But none of them will provide an accurate representation of the total tourism at a destination.

Some more comprehensive inventory of tourists is necessary to get the overall picture and this has to be undertaken by some overarching agency since few individual tourism organizations have the money or inclination to monitor tourism at the national level. This is why the collection/compilation of national and international tourism data is normally the responsibility of governments, national tourist boards and international tourism organizations such as the WTO and OECD. However, even at the international level there is as yet no commonly accepted methodology of inventorying tourists in numbers or total value. Countries use different methods for obtaining data on tourist flows which make comparisons between countries difficult. The data may be based on behaviour (e.g. accommodation occupancy studies, frontier counts) or on reported behaviour, generally derived from questionnaire surveys (claimed visits, etc.).

In an important article on tourism data Edwards (1991) has identified the main data methods for compiling visitor statistics internationally. He identified five major techniques:

- **counts** of all individuals entering or leaving the country at recognised crossings;
- **interviews** at frontiers with samples of people arriving or departing;
- giving all or a sample of arrivals and departures **a self-completion questionnaire**;
- **sample surveys** of the entire population of a country;
- accommodation arrivals and nights **recorded by hoteliers and owners of the accommodation types** covered.

All the methods have their problems.

- **Accuracy**. Arrivals at a frontier are rarely logged with scrupulous accuracy, particularly at peak times when large jams may be forming. Visitor numbers in hotel returns may be underestimated for tax reasons or records may be badly maintained. Where a country uses hotel or accommodation records many visitors will be excluded, particularly people staying with friends and relatives, or in timeshares and second homes (both a growing form of tourism in places like Italy and France).
- **Sampling error**. Exit studies are a common method of recording tourist flows (to and from a country, for example), but the sampling may be variable. Also the sampling frame may change over time. For instance, the Shetland visitor study of 1992 included interviews with airport respondents not included in the previous survey of 1984 which was based mainly on ferry terminal interviews.
- The difficulty of distinguishing day visitors from staying tourists in border surveys where there is a considerable day visitor traffic. For example, two-thirds of US trips to Canada are for one day, and there are also high levels of daily, non-tourist traffic between Spain and Portugal, Switzerland and Italy, and Germany and Austria.
- **Comparability** in tourist definitions and operational measurements. The World Tourist Organization (WTO) has standardized a definition of an international tourist as:

  ... A person who travels to a country other than that in which s/he has her/his usual residence, but outside her/his usual environment, for at least one night but less than one year, and the main purpose of whose visit is other than the exercise of an activity remunerated from within the country visited.

(WTO, 1992)

However, despite this common definition countries vary, as the Edwards list suggests, in how they operationally measure tourists. For example, in December 1992 tourism to Canada was measured by counts of frontier visitor arrivals; to South Africa, by tourist arrivals; to Austria and Switzerland by international tourist arrivals at hotels and similar establishments; to Yugoslavia by international tourist arrivals at all accommodation establishments.

Overall the problem of understanding tourist demand begins with the difficulty of knowing what is going on, let alone why and what will happen in the future. Tourism analysts need to be aware of the variable methods of reporting tourist flows in different countries.

The time gap problem

Once visitor data has been obtained there is a further problem of knowing what to make of it for the future. Tourism data is always out of date, simply because there is a gap between its collection and its analysis, interpretation and publication. This may not be a serious drawback since most tourism data collection is compiled for planning the future, rather than dwelling on the present, except in those instances where a tourism organization is using current data to measure the success of its marketing efforts. In the main, however, tourism planners use data as a springboard for future forecasting. As one writer has put it: 'The main use of aggregated descriptive analyses of tourist flows is in predicting future flows on the basis of those observed in the past' (Mansfield, 1990: 379).

Many methods exist for the analysis and forecasting of tourist trends. Calanton, di Benedetto and Bojanic (1987) have grouped forecasting methods into into four categories:

- **Exploratory forecasting:** an attempt to predict what will happen in the future through extrapolation of past trends and identification of relationships between independent and outcome variables. It is normally undertaken for relatively short-term planning (six months to two years) and is widely used by organizations trying to produce concrete business plans which will enable them to anticipate the likely number of their customers and the size of their revenues. Most attractions, big hotels and airlines annually produce marketing plans which include extrapolations from past to future based on 3–5 year trends.
- **Speculative forecasting:** a qualitative approach oriented to longer-term demand analysis and forecasting. It involves using general predictions based on the (presumably) informed judgement of experts by asking for their opinions about the key factors influencing aggregate demand and then predicting future trends from these assumptions. Normally

the predictions are expressed in general terms of broad developments rather than specific quantified data.

- **Normative forecasting:** an approach involving the identification of methods required to attain prescribed levels of demand. The tourism organization sets visitor targets (in terms of number of visitors, levels of accommodation occupancy or revenue) and then attempts to map out tactics for achieving them. In the early 1980s the Northern Ireland Tourist Board set itself the normative goal of doubling its visitor numbers as a strategic objective and then set about developing means of implementing it. Normative forecasting is required wherever it is necessary to market an event, a programme, or put into effect a management plan that depends upon achieving a given volume of visitors or revenue. Hallmark events such as the Olympics, Expos and many kinds of festival normally involve forecasting of visitors and then programmes to accomplish them.

- **Integrative forecasting:** an attempt to integrate the results from several techniques. At its most ambitious it might involve a systematic programme of research in which the future demand for tourism over a given period is investigated through a variety of forecasting techniques including: trend analysis, econometrics, a range of different 'expert judgement' techniques, as well as being combined with normative business predictions.

Analysis and forecasting of tourism trends is an essential task for destination marketers whatever their size. They need to know what proportion of their visitors will be day trippers (and what catchment areas they will come from), and how many visitors will come from outside the area and what proportion will be international visitors from overseas (and what countries they will come from). All of this means that tourist monitoring and forecasting is a central responsibility of destination marketers:

> Forecasting is more art than science and cannot be relegated to a mechanical data-crunching activity. A forecaster needs to become involved with the data and monitor the data to detect changing patterns as well as atypical data.

> (Geurts, 1982: 21)

The destination life cycle

A concept that emerged in tourism through the 1980s and 1990s (Butler, 1980; Cooper, 1994) which has a direct bearing on visitor analysis is that of the destination lifecycle or tourism area lifecycle (TALC). The TALC postulates a six/seven-stage development pattern for destinations:

- exploration;
- involvement;
- development;
- consolidation;

- stagnation;
- decline or rejuvenation.

Each of the phases are said to be associated with different levels of visitation, different kinds of visitors and different host reactions. The idea is that destination marketers should attempt to identify what stage their destination is at before attempting to plan for the future.

As with the product lifecycle discussed in Chapter 5 there are many problems with TALC. Do all resorts conform to this cycle of inevitable pattern of growth and decline? What can be done about it by tourism marketers to activate the key growth phases and arrest the decline? How can a planner identify at what stage a resort/destination is in? What span of time is required to identify a definite pattern? Can patterns be predicted as opposed to merely recorded with hindsight? (Many examples of TALC were identified after the damage had been done and destinations were in decline.) Should visitor numbers, bednights or spending be used as data for measuring a destination's patterns of growth? (A destination with a growing number of day excursionists may be declining in revenue terms while a resort with a smaller number of high-spending international tourists may be economically better off.)

The only way of answering these questions is through careful comparative studies of lifecycles in several destinations. There have been few studies that use **comparative** data to investigate TALCs over any considerable time span. One that does is a four-resort study by Soane (1993) which showed that the development of Bournemouth, Wiesbaden, Nice and Los Angeles were far more complex than simple rise and fall models would suggest. Smith (1991) has studied the evolution of beach resorts in Malaysia, Thailand and Australia over a more limited period since the war.

Another question about TALC is the possibility that different lifecycle patterns might exist in the **same** destination for **different tourist segments**. In South Africa, since Nelson Mandela came to power, a major sun, sea and sand market has developed almost overnight among black populations, alongside that which has existed for years for white populations. In the four destinations Soane studied there were different patterns of growth among visitors, migrants and residents.

Finally, TALC largely excludes the impact that marketing actions might have in intervening in 'natural' patterns of growth and decline, assuming that such patterns exist. When a destination is seen to go into decline remedial action may be possible, which may include efforts to:

- diversify the base of visitors;
- environmentally upgrade the destination;
- diversify the geographical base of tourism;
- engage in heavy promotion.

Despite these problems TALC is a useful concept for destination marketers to be aware of. One does not have to believe in it in every detail to realize the importance of identifying trends in a destination's visitor and revenue base, particularly in relation to substitute destinations within the same tourism market. Blackpool in the UK has, for instance, maintained its popularity while many other traditional seaside resorts have declined.

In a recent review of the whole subject, Cooper (1994: 341) suggests that TALC can be used in three ways:

- as an applied model of destination evolution;
- as a guide for marketing and planning;
- as a forecasting tool.

In practice the second and third ways both involve marketing since forecasting is integral to effective marketing planning.

DESTINATION AUDITING

Once some idea of past and present visitor demand has been established and forecasts for the future derived from them arrived at marketers need to appraise their capacity to satisfy it. The essential task is to decide what a destination offers that might attract and provide services for target audiences, particularly those that are distinctive from others. Destination marketers should try to identify the **competitive advantage** of their destination. This involves answering three main questions:

- What **is** there?
- What is **thought** to be there?
- What has been **represented** as being there?

What is there – destination resources

A destination is made up of a complex mix of physical phenomena – natural and man-made – which are primary tourism resources. Any destination marketer should have a thoroughgoing knowledge of what they are, to whom they are likely to appeal, and what quantity/quality of tourists they already attract or may attract in the future. Destination resources can be divided into four categories.

Physical attractions

What are the principal natural and man-made attractions? This should include climate, landscape and all other natural and man-made features that might be tourist motivators. One way of inventorying attractions is to enumerate all of them by category, express them as a percentage of total attractions, and, if visitor numbers and profiles on them are available, assess their comparative tourist appeal in tourist numbers. Case 14.3 illustrates the process.

The table in the case study gives a quick overview of the principal attractions of Gloucestershire in type and number and a very rough

CASE STUDY 14.3

Inventorying attractions

In 1992 planners for the English county of Gloucestershire published an inventory of its principal tourist attractions and their visitors:

	Number of attractions	As % of total attractions	Average number of visitors to each (number of attractions surveyed in brackets)
Countryside sites	57	23	na
Historic houses and sites	46	18	67 027 (4)
Cathedrals, abbeys and churches of note	17	7	217 713 (3)
Museums and art galleries	40	16	40 745 (12)
Gardens and arboreta	19	8	38 844
Farm/wildlife attractions	27	11	78 975 (6)
Arts and crafts attractions	20	8	180 909 (3)
Industrial and transport attractions	7	3	53 500 (2)
Others: caves, vineyards, etc.	15	6	na

Source: Gloucester Tourism (1993).

indication of their visitor figures. (The figures are very rough because the averages are based on a limited number of visitor studies which tend to have been carried out by the bigger attractions. For example, Gloucester's main visitor attraction is its cathedral with 450 000 visitors which dramatically inflates the average visitor figure in the 'cathedrals, abbeys, churches' sector. The table also omits the fact that many of the attractions are free and, for those which are not, it does not reveal what average daily spend is.)

Socio-cultural resources

A destination is more than the sum of its physical, tourist-specific features. It also includes social and cultural features (many of them related to its natural and built environment) which give a destination its total ambience. These are harder to inventory and may include its people (their way of life in the widest sense of the term), history, folklore, literature, commercial institutions (eastern bazaars and 'shop-till-you-drop malls'), political institutions, even its distinctive mass media (American TV is a mind-blowing tourist experience for those who have never seen it before).

Infrastructure

How easy is a destination to get to and travel within? What are basic services like? How good are rail, road, sea and air communications? These facilitating factors are not the principal ones which motivate people to visit places but they can have an important bearing on whether the final decision is made and, even more, upon the nature of the tourist experience once it is begun.

Accommodation

Accommodation can be seen as part of infrastructural provision but it is such an important one it demands separate consideration. Destination marketers need comprehensive data on how tourists will be housed during their stays. What is the total accommodation stock and what are the main categories that comprise it (hotels by grade, self-catering, bed and breakfast, camping and caravan, timeshares, etc.)? How does the accommodation stock vary geographically within a country or region and what are occupancy levels? Case 14.4 indicates how a destination marketer might attempt to quantify the different kinds of accommodation-specific tourism in an area.

What is thought to be there – destination image

Analysing a destination's resources only reveals what is there. In destination marketing it is equally important to know what is **thought** to exist. Tourism planners need to know how people perceive destinations and understand what the factors are that make them do so. A destination image is the sum of ideas and impressions that a tourist prospect holds about a destination. It may include information about its geography,

---

CASE STUDY 14.4

Accommodation audit of UK county of Gloucester 1991

	Serviced accommodation	Self-catering	Camping/ caravan	VFRs	Day trippers
Total income	£63 m	£7 m	£28 m	£19 m	£104 m
Total bed-spaces	11 319	449	3 210	na	—
Visitor nights	1 404 688	306 632	1 576 752	685 211	—
Visitor trips	759 292	51 105	525 584	241 822	—
Average length of stay	1.85 (all) 1.94 (overseas)	6	3	2.7	—
Average bed occupancy	34%	70.8% (High season) 56% (Low season)	56% 33%	na	—
Average spend per day	£45.01	£21.66	£17.42	£14.84	£11.03

Source: ETB (1992/3).

people, infrastructure, climate, costliness and history, and *evaluations* of its attractiveness, safety, etc. Destination image is thought to be a decisive factor in influencing vacation choice which is why the concept has received considerable discussion in tourism theory and research. Much of this research has focused on ways of theorizing and measuring destination image (see Echtner and Brent Ritchie, 1991, for a good review of the issues).

For the tourism planner appraising destination image involves answering four key questions:

- What is the perceived destination image held by the customer or potential customer?
- Is it favourable?
- Is it different from perceptions of what is thought to exist in competitive destinations? On average vacation travellers are thought to seriously consider three or four destinations (Woodside and Sherrill, 1977: 14–18), thus to be on the 'shopping list' of potential destinations for a particular category of vacation is essential.
- How can it be affected? Once a destination's image has been determined among its key segments, and its comparative attractiveness relative to substitutes assessed, planners must decide to what extent they need to take action to consolidate, modify or change perceptions.

The answers to the first three questions can only be determined by research carried out with samples of relevant visitor segments. There are two main methodologies:

- Quantitative surveys with representative samples of respondents based on structured questionnaires which normally include a variety of bi-polar, attitude and opinion statements about a destination which can be scored and measured to produce an aggregate image of a destination based on a given number of discrete attributes. Tourist

CASE STUDY 14.5

The destination image of American cities

Lowenthal and Riel (1972) developed a method of investigating differences in people's image of Boston, New York, Cambridge and Columbus. This involved picking a bi-polar scaling technique based on 25 paired attributes that had been chosen as salient for comparing environments, and then getting respondents to rate the four places after having taken several half-mile walks in each. The results showed that there were wide differences between them. New York came out as high-class, fashionable, lively, exciting, entertaining, full of tourists, vulgar, foreign and dangerous. Boston was rated as quaint and 'different'. Columbus and Cambridge were considered green, park-like, neat and tidy but also run down and messy.

Source: Lowenthal and Riel (1972).

boards often include attitude and opinion questions in their visitor studies which can later be used to infer the image.

- Qualitative, open-ended studies which normally involve group discussions or depth interviews with much smaller numbers of people, designed to elicit their images, feelings and attitudes to destinations. The key difference between the first and this second approach, apart from the numbers of people involved, is that here respondents can offer a much wider range of associations instead of simply scoring destinations on a limited number of attributes pre-selected, and thus limited, by the researcher.

The fourth question – what action a destination marketer takes to influence destination image – depends on the strengths/weaknesses revealed by research. It also depends on a realistic assessment of the practical limits within which a destination marketer must work in trying through promotion to affect perceptions of a destination, given the relatively small influence promotional campaigns can make. The tourism planner needs to be aware that destination images are formed from many kinds of information. Theorists have differentiated between two kinds of destination image sources:

- **organic image sources** which are those general, barely recognized information sources including personal experience, word-of-mouth report (e.g. by friends, relatives, associates, etc.), education and the media, and many other kinds of information, most of which are beyond the direct influence of tourism planners;
- **induced image sources** which constitute that comparatively narrow spectrum of destination image information specifically designed by promotional agencies such as tourist boards and public sector organizations in the form of advertising and publicity.

Over the years that tourism organizations and academics have been researching destination image issues a number of general findings have emerged about their nature and formation:

- **Destination images are usually stereotyped, selective notions of place characterized by expectations of the 'other'.** The 'other' is the social anthropologist's term for difference, the exotic, the contrasts with everyday life supposed to exist abroad compared with home (see Chapter 3). The pursuit of the 'other' is a principal motivation in tourism, which is why destination marketers commonly promote those stereotypical features of their destinations most likely to seem attractively different (quaint, traditional, romantic) even though in reality, as cultures become more and more alike through processes of modernization and industrialization, the differences between destinations may be decreasing. The stereotypical effects of much tourism promotion has been criticized from two quarters. Host groups often resent the image of their culture promoted by tourism organizations and held by tourists (Scots don't necessarily see themselves as kilted, haggis-eating bagpipers; modern native Americans resent having their traditional culture served up as a spectator tourist-attraction which conceals the economic hardships of their present life). Academics have also analysed the discrepancy between the constructed, exotic images of faraway places, particularly in the developing world, and some of the other socio-political realities (poverty, political repression) which may exist in them. It is difficult for tourism planners to reconcile these two kinds of critique with the requirements of attracting tourists. Destination promotion from Scotland and London to Fiji and the Seychelles[1] is centrally concerned with evoking a tourist-pleasing dream-world, rather than starker, sociological documentary realism. The key question is not whether promotion represents the destination the way its residents 'see' or 'experience' it but whether it fairly represents what the tourist will see/experience.

- **Destination images are more differentiated and complex to previous visitors than non-visitors**. First-time visitors arrive with a more stereo-typed view of a place than those who have visited previously.

- **Destination images are more affected by non-promotional communication than the efforts of tourism agencies, except in the case of new, little known places**. The impact of induced image attempts by tourism agencies is comparatively weak for well-known destinations (Paris, Miami, Blackpool), compared to the cumulative weight of non-commercial sources which will have established powerful organic images in people's minds. For new destinations where people have less initial information (Belize, for example) the efforts of tourism promotion may be more influential.

- **Destination images are more affected by word of mouth report than most other influences**. Numerous studies have shown that the holiday decision, including destination choice, is often more influenced by informal information networks (friends and relatives, peer groups, etc.) than media sources.

- **Destination images vary in strength and susceptibility to change**. Well-established images are hard to change and require heavy investment to do so, which is why Spain has had to engage in costly promotional efforts to counter the negative images it acquired in the 1970s and 1980s.

- **Where promotion is important it may be public relations, especially media relations, rather than advertising which most influences destination image**. Stories in the press and broadcasting media have been known to influence tourism patterns (Seaton, 1994), e.g. the film

---

1. London is no more full of the postcard-portrayed Beefeaters and punks with Mohican haircuts, and Scotland no more inhabited by kilt-wearing bagpipe players than Fiji and the Seychelles are by grass-skirted natives drinking coconut milk under palm trees. It is naive to judge tourism advertising, or indeed any advertising, by standards of documentary realism. The main issue is whether the destination as depicted to tourists will live up to its promise, regardless of whether what they see is typical, representative, or, as is increasingly the case, a show of 'staged authenticity' specially packaged for tourists.

Crocodile Dundee and a number of soap operas made in Australia have been thought to increase tourism to that country, and the films *Braveheart* and *Rob Roy* increased tourism to Scotland in the summer of 1995.

- **Destination image may be a more important factor for individuated destinations than generic tourism destinations.** For sun, sea and sand holidays where a number of destinations may be close substitutes (Cyprus, Spain, Portugal and Greece in the brochures of British travel agents, for instance) differentiated image may be less critical than for other destinations chosen for their unique, individual features, particularly cultural and heritage destinations such as Florence and Paris.

- **Destination images vary with different audiences and thus there may be several destination images not one.** Destination images are always specific to particular groups of visitor. A destination may be perceived differently depending on the nationality, education and age of tourists, and their purpose of travel (e.g. business vs. recreational travellers).

- **Destination images vary inter-regionally.** Destination images are always geographically selective both in promotional terms and also in people's minds. Some areas within a country may receive little promotional focus and barely exist perceptually for many audiences. Most international recreational tourists do not think of Italy as an industrial country, while for many Spain is more thought of as a sun, sea and sand rather than a cultural destination. One of the problems for destination marketers at the national level is deciding what features of a country to select for promotion, a decision which always involves excluding many features and places and causing resentment among those with a regional interest in them. In some instances a destination promoter may fix upon one attribute of a place and promote it as symbol for the whole area (e.g. the Eiffel Tower as a symbol of Paris).

CASE STUDY 14.6

The BTA's 'Tea and Roses' campaign

In 1993 the British Tourism Authority targeted a campaign at Japanese women who account for 80% of Japanese holidaymakers to Britain, with particular emphasis on those over 40 (7% of the population). The thinking behind the campaign was described by Keith Beecham of the BTA as follows: 'The Japanese tend to associate Britain with heroic, masculine castles. Our campaign is designed to create a softer and more feminine feel – quaint country house hotels, green landscapes and Laura Ashley. Afternoon tea is the ideal vehicle because it has become very fashionable in Japan.'

Source: BTA Annual Report (1994: 10–11).

Can destinations be branded?

The recognition that destination image is a major factor in destination success has recently led some tourist boards and resort marketers to talk about applying branding to destination marketing. In Spain branding has been used to communicate the country's unique identity for cultural diversity and sun. The branding involved the development of a logo designed by the painter, Miro, in red and yellow (the Spanish colours) with the caption, 'Spain. Everything under the sun'. The branding campaign ran for seven years and in 1992 was modified to 'Spain – Passion for life'. Spain's excursion into branding has been summarized as follows:

> The fundamental values of the brand were diversity, dynamism and creativity, which, although not in contradiction with the previous campaign, did require a repositioning in consumer perception . . . The campaign aimed to emphasize the creativity and dynamism of the country, and the variety it offered, which differentiated it from competitors. The objectives of the campaign were to show the country with growing and intense development, capable of providing for the various needs of tourists, to communicate a country with great traditions, culture, history and natural resources, and to manifest a country with personality and enthusiasm for life.
>
> (Camison, Bigne, and Monfort, 1994: 450)

Despite the superficial attraction of destination branding as a way of creating a differentiated image, the concept has a number of fundamental problems because of the intractable differences between destinations and other kinds of tourism product. Branding to be successful involves mobilization of the whole marketing mix. A successful brand emerges from the design of a homogenous product, correctly priced, distributed and promoted **to a defined market segment**. Most of these requirements are impossible for destination marketers because of the following.

- They do not have a homogenous product – a destination, as we have seen, is a complex mix of diverse elements. For most visitors, the physical experience of a destination is not as controllably homogenous as that of, say, a tin of cat food, or even a hotel chain or airline product, which can be made to look similar to all consumers **wherever the product is seen**. Nor do destination marketers have much control over the design of the product, which is mainly determined by pre-existing factors (climate, geography, infrastructural development, etc.).
- Destination marketers cannot set prices in a destination or control the distribution system through which the various components of a destination (accommodation, attractions, etc.) are marketed. In reality destination branding has to rely almost entirely on promotion or publicity.
- Most important of all, branding involves marketing **different products to discrete market segments** (business travellers, young families, etc.), whereas destination promoters must market destinations to all-

CASE STUDY 14.7

The brands of Austria

A variation of destination branding was introduced in Austria in the late 1980s and early 1990s. It was based upon creating marketing associations between groups of hotels specializing in single benefit/interest tourism products developed after an analysis of benefits sought from Austria's major markets. Marketing association made sense in a country where most hotels were small (average of 36 beds). The hotels grouped themselves into 16 named, brand/product consortia, each of which specialized in one type of holiday, including sports products (Multi-tennis Austria, Golf Green Austria, Fishing Ground Austria, Horseback Riding in Austria), products targeted at specific nationalities (L'Austria per Italia, Autriche pro France), family products (Country-style Holidays in Austria, Farmhouse Holidays in Austria), and interest-based products (Vinoveritas Austria, Slim and Beautiful in Austria). In effect the hotel groups had formed a branding partnership offering a highly differentiated product to defined benefit segments which were promoted as distinct Austrian brands. The success of the branding operation has been proven by the fact that average occupancy rate is about 10% higher than for hotels which have not joined the product/interest groupings, and consortia hotels are able to charge on average about 16% more than other hotels from the same region and class.

Source: Muller (1994: 198–216).

comers, often through a single campaign. It is difficult to see how one brand can be made to appeal to all. To apply branding coherently to a destination might involve presenting it in different ways to different groups in which case the destination becomes not one brand, but many. One of the most innovative attempts to create multi-product destination branding, based on benefit segmentation, has been developed in Austria (see Case Study 14.7 above).

What has been represented as being there

In addition to inventorying what exists and is thought to exist at a destination it is also useful to inventory what has been **represented** as existing at a destination. Representation is a term that covers all the ways in which a place has been depicted through the media of human communication, including books of fiction and non-fiction, TV, film, poetry, art, music, etc., and it includes media of both high culture and popular culture. Representation is important because a destination is as much a product of myth as actuality – its appeal may lie in its associations with literature (Hardy's Dorset, Brontë Country, Burns Land, Shakespeare's Stratford), music (Route 66), art (the Piero della Francesca trail in Tuscany and Umbria), popular TV ('Emmerdale Farm Country' and 'James Herriott Country', both named after TV series in the UK, have been used by regional tourism planners in Yorkshire in England as 'packaging' concepts for promoting their regions). Destinations can also be promoted through their associations with people who were the creators working in representational forms (i.e. writers and artists who were born, lived or stayed in particular destinations). Few tourism organizations **systematically** inventory the representational features of their destinations. This can be done through a representational scan, which is an inventory of the ways in which a destination has been represented in literature, film, TV, art, etc., and the famous people who have been born, lived, worked, travelled and died at a destination. The representational scan may involve local historians, literary and artistic experts and others with specialist knowledge (Seaton, 1994).

Summary

At the end of the destination inventory a SWOT analysis should be produced (see Chapter 5). This also includes an appraisal of the various environmental influences likely to affect destinations which were analysed in Chapter 1.

DEVELOPING MARKETING STRATEGY AND A MARKETING MIX

Having determined market trends, forecast future targets and inventoried a destination's appeals, the third step for the destination marketer is formulating strategy and developing a marketing mix that implements it. It is here that one must return to a major problem in destination marketing – the fact that destination marketers have little direct control over the product and price, and only partial influence on distribution, even though publicly funded tourism organizations may advise and make recommendations on them, and, in some instances, grant-aid new developments (as the French government did in the development of Languedoc).

For most destination marketers their prime input into the marketing mix is promotion. Once the principal markets and market segments have been identified and the main appeals necessary to attract them have been determined, destination marketing primarily involves **communication** – linking tourists with the destination in order to achieve the targeted demand. The main elements of promotion have been described in Chapter 7.

ORGANIZATION FOR DESTINATION MARKETING

Public and private sector support and partnership

One of the key differences in destination marketing from other kinds is the role of public sector support and/or the creation of private sector partnerships to market a destination. Since image is such an important factor in destination appeal promoting the identity of a region or country is a central necessity but it can rarely be done by private sector organizations unaided – they do not have the resources to market a country or a region to all the markets that may be involved. This phenomenom has sometimes been called 'market failure' – the inability of market forces in tourism to generate the resources for marketing a destination. Two options are available, either singly or in combination, to overcome the problem.

The first option is public sector intervention. This may take the form of publicly funded tourist boards, enterprise companies, local authorities or other organizations which effectively assume responsibility for the overall marketing of a destination. At national level tourism is normally supported through some kind of national tourist board (NTO). The general roles of the NTO have been described as follows:

> The major objective of an NTO is to optimize tourism revenue and share of earnings for visitor spend (optimize number of high spenders and length of stay) from key international travel markets, weighted for regional and seasonal spread (both objectives geared to maximize the economic benefits of tourism over as wide an area as possible and over as long a season as possible). Other important objectives or key tasks are to maintain a broad spread of markets, to maintain/increase market share in established/growing markets, to sustain/increase volume of traffic (arrivals/bednights) and to increase the number of jobs created by tourism.
>
> (Rita and Moutinho, 1993: 5)

The World Tourism Organization has identified four principal functions of NTOs:

- **identifying markets and audiences:** this is why the research function is a crucial one since markets can only be determined through rigorous analysis of visitor trends, tastes, social change, etc.;
- **communicating with them:** this is the promotional function discussed earlier;
- **improving visitor figures;**
- **promoting destination images**.

Jefferson and Lickorish (1991) have described the roles of tourist boards more vividly as:

- guardian of the image;
- scene setter (research into current demand factors);
- trail blazer (developing new markets in time, space, product sectors, customer groupings, etc.);
- marketing coordinator;
- monitor of visitor satisfaction.

The second option, where public funding is not available, is for private sector tourism industry organizations operating in the same region or country to form their own marketing agencies, funded by contributions from each member. Until the 1960s much of the promotion of destinations internationally was undertaken by chambers of commerce, hotel groups, airlines, railways, etc.

In many countries permutations of both forms of funding may be adopted with considerable cross-fertilization between them. The London Arts Board is a good example of a public-sector led body which collaborates widely with the private sector (Case Study 14.8).

Tourist information/welcome centres

The tourist information centre (or welcome center, as it is called in the USA) is a promotional medium unique to destination marketing. The main purposes of TICs include: making people aware of attractions, providing route information and broadening travel itineraries of visitors, increasing staytime in a region, increasing spend in a region and advising on accommodation.

As destination marketing gets more competitive it is unlikely that many destinations will achieve dramatic tourism revenue increases. Incremental gains will be the order of the day. TICs can have a moderate but worthwhile role in this through the information provision they make available once a

---

CASE STUDY 14.8

The London Arts Board: promoting cultural tourism to London

The London Arts Board was established in 1991. Its main goals were:

- promoting and supporting artistic excellence and innovation throughout London;
- developing access to the arts for the enjoyment, education and benefit of all who live and work in, or visit, London;
- celebrating the richness of London's cultural diversity;
- seeking to enhance London's quality of life, reputation and economy.

Between 1992 and 1993 the LAB spent £2.2 million on promoting tourism to London, targeting ABC1s in Britain and upper income groups in America, particularly first-time visitors. The campaign included advertising in travel publications in the US and weekend publications in Britain, as well as direct mail to 8000 travel agents in the US and database marketing from British Tourist Authority offices in New York, Chicago, Los Angeles and Atlanta. Using the message, 'It's not only Londoners who love London' the advertising featured celebrity endorsement by international stars including Alan Alda, Phil Collins, Sophia Loren, Roger Moore and Elizabeth Taylor.

The Board, linking with hotels, coordinated inclusive accommodation packages for overseas visitors, offered an attractions booking service and inaugurated a £200 000 Industry Training Scheme to ensure a warm welcome which was supported by 40 private and public sector tourism organizations. The LAB is funded by the Arts Council and the Craft Council.

Source: LAB publicity.

CASE STUDY 14.9

Who uses TICs, and why and how does it affect their travel behaviour? Welcome centres in Indiana State, USA

A study reported by Fesenmeier and Vogt (1991) looked at the usage of three welcome centers in Indiana. Two studies were carried out. The first consisted of interviews with people arriving at the centers. The second consisted of a postal follow-up survey with 560 of the original visitors who had agreed to participate after they had returned home.

Study 1: Who stopped at the TICs and why?

The results showed that 82% were married and few had children at home. Most visitors were middle aged (29% were 30–44 and 43% 45–64). They were generally affluent (69% had incomes of $30 000 or more). Main reason for stopping was rest rooms (61.5%) and only 10% had stopped to get information about travel routes. However, 71% picked up information, with maps and attraction data being the main kinds of materials.

Study 2: What effect did the welcome center have?

The follow-up survey was designed to find out how the stop had subsequently influenced the trip: 29% visited places they hadn't planned to visit; 31% extended their trip 1–3 hours longer than planned; 38% indicated that they stayed at least a day longer; 33% said they spent additional money as a result of the welcome center; 68% said they spent more on meals and food; and 58% spent more than planned on petrol. Overall the researchers calculated that approximately $21 000 extra was spent for every 1000 visitor groups receiving information at the three Indiana welcome centers.

Source: Fesenmaier and Vogt (1991).

tourist is in an area. In America attempts have been made to quantify the impact of welcome centers on tourist behaviour as in case 14.9.

CAN ANYWHERE BE MADE A SOMEWHERE?

In the last two decades tourism has come to be seen as a passport to development for poor countries and, at the regional level, a force of potential salvation for post-industrial regions in the West which have lost their former economic base in extractive and manufacturing industries. The growth of tourism in destinations in South East Asia, Eastern Europe and Turkey and urban marketing initiatives in cities once regarded as outside tourism such as Bradford, Stoke, Glasgow and New York have tended to create the impression that tourism can be a ready-made solution to the economic needs of anywhere. What is the truth?

In assessing the tourism potential of a destination the first requirement is to realize that tourism is not one thing but many, and to identify what kind is realistically possible in a particular destination. To the inexperienced national or regional planner tourism is often seen, consciously or unconsciously, as a high revenue-generating, gravy train made up of large quantities of long-staying, pleasure-seeking, free-spending, mass holidaymakers originating from the world's richest countries. For most destinations, particularly urban locations and those without obvious climatic and scenic attractions, this is unlikely to be the case. For these destinations, particularly inland, regional ones, markets are, at best, likely to be made up of domestic visitors, taking day trips or short-breaks, and often stopping with friends and relatives, rather than the jackpot main holiday, mass, international market.

Some destinations, urban ones in particular, are so limited in both natural and cultural attractions that they are unlikely to become 'honeypot' centres even though heavy promotion and new product initiatives such as festival staging, industrial heritage attractions, and business and convention development may improve their tourism appeals. In the 1980s and early 1990s city marketing became a high-profile tourism sector that apparently offered any old industrial city the opportunity to be a big tourism player, but despite a few well-publicized short-term successes (Bradford in the 1980s and Glasgow in 1990 when it was chosen as European City of Culture) the results have not lived up to the hype. There is no post-industrial city anywhere which has successfully generated a new tourism industry comparable in value or employment terms to industries lost from manufacturing. A 1994 symposium in Rotterdam on city tourism concluded that, among eight major European cities, only Edinburgh and Copenhagen had strongly developed urban leisure products and that Lyons, Genoa, Antwerp and Rotterdam had been comparative failures (Berg, Borg and Meer, 1994). Moreover, city marketing is likely to get more difficult due to competitive factors now that there are few cities or towns of any size in the Western world which do not have tourism strategies, most of which are essentially similar. The main impact of city marketing may be upon local residents with improved perceptions of their locality, rather than the generation of a major tourism market from outside it.

So what are the realistic limits of destination marketing? Once the procedures described in this chapter have been carried out (market assessment, destination auditing, etc.) the key question the destination marketer must ask is: 'What kind of tourism destination is possible given our knowledge of our resources and our potential customers?' A useful framework for addressing this question is that devised by Lue, Crompton and Fesenmaier (1993). It is based on a basic insight that destinations differ in their relative importance to tourists, depending on the part they play in the overall trip. They identify five spatial trip patterns associated with five kinds of destination use:

- **Single destination pattern:** where the tourist stays in one place and where the destination factor will be paramount.

- **En route pattern:** where destinations are seen as transit points on the way to somewhere else. The Pas de Calais in Northern France is a good example of a region that most people pass through on their way south.
- **Base camp pattern:** where a destination is simply a convenient starting point for other places. Bradford in the UK has promoted itself as a 'gateway' to the more scenic and cultural attractions of the Brontë country.
- **Regional tour pattern:** where a destination is seen as one of several within a total itinerary.
- **Trip chaining pattern:** where a destination is seen as joint equal with another destination, e.g. a Jules Verne package to Russia and China.

This typology is useful because identifying the relative importance of a destination in a total trip is likely to produce a more realistic assessment of a destination's potential than considering it in isolation. Some destinations may never be capable of achieving main destination status but they may lend themselves to promotion as 'base camps' or 'trip chaining'. Similarly, accepting that a destination is mainly a transit destination may save a marketer a lot of wasted effort trying to position it as a main-stay destination and enable him or her to concentrate on marketing ideas relevant to its transit character.

A related concept which is also useful to destination analysis is the trip index (Pierce and Scott, 1983) which measures what proportion of a trip is spent at a particular destination. It is arrived at by dividing the length of time spent at a single destination by the length of the total trip and multiplying by 100, e.g. if a trip lasted eight days and a stay at one destination lasted two days the trip index for that destination would be:

$$\frac{2 \times 100}{8} = 25$$

Establishing a trip index for a destination (which must be based on visitor survey data) allows a marketer to assess the realistic length of stay likely to be achieved by a destination.

So can tourism be marketed at any destination – can anywhere be made a somewhere? The answer is probably, 'yes to some extent', but the marketer must produce a realistic assessment of the destination's potential, derived from a proper marketing audit and a clear vision of what kind of destination is feasible given the findings of the audit. Few destinations will find that they are in a position to achieve very high levels of tourism if they have not had them before. For most destination marketers the trick is identifying niche markets, often based on day trips and short-breaks, that can **augment** a region's economy, rather than imagining that tourism will be the principal element of it.

SUMMARY

This chapter has provided a discussion of the specific features of marketing tourism destinations. It has highlighted some of the ways in which the destination differs from other tourism products, exemplified concepts useful for destination analysis, and appraised some of the organizational forms possible for destination promotion. At the end of the day, destination marketing involves the same basic procedural and analytical steps as those summarized in the first chapter – with some additional elements relevent to the particular features of destinations as products.

REFERENCES

Berg, L. van der, Borg, J. van der, and Meer, J. van der (1994) *Urban Tourism*, Conference Proceedings, Erasumus University, Rotterdam.

British Tourist Authority (1994) *Annual Report 1994*, BTA, London.

Butler, R.W. (1980) The concept of a tourist area cycle of evolution: implications for management of resources, *Canadian Geographer*, **XXIV** (1), 5–12.

Calanton, R.J., Di Benedetto, C.A. and Bojanic, D. (1987) A comprehensive review of the tourism forecasting literature, *Journal of Travel Research*, Fall, pp. 28–39.

Camison, C., Bigne, E. and Monfort, V.M. (1994) The Spanish tourism industry, in Seaton, A.V. (ed.), *Tourism: The State of the Art*, Wiley, Chichester pp. 442–52.

Cooper, C. (1994) The destination image: an update, in Seaton, A.V. (ed.), *Tourism: The State of the Art*, Wiley, Chichester.

Echtner, C. and Brent Ritchie, J.R. (1991) The meaning and measurement of destination image, *Journal of Tourism Studies*, **2**(2), 2–12.

Edwards, A. (1991) The reliability of tourism statistics, *Travel and Tourism Analyst*, No. 1, Economist Intelligence Unit.

English Tourist Board (1992/3) Tourism Trends Survey, UK Tourism Survey.

Fesenmaier, D.R. and Vogt, C.A. (1991) Exploratory analysis of information use at Indiana State Welcome Centers, in 'Tourism: Building Credibility for a Credible Industry', *Proceedings of 22nd Annual Conference of the Travel and Tourism Research Association*, Bureau of Economic and Business Research, Graduate School of Business, Utah, pp. 111–22.

Geurts, M.D. (1982) Forecasting the Hawaian tourist market, *Journal of Travel Research*, Summer, pp. 18–21.

Gloucester Tourism (1993) *Survey of attractions*.

Heath, B. and Wall, G. (1992) *Marketing Tourism Destinations*, John Wiley, USA.

Jefferson, A. and Lickorish, L. (1991) *Marketing Tourism: A Practical Guide*, Longman, London.

Lowenthal, D. and Riel, M. (1972) Environmental structure: semantic and experiential components, *American Geographical Society Publications in Environmental Perception No. 8*, New York.

Lue, C.-M., Crompton, J.L. and Fesenmaier, D.R. (1993) Conceptualization of multi-destination pleasure trips, *Annals of Tourism Research*, **20**(2), 289–301.

Mansfield, Y. (1990) Spatial patterns of international tourist flows: towards a theoretical framework, *Progress in Human Geography*, **4**, 379.

Muller, K.-H. (1994) Behavioral segmentation as a national strategy, in Gasser, R.M. and Weiermair, K. (eds), *Spoilt for Choice*, Kulturverlag/University of Innsbruck, Austria, pp. 197–216.

Pierce, D.G. and Scott, J.M.C. (1983) The trip index, *Journal of Travel Research*, Summer, pp. 6–9.

Rita, P. and Moutinho, L. (1993) Allocating a promotional budget, *International Journal of Contemporary Hospitality Management*, **4**(3), 5.

Seaton, A.V. (1994) Tourism and the media, in Witt, S.J. and Moutinho, L. (eds), *Tourism Marketing and Management Handbook*, Prentice-Hall, London, pp. 135–9.

Smith, R.A. (1991) Beach resorts: a model of development evolution, *Landscape and Urban Planning*, **21**, 189–221.

Soane, J.V.N. (1993) *Fashionable Resort Regions: Their Evolution and Transformation*, CAB International, Wallingford, UK.

United States Department of Commerce/University of Missouri-Columbia (1991) *Tourism USA: Guidelines for Development*, US Department of Commerce, Washington DC.

Woodside, A. and Sherrill, D. (1977) Traveler evoked, inept and inert sets of vacation destinations, *Journal of Travel Research*, **16**, 14–18.

WTO (1992) *Travel and Tourism Barometer 1992*, December, p. 4.

REVIEW QUESTIONS

1. Why are destinations 'peculiar animals' for a tourism organization to market?
2. What are the main questions that need to be answered in determining the tourism potential of a particular destination?
3. Attempt to apply the TALC as a framework for analysis of a destination of your choice.
4. To what extent do you think it is possible to market any place as a tourism destination?

Airline marketing

M.M. Bennett

15

OBJECTIVES

By the end of this chapter the reader should:

- be able to differentiate between strategic and tactical marketing;
- understand the importance of marketing in the airline industry;
- appreciate the context in which marketing in the airline industry has developed;
- understand how the different marketing techniques are employed.

INTRODUCTION

To illustrate the use of marketing within the travel and tourism industry there can be no better example than that set by airlines. From a sector which began life dominated by restrictive regulations it became one which embraced, if not at times strangled, competition. And it did this through a host of finely-tuned and sophisticated marketing techniques, the end results of which did not always match initial and often innocuous intentions. It is these strategic marketing tools together with more established tactical techniques which have combined to make this sector one of the most marketing-led in the business and it is these techniques which form the subject of this chapter.

BACKGROUND TO AIRLINE MARKETING

To understand airline marketing it is necessary to appreciate the complex institutional framework from which it has developed. Prior to 1978 virtually all air transport was heavily regulated. Fares, routes, capacity and carriers were all subject to government approval on a bilateral basis. The reasons for this are embedded in the development of airlines. Historically, governments have owned airlines for the purposes of national defence and security in order to be able to requisition aircraft in the event of war.

Table 15.1 The Five Freedoms

1st Freedom: The right of an airline to fly over a state to land in another state.

2nd Freedom: The right of an airline to land in a state for fuel and maintenance purposes.

3rd Freedom: The right of an airline to carry traffic from its own country and discharge it in the country party to the bilateral.

4th Freedom: The right of an airline to carry traffic back to the country of origin.

5th Freedom: The right of an airline to collect and discharge traffic in another state on route to a final destination.

Source: Feldman (1988).

Through the provision of state subsidies (a contentious issue today as a result of relaxing regulations) governments have been able to ensure a national transport network, the threat being that without regulations certain services, especially those of low load or low yield, would disappear. The subsequent emergence of national flag carriers resulted in the elevation of airlines to a position of national prestige. The Chicago Convention in 1944 and the Bermuda bilateral agreement in 1946 are probably the most significant events in international civil aviation history in that together they established the 'Five Freedoms' which are effectively the rules of the air and which formed the basis of thousands of bilateral agreements which followed (see Table 15.1).

The result was that organizations such as the International Air Transport Association (IATA) and the International Civil Aviation Organization (ICAO) together with governments became the key parties making the decisions about the operation of airlines. And a consequence of that was that airlines were part of national politics, not market forces. Competition in any real sense was non-existent, bilateral agreements ensured that capacity was shared equally on a 50:50 basis, and fares were identical. Furthermore, state ownership and associated subsidies together with a lack of competition meant that customer service was not given a high priority. In short, the airline industry reflected a civil service as opposed to a service industry mentality and the results were plain for all to see. From an airline marketing perspective the opportunities for product differentiation were few and motivation for attempting it was absent. Uniformity was the order of the day, the corollary of which was a virtually non-existent need for or presence of a marketing strategy.

The Airline Deregulation Act of 1978 this situation irrevocably altered in the domestic market of the United States. This provided the first real evidence of what could happen once regulations were removed and opened up the way for the introduction of marketing techniques on an unprecedented scale. The aims of the Act's instigators were sound: to open up competition by exposing airlines to market forces which would help promote greater choice and lower fares for customers. In the short term, exactly this happened: new carriers proliferated, fares were lowered and new routes were opened up. For example, it is estimated that between 1978 and 1984 a total of 26 new entrants emerged while in relation to fares the number of people flying on discounted tickets rose from 48% in 1978 to 85% in 1985 with discounts representing as much as 50% and over in real terms (Wheatcroft and Lipman, 1986). In the longer term, however, what transpired has been a rather different picture and one which has been the subject of countless articles and books. Without wishing to repeat what has already been stated elsewhere (see Wheatcroft and Lipman, 1986; Button, 1991, 1993; Feldman, 1988; and Williams, 1993 for a fuller account of deregulation and its effects on the airline industry), the aim here is simply to provide a synopsis in a way which relates to the points made later which form the subject of this chapter – that of marketing.

A key theory underpinning deregulation in the United States was that of **contestability**. Unfortunately for the administrators the practice disproved the theory. The assumption upon which this theory is based is that the threat of competition would prevent incumbent airlines from exploiting a monopoly position as another airline could enter the market and undercut prices. The theory failed for a number of reasons. A number of anti-competitive practices were introduced, some of which form the subject of this chapter. One such practice was predatory pricing whereby major airlines used discriminatory price-cutting as a means of driving out low-cost new entrants offering lower fares. Contentious in that it is difficult to prove, the issue is nevertheless recognized as a major factor in undermining deregulation.

Chapter 11 of the US bankruptcy laws caused further problems. This US court mechanism provides protection for companies against bankruptcy and has become a feature of the industry (see Table 15.2). Major airlines including TWA, Continental and Pan Am have operated under it. The root of the problem is that while deregulation offered freedom of entry, it did not permit freedom to fail. And by allowing what are in essence bankrupt airlines to continue operating, it interfered with market forces and adversely affected the operations of the non-bankrupt airlines. As one source at American Airlines stated: 'American does not believe that a successful deregulated industry can coexist with the only bankruptcy laws in the world that permit bankrupt airlines to operate indefinitely and so threaten the financial viability of the healthy carriers' (*The Times*, 25 February 1993).

Table 15.2   Chapter 11

- Debts are frozen
- Payments into company pension schemes are postponed
- Contracts on leased aircraft are renegotiated
- Staff schemes are cut
- Defaulted payments on airport fees are divided among other carriers

Source: *The Times*, 25 February 1993.

CASE STUDY 15.1

Airlines in Chapter 11

In February 1993 more than one-fifth of the total capacity of US-based airlines operated under Chapter 11 protection, including America West, Continental and TWA. According to American Airlines, these airlines' costs are 17% lower than solvent carriers.

Source: *The Times*, 25 February 1993.

Airport slots and gates added to the difficulties. Free entry to the market was only possible where slots and gates were available. In the absence of a slot to land your aircraft and a gate to 'park' it, the problem of operating a service to a destination becomes acute. In addition to limited airport expansion (it can take up to ten years to build an airport) due in part to environmental protestation, the procedure for slot allocation is antiquated and iniquitous. 'Grandfather rights', whereby the incumbent airline has first choice on whether to keep the slot the following year, has dominated the industry. The result is that in practice it is very difficult for a new airline to succeed.

The problem has been exacerbated by hub and spoke networks which have provided economies of scope again for the major airlines. Prior to deregulation in the US flights operated on a city pair basis, in other words flying from one major city to another. However, this disadvantaged people living outside the major cities. So by feeding in planes from various locations (spokes) into a major airport (hub) airlines were able to tie in more people. Flights are geographically synchronized in an east to west or north to south direction such that transfer times for passengers at hubs is minimized. The result has been that hubs are dominated by one or two airlines (see Table 15.3) and commuter or regional airlines have become tied to the majors and form the spokes of the network. Again, the scale of the operation is such that it works against new entrants.

Table 15.3 Ten major US hubs, 1988

Hub city	Dominant airline	Market share (%)
Pittsburgh	USAir	85
St Louis	TWA	83
Salt Lake City	Delta	80
Minneapolis	Northwest	78
Houston	Continental	77
Dallas	American	64
Detroit	Northwest	60
Nashville	American	59
Atlanta	Delta	58
Chicago	United	51

Source: Wheatcroft and Lipman (1990).

The foregoing account demonstrates how deregulation in the US altered the operations of the industry. It also set the precedent for a move away from tight regulation in other parts of the world towards a relaxation of the rules and ultimately an 'open skies' policy. Europe is one such example. Liberalization, as it is termed, represents less a complete removal of all restrictions but more a progressive removal of regulations. While it is recognized that there are fundamental differences between the two areas (Poole, 1989), it is also acknowledged that lessons can be learned from the US. The idea is that by removing restrictions in stages the results of each action can be assessed more easily. Consequently, cabotage rights for each EU member state (i.e. BA flying London–Paris–Nice) will not be permitted until April 1997. However, available now under the European Union's liberalization package is the opportunity for carriers of member states to operate domestic services on intra-European routes. As well as smaller airlines taking advantage of the new freedoms, large carriers have also grabbed the gauntlet. British Airways, for example, in an effort to create a more comprehensive airline network, has become affiliated to secondary airlines in other member states including Deutsche BA in Germany and the French regional carrier TAT. (For a fuller account of liberalization, see Button, 1991; French, 1992; Humphreys, 1992; Wheatcroft and Lipman, 1990.)

A more recent development of deregulation in the US has been the introduction of new low-cost airlines which concentrate on the short- and

---

CASE STUDY 15.2

Southwest Airlines

In 1993 Southwest Airlines was the most profitable airline in the US making profits when the big airlines made losses and in a year when the combined losses for the industry totalled more than $4 billion. Based in Texas, Southwest operates short-haul routes in the south-west and is the largest flight operator within California. With a standard class only, a bag of peanuts for a meal and a glass of orange juice for a drink, it provides a new dimension to the concept of service within an airline environment. Seats are not allocated, operating instead on a first come, first served basis, and if a flight is missed no penalties are incurred as flights are so frequent. With this formula, Southwest's operating costs per available seat mile are 22% below the average for the big carriers and as a result its popularity has soared. As Tomkins (1994) states:

> Southwest's fares are a fraction of those offered by other airlines for comparable distances, a feature that has proved highly addictive to cost-conscious US companies. Business travellers are not only deserting other airlines to fly by Southwest, they are also choosing to fly with the airline rather than drive or to take journeys that their budgets would not previously have allowed them to make.

Source: Tomkins (1994).

medium-range domestic routes and which are proving to be an untimely threat to the big American airlines. They are characterized by fast turn-around times, intensive shuttle services on busy routes and no frills which means that baggage transfers, in-flight meals, free newspapers and first/business class accommodation are all eliminated. The result is that these small airlines operate at a fraction of the big airlines' costs and offer prices to prove it. Consequently, the big airlines are facing competition from such newcomers as Valujet and Southwest. In response and to compete in this increasingly popular no-frills marketplace, the big airlines are following suit. Continental airlines has set up Continental Lite which offers 'peanut fares' on 875 routes, United is planning to set up a similar operation (U2 has been mooted as a name) and Delta is considering the possibility.

While deregulation dominated all discussions on the airline industry in the 1980s, it could be argued that **globalization** is having a similar effect in the 1990s. The idea stems from an increasingly widespread belief that by the turn of the century there will be only a handful of megacarriers which will serve all parts of the globe. The race is now on among the major airlines throughout the world to achieve that goal – or at least survive. Not surprisingly – and as we shall see in the course of this chapter – such a strategy is having a major impact on the industry.

STRATEGIC VERSUS TACTICAL

Before going on to review the different marketing techniques that have been employed, it is worth making a distinction between strategic and tactical marketing. Strategic marketing, as the name suggests, takes a long-term approach. It involves developing a mission statement and treating that as the goal. Consequently, the marketing campaigns are proactive and undertaken over a long period of time. Tactical marketing is the opposite. Programmes are developed on a short-term basis often as a reaction to new information or as an attempt to alter the sales of a specific part of the business. The two types of approach complement each other in fulfilling both short- and long-term objectives. The techniques employed by the airline industry will be categorized according to these headings.

STRATEGIC MARKETING

Techniques to be considered under this heading include brand/image, frequent flyer programmes (FFPs), computerized reservation systems (CRSs), code-sharing, alliances and external linkages. Each will be looked at in turn.

Branding

A major problem facing airlines has been differentiating their product from that of their competitors as the basic product is essentially the same.

Furthermore, the product itself is a means to an end in that a flight is taken to enable the traveller to undertake a purpose at the destination, the flight therefore being of secondary importance to the purpose for travel. Consequently, the problem of attracting passengers in the first instance over and above them using competitors is not an easy one to solve. One solution is branding. British Airways was the first airline to adopt branding and it has proved highly successful. Recognized and respected are Concorde, First Class, Club World, Club Europe (equivalent to business class), World Traveller, Euro Traveller (equivalent to economy) and Super Shuttle. Virgin Atlantic has three brands: Upper Class and Economy were the original two but these have been followed by Premium Economy which is priced at full economy fare but offers a service comparable to a short-haul business class. Virgin's Upper Class service offers first-class sleeper seats with extra legroom for the price of a business class ticket, an idea born in 1984 with the introduction of the service and only now catching on elsewhere in the industry. British Midland has adopted a similar strategy. The key factors, then, differentiating these products are price and the associated level of service. Certainly, it is acknowledged that service levels in business and first are of a high standard but what is more contentious is whether they justify the equally high prices attached to them.

The policy adopted by airlines has been to overcharge Business and First passengers (largely company travellers) and use that revenue to subsidize Economy to compete with their competitors and get 'bums on seats'. Indeed it is a well known fact that high-yield passengers (business and first) generally constitute one-fifth of passengers on an aircraft yet provide two-thirds of the revenue if the seats are filled. While this was satisfactory in the sense that it worked in the boom years when companies were prepared to pay the exorbitant fares as a perk for their industrious employees, in recessionary times business travellers have fled or been forced to the back of the plane. So not only did the world recession result in fewer people travelling but it also meant that those that did travel moved down a class or two. Airline profits were thus squeezed twice as hard. This has happened to such an extent that Sabena, KLM, Swissair and Continental have removed first class altogether (*The Times*, 28 April 1994). That said, the trend away from first class began in the 1980s when brands multiplied so fragmenting the market and resulting in First occupying a smaller niche, and has since been compounded by the recession in the 1990s.

CASE STUDY 15.3

Glasgow to Chicago

On a flight between Glasgow and Chicago, a First Class return ticket costs £4500, a Business Class return costs £2500 and a full Economy ticket £900. A midweek Apex fare can be obtained for £450.

Source: *The Times*, 2 September 1993.

Table 15.4 Intercontinental airlines' business class product features (major airlines serving the UK), 1992

Airline	Name given to business class product	Special features
Aer Lingus	Premier Service	US Immigration preclearance at Shannon. Free helicopter/limousine in US.
Air Canada	Executive Class	45-inch seat pitch. Complimentary chauffeur drive in Canada.
Air France	Le Club	Free stopovers. On board cordless telephone service.
Air Mauritius	Business Class	Wide choice of menus.
Air New Zealand	Business Class	Complimentary money belt. 15 minute baggage retrieval target.
Air Seychelles	Pearl Class	56-inch seat pitch.
All Nippon Airways	Club ANA	Complimentary limousine service in London. Personal TV.
American Airlines	Business Class	Three choices of main course, including 'destination feature' option. Choice of US or European breakfast.
British Airways	Club World	Express parking at Heathrow Terminal 4. Four choices of main meal entrée.
Canadian Airlines International	Business Class	45-inch seat pitch. Special stopover rates. Free 'Speedlink' coach Heathrow to Gatwick.
Cathay Pacific	Marco Polo	Free limousine service in UK. 'Shop over Hong Kong' package.
Delta AirLines	Business Class	—
Emirates		Free limousine service throughout Dubai. Individual in-flight video units.
Japan Air Lines	Executive Class	Ten days free parking at Heathrow. Sony Walkman or personal video system.
KLM	Business Class	Four-course menus. Free stopovers in Amsterdam.
Lufthansa	Business Class	Free New York helicopter transfer.
Philippine Airlines	Mabuhay	Free first-class rail tickets to Gatwick. Free upgrade to First Class.
Qantas		Stopover programme. Free limousine service in UK.

Table 15.4 *(continued)*

Airline	Name given to business class product	Special features
SAS	EuroClass	52-inch seat pitch. 'Eurosleeper' seats. Personal video player.
Singapore Airlines	Raffles Class	Stopover programme. 'Personal cinema' system.
Swissair	Business Class	Free helicopter transfer in New York. Meals served course by course.
United Airlines	Connoisseur Class	Choice of three entrées.
Virgin Atlantic	Upper Class	55-60 inch seat pitch. Free chauffered cars in UK, US and Hong Kong. Sleeper service on all night flights. Free first-class rail tickets to Gatwick. In-flight beauty therapist on selected flights.

Source: Key Note (1993).

Furthermore, the importance of business class is such that airlines are striving even harder to differentiate their product from that of their next competitor. Consequently, service features in both the air and on the ground are heavily promoted to entice the traveller to fly with the airline. Table 15.4 shows the special features offered by leading airlines. Items such as toilet bags, newspapers, footrests and complimentary drinks are excluded from the list as these are largely standard features of any business class product.

Although most airlines offer brands which represent first, business and economy categories, there are those that offer a standard service. South-west Airlines, an example which has already been given, specializes in no-frills, low-cost flights and has been highly successful – in 1993 it was the the most profitable airline in the world (*Financial Times*, 12 June 1994). The evidence suggests that this may well become more widespread.

In an effort to woo passengers to fly with their airline, advertising plays a major role. Levels of advertising as well as the nature of it varies between airlines. For example, main media advertising expenditure by airlines in the UK for 1991–2 show that BA held 18.3% market share with the next contender, American Airlines, on 9.5%. Interestingly, Virgin, which is so often under the spotlight of media attention, held only 3.3% (Key Note, 1993). For a list of advertising expenditure by the major airlines see Table 15.5. Strategies used vary according to airline but television and newspaper media are heavily used. (For examples of press advertisements used by various airlines, see Figure 15.1.)

Customer service is a key factor. The better the class, the greater the service provision. Although the tangible material service has already been discussed, there is also the personal service component. Singapore Airlines (SIA), for example, has an enviable reputation for service. And such

Legrooooooooom.

Upper Class costs no more than ordinary business class. But you get fifteen inches more legroom. Call 0293 747 500 or your travel agent. virgin atlantic

ends. A chauffeur at both

Upper Class includes a chauffeur to the airport (home counties only), and one to greet you at the other end. Outward bound and on your return. Call 0293 747 500 or your travel agent. virgin atlantic

Fly to the States from £229 return.

It's enough to make you leave the country. Before you start packing call us on 0345 222111 or visit your local travel agent.

BRITISH AIRWAYS
The world's favourite airline

*From October 1st you can fly to USA from only £229 Monday to Thursday if you book 21 days in advance

You know it makes cents. £1=$1.96.

America, land of the free. Okay, okay, it isn't free. But there's at least a third off everything from CD's to mountain bikes. God bless America.

BRITISH AIRWAYS
The world's favourite airline

*Exchange rate subject to fluctuation

Figure 15.1 Examples of airline press advertisements.
Reproduced with permission courtesy of British Airways and Virgin Atlantic.
VIRGIN is a registered trademark of Virgin Enterprises Limited.

Table 15.5 Airline main media advertising expenditure in the UK (£000), 1991 and 1992

Airline	1991	1992	% change 1991–1992	% share 1992
British Airways	8 088	10 444	29.1	18.3
American Airlines	10 804	5 685	–47.4	9.9
United	4 428	3 060	–30.9	5.3
Delta	2 618	3 117	19.1	5.4
Qantas	2 435	1 234	–49.3	2.2
British Midland	2 384	2 616	9.7	4.6
Air Canada	1 608	2 453	52.5	4.3
Virgin	1 529	2 095	37.0	3.7
Lufthansa	1 649	2 304	39.7	4.0
Malaysia	—	1 541	—	2.7
Air UK	1 791	1 247	–30.4	2.2
Cathay Pacific	1 939	1 636	–15.6	2.9
Singapore	1 284	1 370	6.7	2.4
North West	1 339	865	–35.4	1.5
SAS	542	1 850	241.3	3.2
Dan-Air	83	877	956.6	1.5
Swissair	731	1 058	44.7	1.8
Other	17 598	13 753	–21.8	24.0
Total	60 850	57 205	–6.0	100.0

Note: figures may not sum due to rounding.
Source: Key Note (1993).

is the level of importance attached to service that BA has introduced programmes including Putting People First and Winning for Customers to instill the service mentality into all their staff. This, in turn, adds another dimension to the brand, the importance of which is not to be underestimated.

Frequent flyer programmes

Having attracted the passenger (business or leisure traveller) to fly with that airline in the first instance, the next objective is to maintain that passenger's custom. One way of doing this is through a loyalty-based scheme which provides upgrades, bonuses or free flights based on the number of miles flown. Although the first frequent flyer programme (FFP) was introduced in 1981 by American Airlines, today the FFP is as much a part of the airline industry as the actual airlines. For example, it is estimated that 10% of the US population are members of FFPs (Verchere, 1993).

As a marketing tool FFPs have proved highly successful. Mainly aimed at the business traveller, they attract the high-yield passengers which are the profit-generating ones. They also enable seats on low-load flights, which would otherwise remain empty, to be filled as rewards to frequent

CASE STUDY 15.4

Frequent Flyer Programmes

According to the Carlson Marketing Group, the 32 million frequent flyer members in the United States have earned more than 620 billion miles worth of free travel which is enough to fill more than 590 000 fully loaded transatlantic Boeing 747s.

Source: Taylor (1994).

flyers. The CRS is all important here in determining the low-load flights such that revenue is not diluted. The synergistic element is the competitive advantage gained from passengers going out of their way to fly with that airline even though another's flight might be inherently more suitable. FFP involvement has become almost as important as punctuality and in-flight service in determining choice of airline and flight. And in an effort to be one of the best, FFPs are now tied into other products often non-travel related including telephone companies, credit cards, car rentals, tour operators, hotel chains and even stocks and shares (Verchere, 1993). Information collected from FFPs can be compiled on a database and can be used for direct mailshots and for fine-tuning/tailoring services.

However, like any innovation, FFPs have not been without problems. For the airlines involved, one such problem is the amount of FFP mileage accrued that has not been redeemed. This is known as contingent liability. While it is acknowledged that redemption of FFPs on low-load flights will minimize revenue dilution, on a busy or full flight the result is very different. Consequently, by using the CRS to monitor flights, restrictions can be introduced limiting redemption on full flights, and similarly expiry dates can be set such that airlines can confidently balance their books without having loose ends. Currently, there is no legal requirement for this liability to be declared on the balance sheet. Should the law change then the future of FFPs could be brought into question.

For airlines not involved in FFP schemes the problems are even greater. FFPs have been seen as an anti-competitive weapon and a barrier to market entry. Such is the popularity of FFPs that airlines are frequently chosen on the basis of their FFP. As such, it becomes very difficult for a new airline or one not linked to an FFP to succeed on a route which is served by an airline with an FFP. As a result, smaller airlines, disadvantaged for not having an FFP, have had little option but to become involved in a scheme through code-sharing agreements and other affiliations with the major airlines in the US based on complementary route networks. The effect of FFPs has spread into the global marketplace (see Table 15.6). Significantly, in the Far East, SIA, Cathay Pacific, Malaysia and Thai are combining forces to set up an FFP. In wanting to compete in the global market it has become necessary to set up an FFP to reduce competitive disadvantage. This in itself is interesting in that it was once the case that

Table 15.6 Frequent flyer programmes

Air Canada	Aeroplan programme with basic, prestige and elite tiers.
Air France	Frequence Plus scheme based on miles for free tickets or upgrades.
Alitalia	Club Ulisse: free economy return ticket for every ten club boarding passes.
American	AAdvantage has basic, gold and platinum tiers.
British Airways	Executive club has blue, silver and gold tiers. Premier tier is by invitation only.
British Midland	4 flights to qualify for diamond club membership, 10 for silver.
Continental	One Pass scheme has elite bronze, silver and gold tiers.
Czech Airlines (CSA)	OK Plus Scheme is the only one of its type among central European airlines.
Delta	Frequent Flyer is a mileage based scheme; upper tier is known as Medallion.
El Al	Frequent Traveller Flyer is a point based mileage system requiring residence in Israel, South Africa and America.
Iberia	Iberia Plus scheme; flights with Aviaco and Viva Air qualify.
Japan Airlines	Mileage Bank scheme; in addition to upgrades and free flights, vouchers towards European holidays offered.
KLM	Flying Dutchman scheme has blue, silver and royal tiers; qualifying carriers are Air UK, Transavia and Northwest.
Lufthansa	Miles and More is a mileage based scheme.
Northwest	World Perks has basic, silver and gold tiering.
Sabena	Welcome programme with plus, first and royal tiers which includes Air France flights.
SAS	EuroBonus offers basic, silver and Royal Viking tiers.
Swissair	Qualiflyer scheme incorporates Crossair, Austrian Airlines and Singapore Airlines.
Singapore	Priority Passenger Service.
South African Airways	Prestige Club programme.
United	Mileage Plus programme has basic and premier tiers.
Virgin Atlantic	Freeway scheme has a Gold tier and a separate corporate scheme.

Source: McWhirter (1993) and Gregory (1993).

FFPs provided a competitive advantage, but due to the widespread adoption of such schemes, becoming involved in one is now merely a means of erasing an inherent disadvantage.

Computerized reservation systems

Like FFPs, computerized reservation systems (CRSs) have become a powerful marketing tool within the airline industry. In particular, they have become notorious for their in-built bias which has led to valuable revenue gains for the CRS owner. Following deregulation in the US, these

CRSs which began life as internal systems were installed within travel agencies and it was this development which encouraged the exploitation of their marketing potential. By owning the CRS, the airline was able to manipulate screen displays to their benefit thus ensuring that more of their airline's tickets were sold over those of their competitors. Known as the 'halo' effect, the incremental revenue gained in this manner is considerable.

Further advantages accrued through renting out space to other carriers unable to set up or market their own CRS. At the same time as charging a fee for every ticket booked on another carrier, that carrier was also being unfairly discriminated against on screen displays. Indeed, it was known that there was discrimination in the fees that were charged. So, in other words, a competitor was paying a higher fee to be part of the CRS and simultaneously faced a higher degree of bias. This was tested in a court case in 1988 between Sabre and BA although the dispute was finally settled out of court. A further benefit of renting out space to other airlines, borne out in the 'dirty tricks' campaign waged against Virgin by BA, is that of the illegal use of another company's information. Having access to such information provides a competitive if unfair advantage.

Another function of CRSs – and frequently that of revenue management systems (RMSs which are private systems, unshared) – is the ability to fine-tune yields such that loads and prices are maximized. The CRS or RMS can track which flights are selling well and which are not and thereby exercise price discrimination on the seats sold on the CRS through travel agents.

Accrued, the advantages for the CRS owner are synergistic. Indeed, so prodigious are the benefits that Robert Crandall, President of American Airlines, is reputed to have said that he would sell the airline before the CRS. Not surprisingly, the power of the CRS has led to suggestions that the CRS is anti-competitive and has erected rather than lowered barriers to entry for new airlines. This, however, has been tackled by authorities in both the US and Europe by the introduction of codes of conduct. The criteria that can be used by travel agents to select a flight include departure time, elapsed flight time (the time it takes to get from A to B) and the minimum number of en route stops. This, together with the emergence of global distribution systems (GDS) comprising a number of airlines rather than just one or two, has helped to eliminate the most blatant forms of bias. While this may reduce the more contentious aspects of CRSs, it will do little to diminish the marketing power gained from owning one.

Code-sharing

Linked to both CRSs and FFPs is code-sharing. This enables airlines to market a service as a through one even though it may involve a change of both aircraft and airline. As a marketing device, it came to prominence following deregulation in the US. With the emergence of hub and spoke networks the major airlines wanted to serve as many locations as possible. So agreements were struck with regional and commuter airlines serving shorter distances out of the hub. There were benefits for both parties: the

Table 15.7   Major US code-sharing agreements, 1988

Major airline	Regional airline	Connecting point
American	Metro Airlines	Dallas/Fort Worth
	Air Midwest	Nashville
	Command Airways	Boston and New York
	Wing West	Los Angeles and San Francisco
	Simmons	Chicago
Continental	Royale	Houston
	Rocky Mountain	Denver
	Mid Pacific	Honolulu
	Gull Air	Boston
	Britt	Chicago
	PBA	Newark
Delta	Atlantic Southeast	Atlanta
	Comair	Cincinnati
	Business Express	Boston
	Skywest	Salt Lake City
Eastern	Metro Airlines	Atlanta
	Air Midwest	Kansas City
	Bar Harbour	Boston
	Britt	Philadelphia
Northwest	Express Airlines	Minneapolis
	Simmons	Detroit
Pan Am	Pan Am Express	New York and Washington
TWA	Air Midwest	St Louis
United	Air Wisconsin	Chicago
	Westair	San Francisco
	Aspen Airways	Denver
US Air/ Piedmont	Henson Aviation	Baltimore
	CCAir	Charlotte
	Brockway	Syracuse
	Crown	Pittsburgh
	Suburban	Pittsburgh
	Pennsylvania	Pittsburgh
	Chautauqua	Pittsburgh

Source: Wheatcroft and Lipman (1990).

major airlines benefited from penetrating a greater number of markets. This together with FFPs attracted additional passengers which in turn translated into greater revenue. For the smaller airline, it meant a better display position on the CRS but it also more importantly meant survival as they were complementing not competing with the majors. Consequently, by 1985 in the US the largest commuter carriers had all formed code-sharing agreements with a major airline, and equally every major airline had formed such an alliance with a commuter airline (Williams, 1993) (see Table 15.7).

As regulations are being relaxed across the entire industry and as alliances (see following section) are being formed on a global scale, code-sharing is fast becoming a universal feature of the industry. In the race to become a global player, agreements are being struck on an increasingly frequent basis. BA, for example, has formed a code-sharing agreement with US Air linked to their 24.6% stake in the airline. Of importance too is the link to FFPs. A larger network facilitated by code-sharing makes the FFP more attractive to potential passengers thus providing incremental revenue. For example, as part of KLM's Flying Dutchman scheme miles can be earned on Northwest Airlines, Air UK and Transavia. One marketing device is thus assisting another and in so doing is helping to consolidate the airline's position.

So the airlines involved benefit from code-sharing but what of the consumer? Described by United Airlines before Department of Transportation approval as 'consumer fraud', and referred to as a 'marketing device that also relies on deception' by *The Economist* (Markillie, 1993), code-sharing would appear to be less than fair to the consumer. The problem is simple: most passengers if flying from A to B would prefer to go direct, but with code-sharing a flight involving a change of plane/aircraft which has a shared code will be given a better position on the CRS screen display because CRS logic favours single codes above those involving more than one code. However, if a code-sharing flight is chosen when a direct flight may well serve the two points, the consumer can be considered to be deceived. Furthermore on a transatlantic flight to the US involving a touchdown at a US gateway, passengers are required to clear customs at the first entry point thus making the flight less convenient than a direct one.

But code-sharing is not all bad news for the consumer. A single boarding pass and ticket can be issued to cover the entire journey and baggage can be transferred through to the final destination. Furthermore, dovetailing

---

CASE STUDY 15.5

Code-sharing

'You finally decide on an XYZ flight at 2.30 to London which connects you to an XYZ flight onto Mexico. But again you are being misled. XYZ doesn't actually operate the flight to London. It has agreed to "share codes" with another airline, *Dod-G* (a one-horse operation if ever there was one). By doing this, XYZ can attract more passengers onto its flights out of London, and *Dod-G* get more passengers for their flights. You once flew with *Dod-G*, and have sworn never to touch them again. But if you book this flight, even though it's shown as an XYZ flight, it will be a *Dod-G* aircraft you'll be stepping into.'

Source: *Holiday Which?* (1988).

connections can reduce the time a traveller has to spend at the airport awaiting an onward flight.

Alliances

Bringing together code-sharing, CRSs, FFPs and branding is the topic of alliances. Linked also to globalization, the rationale is to obtain a larger presence in the global marketplace and to achieve various economies through linking reservations, undertaking joint sales and marketing, offering special fares, sharing facilities and joint purchasing/maintenance agreements.

Airline alliances usually incorporate the following features (*Financial Times*, 13 April 1994):

- shared airport facilities;
- reciprocity on frequent flyer programmes;
- marketing agreements;
- improved connections;
- freight coordination;
- package tour links.

Further economies are gained through reduced competition (through working to some extent with another airline rather than competing head on against it), code-sharing and FFPs, which together result in incremental revenue.

Alliances are not the only way of expanding – mergers, acquisition and internal growth are other avenues. But it is through alliances that many of the key marketing strengths are to be gained which provide the clout arising from size but which also enables them to maintain their independence.

Inter-sector linkages

Airlines gain marketing benefits from becoming involved with other sectors in the chain of distribution. Vertical integration has fostered this trend.

CASE STUDY 15.6

SIA/Delta/Swissair

The tangible link between the three airlines is a 5% equity held by each airline in the other two. The combined network covers all continents, 237 destinations and 64 countries. The synergy of the alliance derives from a combination of the airlines serving different parts of the globe. SIA and Swissair serve the Asian/European market, Delta and SIA the Pacific region, and Delta and Swissair the Atlantic. In addition to these benefits the alliance features blocked space arrangements whereby an airline leases seats on another airline which is then marketed as a through service, reservations linkage, joint sales and marketing, through fares, shared check-in facilities, freight cooperation and aircraft maintenance.

CASE STUDY 15.7

British Airways and US Air

BA's original intention to buy a 44% stake in US Air for £750 million was announced on 21 July 1992. After protracted negotiations with the US Administration and bitter opposition from US airlines, BA withdrew its offer and submitted a revised one early in 1993, finally securing a 24.6% stake in the sixth largest carrier in the US. The alliance was contentious in that it allows BA (as a foreign carrier) a foothold into the lucrative domestic market of the US. The other US airlines opposed this bitterly not only because it would provide them with further competition but also because they were not given equal access to the UK or more specifically Heathrow. The deal, as it stands, gives BA the opportunity to provide a seamless service across the Atlantic by coordinating flights and computer reservations and by refurbishing aircraft in BA's livery. However, there are drawbacks, most notably the anti-trust laws in the US which prevent, in the interests of competition, airlines from colluding on pricing. Coordination is further hindered by the use of different airports; for example, BA flies into Kennedy airport in New York while US Air uses both Newark and La Guardia. A similar problem occurs in Washington.

A natural development for airlines then is to form links with hotels or even own them at airports on the basis that there will be a demand for accommodation once the traveller has reached the destination. At one time, for example, BA was linked with the Penta chain. However, the drain on capital, particularly in recessionary times, has made this a less viable option.

Airline promotion has extended into tour operation. This has two facets: the development of a charter fleet and a tour operator programme. The former can be used either for their own tour operator programme or leased to other companies. Developing their own tour operator programme has proved a particularly useful tool in filling up empty seats. BA has both its own charter wing (Caledonian Airways) and its own tour operator programme (BA Holidays) which uses the scheduled service.

CASE STUDY 15.8

British Airway's globalization strategy

Since 1992 British Airways has embarked upon a campaign to become a global airline by forming a series of alliances with airlines in different parts of the world:

- July 1992 BA acquires a 49% stake in Deutsche BA;
- October 1992 BA acquires Dan-Air;
- December 1992 BA secures a 25% stake in Qantas for £290 million;
- December 1992 BA acquires a 49.9% shareholding in the French airline TAT;
- March 1993 BA secures a 24.6% stake in US Air.

Finally, there is the link with other travel-related companies such as credit cards which put together special offers encouraging spending on the card and promotion for the airline. For example, American Express has formed links with Virgin and the US airlines, BA with Diners.

TACTICAL MARKETING

Tactical marketing, as stated earlier, is concerned with short-term programmes. These are usually either reactive in nature or may focus on a specific segment of the market. The more common approaches adopted in the airline industry will now be outlined.

External factors

Events, the economy, political troubles, etc. are all external forces which wield a heavy influence on the industry. For example, the Gulf War and the recession have had perhaps the most powerful effect on airline revenue in the history of aviation. The increase in capacity based on long-term growth forecasts in the booming 1980s combined with reduced demand resulted in the well publicized losses of the 1990s. The major airlines, faced with unprecedented losses – $12 billion in the three years up to 1993, which is more than all the profits made in the history of international civil aviation (Alexander, 1994) and a threat to their existence – undertook a major promotional effort.

In an effort to get 'bums on seats' given the high fixed costs and perishable nature of the product, airlines are increasingly linking up with everyday consumer products. BA, for example, in the winter of 1992/3 introduced a 30% discount off flights if a consumer spent £200 at Sainsbury's. The success of this promotion led to a repeat of it in the winter of 1993/4. Such an example illustrates how through a series of tactical campaigns one airline has chosen to tackle the recession.

CASE STUDY 15.9

World's Biggest Offer

In an attempt to kick-start the market following the Gulf War and in the midst of the worst civil aviation recession ever, the World's Biggest Offer was launched by the 'World's favourite airline', British Airways, in February 1991. The offer consisted of a massive draw which gave away virtually every seat on British Airways on 23 April 1991 (St George's Day) including Concorde, first, business and economy class travel on all routes except domestic. The offer of 50 000 free seats was simultaneously announced in 67 countries. The cost to the airline was estimated to be £10 million lost revenue on the day and £6 million in advertising.

Source: *The Times*, 22 March 1991.

Types of ticket

The setting of different types of fares, each with their own set of conditions and restrictions attached to them, is well practised. EXECUTIVE, SAVER, PEX, APEX, SUPERAPEX and SEATSALE all differ in the flexibility they offer the traveller and the price. The greater the flexibility, the higher the price. The lower fare tickets are designed to fill up empty seats so that some revenue is gained. The whole idea of attaching restrictions is to enable control to be exercised and to ensure that full-fare paying passengers continue to pay the higher fares. The importance of the CRS and RMS should be emphasized here since it is the combined work of these two tools which ensures that the yield can be manipulated to the airline's advantage.

Inclusive tour by scheduled services (ITXs)

To some extent, the use of scheduled seats/airlines as part of inclusive tour packages can be considered a strategic tool in that it is frequently a long-term arrangement. Many scheduled airlines such as BA offer a block of seats to a tour operator on the understanding that the seats are only sold as part of the package. For the tour operators concerned, i.e. Kuoni, offering a seat on a scheduled airline enhances the upmarket reputation of the product and company and is a particular selling point for long-haul travel. The tactical slant to this tool is the introduction by certain airlines of upgrades to business class at a set price, the rationale being to boost the business class market. A limited upgrade promotion at a time when seats are flying empty assists marginality, increasing revenue and promoting the product to potential business class travellers.

IMPORTANCE OF SIZE

The preceding discussion, in highlighting the strategic and tactical marketing tools adopted by the airline industry, also made reference to the size of company. Indeed, one of the key lessons learned from deregulation in the US was that of the marketing advantage secured by the large airlines. Evidence of this is rooted in loyalty schemes (FFPs), control of distribution (CRSs, code-sharing), branding and associated large-scale advertising, and price leadership. This has been followed by alliances in the quest for globalization – or at least survival – and by inter-sectoral linkages which have provided additional synergy. In the US the result has been the domination of the industry by only a handful of carriers – in 1990 the eight major airlines carried over 90% of domestic passenger traffic (Wheatcroft and Lipman, 1990). With a relaxation of the rules gradually being introduced on a global transnational basis, consolidation within the industry is also reaching global proportions. It has been suggested by more than one industry source that by the turn of the century the global airline industry will comprise only a handful of megacarriers. Certainly globalization strategies among the current major airlines are apparent in the number of alliances that have emerged in the 1990s.

If the marketing advantages are so great for the larger airline in a non-regulated environment, what will this mean for both the smaller airline and consumer? For the smaller airline it will mean becoming strategically attached to, if not a whole part of, a major airline and serving on shorter-haul routes. For the consumer, with less competition and less hope of new competition entering the market place, choice will be limited and prices are more likely to be held at a steady rate. Whether it will be any worse for the consumer than in a highly regulated environment is debatable. Naturally, there are pros and cons but the key is to ensure that the market advantage gained by airlines is not used unfairly. The teething problems for the authorities with tools such as FFPs and CRSs should be long sorted out such that fair play is ensured. As in other sectors, even with deregulation on a global basis, past experience shows that there is a need for some regulatory body to monitor the situation and ensure that the consumer does not suffer. Perhaps the epitaph to this discussion of size and the advantages it conveys is to remember Pan Am. It is a salutary reminder that size alone does not guarantee success.

SUMMARY

In the context of an industry which has been transformed from one which was highly regulated to one increasingly less regulated there has emerged a marketing culture. This has been enforced by the intrinsic similarity of the product and the fact that the product itself is a means to an end, enabling the traveller to undertake their purpose at the destination. Consequently, airlines have turned to marketing to differentiate their product from the competition, not only to attract travellers in the first place, but also to maintain their loyalty. A variety of strategic and tactical marketing techniques have been employed which all, to a greater or lesser extent, have had an impact on the industry. What is clear, then, is that marketing within the airline industry is both heavily and sometimes cleverly used and acts as a prime weapon in the ongoing competition war.

REFERENCES

Alexander, G. (1994) Fare wars push US airlines to edge, *The Sunday Times*, 9 October.

Button, K. (1991) *Airline Deregulation: International Experiences*, David Fulton Publishers Ltd, London.

Button, K. (1993) International interdependencies between deregulation of domestic service industries: a case study of aviation in North America, *The Service Industries Journal*, **13**(3), July.

Feldman, J. (1988) *Development Strategies for the World's Airlines*, Economist Intelligence Unit.

French, T. (1992) The European Commission's Third Air Transport Liberalization Package, *Travel and Tourism Analyst*, No. 5.

Financial Times (1994) Virgin–Delta link follows trend to cope with global forces, 13 April.

Gregory, C. (1993) Frequent flyers can log rich haul of perks, *The Sunday Times*, 22 August.

Humphreys, B. (1992) Deregulating Europe's air services, *Insights*, A37, ETB.

Holiday Which? (1988) Airline Booking Systems, September.

Key Note (1993) *Key Note Report: Airlines*, Key Note Publications Ltd.

McWhirter, A. (1993) Where you can claim your freedom to the skies, *The Times*, 25 February.

Markillie, P. (1993) Airlines: losing their way, *The Economist*, 12–18 June.

Poole, C.H. (1989) *US Airline Deregulation: The Lessons for the European Community*, Department of Transport.

Taylor, P. (1994) Loyalty gets its reward, *Financial Times*, Survey: Business Air Travel, 20 April.

Tomkins, R. (1994) Heavy toll of deregulation, *Financial Times* Survey: Business Air Travel, 20 April.

The Times (1991) Airline offers 50 000 free flights to beat recession, 22 March

The Times (1993) First Class is on the retreat, 2 September.

The Times (1994) Grab a seat for the flying circus, Business Air Travel 4, 28 April.

Verchere, I. (1993) Frequent flyer programmes, *Travel and Tourism Analyst*, No. 3.

Wheatcroft, S. and Lipman, G. (1986) *Air Transport in a Competitive European Market*, Economist Intelligence Unit.

Wheatcroft, S. and Lipman, G. (1990) *European Liberalisation and World Air Transport*, Economist Intelligence Unit.

Williams, G. (1993) *The Airline Industry and the Impact of Deregulation*, Ashgate Publishing Ltd, Aldershot.

REVIEW QUESTIONS

1. Why is it important to appreciate the broader context within which the international airline industry rests?
2. How does strategic marketing differ from tactical marketing?
3. Which strategic marketing techniques have airlines employed and why?
4. How has tactical marketing been employed in the airline industry?
5. What is the relationship between company size and marketing in the airline industry?

Marketing the small tourism business 16

A. Morrison

OBJECTIVES

By the end of this chapter the reader should:

- be able to define what constitutes a small tourism business;
- be able to identify the nature and characteristics of the sector;
- understand the influences on marketing in small tourism businesses;
- be able to illustrate the role of marketing within the context;
- be able to identify appropriate marketing approaches.

DEFINITION: WHAT IS A SMALL TOURISM BUSINESS?

Before the subject can be discussed in depth, it is necessary to identify what exactly is meant by a 'small tourism business'. Building on that foundation, the specific features of small tourism business marketing can be explored. However, definition is not an easy task, for to date there has been little agreement among industry, government or academic sources on what is acceptable. The most quoted study into the small business sector is that of the Bolton Committee (1971) which confirmed that the sector as a whole was both 'extensive and diversified'. More than twenty years on, this still holds true, particularly within the tourism industry where a wide range of people are served by small businesses which themselves vary in terms of the range of physical facilities and services provided, the markets in which they operate, geographic location and ownership arrangements. These are now discussed in turn.

- **Range of physical facilities**. A 'tourism business' may be one of five different types of business: related to transport, accommodation, catering, recreation or cultural activities. Examples of each would include a tour operator, a country house hotel, a restaurant, an equestrian centre and a visitor attraction, each of which requires a different range of physical facilities.

- **Markets of operation**. The small business in the tourism industry serves a wide spectrum of market segments from budget-conscious backpacking students to affluent, well-travelled professionals, all with their own sets of educational, business and pleasure needs to be satisfied.
- **Geographic Location**. This has a bearing on the type and characteristics of the market served. For instance, a city heritage centre will differ from a rural agricultural museum in terms of visitor expectations and the times of year when the tourist visits. Thus, expectations and seasonal spread of trade will vary depending on geographic location.
- **Ownership arrangements**. These will affect the way in which the operation is managed. The various legal formats of business such as sole trader, partnership, company and community business place different responsibilities on the owners. Moreover, the owner's business priorities will impact on the manner in which the operation is managed. In this respect, the business may represent a primary source of income for the owner; as such he or she would be actively involved in the operation on a day-to-day basis. Conversely, the business may be part of wider business interests and it is likely that the owner would be further removed from the daily running of the business.

Bringing together this wide range of small business descriptions, approaches and tourism sector features, the following definition emerges:

> A small tourism business is financed by one individual or small group and is directly managed by its owner(s), in a personalized manner and not through the medium of a formalized management structure. In comparison to the largest unit of operation within its particular tourism sector, it is perceived as small, in terms of physical facilities, production/service capacity, market share and number of employees.

EXAMPLE 16.1

The bed and breakfast

If we apply this definition to a small tourism business – a bed and breakfast operation – it can be seen that compared to a Travel Inn, owned by the large Whitbread corporation, the bed and breakfast operation welcomes a much smaller number of customers. The owner manages and operates the property himself, on a daily basis. He does not employ managers and assistant managers to do the job for him. The bed and breakfast is not part of a chain of similar establishments; it is privately owned and operates as an independent business. As such, the owner is totally responsible for making all business decisions.

WHY SO MANY SMALL BUSINESSES?

Traditionally, the tourism industry has been dominated by the small business and this still remains true in the 1990s. Currently, in Ireland, for instance, the tourism industry comprises many small business and relatively few large firms. Indeed, firms with less than fifteen employees account for around 79% of all Irish tourism businesses. The Welsh Tourist Board (1993) similarly describes the Welsh tourism industry thus:

It is customary for textbooks to describe tourism as a fragmented industry, dominated by small independent operators. That description is especially apt for Wales, which has a relatively high incidence of family-run enterprises and a corresponding lower proportion of group-owned businesses.

This picture can be illustrated through using one hotel establishment as a unit of measurement. In this case, an international sample of estimates of hotel stock having less than 50 bedrooms is shown in Table 16.1.

This domination by the small business of the tourism industry has historically arisen from the sector's key characteristics which can be broadly defined as low entry barriers into the industry and the nature of the operation. These will now be discussed within the context of the trading environment of the 1990s as it recovers from the 1990–93 economic recession.

Low entry barriers

Providing a business person has the required amount of finance, the barriers to entering the tourism industry are not particularly high. For instance, relative professional requirements are minimal and the legislative constraints are lower than in other professions, e.g. medical, legal (Hughes, 1992; Boer, 1992). In addition, while the developments in the tourism industry structure over the past four decades have put the large corporate groups to the forefront, it is still relatively easy for the small business to enter the tourism industry and compete in the marketplace.

However, the barriers to entry are gradually rising as banks have

Table 16.1 Percentage of hotels with less than 50 bedrooms

France	90%
Finland	50%
Germany	75%
Ireland	79%
Switzerland	76%
United Kingdom	75%

Source: Harrison and Johnston (1992); Morrison (1994).

become more cautious in their lending practices due to the lessons they have learnt during the economic recession. In addition, national and European legislation has increased constraints on tourism businesses in the form of social, health and safety, and travel directives. Furthermore, it is predicted (Kleinwort Benson, 1994) that the corporate groups will continue to expand to meet the ever-changing demands of the marketplace thus raising the level of competitive barriers.

Nature of operation

Most major companies are well represented at the primary city centre or resort locations. This strategy is due to their ability to service large concentrated markets and the high capital cost of investment at these locations. As a result, operations outside these major centres tend to be smaller as it is logical that this diversity of supply and demand in rural and coastal locations may be best satisfied by a number of distinctive small businesses, rather than by a large one. Such operations have the potential to provide the special, personalized services which add quality, variety and authenticity to the products and services offered to the tourist. In the past, such businesses have been considered viable propositions as they generally offered a means of achieving a satisfying way of life, and the necessary income to enjoy it.

However, a consequence of the nature of the operation is that the rural and coastal small businesses tend to suffer from seasonality and demand fluctuations, and as a result produce lower trading profits. In addition, during the 1990–93 economic recession small business profit margins fell dramatically causing failure rates to increase substantially. Consequently, in the severe trading environment of the 1990s, many independents are now being forced to reassess the benefits of a quality way of life versus a declining income.

From these two characteristics, it can be seen why the small business has traditionally dominated the tourism industry, but it also sounds a warning bell. It would appear that the trading environment is conspiring against the survival of the small business.

In order to illustrate these pressures upon the small tourism business in the 1990s, refer back to Table 16.1. In the UK the 75% of hotels shown represent 55% of all rooms, with the majority of this stock (78%) having the following profile (Harrison and Johnston, 1993; Kleinwort Benson, 1994):

- situated in low demand rural and coastal locations;
- operating at the unclassified or lower market levels;
- frequently trading at levels which are below financial breakeven point;
- funding dependent on long-term loans and overdraft facilities rather than equity capital;
- lacking the financial, marketing and purchasing economies of scale enjoyed by the large corporate groups.

INFLUENCES ON SMALL TOURISM BUSINESS MARKETING ACTIVITIES

These difficult trading conditions are further compounded by influences from the internal and external operating environments which have an impact on small tourism business marketing activities. The six most dominant of these influences are: mature/declining domestic market; communications technology developments; changing patterns of consumer behaviour; governmental support; lack of power and resources; and high levels of uncertainty.

- **Domestic market**. In general, economic growth has slowed in most countries worldwide. This has led to financial worries and a lack of purchasing confidence among consumers. When this is combined with a mature, often declining, domestic market the small tourism business is forced to look internationally for new markets.
- **Communications technology developments**. Developments in communications technology have transformed the way in which the small tourism business distributes its product, and has assisted in the flow of information and transactions on a global basis, using sophisticated computerized reservation systems (CRS). Already it is estimated that worldwide over 40% of business travellers and over 70% of leisure travellers book their hotel accommodation through travel agents (Sloane, 1990). In addition, the cost and complexity of developing and maintaining a presence on CRSs is financially prohibitive to the small business.
- **Consumer behaviour**. The more sophisticated and knowledgeable consumer of the 1990s is demanding a hassle-free method of purchase and, in line with other purchasing habits, the 'one-stop-shop' approach (Dicken, 1992). Features such as time and place accessibility, convenient payment procedures and comprehensive information provision are becoming crucial elements in the marketing of the tourism product. The small tourism business must identify a means of making its product more readily available to the consumer.
- **Governmental support**. Historically, the role of national tourist board activities in the area of handling sales transactions has been minimal, with a reluctance to enter into what was seen as the 'commercialization' of a public sector body (Archdale, 1992). However, the current move is towards a leadership role, coordinating the activities of the large number of small businesses through destination database development and administration of CRS resources (Bord Failte, 1993; FTB, 1993).
- **Power and resources**. Small business exploitation of market opportunities is severely limited by lack of power, time and financial resources. These limitations obviously constrain the scale and scope of marketing activity in which the small business can usefully participate. The local pub, riding centre or craft shop does not enjoy the economies of marketing and financial scale of the large group-owned business. As

such, the small business must develop cooperative linkages designed to maximize the return on scarce resources.

- **Levels of uncertainty**. The small business is uncertain about the wider influence of social, political and economic factors. This is due to the weaker position they occupy relative to large groups which can afford to work at reducing uncertainty levels through activities such as research, new product development and lobbying bodies. In addition, many of the small businesses operate within the context of uncertain return on facility capacity. This uncertainty makes it difficult for the small business to plan and implement effective marketing activities.

It is clear that the combination of industry sector characteristics, structure and influences arising from the environment in which it operates seriously challenge the capabilities of the small business owner. In addition, it is difficult to see how the small business can maintain overall independence of action without becoming less visible to the public and travel trade. The combination of these factors serves to heighten the importance of effective marketing if the business is to survive into the next century.

MARKETING AND THE SMALL TOURISM BUSINESS

In favourable market conditions, it is possible for small businesses to survive, even prosper, with a passive attitude to customers and the market. However, in an unstable trading environment a passive marketing stance can only result in business failure.

EXAMPLE 16.2

No marketing – run downhill

A lack of commitment to marketing activity by a small business owner has been compared to having a car with no petrol. It can do one of two things: sit there and rust, or run downhill out of control. If that is applied to the business, then you have a visitor attraction without visitors, a hotel without guests, a restaurant without diners. The owner may have invested a lot of time and money in the design and development of superb quality facilities, but without customers it will rust and run downhill at a steady pace.

Whether a business is large or small, basic marketing principles and theories apply. However, fine-tuning of strategies, taking into account the characteristics of the small business, is required if they are to be effective. From the many definitions of what marketing is all about (Kotler, 1991; Waterworth, 1994) the focus of marketing activities can be identified as: market orientation; customer satisfaction; sustainable profit; and dynamic business. These are now defined and then applied to the trading environment of the small business.

Market orientation – jack of all trades

EXAMPLE 16.3

Market orientation

The marketing oriented business ensures that all members of staff share the same philosophy, from the cleaner to the owner. Marketing is a team effort, with complete involvement of all levels of staff as a key objective.

Market orientation in the small business often suffers from the fact that the owner must be a 'jack of all trades' as there is a wider spread of management responsibilities than in a larger business. The owner is trying to be a specialist in all areas of management such as administration, entertaining tourists, accounting, personnel recruitment and training, *and* marketing. Time, resources and expertise are understandably stretched to the limit. As a result, there is a danger of adopting a DIY approach to marketing, which often projects an unprofessional image. Thus, market orientation and the small business is a balancing act between conflicting demands on the owner's time and resources. However, in theory, marketing is much more easily achieved in a smaller business, where the management style can often be termed as parental, with the staff representing an extended family. As such the team is already in place, loyal and willing to respond to marketing oriented directives.

Customer satisfaction – cherish your customer

EXAMPLE 16.4

Customer satisfaction

The continued satisfaction of the customer must be the main purpose of the business. It is essential to identify what they require currently, and research and anticipate what they will require in the future.

The customer base of the small business tends to be more vulnerable than that of a large, multi-unit business, with a smaller market share and lower profit margins. This elevates the need to take care of, to cherish, the existing customer base. Here is an area where the small business can win against the larger more bureaucratic due to the closeness of the owner to the customer. This closeness is a tremendous strength, which facilitates rapid response and ultimate customer satisfaction, encouraging repeat business through word-of-mouth and helping to generate new customers.

Sustained profit – no profit, no living

EXAMPLE 16.5

Sustained profit

Profit keeps the business going. However, it needs to be sustained, built upon year on year. The most valuable contributor to achieving this solid profit base is repeat business. Marketing must therefore aim at keeping the loyalty of the existing customer.

As an independent business, the small business owner is dependent on the profit generated by it to live. This is unlike large companies, where if one unit is a loss-maker a more profitable unit will subsidize it until a time when it can move into profit. Thus, for the small business owner, it is absolutely essential to build on the loyalty and return trade of existing customers in order to generate the vital sustained profit.

Dynamic business – 'lifecycle'

EXAMPLE 16.6

Dynamic business

No successful business is static. It changes and develops according to a variety of factors. It is vital that the business is constantly reviewed so that it can react to changes in the marketplace. This process needs to be managed and planned in a logical, systematic manner.

Appropriate marketing strategies vary over the lifecycle of the business as it moves through pre-start, start-up, breakeven, growth, expansion and maturity. For instance, at the start-up stage the priorities are to let the tourist know that you exist, and to establish a reputation for a good quality product. However, once the business is established priorities move to developing new markets and building on existing market share. For the small business owner with limited marketing expertise and resources this is a complex, somewhat intangible, concept to grasp, never mind apply to the business. However, it is essential that the process is managed and planned in as logical and systematic a manner as if it were a large corporation such as Thomas Cook.

MARKETING APPROACHES FOR THE SMALL BUSINESS

Particular themes which have been identified above within the external environment are concerned with the need for exposure in the international marketplace, changes in the way customers purchase tourism products through computerized booking systems, and high levels of uncertainty regarding trends and demand. Internally, the small business owner is struggling against the fact that he or she is a 'jack-of-all-trades' who needs to 'cherish the customer' with limited resources in order to generate the sustained profits which are necessary for the business to survive over its lifecycle. Based on this knowledge a range of six marketing approaches are presented.

Place – co-operative distribution

There is an obvious move within the tourism industry towards a consolidation of activities which has been triggered in particular by competitive pressures, government initiatives and developments in communications technology. This has resulted in the range of providers of the total tourism product being brought together and requiring small businesses to consider cooperative approaches to marketing as a way to profit from the challenges facing them in the marketplace.

Such cooperative marketing approaches are not new. What is new is their current scale, proliferation and the fact that they have become central to the domestic and international marketing activities of many small tourism businesses (Dicken, 1992). Also of note is their visible success in increasing tourist demand, coupled with the fact that they give the small business access to quality marketing management which they have traditionally lacked. In this way, independent businesses can group together, pool resources and achieve marketing economies of scale, bringing the benefits and strengths of large businesses combined with the advantages of being small (Buttle, 1994). As such cooperative partnerships have the potential to improve performance materially.

As a result, membership of cooperative marketing groups is growing within all areas of small tourism businesses. For example, the world's 25 largest voluntary hotel cooperative groups account for 19 041 hotels, which house 2 412 596 bedrooms (Anon., 1993). The top five groups relative to the number of hotels which are members are: Utell International, Logis de France, Minotels International, Neotel-Trans Europe Hotels and Eurostars.

Such voluntary marketing cooperatives may be based on location, activity or market or are package specific. Their aims can be described as follows:

- **location** – to inform customers about the benefits of the region and to sell its unique tourist qualities, e.g. unspoilt Greek islands, quality assured Italy, Scottish scenic splendour;
- **tourist activity** – to present a comprehensive range of similar activities to a specialist market segment, e.g. golfing holiday, snowmobile safaris, white water river rafting;
- **market** – to group businesses of a similar market level, thus establishing

an easily identifiable brand of services, e.g. wilderness cabins, farm accommodation, country house hotels;

- **package specific** – to pull together all the elements of the tourist experience into convenient, easy to purchase packages, e.g. accommodation, activity and transport inclusive product offerings.

Such cooperative marketing approaches are led by both private and public sector organizations, as can be seen from the following two cases.

CASE STUDY 16.1

Ireland

The Irish Tourist Board has produced a comprehensive guide on cooperative marketing. Basically, several producers of similar tourist products pool part of their marketing budgets to form a Region/Product Marketing Group. Members support each other through market intelligence, operating and visitor handling standards, and group promotions. Such groups include game and sea angling, golf, heritage, walking, watersports, rural tourism and various accommodation sectors. 'Irish Country Holidays', for example, is the brand name for 13 rural tourism centres which are off the traditional tourism route and which enable visitors to experience aspects of rural life which are hard to find in their own countries.

Source: *Co-operative Marketing Guide 1993*, Bord Failte, Dublin.

CASE STUDY 16.2

Scotland's Commended Hotels

Scotland's Commended Hotels (SCH) was founded in 1990 and is now Scotland's largest hotel marketing consortium with 66 members. It describes itself as 'an association of country and town houses of distinction throughout Scotland, all of which are individually owned and managed'. The grading and classification of the hotels by the Scottish Tourist Board is from 3 Crown Commended to 5 Crown Deluxe.

Members pool resources and expertise, thus consolidating and increasing effectiveness of marketing activities in the areas of:

- brochure production and distribution;
- centralized reservations office;
- overseas representation by agents;
- special low season sales promotions;
- inter-hotel referral business;
- representation at major travel trade fairs;
- quality assurance and branding.

SCH is also associated with similar independently owned properties, through other regional marketing consortia, in England (Thames Valley Hotels), Wales (Welsh Rarebits) and Ireland (The Blue Book).

For the small business, the specific choice of a cooperative marketing strategy should reflect the identification of more efficient ways to combine separate economic functions that must be carried out to provide a meaningful assortment of product to target customers (Kotler, 1991). Its success is dependent on the collective, coordinated action of a diverse group of business.

Product – differentiate

Differentiation is all about identifying which target market the small business wishes to attract and developing product features that set it apart from the competition. This strategy is particularly appropriate for the small business since it offers a better chance of selective and sustainable operation. In addition, such differentiation represents a low-risk strategy. It entails finding out what elements of the marketing mix make the business different from the competition, then specializing, emphasizing the non-price elements of the marketing mix such as quality, and stressing the inherent strength of the small tourism business – that of personalized service. In doing this the small business must single out the key selling features of the product which provide a purchasing incentive for the tourist.

Heskett (1984) states:

> The most successful service firms separate themselves from the 'pack' to achieve a distinctive position in relation to their competition. They differentiate themselves . . . by altering typical characteristics of their respective industries to their competitive advantage.

Greene (1993) urges operators to try and find an aspect of their business that rates high on the 'WOW' factor, something that makes an immediate impact, for instance the warmth of the welcome, the gents toilet in which audio tapes of famous comedians are broadcast, the special care for an elderly traveller. In this way the small business is filling a gap in the market that the corporate groups find difficult to emulate. Thus, barriers to entry in a particular market segment are raised and a profitable niche position established.

One apparent problem with niche strategy (Burns and Dewhurst, 1989) is that it is based, by its very nature, on a limited market. However, what might be limited for the corporate groups often offers wide opportunities to the small business. Thus, the competitive advantages of a niche or location will continue to be exploited by the small tourism businesses. Indeed, many small businesses continue to exist by virtue of their niche or their convenient position where a specialized local need is supplied by a local business. The following case study illustrates this approach.

CASE STUDY 16.3

The Lancashire Lodge country house

The Lancashire Lodge has been providing hospitality since the seventeenth century, but longevity is no help when there's a recession on and everyone is chasing a decreasing market. The 40-bedroom hotel offers guests a typical country house style with plenty of relaxing lounges, antique-filled bedrooms and friendly, attentive service. But the country house hotels have to come up with new ways of differentiating themselves and attracting customers.

At the Lancashire Lodge they have developed a number of weekend-break products and special activities as part of the marketing programme. One of those activities is probably a first in the country house hotel market. They have a collection of Morris Minor classic cars. They are old, carefully restored and do not go very fast. The hotel offers four cars for hire. The car hire scheme is supported by other more traditional activities such as group helicopter tours of the Cotswolds, watching cricket on the village green, fly-fishing on the hotel's five-mile stretch of fishing rights or exploring a local ruined monastery. They aim to develop niches which have a long shelf-life and are not passing fads like, for instance, 'Murder Mystery Weekends'.

Promotion – creative

Promotional activity is the visible part of marketing and is concerned with getting positive messages across to customers about the business. However, given the constrained resources of the small business, promotional strategy must seek out creative, low-cost, but nevertheless effective promotional activities. Some of the best examples of these are discussed below.

- **Personal selling and sales promotions to targeted markets**. It is important that the small business achieves a balance in activities between developing new business and cherishing existing customers. Given the many demands on the owner's time, it is important that sales activities are systematically planned and implemented. A profile of the target market needs to be developed, its geographical locations identified, the sales message targeted, appointments arranged, a standard follow-up procedure devised, and measures to monitor the effectiveness of the whole process implemented.

CASE STUDY 16.4

Wildlife centre

In March, Claire an owner of a wildlife centre, did a tour of the schools in the region. She had telephoned beforehand to alert school secretaries to her visit. Most had objected, saying that they would be too busy to speak to her. Claire assured them that it would only take a few minutes to drop off some brochures about the centre – and a gift. She duly arrived, deposited the brochures on the secretary's desk and handed over the gift. This turned out to be a kit to make a potato clock – a clock which was powered by the juices of a potato. Work on the secretary's desk was pushed aside, and full attention focused on how to put the clock together.

Claire participated in this activity, all the time telling the secretary how interesting and educational her wildlife centre was, particularly for school children. The clock was completed, perched in a prominent position, complete with the wildlife centre's logo on the front. Claire left the office. Behind her was the wildlife park's brochures, a secretary whose awareness of the benefits of the park had been raised, and of course the clock. Claire went off to continue her tour of the school secretaries. For the next week, until the potato ran out of juice, everyone who came into all those school offices wanted to know where the secretaries had got that silly potato clock, with the name of the local wildlife park on it.

But what of Claire? Following her visits she mailed all the schools with educational visit information packages. As a result of her efforts, the month of June saw the number of visits by school parties on educational trips to the centre increase by over 100%, compared to the previous year.

- **Newsworthy press releases directed to all relevant publications**. Whenever a small business has some story which is considered newsworthy, it should be encouraged to send it to all relevant publications. Whenever possible, the story should be accompanied by a clear black and white photograph showing a scene of human interest. A good newspaper story is free and often worth a dozen advertisements in terms of capturing the public's attention and raising awareness.

CASE STUDY 16.5

Special activity weekend breaks

The owner of Rosslea Hotel was launching special activity horse-riding weekend breaks. He persuaded the owner of a famous race horse to bring it into the reception desk of the hotel. The horse was then photographed 'checking in' for his riding weekend break! It was an interesting photo and story. As a result it appeared in every local and selective national newspapers as well as tourist trade journals.

- **Sponsorship of activities within the local community**. In the main, small businesses involve themselves in sponsorship as part of building respect within the local community. In sponsoring a particular group, the owner puts the name of the business in front of the public with whom he or she wishes to communicate. The business is seen as generous or socially responsible, and this can create considerable goodwill – which translates into sales turnover.
- **Merchandising of consumer goods with the business logo**. The tourism industry particularly lends itself to the merchandising of a range of

consumer goods with the business logo and message, for instance own-label wines, toiletries, T shirts, hats and travel bags. The tourist is always looking for a souvenir and will be willing to purchase a momento of a tremendous holiday. The costs involved in these items can be offset against income from their sale, increased awareness of the tourist facility and added customer value.

CASE STUDY 16.6

Classic Travel

Classic Travel, an independently owned, small travel agency sponsored the town's junior football team. Costs involved were the purchase of the football strips, boldly embellished with the travel agent's name. These 'adverts' ran about football pitches in the region for the whole football season. As a result, the profile of the business and the goodwill felt towards it was substantially raised. While not many of the young footballers would be purchasing from Classic Travel for some years to come, the purchasing power of the spectators and parents, for both business and pleasure travel purposes, is substantial.

- **Spreading by word-of-mouth of the qualities**. This represents a form of advertising that money cannot buy. If the small business is offering a service, word-of-mouth is likely to be very important indeed, especially where a personal or specialized service is being offered, such as farm accommodation or golfing breaks. However, the question is how to generate word-of-mouth? The answer goes back to the importance of 'cherishing the customer', building a good reputation and protecting it. In fostering good relationships with the tourists who visit, happy ambassadors will be created, eager to share the stories of their happy holidays with other potential customers. Creating word-of-mouth is hard work, but if it is achieved and maintained it will have created more powerful advertising than money can buy.

People – personalize

The personalized nature of the small business is recognized as a tremendous strength which the large corporate groups find difficult to emulate. It is to this area of personalizing market activity that we now turn, in particular focusing on the role of direct database marketing within the small business.

Direct marketing is one of the fastest growing marketing functions within all sizes of business. It is an advertising activity that establishes a direct link between the business, existing and potential customers, aiming promotional messages directly at individuals by post and telephone, at home and at work. The common factor is that it is precisely targeted to specific people. This enables the small business to communicate directly with the existing customers, to remind them of its existence and to encourage them to return, perhaps through the offer of special sales promotions.

In addition, it is a means of cutting out the intermediary retailing organizations and their 18 to 30% commission rates which have become a financial drain on many small businesses.

To carry out this activity information has to be gathered and stored in an easily retrievable database which is increasingly being facilitated by computerization. This leads to the introduction of the term 'database marketing', for which there appears to be no universally accepted definition. Davies (1992) provides the following simple attempt:

> A marketing database is a collection of all available information on past, present and prospective customers, structured to achieve maximum usefulness.

While Kotler (1991) presents a more complex description:

> A marketing database is an organized collection of data about individual customers, prospects, or suspects that is accessible and actionable for such marketing purposes as lead generation, lead qualification, sale of product or service, or maintenance of customer relationships.

Customers of today want to be treated as individuals, with different needs and interests, rather than as one of the mass market. In this respect, database marketing demonstrates a strong, flexible, selling power, where there is the potential to develop positive business/customer relationships and produce highly personalized product offerings. Deep rooted in this approach is the philosophy of getting closer to the customer, which by its very nature is what the small tourism business does best. Furthermore, building relationships with customers is no longer simply good business practice, but a means of survival within the highly competitive tourism industry.

Features of the marketing relationship which can be developed through well constructed databases include:

- focus on customer retention;
- orientation on communicating product benefits;
- long timescale;
- high customer service emphasis;
- high customer contact;
- quality is the concern of all.

There are few industries where customers divulge so much critical information about themselves in the course of booking and consuming the product, e.g. name, address, length of stay, preferred leisure activities, purpose of travel, average spend. As a result, in the tourism industry it is relatively easy to build up a database of customer details. This marketing approach allows the small business to segment its own customers into the finest divisions. There are basically two ways of analysing customer profiles: firstly, through customer characteristics such as geographical location, demographic profile and psychographic features; secondly, features such as purchasing power, reasons for purchasing, price sensitivity and growth potential can be used.

CASE STUDY 16.7

The Grape Vine

The Grape Vine is a 50-seat restaurant and bar located in a conservation village near Hamilton Racecourse. It is on the outskirts of Glasgow, close to main motorways linking Glasgow to Edinburgh. The business has been trading for eight years and during this time has built up a database of around a thousand regular customers. The information stored includes the usual contact details, along with a classification according to the type of group they can be identified with. Such groups include: school teachers, Friends of Scottish Opera, office workers, horse race goers, wine lovers and exhibition organizers. This information is regularly checked and updated to ensure accuracy.*

In identifying these groups, it is possible to predict what time of year they are liable to be motivated to visit the restaurant:

- school teachers: June and December prior to the school holidays;
- Friends of Scottish Opera: one Saturday a month October to May;
- office workers: Friday lunch time and Christmas parties;
- horse race goers: all the meetings on the racing calendar;
- wine lovers: May for light summer wines, November for more robust winter wines;
- exhibition organizers: August and September.

In this way, specially targeted promotional messages can be precisely communicated to each of the groups at the right time, thus achieving maximum impact. Response rates, types of reactions and sales achieved are carefully monitored and the lessons built into successive efforts.

---

* It should be noted that if a business is keeping personal customer information on a database, the business needs to register under the Data Protection Act 1986.

Price – marginal

Establishing the most appropriate pricing policy represents a critical strategic decision for all small business owners but it is a task they seldom do well. Pricing must take into account costs, profit targets, competitor price levels and the customer. The first three areas are reasonably easy to calculate; however, the customer element is more complex. The business is selling an 'experience' to tourists and how this is valued will decide what level of price they are willing to pay based on their perceptions of value for money. These perceptions reflect the desire of certain types of customers to own the benefits, real or imaginary, they perceive in the tourist offering. Within the current economic recovery climate, successful marketing often depends on providing what the customer perceives as 'affordable quality'.

The seasonal pattern of tourist trade also means that pricing must take into account that the operation will not be functioning at consistent utilization rates throughout the year. However, this factor can be advantageous for it means that due to high demand in peak season more can be charged for the product, while in the low-season months discounted prices can be offered to encourage the seasonal spreading of trade.

Examples of ploys to address the 'affordable quality' and seasonality effects are:

- the family which selects a restaurant because it offers children's menus, or 'children eat free' schemes;
- short, city winter breaks packaging air flight and accommodation for £129.00;
- family ticket entrance to a themed amusement park;
- Spring Country House Champagne Weekends.

There are three main methods of price setting which can be used by the small business. The first is cost-plus pricing in which the percentage net profit desired is identified and the unit cost of the product is then inflated accordingly. The second, is to follow the competition which ensures that the price is in line with other similar operations in the marketplace, but takes no account of business costs and profit targets. Thirdly, there is marginal pricing applicable during the low-season months and economic recessionary times, when it is often better to reduce prices and attract some tourists rather than have no tourists. The reasoning behind this is that a reduced profit margin, contributing to the fixed costs, is better than no margin at all. Today, discounts are common and are of various types, including seasonal, volume and preferred guest.

For the small tourism business, the pressure to discount or to provide affordable quality, is likely to come from three main areas: the customer, the distribution channels and the bank.

- **The customer**. During the main season, when demand for the tourist facility is high, price will most likely be accepted without much questioning. However, during the less popular holiday months, visitors may need a little more encouragement to spend money. Moreover, during recent years the customer has become accustomed to reduced prices and is now conditioned to seek out the 'deal'. Thus, if customer expectations are to be met then the business has to consider the current purchasing motivations of the tourists relative to price.
- **The distribution channels**. Very often tour operators, travel agents and hotel reservation companies will offer to 'sell' the tourism product through their retail outlets which have the potential to reach a large volume of national and international customers. This enables the small business to reach a far wider audience than the individual property could manage itself. The reason for entering into this relationship is the expectation that it will generate more business and profit than it will cost. However, there is a cost. Such organizations will expect to be paid commission on the 'sales found' of between 18 and 30% of regular tariff.
- **The bank**. It has been identified as a feature of small tourism businesses that they often operate at financial levels below the breakeven point. This can result in a precarious financial gearing situation, heavily

reliant on overdraft facilities and the goodwill of a friendly bank manager to see the business through difficult trading patches. In such situations the flow of cash through the business and the bank accounts represents the lifeblood of that business – without it it will die and go into receivership. This is where the use of marginal pricing as a technique to encourage the flow of business at times where normally there is none, or it is at low volume, has been proved to be the very factor that has kept many of the small tourism enterprises in business over the low seasons during 1990–93.

Marginal pricing is not recommended as an all year round approach but as a tactic designed to maximize utilization and financial return of the tourist facility during periods of low demand. Thus, price setting for the small tourism business can be seen as a precarious balancing act where it is necessary to take account of:

- associated costs of production and service;
- the desire to make a profit and stay in business;
- the need to be competitive;
- accurate image projection;
- satisfying perceptions of affordable quality;
- seasonality influences;
- social, economic and political environmental factors.

CASE STUDY 16.8

London Restaurants

In April 1993 55 London restaurants proved through the Evening Standard *ES* magazine the power of providing the right product offering at the right price through the right advertising medium

Objectives:	To help the restaurants involved fill Monday and Tuesday evenings, and offer *ES* magazine readers the opportunity to dine out at top restaurants for an affordable price.
Offer:	For £10 diners were offered a two-course dinner with coffee on a Monday or Tuesday evening at some of London's top restaurants. The price included VAT, service and cover charge. .
One-stop-shop:	One telephone call to the restaurant meant that potential customers didn't have to collect vouchers or send away for tokens to reserve their tables.
Marketing by:	Sales promotion featured in *ES* magazine and 'flashed' on the front cover supporting a mention on Capital Radio.
Target:	*ES* readers, predominantly ABC1, 15–44 age group.

Example results offer: Alexanders in Wellington Street was fully booked by 3 pm on the day of the *ES* and received a further 200 calls afterwards.

The Parsonage received 600 calls in one afternoon and an increase of business of about 200% on Monday and Tuesday nights for its 70-seat restaurant.

The Pig and Whistle saw an average increase in business of 50%, and in the first week were full on Monday and Tuesday.

Growth routes

The majority of small tourism businesses choose to stay small, with very few aiming for the sky with shooting star type of operations. Burns and Dewhurst (1993) suggest that the lack of growth motivation may be due to owners placing a great value on independence and the fact that embarking on a high growth strategy may lead to that independence being threatened. Other small business owners have argued that they are aware that they lack the management skills needed to cope with growth and this also acts as a disincentive. What does seem true is that in most countries the majority of businesses grow only in the first few years after start-up and then stabilize to provide the owner with an acceptable independent lifestyle with sufficient income.

However, there are a few ambitious entrepreneurs who test the market with a small business concept and, based on initial success, expand into multi-unit ownership or franchising. This represents an exciting and challenging phase of development for the small business which requires professional management and a strong team of employees to carry it forward.

Broadly speaking, the business has five main market growth strategy alternatives. Each alternative has a different degree of risk attached to it moving from a safe, familiar environment to a higher risk and unfamiliar one.

- **Penetration:** fighting to improve the performance of current products or services in existing markets.
- **New product development:** using knowledge of the market to increase range of product offerings.
- **New market development:** taking existing product to new markets, areas or countries.
- **Diversification:** going beyond existing markets and existing products into wholly new situations.
- **Franchising:** becoming a master franchise holder for the small business concept.

The following two cases illustrate these alternatives.

CASE STUDY 16.9

Oyster bars

John Noble, owner of the Ardkinglas Estate, and Andrew Lane, fish farmer, founded Loch Fyne Oysters in 1978. Local conditions appeared to them ideal. The water is pure and unpolluted, the Loch is fertile and the Gulf Stream warms the sea water and assists in the growing conditions for shellfish.

Inspiration derived from the tradition of the old 'howfs' (cellars) in eighteenth-century Edinburgh where oysters and wine were enjoyed by all classes. The company decided to open an oyster bar where oysters would be sold at reasonable prices in simple surrounding. The aim was to meet the renewed and growing popular demand for oysters. Loch Fyne Oysters opened its first oyster bar in a converted farm building at Cairndow. This proved so successful that another was opened in the centre of Nottingham. A third was then opened in the fine old dairy building at Elton, some ten minutes from Peterborough.

It then occurred to the owners that it would be logical to locate retail outlets at each of the oyster bars, offering the range of menu items and their own Loch Fyne label wines for the passing tourists to take home with them. This venture also proved to be an immediate success, so much so that customers wanted to know how they could get hold of the produce to enjoy in their own homes all year round. Again John and Andrew came up with a money-making solution – offer customers a home-delivery service.

The owners of Loch Fyne Oysters have successfully grown their small business into one which enjoys a substantial financial turnover. They have successfully moved through the four growth alternatives identified above, but with careful management and astute market research accompanying each stage.

CASE STUDY 16.10

Pierre Victoires

Pierre Levicky opened his first eating establishment in Scotland in 1988 and incurred the wrath of some members of Edinburgh's eating community for charging too low prices for high quality food. The restaurants exude minimalism in every respect but customer numbers. They are cramped, the decor is austere and the wooden furniture second-hand, deliberately mismatched. According to Levicky, that is how it would be in many rural French restaurants – bags of atmosphere, and cheap. However, the public response was huge. People queued and booked months ahead for tables, forcing him to make the decision either to put the prices up or to open a second place. Hostile to the first option and having decided early that franchising would play a major role in his future operations, he opened a second restaurant in the city, and a third in 1991. He then decided to franchise the restaurants and in 1993 had expanded the Pierre Victoire chain to 25 wholly owned or franchised units, with a group turnover of £12.5 m. Future plans include the development of three distinct restaurant concepts with a target of 125 units across Britain by 1995.

SUMMARY

The small business within the tourism industry clearly represents a substantial sector and is likely to remain so for the next decade at the very least. There is no doubt that they are operating within an extremely turbulent environment that is forcing those which want to stay in business to reconsider their traditional marketing approaches.

The aim throughout this chapter has been to get closer to understanding the specific characteristics and marketing needs of the small tourism business. This is of particular importance as, unlike some corporate groups, the small business has little hope of changing the rules of the competitive game. Therefore it pays to understand in depth the specific implications of this sector's characteristics, competitive pressures, trends and internal organizational constraints on small business marketing.

The main objectives of marketing activity were identified as: market orientation, customer satisfaction, sustained profit and coping with a dynamic business. The key influences on small tourism business marketing activities were identified as: a mature domestic market, communications technology developments, consumer behaviour, government support, constrained power and resources, and high levels of uncertainty. The marketing approaches selected do not represent a definitive group, but are examples of ways to combat the negative features and accentuate the positive. Those selected for discussion were: cooperative distribution, product differentiation, creative promotion, personalization of communication, marginal pricing and routes to growth.

REFERENCES

Anon. (1993) Consortia enter the electronic age, *Hotels*, July, pp. 68–9.

Archdale, G. (1992) Marketing tourism internationally: developments and techniques for the future, *Tourism*, No. 75, August, pp. 10–11.

Boer, A. (1992) The Banking Sector and Small Firm Failure in the UK Hotel and Catering Sector, *International Journal of Contemporary Hospitality Management*, Vol. 2, No. 2, pp. 13–16.

Bolton Committee (1971) *Small Firms: Report of the Committee on Small Firms*, HMSO, London.

Bord Failte (1993) *Delivering Sustainable Growth: Tourism Marketing Plan 1993–97*, Dublin.

Burkart, A. and Medlik, S. (1986) *Tourism Past, Present and Future*, Heinemann, London.

Burns, P. and Dewhurst, J. (1993) *Small Business Management*, 3rd edn, Macmillan, London.

Buttle, F. (1994) *Hotel and Food Service Marketing*, Holt, Rinehart & Winston, Eastbourne.

Davies, J. (1992) *The Essential Guide to Database Marketing*, McGraw-Hill, London.

Dicken, P. (1992) *Global Shift*, 2nd edn, Paul Chapman Publishing, London.

Finnish Tourist Board (1993) *Annual Report*, Helsinki.

Greene, M. (1993) Stand out from the crowd, *Caterer and Hotelkeeper*, 25 March, pp. 39–42.

Harrison, L. and Johnston, K. (1993) *UK Hotel Groups Directory*, Cassell, London.

Heskett, J. (1984) *Managing in the Service Economy*, Harvard Business School Press, Boston.

Hughes, (1992)

Kleinwort Benson Securities (1994) *UK Hotels Plc*, London.

Kotler, P. (1991) *Marketing Management: Analysis, Planning, Implementation and Control*, 7th edn, Prentice-Hall, Englewood Cliffs, New Jersey.

Lewis, J. (1990) *Partnership for Profit*, Free Press, New York.

Lovelock, C. (1991) *Services Marketing*, Prentice-Hall, Englewood Cliffs, New Jersey.

Morrison, A. (1994) *Strategic Alliances: Theory and Practice in the Hotel Industry*, Paper presented at the 16th National Small Firm Conference, Nottingham, November.

National Economic Development Council (1976) *Hotel Prospects to 1985*, Hotel and Catering EDC.

Pickering *et al.* (1971) *The Small Firm in the Hotel and Catering Industry*, Research Report No. 14, HMSO, London.

Sloane, J. (1990) Latest Developments in Aviation CRSs, *EIU Tourism and Travel Analyst*, No. 4, pp. 5–15.

Waterworth, D. (1994) *Marketing for the Small Business*, Macmillan Education, London.

Welsh Tourist Board (1993) *Tourism 2000: A Strategy for Wales*, Cardiff.

REVIEW QUESTIONS

1. Identify how marketing the small tourism business differs from marketing a large corporation.
2. Consider ways in which a family-owned and run visitor attraction could successfully market their product.
3. Discuss the role of marginal pricing as a marketing tactic within the current trading environment.

Information technology and databases for tourism

M.M. Bennett

17

OBJECTIVES

By the end of this chapter the reader should:

- understand the role played by information technology in the travel industry;
- appreciate the significance of information technology as a competitive tool;
- be able to identify the different types of technology that are employed;
- be able to recognize the trends in information technology developments;
- appreciate the potential impact of developments in information technology.

INTRODUCTION

To say that information technology (IT) has played a significant role in the development of the modern-day travel industry is to understate its importance. Linked to distribution, IT has radically altered the way in which information is transmitted throughout the industry. While this has resulted in many positive benefits such as increased efficiency in the reservation process and the ability to react more quickly to changes in the market, it has also brought a number of issues to the fore including competitive advantage, customer service and the role of IT in effecting change in the tourism industry. It is these issues together with a review of the actual technology which will be discussed in this chapter.

INFORMATION TRANSMISSION

To appreciate the importance of IT in tourism it is first necessary to grasp the role of information within the industry. The tourism industry is essentially fragmentary comprising a variety of different sectors and a whole host of companies ranging in size from the very large to the very small. Communication between the different sectors and companies is required. For example, a consumer will frequently require more than one product such as a hotel and airline reservation or a whole series of flights, i.e. one product but several different companies involved. The need for communication between companies is exacerbated by the perishable and intangible nature of the tourism product, characteristics which are outlined in Chapter 7. The importance of information in relation to the different sectors in the chain of distribution will now be reviewed.

Principals, whether they are tour operators, hotels or airlines, need information on how well the business is performing in terms of what is selling well, where and to whom. Such information is necessary for control and planning purposes. The perishable nature of the tourism product is such that principals have the problem of wanting to discount the product at the last minute to ensure a sale but at the same time of wanting to minimize the effect on the bulk of their sales which are made in advance. This, for example, has been a problem for tour operators in discounting holidays in that the public has tended to adopt a 'wait and see' approach to see how far a holiday will drop in price, safe in the knowledge that they will not lose out on a holiday even if it is not their first choice. Price has thus become the determinant. This has been exacerbated by frequent over-capacity in the marketplace rendering price competition essential which has been in the consumer's, not the principal's, favour.

Travel agents require information on products to know what is available for selling purposes. Other required information related to this is product prices which are constantly changing, associated regulations and restrictions such as those relating to some lower priced air fares, and the reservation methods. Travel agents too need to monitor what products are selling well for their own marketing purposes.

Consumers vary in their information needs. An essential division is between business and leisure travellers. In business travel finding the right product to suit the business person's schedule has always required a high information content because of the individual nature of the trip. The plethora of options in terms of air schedules, types of ticket, class, hotels, etc. have to be sifted through to ensure that the most appropriate ones are chosen. Within leisure the emergence of a 'new' tourism based on flexibility, variety and individualism (Poon, 1993) has been well charted. While talk about the demise of mass tourism has been premature, this 'new' tourism is nevertheless becoming more significant. Independent travel involving custom-made itineraries requires a tremendous amount of information. Without this information the growth of this segment of the market would be hampered. Perhaps what is most important for consumers in general is having access to information on travel. A principal source of information has always been the agent but with developments in electronic media the way in which consumers access such information is changing.

METHODS OF INFORMATION TRANSMISSION

So far the discussion has concentrated on the varying information needs of each sector in the chain of distribution. What we need to do now is look at the methods used for transmitting that information. Until the advent of information technology (IT) the methods used were cumbersome and inefficient. Essentially the telephone was used to contact suppliers and make reservations while post was the mechanism employed by travel agents to settle accounts and order brochures and by tour operators to despatch tickets and send confirmations etc. to clients via travel agents.

Brochures have always been the prime method for suppliers wanting to display products and that is still the case today. Similarly, directories have provided agents with times, dates and prices – the *Official Airline Guide* (*OAG*) is a prime example of how agents accessed information on flights in the past. Of course, this was frequently out of date almost as soon as it was printed due to constant changes being made by airlines to flight schedules and prices, etc. Indeed, deregulation in US rendered useless such forms of information transmission overnight.

Face-to-face contact is still an important method of information transmission at the travel agent/consumer interface. As outlined in Chapter 7 on distribution, the travel agent acts as the reassuring face of the travel industry: it is the human link in the chain of distribution. Yet its future is not secure. There has been much debate on whether it will survive in its present form or whether its role will be usurped by other means. This will be considered in greater detail later in this chapter. For a synopsis of the different methods used at each interface in the chain of distribution see Table 17.1.

Although the emphasis has been on holiday availability and booking, information distribution does not end here. Communication between principals and travel agents extends to tour operator representatives and travel trade fairs, highlighting a major human input which is important in cementing relationships between principals and travel agents.

More generally, with the growth of tourism, an increase in competition and the associated enlarging process of the 'big' companies, television and press advertisements have become a vital tool in marketing products to the consumer both by principals and travel agents alike.

ADOPTION OF INFORMATION TECHNOLOGY

With the growth in tourism and its importance, increased emphasis is placed on efficient and effective communications between the different sectors of the travel industry. Since information represents the intangible product and since the industry's functionality depends upon accurate and reliable information, the mechanism used to convey the information becomes vitally important.

Information technology has proved to be the most effective mechanism

Table 17.1 Methods of information transmission within the travel industry

Interface	Transmission Mechanism
Hotel/principal	Face-to-face contact
	Telephone
	Mail
	Facsimile
	CRS
Principal/travel agent	Face-to-face contact
	Tour operator representative
	Travel trade fairs
	Telephone
	Mail
	Viewdata
	CRS
	Brochures
Travel agent/consumer	Face-to-face contact
	Telephone
	Brochures
	Mail
Principal/consumer	Telephone
	Mail
	Brochures
	Teletext

yet and consequently it has been widely adopted to perform an array of functions. The importance of IT warrants a definition and one of the most comprehensive is given by Poon (1988):

> IT is the collective name given to the most recent developments in the mode (electronic) and the mechanism (computers and communication technologies as well as the software which drive them) used for the acquisition, processing, analysis, storage, retrieval, dissemination and application of information.

Before reviewing IT in the travel industry it is worth remembering that technology *per se* has played a key role within the industry. For example, while railways were the key to the development of Thomas Cook as a company, it was the advent of jet aircraft which facilitated the birth of the

CASE STUDY 17.1

UK television

The four main television channels in the UK all have or have had a holiday programme – *Wish You Were Here?* (ITV), *Holiday* (BBC1), *The Real Holiday Show* (BBC2) and *Travel Log* (Channel 4).

inclusive tour and worldwide travel. This generated an increase in the number of tour operators which affected the size and structure of the industry. And technology today is shaping the airline industry. For example, the prospect of a super-jumbo carrying 600–800 passengers is only a matter of time away as is FANS, the Future Air Navigation System, which should substantially improve air traffic flow and FAST, the Future Automated Screening of Travellers, linking biometric identification with data digitalization and satellite communication making customs clearance a far more efficient procedure (Lipman, 1994).

IT too has had a dramatic impact on the industry. Indeed, it has been suggested that it is not just one type of IT which is being diffused but a 'whole system of information technologies' (Poon, 1988). Airlines, for example, use information for a whole host of internal functions including flight and crew scheduling, arrival and departure times, catering and cargo control. This is an **intra-organizational** system whereby information is collected and analysed from each part of the business and used in other ways for strategic planning and marketing. In addition, basic administration and accountancy functions need to be undertaken as part of the management of the firm. Principals and travel agents alike will adopt systems to perform such functions.

All companies regardless of size and type will monitor sales; whether it is undertaken manually or technically will depend on the individual firm. The larger firms will have the advantage of being able to build up sizeable databases. BA is a prime example – the information BA has collected from marketing campaigns such as the highly successful 'World's Biggest Offer' has helped provide them with an enormous database of information on the market which can be used to streamline the marketing of products. Vertical integration too assists in this matter in that information can be readily collected from different parts of the business and transferred to other parts as and when necessary. What is clear, then, is that all businesses will adopt systems (manual or technical) to perform the inter-organizational functions. While the larger firms will have in-house IT departments, the systems being tailored for the specific needs of the firm, the smaller companies will rely on off-the-shelf systems. A key problem facing such companies is knowing which system to choose from the multitude available which suits the needs of their company. Such a problem is not to be underestimated, particularly given the tourism industry's overwhelming composition of small companies.

The other type of system is the **inter-organizational** system. This involves communication between the different sectors of the distribution chain. For example, travel agents need information on products and need to be able to make reservations; tour operators need to know which holidays are being booked as well as needing to be able to coordinate packages with other principles; airlines and hotels require a system of communication with travel agents for the purpose of fare changes, special offers and reservations. And consumers too require access to information. Consequently, a number of systems have emerged within the travel industry:

viewdata is a specialized and anachronistic form of technology used, for example, in the UK and forms the main link between travel agents and tour operators; computerized reservation systems (CRSs) form the main communication channel between travel agents and airlines, hotels and other vendors such as car rental firms and are a global phenomenon; destination marketing systems (DMSs) assume a variety of forms including reservations and information which commonly are consumer oriented – they too are a global phenomenon.

Viewdata

Viewdata – or videotex as it is also known – is the generic name for screen-based information systems and it appears in two forms. Broadcast teletext is a one-way service, technically described as 'receive only page capture' while viewdata is an interactive two-way service and is used by travel agents.

Viewdata technology has found a niche in leisure travel although it is not a global phenomenon; examples of countries using viewdata include the UK and the Netherlands. With the growth of inclusive tours, the large tour operators turned to IT to manage their internal operations. It was then discovered that by installing 'dumb' terminals in travel agents a link to tour operators was possible. Consequently, travel agents were able to make reservations because of viewdata's interactive nature. Adoption of viewdata in the UK was facilitated by a number of factors:

* the cost advantages to be gained by both travel agents and tour operators: travel agents gained from dialling into a local node to gain local call access while tour operators gained from reducing the size of their telephone reservation departments;
* the emergence of competing network bureaux (a third party) providing links to the main tour operators;
* the step taken by the Thomson organization in the UK only to accept holiday bookings via viewdata – so in other words if a travel agent did not possess a viewdata set it would be unable to make a booking with the largest tour operator in the UK market.

Although simple in technological terms by today's standards (viewdata comprises a screen to display information and the public telephone network to transmit information from a central computer), at the time of its introduction it represented a significant leap forward in operational terms for the travel industry. By 1987 85% of all package holiday bookings were made through viewdata (Bruce, 1987) and it is estimated that there are 23 000 terminals distributed among the UK travel agency network (Hitchin, 1991).

Three principal networks have emerged in the UK market: Istel, Midland Network Services and Prestel, although it is the former two which feature the main tour operators and thus dominate the package tour reservation market. In addition to holiday reservations, these networks offer a variety of other services including hotel and airline booking facilities and a whole variety of other information services.

Computerized reservation systems

There can be little doubt that CRSs are one of the most technologically advanced forms of software in the travel industry as well as one of the most controversial. CRSs enable travel agents to interface with a variety of principals' computers to book, in the main, airline seats, car hire and hotel rooms but also numerous other information and reservation services.

Today CRSs have become an essential tool for the business agent and are mostly airline owned. This is significant in that CRSs are born out of internal airline systems. Each carrier must keep a record of a whole host of information including flight schedules, fares, seat availability and passenger reservations. The sheer volume of information and the rate at which it can change led carriers to turn to computers in the 1950s. Sabre, American Airlines' system, was the first CRS to emerge in 1964. Although developed for internal purposes, it was common practice to include information on other carriers, the main reason being that it facilitated interline ticketing with those other carriers.

It was then realized that such CRSs could be used by the retail travel agent. Prior to the introduction of CRSs, the agent relied on the OAG for the necessary information and then used the phone to contact the airline(s) concerned to make the reservation. Such a cumbersome system today would lead to chaos. A highly complex market exacerbated by the Deregulation Act in the US in 1978 has carved out an important role for the CRSs in providing an efficient means of conveying and displaying information for retailers and airlines. For the latter, they have become a powerful marketing tool.

A number of competing systems exist (see Table 17.2). The Americans have been the torch carriers and they have produced an array of different systems, the fortunes of which have largely reflected those of their airline parent owners. However, a key change is taking place and that is the move towards multiple airline ownership, a development initiated in Europe with

---

CASE STUDY 17.2

TOP

Thomson Holidays, the largest tour operator in the UK, launched TOP, the Thomson Open-line Programme, in 1982. The success of TOP derived partly from the fact that for many years it was not available on any of the main network bureaux. Its position was consolidated in 1986 when the decision was taken to withdraw bookings by telephone thereby forcing travel agents to use TOP.

Table 17.2 CRSs worldwide

Name	Owner(s)	% ownership
Sabre	American Airlines	100
System One	Continental Airlines	100
Worldspan	Delta Airlines	38
	Northwest	31.6
	TWA	35.7
	Abacus	5
Gemini	Air Canada	—
	Canadian Airlines	—
	Galileo International	30
Amadeus	Air France	33.3
	Iberia	33.3
	Lufthansa	33.3
Galileo	United Airlines	38
	US Air	11
	Air Canada	1
	British Airways	14.7
	Swissair	13.2
	KLM	12.1
	Alitalia	8.7
	Olympic	1
	TAP	1
	Aer Lingus	1
	Australian Airlines	1
START	Lufthansa	30
	Deutsche Bundesbahn	30
	TUI Hannover	30
	Amadeus	10
Infini	All Nippon Airways	60
	Abacus	40
Fantasia	Qantas Airways	50
	Ansett Airlines	25
	Air New Zealand	25
Abacus	Cathay Pacific	13.5
	Singapore Airlines	13.5
	Malaysian Airlines	13.5
	China Airlines	13.5
	Royal Brunei Airlines	13.5*
	Dragonair	2.5*
	Silk Air	2.5

Table 17.2 *(continued)*

Name	Owner(s)	% ownership
	Worldspan	4.5*
	Infini	13.5
	Philippine Airlines	9.5*
Axess	Japan Airlines	100
Southern Cross	Qantas Airways	50
	Ansett Airlines	25
	Air New Zealand	25

*Estimate.

the formation of Galileo and Amadeus, two global distribution systems comprising an assortment of European airlines. To a large extent, such links at CRS level parallel similar alliances taking place at the airline level in the quest for globalization although such alliances have not always been in tandem with CRS links. An obvious exception to this increasingly general rule is that of Sabre which has remained under the complete control of American Airlines. One thing is certain – further alliances and regroupings will take place which will probably lead to rationalization within the CRS sector, but quite what those ways will be and which will survive in the longer term remains to be seen.

Destination marketing systems

Destination marketing systems (DMS) are referred to in a variety of different ways: destination databases (DD), destination management systems (DMS), travel information systems (TIS) and destination information systems (DIS) to name but a few (Haines, 1994). In addition, they encompass information and reservations, although not necessarily both together, and they operate at national, regional and local levels. Some address particular aspects such as pre-trip information, post-arrival

CASE STUDY 17.3

Sabre

Sabre was the first CRS to be developed some forty years ago by its parent company American Airlines. It has computer terminals in 26 000 travel agencies in 184 countries. In addition to housing world airline information, it also services 200 hotel companies and 60 car hire firms. Its IBM computers are located in Tulsa, Oklahoma and process approximately 150 million travel requests per day.

Source: *Sunday Times*, 24 April 1994.

information, reservations and product databases. Consequently, some are accessible by consumers while others are not. Hence a definition of this type of technology is difficult to say the least as there are so many potential forms. What can be said with more clarity is that these systems tend to cater for the smaller companies to enable them to compete with the larger ones as far as marketing their services electronically is concerned. Ownership is variable although the tourist boards are common users of this form of technology. As an umbrella term, DMS can incorporate the following features (although it should be emphasized that not all features will be found in every DMS) (see Haines, 1994):

- product database;
- client database;
- marketing facilities;
- information retrieval;
- reservations;
- distribution.

Examples of DMS can be drawn from across the world: Queensland Travel and Tourism Commission can boast the largest public destination database known as ATLAS; New South Wales in Australia has NEWTRACS, an information-based service which is moving into reservations; Gulliver is based in Ireland; and the Tyrol Information System (TIS) is in Austria (Archdale, 1994).

CASE STUDY 17.4

Tyrol Information System (TIS)

The TIS was set up in 1991 as an information-based system with a dual purpose to:

- provide information to clients about the Tyrol as a tourist destination; and
- provide marketing/management information for the local tourist boards and local suppliers.

The information component comprises: traffic and weather information; tourist products and services; events; restaurants and accommodation; family products and services; public transport and timetables; and local information. The marketing/management component includes: addresses; organizational charts; subsidies; promotional materials; media data; promotion groups; press conferences; media advertising schedules; trade fairs; marketing diagrams; statistics; mail box; educational programmes and courses; literature; dictionary; and decision support tools.

Future enhancements planned include: a multi-media system based on touch-screen technology for use by tourists; TIS data to be made available to international distribution systems and home computer networks, i.e. Mintel; and development of TIS into a nationwide system called TIS Austria.

Source: Ebner (1994).

INFORMATION TECHNOLOGY: A COMPETITIVE TOOL

Competition is a feature of any industry and the travel industry is no exception. What has become apparent is that as technology has permeated the different sectors in its capacity as information conveyer and manager, it has also been used as a competitive tool. Several examples can be cited.

Publicity surrounding **CRSs** has concentrated on bias. Defined as 'the inclusion of parameters in software packages to favour the services of the CRS owner and certain carriers over other carriers', bias has manifested itself in a number of ways. Boberg and Collison (1985), for example, distinguish between structural, carrier, connection point, display and screen bias. Furthermore, research has shown that 75–80% of bookings are made from the first flight or list. All of this adds up to what is known as the 'halo' effect whereby the CRS owner sells more of its own airline tickets. The CRS is thus a powerful sales tool. But the advantages for the principal extend even further. As most airlines do not have their own CRS, it is common practice to be included in existing CRSs. So CRS owners earn extra revenue from charging fees to competitor airlines. A bone of contention in the past has been the higher fees charged to non-owning vendors and the associated bias in the CRS display. The revenue gained from such higher fees was then used to tie in more travel agents to the vendor CRS and so gain more incremental revenue from the 'halo' effect. So in other words, the non-vendor airlines paid a higher fee to effectively subsidize travel agency incentives to steer business away from them. The very lucrative nature of such CRSs is summed up in a frequently quoted statement by the President of American Airlines, Robert Crandall, who is reported to have said that he would sell the airline before the CRS.

Linked to CRSs is the issue of code-sharing. By entering into alliances with smaller airlines, major airlines can extend their network of services. By sharing the larger airline's code, both parties achieve a higher position on the CRS display as a single airline code is given a higher priority than one involving a connection showing two codes. This has proved particularly popular in the US due to the hub and spoke style operation. The result is that every major US airline is tied to regional or commuter airlines in the domestic market. It is a habit that has caught on and is being witnessed on a global scale as worldwide alliances abound.

Affiliated to the CRS is the RMS (revenue management system) which is unshared for good reasons. It is the intelligent counterpart of the CRS monitoring sales and calculating fares accordingly. Given the fact that competing airlines are in the CRS, the RMS will monitor them too and use that information in its fare calculations. All of this gives the CRS owner an unprecedented competitive advantage in the marketplace, or, as some might argue, an unfair advantage.

Competition between CRSs in the US in the past has led to travel agents becoming tied to CRSs through what was termed 'golden handcuffs'. Travel agents were offered special incentives to use a CRS exclusively because of the lucrative benefits conferred to the CRS owners. In the 1970s

CASE STUDY 17.5

British Airways versus Sabre

In 1987 a court case between BA and AA in which AA alleged that BA refused to sell BA tickets through the Sabre system in the UK hit the national UK papers. The crux of the matter was that travel agents in the UK would not be interested in using Sabre as they were unable to issue the national carrier's tickets. BA, meanwhile, claimed that Sabre discriminated against it on screen displays. What was also inferred but never stated was that BA disliked paying American Airlines for selling BA tickets in the UK. The dispute ended in a less dramatic out of court settlement in which BA agreed to sell tickets through the Sabre system in the UK and American Airlines promised to alter the display logic.

Source: *The Independent* (1988).

and 1980s this resulted in a proliferation of lawsuits involving travel agents and CRSs following attempts by rival CRSs to convert travel agents to their system by invoking penalty clauses and paying the penalties.

Blatant bias of the type referred to in this chapter has largely been eradicated through codes of conduct implemented in both the US and Europe. Furthermore, multiple ownership as in the cases of Amadeus and Galileo further weakens the potential for bias.

The sharing of **databases** by rival companies has also created problems where only one company owns the system. This results in the owning

CASE STUDY 17.6

Dirty Tricks

'Dirty Tricks' was the name given to a campaign waged by BA against Virgin and brought to a head in January 1993. The thrust of the campaign was to discredit Richard Branson and undermine his airline Virgin. A number of techniques were used including BA's booking system, BABS. As with CRSs, many airlines, particularly smaller ones, cannot justify setting up their own reservation system and so they rent space on an existing one. In this case, Virgin rented space on BABS. In spite of assurances of confidentiality by Sir Colin Marshall, BA staff were able to access information on Virgin including the number of passengers on each Virgin flight, class of seat and corporate account details. With no audit trail to show who has entered and used BABS and an infrequent changing of passwords on Virgin's part, BA staff were able to use this information to contact Virgin customers to persuade them to switch to BA. This, together with other techniques, culminated in the highly public court case in January 1993 in which Virgin Atlantic was awarded £610 000 in damages while BA faced public humiliation. What the case also showed was the power of IT and how, through competition in the marketplace, it can be greatly and sometimes dramatically abused.

Source: *Financial Times*, 12 January 1993.

company having potential access to competitor information so conferring an unfair competitive advantage.

Databases enable principals and travel agents alike to acquire information on the market. Information gained in this way can be used for target marketing and improving customer service. For example, by storing information on the client, the principal or travel agent is able to customize their service by referring to the individual by name and attending to their requirements.

Information technology has been used to provide an advantage in **pricing**. By monitoring other competitors' pricing, principals are able to alter their own accordingly and quickly. Thomson, for example, was able to do just this by using a competitive pricing system which formed part of TOP. Given the price elastic nature of the package tour in the UK such a system has proved particularly useful, especially in its fight for market share with ILG in the late 1980s which was based on price and which culminated in the demise of ILG and Harry Goodman's empire.

IT has assisted also principals in offloading unsold products close to departure. The result is that they are able to secure some revenue albeit at a lower yield.

Consumer choice is limited by both travel agents and principals. Tour operators in the UK, for example, pay to subscribe to the different network bureaux. Costs tend to prevent them from joining every network. Travel agents too, for similar reasons, will select which networks they wish to subscribe to. Consequently, travel agents are potentially limiting choice by only selling the products available on the networks they are linked into.

Ease of use of different systems has become a means of differentiating between principals and has been used to gain competitive advantage. Travel agents instinctively opt for certain products if the system is easy to use. The result is that products are in part being differentiated on the basis of the system or distribution mechanism.

Quite clearly, customer service and IT do not always go hand in hand (Bennett, 1993). While IT has the potential to improve service in any number of ways, the fact that competition exists and will continue to exist

CASE STUDY 17.7

Late availability holidays

In the price-wars of the 1980s in the UK, tour operators frantically reduced holiday prices in the belief that volume of sales would result in greater market share. Late availability services proliferated in number thereby assisting this trend. Initially good news for the tour operator, it led to consumers adopting a 'wait and see' approach confident in the knowledge that they would secure a holiday. Consequently, the consumer trend towards late booking became established resulting in lower profits for the tour operator. For the travel agent this was detrimental as lower prices equated with lower commission.

between principals means that IT will always be used as a competitive weapon thus hampering, if not preventing, its ability to improve customer service. In so doing, it also affects the travel agent's role.

DEVELOPMENTS IN INFORMATION TECHNOLOGY

The developments in IT are such that a number of trends are becoming discernible. The permeation of computers into every aspect of our daily lives is becoming a reality. Indeed such is the growth of telecommunications and computers that the world is witnessing the development of the 'information superhighway'. This term refers to a mother network providing the capability of linking together the world's vast number of computers. This is facilitated by broad bandwidth which in simple terms means the capacity to transmit and process data. Most of the actual highway exists in the form of phone lines, fibre-optic cables, satellites and cellular networks, the first phase of which is represented by the Internet.

The importance of the information superhighway is demonstrated in its potential to revolutionize not only the way information is transmitted but also the manner in which we as individuals go about our daily lives.

A second major IT development is that of multi-media technology. As the term suggests multi-media brings together a variety of different media including graphics, pictures, video and sound. One or more of these media are usually combined with text using a personal computer. This form of technology together with the information superhighway provides the technological infrastructure to facilitate numerous developments including video-conferencing, home shopping and point-of-sale developments, and virtual reality.

Video-conferencing

Like so many technologies in its early stages video-conferencing has been the subject of much discussion but in practice there are relatively few

---

CASE STUDY 17.8

The Internet

The Internet was created in the 1960s to serve government research laboratories. Today it has become a global cooperative known as 'The Net'. It comprises a host of small computer networks and mainframes which are connected by long distance telephone lines. In 1994 there were 30 million users connected to The Net covering 140 countries. Such is the growth in users that it is estimated that there will be 100 million by 1998.

Source: *Financial Times*, 17 October 1994; Roberts (1994).

examples. That is not to say, however, that its potential is limited. What video-conferencing offers is the opportunity for businesses to cut costs by replacing the need for travel. The area of application is therefore that of business travel. When profits are being squeezed it is only natural for companies to look for cost-cutting alternatives to conduct business.

Video-conferencing is a hybrid of multi-media technology and the information superhighway. It uses real-time video and audio transmission to show live images of users allowing them to see by way of a personal computer the person they are talking to. In this way face-to-face meetings can be held with people at a distance without the need to physically travel.

The market potential for video-conferencing is enormous. By removing the need to travel and by enabling faster transactions, video-conferencing could save companies serious sums of money in travel costs. Business travel as a segment of the market could become far less significant than it is currently, a trend which would have serious implications for airlines and hotels, two sectors in particular which largely subsist on business travel.

But video-conferencing does have its limitations, both technical and social. The technology is not perfect in that images can be jerky and the audio non-synchronized resulting in conference participants talking over each other. From a social perspective, video-conferencing does not allow body language signals to be picked up. In meetings where individuals actually meet, such signals can implicitly steer the discussion towards a consensus decision. Without such signals those same meetings could take a lot longer to reach a decision. Furthermore, being introduced to someone for the first time via a video-conference link is not ideal as the actual personal contact is absent. On this basis video-conferencing is better suited to follow-up meetings.

While the social limitations are largely insurmountable, the technological ones are not so, and improvements in this form of technology are inevitable. The likelihood, then, is that the adoption of video-conferencing will become more widespread in the future.

Home shopping

The idea of shopping from home is not a new one. Although there has been much talk of a revolution in the way we shop, in practice it is rather more

---

CASE STUDY 17.9

Hilton

The hotel chain Hilton is piloting a video-conferencing service at three of its hotels in Watford, Bristol and Leeds. The Hilton National commercial marketing director states: 'A one-hour video-conference generally costs less than an international air fare enabling companies to make significant savings.'

Source: *TTG*, 21 September 1994.

evolutionary with trials occurring on a piecemeal basis. Part of the problem lies not in the technology but in the habits of the public. People like to go out to shop; it is in essence a sociable activity, and they like to compare items in terms of quality, colour, price, etc. So in other words, the social obstacles are in many ways of greater importance than the technological ones.

In travel the situation is rather different. As the travel/tourism product cannot be seen, the only way of comparing products before purchase is by way of information. And such information can be just as readily consumed in the home. Indeed, in many respects, particularly in leisure, this is preferable as time is required to read and digest information and possibly compare views with other people, such as members of the family. Indeed the taking home of brochures from travel agents is testimony to this activity. Rarely, apart from in the booking of late availability holidays, is leisure travel a spontaneous purchase. Given the expense involved and the relatively infrequent nature of the experience, the natural tendency is to deliberate for a time before making a purchase. So the social factors which are so important in convenience shopping are less relevant in travel shopping.

In technological terms the key developments facilitating this trend are multi-media, combining sound, graphics, pictures, video and text onto a screen with fibre-optic cabling permitting large volumes of information to be transmitted quickly. Combined, the technology will provide consumers with all the information necessary upon which to base a decision about travel.

While the revolution in shopping is still some way off, there are clear indications of a shift in the habits of the public. In particular there is evidence of consumer willingness to access information themselves without the aid of a human interface. A number of examples can be cited:

- **The proliferation of multi-media kiosks**. These are being increasingly adopted by tourist boards showing video clips of destinations and places of interest as well as images of hotels and location maps. Thomas Cook's experimentation with a multi-media kiosk in their Marble Arch outlet is evidence that travel agents too are aware of the benefits such technology can bring.
- **Self-ticketing machines** can be found at airports and train stations enabling consumers to avoid the long queues for a personal ticket service. British Airway's Timesaver machines at the main UK airports is a good example whereby tickets can be purchased for travel within the UK. The success of such machines stems from the simplicity of travel in that there are a limited number of destinations, routes and prices to choose from. It also serves the business traveller well who will most likely be a frequent traveller perhaps needing to buy a ticket at the last minute.
- **Teletext** has become an important media for holiday sales, in particular for late availability. Typically only the most essential information

---

CASE STUDY 17.10

Welcome to London

'Welcome to London' was set up by the BTA in association with a company called Open World to provide an interactive guide to a variety of tourist attractions encompassing heritage, hotels, shops, restaurants, sights and arts. In addition to location maps, text-based information and a print-out facility, there are 130 movies which take you inside various places. The program exists in two forms: multi-media kiosks which are currently up and running in the BTA travel centres of London and New York with plans for other centres including Paris, and CD-Rom allowing the consumer to view the destination from the comfort of their own homes; the latter facility costs $19.95 or £19.95.

Source: Bennett (1995).

---

is provided, i.e. dates, length, price and accommodation style together with a contact number, normally that of a travel agent, so that a holiday or flight can be booked. Teletext can be viewed as a forerunner to interactive television which uses telephone lines to transmit information to the consumer via the television.

These examples demonstrate the increasing trend towards self-service as consumers become increasingly familiar with both technology and travel. However, there are limitations. Complexity is a key issue. Where the travel involved is relatively straightforward, such as in the purchase of a package holiday, a domestic flight, etc. or where the travel has been undertaken before, the consumer will feel more comfortable with organizing the arrangement or making a choice about travel with little advice.

CASE STUDY 17.11

Touch

Touch is the name given to a multi-media kiosk Thomas Cook is piloting. It provides consumers with travel information, electronic brochures (using video, still images and sound) and the opportunity to make a booking by way of a 17 inch touch screen, videolink handset, credit card reader and laser printer. If a reservation is requested, a Thomas Cook sales representative appears on the screen as a live image and talks the consumer through the process. By inserting a credit card into the terminal the transaction can be completed and a receipt and confirmation issued internally. The kiosk was initially piloted at Thomas Cook's Marble Arch branch between May and September 1994 and such was its success that the trial was extended in January 1995 to five other locations, three of which are at branches of the National Westminster Bank. The trial incorporates Cook's Own Label Flights, City Breaks, Disneyland Paris, Summer Sun, late availability sales and a brochure ordering facility.

Source: Bennett (1995).

CASE STUDY 17.12

BT Interactive TV

BT Interactive TV is an interactive multi-media television service set up and piloted by BT. It was tested from March 1995 on 2500 residents of Ipswich and Colchester in East Anglia using standard telephone lines. Services on offer included Thomas Cook (holidays and travel), Sears (Olympus Sports), WH Smith (books, CDs and videos), Safeway (groceries), National Westminster Bank (personal finance and banking), interactive magazines and movies on demand (BBC, Carlton, Granada and Hollywood Studios). These services were available by plugging the TV set into the telephone socket via a connector box and using the remote control to access each of the services. The travel services offered by Thomas Cook included a range of summer and winter holiday packages, Disneyland Paris, flights, foreign exchange and a range of guidebooks and destination videos.

Source: Bennett (1995).

Where travel is more complex and more expensive, it is more natural for the consumer to want advice from an expert. So even if technology facilitates increasing self-service in travel, the social limitations will restrict its adoption. Nonetheless, IT will almost certainly continue to encourage the trend towards home shopping, albeit not always from 'home'.

Virtual reality

Virtual reality (VR) is, as the name suggests, something which resembles or emulates reality. It provides an impression of reality without being real. It has been likened to Alice's Adventures in Wonderland, moving from the realms of fiction and imagination to actual simulation. Heim (1991), for example, states: 'VR needs to be not quite real or it will lessen the pull of imagination . . . which allows us to take what we need to hear and reconstitute the symbolic components into a mental vision.'

So how is reality simulated? The answer lies in technology, in particular that of mult-media technology (combining visual and audio) which is used to create a virtual image in three dimensions. A key development is that of the head-mounted display (HMD) which enables a person to look around a virtual place. Further developments which are still evolving are the dataglove and datasuit which will allow movements of the arm and body to be detected. A development in the future is the sensory floor which will sense the location of the person within the virtual place (Williams and Hobson, 1994).

Two features in particular characterize the VR experience:

- **Immersion**. This creates the feeling that the person is 'actually there'. It is an illusion created and sustained by the technology on the basis of its audio, visual and kinetic sophistication. Logical developments in sensory immersion include temperature, smells and tactile sensations (McClure, 1994).

- **Interactivity**. Effectively this is the degree of involvement of the person in the experience. There are three levels: passive, exploratory and fully interactive (McClure, 1994). A passive system is one whereby the person has no control over the image presented; an OMNIMAX theatre consisting of a panoramic screen (usually found in theme parks) is one such example. An exploratory system would allow the person to move through the environment by giving commands to the computer. Finally, a fully interactive system would enable the person to interact with the environment by, for example, picking up objects.

Given these developments there are a number of ways in which VR technology could be applied to the travel industry:

- One of the earliest applications of virtual reality technology rests with the travel industry in the form of flight simulators which enable pilots to be trained 'safely'.
- Linked to this is the role of VR in high-risk activities, in particular that of adventure/activity holidays. The marvellous advantage of VR is that high-risk activities such as rock climbing etc. can be undertaken without the actual risk of physical harm involved. This would be especially useful for people wanting to 'try out' something new safe in the knowledge that if they are uncomfortable with the experience they could extricate themselves from it more readily than if the experience were real.
- VR will provide the opportunity to 'see' places as a forerunner to an actual visit, perhaps aiding the decision-making process of choosing a holiday. Taken to the ultimate conclusion, VR may act as a surrogate to travel altogether ensuring that the experience is safe and secure. It will enable the individual to fulfil a fantasy, albeit on a surrogate basis.
- Probably the application with the greatest potential is that of theme parks. VR could replace the need for actual theme parks by offering virtual theme parks which enable the individual to simulate all the experiences associated with a 'real' park but without the hassle of queuing for rides or relying on weather.

But there are limitations, both social and technological, to the advancement of VR in tourism. First, the technological problems include the following:

- The HMD currently only allows for the head not the eyes to be monitored, so if the person wished to take a side view, they would have to move their whole head.
- Movement in VR is restricted resulting in a less than authentic experience.
- Tactile feedback is still in the early stages of development and is yet to be perfected.

The social limitations are twofold:

- VR is currently a non-social activity undertaken in isolation, which is in stark contrast to real tourism which is highly sociable.
- The fact that VR is not real means that it will never be able to fully replicate the senses of smell, sound and sight in a real environment.

While developments in technology are such that many of the technological limitations may be surmounted in the future, the social limitations are rather more entrenched and it is therefore these factors in particular which will determine the future potential of VR in tourism.

IMPLICATIONS OF TECHNOLOGICAL DEVELOPMENTS

Developments in video-conferencing, home shopping and VR have the potential to radically affect the travel industry. If video-conferencing were to be adopted on a widespread basis it would seriously reduce the amount of business travel. One estimate by a member of the trade is that of a reduction in travel of between 10 and 15% 'eventually' (*TTG*, 7 September 1994). This may be a conservative estimate in which case the impact may be much greater, but even at 15% the effect would be felt by hotels, airlines, travel agents and indeed all the services involved in business travel on a worldwide basis. Some business travel agents are already adapting to the potential change by moving towards travel consultancy such that video-conferencing may be offered as an alternative to travel. Hotel chains too are considering offering video-conferencing as a facility for business customers. So the industry is not shying away from the development, rather it is acknowledging that it has a role to play and is accommodating it accordingly, albeit reluctantly.

The trend towards self-service and home shopping could also have major consequences. Indeed it could potentially eliminate a whole sector of the chain of distribution, that of the travel agent. This is known as disintermediation, i.e. the removal of the intermediary, which in the case of the travel industry would have an enormous impact on distribution. Given that the travel agent relies on information to sell products due to the intangible nature of the tourism product, the need for the travel agent can be questioned, especially if another mechanism can provide the same information in a more convenient form. Consequently speculation in the trade and in academic literature on the future role of the travel agent has been rife with many predictions about its eventual demise. Certainly the trend towards self-service is a step along this path but as yet there is no firm evidence to either refute or confirm such a prognosis.

So what will prevent IT from eliminating the travel agent? The answer lies with the travel agent's role in providing advice to the traveller. Whether it is called high-touch, the people factor or the human element, they all mean the same: someone to advise and counsel the consumer. As travel is costly relative to other purchases and as the nature of travel is often complex, the need for someone to offer advice is heightened. Furthermore, the role of the travel agent in reassuring the client and in being able to provide additional information perhaps stemming from their own experience of a place, all point to the need to a travel agent, therefore reducing the omnipotence of IT. It is possible that in future a role for the travel agent could be carved out in conjunction with the technology. The travel agent could, for example, feature as a live image in the home assisting with the decision-making and reservation process, as demonstrated in the Thomas Cook 'Touch' project. Whether this proves to be a common trend remains to be seen.

VR has the potential to alter the shape of tourism. In the worst case scenario it could replace tourism altogether by enabling people to experience places and activities on a surrogate basis. While being environmentally friendly, risk-free and secure, the limitations of VR are such that it is unlikely to actually replace tourism. Rather it is more feasible that it will find a niche such as in virtual theme parks. Of course it could be argued that virtual tourism itself is a contradiction in terms in that by definition tourism involves some sort of travel (Williams and Hobson, 1994). That said, while VR may augment certain forms of tourism, it is difficult to envisage it actually replacing it altogether. Ultimately it will more probably be conceived as a poor substitute or second best to the real thing.

It is all too easy to speculate on futuristic technological innovation without taking account of social, economic and even political factors. In reality, such factors are every bit as important as the technological ones and they provide the context within which IT will either flourish or wither. So while IT will undoubtedly have an impact on the industry, the nature of the impact will depend upon numerous factors of which technological capability is but one.

SUMMARY

The importance of information within the tourism industry has been demonstrated. The intangible nature of the tourism product together with the array of companies involved renders communication of information vital. Consequently, information technology has been adopted to perform a variety of functions. Three principal forms of technology were focused upon, namely viewdata, CRSs and DMSs. As well as serving a communications role, IT has also assumed a more contentious role as a competitive tool. This has raised several issues, in particular with regard to the effect on customer service. The chapter then turned to developments in IT concentrating on video-conferencing, home shopping and virtual reality. While it is acknowledged that such technology could have far-reaching implications, its potential is tempered by social constraints.

REFERENCES

Archdale, G. (1994) Non-European initiatives and systems, in Schertler, W., Schmid, B., Tjoa, A.M. and Werthner, H. (eds), *Information and Communications Technologies in Tourism*, Proceedings of the ENTER international conference in Innsbruck, Austria, Springer-Verlag, Vienna.

Bennett, M.M. (1993) Information technology and travel agency: a customer service perspective, *Tourism Management*, August, pp. 259–66.

Bennett, M.M. (1995) The consumer marketing resolution: the impact of IT on tourism. *Journal of Vacation Marketing*, **1**(4), 376–82.

Boberg, K.B. and Collison, F.M. (1985) Computer reservations and airline competition, *Tourism Management*, **6**, September, 174–83.

Bruce, M. (1987) New technology and the future of tourism, *Tourism Management*, June.

Ebner, A. (1994) TIS Tourism Information System for the Tyrol, in Schertler, W., Schmid, B., Tjoa, A.M. and Werthner, H. (eds), *Information and Communications Technologies in Tourism*, Proceedings of the (ENTER) Springer-Verlag, Vienna.

The Financial Times (1993) BA to pay Virgin £610 000 in 'dirty tricks' case, 12 January.

The Financial Times (1994) Home shopping buys its way into Internet, 8 September.

The Financial Times (1994) Surprising collaborations emerge, 17 October.

Haines, P. (1994) Destination Marketing Systems, in Schertler, W., Schmid, B., Tjoa, A.M. and Werthner, H. (eds), *Information and Communications Technologies in Tourism*, Proceedings of the (ENTER) international conference in Innsbruck, Austria, Springer-Verlag, Vienna.

Heim, M. (1991) The metaphysics of virtual reality, in Helsel, S.K. and Roth, J. (eds), *Virtual Reality: Theory, Practice and Promise*, Meckler, Westport, CT.

Hitchin, F. (1991) The influence of technology on UK travel agents, *Travel and Tourism Analyst*, No. 3.

The Independent (1988) BA resolves feud with US airline, 27 June.

Lipman, G. (1994) Tourism: the world's largest industry, in *Information technology for Travel and Tourism Marketing: A Tool for Profit*, Conference proceedings, PATA, San Francisco.

McClure, M. (1994) The travel experience: technology as threat or opportunity, in *Information Technology for Travel and Tourism Marketing: A Tool for Profit*, Conference proceedings, PATA, San Francisco.

Poon, A. (1988) Tourism and information technologies, *Annals of Tourism Research*, **15**.

Poon, A. (1993) *Tourism, Technology and Competitive Strategies*, CAB International, Wallingford, Oxon.

The Sunday Times (1994) Airline war moves to reservation systems, 24 April.

Travel Trade Gazette (1994) Will business travellers prove camera-shy?, 7 September.

Travel Trade Gazette (1994) Hilton pilots video networks for meetings, 21 September.

Williams, A.P. and Hobson, J.S.P. (1994) Tourism – the next generation: virtual reality and surrogate travel – is it the future of the tourism industry?, in Seaton, A.V. *et al.* (eds), *Tourism: The State of The Art*, Wiley, Chichester.

REVIEW QUESTIONS

1. What are the functions of IT in the travel and tourism industry?
2. Why has IT been adopted by the travel and tourism industry?
3. How has technology been used as a competitive tool?
4. What applications are possible from more recent developments in technology?
5. What impact will these developments have on the tourism industry?
6. How can developments in home shopping affect distribution of the tourism product?

18 Service, quality and tourism

M.M. Bennett

OBJECTIVES

By the end of this chapter the reader should:

- understand the concepts of service and quality;
- appreciate the difficulty associated with defining service and thus measuring service;
- understand the importance of service within the tourism industry.

INTRODUCTION

Everyone appreciates good customer service when they see it or experience it. Similarly a poor service is equally instantly recognizable. The quality of service provided in any given situation is thus appraised very quickly indeed. Nowhere is this more pertinent than in tourism. By its very nature the tourism product is service driven making the quality of the product intrinsically linked to the level of service provided. The aim of this chapter therefore is to consider the role of customer service within the tourism industry. First focusing on the concepts of quality and service, the chapter will then introduce tourism and consider how the three intertwine.

QUALITY

Quality and service are closely linked but for the purpose of understanding the link it is first necessary to distinguish between the two. Horowitz (1990) defines quality as:

> ... the minimum level of service which a firm chooses to provide in order to satisfy its target clientele. At the same time it is the degree of

consistency the firm can maintain in providing this predetermined level of service.

So in other words the level of service provided is related to who the consumers are who will purchase the product or service. And consumers will vary in their expectations. For example, a business person will have very different expectations to a leisure traveller when booking a seat on a plane. Similarly the level of service expected from a consumer staying in a five-star hotel will vary from one staying in a two-star. Clearly price is also a factor here in that the higher the price of a service the greater the quality expected.

Consistency is the final factor in the quality equation. The same degree of service quality must be provided at all times and in all sectors of the company. For example, a traveller flying on a domestic flight should experience the same standard of service as one on a long-haul flight. Meals served in one restaurant forming part of a chain should be of the same standard as those served in another. The staff will be different in each case but the level of service should be the same. The human element therefore plays a crucial part here adding to the difficulty of achieving consistency. Furthermore, where the service is more widely dispersed or where the product/service is distributed through intermediaries, the greater the difficulty of ensuring consistency in quality (Horowitz, 1990).

SERVICE

Service as a concept is more difficult to define. This is because it relates to different factors, principally that of price and and the expectations of consumers. It is therefore by its nature subjective. The perception of a service level will vary according to an individual's socio-cultural grouping, age and lifestyle. These factors combined with the price of a product/service and the reputation of the company will influence the individual's expectations which in turn will determine the perception of a service in terms of how it rates on a good and bad scale (Gnoth, 1993; Bennett, 1993). The subjectivity of service is further compounded by its intangibility. Service cannot be seen, touched or taken away to show someone else. It is a short-lived phenomenon pertinent only to the moment. Table 18.1 outlines the characteristics of service.

All too often the perception of service differs from the expectation thereby creating a gap and a problem for the provider (Gronroos, 1988; Horowitz, 1990). This thesis was expounded by Zeithaml, Parasuraman and Berry (1985) and led to the development of a service model. This model was further developed by Gilbert and Joshi (1992) who identified five gaps in service delivery (see Figure 18.1):

- gap between consumer expectation and management perception;
- gap between management perception and service quality specifications;
- gap between service quality specifications and service delivery;

Table 18.1 Characteristics of service

- It is intangible. It cannot be easily measured.
- It cannot be taken away to show someone else.
- On being provided service, the customer has not acquired anything. It does, however, have added-value importance by way of after-sales support, pre-sales service and financial assistance.
- It is difficult to standardize service.
- Service is perceived differently by:
  - different people in the same group;
  - the same person at different times;
  - people from different social/cultural groups;
  - people with different levels of knowledge/experience.
- Perceptions relate to expectations.

Source: Adapted from Time Management International (1983).

- gap between service delivery and external communications;
- gap between perceived service and delivered service.

Such gaps need to be bridged if the service potential is to be fully exploited.

Technical versus personal service

The broad term 'service' can be subdivided into two thereby assisting the quest for a definition.

Technical service

This form of service is also known as 'material' and relates to tangible aspects which include equipment, resources, staffing, information, etc. In turn these factors can be assessed on the basis of price, quantity and timing. For example, the length of time taken to answer a telephone can be monitored and quantified. Targets are readily set among service-driven companies such as American Express. This is one physical aspect among many which can be more objectively assessed.

Personal service

Also referred to as 'functional', it is this type of service which is most readily associated with customer service. It is, in essence, the human interface between consumer and producer whereby the service provided attends to the needs of the individual. Various factors are at work here including promptness, knowledge, courtesy, accuracy and, of course, personal attention. It is these features which are characteristically intangible and subjective making assessment considerably more hazardous.

Combining the two types of service results in a more holistic approach. Parasuraman, Zeithaml and Berry (1990) define service quality on the basis of ten dimensions used by consumers in evaluating service: tangibles,

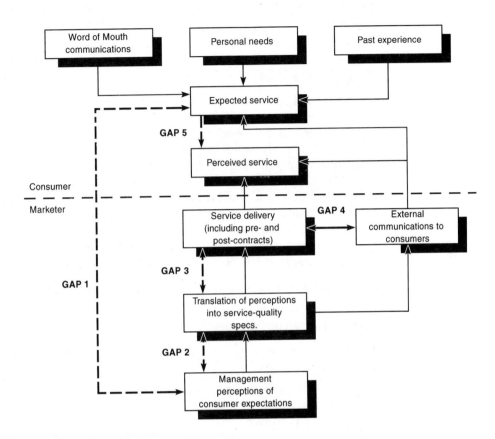

Figure 18.1 Service quality model.
Source: Gilbert and Joshi (1992) after Zeithaml, Parasuraman and Berry (1985).

responsiveness, competence, courtesy, credibility, security, access, communication and understanding the consumer. Lehtinen and Lehtinen (1985) suggest the use of three components in measuring service quality: physical quality (tangible aspects), corporate quality (company image/reputation), and interactive quality (interaction between service providers and recipients). Along a similar line of thought Sasser, Olsen and Wyckoff (1978) identify three dimensions of service performance: levels of materials, facilities and personnel. Both forms of service therefore need to be recognized and measured for a complete appreciation of service.

While both forms of customer service are undoubtedly important it is the personal service which is critical (Bitner, Nyquist and Booms, 1985; Bennett, 1993). This partly stems from the fact that it is generally assumed that the material service will be up to standard while the personal service is more variable involving individual responses to individual requests. The importance of front-line staff in any organization cannot therefore be overstated as it is these people who communicate either face to face or voice to voice with the consumer, and so it follows that these people who represent the company largely determine the type of service which is offered.

The importance of service

There can be little doubt that the role of customer service within any organization has assumed major importance. Consumers increasingly expect a better service from organizations they interact with and as competition is inexorably increasing, it is service which can make the difference between one company and the next. Nowhere is this more important than in service industries.

The implications of poor service are serious. A person dissatisfied with the service received will not only be unlikely to return to the company but will more readily communicate their dissatisfaction than one who is satisfied. Hence the old adage about bad news travelling fast is an appropriate one. For example, it has been suggested that a dissatisfied customer will tell 11 people about their experience while a satisfied one may only tell three people (Horowitz, 1990). This relates to the fact that people increasingly expect to receive good service so when it is not delivered their dissatisfaction is exaggerated. There are, however, 'zones of tolerance' which Lewis (1993) defines as the difference between desired and adequate expectations. While an adequate level of service may not be a desired level, it may fall within the bounds of acceptability on the part of the recipient therefore mitigating feelings of consternation. Such tolerance zones will vary according to the individual so making the task of bridging the gap between conceived and perceived service delivery difficult.

However, there is scope for a company turning a negative situation into a positive one. This is referred to as recovery. If a complaint is handled well and a dissatisfied customer is transformed into a satisfied one, then he or she is more likely to return to the organization again (Ostrowski and O'Brien, 1991). The damage limitation exercise is therefore assisting the company. Although this is a valid point, it is not a strategy to be encouraged. It has been suggested, for example, that the cost of replacing a customer is five times that of keeping one (Lewis, 1993). Rather, there is a very real need to get it right first time so that not only are customers won, but they are also maintained.

Customer service is therefore a competitive weapon which, if used well, can become a competitive advantage for a company in an increasingly competitive world.

QUALITY SERVICE AND TOURISM

As a service industry the tourism industry has no product as such to promote. The product is a service and has a number of associated characteristics. These characteristics were outlined in Chapter 7 on

---

CASE STUDY 18.1

American Express

In research conducted by American Express it was found that:

* 96% of dissatisfied customers do not complain;
* 65–90% of non-complainers will not buy from you again;
* 54–70% of complainers can be won back by showing you care;
* 95% of complainers will become loyal if you handle their problem well and quickly;
* a customer who has had an unpleasant experience will tell about 12 people while a customer who has had a pleasant experience will tell only three people;
* it costs five times more to get a new customer than to keep an existing one.

Source: American Express in-house literature.

---

distribution but it is worth reiterating them here in the context of service provision.

* **Intangibility**. As the product cannot be touched, it is experience which matters. A person's holiday, flight, ferry crossing, short-break, etc. all involve service from actual booking through to the experience itself. Indeed, at almost every stage of the experience an element of service will be required. For example, a seat on an aircraft will have been booked either direct with the airline or through a travel agent. Arriving at the airport will require service at the check-in desk, followed by a period of waiting in the departure lounge. Service on the flight will encompass meals and drinks, comfort, entertainment and information provided. And finally arriving at the destination the consumer will be faced with baggage retrieval. If at any stage in the consumer's experience the service is poor then this will affect their level of satisfaction and future behaviour, i.e. by changing airline, flying from a different airport, booking in a different manner.
* **Perishability**. Although a service, such as a flight, may be experienced by the same person numerous times, each experience is unique. Therefore, there is great emphasis on the need to provide a consistently good service such that every experience is a pleasant one. There are no second chances. This is heightened by remembering that in many situations tourism is simply a means to an end. For example, a flight followed by a night in a hotel room may be necessary for a meeting the next day. So if a flight is delayed or a night spent in a hotel room is an uncomfortable one then the consequences can be far-reaching.
* **Heterogeneity**. The problem of providing a consistently good service arises out of the fragmented nature of both the product and the industry. So, often more than one company will be involved in delivering the service (Carlzon, 1987; Laws and Ryan, 1992). For example, in taking a flight, a travel agent may have been used to book the flight,

the airline will host the check-in desks and take full responsibility during the flight, while a baggage handling company will assume baggage responsibility upon landing. Given that there are so many companies involved in providing a single service, consistency in the provision of that service becomes all the more difficult to guarantee. The need to identify the cause of any dissatisfaction on the part of the consumer is also heightened.

- **Volatility**. Tourism is a dynamic industry. Changes either internally generated by companies supplying the product or externally generated by political or economic factors etc. have an effect on supply and demand. For example, if a flight is delayed due to air traffic control problems, the airline must ensure that the discomfort and inconvenience caused to passengers is minimized. Similarly if a hotel is overbooked arrangements must be made quickly to find other suitable accommodation at minimum inconvenience to those affected. Prompt action is required in such cases to limit the potentially damaging effects. It is the service offered at such 'moments of truth', i.e. the recovery strategies employed, which distinguish the companies which are service orientated from those which are not.

Three further factors emphasize the importance of service in tourism:

- In much of tourism the essential ingredients making up the service are the same. For example, the typical package holiday comprises a charter flight and transfer at the destination to a hotel, as well as virtually guaranteed sun, sand and sea at a low cost. This has been termed substitutability whereby one holiday can be readily swopped for another. In such a situation the quality of the service provided throughout the consumer experience can differentiate one company from the next.
- The second point relates to tourism as a means to an end. A flight undertaken is almost certainly of secondary importance to the activity conducted at the destination. The same may be said of a person staying overnight in a hotel on business. In such situations the ingredients of the product are basically the same but what will distinguish one company from the next is the type and quality of service offered. Hence, airlines go to great lengths to attract the business traveller by way of separate check-in facilities, separate departure lounges, larger seat pitch and the provision of business services, i.e. fax machines, telephones, etc. It is these elements of service which form the marketing strategy which determines firstly whether customers are won and, depending upon service execution, whether they are kept.
- The latter point raises a final issue. In tourism, both the technical and personal components of service are important. The personal service, as we have already seen, pervades virtually every situation in tourism making its importance undisputed. Technical service too plays a vital role. The quality of a meal served in a restaurant, the comfort level on an aircraft, the hygiene in a hotel and the facilities provided are all

tangible aspects. Evidence of the importance of technical service is provided by way of complaints. In an ABTA survey of complaints made by holidaymakers while on package holidays the majority of complaints referred to such tangible factors as substandard accommodation, poor standard of food, poor in-transit facilities, noise, etc. (ABTA, 1985, in Gilbert and Joshi, 1992). This endorses the point made earlier that it is generally expected that technical service will be up to standard. Also, it should be recognized that it is easier to complain about something which is tangible as this can be more easily qualified.

IMPLEMENTING QUALITY

Given the clear importance of quality service there is a clear need to ensure that organizations implement customer service programmes. These can take many forms and have given rise to such terminology as quality circles and total quality management (TQM), but perhaps the overriding point is that their penetration throughout an organization extends beyond that of a mere programme. In essence the focus on service must form part of the management ethos or philosophy of the company (Ostrowski and O'Brien, 1991).

In formulating a customer service programme Mansfield (1990) suggests that the following principles be incorporated.

1. It starts at the top

For quality to be taken seriously it needs to form part of the organizational culture. As highlighted earlier one of the key variables in the quality equation is consistency. For this to occur there must be a belief in quality beginning at the very top of the management hierarchy. In

---

CASE STUDY 18.2

British Airways

In BA's list of goals, two are service driven:

- Service and value – to provide overall superior service and good value for money in every market segment in which we compete.
- Customer driven – to excel in anticipating and quickly responding to customer needs and competitor activity.

The success of BA is partly reflected in its commitment to serving its customers in the best possible manner.

Source: British Airways (1993).

CASE STUDY 18.3

Trailfinders

Trailfinders is an expanding travel agency specializing in tailor-made independent holidays and itineraries. It has grown from a staff of four on opening in 1970 to a staff of over 400 today with offices in London, Glasgow, Bristol, Manchester and Cairns (Australia). Among a list of reasons presented for why anyone should choose to travel with Trailfinders, the following are of note:

- Trailfinders has as unmatched reputation for friendly service and efficiency.
- Trailfinders has a full time Customer Relations Manager so that in the unlikely event that you experience any difficulty you are assured of a prompt, courteous and understanding reaction on our part.

Emphasizing the service point further, Mr Gooley, Managing Director, states:

I would like to say that complete client satisfaction is, and always has been, paramount in Trailfinders' way of doing things. The Trailfinders team and I give you, our client, a personal and sincere guarantee to honour your custom with the highest levels of service and professionalism.

Source: Trailfinders (1994).

companies which have succeeded in being associated with quality, the CEO is usually an exponent of quality, as in the case of Sir Colin Marshall of BA, for example, who has been quoted as saying: 'In the end the success of an airline depends on service to the customer' (Elliott, 1994). If management are active in promulgating quality then it is more likely that their commitment will filter down through the company to the front-line staff.

2. Customer care involves everyone

For the quality message to pervade the company it must involve every member of that company. Again it relates to the point about consistency but it also relates to the culture of the organization. Where quality service is a top priority, programmes are implemented which require participation by every company member. Probably the best known programme is 'Putting People First' which has been run, among others, by British Airways, Sheraton Hotels, SAS, Thistle Hotels and American Express, all companies with a very strong commitment to quality.

3. Care for your staff and they will care for your customers

In any organization the human resource is probably the most important of all the resources available. If time and effort is invested in recruiting, training and rewarding staff then the company will benefit in numerous ways from customers receiving a better quality of service at those 'moments of truth' in the service encounter.

4.   *It is a continuous process*

A one-off programme is not the solution. For quality service to be maintained, training must be ongoing, new initiatives must be implemented and the company must be prepared to adapt. We thus come full circle in that for quality to penetrate an organization it has to be part of the company ethos and for that to occur it must start at the top.
It can be argued that there is a further principle worth adding:

5.   *Empowerment*

In the 'moment of truth' of the service encounter it is usually the front-line staff who provide the service to the consumer. It therefore follows that it is these people who leave the lasting impression on the consumer, an impression which supersedes any preconceived notions concerning the reputation of the company and associated service expectations. It is when problems arise that the role of these frontliners is heightened. It is therefore vital that such staff are given the power to act on and resolve a problem instantaneously without recourse to a higher authority for advice (Hart, Heskett and Sasser, 1990; Partlow, 1993). In this way a solution is found and the customer's dissatisfaction is dissipated. Dithering on the part of the customer contact staff or an inability to take action only exacerbates an already fractious situation. In research conducted by BA on the factors most important in people's flying experience, it was found that spontaneity, i.e. front line staff having the authority to deal with problems, and recovery, i.e. staff apologizing and ameliorating a situation, were ranked within the top four in importance (Lewis, 1993).

Assessment

To ascertain the value of a customer service programme some form of assessment must be introduced. However, as with anything intangible, this becomes an acutely difficult task (Stabler, 1993). The two forms of service referred to earlier, technical and personal, are important here. Personal service encompassing courtesy, knowledge and empathy are subjective, totally intangible and therefore difficult to measure in a way which is both consistent and meaningful (Witt, 1993). Meanwhile technical service which relates to more tangible aspects, including resources, equipment and staffing, can be more readily qualified on the basis of price, quality and speed. For example, the number of reservations made by a member of staff in a travel agent does not reflect the quality of the advice offered. If consumers return from their holidays dissatisfied as a result of poor advice or insufficient information upon which to have made a decision then the previous statistic is meaningless. Furthermore, the consumer is unlikely to return to

CASE STUDY 18.4

British Airways

British Airways began implementing customer service programmes a decade ago in an effort to transform the company culture into a customer orientated one following privatization. All of the airline's staff have attended four programmes:

- **Putting People First:** introduced in 1984, the programme, as the name suggests, focused on the ways to enhance customer service.
- **A Day in the Life:** built bridges between different departments by helping people to understand the work undertaken in other departments by other staff.
- **To Be the Best:** focused on ways in which performance could be improved in the context of increasing competition.
- **Winning for Customers:** a one-day programme which brought staff together in groups to tackle cases, in particular focusing on recovery strategies when problems are encountered.

BA's commitment to service is ongoing and penetrates the entire company. As Lewis (1993) states: 'Service quality is a journey, not a destination.'

Source: Churchill (1994).

the travel agent thus resulting in lost business. The tendency is, however, for service to be assessed in this way because it is more easy to do so (Lockwood, 1993).

One aspect of service which can be measured is the cost of getting things wrong. For example, an overbooked plane will require cash compensations or upgrades being granted. A cancelled flight may require passengers being accommodated overnight in hotels. These sorts of costs can be quantified and thus measured. What is more difficult to assess is the longer-term effects of such service strategies. While it has already been noted that recovery strategies can act in the company's favour by securing consumer loyalty, the opposite can also occur resulting in lost business and a detrimental effect on the health of the company.

Benefits

Getting customer service right can provide a whole host of benefits. For the organization this can include;

- enhancing the company's reputation through word of mouth;
- improved customer loyalty resulting in increased repeat business;
- more first-time customers arising out of personal recommendation;
- fewer complaints.

For the employee too there are benefits including:

- improved morale and job satisfaction;
- increased loyalty to the company;

- better employer/employee relationship;
- greater cooperation among employees.

A further benefit arising out of a combination of the above is that of a reduction in staff turnover. Not only does this have a financial payoff in terms of lower recruitment costs but it also has a beneficial service spin-off by way of increased consistency and a higher quality of service provision.

Counterbalancing the benefits are the disadvantages of not getting it right first time. The cost extends beyond the loss of one individual. As noted earlier, dissatisfied customers tend to be more vociferous in their complaints to others than those that are satisfied. Where such complaints are directed at other people rather than the organization, it has an adverse effect on first timers and provides no opportunity for the company to redeem itself. The need to get it right first time is thus heightened.

Information technology

In considering customer service and how best to provide it, the link with technology is not an immediately obvious one. Yet the penetration of information technology (IT) throughout the tourism industry is having an impact on service provision. This includes:

- electronic data interchange (EDI) at the supplier/supplier and supplier/intermediary interface;

CASE STUDY 18.5

American Express

American Express, a company renowned for its emphasis on quality, cites the following benefits to be gained from providing good customer service:

- greater customer loyalty – those that have received good service in the past will want to return;
- free advertising – a satisfied customer will recommend you to others;
- new markets – cross-selling opportunities arise as satisfied customers return to buy alternative products;
- increased efficiency – fewer complaints reduce handling and rectification costs;
- improved morale – front-line staff enjoy working with happy customers;
- good company image – becomes your most effective corporate advertising;
- responsive suppliers – employee expectations will increase and inefficient suppliers will no longer be tolerated;
- increased sales – without the necessity to reduce prices;
- safer future – your local clients become your future.

Source: In-house literature.

- management information systems;
- revenue management systems (yield/inventory control);
- reservation systems;
- consumer information systems (TICs);
- databases of consumer information.

Such systems generally result in a more efficient and speedier operation. Yet the benefits of IT extend beyond the technical service. IT can and does complement the functional/personal service. For example, databases enable travel agents handling frequent travellers to know their preferences. Furthermore, technology is usurping many of the more routine administrative tasks, enabling staff to concentrate on providing a better service by tailoring advice and matching products to the individual (Bennett, 1993; Lewis, 1993).

However, as well as having a beneficial effect on customer service provision, equally IT can have a more pernicious effect. In the quest to gain a competitive advantage, many companies have turned to IT. Consequently, IT is being used to manipulate the manner in which information is provided to encourage sales. The CRS is a prime example. Bias in CRSs has resulted in increased sales for the CRS owner to the disadvantage of non-owning carriers in the CRS. This has been effected by screen displays and in particular code-sharing. A flight given a higher listing on screen due to a marketing alliance with another airline may be booked but it may involve a change of aircraft and airline and thus may not be the best option for the consumer. In such a situation the travel agent is providing poor customer service (Bennett, 1993).

SUMMARY

Quality service is of vital importance to any organization today. Yet the difficulty of providing consistent quality service is matched only by the

---

CASE STUDY 18.6

Code-sharing

Not only can code-sharing lead to the inconvenience of having to change planes but it can also result in the equally annoying inconvenience of changing terminals. For example, the route between London and Bergen is code-shared between British Midland and SAS although all flights are operated by British Midland which depart from Terminal One at Heathrow. SAS's flights, however, leave from Terminal Three. So on a multiple-legged journey with SAS destined for Bergen via Heathrow, the chances are that passengers will be forced to transfer to another terminal which is more time-consuming and definitely less convenient.

Source: Wickers, (1994).

CASE STUDY 18.7

The Lanesborough Hotel

The Lanesborough is said to be one of the most technologically advanced hotels in London, if not the world (Jones, 1992). Of $100 m spent on development costs, it is estimated that $10 m was spent on technology to improve service. The services offered through this technology are:

- a direct dialling system providing guests with individual phone and fax numbers before they arrive. Regular guests can therefore request the same number enabling callers to bypass the switchboard;
- a property management system hosting guest information including preferences allows butlers to greet guests by name on arrival;
- a call and room management system enabling staff to know whether the guest is in their room;
- an energy management system controlling temperature and lighting such that as a guest leaves a room the temperature drops to 10°C and the lighting dims.

The managing director states: 'The whole idea is to make their (guests) life easier. The hotel does not say high-tech when you walk in – it's very much a residential feel. We have put in the latest technology to inform the employee and to make sure the guests get what they want more quickly than normal.'

Source: Jones (1992).

difficulty in defining and measuring it. The problem stems from its intangible nature, its subjectivity, and the gap between expectation and perception in service delivery which itself is variable and dependent on the individual. Two types of service exist, technical and personal, both of which are important, although it is the latter which is most usually associated with service and which is the most difficult to define.

Service and tourism are intrinsically linked not least because of the tourism product's intangibility. The fragmentation of the industry further exacerbates the task of providing a consistently good service. Given the often limited differentiation of products in tourism, it is the quality of service which can distinguish one company from the next.

Commitment to service provision is demonstrated through a management ethos which embraces service and the implementation of various programmes. Assessment of such initiatives is of equal importance but more difficult to undertake. Yet the benefits of providing the right service quality are undisputed. Finally, the chapter turns its attention to information technology showing the ways in which service provision can be both positively and negatively affected by IT.

In conclusion it is found that customer service is of vital importance to the long-term health of companies involved in tourism. Those that demonstrate a commitment to service provision will almost certainly be the survivors in an increasingly competitive world.

REFERENCES

ABTA (1985) *Report on Holiday Complaints*, ABTA, London

Bennett, M.M. (1993) Information technology and travel agency: a customer service perspective, *Tourism Management*, August, pp. 259–66.

Bitner, M., Nyquist, J. and Booms, B. (1985) The critical incident as a technique for analysing the service encounter, in Block, T. *et al.* (eds), *Service Marketing in a Changing Environment*, American Marketing Association, Chicago, pp. 48–51.

British Airways (1993) *Annual Report and Accounts.*

Carlzon, J. (1987) *Moments of Truth*, Harper & Row, New York.

Churchill, D. (1994) Training policy puts people first, *The Times*, 25 August.

Elliott, H. (1994) Leading right from the front, *The Times*, 25 August.

Gilbert, D.C. and Joshi, I. (1992) Quality management and the tourism and hospitality industry, in Cooper, C.P. and Lockwood, A. (eds), *Progress in Tourism, Recreation and Hospitality Management*, Belhaven Press, London.

Gnoth, J. (1993) Quality of service and tourist satisfaction, in Witt, S. and Moutinho, L. (eds), *Tourism Marketing and Management Handbook*, Prentice-Hall, Englewood Cliffs, New Jersey.

Gronroos, C. (1988) *Assessing competitive edge in the new competition of the service economy: the five rules of service*, Working Paper No. 9, First Interstate Centre for Services Marketing, Arizona State University.

Hart, C.W.L., Heskett, J.C., and Sasser, W.E. (1990) The profitable art of service recovery, *Harvard Business Review*, July–August, pp. 148–56.

Horowitz, J. (1990) *How to Win Customers: Using Customer Service for a Competitive Edge*, Pitman, London.

Jones, W. (1992) Lanesborough Luxury, *Caterer and Hotelkeeper*, 16 January, pp. 42–5.

Laws, E. and Ryan, C. (1992) Service on flights – issues and analysis by the use of diaries, *Journal of Travel and Tourism Marketing*, **1**(3).

Lehtinen, V. and Lehtinen, J.R. (1985) *Service Quality: A Study of Quality Dimensions*, Helsinki Service Management Institute, Finland.

Lewis, B.R. (1993) Quality of service and customer care, in Witt, S. and Moutinho, L. (eds), *Tourism Marketing and Management Handbook*, Prentice-Hall, Englewood Cliffs, New Jersey.

Lockwood, A. (1993) Quality management – hotels, in Witt, S. and Moutinho, L. (eds), *Tourism Marketing and Management Handbook*, Prentice-Hall, Englewood Cliffs, New Jersey.

Mansfield, S. (1990) Customer care in tourism and leisure, *Insights*, ETB, November, A65–70.

Ostrowski, P.L. and O'Brien, T.V. (1991) Predicting customer loyalty for airline passengers, *Tourism: Building Credibility for a Credible Industry*, TTRA, University of Utah.

Parasuraman, A., Zeithaml, V.A. and Berry, L.L. (1990) *Delivering Quality Service*, Macmillan, New York.

Partlow, C.G. (1993) How Ritz-Carlton applies TQM, *Cornell Hotel and Restaurant Administration Quarterly*, **34**(4), pp. 16–24.

Sasser, W.E., Olsen, R.P. and Wyckoff, D.D. (1978) *Management of Service Operations*, Alwyn & Bacon, Boston, Mass.

Stabler, M.J. (1993) Quality assessment of tourism developments, in Witt, S. and Moutinho, L. (eds), *Tourism Marketing and Management Handbook*, Prentice-Hall, Englewood Cliffs, New Jersey.

Time Management International (1983) *Putting People First*, Scandinavian Service School, Hillerod, Denmark.

Trailfinders (1994) *Trailfinders Magazine*, Autumn, Trailfinders, London.

Wickers, D. (1994) What's in a name, *The Sunday Times*, 21 August.

Witt, C.A. (1993) Total quality management, in Witt, S. and Moutinho, L. (eds), *Tourism Marketing and Management Handbook*, Prentice-Hall, Englewood Cliffs, New Jersey.

Zeithaml, V.A., Parasuraman, A. Berry, L.L. (1985) A conceptual model of service quality and its implications for future research, *Journal of Marketing*, **49**(4), pp. 41–50.

REVIEW QUESTIONS

1. How does quality differ from service?
2. What is the difference between technical and personal service?
3. How do the characteristics of services relate to tourism?
4. What principles might a company consider employing in formulating a customer service programme?
5. What are the problems associated with assessing service quality?
6. What are the potential benefits of a successful customer service strategy? What are the consequences of not 'getting it right first time'?
7. How has IT been used to influence service provision in tourism?

Part 3
Cases

This section comprises five specially written case studies which represent five main tourism product categories: airline marketing (Northwest Airlines), hotel marketing (Canadian Pacific Hotels and Best Western), travel agency marketing (Thomas Cook), tour operator marketing (Direct Holidays) and destination marketing (Florida).

Airline marketing: Northwest Airlines 19

M.M. Bennett

NORTHWEST AIRLINES

The mission: to build together the world's most preferred airline with the best people, each committed to exceeding our customer's expectations every day.

BACKGROUND

Northwest Airlines is America's oldest carrier with an identifiable name. It began operations in 1926 flying mail between Minneapolis/St Paul and Chicago. A year later it began passenger services. A notable feature of its development was the introduction of the 'Great Circle' or polar route to the Orient. Indeed Northwest has operated in the Pacific region longer than any other airline.

Today Northwest is the world's fourth largest carrier with a fleet size of 355 aircraft serving 242 cities across 21 countries (see Table 19.1). With hubs in Minneapolis/St Paul, Detroit and Boston, Northwest has a market share of 12.5% in the United States.

In profitability terms, Northwest has suffered losses like many of the world's major airlines. In 1993, for example, Northwest made a loss of $115.5 m, a situation engendered by reduced business travel which was a result of both the Gulf war and the worldwide recession. Financial pressures were exacerbated by problems in the Pacific region, namely a simultaneous increase in capacity and competition concurrent with a contraction in demand, the latter stemming from the worst recession ever experienced by the Far East. For Northwest the situation was serious as the airline was enlarging and increasing capacity while the market was contracting. By 1993 Chapter 11 had become a very real possibility. To prevent such an outcome Northwest undertook a major restructuring exercise of its benefit package to employees, an action more usually conducted once the airline has declared Chapter 11 status. In return for an

Table 19.1 Northwest Airlines in numbers – 1993

Total revenue	$8.60 billion
Total profit (loss)	($115.3 million loss)
Total number of passengers carried	41 828 000
Total number of passengers carried daily	114 597
Total revenue of passenger miles	58.130 billion
Total available seat miles	87.212 billion
System load factor	66.7%
Total number of daily flights	1390
Number of cities served by Northwest and Airlink partners	242
Total number of meals served	38.8 million
Total number of employees	43 000
Total number of pilots	5316
Total number of flight attendants	9539
US market share	12.5%
On-time performance in US	86.1%*
Fleet size	355 aircraft
Aircraft on order or option	60 aircraft

* Ranked number one for fourth consecutive year.
Source: Northwest Airlines.

equity share in the company the employees agreed to relinquish 15% ($900 m) in concessions over three years. This proved to be the catalyst for reaching agreement with the banks enabling Northwest to restructure its debt repayments alongside aircraft deliveries. The pay-off has been a return to profits which amount to $210.8 m for a 12-month period running up to and including the second quarter of 1994. Consequently, Northwest has managed to escape Chapter 11 and its pernicious publicity and continue business with an altogether healthier outlook.

STRATEGIC MARKETING

Alliances

The importance of alliances between airlines was discussed in Chapter 15. In fact the early roots of globalization can be traced to Northwest and its link-up with KLM. Indeed, the importance of this alliance is such that it dominates the discussion of strategic marketing. The origins of this particular alliance lie with the buyout of Northwest by a company called Wings formed for such a purpose. The resultant buyout happened in 1988 and it represented the last of the major corporate raids. KLM contributed equity thus providing them not only with a stake in an American airline but also with a valuable foothold in the US domestic market and opportunities for building an alliance. For both carriers the alliance has meant the opportunity to market a far greater number of destinations than possible on their own strength, a feature originating with code-sharing agreements.

So what are the features of this particular alliance?

- **Code-sharing**. KLM and Northwest code-share the following cities: Copenhagen, Stockholm, Oslo, Munich, Geneva and Zurich. Approximately 60 cities in Europe, Africa and the Middle East are linked into a code-sharing service.
- **Anti-trust immunity**. Linked to code-sharing this allows Northwest and KLM to price, market and sell as one airline. This is significant because they are the only two airlines to be granted anti-trust immunity by the US Department of Transportation. Anti-trust immunity also provides a firm foundation for joint marketing arrangements.
- **Route system**. The global airline alliance serves more than 350 cities in at least 80 countries in six continents. Schedules are synchronized and check-in is required only once.
- **Frequent flyer programme**. Both airlines offer separate free travel plans, Northwest's is called 'World Perks' and KLM's is called 'Flying Dutchman'. The two programmes are linked such that full mileage reciprocity operates enabling members of either scheme to accrue mileage on both airlines. Membership of both programmes is free with members receiving a free round trip domestic ticket after 20 000 miles flown. Bonus miles accrue when members fly in First or Business Class. World Perks members also earn mileage from staying at hotels, renting cars and using the World Perks Visa card. As a further incentive to clock up miles with the same airline, both schemes offer different levels of membership. The top tiers for Northwest and KLM, World Perks Gold and Royal Wing respectively, provide members with a priority service at all Northwest and KLM airport check-in counters.
- **Joint advertising**. The introduction of a new joint business class service called 'World Business Class' was jointly and heavily promoted. The global advertising campaign consisted of radio, television and print advertisements in every market where Northwest and KLM operate. Introduced on 15 February 1994, it represented a major step forward in the development of the alliance, further consolidating the link between these two carriers. An example of the type of advertising undertaken is displayed in Figures 19.1 and 19.2.

The alliance between KLM and Northwest is one of the longest established international alliances in the airline world as well as one of the most successful. It could be argued that it provided the model which other international carriers are following. In an industry where size is equated with marketing strength, the importance of such an alliance is clear. Economies gained from the practicalities of coordinating the two operations are complemented by enhanced marketing power.

However, alliances are not without their problems and this one is no exception. Given that the alliance is formed from two separate companies, the main problems arise from ensuring that the benefits are shared equally.

Figure 19.1 Northwest/KLM joint advertising: *World Business Class* brochure front cover.

On May 21, 1946, a KLM DC4, bearing the registration PH-TAR Rotterdam, with Captain Evert van Dijk at the controls, touched down at New York's Idlewild Airport, completing the first post-war commercial flight across the Atlantic. ▼ On July 16, 1947, just after dawn, a Northwest Airlines DC4, in the hands of Captain Ed La Parle landed at Tokyo Field, completing history's first commercial flight across the North Pacific. ▼ It is fitting that these two pioneer airlines have joined together to form the first truly global airline alliance; which can now take you to more than 380 cities in 81 countries on 6 continents with an integrated flight experience on our worldwide system. You fly on one ticket. You check luggage only once—providing the assurance of a one-airline experience. ▼ It is also fitting that they introduce you to World Business Class service, available on intercontinental flights worldwide. It offers you a combination of passenger Comfort, Choice and Control that has no equal in the sky.

World Business Class

Figure 19.2 Northwest/KLM joint advertising: *World Business Class* brochure inside right-hand page.

From a purely marketing or, more specifically, advertising perspective, the two airlines benefit equally, but in terms of practicalities differences exist. For example, reciprocity in mileage terms on the FFP plans is fine in principle but in practice the cashing-in of miles is unequal. The problem arises out of different mileage structures in Europe and the US such that it is easier to accrue free tickets in the US as fewer miles are required. Consequently Northwest is disadvantaged as mileage is earned on KLM and spent on Northwest. The result is that KLM benefits from increased revenue while Northwest suffers from increased contingent liability. Such a problem highlights the practical intricacies of alliances which need to be resolved if they are to benefit all companies concerned and thus work in the long term.

The difficulties of making alliances work are perhaps better explained by looking at those that have failed. In relation to Northwest there are two notable examples:

- a proposed tripartite alliance between British Airways, KLM and Northwest; and
- a quadruple airline alliance known as Alcazar.

British Airways and KLM/Northwest

In this proposed merger the discussions which began in 1991 were princi-pally between BA and KLM although a key attraction of the deal for BA was KLM's share in Northwest (20% of the voting rights). A merger would have fully incorporated Northwest into the group subject to a relaxation of US restrictions which limits foreign ownership (voting rights) to 25%. The proposal extended beyond a marketing alliance to full merger such that the two principal airlines involved (KLM and BA) would have been replaced by another name – 'World Airlines' was mooted as a possible title. If the merger had been agreed it would have resulted in the following:

- the creation of the world's first global airline;
- enabling the merged airline to dominate the European scene;
- the development of a hub and spoke network based on Schipol, Detroit and Heathrow;
- a seamless service for passengers flying from both regional and capital city airports.

The talks failed in February 1992 over the equity issue. KLM wanted 40% while BA wanted 75%. The entrenched position of these two airlines stemmed partly from nationalism. KLM is 38% government owned, and from a purely political standpoint, it did not want to be seen to be selling the national airline to the British.

Alcazar

The proposed alliance named Alcazar – a four-towered Moorish fortress built to keep predators at bay – centred on four European airlines: Austrian

Airlines, KLM Royal Dutch Airlines, Scandinavian Airlines System and Swissair. Talks which began in the autumn of 1992 and became public in February 1993 arose out of the need to develop global reach and thus effectively compete with other European alliances such as that between BA and Lufthansa and the big American carriers. The complexity of merging four separate airlines, a gargantuan task in itself because of four prevailing and distinctive cultures, was exacerbated by existing alliances between KLM with Northwest and Swissair with Delta. Effectively then the proposed airline involved not just four airlines but six as the two existing alliances are founded on equity rights. Interestingly, it was this issue which formed the toughest stumbling block. While it was acknowledged that an American partner was needed, the choice between Northwest and Delta created tension. KLM's stake in Northwest was greater than that of Swissair's in Delta but Northwest had been in the weaker financial position. It is perhaps ironic, though, that all four principal airlines involved in the alliance were loss-making. In spite of this the two key airlines concerned became entrenched in their respective positions rendering an agreement virtually impossible.

In addition to the problem of deciding upon an American partner, the actual mechanics of formulating an alliance were complicated. A number of issues had to be addressed including:

- how to unify four corporate cultures;
- how to form a single multinational management structure and flight network against the backdrop of a rigid bilateral institutional framework;
- where to locate the headquarters given a choice of six countries.

To answer some of these questions, approximately 17 committees were formed comprising representatives from each airline. In addition to focusing on technical matters, such as passenger and cargo systems and fleet maintenance, three of the committees worked on corporate and political matters including the equity issue.

Ultimately idealism gave way to realism. For example, the intention of forming a joint management company under which the four airlines preserved separate tax and corporate structures proved unacceptable due to EU and US anti-cartel regulations. Added to this was the unresolved problem of the American partner, and so the final death knell was rung. In November 1993 Alcazar failed, bequeathing more than a note of caution to other airlines blazing a similar trail.

Distribution

Like most major airlines Northwest distributes its products through both travel agents and its own airline offices although the predominant channel is the former. As seen in Chapters 7, 15 and 17 technology is playing an increasingly important part in the distribution of the travel product and among airlines CRSs have become crucial.

Northwest's involvement with CRSs lies with Worldspan, the marketing umbrella for three separate systems: Pars, Datas II and Abacus. Northwest bought into Pars, the TWA system, in 1986 so that it could compete with United Airlines and American Airlines and their respective systems Apollo and Sabre. This was necessary on both economic and competitive grounds as Northwest objected to paying its competitors for Northwest flights being booked on their systems. By buying into Pars it meant that not only did Northwest open up a channel whereby tickets for their flights could be booked but also it enabled them to generate revenue from tickets being booked on competitor's flights. In other words, it put Northwest on an equal footing with its competitors.

A further advantage relates to code-sharing. Northwest has code-sharing agreements with both KLM and its Airlink partners in the US. By using through-flight numbers, Northwest and its code-sharing partners benefit from a higher priority ranking in screen displays. The CRS will, however, stress a stopover or plane change en route thus placing the onus on the travel agency clerk to alert the consumer accordingly. Admittedly, this is a benefit to Northwest no matter which CRS is used, although a travel agent with a Worldspan system will be more inclined to book the Northwest/KLM flight. This is known as the 'halo' effect and it is a well recognized advantage of owning a CRS. Although difficult to quantify, the incremental revenue gained by this means was estimated by Robert Crandall, head of Northwest, to be 8–12% if a travel agent used the host system, with an equivalent loss if the travel agent used an alternative system. This exemplifies the importance of airlines encouraging travel agents to adopt their system over that of their competitors.

The benefits of owning a CRS extend to the RMS, the revenue or inventory management system, which analyses information provided by the CRS. Like other airlines, Northwest has a range of seat prices. Flights are monitored every other day according to how well seats are selling at given prices. Those selling less well at the higher price band may be released to a lower band and conversely those selling well at a cheaper band can be closed altogether. Management information originating from the CRS is crucial for Northwest's operational effectiveness.

Product branding

Northwest has three major brands: First, Executive and Economy. In Europe flights operated by Northwest comprise a two-class configuration of Executive and Economy due to the type of aircraft flown, namely DC10s. On 747s, a three-class configuration is maintained.

Northwest is a prime example of how airlines are responding to changes in the marketplace. Due to depressed loads stemming largely from the recession, demand for First Class in particular has subsided. Consequently, many airlines are either abandoning First Class altogether, such as KLM, or reducing the number of seats available. Northwest opted for the latter by reducing the number of first-class seats on their 747s from 18 to eight at the end of 1993. The space released from first class has been used to expand Business Class.

It is business class which generates the largest amount of revenue. Although Business Class usually only constitutes one-fifth of the aircraft, it generates two-thirds of the revenue if the seats are filled. As a result, it makes commercial sense to concentrate on this sector of this market, and it is for this reason alone that all major airlines, almost without exception, ardently woo the Business Class passenger. Product differentiation is the key and airlines go to great lengths to distinguish their business class product from that of their competitors. This is reflected in advertising expenditure. Northwest's emphasis is on seat pitch (leg room) which on services from Glasgow (these services were withdrawn on 25 October 1994) was said to be greater than on any other airline across the Atlantic.

The marketing of Northwest's Business Class product has been boosted by the introduction of a new international service with KLM called World Business Class. Introduced in February 1994, the new service offers enhanced amenities available on both KLM and Northwest (Table 19.2).

Frequent flyer programme

Although this has already been discussed in relation to Northwest's partnership with KLM, it is worth raising as a separate issue to highlight several points:

* Firstly, Northwest operates an FFP called World Perks. This is essential for Northwest's competitive position within the industry. Initially viewed as a competitive advantage in encouraging passenger loyalty to an airline, the emergence of so many schemes has made the FFP a standard feature of the industry and has resulted in airlines being competitively disadvantaged without one.
* Secondly, Northwest has a mileage reciprocity agreement with KLM and its FFP, the Flying Dutchman Programme. However, as previously stated, there is an imbalance between the two airlines in the spending of mileage accrued to the disadvantage of Northwest. Not only does this highlight the practical difficulties associated with

Table 19.2 World Business Class amenities

---

* Full size blankets plus custom-contoured pillows for neck support
* International selection of publications
* Amenity kit for every passenger
* Thank you mementos: a compact disc from a selection of six
* Menus developed by renowned chefs
* Meal services adapted to meet the needs of the business traveller, i.e. reduced length of meal service on night flights; mid-flight fare (availability of food throughout flight) on selected flights in the Pacific
* State-of-the-art passenger video entertainment systems installed at every seat offering video and audio entertainment, on-board shopping and video games.

---

alliances but more specifically it provides Northwest with the problem of contingent liability. Efforts to resolve this problem such that a level playing field emerges are a priority.

- Thirdly and finally is the future of FFPs. Given expiry dates of approximately three years, together with the liability issue, the future of FFPs in the longer term has to be questioned. Currently, this liability is not written into the balance sheets but if this situation were to change then an airline's profitability statement could alter radically. And if that were to happen a change in the structure of FFPs, if not their actual demise, would seem inevitable.

Code-sharing

Code-sharing is a major marketing weapon and has already been discussed both in Chapter 15 and in relation to Northwest's alliance with KLM. To recapitulate, code-sharing provides an airline with a better position in the screen displays of CRSs which translates into a greater number of its own flights being booked which in turn equates with increased revenue.

Apart from the main code-sharing agreements with KLM, Northwest also has agreements with niche/regional carriers in the US. These are called Airlink partners and they were brought on board from the mid-1980s onwards. They include Express Airlines, Alaskan Airlines, America West Airlines, Business Express, Mesaba Airlines, Big Sky Airlines of Montana and Fischer Brothers Aviation of Detroit. The marketing alliance with these feeder carriers extends beyond shared flight numbers to the actual livery of Northwest, although the operational responsibility of these airlines remains in their hands and not with Northwest. The development of these mutual feeder arrangements is intrinsically linked to the hub and spoke arrangement in the US.

Inter-sectoral linkages

It is not uncommon for airlines to diversify into other sectors of the industry. Buying into companies lower in the chain of distribution, namely travel agents and tour operators, is known as forward vertical integration. Northwest has not embraced integration on any great scale although in 1985 it purchased a tour operator – Mainline Travel Inc. (MLT) in Minnesota, including its affiliate Sun Country Airlines Inc. MLT operates charter flights using Northwest aircraft which form packages to Europe and the Far East aimed at the US market. In addition Northwest has links with other tour operators for the purposes of operating fly-drives in various countries.

TACTICAL MARKETING

The discussion so far has focused on strategic marketing. However, as outlined in Chapter 15 tactical marketing is also significant. To recapitulate, tactical marketing is concerned with short-term programmes to promote the airline. For Northwest, three cases can be presented.

Northwest and KLM's World Class international business service

Although this is part of a long-term strategy, the advertising campaign falls within the tactical 'heading' as it is focusing on the actual launch of a new service which by its nature is short term. The new service, which began in February 1994, was jointly promoted through a global advertising campaign using a variety of media. Markets targeted include the US, Canada, Europe, Africa, the Middle East, Latin America, Asia and Australia which are all markets served by either Northwest or KLM. The advertising was adapted to specific markets and presented in 12 languages. A combination of international and local media were used to support and reinforce the message. The campaign was themed on offering the business traveller greater comfort, choice and control. The slogan adopted was 'World Business Class service is so good you can sleep through it'.

Clydesdale/Northwest promotion

This is an example of a more local promotion based in Scotland. In 1992 Clydesdale, an electrical goods retailer, approached Northwest with an idea for a promotion whereby if the consumer purchased certain goods to a given value in Clydesdale they would be offered two tickets with Northwest for the price of one. The benefits to Northwest were:

• free advertising – Clydesdale spent a reputed £750 000 on advertising the promotion;
• the promotion generated incremental revenue for Northwest at off-peak periods albeit at lower yields.

The promotion ran from 1 November 1992 to 31 May 1993. In that period, 5000 seats were sold of which 2500 generated revenue. Overall, the promotion was viewed as a success such that it was repeated in 1994 prior to Clydesdale going into liquidation. The main drawback was that it ran at the same time as the Hoover débâcle which caused a certain amount of confusion among the general public thus detracting from the success of the Clydesdale promotion.

Boston Flyers Club

As a gateway city to the US and a hub of Northwest, the airline launched a club aimed primarily at the business traveller. Titled the Boston Flyers Club, it provides the business traveller with added benefits including free hotel upgrades at 19 of Boston's hotels, guaranteed tables at top Boston restaurants and free entrance to the best night clubs. Quarterly mailings provide updates on benefits available to club members.

The Club has been set up in conjunction with the Massachusetts Port

Authority, the Greater Boston Convention and Visitors Bureau and the Massachusetts Office of Travel and Tourism with membership free to every Northwest passenger travelling to and through Boston on a First, World Business Class or Full Economy fare ticket. As part of this membership travellers will receive a membership pack containing a leather personal organizer, individual membership card and member information. Colin Barette, Northwest's European Marketing Programme's manager, said:

> We want to show European travellers, particularly those on business, that Boston is not only a great commercial destination but also a fun place to enjoy. We will continue to offer members added benefits throughout their membership of the club. These benefits will extend to include vacation travel in Boston, Massachusetts and New England.

SUMMARY

Like most of the world's major airlines in the 1990s Northwest has suffered from depressed loads and financial losses. Yet from being on the brink of bankruptcy, the airline has managed to turn the situation around such that it is now producing healthy profits.

From a purely marketing perspective, Northwest has been innovative at both a strategic and tactical level as demonstrated by its alliance with KLM and the Clydesdale promotion. While the alliance with KLM is one of the longest established in the business and generally works well, there are numerous practical difficulties which are yet to be resolved.

Although the future success of Northwest cannot be guaranteed, the fact that the airline has proved itself capable of adapting to changing market conditions places it in a stronger position to meet the challenges ahead.

REVIEW QUESTIONS

1. What are the main components of the alliance between KLM and Northwest?
2. Which distribution channels has Northwest employed to sell its products?
3. What changes has Northwest introduced to its product branding?
4. What examples can be cited as evidence of tactical marketing?

Hotel marketing: marketing planning in the Canadian hotel industry

20

D. Anderson

The following case contains five parts as follows: a current overview of tourism and specifically the hotel industry in Canada; a property profile of two comparative Canadian hotels including their affiliations to a chain-owned and a franchise system; an account of their marketing planning process; a brief analysis of their distinct competitive advantages in marketing; and final conclusions with case questions.

INTRODUCTION

A tourism overview

Tourism generated Can $26 billion in total revenues for Canada in 1994. This amount represents approximately 5% of the country's gross domestic product. Tourism is a major employer responsible for an estimated 600 000 jobs and is the third largest foreign exchange earner. In the 1980s, high interest rates and a relatively strong Canadian dollar value depressed the Canadian economy and the ability of Canadian tourism to compete globally. With these circumstances prevailing throughout the latter part of the decade and the early 1990s, Canada's position as a major destination of international tourists increased volume wise, but as a percentage of worldwide market share of foreign tourist receipts it slipped from sixth place to twelfth. Tourism in Canada, like many countries, is dominated by the domestic market, equivalent to approximately 65% of total visitor revenue. Internationally, the proximity of the large US travel market has resulted in a 20% income share with the remaining 15% overseas visitors. The strongest growth over the past decade has been from offshore markets, particularly the United Kingdom, Germany, France and Japan, while US and domestic visitation has shown minimal 1–2% annual increase. Most tourism revenues in Canada are generated in the four key provinces of Ontario, Quebec, British Columbia and Alberta with visitors participating in one or more of Canada's four main tourist products of touring, adventure and recreation holiday, urban or resort destination vacations.

Outbound Canadian visitors continue to have a high propensity to travel with the national travel trade deficit reaching a peak of $8.2 billion in 1992. With the devaluation of the Canadian dollar over the past few years, the deficit has declined to a projected level of Can $6 billion for 1995. With the emergence of the new private-public marketing agency, the Canadian Tourism Commission, by mid-1995, replacing Tourism Canada, and with a tripling of the budget to Can $50 million by the federal government supplemented by a similar amount from private industry, a more focused and stronger promotional effort should exist in increasing international tourists to Canada. All indications show that tourism, as a major business sector in the country, will continue to grow in the twenty-first century.

The Canadian hotel industry

Between 1984 and 1990, the hotel industry in Canada experienced unprecedented growth in supply, much of it being driven by domestic and international demand for real estate. With the recession concluding in 1983, consumers and business began to spend more on travel and the accommodation sector enjoyed an overall rise in occupancy. The decline in demand, once again as a result of the 1989–1990 recession, commenced in late 1990 for most key hotel market areas in Canada. This most recent recession had a much more severe impact on the hotel industry, due in large part to the increased room supply over the 1980s. The majority of hotel rooms in Canada are concentrated in the seven urban centres of Vancouver, Calgary, Edmonton, Toronto, Ottawa, Montreal and Halifax. Between 1990 and 1992, occupancy rates fell by 8 to 10% in many of these locations. With a national average occupancy of 64% in 1990, this rate declined to an uneconomic level of 58% in both 1991 and 1992. The present economic recovery has been somewhat hesitant, but much of the industry is recovering with occupancies returning to the low 60s percentile range. Much of the supply base is now represented by new or upgraded properties, varying from limited service budget facilities to full service luxury hotels. Canada has a full range of one to five star accommodation types from downtown first-class hotels, roadside motels and highway motor hotels to resort lodges. Canada's hotel industry is in a relatively good position to take advantage of the new demand growth projected to occur in the last half of the 1990s.

PROPERTY PROFILE

The two hotels chosen for comparative purposes are the Palliser Hotel and the Village Park Inn, both located in Calgary, Alberta. The former is a

Canadian Pacific ⬛◀ Hotels & Resorts

MISSION STATEMENT

We will earn the loyalty of our guests by consistently exceeding their expectations for personal service and warm hospitality and by welcoming them in distinctive surroundings.

After more than 100 years of operation, Canadian Pacific Hotels and Resorts has become the largest hotel chain in Canada. The company owns or manages 26 properties with total number of rooms exceeding 11,000. Over the past decade, a renovation plan of over Can $600 million was undertaken and has made CP Hotels one of the largest restored collections of landmark, heritage hotels. The Palliser Hotel is one of these properties.

Corporate Head Office

Canadian Pacific Hotels Corporation, One University Avenue, Suite 1400, Toronto, Ontario, Canada, M5J 2P1

Figure 20.1 Mission statement, Canadian Pacific Hotels and Resorts.

Best Western International was founded in California, USA in 1946 and was the first lodging company to realize the advantages of the referral system, or as it is known today, chain operation.

Best Western is the largest individually owned and operated franchise chain in the world. It has over 3,300 inns, resorts and hotels in 48 countries and 1,230 cities. The Village Park Inn is one of Best Western's franchised properties.

Corporate Head Office

Best Western International, PO Box 10203, Phoenix, Arizona, USA, 850604-0203

Figure 20.2 Information, Best Western Worldwide Lodging.

wholly owned member of Canadian Pacific Hotels and Resorts chain (Figure 20.1) while the latter is an independently owned member of the Best Western franchise group (Figure 20.2).

The Palliser Hotel

The seven-floor Palliser was originally constructed in 1914 at a cost of Can $1.5 million with a further four-storey expansion in 1929. The hotel was named after Captain John Palliser, a renowned Western explorer and surveyor of the then British North America in the mid-1800s. Located in the urban central district, on 9th Avenue, and within close proximity to the Calgary Tower and the Calgary Convention Centre, the hotel has undergone extensive renovations over the years. The most recent between 1989 and 1993 was a Can $28 million restoration programme of all guest rooms, public areas and various function rooms. This full-service, corporate and convention hotel houses 406 guest rooms, 15 meeting rooms (20 000 square feet) and two food and beverage facilities. With over 80 years of operation, The Palliser has regained its 'grand hotel' status as Calgary's premier hostelry, and is a prime example of a Canadian Pacific heritage railroad property.

The Village Park Inn

The five-storey Village Park Inn was built in 1982, at the end of Alberta's energy boom, for approximately Can $4 million. Wholly owned by the De Gagne family, which have had over 30 years experience in the provincial hotel and motor hotel industry, the hotel attained a Best Western franchise at time of opening. Situated in the suburban northwest area of Calgary, it is specifically part of the Motel Village service centre which is adjacent to two major arterial roadways, the Crowchild Trail and the TransCanada Highway. The hotel also has a sister property in the south region of the city, the Hospitality Inn.

As a full-service motor hotel, it has 162 guest rooms, six meeting rooms (9000 square feet) and two food and beverage facilities. Operating for 14 years, the Village Park Inn is a well-run accommodation facility that has developed specialized market niches.

In summary, the two hotel properties have been contrasted as to location, size, amenities, length of operation, ownership and general style. Both are profitable establishments and have adapted well to satisfying their key customer market needs.

THE MARKETING PLANNING PROCESS

For hotels to survive in today's competitive environment, a systematic approach to the development of a business/marketing plan is a necessity to yield best results. Both subject Canadian properties have prepared written plans to guide in this respect.

The Palliser Hotel

The Palliser generated almost Can $19 million in revenue in 1993, with a marketing budget set at 5% of sales. The hotel achieved an overall occupancy of 66% and a Can $102 average room rate. Its visitor market mix as a percentage of room demand shows 43% corporate, 18% convention/meeting, 5% government, 16% leisure tourism, 11% tour group and 7% other sources. Similarly, guest origins indicate 75% Canadian (20% Alberta based), 15% US and 10% international. Of the almost Can $1 million spent on marketing, including related payroll, approximately 36% was allocated to entice corporate, 33% convention and 31% leisure tourist markets. Of additional interest, about 40% was expended on direct sales activities (which are growing in importance) along with public relations at 10%, and the remaining 32% and 18% on sales promotion and advertising respectively (the latter of which is decreasing).

The Palliser's annual business plan is compiled by the hotel general manager typically by late July or early August, and then approved by the president and board of CP Hotels later in the year. The plan includes elements on marketing, financial projections and variances, staffing and a capital plan. Approximating this same time frame, the hotel marketing plan is prepared by the director of sales and marketing and is available to the general manager for review by May or June. This plan contains sections on situation analysis, competitive property profiles, market segments and respective strategies, room rate analysis, key account reviews, sales/promotional activities action plan and staffing/organization.

The Village Park Inn

The Village Park Inn had approximately Can $6 million in revenue in 1993, with a marketing budget of 5.5% of sales. The motor hotel averaged an 80% annual occupancy rate and a Can $75 room rate. Its visitor market mix as a percentage of room demand shows 46% corporate, 8% meeting, 12% government, 21% leisure tourism and 13% other sources (predominantly sports groups in the off-season). Similarly, guest origins indicate 86% Canadian, 8% US and 6% international. Of the Can $330 000 spent on marketing, close to half is allocated to increase corporate/government, 12% meeting, 10% leisure and 30% to other tourist markets (sports groups). Of note, 50% is expended on direct sales activities, 10% public relations and the remaining 20% each on sales promotion and advertising.

The hotel's annual business plan is completed by the hotel general manager by the first quarter (fiscal year end being March 31) for local ownership approval. This plan provides sections on marketing, budgets/financial projections, organization/staffing and proposed capital improvements. The hotel marketing plan is prepared by the director of sales and is available to the general manager for review by January. It contains a situation analysis, current business assessment, key customer segments, competitive analysis, programme objectives and strategies and a sales/promotion action plan with measurements.

Hotel marketing comparisons

An evaluation of both hotel marketing planning processes and related plan information demonstrates key attributes as shown in Table 20.1.

In summary, the two hotel properties recognize the value of a business plan and, in particular, the marketing plan component. Acknowledging hotel guest needs through research and analysis assists each hotel in their overall performance within a more competitive marketplace.

COMPETITIVENESS IN MARKETING

Both hotel properties have developed solid competitive positions through the vigorous exercise of annual marketing planning as depicted in Table 20.2. They are indirect competitors (location and style notwithstanding) but share key advantages across their accommodation types.

In summary, the marketing planning process lends to the identification of key customer sales advantages and to the contribution of long-term competitiveness to hotels which seriously undertake it.

CONCLUSIONS

Some of the major challenges facing the hotel industry in Canada – and specifically in the area of marketing planning – as derived from the case

Table 20.1 Key attributes of hotel marketing planning process

- A comprehensive business plan and a separate marketing plan are prepared annually.
- Contents of both plans are similar between the two properties.
- Both plans are compiled by the general manager with direct assistance from the director of sales and marketing on the marketing plan.
- Plans are approved by owners and/or representative boards.
- Five per cent of revenue is typically spent on marketing and sales.
- More attention and budget are devoted to a qualified direct sales promotional programme and less generally on awareness advertising.
- Chain properties can 'buy in' to regional/national promotional campaigns which assist in brand marketing presence.
- Both hotels are largely dependent on corporate business with the city centre hotel also catering to conventions and the suburban hotel more to leisure tourism.
- Majority of hotel guests are domestic travellers with strong future growth in international tourists.
- Less capacity for food and beverage seating while more need for meeting space has occurred.

Table 20.2 Competitive positioning through marketing planning

The Palliser Hotel (chain)	The Village Park Inn (independent franchise)
• Unique downtown heritage hotel	• High quality suburban motor hotel
• Substantial marketing/ promotional impact	• Quick marketing opportunity responsiveness
• High product/service programme standards	• Close guest relationships
• Fully integrated GDS reservation system	• Franchise reservation system
• HQ advisory assistance	• Local ownership reporting
• Easier acceptance of capital improvement requests	• Low overhead costs with no HQ allocation
• Value pricing for more focused market segments	• Positive value/price perception

study are as follows: more focused marketing plans, including better competitive and market segmentation analyses; further emphasis on the implementation of yield management practices; broader acceptance of new technology, especially the global distribution system (GDS) and its implications for customer information and reservations; the use of database/personal marketing techniques; and the value and determination of return on investment (ROI) analysis as it applies to future market segments and promotional programmes.

REFERENCES

Economist Intelligence Unit (1991) Canada *International Tourism Reports*, No. 3.

Pannell Kerr Forster. (1993) *Trends in the Hotel Industry*, Canadian edition.

Powell, Ian. (1994) Personal interview with the General Manager, The Palliser Hotel, September.

Rheaume, Marc. (1994) Personal interview with the General Manager, The Village Park Inn, September.

REVIEW QUESTIONS

1. How does this case relate to the typical framework of hotel marketing planning?
2. Identify and discuss the differences in marketing planning between a downtown and a suburban hotel property.
3. Describe the advantages and disadvantages of preparing a marketing plan for an independent, non-franchised hotel in comparison to a chain property.

4. Are there any marked differences in hotel marketing planning among Canadian, American and European properties? Advise with examples.
5. Identify and explain briefly additional broad-based marketing challenges confronting the UK and European hotel industry.

Travel agency marketing: Thomas Cook, UK* 21

M.M. Bennett

INTRODUCTION

The main objective of this case study is to review the operations of a travel agent particularly in relation to the marketing issues presented in Chapter 7 on distribution and place. However, as the focus of this case study is Thomas Cook this exercise becomes rather more complicated. Given that Thomas Cook is a worldwide travel company with a variety of different travel interests/concerns, it is not altogether easy or, one could argue, wise to disentangle the travel agency part of the business from its other interests. Therefore in presenting this case study, all of Thomas Cook's activities will be reviewed to provide the context for understanding distribution via travel agency.

HISTORICAL DEVELOPMENT

The roots of Thomas Cook date back to 1841 when a 33-year-old printer on a journey from Market Harborough to Leicester to attend a temperance meeting considered how railways could aid the temperance cause. At the meeting he proposed a trip from Leicester to Loughborough which he subsequently organized at a cost of one shilling (per person). The date was 5 July 1841 and the printer's name was Thomas Cook.

With philanthropic zeal, Thomas Cook began running excursions in 1845 to Liverpool and North Wales. As well as planning the route, he printed a handbook and led the tour in person. A year later he introduced organized trips to Scotland and in 1851 escorted 165 000 people to the Great

* The author would like to acknowledge the following people from Thomas Cook who assisted with the production of this case study: Rhona Mennie, Senior Product Manager Own Label; Fiona Ferguson, Head of UK Retail Marketing; and Nicola Holgate, Public Relations Manager.

Exhibition at Crystal Palace. Four years on, trips to the Continent were introduced as were tours to the USA after the American Civil War. The year 1869 saw the first tour to Palestine and Egypt leading later to the development of luxury cruises for the Nile which became known as 'Cook's canal'. Then in 1872–73 Cook initiated the first round-the-world tour. By 1880 Thomas Cook had become a worldwide network of offices and services.

Two further events are significant in the development of Thomas Cook. In 1867 Cook introduced a hotel coupon system which depended upon the trust of hoteliers in Thomas Cook as it was used in lieu of payment for accommodation. As well as proving to be the foundation for a similar system still operational today, it also facilitated the introduction of the Circular Note in 1874 which was the first form of the traveller's cheque.

The early origins of Thomas Cook are still in evidence today. The name Thomas Cook has become an international brand of high repute. Today it has three core businesses: leisure travel, foreign exchange and traveller's cheques. Thomas Cook has the largest network of foreign exchange centres and is the world's largest supplier of traveller's cheques outside the US. The company has grown in size to approximately 2000 offices in more than 100 countries. In spite of such growth and the death of the founder in 1892, the company has maintained the original brand values and vision in its current operation. Indeed, in commemorating its 150 years, the company organized special trips mirroring in part the essence of the first tours.

Events of more recent importance include the integration of Thomas Cook into the Midland Bank Group in 1972. Twenty years later (1992) Midland Bank sold Thomas Cook to Westdeutsche Landesbank (90%) and the LTU Group (10%). In 1977 the current UK headquarters of Thomas Cook were established in Peterborough. Today the worldwide headquarters of Thomas Cook are based in London. Table 21.1 provides a list of key dates in the history of Thomas Cook.

THOMAS COOK OPERATIONS

Thomas Cook today is an organization of considerable size as Table 21.2 demonstrates. It is also a company which has proved to be highly successful. In 1993 the group made record profits achieving pre-tax profits of £31.6 million, a turnover of £595.6 million and gross sales of £15.8 billion. Set in the context of a worldwide recession such results are impressive. The company's mission is to be the best and most profitable travel-driven service business in the world. To this end, Thomas Cook is focusing upon:

- being customer driven;
- investing in staff development;
- continuously improving processes;
- improving profitability.

As an international travel service provider Thomas Cook provides a wide range of services. However, following a strategic review of the

Table 21.1   Thomas Cook – 150 years of history

1841	First excursion, Leicester to Loughborough.
1845	Trip to Liverpool with extensions to North Wales.
1846	Tours to Scotland begin.
1851	Cook takes 165 000 people to the Great Exhibition.
1855	First continental tours.
1863	Beginning of tours to Switzerland.
1865	Thomas Cook opens London office.
1866	First tours to North America.
1869	First tours to Holy Land and Egypt.
1872	Thomas Cook pioneers round-the-world tours.
1874	Traveller's cheques launched under the name of Circular Notes. Publication of Thomas Cook Timetable begins.
1884	Thomas Cook provides transport for the General Gordon relief expedition.
1887	Thomas Cook arranges pilgrimages for Indian Moslems and transports maharajahs to Queen Victoria's Golden Jubilee.
1892	Thomas Cook dies.
1898	John Mason Cook, Thomas's son, arranges tour to Jerusalem for the German Kaiser and his court.
1902	First winter sports brochures. First motor car tours.
1919	Thomas Cook advertises air tours.
1927	First air charter, New York–Chicago, for Dempsey–Tunney fight.
1939	First package tour to South of France.
1940	Thomas Cook involved in evacuation of children and handling enemy mail.
1959	First meeting of the British Guild of Travel Writers held in Berkeley Street, London office.
1966	First real-time automated holiday reservation system installed.
1972	Thomas Cook becomes part of Midland Bank Group.
1974	Thomas Cook 24-hour money back guarantee launched.
1977	Princess Alexandra opens Thomas Cook's new headquarters in Peterborough.
1980	The Travel Information Bank is automated.
1981	Thomas Cook reaches agreement with European banks to launch Euro traveller's cheque.
1983	Thomas Cook joins the Mastercard traveller's cheque programme.
1985	The ECU traveller's cheque is launched.
1988	Thomas Cook Holidays cease operating in short-haul market.
1989	£36 million invested in a three-year project to transform all Thomas Cook shops into superstores.
1990	Installation of CRS back-office automation system. Development of worldwide office network begins.
1991	Thomas Cook celebrates its 150th anniversary. To commemorate this occasion, a round-the-world trip taking in seven wonders of the world.
1992	Thomas Cook is sold by Midland Bank to Westdeutsche Landesbank (WestLB) and the LTU Group.
1994	Thomas Cook acquires Interpayment Services, the traveller's cheque subsidiary of Barclays Bank plc, to make Thomas Cook the largest supplier of Mastercard and Visa traveller's cheques in the world.
1994	Thomas Cook sells its corporate travel management business and USA franchised travel offices to American Express.

Table 21.2   Thomas Cook: facts and figures*

Thomas Cook comprises:

- 385 retail shops;
- 150 foreign exchange bureaux de change;
- 7500 staff in the UK and Ireland;
- over 10 000 staff worldwide;
- over 2000 offices worldwide in over 100 countries;
- over 1200 staff in the Peterborough head offices.

* These figures were compiled prior to the sale of Thomas Cook Travel Management.

company's operations in 1994 it was decided that the focus of the company in the future should be leisure travel, foreign exchange and traveller's cheques. Indeed, in 1993 leisure travel accounted for over 50% of Thomas Cook's revenue. As a result, Thomas Cook Travel Management (TCTM) which offered a business travel service was sold to American Express in September 1994 for $375 million. This was a significant move which attracted considerable media coverage and which underlines the very different nature of business and leisure travel.

The Thomas Cook strategy as of September 1994 encompasses the following:

- **Leisure travel:** to expand methods of leisure travel distribution in key worldwide markets and to exercise greater control over the products distributed to customers. Thomas Cook's investment in Thomas Cook Direct, its expansion of the UK retail branch network and the acquisition of leisure travel companies Auto-Fischer and Paco-Reisen in Germany are testimony to this.
- **Foreign exchange (FEX):** to develop Thomas Cook's FEX network in key travel markets and to increase its presence at international gateways. In June 1994 Thomas Cook doubled its FEX network in France by acquiring a major retail FEX operation.
- **Traveller's cheques:** to continue to be a major player in the international traveller's cheques market with the highest standards of customer service and lowest processing costs. In August 1994 Thomas Cook announced its acquisition of Interpayment Services Ltd, the Barclays Bank traveller's cheque subsidiary, making Thomas Cook the world's largest supplier of Mastercard and Visa traveller's cheques and increasing its share of the Thomas Cook market from 17 to 30%. After a preliminary investigation by the Office of Fair Trading, the decision was taken not to refer the sale to the Monopolies and Mergers Commission. The sale was completed on 24 November 1995.

In terms of actual services offered, Thomas Cook provides the following:

- Thomas Cook (TC) travel shops;
- TC Holidays (own brand);
- TC Holidays (own label);

- TC financial institution services;
- TC travel archive;
- TC travel clinic;
- TC Direct;
- TC publications;
- TC performance;
- Flightsavers;
- national hotel desk;
- airport services;
- business centres;
- long-haul leisure rail;
- passports and visas.

In the course of this case study several of these services will be looked at in greater detail.

RETAILING

Although the origins of Thomas Cook lie in tour operation, today Thomas Cook is most commonly associated with retailing. At the time of writing (November 1994) Thomas Cook had 385 shops located throughout the UK. In 1989 Thomas Cook introduced its 'Superstore' concept which consisted of four stores or services within each shop. These comprise:

- **travel centre:** a range of package holidays and cross Channel ferry tickets are provided;
- **flight centre:** a range of charter and schedule air fares are offered;
- **bureau de change:** foreign currencies in traveller's cheques are available on demand in addition to a rapid money transmission service, currency drafts and telegraphic transfers;
- **world travel service by appointment:** this service caters for individual tailor-made holidays by offering one-to-one private consultation with 'highly trained consultants in classically designed private travel lounges'.

The division of each store into four distinct operations is a reflection of the different types of service required by consumers. It is customer focused and helps to overcome the problem of a customer wanting to organize a round-the-world trip standing in a queue behind someone wanting to book a charter flight to Palma.

PRODUCTS

Thomas Cook further differentiates itself from the competition on the basis of the products it offers. Unlike other companies that have acquired travel agents for the sale of its products, Thomas Cook has remained rather unique in offering Thomas Cook Holidays through Thomas Cook shops. This policy can be traced back to the origins of Thomas Cook and the emergence of tours. What is significant is that Thomas Cook has actively developed the brand name of Thomas Cook and has made it exclusive by only permitting the sale of its products through its own outlets. As the brand has become synonymous with quality so its appeal has endured.

Thomas Cook Holidays can be distinguished according to own-brand and own-label brochures. Thomas Cook Holidays **own-brand** consists of ten brochures specializing in long-haul holidays. These holidays are principally organized by Thomas Cook in its capacity as tour operator although outside tour operators are not totally excluded (see Table 21.3). Incorporated within the Faraway collection is the 'Cook's Tours' programme which reflects the origins of the company when Cook led tours around the globe.

Thomas Cook holidays **own-label** differs from own-brand in that it involves other tour operators in the industry. Selected operators in specific market sectors are chosen on the basis of product and customer care. The products are branded as Thomas Cook Holidays and the synergy between the respective brands must be close. In this sense, the operator is the manufacturer and Thomas Cook is the retailer. This method has been well practised in other forms of retailing, most notably by Marks and Spencer, Boots and major supermarket chains. Own-label holidays was set up in 1988 and mostly focuses on the short-haul and specialist markets although the US is included. A list of the brochures offered and the operators involved are shown in Table 21.4.

Thomas Cook therefore has an advantage over other retailers in that it is able to sell not only its own products but also those of other operators under the Thomas Cook name so strengthening the brand further.

Table 21.3 Thomas Cook Holidays (TCH) – own brand 1994

Brochure	Operator
Worldwide Faraway Collection (incorporating) Tours Worldwide)	TCH
China and Beyond	Jules Verne
Tauck Tours	Tauck Tours with TCH
Cook's Tours Canada and USA	TCH
Egypt	TCH
AustraliaJetabout with	TCH
New Zealand	Jetabout with TCH
Australia and New Zealand Flights and Fares	TCH
South Africa for the Independent Traveller	TCH
Canada for the Independent Traveller	TCH

Table 21.4   Thomas Cook Holidays – own label 1994/1995

Brochure	Operator
UK Short Breaks and Airport Hotels	Superbreak
Paris and Amsterdam; Cities	Travelscene
Premier Collection – Winter	Sovereign
Premier Collection – Summer	
Winter Flights	Falcon
Summer Flights	
Villas Premier Collection	Meon
Florida	BA Holidays
France – Camping and Mobile Homes	Sunsites
European Escorted Journeys	Insight International
America Fly-Drive	American Holidays
Jersey and Guernsey	Premier Holidays
UK Airport Parking	BCP
France – Hotels and Apartments	Cresta
Wintersun and W'sun Price Busters	Enterprise
Ski	Enterprise
Club Med Choice	Club Med
Summersun and S'sun Price Busters	First Choice
Disneyland Paris	Paris Travel Service
Holiday Car Hire	Hertz

DISTRIBUTION/PLACE

As a major travel company Thomas Cook has been a leading light among retailers in experimenting with ways to distribute their products into the marketplace. In addition to having 385 retail shops located throughout Britain, Thomas Cook also operates a telephone holiday booking service known as Thomas Cook Direct. Set up in 1989 with four telephone lines and four members of staff, it has grown in five years to more than 150 telephone lines and 150 employees. The rationale for the introduction of the service is the convenience and flexibility offered to the consumer enabling calls to be made Monday to Saturday from home or work. The service offers information or bookings using a credit/switch card on holidays, cruises, flights, hotels, car hire and independent travel.

A second and more recent key development is that of a 'Travel kiosk' which utilizes state of the art multi-media technology to provide consumers with travel information, electronic holiday brochures (using video, still images and sound) and the opportunity to make a booking. If the latter is activated, a Thomas Cook sales representative will appear on screen as a live image who will talk the consumer through the process. On completion of a transaction, the consumer is requested to insert a credit card into the terminal. A printed receipt and booking confirmation is then issued. The kiosk is a self-service system which was piloted in the Thomas Cook Marble Arch shop between May and September 1994. It is viewed by Thomas Cook as a complementary distribution channel which will extend the range available to the consumer and not one which will replace the travel agent. As Tony Bennett, Strategic Marketing and Development Director, Europe, states:

> Over the next decade, we firmly believe that the majority of consumers will continue to book their holidays face to face or by telephone . . . However, we recognize that we can only hope to stay at the forefront of the travel industry by developing new products and services which give customers complete flexibility and convenience. Therefore we have developed the 'Travel Kiosk' in line with our strategy of giving first-class customer service and staying one step ahead of our competitors.

In January 1995 Thomas Cook announced that it would be extending the trial to five locations in London, three of which will be at branches of the National Westminster Bank, the other two being at travel agency locations. The latter will broaden the service beyond Thomas Cook sites highlighting the potential of this development to extend considerably in the not too distant future. Incorporated within the trial are Cook's Own Label Flights, City Breaks, Disneyland Paris, Summer Sun, late availability sales and a brochure ordering facility.

A third and final development in distribution is Thomas Cook's involvement with British Telecom's home shopping trial through which Thomas Cook will sell travel services via television and telephone. These services will include a range of winter and summer holiday packages, City Breaks, Disneyland Paris, flights, foreign exchange and a range of guidebooks and destination videos. Bookings can be made by phone. Tony Bennett, Strategic Marketing and Development Director, Europe, states:

> Although interactive TV is very much at the research stage, it may well lead to the biggest change to people's lifestyles since the introduction of television. One of the major benefits will be a massive improvement in the quality of information available to assist in the choice of holiday and the creation of an additional, highly convenient method of booking.

The British Telecom scheme, which will incorporate a selection of other services including home banking, shopping, movies and information, will be tested from mid-1995 in 2500 households in East Anglia.

All three developments outlined are evidence of a move towards home shopping. While only the kiosk is representative of technological innovation, all three point to a shift, albeit a gradual and incomplete one, in consumer attitudes. The fact that consumers are willing to access information and make bookings without face-to-face contact reveals an increasing confidence on their part and is a reflection of a commensurate rise in familiarity with travel. It is a trend which is set to continue which can only lead to more developments of this type. Their potential to infiltrate the marketplace longer term remains unknown.

PROMOTION AND PRICE

As a long-established major travel company, Thomas Cook's marketing strategy is well developed. This is reflected in the range of media used to promote the company, including national press, television, radio, cinema, posters and point-of-sale material within Thomas Cook shops, and the way in which the marketing functions are organized. The marketing strategy is based on a three to five year rolling strategic plan with marketing programmes developed to meet strategic objectives. The current strategy is to promote Thomas Cook as a price relevant and price aware retailer of holiday products. The route chosen to achieve this objective has been through price discounting.

Thomas Cook uses the Bainsfair, Sharkey, Trott advertising agency to produce their above-the line material. The company also uses a media specialist Booth Lockitt Martin (BLM) to select and purchase advertising space. Thomas Cook works with these two companies as a team to formulate long-term marketing strategies and to execute campaigns. In addition, all point-of-sale is produced by Promotional Campaigns Ltd. These promotions can be both product specific and broad based. Joint promotions may also be undertaken with other tour operators. Reflecting the different nature of direct marketing, Thomas Cook uses a separate agency, Barraclough Hall Woolston Gray. A database of previous customers is maintained which forms the basic tool for targeting specific customers with specific product promotions.

National advertising campaigns are marketed in several different ways involving press, television, point-of-sale (mainly posters), sponsorship, direct marketing and radio. As a major travel company, Thomas Cook has made extensive use of television and press. In the frenzy of discounting which accompanied the new brochure launches in August 1994, Thomas Cook relied heavily on the national press and television to promote the discounts on offer. Up to 15% discount was available on selected summer 1995 brochures in August while up to 30% discount was offered on selected summer cruises. A selection of the advertisements used at this time can be seen in Figure 21.1. What is significant is that the discounts are selective in the operators available; not surprisingly Thomas Cook Holidays is on offer while Thomsons, although not advertised, was discounted at 5%. This is linked to the issue of vertical integration in that discriminatory discounting has reflected tour operator/travel agency alignments resulting in heavy directional selling. This was in evidence among the top travel agents in the summer 1995 product launches. Rhona Mennie, Senior Product Manager, states:

> The way the market is going is all about vertical integration . . . What we are seeing particularly in August this year with the summer '95 product launches is vertical integration being mirrored in high street marketing campaigns . . . I imagine that will continue to be the trend – that the retailer and tour operator will become more and more aligned to selling their own products.

Figure 21.1   Selection of Thomas Cook advertisements to promote discounts.
Various sources. Reproduced with permission courtesy of Thomas Cook, UK.

Figure 21.1 *(continued)*

Figure 21.1 *(continued)*

Figure 21.1 *(continued)*

Furthermore, as with discounts offered by any tour operator, the offers are subject to the retailer's insurance being taken out. This is linked to the level of commission which at 30–40% helps to fund such discounts.

Significant too is the price guarantee in the small print on some of the advertisements. One advertisement states: 'Should you find exactly the same winter holiday, cruise or brochured flight, with the same operator, from another ABTA high street travel agent for less within 48 hours of booking, we will match the lower price.' This is a reflection of a shift in price consciousness on the part of Thomas Cook. In the past Thomas Cook gained a reputation for offering quality products with high prices attached. In an attempt to broaden its appeal Thomas Cook has focused its marketing on price to show that it is price competitive and affordable. The theme of the advertisements endorse this further by the adoption of the slogan 'Take a Thomas Cook at that' and variations on it which actively draw attention to the discounts on offer. Fiona Ferguson, Head of UK Retail Marketing, states,

> We're repositioning the brand to make it more of a place where people want to shop rather than them thinking Thomas Cook's not for me, it's boring, staid or too expensive. So we're having to do alot of work to promote price to make up for 150 years of heritage that doesn't mention it.

All of the advertisements also promote ways in which the offers can be taken up highlighting the Thomas Cook shops and significantly the Direct Booking Service. So in other words the advertisements not only promote the discounts but also the Thomas Cook Direct service.

An area requiring promotion was that of foreign exchange (FEX). Up until 1992 FEX was not promoted as it was assumed that people would use it. Customer research showed that this was not necessarily the case. The research revealed that consumers did not think about FEX until they purchased other items for the holiday. The window for promoting FEX was therefore seen to be 7–10 days before departure. The marketing strategy adopted was three-pronged:

- The database of Thomas Cook customers was used to target market them two weeks before departure with a mailshot on FEX offering a free roll of photographic film.
- The same offer was used in the national press. The advertisement was shaped in the form of a roll of film which acted as a coupon for the customer to take into a Thomas Cook shop and exchange for a film (see Figure 21.2). This provided an additional set of names and addresses to add to the database.
- The promotion was backed by an awareness building television campaign.

The benefit of being vertically integrated means that the marketing department is able to assess the number of consumers booking own-label/brand holidays who purchase FEX as well as those who buy FEX but do not book their travel through Thomas Cook. In this way a cross-sell ratio

Figure 21.2 Promotional advertisement of Thomas Cook's foreign exchange services. Reproduced with permission courtesy of Thomas Cook, UK.

is generated which provides additional information for engineering the marketing strategy.

Promotional activity is determined a year in advance and is planned on the basis of product area, i.e. long haul, cruise, etc. Budgets which vary from year to year in accordance with the business strategy are allocated to each product area.

All campaigns undertaken by Thomas Cook are monitored to determine their effectiveness in achieving the original objectives set. The advertising tracking monitor mentioned above is one such example. Specific promotions such as two for one offers or discounts are monitored to assess uptake. What is more difficult to evaluate is the effectiveness of individual media where more than one medium has been used in a promotion such as in the case of simultaneous television and press campaigns. In these situations sales figures are monitored on a weekly basis.

Market research is conducted both internally by a team of four people at head office and by outside agencies. Four activities are undertaken on a regular basis:

- Twice a year research is carried out at selected Thomas Cook shops asking customers upon departure what they purchased, why they chose Thomas Cook and what they thought about the service received. Among other things this allows for transaction values to be gauged.
- Advertising is tracked on a monthly basis. Every week 80 interviews are conducted with consumers (including those that use Thomas Cook and those that do not) to assess awareness of Thomas Cook's advertising.
- Customer service questionnaires are placed in every shop.
- Thomas Cook participates in omnibus surveys adding questions to other organizations' research.

VERTICAL INTEGRATION

Vertical integration has become a common feature of the UK travel industry. Major travel companies have vertically integrated to ensure an outlet for the sale of their products. This helps to overcome the problem of brand loyalty among travel agents and ensures that flights can be organized to transport passengers to their destination as part of a package.

As Thomas Cook is both a retailer and a tour operator it has not had the same need to affiliate itself with another retailer as it already has an avenue for the sale of its products. Through its own organic growth it has become forwardly integrated.

In 1992 Thomas Cook took a 21.6% shareholding in First Choice at a time when Owners Abroad, as it was then known, was facing a takeover bid from its rival Airtours. The strategic alliance formed with Owners Abroad provided Thomas Cook with a link to a tour operator which was useful for the Own Label division as well as providing it with access to Air

2000, the airline owned by First Choice. It should be emphasized that the link with First Choice is viewed as an alliance and as such differentiates Thomas Cook from other major companies where vertical integration involves total ownership.

CUSTOMER SERVICE

Earlier it was stated that Thomas Cook's mission is to be the best and most profitable travel driven service business in the world. One priority in achieving this goal is to be customer driven. Indeed the group's philosophy is that the customer comes first and as result all company policies are formulated with customer service in mind. Indeed Chief Executive Christopher Rodrigues states in the 1993 Annual Report: 'Only if we can transform Thomas Cook into a dynamic, customer-driven organization will we be fit to survive in the 21st Century.' Certainly Thomas Cook has developed a reputation for providing quality in both products and service. Undoubtedly this has been a key factor in the group's enduring success.

Thomas Cook's commitment to customer service is evidently company wide and this is reflected at the operational level. In retailing, for example, Thomas Cook has developed a customer service questionnaire which is available at all branch shops. The questionnaire asks about the service the customer received at the branch using a Likert scale to record the answers. Space is also provided for the customer to write additional comments. Using the business reply service the completed questionnaire can then be sent to the Peterborough offices where the information is fed into a database and analysed. Through this form of market research Thomas Cook is able to monitor the service it provides in its shops and take steps to improve or alter it accordingly. A copy of the six-panel questionnaire is shown in Figure 21.3.

SUMMARY

As an international travel company, Thomas Cook is involved in a variety of different travel services although its historical roots originate in tour operation. In focusing on the retailing division it is necessary to appreciate the full extent of Thomas Cook's operations as these provide the context within which retailing operates. It helps to explain, for example, why Thomas Cook is not fully vertically integrated given the inherent advantages of having an in-house tour operation. Furthermore, the Thomas Cook name is strengthened by operating own-label brochures and by only distributing them and own-brand holidays through their own shops. By concentrating on quality both in service and products, the brand name has endured.

As a retailer Thomas Cook has proved innovative in experimenting with new channels of distribution and harnessing new technology. It has also

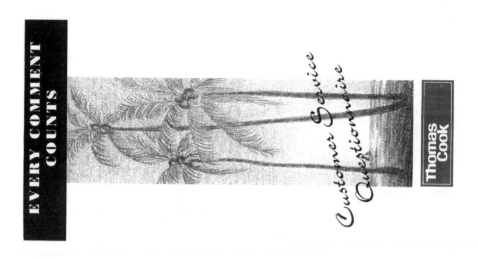

EVERY COMMENT COUNTS

Customer Service Questionnaire

Thomas Cook

Business Reply Service
Licence No PE30

The Thomas Cook Group Ltd
Customer Service Department
PO Box 36
PETERBOROUGH
PE3 6BR

Postage
will be paid
by licence

Do not affix Postage Stamps if posted in
Gt Britain, Channel Islands, N Ireland
or the Isle of Man

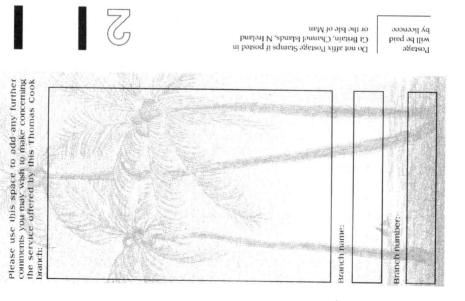

Please use this space to add any further comments you may wish to make concerning the service offered by this Thomas Cook branch:

Branch name:

Branch number:

Figure 21.3   Thomas Cook: customer service questionnaire.
Reproduced with permission courtesy of Thomas Cook, UK.

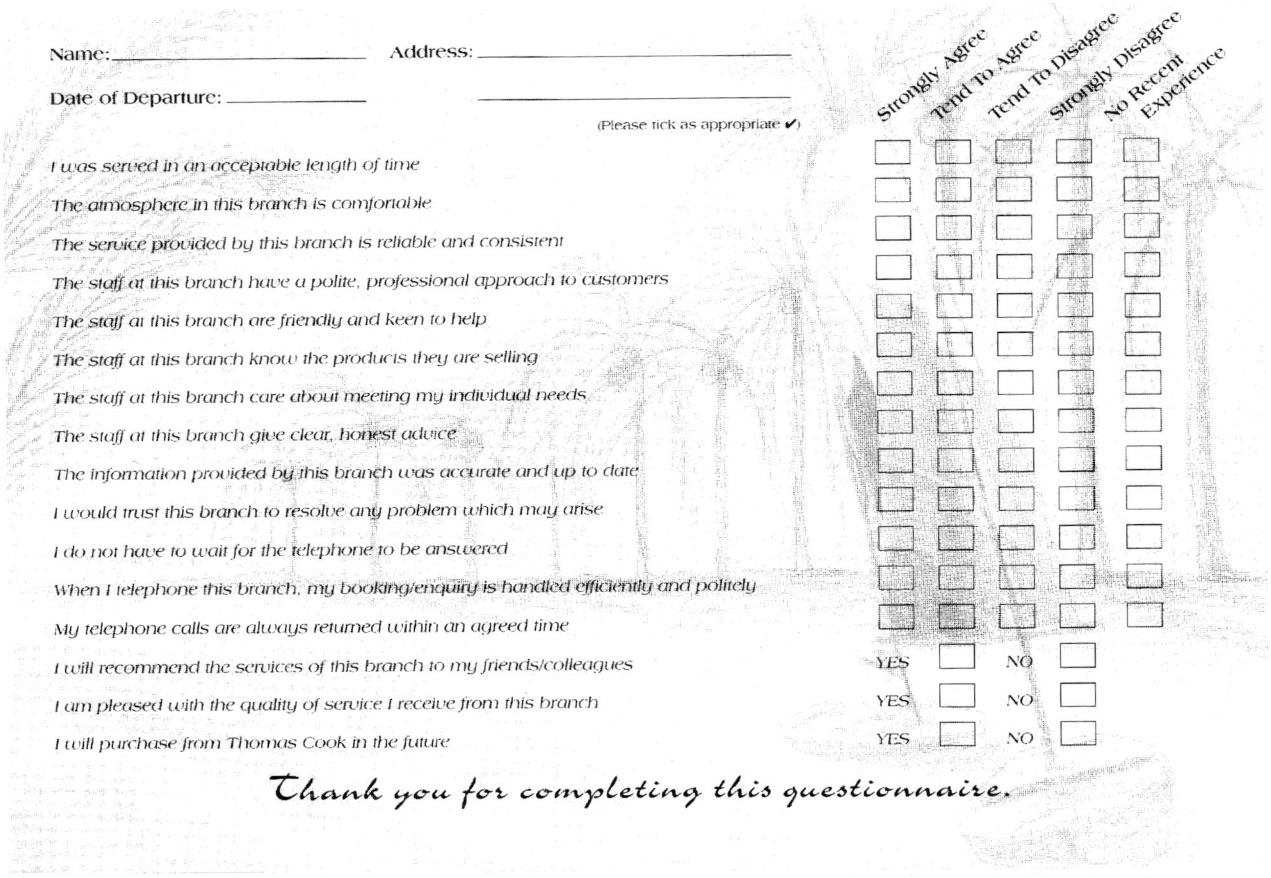

Name: __________ Address: __________

Date of Departure: __________ __________

(Please tick as appropriate ✔)

	Strongly Agree	Tend To Agree	Tend To Disagree	Strongly Disagree	No Recent Experience
I was served in an acceptable length of time	☐	☐	☐	☐	☐
The atmosphere in this branch is comfortable	☐	☐	☐	☐	☐
The service provided by this branch is reliable and consistent	☐	☐	☐	☐	☐
The staff at this branch have a polite, professional approach to customers	☐	☐	☐	☐	☐
The staff at this branch are friendly and keen to help	☐	☐	☐	☐	☐
The staff at this branch know the products they are selling	☐	☐	☐	☐	☐
The staff at this branch care about meeting my individual needs	☐	☐	☐	☐	☐
The staff at this branch give clear, honest advice	☐	☐	☐	☐	☐
The information provided by this branch was accurate and up to date	☐	☐	☐	☐	☐
I would trust this branch to resolve any problem which may arise	☐	☐	☐	☐	☐
I do not have to wait for the telephone to be answered	☐	☐	☐	☐	☐
When I telephone this branch, my booking/enquiry is handled efficiently and politely	☐	☐	☐	☐	☐
My telephone calls are always returned within an agreed time	☐	☐	☐	☐	☐
I will recommend the services of this branch to my friends/colleagues	YES	☐	NO	☐	
I am pleased with the quality of service I receive from this branch	YES	☐	NO	☐	
I will purchase from Thomas Cook in the future	YES	☐	NO	☐	

Thank you for completing this questionnaire.

Figure 21.3 *(continued)*

broadened its market appeal by becoming price sensitive. This is reflected in its approach to marketing which is conducted at national and local levels and employs a wide range of media.

Thomas Cook has proved itself to be forward thinking and proactive in its approach as the sale of Thomas Cook Travel Management to American Express testifies. With a clear strategy for further development and healthy profits being made Thomas Cook is able to face the future with confidence.

REVIEW QUESTIONS

1. Which operations are Thomas Cook involved in?
2. How does 'own brand' differ from 'own label'?
3. Which distribution channels does Thomas Cook employ?
4. Which promotional tools has Thomas Cook employed?
5. Is Thomas Cook a vertically integrated company?

Tour operator marketing: Direct Holidays, UK*

22

M.M. Bennett

INTRODUCTION

The purpose of this case study is to review the operations of a tour operator to illustrate the issues presented in the chapter on distribution and place. As it is common to find case studies on the large mainstream tour operators and as a case study on Thomas Cook is presented in this part, a decision was taken to focus on an independent tour operator. Direct Holidays was selected as it is a young vibrant company which is growing fast. And unlike many other travel companies it is not affiliated to any other companies. Significantly, as its title suggests, it does not use the travel agent for selling its products therefore making it an interesting company upon which to base a case study.

HISTORICAL DEVELOPMENT

Direct Holidays was launched on 24 September 1991 making it Scotland's first independent direct sell company. The company, based in Glasgow but with its head office in London, was founded by John and Hugh Boyle and Paul Chestnutt. John Boyle formed Falcon Leisure in 1975 and played a key role in the development of Owners Abroad, including taking charge of Air 2000. Interestingly, he successfully challenged the government over Prestwick airport's monopoly as the transatlantic gateway which led to an 'open skies' policy in relation to Glasgow airport. Hugh Boyle was also on the board of Owners Abroad responsible for the direct sell operation which encompassed Martin Rooks, Tjaereborg and Sunfare. The brothers left Owners Abroad following a dispute over the direct sell operation.

The decision to set up a direct sell operation was based on a combination

---

* The author would like to acknowledge Robin Parry, Marketing Manager at Direct Holidays, for his assistance in the preparation of this case study.

of the brothers' knowledge of direct sell, competition in the marketplace and more favourable start-up costs. In setting up Direct Holidays £1 million was invested by the founder John Boyle with further backing from the Royal Bank of Scotland. Indeed in August 1994, the Royal Bank of Scotland purchased 22% of Direct Holidays. The first year of operation was summer 1992. Today, with an annual quota of 30 000 package holidays in Scotland, Direct Holidays has 12% market share in Scotland. It plans to increase the number of holidays to 50 000 from the four Scottish airports and thereby achieve a target of 15%. Turnover figures since operations began show considerable growth year on year (see Table 22.1). Direct Holidays has concentrated on Scotland because of the perceived gap in the market in that there is a strong ITC client base but a more limited choice of holidays from Scottish airports. Hugh and John Boyle are also Glaswegian by origin and are therefore familiar with the Scottish market. Boyle states:

> The Scottish market has an extraordinary advantage in that it is not diluted by people who pack up their suitcases in their cars and take the ferry across the Channel. When Scots go abroad they fly; it has been a unique combination of media, homogeneity and effectiveness which combine to make a very attractive marketing package.
>
> (*Marketing Week* 10 October 1991)

The principal sales office is located in Glasgow providing telephone sales and acting as a reservation centre for members of the public. Direct Holidays is a member of ABTA and is licensed by the CAA.

COMPETITION

The competition is viewed to be the mass market tour operators, in particular Thomson, Airtours and First Choice. Both Thomson and Owners Abroad have direct sell divisions represented by Portland Holidays and Eclipse Direct respectively. Eclipse Direct subsumes the previously separate brands of Martin Rooks, Tjaereborg and Sunfare, with the latter catering only for Scotland. Analysis of a question on the customer service questionnaire asking which other holiday companies' clients have travelled

Table 22.1 Direct Holidays: Turnover

Year	£ million (year end 31 October)
1992	9.3
1993	11.5
1994	17.5*
1995	25**

*Estimate.
**Projected.

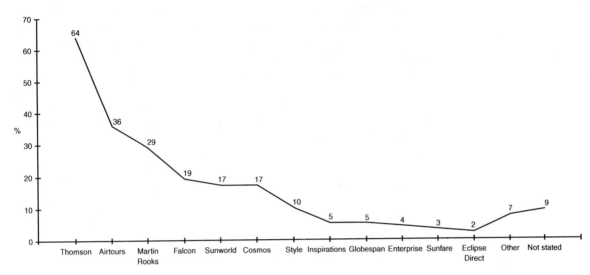

Fig. 22.1 Direct Holidays: competition – travels with other holiday companies 1989–94.

with in the last five years showed that by far the biggest competitor is Thomsons (64%) followed by Airtours (36%) and Martin Rooks (29%) (see Figure 22.1). Competition to Direct Holidays is set to increase with Portland Holidays' planned expansion into the Scottish market. From a positive perspective this will raise general awareness among the public of buying direct.

PRODUCTS

Direct Holidays produces four brochures: Direct Holidays, Direct Greece, Direct Holidays – Private villas with pools and Direct Flights. They differ in the market they each serve and the airports from which they operate. Further information on each product can be found in Table 22.2. Direct Holidays' mass market brochure constitutes the core product with 72% of sales and it is upon this that the case study material is largely based.

It is interesting to note that in terms of departure airports used, Glasgow and Prestwick are both offered although Prestwick has only been offered since 1994. This is particularly significant given John Boyle's role in opening up Glasgow and the current rejuvenation of Prestwick airport. As an incentive for tour operators to operate from Prestwick, the airport's owners offered a £15 discount, free marketing support and free rail travel within Scotland. Further advantages included a guaranteed ten minute check-in and the cheapest duty free in Scotland. As a result, in Direct Holidays' first year of operation from Prestwick it achieved a 50:50 ratio of holidays departing from Glasgow and Prestwick. The addition of Edinburgh and Aberdeen to the summer 1995 brochure is a new venture. Although Direct Holidays has principally operated out of Scotland, the

Table 22.2 Direct Holidays: product range 1995

Brochure	Market	Year began Trading	Season	Departure airport
Direct Holidays	Mass market	1992	Summer/Winter	Glasgow, Prestwick *, Aberdeen,** Edinburgh,** Liverpool**
Direct Holidays Private Villas with pools	Villas upmarket	1995	Summer	All airports offered in other brochures
Direct Greece	Holidays for more select travellers	1992***	Summer	Gatwick, Manchester
Direct Flights	Seat only	1992	Year round	All airports offered in other brochures

*Began 1994.
**To begin in 1995.
***Originated as Jenny May Holidays.

company's success is such that it is expanding into Liverpool. In September 1994 it was announced that Direct Holidays would be operating a programme out of Liverpool airport from summer 1995. With an investment of £7 million the plan is to run 250 flights from Liverpool to the main holiday destinations which include Majorca, Minorca, Tenerife, Lanzarote, Gran Canaria, Costa Dorada, Costa Blanca, Algarve and Turkey. A separate brochure will be produced similar in design to the Scottish brochure but with phone numbers and price panels relating to Liverpool.

The Direct Holidays brochure is a mass market product and as such serves the popular Mediterranean resorts as well as some further afield. For a list of destinations served see Table 22.3. The table highlights an expansion in the range of destinations offered in summer 1995 which include Zante, Cyprus, Salou and the Bahamas. In terms of sales, figures for the period April to October 1994 revealed Palma (17%), Faro (16%) and Las Palmas (11.7%) as the biggest selling destinations. In total for the same period 35 093 holidays were sold from the Direct Holidays brochure.

PLACE

It is no secret that commission rates paid to travel agents for the sale of inclusive tours are usually about 10%. Given that this is a significant sum which reduces the tour operator's potential revenue, it is not surprising that direct selling is an attractive alternative option.

Since the start of its operations, Direct Holidays has traded as a direct sell company. It differs from mainstream tour operators like Thomson who trade both direct and via the travel agency network by trading exclusively

Table 22.3 Direct Holidays: destinations 1995

Islands	Mainland
Zante*	Turkey
Cyprus*	Algarve
Malta	Costa Dorada*
Bahamas*	Costa del Sol
Minorca	Florida
Majorca	Costa Blanca
Gran	Canaria
Tenerife	
Lanzarote	

*Beginning summer 1995.

as a direct sell operator. John Boyle has stated that while other direct sell companies exist 'they belong to large groups which also sell brands through travel agents and their dependence on the goodwill of travel agents means they are fighting with one hand tied behind their backs' (*Scotsman*, 25 September 1991). Cutting out the travel agent has been the thrust of all promotions undertaken and it has been used to good effect. The company's name further enforces the message conveyed to the public.

When Direct Holidays was launched considerable media attention was afforded the company, in particular focusing on its decision to cut out the travel agent. Headlines included 'New travel firm cuts out the middleman' (*Sunday Times*), 'Cutting out the agent' (*Daily Telegraph*), 'Travel agents under fire from new firm' (Scots media), 'Boyle is back with direct sell' (*Travel Trade Gazette*), 'Cut price brothers in arms' (*Evening Times*) and 'Holiday firm cuts out middleman' (*Scotsman*).

By bypassing the travel agent Direct Holidays claims that holidaymakers can save up to 16.2% on the price of a comparable holiday offered by the large tour operators, equivalent to an average saving of £56 on a holiday costing £300. John Boyle states:

> Ten years ago people needed a travel agent for advice on where to go. But now they have been on five or six holidays they know what they want and that need is no longer there.
>
> (Scots media, October 1991)

He also states:

> The travel agent has virtually been reduced to the role of order taker, often staffed by people with less knowledge than the holidaymaker. Why pay him a 15% commission for that?
>
> (*Sunday Times*, 22 September 1991)

The success of Direct Holidays therefore partly derives from the fact that it is selling the tried and trusted package holidays with which holidaymakers are familiar making them more confident in booking direct. Little advice is required and the actual booking is relatively straightforward as complexity is not a feature. The product therefore lends itself to direct booking. This has been made an attractive proposition to the consumer by the incentive of cost savings.

Distribution therefore consists of brochures which are sent directly to people's homes either upon request or on the basis of a targeted mailing list. Consumers can then make bookings by telephone or at one of the company's travel centres. Direct Holidays also has a page on teletext which is used to promote sales and offload late availability holidays and flights.

PROMOTION

To date Direct Holidays has been involved in heavy promotional activity. This is partly attributable to its recent birth and the quest to establish itself in the marketplace but also to the ongoing need to create awareness among the public that selling direct is an alternative option to using a travel agent.

Following its launch Direct Holidays embarked upon a £180 000 television, poster and press advertising campaign which within four months had generated 9300 requests for brochures. The thrust of the campaign revolved around the slogan 'Why travel agent when you can travel direct?', a slogan which is gradually being phased out.

Direct Holidays has consistently employed a wide range of media to convey its message; the success of the company would suggest that this has been done effectively. Marketing campaigns are timed to coincide with brochure launches which occur in January and August. For example, in the summer 1995 brochure launch, radio, national and local Scottish press and television were employed. Figure 22.2 shows percentage spend by newspaper and radio media. (It should be emphasized that all media used focuses only on the Scottish market so even where national media have been employed they have only reached the Scottish market.)

The message conveyed by all the advertising is that of cost-savings from booking direct with the tour operator. One method used to demonstrate this is that of a price comparison between Direct Holidays and other major tour operators offering virtually identical holidays in terms of resort, accommodation and dates to accentuate the difference in price. By providing real examples, it is an effective means of driving home the price message. Furthermore, press advertisements highlight cheaper insurance and do not make it compulsory in contrast to other tour operators who insist on their insurance being taken when discounts are offered. Figure 22.3 shows a selection of press advertisements employed by Direct Holidays between January 1993 and September 1994. A further form of advertising used is that of bus sides. An example of this is shown in Figure 22.4. As television advertisements, posters and bus sides tend to be used to create awareness instead of generating a response, assessment becomes rather more difficult to quantify. Clearly, then, response driven media is much simpler to quantify than awareness driven media.

The effectiveness of marketing campaigns is assessed according to

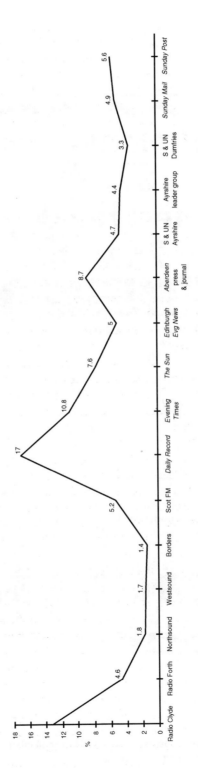

Figure 22.2 Newspaper and radio spend for Scottish brochure launch, August–Spetember 1994.

Figure 22.3 Direct Holidays: press advertisements January 1993 to September 1994. Reproduced with permission courtesy of Direct Holidays, UK.

There's only one thing missing from our holidays – the travel agent's commission.

Holiday	Other Tour Operators	Direct Holidays	Saving per person
ALGARVE Albufeira Jardim 24 July – 2 wks	**Thomson** £514.00 incl. **Lunn Poly** Discount	**Direct** £399.00	**£115.00**
COSTA BLANCA Fiesta Park 14 August – 2 wks	**Sunworld** £511.00 incl. **A.T. Mays** Discount	**Direct** £399.00	**£112.00**
FLORIDA Flydrive 15 Aug – 2 wks	**Cosmos** £498.00 incl. **Pickford Travel** Discount	**Direct** £399.00	**£99.00**
LANZAROTE Plaza Azul 22 July – 2 wks	**Martyn Holidays** £518.00 incl. **Thomas Cook** Discount	**Direct** £409.00	**£109.00**
MAJORCA Pollensa Park 10 July – 2 wks	**Enterprise** £606.00 incl. **Thomas Cook** Discount	**Direct** £529.00	**£77.00**
GRAN CANARIA Broncemar Apts 17 July – 2 wks	**Sky Tours** £436.00 incl. **Pickford Travel** Discount	**Direct** £364.00	**£72.00**
OPEN MON-SAT 8.00am-8.00pm. SUN 11.00am-4.00pm			

When you book a Direct Holiday you cut out the middle man. There's no travel agent, so there's no travel agent's commission. Instead we pass the savings on to you. So you get the same holiday, same hotel, same flight, same ABTA security as you would from the travel agent for less. Phone for a brochure. **Low deposit – £10.**

041-221 0077
8 DIXON STREET, GLASGOW G1

ATOL 2105
ABTA C 6548

DIRECT HOLIDAYS

Figure 22.3   *(continued)*

The most direct route to Florida is not via the travel agents.

Holiday	Other Tour Operators	Direct Holidays	Saving per person
FLORIDA Flydrive 15 Aug – 2wks	**Cosmos** £533.00	**Direct** £399.00	**£134.00**
FLORIDA Villa with pool 20 June – 2wks	**Thomson** £612.00	**Direct** £522.00	**£90.00**
FLORIDA Twin Towers 17 Oct – 2wks	**Thomson** £2,165.00 Family of 4	**Direct** £1,796.00 Family of 4	**£369.00** per family
OPEN MON-SAT 8.00am-8.00pm. SUN 11.00am-4.00pm			

We've cut 2 hours off the flight time by flying wide-bodied jets non-stop to Florida **and** we've cut out the travel agent's commission. So to save both time and money, simply phone us for a brochure. **Low deposit – £10.**

041-221 0077

8 DIXON STREET, GLASGOW G1

ATOL 2105

ABTA C6548

DIRECT HOLIDAYS

Figure 22.3 *(continued)*

Figure 22.3   *(continued)*

**Free Child Places.
First Come. First Saved.**

FREE KID'S CLUB TOO

There is no gimmick. We have genuine Free Child Places available to a wide variety of hotels and apartments throughout the Mediterranean. We've also set up The Dolphin Club, with free carefully supervised entertainment to keep children amused and parents sane!

THIS BROCHURE IS NOT AVAILABLE AT THE TRAVEL AGENTS

PHONE NOW FOR A COPY
041-221 0077

DIRECT HOLIDAYS

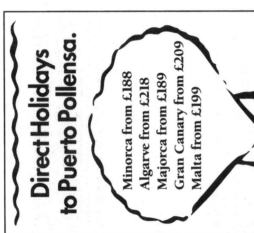

Direct Holidays to Puerto Pollensa.

Minorca from £188
Algarve from £218
Majorca from £189
Gran Canary from £209
Malta from £199

Why shell out more at the travel agents?

For summer '95, Direct Holidays have some of the best hotels and apartments in Majorca's most beautiful beach resort. And, because we cut out all of the travel agent's commission, we have the best prices too.

THIS BROCHURE IS NOT AVAILABLE AT THE TRAVEL AGENTS

PHONE NOW FOR A COPY
041-221 0077
8 DIXON STREET, GLASGOW G1

DIRECT HOLIDAYS

Direct Holidays to Salou.

from £159

Get your claws on our summer '95 brochure.

Miles of sandy beach in the Mediterranean's best value for money restort – Salou on the Spanish Costa Dorada is a new destination for Direct Holidays, in our biggest-ever brochure.

THIS BROCHURE IS NOT AVAILABLE AT THE TRAVEL AGENTS

PHONE NOW FOR A COPY
041-221 0077

DIRECT HOLIDAYS

Figure 22.3 (*continued*)

Figure 22.4 Direct Holidays: bus side advertising.
Reproduced with permission courtesy of Direct Holidays, UK.

individual media. For example, brochure promotion is evaluated on the basis of the cost of the advertisements and the number of responses which combined generates a cost per response figure. The more detailed the information the more cost-effective future marketing campaigns will be as such information will determine the optimum media to employ.

Market research is undertaken, for example on the lifestyle of the Direct Holidays client base. Results show that a high proportion of clients are clerical workers who are married who fall within the 35–64 year age group who have two children aged 11 and over; they tend to own a house with a garden valued up to £60 000. They have an annual household income of £15–30 000 and a main hobby is doing the Pools. Financially they have a bank account, a credit card and a savings account. From this research Direct Holidays is also able to identify categories in which they have an under-representation of clients. Knowledge about the client base clearly assists in developing the business strategy and in formulating appropriate marketing campaigns.

Such information was used, for example, in developing the business and marketing plan for Liverpool airport. An agency brief was drawn up which set out the objectives, target market, product information, features and benefits, offers/incentives, image and media usage, budget, assessment and timing. This was to provide the basis for a marketing campaign to promote a £7 million holiday programme for summer 1995. The thrust of the campaign was to promote the costs savings not only in relation to travel agency commission but also in comparison to holidays from Manchester. John Boyle stated:

> At present the people of Liverpool do not have the choice of travelling from their own city but have to make their way to Manchester or London. With substantially lower operating costs at Liverpool airport, Direct Holiday packages will be around 20% cheaper than similar holidays from Manchester.
>
> (Direct Holidays, 1994)

In addition, by cutting out the travel agent, clients could save approximately 15%. It was therefore estimated that a holidaymaker would save £70 on an average summer holiday which for a family of four travelling from Liverpool could amount to £280. Direct Holidays also intended to promote the benefits to Liverpool, including revitalization of the local airport, employment in the new sales office and employment for overseas representatives.

PRICE

The principal weapon used in Direct Holidays' competitive strategy is that of the cost savings to be gained from cutting out the travel agent. So far in this case study the focus has been on the marketing campaigns used to convey this message. The brochure is also an avenue for promoting price.

As well as offering free child places and a low deposit, a standard feature of the brochure is the promise of 'the lowest prices'. To endorse this Direct Holidays guarantees that if a 'directly comparable holiday is found at a lower price at a travel agent within a month of booking' they will refund the difference. The brochure also offers a 'no surcharge guarantee' after a holiday has been booked. Significantly the brochure also makes reference to the quality of holidays in its heading 'reduced prices not quality' to ensure that the product is not undermined. The emphasis is once again placed on distribution as the reason for lower prices claiming that the product is of the same standard as holidays booked through travel agents. To illustrate these points the front inside cover of the Direct Holidays brochure is shown in Figure 22.5.

CUSTOMER SERVICE

As with all successful companies Direct Holidays places emphasis on customer service. This is revealed in two main ways. First, because Direct Holidays only sells its own products the sales staff are highly knowledgeable about the products and are capable of answering any queries a client may have. Also, as reservations advisers are taken to the resorts to see the accommodation they can advise clients accordingly. The brochure states: 'We promise that you will always be able to talk to someone who's been where you're thinking of going.'

Second, Direct Holidays distributes customer satisfaction questionnaires to every client on the transfer coach at the end of the holiday, information from which is used to 'monitor' holidays and improve the 'standards and quality of future holidays'. In addition to basic classification questions the questionnaire adopts a Likert scale to assess accommodation, the holiday representative, overall enjoyment, car hire, future holidays and holiday choice. The penultimate section is devoted to market analysis which provides additional information about the client, while the final section provides space for the client to write their comments about the holiday and service. It is this section which often provides the most acute insights into clients' views. A copy of the six panel questionnaire is shown in Figure 22.6.

There is also a customer relations department based in Glasgow which handles individual queries and complaints.

SUMMARY

The case study has shown that Direct Holidays differs from most mainstream tour operators in that it exclusively sells direct to the consumer by cutting out the travel agent. It has also targeted only the Scottish market although that is set to the change with expansion into Liverpool. Certainly the strategy has been to focus on regional airports. The thrust of its

WHY DOES BOOKING DIRECT SAVE YOU SO MUCH MONEY ?

Traditionally, people have booked their holiday at the travel agents. However, this is not a free service. Travel agents make their money by charging you a commission of up to 15% of the cost of your holiday. Booking Direct means that you bypass the travel agent and avoid paying this commission altogether. The saving can be quite considerable. For example, a family holiday costing £1000 at the travel agents, would be 15% cheaper if bought from Direct Holidays and would cost about £850 - that's a saving of £150 that comes direct to you.

REDUCED PRICES NOT QUALITY

Booking direct reduces the price of your holiday. It does not mean a reduction in quality. The holidays are exactly the same. You stay in the same hotels, fly on the same airlines and have the same ABTA security as you would if you'd booked your holiday at the travel agents. Apart from the price, the only difference you might notice is our emphasis on personal service. Because we only sell our own holidays (unlike travel agents who sell many different brands of holidays) we have an intimate knowledge of our product. When you phone our reservations advisors, you'll find that they can give you real answers to your questions, not just guesses. We have a policy of taking our reservations advisors out to the resort to look at the accommodation we feature, so they are better able to assist you in your choice. What's more, we promise that you will always be able to talk to someone who's been where you're thinking of going. We know of no travel agent who can promise you that.

SECURITY GUARANTEED

Direct Holidays plc is Scotland's largest direct sell holiday company. It is a member of ABTA and is licensed by the Civil Aviation Authority. This guarantees you complete financial security.

HOW DO I BOOK WITH DIRECT HOLIDAYS?

It couldn't really be easier . All you have to do is pick up the phone and have a chat with one of our reservations advisors. Not only will they know all about the holidays in this brochure, but they will also be able to advise you on any extra savings you might be able to make, such as taking advantage of **free child places**. We are also happy to answer any other questions or queries that you may have, whether they're about getting to the airport, travel insurance, car hire, wheelchair assistance - whatever. You can pay either by credit/debit card or send us a cheque, as always with Direct Holidays, it's whatever you find easiest.

NO SURCHARGE GUARANTEE

Direct Holidays offers you an unconditional guarantee that, once booked, your holiday will not be subject to any surcharges.

WE PROMISE THE LOWEST PRICES

We are so confident that our prices are the lowest, that if you find a directly comparable holiday at a lower price, at any travel agent, within a month of booking with us, we will refund you the difference. This guarantee is only valid for bookings made at least eight weeks prior to departure and applies to adult holidays at full brochure price.

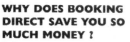

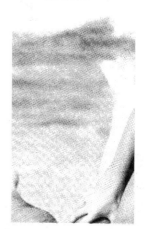

2

Figure 22.5 Direct Holidays brochure: front inside cover.
Reproduced with permission courtesy of Direct Holidays, UK.

SECTION 8 — *Market analysis cont'd*

3. **Please indicate which ONE of the following holiday groups your party falls into?**
   - Travelling alone ☐
   - Travelling as a couple ☐
   - Family/families with children ☐
   - With a group of mixed sex friends ☐
   - With a group of same sex friends ☐
   - As part of an organised group ☐

4. **Which other holiday companies have you travelled with in the last 5 years?**

• Airtours ☐	• Martin Rooks ☐	• Eclipse Direct ☐
• Globespan ☐	• Enterprise ☐	• Sunfare ☐
• Falcon ☐	• Sunworld ☐	• Cosmos ☐
• Thomson ☐	• Inspirations ☐	• Style ☐
• Other (*please specify below*) ☐		

5. **Which of the following daily newspapers do you normally read?**

• Aberdeen Press & Journal ☐	• Evening Times ☐
• Ayrshire Post ☐	• Glasgow Herald ☐
• Daily Record ☐	• Scotsman ☐
• Dundee Courier ☐	• The Sun ☐
• Other (*please specify below*) ☐	

6. **Which of the following Sunday newspapers do you normally read?**

• Sunday Express ☐	• Scotland on Sunday ☐
• The Independent on Sunday ☐	• Sunday Post ☐
• News of the World ☐	• Sunday Times ☐
• Sunday Mail (Scotland) ☐	
• Other (*please specify below*) ☐	

SECTION 9

Please write any additional comments you have about your holiday, or Direct Holiday's services

THANK YOU FOR YOUR HELP AND COOPERATION

We regret we cannot reply to individual questionnaires. If you have any specific comments you wish to make to which you require a reply, please write to our Customer Relations Department, 8 Dixon Street, Glasgow G1 4AX.

2

Hand in or Post NOW
You could win a
FREE HOLIDAY!

Direct Holidays
FREEPOST
8 Dixon Street
Glasgow G1 4BR

DIRECT HOLIDAYS

DH001

Last season's draw winner was Mrs Robertson, Carluke, Lanarkshire

Dear

May I, on behalf of all the staff at Direct Holidays thank you for choosing to holiday with us. I hope you had a pleasant and relaxing time.

As a valued customer, your opinion is extremely important in helping us to monitor our holidays and improve the standards and quality of future holidays.

Please could you spare a few moments of your time to complete this questionnaire, and at the same time, earn the chance of WINNING A FREE HOLIDAY FOR 2 THE FOLLOWING YEAR.

Upon completing the questionnaire, please return it to your representative, or alternatively upon your return to the UK, send it to us by post - no stamp required.

Thank you once again for holidaying with us and I hope that you will travel with us again in the future.

Yours sincerely

Hugh Boyle

Booking Ref No: ☐☐☐☐☐☐

UK Departure date: ☐☐☐☐☐☐

Representative's name: ☐☐☐☐☐☐☐☐☐☐☐☐

Figure 22.6 Direct Holidays: customer service questionnaire. Reproduced with permission courtesy of Direct Holidays, UK.

SECTION 1 — Holiday details

1. Name of resort?

2. Name of your accommodation?

3. How did you book your holiday?
   - Telephone
   - Came into Direct Holidays Glasgow shop

4. Have you travelled with Direct Holidays before?
   - Yes
   - No

5. How long before the start of your holiday did you book?
   - less than 2 weeks
   - 2-4 weeks
   - 1-2 months
   - 3-6 months
   - 6-9 months
   - 9+ months

6. Which UK airport did you depart from?
   - Glasgow
   - Prestwick
   - Other (please specify)

7. Please rate your UK departure airport for the following?

	EXCELLENT	GOOD	FAIR	POOR
The waiting time at the check in counter				
The service at the check in counter				
Personal attention by UK airport staff				
The departure lounge				
The flight boarding procedures				
Facilities (eg. Shops, Bars, etc)				

8. How likely are to fly from this airport again?
   - Definitely
   - Probably
   - Possibly
   - Unlikely

9. How did you travel to the UK departure airport?
   - Train
   - Taxi
   - Taken by friend/family
   - Own car parked at airport

SECTION 2 — Your accommodation
Please rate the following (if applicable)

	EXCELLENT	GOOD	FAIR	POOR
Location of accommodation				
Comfort of sleeping arrangements				
Cleanliness				

SECTION 2 — cont'd

	EXCELLENT	GOOD	FAIR	POOR
Meals (if provided)				
Facilities (eg. bars, lounge etc)				
Helpfulness of accommodation staff				
Entertainment programme (if provided)				
The transfer journey to and from the airport and your accommodation				

SECTION 3 — Your holiday representative
Please rate the following (if applicable)

	EXCELLENT	GOOD	FAIR	POOR
Helpfulness of your representative				
Smartness of your representative				
Availability and punctuality of your representative at times published				
Quality of information available from your representative apart from the welcome meeting				

- Did you attend the welcome meeting Yes No
- If yes, how did you rate the meeting for information
- Did you book any optional excursions through your representative Yes No
- If yes, how did you rate the excursions for
  i) Value for money
  ii) Overall enjoyment

SECTION 4 — Taking everything into account
Please rate the following (if applicable)

	EXCELLENT	GOOD	FAIR	POOR
Overall holiday enjoyment				
Your accommodation overall				
The resort overall				
Value for money of your holiday				
Pre-departure service by Direct Holidays				
The accuracy of our holiday brochure				

SECTION 5 — Car hire

1. Did you hire a car whilst on holiday?
   - No
   - Yes, pre-booked with Direct Holidays in the UK
   - Yes, booked in resort via Direct's representative
   - Yes, other

SECTION 6 — Future holidays
How likely are you to:

	DEFINITELY	PROBABLY	POSSIBLY	UNLIKELY
Travel with Direct again				
Recommend Direct to your friends				
Travel to this country again				
Travel to this resort again				
Travel to this accommodation again				

SECTION 7 — Your holiday choice

1. How many holiday brochures did you look at before choosing this holiday?
   - 0
   - 1
   - 2-5
   - 5+

2. When choosing this holiday, how important were the following points?

	VERY IMPORTANT	IMPORTANT	FAIRLY IMPORTANT	UN-IMPORTANT
Same holiday cheaper with Direct than other tour operator				
Good value for money				
Low price				
Convenient departure airport				
Recommendation of friends				
Previous experience with Direct				
Our reputation for quality and reliability				
Holiday available for date required				
Chosen accommodation available				
Children's prices				
Flight timings				
Ease of booking				
ABTA membership				

SECTION 8 — Market analysis
(all replies are strictly confidential)

1. How many are there in your party?

2. Please state how many members of your party fall into the following age ranges?
   - Under 2   • 17-24   • 45-54
   - 2-11   • 25-34   • 55-64
   - 12-16   • 35-44   • 65+

Please fold, moisten and seal the edge

Figure 22.6 (continued)

marketing strategy revolves around the costs savings to be gained from eliminating the travel agent and the associated commission. In conveying this message the company has been aggressive; a principal method used has been cost comparisons with the competition. The success of the company to date would suggest that the business and marketing strategies have been effective in achieving their objectives. The future is likely to witness further growth with a logical development being the extension of its operations into other regional airports in England and Wales.

REFERENCES

Direct Holidays (1994) *£7 million holiday boost for Liverpool airport*, press release.
Marketing Week (1991) Travels double agent, 10 October.
Scotsman (1991) Holiday firm cuts out middle man, 25 September.
Scotsmedia (1991) Travel agents under fire from new firm, October.
The Sunday Times (1991) New travel firm cuts out middleman, 22 September.

REVIEW QUESTIONS

1. How does Direct Holidays distribute its products?
2. Which markets are being targeted by Direct Holidays?
3. What are the main ingredients of Direct Holidays' promotional activity?
4. What price strategy has been adopted?
5. How does Direct Holidays monitor customer service?

23 Destination marketing: Florida – the uses of research

B.E. Pitegoff

This case is slightly different in format from the previous four. It is an edited version of a speech delivered by Barry E. Pitegoff, Research Officer for the Florida Chamber of Commerce, to the Society of Travel and Tourism Educators' annual conference in Miami, Florida in October, 1993 just after the shootings of two English tourists had attracted worldwide attention. Pitegoff joined the Florida Division of Tourism in January 1981 to administer its tourism research programme. With a staff of eight colleagues, he manages programmes as diverse as estimating the volume of current Florida visitors to developing tourism advertising strategies through attitudinal research with potential visitors. His account offers an inside view into how Florida uses short-range and long-range research in marketing planning, and also provides a fascinating insight into the role of information in the state's 'crisis management' programmes after the shootings.

INTRODUCTION

I had been working on this set of speech notes on and off when the tragedy against the British visitors on 1 October occurred just outside of Tallahassee. I thought I would begin by sharing with you the types of research we are asked for at the time of such a crisis. (In September 1993 two visitors from England flew to Orlando, Florida to begin an excursion of the region. They motored to New Orleans, Louisiana, about 650 miles from Orlando. On their return drive, they stopped at a rest area on Interstate-10, a major highway route which crosses the United States from Jacksonville, Florida in the east to Los Angeles, California in the west. The rest area was outside of Tallahassee, Florida, the capital city of the state. While this couple were at the rest area, one of the visitors was shot and killed in an act of violence still pending trial at the time of the writing of this article. The crime received widespread international publicity).

As soon as the story broke, we had reporters calling from literally everywhere for background information. The first questions had to do with: how large is Florida tourism? what is its impact on the state? how many visitors are hosted from the United Kingdom? what kind of crime rates do our visitors and residents face, and how does this compare to elsewhere? In an emergency, the research office is turned to first for 'the truth', that is the most accurate information for the department to issue and be guided by. This requires a staff with the endless patience to continually teach new reporters the types of data available and how to interpret them.

A day or two later, the press explores questions that are more general, like crime rates in the state and crime rates against visitors as compared with residents. At the same time, the offices of the Governor and the Secretary of Commerce want to know economic impact scenarios, like the amount of economic activity the state might lose if different volumes of visitor spending were seen to be lessened.

A very important lesson to understand is that many types of ratios and statistics can be developed from the same set of data. Often, each summary statistic created is a good description of one situation and might be a poor answer to another question. For example, is the number of potential crime victims in the state on any given day equal to the population, the population inflated by tourists, or the population inflated by tourists less residents travelling? The propensity to be the victim of a certain type of crime does vary with whether the possible victim is a resident or a visitor.

Here is an overview of the types of information we gave out:

- Florida hosts about 40.5 million visitors a year. (The final number for 1993 was 41.0 million.)
- About 20% of our visitors come from outside of the United States, and they account for about 36% of visitor spending in Florida. (The final number for 1993 was 17%, including Canadians.)
- About 1.3 million visitors a year come to Florida from the United Kingdom. That makes the UK our number two source of non-American visitors after Canada, which sends us about 2.5 million visitors a year. (The 1993 volume from the UK was 1.1 million.)
- Florida's tourism adds an estimated 1.3 million persons each day to the state on top of a residential population of 13.4 million. In other words, at any given time, an average of one out of eleven people in the state is a visitor. (The 1993 final figure was 1.4 million, or about one out of ten.)
- Tourism is our largest industry, and contributes about 22% to the state's general revenue collections. (The final 1993 figure was 21%.)
- A 5% decrease in spending by international visitors in Florida, over the course of a year, is likely to result in a loss of about $500 million in sales by Florida businesses and some 8000 jobs in the state.
- A homicide is a terrible situation, whether against a resident or a visitor. The rate of homicides of visitors has consistently been a tiny

fraction of the rate against residents, adjusted for relative populations. For example, in 1992, the state had 16 visitor homicides for every 10 million visitors, or a total of 64 homicides against visitors. Over the past four years, that statistic has stayed in the range of 60 through 93. Equally frightening is the fact that about the same number of visitors each year take their own life while in Florida.

Because more than ever before, tourism is an industry where marketing must be based on sound information, Florida has set up information systems which I shall now describe.

First, what is our research philosophy, what tools do we use, and what have we learned about the positioning of Florida? I shall cover several areas with you. The first is to emphasize how powerful a force tourism is in this state. Next, I shall describe the position of research in the marketing of tourism in Florida. After that, what are the key trends research is telling us to follow, and what do we think that means for Florida in the long run?

First, let me give you an idea of the magnitude of tourism in Florida.

THE NATURE OF TOURISM IN FLORIDA

Our research philosophy is a total marketing research concept. To understand our tourism, you must understand the quantitative and the qualitative sides of it. You need to know how big the industry is, but you also need to know why people come to Florida and what needs Florida satisfies.

Tourism is Florida's largest business. In 1992:

- Florida hosted just under 41 million persons . . . about three times the state's population. (The 1993 figures was just *over* 41 million.)
- Tourism spending, by both residents and visitors, exceeded $31 billion, with most coming from visitors. The taxes collected on these trans-actions exceeded one-fifth of the state's general revenue collections. (The 1993 value was also one-fifth.)
- Over 663 000 persons are employed in our core industries of tourism – about as many people as are estimated to be working in tourism in all of Canada. (The 1993 figure was 699 000.)
- The lodging industry in the state has a total inventory of 350 000 rooms. Just 15 years ago, our biggest single hotel was nearby, on Miami Beach, The Fountainbleau Hilton, with 1206 rooms. Now the Fountainbleau is our sixth largest hotel, and the five ahead of it are all in Central Florida.
- In short, we do tourism on a very big scale in Florida.

On the qualitative side, we need to be constantly aware of why people choose to come to Florida. This helps us to understand the positioning and advertising philosophies needed. Our current thinking looks at the reasons to come to Florida as a core set of five interrelated points:

- First is our favourable outdoor orientation. In Florida, tourism is truly an encounter with the environment, with visitors enjoying our beaches, boating, fishing, diving and theme parks. Because our state's largest industry is critically dependent on a clean environment, the outdoor orientation of our tourism helps us to reinforce the state's goals of environmental preservation.

  As interest in ecotourism increased in recent years, Florida found itself well positioned to respond to this travel motivator. The Everglades and the reef are of particular interest to our international visitors interested in ecotourism experiences.

- Second, we are fortunate to be the leading sun destination with an appeal to families. Our visitors tell us that many of the famous island resorts are just not as viable when it comes to taking the children with them on vacation. Our concern now seems to be on the pitfalls of having a strong image in this area.

  First, how do we handle the fact that there are more (American) households consisting of married couples without children than with children? Second, more and more children are, unfortunately, in single-parent households, where the discretionary income available for leisure travel is usually a lot lower.

- Our third element is hospitality. Over 90% of our visitors tell us they have been to Florida before. This is very impressive. However, on a per trip basis, the first-time visitor outspends the repeat visitor. So, we need to understand how to attract more first-time visitors, or encourage more spending by repeat visitors.

  The approach to selecting which market segments to pursue for more first-time visitors needs to be based on an analysis of the potential long-run stream of revenues from different segments being considered. A visitor is worth the sum of the long-run stream of revenue that visitor can generate for the destination through personal visits and through the visits of others whom that visitor has influenced.

- Fourth, we are proud of the value and variety of the tourism product available to our visitors. Our 5000 hotels and motels range from the economy segment to the resort segment. We have gourmet restaurants and chain restaurants.

  However, recently we are noticing that 'value' is a bit harder to communicate to our prospective visitors than before. We are beginning to study the difference between the median income of the (domestic) traveller to Florida and the median income of the American household, and our travellers have significantly higher income. For example, the median income for our air visitors was $60 000 and the median income for our auto visitors was $40 000. At the same time, the median family income in the United States was $35 225. (These two sets of incomes come from recent years which were not the same, but with minimal effect from change across years.) This could be an indication that the typical Florida vacation is moving out of reach of the typical 'middle class' household.

- Fifth, and last for this short list, is the fact that we are a 'heritage brand'. Florida has been a leader in the vacation destination field for years and years, just as Coca-Cola and Ivory Soap and IBM and Xerox have been leaders in their fields. The great play, *Death of a Salesman*, opens with the lead characters having just returned from a vacation in Florida. New meeting planners have told us, in our research, that they feel comfortable with Florida, safe with the perception that we have done this so well for so long that we will keep them from failing.

The *Christian Science Monitor* newspaper opened an article on the health of 'the American Dream' a few years ago with our statistics on the number of families piling into station wagons and driving down to Florida on vacation. They pronounced the state of the American Dream as being alive and well.

More recent American consumer attitudinal research finds this changing, however. In February 1994, Roper-Starch Worldwide, Incorporated, a well-respected United States polling organization, reported that only one-fifth of the American public was currently saying, 'The American Dream is very much alive today.' Recently, that value was higher, standing at one-quarter in 1990 and at one-third in 1986.

THE ROLES OF RESEARCH IN FLORIDA TOURISM MARKETING

There are four basic types of research:

- understanding the current market;
- scanning for perspective;
- strategic directions research;
- trends watching.

Because the health of this industry is so critical to the health of the state, we do a considerable amount of research to ensure that our marketing programmes are on target.

Aside from emergency research, like the information needed to respond to the 1 October crisis, we have ongoing research for the main purpose of 'understanding the current market'. This is dominated by a continuous tracking model to understand who our current customer is. This research starts with 9300 face-to-face surveys conducted annually with visitors leaving the state, responding to a 15-minute survey instrument. The questions cover the nature of the travelling party, the nature of the trip planning process and the nature of the travel experience in Florida, particularly if it differed from the previous experience in Florida, if there was one. This is combined with a separate system which helps us to estimate the flow of visitors to the state, giving us continuous information on how many visitors we are hosting and their major characteristics.

About half of these interviews are spread across the thirteen major airports in Florida, in a carefully developed stratified sampling design. The other half are administered at five highway locations. In the airports, we are at the departure gates for flights leaving the state of Florida. At the highway sites, we are at the state border or at the rest area closest to the state border. This sampling system is highly respected for its accuracy.

The insights from this tracking model help direct our advertising and promotion programmes by telling us the markets and messages for our advertising efforts, travel agent efforts and consumer efforts. Here are some surprising statistics from this system:

- We are observing that the average length of trip is staying constant, so economic pressures on our tourists are causing them to make trade-offs within their trip itineraries. In a sense, this is a benefit of our diversified tourism product. When budgets are tight, a visitor can move to a high quality, less expensive hotel, or to a high quality, less expensive restaurant, and still preserve a vacation experience in Florida. Destinations more homogeneous in their tourism product are likely to have a greater tendency to lose visitors under those conditions.

- Only about 25% of our visitors pass through a travel agency and less than half of our visitors go to a major attraction or theme park while there. Most think those numbers are higher. However, half of our visitors drive and travel agents prefer to have clients who at least purchase an airline ticket.

  The high repeat visit incidence can offset the motivation to go to the attractions, when they are perceived as having made no changes since the last time the traveller visited them. Many of our attractions have responded to this challenge by continually updating and expanding their offerings. The result is often a rejuvenated sense of value, and as a result, a resurgence in visitation.

- Friends and relatives, of course, are an important variable in the Florida tourism picture. On the average, about 35% of our tourists stay with their friends or relatives. This 'host party' phenomenon has both a 'destination component' and an 'emotional bonding' component. For an analysis of the destination component, we once researched travellers who came to stay with friends and relatives. Using in-depth interviews, we probed to what extent they would travel to visit those same relatives if those same relatives lived in another state, like Arkansas or Oklahoma. It was obvious that very important in reason to visit those friends and relatives was the fact that they lived in Florida.

  Similarly, we once wanted to disaggregate the 'social bond' from the 'economic bond'. We asked travellers who stayed with friends and relatives if they would stay instead at a new nearby motel with a substantial discount, especially if their 'host party' recommended or suggested it. There was a resounding feeling on the part of those travellers that this would mean that their relatives did not want to see them anymore, i.e. they had 'overstayed their welcome'. In effect, they would rather not make the trip. From the opposite side, however, came the feeling from 'host parties' that they had to adapt to family visiting and staying with them instead of in a motel because 'family is family'.

The 'visit friends and relatives' component of Florida tourism is fascinating in terms of how it benefits the entire tourism industry. In 1993, some 37% of the tourists who flew to Florida stayed with friends/relatives, but only 29% of those air visitors reported that 'visiting friends/relatives' was their main reason to come to Florida. Similarly, 34% of those who drove to Florida in 1993 stayed with friends/relatives, but 28% of our auto visitors reported that 'visiting friends/relatives' was their main reason to come to Florida. In each case, we appear to have quite good diversified touristic activity from those coming to stay with friends/relatives.

The second type of research we do in Florida is keeping an eye on the perspective ('scanning for perspective'). The interpretation of our impact from tourism is so much more significant when we know how others are doing, and how overall trends are going. For example, the United States Travel Data Center reported a few months ago that 82% of all travellers were very or somewhat likely to travel for pleasure or vacation during the summer of 1993, the highest value for this variable in the few years it has been recorded.

Hilton Hotels is quite good at keeping up with their understanding of their customer through consumer attitudinal research and then not only applying the results to marketing strategies, but also playing back the research in their consumer advertising. In a recent mail ad campaign, Hilton touted that 'What's Hot . . . [includes] . . . relaxation, romantic getaways, leisurely dining, lots of fun, being pampered, and spending time with someone special.' On the other hand, they reported that: 'What's not . . . [includes] . . . stress, weekends at work, eating on the run, lots of responsibilities, being overburdened, and spending time paying bills.'

The third type of research we do regularly is a set of forward-oriented customer research projects, each heading towards strategic marketing implications ('strategic directions research'). We divide these studies into two areas: those directly involved with our advertising programmes, and those not directly involved with our advertising programmes.

Our advertising research looks at what we should be communicating, then how effective we are at trying to communicate that message. We start with qualitative research, like discovery sessions and focus groups to get campaign platforms. Then, we follow it with testing potential commercials in simulated viewing sessions. This process recently drew our attention to the different, but related, concepts of affordability and value. We actually tested some commercials a few years ago which caused prevailing attitude levels towards Florida's affordability and value to drop. That caused us to critically examine the visual cues in the commercials and how to change them.

We also average about one or two custom research projects a year not dealing directly with advertising programmes. One of those recent studies, our 'Lifestyle Segmentation Study', provides some insights and marketing implications. We saw three challenges facing us from the country's changing demographics. We needed to know what the impacts on us would be and any actions which would be required.

- The recession has been deep and pervasive. The impact on vacationing varied around the country. We began to see that some of our advertising concepts which were successfully communicating in the 1980s were now hitting some obstacles in their ability to communicate the affordability and value messages desired. A major challenge to the industry in the 1990s, we learned, was the need to satisfy the demands of value conscious consumers with better service and a higher quality product.

- A second change we looked at was family composition. Florida tourism has a strong family appeal. Yet, the incidence of households in the US of married couples without children under the age of 18 is about 29%, while the incidence of households of married couples with children under the age of 18 is running at about 22%, a full seven percentage points lower.

- So, how was that affecting us? This was one of the few times we found a bi-modal distribution underlying the data. For childless couples who could afford to vacation in non-child oriented destinations, that surely was their preference. On the other hand, for those who were childless and could not afford to vacation in non-child oriented places, they know how to cope by using child-oriented places off-season, like the Disney complex in October.

- The third lifestyle we looked at was wedding-related travel. America averages about three million marriages a year. In one million of these marriages, at least one partner has been to the altar at least once before. 'Repeaters' are more likely to spend more on the special trip because they are more in control of their budgets, the gown and reception are not as important to them, and they have travelled more extensively for business and pleasure and have a more discriminating taste. This study identified this important segment for us. The remaining challenge is how to find them. We think city-oriented magazines may be a key.

KEY CONSUMER TRENDS WE ARE WATCHING

'Trend watching' – Florida deals in 'mass' tourism. With over 40 million visitors a year, with 15–20% from other countries, with a myriad of reasons to come and places to stay, the Florida tourism product is somewhat like the offerings in a department store. Consequently, we keep a sharp eye on how American consumers behave in all marketplaces to gain insight into how they might be making travel decisions. Here are some examples.

- A major issue of the 1990s is the time crunch. Saving time has become

the critical element. In tourism, popular elements might be express registrations and express check-outs.

- Family, home and building closer relationships are more important in the 1990s than they were in the 1980s. We have seen more hotels plugging into the reunion market and family-oriented packages.
- Consumers **sense** that the 1990s are different from the 1980s. They are more limited in their prospects, and realize they may have to reduce their expectations. Hence, tourism products which will do well are those which will position themselves as 'ideal' for the 1990s lifestyle, like those with obvious good value and affordability and which are less ostentatious.
- 'Scepticism and Fear' are at the core of the (American) in the 1990s, according to DDB Needham Worldwide's 1993 'Lifestyle Study', as reported in *Advertising Age*, 18 April 1994. There has been a significant recent increase in Americans agreeing with 'Our family is too heavily in debt today', and with 'It is hard to get a good job these days'. There has been a marked decrease in agreeing with 'I try to stick to well-known brand names'. These attitudes may be coming to influence more travel preferences towards nature-involved vacations (minimal debt) and small inns and bed and breakfast facilities (not brand name).
- The recent recession has differed from others by giving consumers a profound sense of shaken security. Their shopping is done much more carefully. Bargain bragging is fashionable. So is 'brand dating', or having several favourite brands, depending on value, rather than only one. Add to that, the increasing phenomenon of shopping by the same household being done concurrently from both ends of the price spectrum, and you have a threat to brand loyalty. The tourism industry has thrived on customer loyalty programmes, but even they may have to be modified in the 1990s for companies to retain their markets.
- Another indication of this 'profound sense of shaken security' is in a Bruskin/Goldring telephone survey of Americans in April 1994. In response to the question, 'How's the economy?' 37% said 'getting better', 28% said 'getting worse', and 33% said 'staying the same'. With this three-way split in response, the American public may well be reflecting also its shaken faith in the reporting of economic news.
- Tourism products which play into reality, quality and frugality are poised to do better. Room rates which include breakfast, deep discounts for advance bookings and customer reward programmes which kick in after fewer transactions are all the way to go.
- Consumer behaviour in the 1990s, according to Judy Langer and Associates, a research firm we have much respect for, is being dominated by the desire for 'simplicity'. The consumer has seen too many choices, particularly too many brand extensions. This caused us to test the theme, 'This year, keep it simple. Come to Florida'. It was an attempt to build on the familiarity most travellers have with the

Florida tourism product. The idea tested well, but not as well as some other concepts.

- Families are getting smaller, which is a concern for a major family destination like Florida. From the 1980 national census to the 1990 national census, there was an unprecedented 76% rise in the percentage of women aged 40–44 who had only one child, the actual rate increasing from 9.6% to 16.9%.
- Telematics, a consumer forecasting firm, believes that there is an increasing consumer desire for personalization, especially in a concern with the body. Hotels can play into this with health equipment and more nutritional labelling of many items. They do not have to go as far as converting themselves into health spas to win.
- *American Demographics* magazine is saying:
  - The 'under 5' group will decline in the next five years as the first baby boomer turns 50 on 1 January 1996.
  - From 1980–90, those with any college education had their incomes increase by about 15%, while those without any college education had their incomes shrink by about 15%. It is to our industry's advantage to support education.
- Two other interrelated ways the American population has changed, with likely impacts on tourism, start with the reduced presence of the classic 'nuclear family'.
  - As recently as 1970, about 40% of the total households in the United States consisted of married couples with at least one child under the age of 18, and some 71% of US households were considered to be 'married couple households'. For 1992, only 55% of the households were 'married couple households' and only about 26% were married couple households having at least one child under the age of 18 present. One has to assume that the presence of children in the household significantly affects when and where travel activity occurs, especially when there are theme parks and major attractions involved.
  - Second, this country has seen an explosion in the rate of households headed by single parents. More often than not, that implies lower discretionary income and lower travel expenditure potentials. The rate of single-parent households in the US went from 13% figure comes from averaging a rate of 24% among white families with a rate of 62% among African-American families. Needless to say, targeted marketing programmes, with the best of intentions against selected minority groups, have very difficult obstacles to overcome when they bump up against sociological situations like these:
    - (a) Consumers want more privacy. They increasingly feel that businesses are taking advantage of them more than government. Our industry may need to be even more sensitive in how it uses its mailing lists.
    - (b) Environmentalism, as an issue, is getting more important for consumers but less important for corporations. Therefore,

our industry needs to stay alert to showing our customers that we are sensitive. More are making travel decisions with this in mind.

- The Roper Polling Organization has come out with a report on the major trends of Americans which will shape the future of American business. Some of their relevant highlights include:

  - Americans are increasingly more concerned with paying off their personal debt, or at least making more and more marketplace decisions with a conscious orientation towards their impact on their debt. Directly in line with that, *The Wall Street Journal* reported, on 6 August of this year [1993], that more than one-third of American households have little or no discretionary income after paying for their necessities of life, a profound finding. Quality economy lodging may benefit from this.

  - Today's shopper is being called a 'tactical consumer', expecting and getting the 'best' quality for the most 'reasonable' price. Chain-affiliate operations in tourism, which can afford the type of corporate messaging which creates this image for themselves, may be able to benefit from this change.

    Even before visitor crime situations began receiving as much publicity as they are getting, personal health and safety concerns were becoming dominant consumer themes of the 1990s. The attitude is one of life has risks, but the risks should be known and managed. Our industry is responding to this need through safety brochures, smoke-free restaurants and more nutritious menu selections.

  - Moderation and balance are the new key consumer guidelines. Lifestyles should not be as exhausting and clothes should be more functional. Hotels which were just seen as gateways to attractions may need to build in more quiet time opportunities, like pools, gyms and whirlpools.

  - Although households have moved from the dominance of the nuclear family to the diversity of many lifestyles, there is a greater demand for more family-oriented marketing. In travel, this could mean continuous promotion of special airfares for children travelling with adults, or hotel breakfasts included free for children.

  - The increase in the so-called 'nomadic office' means work can increasingly travel with the employee, even on vacation. Hotels with business centres need to make these options more accessible and affordable.

  - Ethnic tastes in cuisine are broadening, and tourists increasingly feel they want to experience the local flavours.

- In light of all this, we feel Florida is ideally suited to meet the challenges of the 1990s, by being an established brand for quality vacations at good value prices with easy and affordable accessibility. When we develop marketing strategies for tourism at the state level, we know how important it is to use research to shape, guide and evaluate those strategies.

REVIEW QUESTIONS

1. The case describes four types of research used in planning tourism marketing in Florida. How do they differ in content and the usages to which each is put?
2. What role did information provision play in the 'crisis management' following the Miami shootings?
3. Compare Florida's research programmes to those of any other destination agency, national or regional, with which you are familiar.
4. From your reading of this case identify the research elements which contribute to the environmental scanning function described in Chapter 1.

APPENDIX 23.1 STATISTICAL DATA

Table 23.1   Lodging Types used by Domestic Air Visitors Surveyed

Rank	Type	% 1993	% 1992	% 1991	% 1990	% 1989
1	Hotel/motel	47.8	48.5	49.4	49.5	49.1
2	Friends/relatives	37.1	37.5	36.3	36.8	36.2
3	Condo/apt./home (own)	7.8	7.2	7.4	6.3	7.3
4	Condo/apt./home (rent)	4.1	4.1	3.7	4.0	3.8
5	Other	1.6	1.5	1.8	1.5	2.1
6	Timeshare unit	1.1	0.8	0.9	1.1	1.0
7	Campground/RV park	0.4	0.3	0.5	0.8	0.5

Source: Florida Department of Commerce (1993) *Florida Visitor Study.*

Table 23.2   Pre-Trip Planning Activities of Air Visitors Surveyed

	% 1993	% 1992
1. Stopped at a travel agency for brochures	19.6	19.5
2. Had a travel agent make some of the arrangements for this trip	56.8	56.0
3. Had a travel agent suggest some activities which they enjoyed or places they stayed	15.1	13.1
4. Used the services of an auto club to plan this trip	7.8	8.3

Source: Florida Department of Commerce (1993) *Florida Visitor Study*

Table 23.3   Trip Parameters of Auto Visitors Surveyed

	1993	1992	1991	1990	1989
Average no. of nights	15.7	15.1	13.4	14.8	15.7
Long weekend stays	42.0%	48.0%	47.2%	44.3%	39.9%
Size of party	2.5	2.5	2.4	2.5	2.6
Median no. of nights	6.3	6.5	6.1	6.6	6.4
Person-nights (millions)	334.3	319.0	270.0	300.0	325.0

Source: Florida Department of Commerce (1993) *Florida Visitor Study.*

Table 23.4 Florida as the Intended First Address in the United States (For selected Origin Countries, 1992–1993)

Country	Total to Florida 1992	1993	Percent	Total to United States 1992	1993	Percent
Total overseas (w/Mex)	4 299 584	4 619 256	7.4%	19 347 821	20 253 495	4.7%
W. Europe	**2 203 275**	**2 231 128**	**1.3%**	**8 054 871**	**8 397 055**	**4.2%**
France	106 725	110 314	3.4%	795 444	844 644	6.2%
Germany	453 559	455 046	0.3%	1 691 663	1 826 757	8.0%
Italy	85 555	85 754	0.2%	589 837	555 785	−5.8%
Netherlands	79 337	88 214	11.2%	342 034	378 904	10.8%
Norway	24 860	22 162	−10.8%	103 863	106 437	2.4%
Spain	67 924	64 935	−4.4%	348 922	309 695	−9.9%
Sweden	80 595	53 626	−33.4%	261 728	224 281	−14.3%
Switzerland	62 082	63 608	2.4%	321 725	341 591	6.1%
United Kingdom	1 071 401	1 127 739	5.2%	2 823 983	2 999 301	6.2%
South America	**964 510**	**1 124 277**	**16.6%**	**1 770 162**	**2 026 391**	**14.5%**
Argentina	181 923	200 933	10.4%	342 008	387 116	13.2%
Brazil	254 890	294 976	15.7%	475 266	555 102	16.8%
Chile	50 350	58 845	16.8%	104 548	120 901	15.6%
Colombia	108 347	127 329	17.5%	188 808	212 688	12.6%
Ecuador	46 824	49 749	6.2%	87 035	89 554	2.8%
Peru	72 584	82 882	14.2%	114 776	128 216	11.7%
Venezuela	208 477	268 992	29.0%	372 313	444 355	19.3%
Central America	**205 607**	**245 328**	**19.3%**	**481 005**	**544 602**	**13.2%**
Other Countries/Regions						
Asia	138 511	147 444	6.4%	5 096 893	5 165 147	1.3%
Japan	104 537	112 695	7.8%	3 652 828	3 542 546	−3.0%
Australia	15 106	16 601	9.8%	486 851	448 507	−7.9%
Caribbean	473 882	536 177	13.1%	1 004 291	1 098 110	9.3%
Mexico	232 052	230 408	−0.7%	1 556 792	1 591 678	2.2%

Note: This is the official database used by the Department of Commerce for estimates of international travellers to Florida.

*Figures do not include Canadian data.

Source: United States Travel and Tourism Administration, 'Summary and analysis of international travel to the United States, 1992 and 1993', in Florida Department of Commerce (1993) *Florida Visitor Study*.

Index